ETHICAL OBJECTIVISM The view that holds that the truth of an ethical judgment is independent of the person who makes the judgment and of the time and place it is made.

ETHICAL RELATIVISM The view that there are no universally applicable ethical standards but that their applicability is dependent on historical, cultural or other conditions.

ETHICS The study of good and bad, right and wrong in human conduct. Comes from the Greek *ethos* (way of life) and is applied to the study of moral conduct. While some persons use the terms *morals* and *ethics* synonymously, among philosophers *morals* and *morality* usually refer to the conduct or behavior pattern, whereas *ethics* and *ethical* refer to the study of these matters or to a system of ideas about them. We usually speak of a moral act or a moral man and of an ethical system or code.

EUTHANASIA Mercy killing or the deliberate putting to death of persons suffering pain from incurable diseases.

EXISTENTIALISM The attitude and outlook in philosophy, theology, and the arts that stresses the human predicament and emphasizes human existence and the qualities distinctive of individuals rather than of "man" in the abstract, or nature and the world in general.

FATALISM The belief that events are irrevocably fixed so that human effort cannot alter them, although sometimes things appear otherwise. The idea that "what is to be, will be."

FORMALISM Adherence to prescribed forms. In education, formalism has meant the tendency to emphasize subject matter and traditional methods. In ethics, it has meant the view that certain types of acts follow fixed moral principles, so that circumstances do not alter cases.

FREEDOM OF CHOICE, FREE WILL The doctrine that man has some genuine power of alternative choice; the power of self-determination.

GOLDEN RULE The principle "Do unto others as you would have them do unto you."

GOOD The term applied to a thing or an experience that is of worth, possesses desirable qualities, or satisfies some need. Goods are of many kinds, and since the time of Aristotle, philosophers have distinguished between intrinsic goods (valuable in and of themselves, such as health and happiness) and extrinsic or instrumental goods (a means to something else, such as money and medicine).

HEDONISM The doctrine that pleasure (or happiness) is the chief good in life. Psychological hedonism insists that every person seeks his own pleasure in life. Ethical hedonism claims not that he always seeks to gain pleasure, but that he ought to do so.

HUMANISM A doctrine that emphasizes distinctively human interests and ideals. In the Renaissance, it was based on the Greek classics. In modern literature, it stresses a classical type of liberal education. In religion and philosophy, it emphasizes man and abandons all concepts of the supernatural.

INDETERMINISM The theory that personal choices in some cases are independent of antecedent events.

(Continued on back endpapers.)

ETHICS FOR TODAY
Fifth Edition

ETHICS FOR TODAY
Fifth Edition

Harold H. Titus Denison University

Morris Keeton Antioch College

D. Van Nostrand Company
New York/Cincinnati/Toronto/London/Melbourne

D. Van Nostrand Company Regional Offices:
New York   Cincinnati   Milbrae

D. Van Nostrand Company International Offices:
London   Toronto   Melbourne

Copyright © 1973 by Litton Educational Publishing, Inc.

Library of Congress Catalog Card Number: 72-4261

ISBN : 0-442-25803-8

All rights reserved. Certain portions of this work copyright © 1966, 1957, 1954, 1947, 1936 by Litton Educational Publishing, Inc. No part of this work covered by the copyrights hereon may be reproduced or used in any form or by any means—graphic, electronic, or mechanical, including photocopying, recording, taping, or information storage and retrieval systems—without written permission of the publisher. Manufactured in the United States of America.

Published by D. Van Nostrand Company
450 West 33rd Street, New York, N. Y. 10001

Published simultaneously in Canada by Van Nostrand Reinhold Ltd.

10   9   8   7   6   5   4   3   2

PREFACE

While a book on ethics may not "date" as rapidly as a book in the physical or biological sciences, the previous edition of this text written in the mid-sixties seemed dated at various points, reminding us that the time span of significant changes is much narrower than ever before. In the 1970s society faces many problems that were nonexistent even a few decades ago and some others that were acknowledged but were not as urgent as they are today. For the first time in history man can now change his own basic nature, or even blot out history and his own existence. A society that changes as fast as ours demands consideration of ethical problems that take into account the new conditions under which men live, even when the solutions involve the application of ancient and well-tested principles.

As in the earlier editions, we have attempted to keep the Fifth Edition of the book readable and nontechnical. Since we have written it for students, we do not attempt to treat all the technical issues that are of interest to mature philosophers. Our aim is double: (1) to open the field of ethics to those students who ordinarily take only one course in the subject, introducing them to the great systems of moral philosophy of the past and present, and (2) to emphasize normative ethics, presenting principles that need to be kept in mind as men face and attempt to solve the problems of personal and social living in the contemporary world.

The Fifth Edition differs from the Fourth Edition, first, in organization. Whereas the earlier edition has four parts, the present edition has an introductory chapter and two parts. Another difference lies in compactness. The new edition consists of twenty-four chapters as compared with twenty-nine in the Fourth Edition. We have consolidated material from several former chapters into new or different chapters containing material of related interest.

The new edition includes much new material. In a new introductory chapter, we discuss the lost consensus in the field of values and the change from confidence and optimism early in this century to the widely acknowledged fact that we live in the midst of a serious crisis that demands urgent attention to our basic values. Chapter 2, "Steps in Ethical Inquiry," deals mainly with the possible methods of approach and attempts to clarify the approach of this book. Chapter 11, "Additional Types of Ethics," includes Marxism and existentialism and is largely new material. Chapter 22, "The Limits of Life and Abundance," which treats questions of population and the environment, is entirely new. Nearly all the chapters are given a new slant and changes have been made in order to make them relevant for the seventies. The chapters that have relatively the least changes are those dealing with the classical theories which have not changed even though their modern supporters have offered new insights.

In Part 1 we are concerned with the search for a moral philosophy that will be adequate for our changing times. Here we consider the various methods of approach, the nature and development of morality, and how we distinguish between right and wrong. After a brief elaboration of the main ethical systems, we point out the characteristics of a reflective and a mature morality.

In Part 2 the principles treated earlier are applied to numerous problems of personal, vocational, and social living. The discussions generally move from the personal to the more distinctly social and institutional, from such problems as truthfulness and intellectual freedom to questions regarding the professions, business, the mass media, marriage, race, population and environment, the state, wars, and the thermonuclear age. With the rapid increase of specialization and its accelerated rate of change, many people today face problems which older authorities and customs cannot solve. We believe that a text must, as this one does, acquaint students with the problems they will face as they enter the professional and business world. For the philosopher to avoid discussing the application of his principles to the areas of human experience is to miss an opportunity, to shirk a duty, and to leave himself open to the charge that he lives in an ivory tower. A moral problem is never just a moral problem; it is also a problem of personal living, domestic relations, professional responsibility, economic and political affairs, or international relations.

To aid both the instructor and the student, Questions and Projects, Suggested Readings, and a Glossary have been provided. The Questions and Projects at the end of the chapters have in the past brought much favorable comment, and this material has been expanded rather than contracted. Many new books, some published in the early seventies, have been added to the Suggested Readings. The Glossary is a new feature in this Fifth Edition and is included because terms in the field of moral philosophy are sometimes used with special meanings. The definitions and explanations in the Glossary give the meaning that a term has in this book. In general we include most terms used in discussions of moral conduct and ethical systems whose meanings are different from those in everyday conversation and terms that can be defined in a brief space. For convenience the Glossary is presented on the front and back endpapers of the book. Further elaboration of many of these terms is found in the text.

At the request of some instructors who find supplementary readings useful, we prepared a paperbound book of readings for the Fourth Edition, entitled *The Range of Ethics* (New York: D. Van Nostrand Company, 1966). These readings introduce the student to some primary sources. They also appear as the first item of the Suggested Readings sections in all text chapters except one. The Fifth Edition of the text and the reader may be used jointly or separately with other texts and readings.

Some instructors who have used the text in the past have been good enough to make suggestions for revisions. We would like to be able to acknowledge all of these, but obviously that is not possible. We do, however, invite users of the text to write to us.

H. H. T.
M. K.

TABLE OF CONTENTS

In each chapter:

    Questions and Projects
    Suggested Readings

1 A Lost Consensus   **1**

    From Confidence to Uncertainty   2
    What Are the Causes of the Crisis?   6

PART 1 THE SEARCH FOR A MORAL PHILOSOPHY

2 Steps in Ethical Inquiry   **23**

    The Necessity for Decisions   23
    Six Possible Methods of Approach to Ethical Inquiry—
        A Survey   27
    A Comprehensive and Common-Sense Approach   33

3 The Development of Morality   **39**

    Early Group Life and Customary Morality   39
    Statutory Law   44
    The Appeal to External Authority   47
    The Appeal to Conscience   49
    Reflective Morality   53
    Summary   58

4 Nature, Human Nature, and Freedom of Choice — 64

The World beyond Us — 64
Human Nature — 65
Hereditary and Environmental Conditions Affecting Man — 70
Freedom of Choice — 75
Freedom As Self-determinism — 79
How Free Is Man? — 82

5 Why Right Is Right — 88

The Basic Moral Postulate — 89
Some Moral Guidelines — 93
The Generalization and Other Principles — 96
Motives, Means, and Consequences — 98
An Example of Reflective Morality — 102
Three Viewpoints in Contemporary Ethical Theory — 104

6 Do Moral Judgments Express Knowledge or Feelings? — 108

Three Elements in a Judgement — 109
The Historical Relativity of Morals — 111
Language and Emotive Meanings — 114
Basing Criticism and Actions on Working Convictions — 126
Summary Conclusions — 129

7 Kant and Some Later Intuitionists — 133

Immanual Kant, 1724-1804 — 134
Summary and Evaluation of Kant's Ethics — 142
Later Intuitionism and the Ethics of Duty — 146

8 Pleasure and Happiness As the End of Life — 151

Proponents and Types of Hedonism — 151
The Utilitarianism of Jeremy Bentham — 153
The Utilitarianism of John Stuart Mill — 155
An Evaluation of Hedonisms — 157
Conclusion — 166

9 Nature As the Standard — 170

- Darwin's Ethics — 171
- Spencer and Later Evolutionists — 175
- The Self As Power and Will: Nietzsche — 177
- Later Evolutionists — 180
- Summary — 184

10 The Fulfillment of the Individual in Society — 190

- Ancient Greek Contributions — 190
- Medieval and Modern Contributions — 194
- Distinctive Points of Emphasis in Self-realization — 197
- An Evaluation of the Ideal of Self-realization — 202

11 Additional Types of Ethics — 209

- Marxism and Ethics — 209
- Existential Ethics — 213
- Types of Religious Ethics — 218

12 Reflective Morality in a Changing World — 231

- Is Experimentation Possible in the Realm of Morality? — 232
- Why We Need to Experiment in Morality — 234
- Is It Ever Right to Compromise? — 238
- Bringing Our Morals Up to Date — 240
- Principles That Need Wider Application — 243
- Individual versus Group Morality — 245

13 Values, Rights, and Obligations — 251

- The Grounding and Selection of Values — 252
- Values and Rights — 254
- Human Rights — 256
- Obligations — 261
- Concluding Questions — 267

PART 2 SPECIFIC PROBLEMS OF PERSONAL AND SOCIAL MORALITY

14 Physical and Mental Health — 273

- The Importance of Physical Health — 274
- The Use of Alcohol, Tobacco, and Drugs — 279
- The Cultivation of Mental Health — 289
- The Need for a National Health Plan and Program — 292

15 Freedom of Thought and Expression — 298

- Faith in Critical Thinking — 298
- Historic Defenses of Freedom of Expression — 301
- Intellectual Freedom under Attack — 303
- The Invasion of Privacy — 309
- Why Freedom Is in Jeopardy — 311
- Why Intellectual Freedom Is Important — 313

16 Moral Excellence in Everyday Life — 320

- Moral Excellence As Emphasized in the West — 321
- Moral Excellence As Stressed in the East — 324
- The Importance of Truthfulness — 327
- Evaluation and Conclusions — 336

17 Institutional and Professional Ethics — 343

- The Importance and Dangers of Institutions — 343
- Professions and Professional Standards — 347
- Morals, Law, and Professional Ethics — 349
- Three Professional Groups — 352
- A Concluding Question — 367

18 Ethics of Business and the Industrial System — 374

- A Changing Industrial System — 375
- Criticism of the Business and Industrial Order — 379
- Efforts toward Improvement of Business Standards — 385
- Industry and Labor — 389
- For Improvement of Industrial Society — 392

19	**Ethics and the Mass Media**	**399**
	The Newspaper	400
	Broadcasting: Radio and Television	405
	Motion Pictures	411
	Freedom, Control, and the Mass Media	413
	Some Conclusions and Suggestions	416
20	**New Designs for Family and Marriage**	**423**
	Changes in the Prevailing Views of Rights	424
	Technological, Demographic, and Other Social Changes	427
	Changing Practices in Marriage and Sex	431
	What Is and What Ought to Be in Marriage	435
21	**Cultural Pluralism and Racial Justice**	**449**
	Discrimination in America Today	452
	Racial Differences and Sources of Tension	454
	Prejudice: Its Roots and Its Effects	456
	A Challenge to a Racist Social Order	459
	Searching for a Way toward Racial Justice	461
22	**The Limits of Life and Abundance**	**471**
	A Human Predicament	471
	A Matter of Priorities	474
	The Control of Population	476
	Ecological Disasters and Chronic Polluters	484
	What Does It Mean to Choose Life?	485
23	**Government for the People**	**493**
	The Functions of Government	494
	Social Priorities and the Federal Budget	500
	The Government and Moral Standards	503
	The Government and the Individual	508

24 War and the Quest for Peace   **521**
   The Role of Atomic Energy   521
   War As an Ancient Institution   524
   Efforts to Achieve Peace   526
   Is Permanent Peace Possible?   528
   Revolution and Violence   533

Index   **541**

ETHICS FOR TODAY
Fifth Edition

1
A LOST CONSENSUS

Today is a day of frustration and broken lives, of widespread and often violent social conflict, and even of prophecies that both civilization and human survival are doomed. Why? What should be done?

We know many answers to these two questions, but none that are satisfactory—at least not by themselves. In these pages we ask these questions again, not expecting to get completely adequate answers, but to improve our insight, to gain a greater understanding of the human condition, and possibly to contribute to the quality of life among us. This book is organized around a hypothesis which may or may not appeal to you after you have examined it. However, if studying it aids your understanding of the problems and possibilities of contemporary man, our work will have served its purpose. The hypothesis is this: The current doubt, turmoil, and despair reflect a loss of consensus among men about what is good or right and what is better or worse in human conduct for the present time. This loss of consensus arises from many causes. Among them, paradoxically, are changes that enlarge our opportunities—changes that, interacting with other conditions, create unwelcome as well as beneficial effects. One cause of the loss of consensus is the conflict and disagreement about who gains and suffers and about who should gain and suffer as these changes occur. If the same people experienced both the benefits and the costs of each change in similar proportion, and if they were all clear about the linkage between the two, our options for life might be happier than they are. As it is, the benefits and the costs often fall upon different people and in different proportions, and our knowledge of the interconnections among the changes is very limited.

FROM CONFIDENCE TO UNCERTAINTY

Not every society experiences such marked disagreement as ours does about what is good and right, at least not with the sense of crisis so common today in our society. During the late nineteenth and early twentieth centuries, there was widespread optimism, faith, and confidence. A few lonely voices in the nineteenth century warned the West about dangerous trends and possible disaster ahead, but these "prophets of gloom" were largely disregarded. The prevailing outlook was one of tremendous confidence in the future. There was a rapidly expanding faith in education. There was great confidence in science and a belief that it would be able to solve most problems rather quickly. There was great optimism for democracy. While some nations were not democratic, it was believed that they were merely retarded in their development, that in a few more years they too would be free and democratic. Faith in progress and in the future was strong. For several generations Western society took human progress much for granted. Many assumed that all we needed to do was to accumulate more and more knowledge and skill in more and more fields, and a good life would naturally follow. Thus it was said that education, science, democracy, human ingenuity, and a little time would usher in a new and better world.

Since then many things seem to have gone tragically wrong. World War I was followed by the Roaring Twenties, the so-called lost generation, and then the Great Depression. Movements like communism and fascism that denied many Western values rose to power in various countries. Then came World War II, the cold war, and war in Korea, Vietnam, and Southeast Asia. This story is well known and we need not dwell on it. As one moves around the world today, one detects uneasiness, uncertainty, confusion, and fear of the future.

Some years ago the president of the National Association of Manufacturers said that he had traveled fifty thousand miles in the United States, visited every state in the union, and talked with people in all walks of life. He found three fears gnawing at the minds and hearts of the people: fear of spiral inflation, of another great depression, and of a third more terrible world war. Had his trip been more recent, he probably would have said something about violence in the streets, rebellious youth, and the interruption of essential services.

In his book *The State of Siege*, C. P. Snow says that after traveling many thousands of miles around the world in 1967,[1] he returned with "one overmastering impression"—that nearly everyone was worried and uncertain about the future. In spite of the fact that people generally were healthier and richer, and in spite of great scientific and technological achievements, people were turning inward and were afraid that we were headed toward major catastrophes of an unprecedented nature.

In the late 1960s and the early 1970s, writers on the far left as well as those on the far right were highly critical of the society in which we live. Herbert Marcuse, for example, said that the sharp conflict between society's great scientific resources and technological instruments, on the one hand, and the waste and destructiveness on the other hand, simply cannot go on. "I can't imagine," he said, "an intelligent and sincere man who does not feel that opposition to this society is a necessity—not just in political and philosophical terms, but even in moral and biological terms."[2]

The lost consensus is seen most clearly by two extreme and sharply contrasting views of the causes of the crisis we face. According to one view, the country is being undermined by rebellious youth and their allies among older people. These rebels are without respect, loyalty, patriotism, and culture. They have been spoiled by permissive parents and school and college administrators and misled by subversive teachers. According to the outlook at the opposite extreme, the country is ruled by a hypocritical establishment that talks about virtues and law and order but does not practice what it preaches. It talks about a better society while it opposes most reforms. It is racist and imperialistic and supports immoral wars while it puts profits and money above nearly everything else.

Philosophers, psychologists, historians, and others have been warning us for years about the dangerous trends in the modern world. More than a decade ago a psychologist, after pointing out that he was constitutionally an optimist working for man's health of mind and spirit, said that if the present trend continues without being checked, "modern man will become more and more neurotic. . . . Suicide rates will continue to rise. And the psychopathology of the individuals will become the psychopathology of the masses—and inevitably—of their leaders, their governments. There can be only one outcome of such a develop-

---

[1](New York: Charles Scribner's Sons, 1968).
[2]*Time*, 22 March 1968, p. 40.

ment: the holocaust of war and, quite possibly, the extinction of our species."[3]

Many people today are asking how much longer we can retain our type of civilization and indeed how we can even survive if crime, violence, rioting, drug traffic, and disruption of essential public services increase at their present rate. People, especially in the cities, are afraid to walk out at night, and in some areas in the daytime as well. Even businesses are under siege, the targets of professional racketeers, embezzling employees, and political protesters. Office buildings, banks, and department stores have been damaged by stones, fire, and bombs. Car thefts have become big business. Petty thievery and white-collar crime are rising. The demand for guards, watchdogs, alarm systems, safety devices, and identification systems has risen at a rapid rate.

How much longer can we survive and retain our health if pollution of the air, water, and earth continues at the present rate? We cannot mar and destroy our environment without lowering the quality of human life. Man has been upsetting the equilibrium between population and environment and has endangered all nature including himself. The historian Herbert J. Muller says that during the past half-century, the major cities have become increasingly less habitable. In his youth he fell in love with New York and walked all over Manhattan, but his outlook has changed: "I am more keenly aware how woefully New York has deteriorated, and how critical its condition is today. In this respect it is like almost all the big cities in America. . . . Congested, blighted, and polluted, they make some authorities doubt that the central city is worth saving or restoring."[4]

An early voice recording the loss of confidence in this century was Oswald Spengler of Germany whose *Decline of the West*[5] appeared soon after World War I. Spengler forecast an inevitable decline which in the critical stage is marked by certain characteristics including the rise of great cities in which life becomes artificial, fast, and shallow; the dictatorship of money that first destroys intellect and then democracy as the body prospers and the spirit decays; the growth of imperialism and war as warlords seize the citadels of power; the development of skepticism and lack of conviction; the replacement of quality by quantity and

---

[3]Arthur Isenberg, *Reflections on Psychological Insecurity in Modern Man,* Transaction no. 31 (Bangalore, India: The Indian Institute of World Culture, 1961), p. 16.

[4]Herbert J. Muller, *The Children of Frankenstein: A Primer on Modern Technology and Human Values* (Bloomington, Ind.: Indiana University Press, 1970), p. 261.

[5](New York: Alfred A. Knopf, 1945).

of beauty by utility as men become the slaves of the machine and the industrial system. Though at least forty or fifty substantial studies of this problem have since been published, and though they agree that the West is in serious trouble, most of them reject Spengler's prophecy of inevitable decline. Yet recent books show a new measure of fear and doubt. For example, the book section of *Time* magazine of June 1, 1970 reviews four books about America written by a high government official, a journalist, a professor of sociology, and a professor of government. The review says that "the possibility that America has reached its end time haunts the authors of three of these exercises in national self-appraisal. The fourth assumes that an American doomsday is a distinct probability."[6]

There are a number of thinkers in our society who believe that the prophecies of doom are unwarranted. While admitting that there is danger when intelligence is applied without moral insight, they believe that the breakdown of the old order may be at the same time the birth process of a new and better world. Charles A. Reich explained his theories in this vein in *The Greening of America*,[7] a book which skyrocketed to the best-seller list, widely praised by some critics as a deeply thoughtful work and severely criticized by others as an oversimplified and sentimental idealization of the confused culture it represented. Reich speaks of a third consciousness which is emerging and which he thinks offers great promise. Consciousness I is the free enterprise and individualistic outlook of the American farmer and small businessman. Consciousness II was formed by the technological and corporate society of the first half of the twentieth century and is conformist and repressive in nature. Consciousness III is emerging in the second half of the twentieth century and is spreading among wider and wider segments of youth and by degrees to older people who sense the discrepancy between what is and what could be. "A society is mad," says Reich, "when its actions are no longer guided by what will make men healthier and happier, when its power is no longer in the service of life."

Reich feels that a revolution is in the making, but that it will not be like the revolutions of the past. "It will not require violence to succeed, and it cannot be successfully resisted by violence." The new outlook on life is spreading rapidly, and our laws, institutions, and social structure are reflecting this new consciousness. The outcome promises a more human community, a liberated individual, and a "renewed relationship of man to himself, to other men, to society, to nature, and to the land."

---

[6]"America: Going, Going, Gone?" *Time,* 1 June 1970, p. 86.
[7](New York: Random House, 1970; Bantam Books, 1971).

The question now being asked by Reich and others is whether we can develop a consciousness that places man and human values above the machine.[8]

WHAT ARE THE CAUSES OF THE CRISIS?

When we ask why things seem to be out of gear, it is easy to stress symptoms rather than basic causes. Sometimes it is difficult to distinguish clearly between causes and effects. Certain people, the "great simplifiers," find it easy to seize upon some one factor as the explanation: weak laws and a lack of a sufficient number of trained police, racial conflict and hatred, inadequate monetary and taxation policies, neglect of planning in our cities, the breakdown of homes and family life, war and the military-industrial complex, the presence of communism and other radical movements, or a foreign policy that leads to conflict rather than to peaceful solutions.

We agree that war, population pressure, poverty, racial conflict, pollution of the environment, and the like are among the problems that need our immediate attention. They have aggravated the crisis of our time and have led to student unrest and major maladjustments and disturbances. These problems are being widely discussed in our society today and we shall consider them in later chapters. In this chapter we give attention mainly to some of the neglected but basic causes of both the local and the world-wide crises we face.

What are some of the basic causes of our disorders and confusion? We are suggesting that some of our most serious dangers are "creeping dangers" that have come upon us slowly and unawares. This may be the reason for their neglect. A simple example may help us to grasp this point. We are told that if we put a live frog into a pan of water and heat the water very slowly, the frog will remain in the water until it comes to a boil and he loses his life. At any time up to a certain point, he can jump out and save himself. He does not do so because at no particular point does he recognize his danger. He becomes accustomed to a degree of heat and a little more does not disturb him if the increase is gradual enough. Perhaps something like this has been happening to us. Consider the following, more fundamental explanations of the crisis we face.

---

[8]Many books of a somewhat similar nature were being discussed in the early seventies. See the books by Mumford, Revel, Toffler, and others listed in the *Suggested Readings*.

I Scientific and Technological Changes of a Revolutionary Nature

We are in trouble partly because *we live in the most catastrophically revolutionary period of history*—revolutionary in the sense of experiencing rapid and far-reaching changes. Alfred North Whitehead in his *Adventures of Ideas*[9] spoke of the shortening of our time span of significant change. Great changes used to occur slowly, perhaps taking centuries. Now great changes come within the lifespan of single individuals or even within a few years. This creates many new problems not only for individuals but for society and its institutions. We have changed within a few generations from a society predominantly rural and simple in organization to a highly industrialized machine civilization that is becoming increasingly complex, interdependent, and impersonal. Urbanization, automation, the pace of scientific development, and the magnitude of investment in scientific research are creating unprecedented problems. The industrial, technological, and atomic revolutions are producing a society that is mechanically efficient but capable of destroying itself. The danger is that we may have learned how to control nature and split the atom before we have learned how to unite mankind or establish a system of international law with means for enforcement. Continuing discoveries about nuclear energy have heightened the urgency for finding a solution to many of our human problems. Only the future can disclose what the release of new energy may mean for good or for evil. Some fear that we may be creating a monster which is about to devour us.

We have been told that ninety to ninety-five percent of all scientists the world has produced are now living. Our century has witnessed scientific and technological changes as great as or greater than those which appeared during the previous two thousand years. A peasant or laborer from ancient Greece or Palestine could adjust quite easily to the working conditions at the end of the nineteenth century. A farmer or laborer from the nineteenth century would be mystified by the elaborate power machines of today.

At the beginning of this century the United States was a nation of farms, small villages, and towns. Forty percent of the employed were engaged in agricultural pursuits. Now five percent can produce more food than we need. A few automobiles were manufactured in the 1890s, and the thirteen hundred reported to exist in 1900 were regarded as just the playthings of the sporting rich. There were no pavements except in a few cities, and horses were everywhere. There were no radios, for their development took place mainly in the 1920s. There were no televi-

---

[9]"Foresight," ch. 6 (New York: The New American Library of World Literature, 1955).

sion sets, because they developed mainly in the 1940s. And of course there was no air travel. Only six percent of the nation's youths graduated from high school. Young people grew up in the company of adults, watched them work, and took over the culture from them. For many young people today it is difficult to realize that there are men and women living in our society who were born before there were any automobiles, radios, televisions, airplanes, or electronic machines.

Before we had become adjusted to the industrial and technological revolutions of the nineteenth century, we were ushered into the age of electronics, computers, automation, cybernation, mass media, the knowledge explosion, the population explosion, the thermonuclear age, and the space age. Old habits and customs were broken up, and we have had neither the time nor the stable conditions to enable men to construct new ones. Our thinking and social philosophy cannot keep up with the changes, and all too often we have tried to run a complex, interdependent, machine age with the philosophy of the days of the oxcart. Sometime before his death, Albert Einstein, who has had as much to do with bringing in the new age as anyone, said: "The unleashed power of the atom has changed everything except our ways of thinking. Thus we are drifting toward a catastrophe beyond comparison. We shall require substantially a new manner of thinking *if* mankind is to survive."

Over a decade ago, an article appeared in the *New York Times Magazine* entitled "Ten Patents That Changed the World"[10] in celebration of the one hundred twenty-fifth anniversary of the founding of the United States Patent Office and the three-millionth patent. The thing that really surprised many people was that eight of the ten patents described were taken out in this century. They ranged from powered flights (the beginning of the airplane) and the vacuum tube to wonder drugs and atomic power.

An important invention let loose in a society can be compared to a stone dropped into the smooth surface of a pond. Soon the ripples will cover the entire surface. What is happening today, however, is more like handfuls of stones being thrown continuously at rapid speeds on the surface. From one point of view the scientists and technicians are the men who are changing the world.

Recently, a student asked one of the authors, "Is this age really any different—haven't there been changes and serious crises in the past?" We think this age is different because of the remarkably accelerated speed of changes taking place in many areas of life, and because our partial control over nature has enabled us to increase life expectancy by reducing the death rate but not the birth rate. In a decade or so there

---

[10] Stacy V. Jones, *New York Times Magazine*, 17 September 1961, pp. 24–25.

may be a billion people added to the world's population, unless we find better means of population control and greatly increase acceptance of it. The disparity between rising population and available food supply may create a major catastrophe. This age is also different because man has gained the power to change his own nature and even to blot out history. Then, too, there is a new human consciousness today, created in part by the mass media and new electronic devices. The present generation is conscious of and can watch or be present at events that are taking place all over the world. The young who have been born and reared under these new conditions have been affected most drastically.

II Widespread Confusion and Disagreement about Moral Standards and Values

The crisis we face is caused, in part, by the fact that, as individuals and as a society, we have become confused with a welter of conflicting values that leaves us powerless to make the right decisions and to act on them. We have failed to bring our ideals and values into effective use to guide our responses to meet the needs and demands of the new age in which we live. A civilization is a set of ideas, ideals, values, and loyalties that act as the cohesive force or the cement, so to speak, that holds the various parts of society together. When they are weakened or lost, society tends to break up into conflicting groups. Men seek other and less worthy ends and civilization tends to decline. Psychologist Abraham Maslow, editor of *New Knowledge in Human Values* to which scientists, philosophers, and others have contributed, speaks for the group in affirming that "this volume springs from the belief, first, that the ultimate disease of our time is valuelessness; second, that this state is more crucially dangerous than ever before in history; and finally, that something can be done about it by man's own rational efforts."[11]

One explanation of the crisis is that people in general do not have or care about values, that their scale of values has eroded and left them without any. Another interpretation is that people are more deeply concerned than ever before about the problems of morals, ethics, and the lack of consensus that so frequently paralyzes programs of reform. The latter interpretation appears to be confirmed by a Time-Louis Harris Poll taken in 1969 which shows that many people are not valueless but think that other people either are or at least choose the wrong values and priorities. "Men and women, young and old, professionals and laborers, whites and blacks, Christians and Jews, all agree by lopsided

---

[11]Abraham H. Maslow, *New Knowledge in Human Values* (New York: Harper & Brothers, 1959), p. vii.

majorities that morality in the United States has declined over the past ten years."[12] Polls taken abroad indicate that people share a like opinion regarding moral decline in virtually all nations of the Western world. These people are aware as no other generation before has been of the enormous disagreement among people about what is best, and of the vast gap between the ideal conditions we can envisage today and the actual conditions in the midst of which we live.

The sense of moral decline can itself add to demoralization of efforts to live by the best each one knows and to seek for larger areas of agreement and cooperation about what is good. Without some shared sense of direction, the people of a community fail to support one another even in the things they commonly want. Such confusion can undermine not only neighborliness and civic improvement efforts but also the informal pressure that keeps down the exploitation of others. This community pressure underlies the law and its capacity to control delinquency and crime. As Chief Justice Earl Warren said: "In civilized life, law floats in a sea of ethics. Each is indispensable to civilization. Without law, we should be at the mercy of the least scrupulous; without ethics, law could not exist. Without ethical consciousness in most people, lawlessness would be rampant."[13] A society is in danger when intelligence and technology are applied in a moral void.

We have said that civilization is essentially a set of ideals and loyalties that hold the various sections of society together. The most important difference between life in the United States and in the communist countries in recent years and in the fascist countries a few decades ago is not a matter of science, technology, industry, and machines; it is the ideas, ideals, and loyalties around which these are organized.

How are we to explain the moral confusion of our times? At least three developments need to be pointed out. First, our problem stems in part from the fact that our traditional value system grew up in a simple agricultural society that was relatively static. In that form it was associated with an unchanging, authoritarian, ecclesiastical system. Today we live in a complex, interdependent, mechanized civilization with scores of new ways of injuring, killing, lying, and stealing. Our failure to bring our morals up to date, to see their dynamic nature, and to apply them to our modern society is one cause of the crisis we face. This problem is too large and complex a question to discuss at this point and we shall return to it in chapter 12.

Second, in the West until recently the Greek and Judaeo-Christian

---

[12]*Time*, 6 June 1969, p. 26.
[13]From an address delivered at the Louis Marshall Award dinner at the Jewish Theological Seminary, New York City, November 11, 1962.

ethical ideals furnished the loyalties and values that held the parts of society together. At least the educated and cultural leaders generally held them and set the pace. With the rise of the doctrine of sovereignty in the early modern period, the state in a sense broke away and asserted its independence and separate power. Modern national sovereignty at first meant absolute internal authority, as well as freedom from external control. The state was regarded as a law unto itself. It made the laws but, in the early days, was above law and morals. After the industrial revolution in the eighteenth and nineteenth centuries, commercial and business groups wanted to be free even from governmental restrictions on their right to make money as they saw fit. The demand was "laissez faire"—leave us alone, business is business, business ought to be free to make decisions on the basis of financial considerations alone. Soon, workingmen began to feel that they were being left out, and they formed unions to fight for their own interests. Professional groups (doctors, lawyers, teachers) and farm blocs organized to protect their special interests. Artists insisted on "Art for art's sake," and education, too, was becoming independent and stressing neutrality. These developments have brought benefits as well as dangers. The central point is that no one part of society can be a law unto itself and disregard society as a whole without creating conflict and endangering the whole.

Third, curricular changes in high schools, colleges, and universities over the last hundred years have tended to replace the value studies and many courses in the humanities in general with courses that are vocational or more "practical." A large majority of young people, possibly as high as ninety percent, go from matriculation to graduation without any formal study in the field of morality. Alongside the educational system there have grown up in recent decades powerful new means of influencing the behavior, emotions, and cultural life of people. We refer to the mass media which we shall discuss in a later chapter.

The divorce between profession and practice, morality and politics, religion and economic affairs, and the like is one of the real dangers of our rapidly changing world. It is at least one factor behind the protests and rebellion of some of our more idealistic young people. If parents, and society as a whole, give the next generation automobiles, guns, and electronic devices but do not pass on to them the moral and cultural heritage of the race, we are in for more and more trouble.

III A Distorted View of the Nature of Man

Civilization is now in mortal danger because of a distorted view of man that has been growing in recent decades. Methods devised for the study of physical nature, machines, and animals have been applied to the study of man. These methods have given us new descriptive knowledge of many processes, but they have tended to ignore or even deny what is unique in man. The serious division in the world today is not so much on social, economic, or political questions as on the basic question of what or who man really is. Is he a being of worth and dignity with unique powers of creativity and selfhood, powers not found in the rest of the universe as we know it, or is he merely an animal differing from other animals only slightly in degree? Is he a "hollow man" with no distinctive inner life, almost wholly concerned with the external and the material? We have gone to the white rat and the guinea pig and have obtained some useful information. But when a man goes to the white rat and then attempts to tell us just what we are, we should object, should we not? What a man believes in the depth of his being is what makes him what he is, and what he believes about himself is crucial. Let neutrality, indifference, and skepticism about himself become strong and the very springs of life will dry up. He will lose heart, become bitter and cynical, and perhaps give way to violent behavior. The failure or decline in man's image of himself may be an important part of the crisis we face and may explain man's loss of a sense of meaning, dignity, and direction. This question of the nature of man will determine the kind of world he will make and his efforts to build a society and achieve peace and order.

In various writings including his book *The Conduct of Life*,[14] Lewis Mumford has talked about the "bias against the personal" in recent Western society. Western man in his drive for profit and power and his pursuit of objective knowledge in highly specialized fields and in gigantic industrial and military organizations has tended to ignore the unique and the personal. The process of dehumanization has thus spread to almost every segment of society.

This is a large and complex issue, but let us briefly look for some examples in three areas—the sciences, literature, and art. A considerable number of books in psychology, biology, and related fields proceed on the basis of a mechanistic approach to scientific inquiry. There is no objection to eliminating personal factors as a study is set up as long as this fact is not forgotten.

First, in the sciences, let us look at a few psychologists: (1) Donald Hebb says that his *A Textbook of Psychology*[15] assumes "that mind is a bodily process." Modern psychologists "work with this theory only." A mechanistic and materialistic presentation is therefore the result. (2) Charles E. Osgood in *Method and Theory in Experimental Psychology*[16]

---

[14](New York: Harcourt, Brace & Co., 1951).
[15](Philadelphia: W. B. Saunders Co., 1958).
[16](New York: Oxford University Press, 1953).

says that psychologists must eliminate mentalistic constructs—such as thoughts, ideas, and images—from psychological science. If we do admit them, we must at least deny that "they partake of something other than the material world. Otherwise we should be unable to investigate them at all with scientific methods." (3) In a number of books including *Walden Two,* the widely used textbook *Science and Human Behavior,* and *Beyond Freedom and Dignity,*[17] B. F. Skinner rejects the concepts of human dignity, freedom, man's responsibility for his own acts, notions of an inner man (ego, personality, spirit, or mind that is somehow free). He speaks of "man a machine" and "man as an animal" and asserts that "a concept of self is not essential in an analysis of behavior." Or again, "since mental or psychic events are asserted to lack the dimension of physical science we have an additional reason for rejecting them." A scientific analysis, we are told, shifts both the responsibility and the achievement to the environment. There is no inner or autonomous man.

In claiming that the self, which persists through the changing experiences of a person's existence, is immediately known and cannot be completely described in the objective terms of the sciences, we do not intend to minimize the great achievements of the sciences and the value of scientific method. There is no area of life about which scientific methods cannot furnish much information. Scientists may investigate anything with which their methods are capable of dealing. Many sciences, perhaps all of them, ought to employ objective, quantitative, and mechanical methods because of their simplicity and accuracy. Those of us working in the field of moral philosophy and human conduct need all the help we can get from the many special sciences. What we are saying, however, is that when these methods are used the sciences are not telling the whole story.

Quite a number of sociologists, including David Riesman and John K. Galbraith, tell us that something strange and dangerous for the future is happening to the American character: We are slowly changing from inner-directed to outer-directed persons. A society whose members have starved or warped inner lives and are outer-directed tend to build up a need for outward and frequently violent expression. This has been altering not only our personal lives, but our institutions and our cities. The change is related to the sense of doubt, defeat, futility, and emptiness characteristic of so many today.

In a number of books, but especially in *On Being Human,*[18] the anthropologist Ashley Montagu contends that the constructive and cooperative

---

[17]Respectively, (New York: Macmillan Co., 1948, 1951); (New York: Macmillan Co., 1953); and (New York: Alfred A. Knopf, 1971).
[18](New York: Henry Schuman, 1950).

forces in man's nature are biologically more important than the egotistic and destructive forces. Our age, however, has inherited a tradition from some nineteenth-century writers in biology and economics that life is a cruel struggle and competition is the dominant law of life. This outlook seemed to justify the every-man-for-himself attitude as well as competition and even war. While this viewpoint motivates large areas in the Western world, Montagu insists that it is false and dangerous or destructive. He gives many examples, maintaining that this false outlook has made us the disordered, egocentric creatures we have become. He says that without love it is not possible to live, but only to exist in a low form.

Second, let us take just a brief look at the world of literature and the dramatic arts. From the time of the early Greeks and Hebrews to this century, the great literature and drama made a distinction between good and evil, right and wrong, beauty and ugliness. During the nineteenth century, with a few notable exceptions, most literary men were optimistic. Tennyson and many others held to the doctrine of inevitable progress, and men like Emerson and Whitman stressed the importance of the self and personal identity and saw man as a free, sovereign, inner-directed person having a sense of his own significance. Much of the literature of the twentieth century stands in sharp contrast with that of the last century. Many of the most popular novels deal with scenes of violence, sex and lust, cruelty, oppression, and war. Much of modern literature reflects the views of those who feel isolated and at odds not only with society, but with themselves. In fiction and plays many young artists seem to be creating characters that express fury, disgust, and an attitude of alienation toward society. The theater of the absurd reflects life as without sense and meaning. There is often the empty stage, little or no plot, characters that are unconventional and sometimes offbeat.

Edmund Fuller, editor, novelist, and critic, writing on "The New Compassion in the American Novel," speaks about changes that have occurred in recent decades. Starting in the thirties and continuing for some time, there was much emphasis on "the lovely bum," whose place was soon taken by "the genial rapist, the jolly slasher, and the funloving dope peddler." Fuller says that "since their [the writers'] concept of compassion will not permit them to blame anything upon the criminal, the degraded, and the destroyed, they blame everything upon the noncriminal, the nondegraded, and the undestroyed . . ." If you have no values and see no values, "you cannot distinguish between the hypocrite and the virtuous man . . ."[19] Where there are no objective standards it is hard to criticize or condemn anyone and even the state cannot be challenged.

---

[19]*The American Scholar*, Spring 1957, pp. 155–163.

Third, art tends to be a sensitive barometer of the age and the human spirit. We see many pictures of broken statues, disfigured and deformed bodies, sometimes even with dislocated arms, legs, and heads. Fantastic and mystical symbolism portrays the confusions and conflicts of the day. There is relatively less that reflects beauty, harmony, or the expression of love, friendship, and the hope for the future.

Perhaps art is saying something important to our age. It is saying that ours is a segmented and confused era, but one that is seeking meaning and a sense of direction. The question is whether the artist, like so many others, is merely to reflect the distortions of our time and remain uncommited. In this case the artist tends to increase or reinforce the confusion. Does he, like others, have some responsibility in helping our age find a greater sense of balance and direction? Ideas and attitudes have far-reaching consequences.

The danger of this distorted view of man has been stressed, not only because of its damaging effects on the lives of individuals, but because of its equally undermining effect on our Western doctrines of freedom, democracy, human rights, and conceptions of right and wrong. We shall return to these conceptions later in our text. Philosophy bakes no bread, it is true, but a distorted philosophy can lead to the destruction of a civilization.

IV A Serious Crisis of Belief

We can expand upon the last two points with the idea that civilization is in danger because of a crisis of belief. We have said that a civilization cannot maintain its unity, its social cohesion, its sense of purpose and direction unless a large majority of its people hold certain guiding ideas and ideals. Our troubles spring not from a lack of science, of technical education, or of material equipment, but from a lack of convictions sufficiently strong to sustain a great civilization. The reasons for the crisis of belief are many and the issues are complex, but the following have contributed to this condition.

A High Degree of Specialization and Perhaps Over-Specialization. Specialization has brought many benefits and without it we could not develop a high civilization. Yet there are dangers of which we must be aware. The direction of learning during the past century has been toward specialization in thought as well as in technology. This has meant a fragmentation of knowledge. The result has been that the well-rounded men, the men of broad wisdom, have tended to be replaced with narrow, one-gauge men who easily develop blind spots. Biologists have told us that animals that are too highly specialized tend to become extinct because they cannot adjust to life under changing conditions.

Reductionism. This is the explanation of a whole by some simple unit or units. It is closely related to specialization. One example reduces human personality to physiology and then to physics and chemistry or other "real" aspects. It has been called the "nothing but" attitude: Love is nothing but sex, or mind is nothing but a determined mechanism. Francis Crick in *Of Molecules and Men* says that "the knowledge we have already makes it highly unlikely that there is anything that cannot be explained by physics and chemistry."[20]

Positivism. This outlook accepts as true only that which is disclosed by the positive, objective, or natural sciences. It takes many forms, but in its simplest outlook it accepts only what we see, hear, touch, taste, and smell. If one rejects anything beyond what is discovered by the senses, certain disciplines like ethics, theology, and metaphysics (life views and world views) lose their significance. There is likely to be a loss of a sense of the worth and dignity of the self or person.

Subjectivism. This view is quite different from positivism and asserts that conscious beings and their mental states are all we can affirm. Value statements, according to subjectivism, express feeling and have no independent or objective status; there is nothing right or wrong but thinking or feeling makes it so. Subjectivism and the relativism to which it is related will be discussed in a later chapter.

Irrationalism or the rejection of reason is a characteristic of uncertain times and may arise from various false methods of knowing, but more probably from lack of a balanced education. An upsurge of irrationality and an emphasis on sensuality and excitement are seen in the growing use of narcotics, obsession with sex and perversions of sex, increased gambling, and a growing tendency to regard violence as the solution of problems whether domestic, international, ideological, or political and economic in nature. For many of today's youth as well as for older persons there is a new interest in the occult—in the crystal-ball mediums, astrologers, palmists, phrenologists, numerologists, and gurus. Sales in occult books have risen rapidly, and over seventeen hundred daily newspapers are said to carry astrology columns. Horoscopes can be bought in most drugstores and even in supermarkets.

"Today all groups in our national life," says John W. Gardner, "seem caught up in mutual recriminations. . . . The fissures in our society are

---

[20](Seattle: University of Washington Press, 1966), p. 98.

already dangerously deep. We need greater emphasis on the values that hold us together. . . . Back of every great civilization, behind all the panoply of power and wealth, is something as powerful as it is insubstantial: a set of ideas, attitudes, and convictions—and the confidence that those ideas and convictions are viable. . . . If the light of belief flickers out, then all the productive capacity and all the know-how and all the power of the nation will be as nothing, and the darkness will gather."[21]

While testifying before a joint Senate-House subcommittee early in 1970, Barnaby C. Keeney, former president of Brown University and chairman of the National Endowment for the Humanities, warned Congress that American society is in "real trouble" because of the overwhelming emphasis on science and technology in public life and at every level of education. This imbalance is "dividing the nation, destroying its values, and making it impossible to solve society's most serious problems." The result of this neglect of our system of values means that people "now have no real guide for their lives."[22]

An individual who lacks convictions and who has no reasonable basis for making choices is likely to experience a deep anxiety and a sense of alienation. If he turns inward and becomes concerned with his own identity, the next step may be apathy and an attitude of "I don't care." After that, as an individual or in association with others, he may turn to violence, for many individuals find it difficult to live with the continuous numbing experience of their own powerlessness. Repressed emotion and energy are likely to express themselves negatively and violently if constructive outlets are blocked.

V Institutions Grow Obsolete and Resist Change

A number of our leading institutions, whether political, economic, scientific, educational, or religious, must share a part of the responsibility for the crisis we face. When a group of people have some interest or need in common they organize and set up an institution. It is established for specific purposes, to forward this interest or that, rather than just to do anything that needs to be done or to meet new situations. Usually the end or purpose is a noble one. People in groups and in organizations can do what they would find difficult or impossible to do as separate individuals.

Institutions can become problems and create strain and conflict in society for two reasons: 1) As time goes on they tend to harden or become fixed so that they do not adapt to changing conditions. They

---

[21]"But What of the Dream," *Reader's Digest* 92 (January 1968): 37–41.
[22]*New York Times*, 27 January 1970, pp. 1, 31.

may change and become ends in themselves. Keep in mind that many of our traditional institutions grew up under very simple conditions such as existed in rural societies or under primary group relationships. Today we live in a complex, mechanized, highly interdependent civilization in which our actions affect people far away whom we have never seen. 2) Institutions are affected by faults similar to those we find in individuals. Individuals tend to be selfish or at the very least self-centered. This is a part of human nature. But self-centeredness is especially dangerous in groups and institutions, because selfishness can masquerade under the cloak of loyalty to the institution. A worker, business executive, or a professional man may promote a policy or practice that is detrimental to society at large, while he gets a glow of satisfaction from feeling loyal to his union, trade association, or professional group. Vested interests tend to triumph, and a creative minority gives way to a dominant minority whose interest and effort are to retain its position and prestige. When this happens critics become more numerous and there is a loss of social unity and sometimes open conflict.

All too frequently in the past, progress has had to come by means of bypassing obsolete institutions and dominant classes. Revolutions or deep-rooted changes may be of three types: (1) Changes may be brought about by reason and discussion, such as the changes in England during the nineteenth and twentieth centuries when the country moved from aristocratic to democratic control through a series of legislative measures. (2) Changes may steal up on us like the Renaissance and the industrial revolution. Society today is being radically changed by the men who work unnoticed in the laboratories and by the general knowledge explosion and the population explosion. (3) Changes through violent revolution may come because of stupidity on the one hand and resentment on the other hand, or when there are grave injustices which men have come to feel cannot be eliminated by peaceful and rational means. The American, French, and Russian revolutions were of this type.

In this opening chapter we cannot discuss the specific institutions of society, except to note that great masses of people are frustrated and dissatisfied by political institutions which have so frequently led to conflict and to war, by economic institutions which leave so much poverty in the midst of potential plenty, by ecclesiastical institutions that tend to separate rather than unite people, and by educational institutions that fail to prepare men and women to live in and to defend a free society. Once the home, the school, and the church set the standards for most persons in society. The church now has little time even with those it reaches. The schools tend to leave character development to the homes, and the homes are not measuring up to what was once expected of them. Recently the mass media and the drill sergeant have taken over a part of this function. To assert that violence on the screen and training in the arts of war have not seriously affected the outlook on life, the attitude toward other human beings, and the behavior of young and old in our day, seems to be absurd.

This is an exciting and challenging time to be a young person. For people looking for a cause, there are literally scores of important tasks waiting to be carried out. The challenge is to take the products of human genius, the resources, the knowledge, and the skills that are available and use them so that they will create, not human misery, bitterness, and war, but mature and free persons, human welfare, and lasting peace.

QUESTIONS AND PROJECTS

1. Before reading further in this text or in other books, write out your present judgment as to why right is right. This will stimulate your thinking, and you will find it interesting to compare your answer with answers given later in the text.
2. Keep a section in your notebook for cases or problems in morality that come to your attention or that arise in your own experience. It will sharpen your critical faculties, and it will help link your study with your daily experiences.
3. Think about the age in which you live, then indicate some things (events, trends, and the like) that discourage you, and some things that encourage you or contribute to human welfare. Do you think there is a possibility of remedying, reducing, or altering for the better the discouraging events or trends, and why?
4. Some men have asserted that, as a result of the great scientific and technological changes in the twentieth century, we are being led to think mainly in terms of material things, pleasure, and creature comforts. Indicate whether you think there is any justification for this charge.
5. If men are to plan for the future, they need to know the goals and values to be sought (the priorities), so that they will have some sense of direction. List the goals and values you think should be stressed and be ready to discuss them. Later you may want to revise your list.
6. Is this really one of the best of times in which to be alive? After thinking about this question, you may wish to read Mortimer J. Adler, *The Time of Our Lives: The Ethics of Common Sense*, pt. 4 (New York: Holt, Rinehart & Winston, 1970) in which he has much to say on this question.
7. Review one of the following books: John W. Gardner, *The Recovery of Confidence* (New York: W. W. Norton & Co., 1971); Lewis Mumford, *The Conduct of Life* (New York: Harcourt, Brace & World, 1960); Sir David Ormsby-Gore (Lord Harlech), *Must the West Decline?* (New York: Columbia University Press, 1966); C. P. Snow, *The State of Siege* (New York: Charles Scribner's Sons, 1968); James P. Warburg, *The West in Crisis* (New York: Doubleday & Co., 1959).

SUGGESTED READINGS

Barbour, Ian G. *Science and Secularity: The Ethics of Technology*. New York: Harper & Row, Publishers, 1970.
Booker, Christopher. *The Neophiliacs*. Boston: Gambit, 1970.
Clark, Kenneth. *Civilisation: A Personal View*. New York: Harper & Row, Publishers, 1970.
Drucker, Peter F. *The Age of Discontinuity*. New York: Harper & Row, Publishers, 1968.
Gabor, Dennis. *Inventing the Future*. New York: Alfred A. Knopf, 1969.
Gross, Leonard. *1985: An Argument for Man*. New York: W. W. Norton & Co., 1971.
Hacker, Andrew. *The End of the American Era*. New York: Atheneum Publishers, 1970.
Harrington, Michael. *The Accidental Century*. New York: Macmillan Co., 1965.
Helfrich, Harold W., Jr., ed. *Agenda for Survival: The Environmental Crisis*. New Haven: Yale University Press, 1970.
Johnson, A. H. *Whitehead's Philosophy of Civilization*. Boston: Beacon Press, 1958.
Lifton, Robert Jay. *Boundaries: Psychological Man in Revolution*. New York: Random House, 1970.
Milner, Esther. *The Failure of Success: The Middle-Class Crisis*. St. Louis, Mo.: Warren H. Green, 1970.
Muller, Herbert J. *The Children of Frankenstein: A Primer of Modern Technology and Human Values*. Bloomington: Indiana University Press, 1970.
Mumford, Lewis. *The Myth of the Machine. Techniques and Human Development*. Vol. 1. New York: Harcourt Brace Jovanovich, 1967; *The Pentagon of Power*. Vol. 2, 1970.
Reich, Charles A. *The Greening of America*. New York: Random House, 1970.
Revel, Jean-François. *Without Marx or Jesus*. New York: Doubleday & Co., 1971.
Schlesinger, Arthur M., Jr. *The Crisis of Confidence*. Boston: Houghton Mifflin Co., 1969.
Schweitzer, Albert. *The Philosophy of Civilization*. Translated by C. T. Campion. New York: Macmillan Co., 1949; paperback ed., 1960. Pt. 1, *The Decay and Restoration of Civilization*; pt. 2, *Civilization and Ethics*.
Toffler, Alvin. *Future Shock*. New York: Random House, 1970.
Toppin, Don, ed. *This Cybernetic Age*. New York: Human Development Corp., 1970.
Toynbee, Arnold. *The World and the West*. New York: Oxford University Press, 1953.

part 1
THE SEARCH FOR A MORAL STANDARD

2
STEPS IN ETHICAL INQUIRY

The present, we said in chapter 1, is a time of lost consensus with baffling problems facing us as individuals and as a society. While there have always been disagreements among men, especially between those who look toward the past and those who put their faith in the future, the diversity today is caused in considerable part by the unprecedented rate of change in the areas of both thought and action. People, behavior patterns, and institutions are undergoing strain and change. In such a world some men are sensitive or responsive to the new conditions and seek to adapt to them; other men cling tenaciously to the older creeds, forms, and systems that have been declared final and authoritative by earlier peoples.

THE NECESSITY FOR DECISIONS

This is a time when each individual must make many immediate decisions. Some choices are important and cannot be long delayed, otherwise time or other persons make an individual's decisions for him. Many of our choices cannot be settled on grounds that are free of doubt. The evidence is not complete in any area of experience. For example: Shall I enter business or one of the professions? Shall I marry this person or that one? What are the prospects of my successful marriage? For what courses shall I register in cases where I have a choice? In what school activities shall I participate? To what extent shall I let sports and social engagements cut into my study schedule? At election time (national, state, local, or campus government) for whom shall I vote? I am not even sure of some important facts about the persons up for election, and I do not completely agree with any one of them on all the issues. I must make a choice in which the best of my options is athwart some of my convictions. How can I or should I approach the making of such decisions?

Is the study of ethics or moral philosophy of any use to the person who day by day is facing decisions which, even if not always momentous or unavoidable, add up over a period of time to produce a better or a worse life? We do not want to overstate the benefits to be gained from a limited study of ethics or from a course in the subject; neither do we want to minimize them. The benefits may seem small or difficult to trace, but the matters under consideration are so substantial and crucial that the prospect of even modest improvement in handling them makes the effort worthwhile. In technology we are familiar with the enormous effect which small inventions based on improved knowledge can have. In a similar way ethical inquiry can alter the quality of life.

We think the study of ethics is very important in broadening a man's understanding of the problems he faces, in widening the range of his choices, and in improving the process and steps by which he makes decisions. Such a study should help a person to know just what is involved in the available options and to shape his feelings and commitments in greater agreement with his conscious choices. A harmony of thought and action, and of mind and will is desired. Some choices are of truly great significance: What kind of person do I want to become? What type of life is most worth living? What kind of world do I wish to help come into being?

The problems we face cannot be solved by any one specialty. If satisfactory and long-term solutions are to be found, men of broad knowledge, good will, wisdom, and concern will be required to help—men who come from many different backgrounds and areas of interest: the natural sciences, the social studies, the humanities and the arts, as well as religion and philosophy. One thing seems essential, and that is that men and women today must make commitments and choose the set of values, the moral standards, and the kind of world they wish to preserve. To help them do this more intelligently is part of the task of moral philosophy.

Everyone, we believe, needs a moral philosophy if he is going to be mature and make his own decisions. He needs to build up in himself an understanding and inner control so that he can move from a lack of any adequate personal standards, or from a traditional and static morality where the guides are mostly external, to a more enlightened and mature morality where he acts on the basis of conscious and carefully chosen ends. If the controls are merely external, there may be a tendency to resist or evade them. If the controls are internal and self-chosen, they are followed more easily. If a person does what he does merely because of custom or fear of the law, he is not, in the highest sense, moral.

A personally chosen and consciously held moral philosophy will help one rise above his own group or social milieu and enable him to evaluate critically his own conduct and that of others. Only in this way will he be able to live a consistent and meaningful life in a rapidly changing society.

In order to have any orderly social life, we must have agreements, understandings, principles, or rules of procedure. Ethics seeks the most intelligent principles of behavior, or the principles which will make life most wholesome. In every department of life we develop ways of procedure to which we refer individual cases. Any cooperative group activity is founded upon conventions, customs, and agreements. These may be conscious and very much in evidence, or they may be imbedded in the habits of the members and be unnoticed. Morality must not be a mere matter of inheritance, of convention, of impulse or emotion. Men must come to see the desirability of an authentic morality that is the result of applying their intelligence to the facts of life and human experience.

Judging takes place constantly in the lives of all of us as we are faced with the need to make decisions. Some of our judgments are factual or descriptive statements of qualities or relations: "This stone weighs two pounds." Other judgments are aesthetic in nature: "This picture is beautiful." Still other judgments are moral in nature: "Honesty, self-control, and respect for persons are traits to be cultivated." Valuing occurs almost continuously for most people and is present whenever anything—a physical object, a way of acting, or a person—is preferred or chosen. Some choices are trivial, such as whether we prefer coffee or tea. Others may affect our entire lives, for example, a career or a marriage partner.

Ethics or moral philosophy is traditionally called the study of right and wrong in human conduct, and thus it is concerned with some of the most basic issues of life. The philosopher C. I. Lewis in *The Ground and Nature of the Right* has written: "In all the world and in all of life there is nothing more important to determine than what is right. . . . What is right is thus the question of all questions; and the distinction of right and wrong extends to every topic of reflection and to all that human self-determination of act or attitude may affect."[1]

You had to decide whether or not you were going to college and, if

---

[1](New York: Columbia University Press, 1955), pp. 3–4.

so, which college. It was a choice that may significantly affect the quality of your life and future, even though several options might have been appropriate. Suppose you have an opportunity to secure a position during the summer vacation that will pay practically all your expenses for the coming year. You feel that the work you would be required to do is wrong. You think also that it is the only way you will be able to secure enough money for your expenses. Will you be justified in accepting the position? Here, obviously, is a situation in which you will have to consider what is right. Some decisions are easily made because there is no question as to what is the right thing. Deliberate lying and stealing for instance, are considered to be wrong by practically everyone and in practically every circumstance. And nearly every person would agree that being courteous and friendly is commendable. There are many issues, however, that seem involved and that cannot be decided quickly and easily. What shall be the basis for judgment in such cases? A part of our task is to answer such questions.

Consider, for example, a recent problem which seemed at first to be merely a matter of regulating crowds in a public place but ended by raising issues of law and order and of civil rights. In a developing new town with a lake near the central downtown mall, the lakefront became a favorite gathering place in the evenings and on holidays. Some of those who came were people of various ages just whiling away the time and enjoying the lake and the crowd. Some were young people on drugs and pushers trying to make a buck. Others were from city gangs from nearby urban areas where there were no such pleasant surroundings and where racial discrimination made them unwelcome. A restaurant owner operating adjacent to the lakefront began to complain about offenses by youth—drunkenness, obscene behavior directed toward patrons of the restaurant, and sometimes brawling or assaults.

At about this time some merchants in a nearby county seat were also experiencing a problem with loiterers, though in this case mainly from older panhandlers, petty thieves, and the like. To get relief from the loss of business they thought was being caused by this situation, the merchants pressed for antiloitering legislation which would authorize them and the police to order people off their property and away from the area. The lakefront merchants and the new town development authorities asked that the legislation be extended to apply to the quasi-public open spaces in the new town. Some citizens thereupon protested that these spaces were meant for loitering; that is, for leisure use having nothing to do with conducting business with the merchants. Moreover, they argued, to prohibit loafing around would interfere with the right of assembly, the right of free speech, and the equal right of citizens to the use of public places and places of business open to the public.

This dispute not only confronted the County Council with a decision on policy, but also with a problem in determining the merits of the opposing judgments for the good of the community. If you were a member of the community where would you stand?

There is an ever-present necessity for moral judgments. As previously stated, some acts are almost universally condemned. Other acts receive widespread acclaim. Still others are subjects for discussion and controversy. Wherever human groups are found, some practices are approved and others disapproved. Ideally at least, though not always in practice, actions that are approved are considered beneficial to people in general, and these are called right. The practices that are believed to bring injury to people are called wrong. This problem of conduct, which has been so persistent in the history of the race, has taken the name *morality*. Consciously or unconsciously, men try to discover the kind of life which is most worth living.

Obviously, moral judgments do not apply to all behavior. Such judgments are not ordinarily passed on the happenings or processes of inanimate nature, nor upon the behavior of animals. The exceptions to this will be found in figures of speech, or where nature is personified through poetic imagination. In a more positive sense, moral judgments are applied to the actions of human beings and in particular to their voluntary acts.

We want our choices and moral judgments to follow the well-tested methods of reflective thinking. While we cannot give, even in outline, the principles of logic or discuss the problems of knowledge (epistemology), we do want to follow the basic laws of thought which are discussed in formal logic and the proven methods of drawing conclusions which are illustrated in the sciences and elaborated in treatises on the scientific method.

SIX POSSIBLE METHODS OF APPROACH TO ETHICAL INQUIRY—A SURVEY

For more than two thousand years many of the world's ablest thinkers have sought to improve life, that is, to make it better than it would be if they did not try to improve it. In an effort to gain as much help as possible, let us examine the six methods of building a moral philosophy that have evolved. Even though each of the methods outlined below may be inadequate or incomplete by itself, each one may have some insight and evidence that other approaches may neglect.

First, shall we accept the pronouncement of some external authority and make that regulative for our lives? Some persons and groups proceed by this very simple method. In nearly all fields we do accept the opinions of those whom we regard as more knowledgeable than we are. Probably nine-tenths of what most people believe is accepted on faith or from the testimony of their fellowmen. Our knowledge of the solar system and of the structure of the earth or the moon is based on the word of astronomers, geologists, or other authorities. The average man's knowledge of health and disease comes largely from the medical profession and other specialists. He is also likely to accept much pseudo-knowledge, such as "old wives' tales," and his friend's anecdotes about similar cases ("I knew a man who had the same trouble, and he . . .").

The appeal to authority is a method of approach used by some people today and by many people in the past. Is the acceptance of some external authority the method we should use in building a personal moral philosophy? We shall return to this question in the next chapter and ask when the appeal to authority is justified and when it is not justified.

Second, since our morals, like our language and social institutions, are the product of long periods of development and adaptation to changing environmental conditions, shall we place the emphasis on what is known as *descriptive ethics,* that is, on a study of the history of moral standards? This second available step in ethical inquiry involves considering past experience with decisions and choices similar to the ones with which we want help. This mode of inquiry is implicit already in the use of authorities, who derive that status in part from their supposed knowledge of this history of good and bad practice. A direct inquiry into the history of policies, institutions, and social practices can sometimes throw additional light on current decisions. Unfortunately the study of the history of "morals" has in the past been misdirected often by its concentration upon a much narrower or different range of issues of right and wrong than, for example, that broad range of conduct we recognize in this book as crucial for the quality of life. Also, those who have studied past morals have sometimes approached the inquiry assuming that the past practice was likely to be the best practice drawn from a "golden age" of morality.

Instead, we propose that inquiry into past practice is more likely to enlighten current decisions if we focus upon questions such as: To what particular environmental circumstances was this pattern an adaptation? What assumptions about value and obligation were taken for granted as a basis for this practice? What effects in the cultural and institutional life of the time did this combination of practice and circumstance create? This type of inquiry has recently become a matter of great interest among anthropologists and other social scientists. They seek to understand how people, both past and present, feel, think, and behave in different social and physical environments. Their researches can thus help us to understand present questions, even though they always require judgment in synthesizing the experience of the past with the aspirations of today.

In trying to use a knowledge of past moral practice and experience, we may fall into a habit of thinking of primitive man as morally inferior to modern man. Surely early men knew less of the content of our science and technology than do we. They were also presumably less aware of alternative outlooks and therefore of their own unquestioned framework of belief than are we. It does not follow that they were necessarily less mature individuals, or that we have now eliminated the danger of falling victim to unquestioned values or beliefs, or that relative to what they knew they made less astute or well-considered judgments. They certainly had fewer options, in part because of the limitations of resources and knowledge available to them, and possibly as well because of their hesitancy or hostility to the inclusion of as large a circle of mankind within their primary circle of concern. Because of the complexity of judgments and conduct about ethical issues, however, we continue to embody a strange mixture of the "primitive" and the "mature" in our social and individual conduct. Some men continue to try to apply to present problems solutions which worked earlier under different conditions, but which do not apply to current conditions or do not satisfy the enlarged moral consciousness of living men. Some of these anomalies of practice and judgment are more easily understood if seen in the light of the history of morality.

A third step that may help in ethical inquiry is that of asking what light can be thrown upon our choices by a study of ethical theories propounded in the past. This step can suggest alternative standards by which to evaluate the choices open to us, and it can draw upon historic controversy about these theories to show us the merits of different standards. For example, in discussing the bussing of school children to achieve racial integration or the equality of educational opportunity, which of the following options would be most helpful: the standard of custom, a criterion as to the effect of each option upon the "happiness" of different numbers of people, or a criterion of the bearing of the alternative statutes upon the fulfillment of the individual? Or are none of these theories very helpful to such a decision? In his book *Ethics for Policy Decisions*[2] Wayne Leys translated each of a number of historically important ethical theories into a set of questions the asking of which would help evaluate alternative policies. We believe that this treatment of ethical theory is not only valuable for clarifying the

---

[2](New York: Greenwood Press, 1968).

merits of social policies, but also for testing the adequacy of ethical standards. If our most crucial choices and policies in life are to be guided by some comprehensive set of standards as to what constitutes a full and good life, then it is of critical importance that this set of standards include all that enters into the good life, that it be manageably clear in its applicability to the choices we will face, and that it not be marred by internal contradictions among the standards.

In this book we will study, then, the history of ethical theories with an eye to their usefulness to the inquirer who would apply them to his choices. Of what use to this purpose, for example, is Socrates' admonition "Know thyself" or his thesis that "Knowledge is virtue"? Such statements certainly do not indicate a clear result in our effort to decide whether the dangers of air pollution justify a substantial raise in taxes in order to police polluters. It is, on the other hand, a common error of people having trouble with their job supervisors or facing divorce that they have not adequately understood their own personality, psychological needs, and behavior patterns and how these offend or affect other people. Socrates probably had in mind inquiries in self-understanding that were familiar in his own time rather than the kind which modern psychology and sociology enable us to make. He would surely wonder in our time, if he were here, whether in our rush to acquire possessions and entertain ourselves, we are reflecting an understanding of what is most fundamental to the fulfillment of our lives.

The history of ethical theory is not altogether a story of great admonitions and wise pronouncements about the nature of good and evil, right and wrong, or methods of ethical judgment. Some of the great figures in that history have been skeptics about these same wise sayings. Their questions have survived because they were correctives of earlier over-simplifications. What is good and right is not a simple matter. In the rush to get the answers on such important matters, it is easy to close the questions too quickly. In what follows we will seriously consider questions starting with those of the early Greek skeptics through those of Hume to those of twentieth century logical positivists, linguistic analysts, ethical relativists, and emotivists.

Also available in the history of ethical theory are the reflections of thinkers who came upon their ethical ideas as implications of a religious outlook—Taoist, Confucian, Hindu, Buddhist, Jewish, Christian, Islamic, and so on. Currently there are numerous people, both sectarian and ecumenical in outlook, who seek to bring such viewpoints to bear helpfully upon the most distressing of contemporary moral issues. We will ask how these seekers can throw light upon not only particular current issues and policies but upon the endeavor to develop an adequate set of ethical standards.

The study of the history of ethics has in the past often been an exercise in futility for anyone seeking help for today's decisions. The preoccupation has been with what men of other times thought and with haggling about nuances of interpretation which are unresolvable with the evidence in hand. What we propose here seems to us both to take these men more seriously and at the same time to be less captive of their times, their preoccupations, and their outlooks. If, as we believe, they were able inquirers and did indeed discover some things about values and right, then we can save ourselves mistakes by learning what they discovered. If, as we also believe, they got only part way through the enormous task of understanding the potential of life, and furthermore lived in times of less scientific information, of different technology, of smaller population and more isolated cultures, then we must take care not to misapply what they knew. We will try to see both of these sides of their searchings.

A fourth line of inquiry in ethical studies is that of clarifying questions, meanings, and issues by the analysis of language and usage. This type of inquiry has been given great attention by English-speaking philosophers in the twentieth century, though it was also more or less explicitly a part of a number of the earlier traditions which we treat in the history of ethical theory. In this book we do not treat ethical theory as identical with linguistic analysis of the terms, relations, and operations of discourse about matters of right and wrong, good and bad, in human conduct. However, the effort to be clear about what we are saying (for example, "cruelty is wrong") can, we think, contribute to ethical understanding and thereby in time to improvement in human choices. Does the statement "cruelty is wrong" merely express a dislike, make an entreaty, give a command, or assert something that can be shown to be true or false? A. J. Ayer suggested that confusion on these questions was causing people to block fruitful inquiry and impose meaningless and unverifiable conclusions upon one another. Getting the questions straight, on the other hand, is only a step toward getting some kind of answers to them or arriving at some basis for deciding when there can be no adequate answers. The analysis of language and usage will serve as only one of the modes of inquiry essential to the purpose of this study.

A fifth mode of inquiry concerning questions about how to do better or to know and to meet obligations is that of scientific or factual investigation. To what extent or in what respects, we will ask, can we resolve ethical issues by applying the strategies of research common to the physical and social sciences? For example, should a certain type of drug be used in a particular way to treat Parkinson's disease in a particular patient? Given that the parties deciding this issue are in agreement about what they mean to achieve (survival, tolerable unwanted side effects, etc.), the question can be decided by laboratory and clinical investigation. Suppose, however, that the question involves building a nuclear power plant on Calvert Cliffs overlooking Chesapeake Bay. Such a plant would affect many diverse interests of different groups of people. There would be risks of radiation accidents and there would be heat pollution of the waters of the bay. If the plant is not built, there will be either power shortages or more expensive measures to supply power with different consequences in pollution of other types affecting different neighbors. The dispute in this case will turn in part upon the relative value placed by different people upon the dangers of pollution on the one hand and the advantages of enormous power resources on the other. Straightforward scientific research on the physical, chemical, and biological aspects of this question will not wholly resolve the issue.

In this last example, is it possible to apply to the differences of opinion some form of sociological or psychological research as to who wants what and how many hold similar opinions? Certainly such research is feasible. But it raises a further question: By what criterion should one determine what is right or best if perhaps eighty percent of the respondents would favor the development of nuclear power and twenty percent oppose the risk of cataclysmic radiation accident? This does not appear to be a question resolvable by factual investigation of the sort that the sciences do.

A knowledge of science and its findings is important in making moral judgments. Science gives us a knowledge of the world and discloses causal sequences. All action, and this includes moral conduct, takes place in the world of our everyday affairs. If circumstances alter cases (a topic to be discussed later), moral judgments need to take account of the circumstances under which men live. Moral judgments can be made intelligently only when accurate knowledge is available of the effects of action, conditions, things, and the like on human life and conduct. Students of ethics need to recognize the relevance of facts disclosed by the sciences, especially the facts regarding human nature and the influence of environmental, biological, psychological, and social conditions on human behavior. The traditional morality did not recognize these conditions, or at least did not take them seriously into account.

Guidance about facts of the situation is important, but this is not, by itself, moral guidance. Scientific judgments differ from moral judgments. A scientific judgment is always about what is, was, or will be, given certain conditions. It enlarges the scope and possibility of human action but, except in purely technical questions where the end to be sought is given, it does not by itself prescribe or tell men what they ought to do. Science describes and is ethically neutral. A moral judgment, on the other hand, is always about what I, or perhaps people in general, ought to do or to be. It includes a value judgment that is implicit if not always clearly stated. After a person has acquired all the available knowledge of the facts, he still has to decide how he ought to use this knowledge—to save life or to kill, to preserve the beauties of nature or to lay waste a countryside for commercial gain. To identify scientific with moral judgments is to confuse the two fields.

A sixth mode of inquiry in ethics is that of focusing upon quite specific current issues of great social importance and using those as "test cases." While some specific case may prove undecidable, its investigation can throw light upon what is involved in answering an ethical question, what can be done with cases that are not clearly resolvable, and how in the long run they can be brought to resolution. The study of current issues has the advantage of being of immediate interest to many people and the further advantage that many of them may have prior knowledge which can be brought to bear upon the study. This type of inquiry also requires that precept and practice be brought together. Finally, it makes abundantly clear that a moral problem is never just a moral problem. It is also a problem of personal or domestic relations; of sports, business, or professional affairs; of international relations; or the like. This mode of study prevents a meaningless concentration upon abstractions which are left unrelated to life and practice. There is something seriously wrong with ethical inquiry or with a moral philosophy which, in an age such as ours, gives no help in attending to problems of race relations, the population explosion, war and peace, sexual relations and marriage, or business, professional, and political conduct.

An adequate strategy of ethical inquiry will, we think, incorporate the advantages of each of the six modes of inquiry just discussed. To confine attention exclusively to the moral philosophers of the past or to concentrate on technical questions and the analysis of language alone appears inadequate, at least in introductory studies for the general reader. While some particular ethical questions may be resolved by the use of a single mode of inquiry, the overall strategy must include ways of deciding what method or methods will best function with the particular problem we face.

A COMPREHENSIVE AND COMMON-SENSE APPROACH

The approach of this text, as the preceding paragraph indicates, is not confined to any one of the six possible approaches just sketched but draws insights from each. Our approach is comprehensive, synthetic, or integrative and, we hope, balanced, in that the aim is to examine man's moral experience as a whole in so far as this appears possible. We begin with human experience and with what to us is a common-sense approach. This outlook is not new, but it is one that needs emphasis in this day of a high degree of specialization with corresponding limited points of view. It attempts to study some aspirations that seem almost universal. Men everywhere want certain things and dislike or condemn other things. There is a vast difference between just living and living well.

There are times when we need to appeal to authority, especially in those situations where our experience is limited and where we know that others have information and insight not readily available to us. But here we need to proceed with caution. We expect to gain information about the nature of morality through a brief examination of the long story of the development of morality and the behavior of peoples past and present. The great ethical theories of the moral philosophers can sharpen our thinking and bring to our attention questions which might otherwise escape us. The analysts have taught us to be more careful in the use of language, and this has made us aware of some mistakes into which we easily fall. The natural sciences can furnish many facts that need to be taken into account as we formulate moral judgments and make decisions. After considering all this information and clarifying our moral principles, we need to apply our insights to the pressing personal and social problems of today. Following this order, therefore, part 1 of this text discusses the nature of morality, whereas part 2 deals with applied ethics.

The comprehensive, common-sense approach which brings together the quest for truth and the concern for human welfare is not a radical departure from the outlook of many of the outstanding moral philosophers East and West.

Throughout the centuries higher education in the Western world as well as in Oriental civilization has been motivated by two main impulses. First is the desire to know for its own sake. This is the quest for truth: "to seek knowledge and yet more knowledge." Sometimes this urge has the legitimate desire of mainly satisfying one's curiosity. Sometimes there is the questionable assumption that if knowledge is accumulated, it will inevitably be used for good ends. Second is the concern for the good life, the full life, and the welfare of the community. This is the desire to improve man's life through the wise use of his knowledge and skills.

These two impulses, the desire to know and concern for the welfare of the person and the community, existed side by side in Graeco-Roman culture. Most of the great thinkers and leaders, from Plato, Aristotle, and the Hebrew prophets and scholars to Dewey and Whitehead, have insisted that formulation of a moral ideal, or some aim that transcends knowing merely for its own sake, is essential to the education and development of free men. During the early Christian and medieval periods, education was organized within a Christian framework and world view. A study of the charters and declarations of aim of the early universities in Europe and America makes it clear that knowledge was not merely for its own sake but for the enrichment of man's life through the professions and other activities. That is, there was a dual quest for truth and for goodness through the cultivation of character and the growth of concern for the common good. There has sometimes been a tension between these two impulses. The Greeks tended to stress the intellectual, man as a thinking being, though interest in man and the good society was never absent. The Hebrews tended to stress righteousness and man's relation to his fellowman and to God. In both Chinese and Hindu thought, the aim of studying philosophy is not merely to gain knowledge for its own sake, or just to satisfy one's curiosity, but to discover and to live the highest and richest life, which brings permanent satisfaction. In the West, culture and educational institutions have been most healthy and have moved forward more consistently when and where these two impulses have found harmonious expression.

In the West, the two impulses have fostered formal education, especially in its higher branches. During the last hundred years, however, they have been growing apart, or rather, the second impulse, the concern for values, has been neglected in many educational institutions and in society in general. The pursuit of knowledge either for its own sake or merely for its immediate practical utility has been encouraged and strengthened by a number of trends including the following: (1) The increasing departmentalization and specialization of knowledge that has accompanied the multiplication of new subjects and the introduction of a large number of new courses in all educational institutions. (2) The separation of many of the older colleges and universities from their church connections and the rapid rise of state and municipal institutions of learning with emphasis on "useful" and vocational training. A hundred years ago moral philosophy, biblical studies, or other courses in religion were required in most colleges and universities. Now probably more than ninety percent of college students go from matriculation to graduation without any study of moral standards. (3) Funds available for research have been heavily weighted on the side of the physical sciences and the immediately useful. For example, in the sixties in the United States, about seventy percent of federal expenditures for research went to the physical sciences; about twenty-six percent to biology, medicine, and agriculture; about two percent to the psychological sciences; one percent to the social studies; and practically nothing to the humanities. This is leading to a dangerous imbalance of emphasis in many institutions of higher education. Furthermore, many courses in general literature have changed in outlook and tone from a positive attempt to stimulate high standards of living to a tendency to be cynical about all standards.

We need an education in which facts and values, critical analysis and concern for human welfare, the sciences and the humanities develop hand in hand. If there is a great imbalance and the emphasis is largely on "truth for truth's sake," in which objectivity and neutrality alone are stressed, scholars may refuse to commit themselves on any issue and "practical men" may come to prize knowledge only if it leads to a job and a higher income. When this condition exists, the civilization is in danger.

Morality is the attempt to discover the nature of the good life and then to live it. The task of this book is to seek those attitudes, ways of living, and principles which enable men to live at their best in their personal lives and in their community relationships. This is a task that the individual will face throughout his life. While gaining help from all the six approaches set forth above, a mature and reflective morality is one which the individual person accepts and understands, and one for which he can give good reasons. In the succeeding chapters we attempt to think together in the hope that each reader will work out for himself a moral philosophy by which he can live.

QUESTIONS AND PROJECTS

1. Before proceeding further in your reading, you need to clarify the meaning and use of certain frequently used terms such as *morals, ethics, right, good,* and *value.* Consult the *Glossary* which begins inside the front cover of the book and is continued inside the back cover.
2. When the word *moral* is used, what do many persons take it to mean? Do you find the term used in ways other than those given in this chapter? For example, what do some court officials mean when they talk about a "morals case"?
3. Is there any difference morally between a disapproved action in which you are caught and the same action that never becomes public? Do many persons in our society make a distinction between these two situations? How do you explain this difference in attitude?
4. In your opinion which of the following are issues of moral concern, and why?
    (1) Driving faster than the speed limit.
    (2) Driving your car with defective brakes.
    (3) Eating food your doctor has advised you to avoid.
    (4) Wearing a loud necktie that does not match your other clothes.

(5) Writing your initials or name on public monuments.
(6) Voting at election time.
(7) Using torture in an attempt to get a prisoner to talk.
5. In this chapter we have said that there is an ever-present necessity for making moral decisions or moral judgments. Consider the following cases or problems. Think over each carefully. Then decide what is the right thing to do in each case, and why.
  (1) A young woman who is a domestic servant in a family comes to see the local physician. He finds that she is suffering from a communicable skin disease. If the family is informed, she will undoubtedly lose her position. She is unwilling to make the facts known. Is it the doctor's duty to tell her employer?
  (2) The members of the executive board of a corporation are anxious to show larger earnings for their company, which is now making moderate profits. They control most of the milk supply and hence the price of milk in the city in which they do business. They are contemplating raising the price of milk two cents a quart. While this will mean greater profits, it will also mean a reduced consumption of milk in the city. One of their members who does not favor the proposed action points out that the higher price and the reduced consumption of milk will mean that some babies will die who otherwise would live. Should the decision be influenced by considerations of social welfare or only by those of business interests?
  (3) As part of the condition for attendance at a particular college, a student has agreed to abide by college regulations and be law-abiding, yet on one issue he now feels strongly that the local law is wrong and incompatible with the national constitution. On another issue he agrees with the law, but is disturbed because the law is not being enforced by the local authorities. Is he justified in either case in joining a "sit-in" or a protest march if such action has been forbidden by the city council or by court action?
  (4) In a community in which there is much unnecessary noise that disturbs many people, the city council is considering passing an anti-noise ordinance. Some people say that this action would interfere with their personal freedom. Do you think it right or wrong to pass laws of this type?

SUGGESTED READINGS

Adler, Mortimer J. *The Time of Our Lives: The Ethics of Common Sense.* New York: Holt, Rinehart and Winston, 1970.

Aiken, Henry David. *Reason and Conduct: New Bearings in Moral Philosophy.* New York, Alfred A. Knopf, 1962.

Burtt, Edwin A. *In Search of Philosophic Understanding.* New York: New American Library of World Literature, 1965; Mentor Book, MY765, 1966.

Cahn, Edmond. *The Moral Decision: Right and Wrong in the Light of American Law.* Bloomington: Indiana University Press, 1955.

Caws, Peter. *Science and the Theory of Value.* New York: Random House, 1967.

Frankena, William. *Ethics.* Englewood Cliffs, N.J.: Prentice-Hall, 1963.

Hudson, W. D. *Modern Moral Philosophy.* New York: Macmillan Co., 1970.

Hyde, W. DeWitt. *The Five Great Philosophies of Life.* New York: Collier Books, 1961.

Lewis, Clarence Irving. *The Ground and Nature of the Right.* New York: Columbia University Press, 1955.

Leys, Wayne A. R. *Ethics for Policy Decisions.* Westport, Conn.: Greenwood Press, 1968.

Means, Richard L. *The Ethical Imperative: The Crisis in American Values.* Garden City, N.Y.: Doubleday & Co., 1969.

Rice, Philip Blair. *On the Understanding of Good and Evil.* New York: Random House, 1955.

Sprague, Elmer. *What Is Philosophy?* New York: Oxford University Press, 1961.

Stace, W. T. *The Concept of Morals.* New York: Macmillan Co., 1962; paperback reprint, 1962.

3
THE DEVELOPMENT OF MORALITY

The person who disregards or does not know the past is likely to repeat the mistakes of the past; he is also likely to fail to understand the nature of the problem he is studying. This is especially true in the area of morality because moral standards grow out of the conditions under which men live. The origin and development of morality is closely connected with the general development of social life and social institutions. Wherever human beings live there are decisions to be made, right and wrong ways of acting, and problems of conduct. Wherever people live in orderly social life there are agreements, understandings, and regulations of some sort backed by the approval of the group. The regulations, however, have varied from time to time and from place to place, as we shall see.

EARLY GROUP LIFE AND CUSTOMARY MORALITY

The question "When did morality begin?" cannot be answered with any finality because our morals, like our language and our social life, are the product of long periods of development and of adaptation to changing needs and environmental conditions. But we can assume that morality was not at first the outcome of a conscious thought process; its rudiments were perhaps of prehuman origin. Among animal social groups we find the rudiments of such social virtues as self-sacrifice, sympathy, mutual aid, and cooperation.

Thus when man became man, there were probably well-established ways of doing things which primitive man very naturally followed. Such uniform ways of acting are called *customs*. Customs are passed from generation to generation by imitation and by precept. Students of group life agree that the individual is almost completely submerged in the life of the group. The individual's ways of acting, feeling, and thinking are controlled by the group. Men tend to do the things that the group they respect expects them to do. What is custom in the group becomes habit in the individual.

Customs ordinarily arise out of the needs of human life under specific conditions. The first demand of life is to continue to live. Human beings begin to live with acts, not with thoughts and theories—these emerge later. Men need food, drink, shelter, protection from enemies of various kinds, and the like. Since most needs are common needs, there is considerable similarity in the behavior patterns of peoples living at the same general level of culture. Regulations grow up regarding the food supply, patterns of mating, and ways of making a living, of dealing with friends and foes, and of coping with sickness, old age, and death. A group that does not satisfy these and other basic needs may cease to exist. There are significant agreements as well as differences in the ways of meeting these needs.

Some customs arise because of special incidents, historical accidents, or peculiar conditions. For example, some customs regarding food and clothing arise from geographical conditions. Customs tend to represent the funded experience of men in the past who live under these special conditions. They save time and energy in that they are ready-made programs of action and adjustment. As an integrating force in the life of the group, they tend to promote satisfaction and moral goodness. To act contrary to the customary mode of conduct in a community, especially for the young or the inexperienced, is to incur serious risk of injury to one's person or career. Custom is one basis by which the moral life of the individual is sustained and developed. It often preserves a certain unformulated wisdom that has accumulated in society. For thoughtful and informed people, however, it is not the standard for a distinction between right and wrong, as we shall see later.

The early group was a kinship group—a family, clan, or tribe—whose members believed that they had sprung from a common ancestor or ancestors. The ancestor was usually believed to be a god, some hero, or even an animal (as in a totem group). Birth into such a group usually determined for early man his standing in life. It determined where he was to live, how he was to make his living, the group or groups from which he must take his wife, what religious ceremonies he must observe, and the way in which he was to be ruled. The early kindred group was an economic, political, religious, and moral unit.

Students of early group life agree that in such societies, a person's rights and responsibilities are fixed by the group of which he is a part. As an individual apart from the group he has no rights or privileges that anyone is bound to respect. Within his own kinship group, if he breaks the tribal code, he is treated more or less as an individual; but aside from this he stands as a member of the group. In dealing with outsiders, the primitive group is a unit. If a member is killed or injured, his group holds the group of the offender responsible. It may demand satisfaction or the life of the offender. In such cases, if the offender's group defends him or offers resistance, a blood feud may be started. Thus, there is joint responsibility and mutual support.

The fact of joint responsibility and rigid social solidarity is well illustrated by numerous accounts that have come down to us from earlier times. The story of Achan as told in the Old Testament is probably the best known. When Achan sinned, not only Achan but his kin, his herds, and all his possessions were destroyed. Similar accounts are available from nearly all primitive groups of which we have records.

Each primitive group feels that it is superior to all other peoples. This helps explain its lack of a sense of obligation toward outsiders. If other people are inferior, perhaps not even real men, why should there be any obligation to respect them? Ethnocentrism (regarding one's racial or ethnic group as the center of culture) seems to be a common human trait. Each group tends to think that it is the center of the world and therefore that its own folkways are right.

The system in which moral standards are based on customs accepted without reflection is called *customary morality* or *group morality*. This system was especially prevalent among kinship groups. Among all peoples, ancient and modern, the power of custom is strong in the determination of conduct. And early man showed very little tendency to guide conduct on the basis of a consciously chosen ideal of life.

In the stage of customary morality, there are certain acts which are almost universally forbidden, such as murder, especially of the members of one's group; cruelty to and neglect of offspring; and disloyalty to the group. There are certain acts that are almost universally required, such as parental care, respect for the life of one's fellowmen, loyalty to one's group, and some curbing of the sexual impulse. Among all groups we find some regulation concerning the proper relations of the sexes and marriage. These regulations vary widely, however, and they operate through custom and habit and not by edict or conscious choice on the part of most members of the group.

Customs arise in various ways, as we have seen. In order to live, men must adjust themselves to one another and to the situations in which they find themselves. Out of these needs of life develop habits in the individual and customs in the group. Once these customs are formed, they are passed on from parents to children by instruction, imitation, and tradition, and they become a powerful societal force. Changes in custom come when strain appears. At such times conscious reflection on the part of some members of the group may lead to a search for ways to remove the strain and possible conflict. These changes are ordinarily in the direction of better adaptations to the conditions and purposes of life.

The strength of customary or group morality is its tendency to develop a stable character that functions with little friction in a relatively unchanging environment. Under such conditions, customs give what the sociologist calls "a definition of the situation." The average man and weaker individuals are held in line. Customs that have come from the past are to be accepted, not because they are old and venerable, but because they are felt to serve the needs of living generations. When many routine affairs can be left to custom and habit, there is less strain and man can turn his attention to other issues. The problem, however, is that social conditions are never entirely static. Some change is always taking place.

In the twentieth century widespread and rapid changes are occurring, and the inadequacies of customary morality are very evident. Such morality tends to formalism, literalism, and an emphasis on a fixed scheme of "Do's" and "Don'ts." Its appeal is to an external standard rather than to the development of understanding and self-control. With changing conditions, it may be so ill adapted to the needs of life that harm may result. To take custom alone as the standard submerges the individual in his society to a greater degree than experience has shown compatible with the greatest good of the individual and society. While the average man may be held in line, the exceptional man, who might forge ahead into new and better ways, is kept behind.

Moral evolution has moved in the direction of increasing emancipation of the individual from the control of his culture. The fact that a majority, or even all, of the members of a group declare an action right or wrong does not make it so. While customs and moral demands often coincide, to accept all social customs as moral obligations and to recognize no duties except those laid down by the group is to surrender the main task of morality. Progress has come in large part through the individual's challenging the customary actions and ideals of his group. If there are good customs and bad customs, then custom cannot be the standard of right and wrong.

Nor can customary morality tell us what to do in novel situations. While there are usually some areas of life in which custom speaks clearly and accurately, indicating what is best for the individual and members of the group, there are other areas, usually the new ones, in which it does not give any clear guidance. For example, when does a pilot flying his plane trespass on one's property? If custom alone is the standard, does this mean that there are no standards or principles that apply in this situation or in other new situations, such as the introduction of thermonuclear energy and the use of atomic bombs? Does it mean that the pattern set by the first users of these devices sets the custom and is then an adequate guide to others?

A moral code that is satisfactory must provide for criticism and for some form of revision under changing conditions. Customs grow up under all sorts of irrational influences, including chance, historical accidents, and superstitions; under the pressure of human needs; and sometimes through human reflection. Reflection is one form of revising custom, but custom by itself has no way of settling issues when conflicts arise. A conflict may occur when more than one custom—each implying different judgments—is thought to apply to the same dispute. For example, industrial disputes arise when the same act is considered insubordination from the point of view of managers, but obedience to the rules of health from the point of view of the employees. In such a case custom often does not supply a way of deciding the outcome, and so industries provide a mechanism of arbitration or mediation to settle the matter. This solution amounts to supplementing an ineffective custom with a reflective process.

Conflicts may also arise when the prevailing custom in a small community (village, town, state) differs from that in a larger community (state, nation, and the like). To speak of custom at all is to refer implicitly to a group or society whose custom it is. The fact that each small community is part of a larger one creates the possibility that conflict may arise between local, national, and international precedents and common practices.

An example of this type of conflict in the United States in the 1960s and 1970s is the issue of racial segregation and desegregation. The prevailing pattern is that children of all races attend the same schools in their districts; but a different pattern has prevailed in some areas. The fact that the issue required the use of legal means illustrates the inadequacy of custom to deal with this particular discrepancy between local and nonlocal customs. Such discrepancy is not always settled by having the larger community's habits overrule the smaller. Sometimes it is decided to let different customs prevail in different regions. Thus, in many large countries today, it is viewed as desirable to encourage diversity of language, arts, and even requirements of decorum and good conduct in different provinces as long as these diversities do not adversely affect fundamental rights. To reach this policy, however, requires a standard or procedure other than adherence to custom itself.

An important difference between primitive and modern man is that, when necessary, modern man may critically examine the customs of his day and modify them in the light of experience and reflection. Only in the later and higher stages of morality do moral judgments come to take an important place in modifying customs and external conditions. Conceptions like morality, duty, and right and wrong were late in appearing.

While primitive man was rather completely bound by the customs of the tribe or group of which he was a part, modern man is likely to belong to a number of groups. He is born into a family, but he may leave it as he grows older. He may choose his own vocation, wife, place of residence, and friends as well as his religion and political affiliation. He may rent or buy a home of his own and will it to a person or persons of his own choosing. He may travel abroad and even change his national allegiance. But while modern man, in comparison with primitive man, is free to a considerable extent from the type of stifling group restrictions that tend to retard the development of individuality, he is apparently still bound too much by custom. Too large a part of our present morality depends on where we were born or reared and not on principles that will stand up under critical examination. Patriotic allegiance, the attitude toward property, marriage, other racial groups, and standards of personal honor are set for us largely by our social circle and by the trade and professional groups of which we are a part.

STATUTORY LAW

In early society customs are all-pervasive, or at least predominant. With the growth of society, custom is forced to share its influence with other guides to conduct. One of these is statutory law.

While the influence of custom has continued to be strong from an early period to the present, as population increases and society changes and becomes more complex, custom alone is not enough. Laws are formulated and promulgated officially that either crystallize previous customs and make them more specific or change them to meet new conditions.

The historical development from custom to statutory law may take place in the following manner. Conflicts between kinship groups or tribes may continue until some leader succeeds in gaining control of an entire area. He may refuse to relinquish his power after the conflict has ceased, thus becoming the ruler. He may even succeed in establishing his family in power as the royal family. As he gathers military and civil aides about him, a nobility, as distinct from the common people, comes into existence. If there are captives or conquered peoples, they may be forced to occupy the position of slaves, serfs, or low-caste persons.

Gradually the decrees of the ruler and his court, or of some lawmaking body, take their place along with customs in the conduct of affairs. The distinction between what must be done and what must not be done is clearly and specifically stated, and definite penalties are specified for violations of the law. The law consists of those regulations which are laid down and enforced by the rulers or by the people through their elected representatives: the government. A law defines a situation and aims at making uniform the conduct of all members of society. When a law is clear and reasonable in its demands, most persons support it.

In democratic societies, law tends to follow and reflect the growing moral consciousness and the opinion of the majority (or of the most vocal group) in the society. However, it also tends to lag behind that consciousness. Furthermore, the law does not cover all cases of conflict, personal or social, that arise. At least in a rapidly changing society, laws become antiquated and reform is needed. If the courts interpret and decide new cases on the basis of precedent, as they frequently do today, the law will tend, as time goes on, to embody the policy of the past rather than the mature judgments of living men.

In contemporary society, law is a far more refined guide than custom. First, the scope of applicability of elements of the law (constitutions, statutes, precedents, the discretion of judges, and so on) is more carefully defined. The definitions of offenses and of appropriate awards and punishments are clearer than is generally the case with custom. There is provision for decision procedures for cases that are not specifically defined in statutes; courts of equity and courts of appeal are available for different types of difficulties in interpreting and applying the law. The people who decide and the procedures for deciding different types of issues are many and must therefore be defined more explicitly, precisely, and systematically. These characteristics of law tend to give it greater impartiality than custom provides.

But the claim that law supplies an adequate standard for all ethical conduct is rarely, if ever, seriously made by a legal scholar. While there are different philosophies of the nature and functions of law, students of jurisprudence generally hold that law is only one of the elements involved in defining what ought to be done in society. The questions as to what the precise functions of the law ought to be and how well they are being discharged are issues in social ethics that are not fully answered by law itself. We can give some guidance on these points, however.

Law will not pretend to say how friends can best conduct their friendship; it will say only that certain kinds of exploitation are not permitted between friends—or any persons. In our culture the law refrains from intervening in the internal affairs of churches. Our legal position is that the state and the church are to be separate in these respects, and the state intervenes in church affairs only in exceptional circumstances. In other cultures this question is decided differently.

There are some matters in which the law attempts only a rough approximation of justice, not because this is thought to be ideal, but for other reasons: (1) It may be contrary to public interest to encourage people to bring cases to court merely to get a small refinement on the degree of justice they could obtain without such costly litigation. (2) Sometimes to make a more refined judgment would require elaborate investigation and even then would produce uncertain results. (3) Some relationships cannot be made ideal by enforcement—for example, the courts will not enjoin the continuance of a personal service contract when one party is adamant, because the whole point of the relation depends on its being voluntarily and mutually carried out. While it may be argued that in such cases the courts do prescribe the best course of action possible in view of the litigants' attitudes and behavior, for the great majority of cases the standard is found, and ought to be found, independently of courts and law.

The law represents a refinement on the total body of custom in several respects. It often provides procedures for settling novel cases, even though it does not provide a definition of the content of right action. It gives, so to speak, a procedural definition of right. Like custom, however, it does not provide procedures for all novel cases. Consider, for example, the question of how peace-keeping operations by police forces of the United Nations ought to be instituted and supported. While conflicting precedents, conflicting dicta, and conflicting judgments are rendered by different legal bodies, the law often provides means of getting an authoritative decision. The law, as compared with custom, provides a better systematized "memory" for the reasons for the judgments it provides and thus for determination of new cases on relevant grounds. In many matters the law gives the clearest available guidance to wise conduct—for example, the considerations to weigh and the forms of definitions to use in making a will or in establishing responsible management of a trust.

In a changing industrial society a constant and complex set of interactions go on that we cannot discuss in detail. The courts apply the law not only to clear cases that come before the judges, but also to cases calling for new interpretations of the law. In this way we get an expansion of the law through judicial decisions. From time to time legislators reexamine the adequacy or inadequacy of current laws and make such changes as appear advisable.

In many matters our legal institutions and practices provide a clarity, consistency, impartiality, and economy in the making of ethical judgments that are lacking in custom. However, when a dispute arises as to whether in any of these respects or in its overall rendering of justice its task is adequately done, the law cannot be the standard by which its own merits are appraised. This is no depreciation of law. It is no more than the observation that law is but one of the instruments of ethical endeavor. Morality is more than legality.

THE APPEAL TO EXTERNAL AUTHORITY

Before we leave the fields of custom and law and turn from external to internal sources of authority, such as the appeal to conscience, to reason, and to reflective morality, let us consider the appeal to external authority. We pointed out in chapter 2 that the appeal to authority is one of six possible methods of approach in the realm of morality.

The reliance upon some external authority for moral guidance has been widespread in the past among nearly all groups of people. The number of authorities to which one might appeal for guidance is legion: parents, companions, teachers, custom, the law, political leaders, religious institutions and their literature or spokesmen, some fixed "natural law," the "will of God," and so on.

There are situations in which the appeal to authority is justified. This is the case when the person whose testimony we follow has had more opportunity than we have to know the facts and the problems in question, when we feel that he has used the best method in facing those problems, and when he is a person of integrity. Even in scientific research, present investigators accept the findings of past investigators if there is no evidence calling for a revision of these findings. They do not assume, however, that the findings are so final that they must never be questioned or modified. We must leave the answers or the solutions of many problems to experts in whose knowledge and skill we have confidence. This is true even though we realize that their conclusions are only relatively final and that we may have to modify them at some later time.

In the field of morals our views of right and wrong are first implanted in us by our parents, companions, and teachers before we develop our own critical faculties. As children our experiences are limited, and we tend to believe what we are told. As adults we are only slightly less suggestible and credulous, and we tend to believe what we hear or read unless we have reasons for doubting. There is a presumption in favor of principles and practices that are widespread in time and in space and that have been approved by men of insight. Such principles and practices are no more to be discarded without sound reasons than are the scientific principles discovered in the past.

The appeal to authority is not well justified under certain conditions and may even be dangerous for the welfare of the person and the society. The true authoritarian is one who feels secure only when his convictions are certified by some authority that he accepts as final and infallible. A system of morals that is authoritarian in this sense tends, first, to be prohibitive and negative and to tell us what we must not do rather than what we ought to do. The "Thou shalt not" is much in evidence. This is part of the reason why some persons have come to resent terms like *morals* and *ethics* as being repressive. Second, authoritarianism in the realm of morals is destructive of moral perspective in that it tends to put the fundamental values and the less important or even trivial on the same level. It considers acts wrong if they violate the moral code. To urge obedience on the ground of authority rather than on the effect of the conduct on persons and human society is to endanger the whole moral life. Furthermore, we live in a rapidly changing social order—one in which a rigid or fixed code tends to delay social progress. Over the centuries slavery, witchcraft, dueling, and a host of other evils have come to be banned even though they were once approved. True morality seeks for the positively good or for that which brings a more abundant life under present conditions.

The appeal to some religious authority has been fairly widespread. Almost all peoples have attributed their moral codes to their gods or to God. Yet these codes have been most diverse and have changed through the centuries with the development of the group and with changed conditions. A knowledge of history would seem to indicate that there is no infallible church, bible, state, or science.

The reign of authority has been growing weaker. Customs and traditions, including political and ecclesiastical decrees, are not accepted without question, at least by the majority of younger people today. This weakening of authority has been the result of a number of influences including the Renaissance, the Reformation, the rapid development of science, the growth of the democratic spirit, the use of historical criticism in examining many ancient documents and codes, and the rise of social studies that have thrown new light on the variety of human customs and standards. Many of the basic assumptions which an older generation took for granted are being questioned. The prevailing attitude among many people is to "prove all things" and to hold fast only to that which is discovered to be good.

THE APPEAL TO CONSCIENCE

The conflicts that occur between one custom and another, between one law and another, and between custom and law lead men to search for some other standard of judgment. From experience men acquire the strong sense or feeling that some things *ought* to be done, and not others. This sense of an inner prompting or inner law—a sense of obligation that must be obeyed—is called *conscience*. This capacity to feel a moral obligation has been interpreted in many different ways and its relation to moral conduct has not always been clear.

Some people appear to believe that conscience is a faculty (ability or natural aptitude), or a built-in signal within them, that distinguishes between right and wrong in a fairly clear-cut fashion. What is built in, however, is a human capacity for conscience that can be filled with many different kinds of social content. The consciences even of very conscientious people are known to vary widely.

In this appeal to the conscience of the individual, there are at least four strands of human experience. These strands are closely related but can be distinguished for purposes of analysis. On occasions one or another may be dominant. First, there is the memory of the past experiences of the individual. In the past some acts have resulted in pain or other unpleasantness, others in pleasure or keen satisfaction. The memory of this lingers on below the level of consciousness, if not in our conscious memory. These experiences exert a vague but very real pressure against the antisocial impulses which occasionally arise. An additional factor is the conscious or partly conscious fear of punishment for infractions of the law. Uneasiness may accompany violation, even if the act is not detected. Knowledge that the act is condemned and that the individual may be brought to task at some time adds its weight to the inhibitions we have already discussed. Conscience, it is well to keep in mind, may act to sustain outmoded attitudes and ways of doing things. A segregationist, for example, may be prompted by conscience to violate a progressive law or an emerging and new moral obligation. On the other hand, conscience may be the expression of some mature moral insight.

A second element in the development of conscience is the individual's awareness of the group or groups of which he is a part. In this sense, conscience is in part the voice of the group or community expressing its approval of some actions and the disapproval of others. These judgments of the group are a part of his tribal or community consciousness. Since the individual as a member of the group is likely to share in the judgments of the group, a strong pressure is felt to conform and to avoid group censure or punishment. This self-judgment made by an individual in line with the practices of the group is an important element in conscience.

Combining the personal experience of the individual with the awareness of the group, we see that conscience is in considerable part the result of the experience and training we have had during our most impressionable years. Strong feelings that some things are right and ought to be done and that other things are wrong and ought not to be done are built up in us by our parents and associates at a time when we are most plastic and receptive. We accept these moral standards, usually without question. Once the feelings or attitudes are established, we internalize them—they become a part of us. Their influence is present even when we are alone and when our acts are known only to ourselves. Violations of these standards are accompanied by unpleasant emotional reactions, possibly by worry and a sense of guilt, which may make us exceedingly unhappy. We do need to respect the teachings of our elders, the moral codes of society, and the sense of moral obligations in us which we call conscience. Such respect, however, does not require conformity to old ways if we think they do not meet the needs of men living under changed conditions.

Sigmund Freud and his followers have made much of the past experiences of the individual and the pressures exerted on him by the social group. They have emphasized the superficial role of reason and the depth of the irrational in man's life. The Freudians have identified three elements in the structure of the personality. There is the *id*, the subconscious realm of instinct, impulse, and passion; the *ego*, the element of individuality, which is capable of deliberation and may at times exercise some control over the subconscious drives; and finally the *superego*, the internalization of the demands of society called conscience. Conscience, from this point of view, is the "inner perception of objections to definite wish impulses that exist in us." These inhibitions were originally given us by our parents and others with whom we have been in close contact. They may express or conceal a desire and they are often accompanied by some uneasiness or anxiety.

A third element in this inward development is the tendency in the human being to feel revulsion against acts believed to be injurious to himself or his fellowmen. This has been called the "uneasy conscience," the "experience of the divine," the "Voice of God," which calls on man to respect the rights of other men and restrains and prompts him to act in the light of an ideal. One philosopher says that in this area "social conditioning plays only the secondary role of helping to determine what actions shall be thought injurious or beneficial. . . ."[1] Hence he attributes conscience to something in the nature of the structure from which personality develops. The traditional or uncritical conscience may merely reflect social pressure, but the critical conscience becomes uneasy and resists the social tradition when its demands tend to undermine rather than support human well-being. Conscience as a sincere attempt to maintain the integrity of a man's moral convictions or sense of duty is central in the moral life.

A fourth element in conscience, especially in more mature persons, is the element of reflection which accompanies moral judgments made in the light of some accepted moral standard. Thus rational and emotional factors are fused in the feeling of moral obligation. Intellectual elements are important aspects of the critical conscience mentioned before. The fact, however, that conscience functions immediately when faced with familiar situations and problems and is so frequently absent or confused in new and complex situations seems to indicate that social experience and habit play the dominant roles. We shall consider the reflective elements in morality more fully in the next section.

As a procedure for identifying appropriate moral standards and determining their implications for action, the appeal to conscience clearly is a call on the individual's own judgment or habit. This judgment or habit may be informed by divine insight, by adherence to custom, by the unusual knowledge and wisdom of the individual, or by faithfulness to an authoritative code. But it may also be shaped by caprice, immaturity, ignorance, stubbornness, or misunderstanding. To determine the quality of a particular person's conscience requires knowledge of that individual. The very recital of these last possibilities indicates that consciences may fail to show the consistency, clarity, practicability, impartiality, and adequacy of standards sought. We will focus here on identifying the part that conscience can best play in the search for moral standards.

Some moralists have conceived of *conscience* in such a way as to avoid the difficulty just stated. In effect, they have said: "Conscience is the divine speaking through the individual" (Butler); or "Conscience is reason speaking for the universal imperatives that all right action should follow" (Kant); or "Conscience is the wise restraints of the culture ingrained into the individual by social conditioning" (Westermarck). Each of these three definitions assures us that conscience will

---

[1] A. Campbell Garnett, *Religion and the Moral Life* (New York: Ronald Press Co., 1955), p. 75.

be right, but it leaves us without a way of distinguishing between the dictates of our conscience and the impulsions of our mistaken wishes and judgments.

Some advocates of conscience as a source of moral standards mean simply to insist that we act according to the best light that we recognize, remembering that even our best, of course, is not infallible.

We do need conscientious people, but we need to recall that conscience can support bad as well as good causes. Pascal's discerning observation also needs to be kept in mind: "Men never do evil so fully and so happily as when they do it for conscience's sake." If it were advisable for parents to have smaller families in order to alleviate the population problem, something more would be needed than an appeal to conscience, for those who have large families would produce a larger proportion of the next generation than those with more sensitive consciences. Conceivably this might set up a selective system the result of which would be the elimination of conscientious people from society. Other means of restraint will need to be added if this and other issues, such as support for public education, are to succeed.

The appeal merely to the conscience of the individual will not be permanently satisfactory. The conflicts that occur in the life of action are likely to be found also in the inner life. The demands of conscience carry no valid claim upon anybody except the person whose thoughts and feelings they express. Such a person, however, is likely to feel that others should recognize the same demands of conscience, and that he may rightly speak out in defense not just of his sense of what he ought to do, but of his sense of what others should recognize and do. Thus, the sharing of conscientious convictions may play a part in the reform of custom, law, and moral sentiments. Like other human capacities, conscience is in considerable part the outcome of growth and education, in that emotions are trained to approve some actions and disapprove others. Even the desire to do the right thing does not necessarily imply an insight into what is right.

Those among us in need of revision of major ethical convictions are much more numerous than we might suspect. They include children in many of their selfish moods, students whose only concern is for what they personally can get out of college, hardheaded politicians who feel that they must decide on the basis of local interests or local vote producing, a college counselor's clients who cannot break out of perspectives which are frustrating their own fulfillment, and new officials of a small country who must perforce be skeptical of the suspected biases of their foreign advisers on economic and social development. All of these are examples of restricting the in-group, of limiting primary concern to a narrow circle.

REFLECTIVE MORALITY

We have seen that, with the growth of law as distinct from custom, and the emergence of conscience or a personal sense of obligation, conflicts inevitably arise. Such tensions stimulate the growth of reflective criticism. The precepts of the parts are too rigid to guide conduct under new situations. As exceptional circumstances, strain, and new problems occur, men are aroused to reflect on the principles underlying custom, law, and conscience in general. In this way men ask not merely what was done in the past, but what the present demands. When the stage of reflective morality has been reached, men begin to formulate moral judgments and control their conduct on the basis of a reflective evaluation of principles and a careful examination of facts in their relation to human life.

Whereas the customs and laws of a community or state are in the main directed against external acts that are believed to be detrimental to the welfare of society or of the individual himself, mature and reflective moral judgments take into account the motives and character of a person. We need to keep in mind, however, that the part played by reflection, even among modern men, can be easily exaggerated. The conduct of even the most thoughtful men is guided to a large extent by custom, convention, and by legal enactment as well as by ideas that are contributed by the intellectual atmosphere of the day. Yet the development of the highest morality depends on the addition of reflective thinking to those factors already mentioned in its development. A statement made some decades ago by Dewey and Tufts states this point clearly: "Complete morality is reached only when the individual recognizes the right or chooses the good freely, devotes himself heartily to its fulfillment, and seeks a progressive social development in which every member of society shall share."[2]

Our treatment of reflective morality at this point is introductory since the rest of the book is an attempt to expand or put content into what we might call a mature and reflective morality. If men do what they do merely because of custom or the law or outside pressure, they are not moral in the highest sense.

Of the many fields from which examples of the development of morality might be taken, we have selected for presentation the administration of justice and moral progress among the Hebrews.

---

[2] John Dewey and James H. Tufts, *Ethics*, rev. ed. (New York: Henry Holt & Co., 1932), p. 18.

The Administration of Justice

1. *Primitive Vengeance.* We may go back in human history to the time when we find primitive tribes with scarcely anything that can be compared to our modern administration of justice. Private wrongs were avenged by the individuals wronged or perhaps by a close kinsman. Each man took vengeance as best he could. If the members of his family came to his assistance and if the offender were also given aid, a blood feud might develop. While there was no attempt to render to each man a just punishment as judged by impartial authorities, there was a rough sense of justice in operation. "Whoso sheddeth man's blood, by man shall his blood be shed."

2. *The Law of Retaliation.* One of the early attempts to curb primitive vengeance is the famous *lex talionis,* or law of retaliation: "An eye for an eye; a tooth for a tooth." It is found in codes as early as the code of Hammurabi, formulated nearly two thousand years before Christ, but it has been made most familiar through the Book of Exodus. This way of administering justice is found not only among people of early historical periods but also in modern times among people living at a low stage of social and moral development.[3]

3. *Compensation for Offenses.* Retaliation did not always end the quarrel, and it was destructive and tended to weaken or destroy the group. Slowly a stage of compensation for offenses came into existence. So much compensation must be given for an eye, so much for a hand, and so much for a life. Distinctions of status, rank, age, and sex were usually taken into consideration. A free man was worth more and had more rights than a slave, an adult took precedence over a child, and usually a man over a woman. This stage often accompanied the growth in power of a chieftain and the settling down of tribes in a more peaceful and stable type of life.

Another characteristic of this early stage of the administration of justice is found among the Hebrews. Collective responsibility at times extended to the point where the whole family of the offender might be destroyed. If the offender could not be found, vengeance would sometimes be satisfied with the life of his brother or son. A practice that seems especially strange to modern man is the punishment of animals for offenses of their owners. Such practices continued in Europe as late

---

[3]For control of in-group aggression and retaliation among various tribes and peoples, see Mary Edel and Abraham Edel, *Anthropology and Ethics* (Springfield, Ill.: Charles C. Thomas, 1959), pp. 53–67, 174–178.

as the sixteenth century and were often associated with belief in witchcraft, possession, and various magical ideas.

4. *The Growth of Independent Courts.* The growth of the administration of justice by a group not directly involved in the offense happened in long and slow stages. We do not have space to relate these stages or to explain the various uses of the duel, the oath, or the ordeal (walking through fire, dipping one's hands in boiling water, and the like). With the development of society and the growth of a central authority, an independent and impartial group was formed to administer justice. Serious offenses against the individual came to be considered as injuries to the community. At first the council or "court" acted more as peacemaker than as judge. Later the function of the court came to be to try and then to punish the criminal and to protect the rights of both innocent and guilty individuals. Another advance was the distinction between civil justice, whereby restitution or compensation may be given to a complainant, and criminal justice, whereby punishment is assigned by society through the pronouncement of a judge or jury. The long struggle to improve the courts, prisons, penal codes, and practices in general has not ended, but great improvements have been made.

Today men are coming to recognize that the criminal, as well as society, has rights which must be respected. Punishment is ethically justified only when it helps reform the wrongdoer and leads him back to honest, wholesome ways of living. Simply to make the offender suffer, without asking questions regarding the intent and the effect of such punishment, may further degrade the recipient. To inflict pain with no healing intent is probably immoral.

While many advances in the administration of justice have been made in the past, we still have a long way to go. The quest for justice and improvement in the administration of justice continues to be one of our major domestic problems.

Moral Progress Among the Hebrews

A second illustration of the development of morality is taken from the history of the early Hebrews. Probably no other group of people has made such rapid progress in ethical insight in so short a period of time. The evidence of this development is found in the Hebrew literature, especially the Old Testament, when the passages are arranged in chronological order. We shall trace this growing moral insight in (1) the growth of the idea of God, (2) the development from group or customary morality to personal morality, and (3) the treatment of slaves and foreigners.

1. *Growth of the Idea of God.* The ethical ideas attributed to God by a people are a clear reflection of their own moral conceptions. The moral aspirations of the Hebrews are set forth in the words of Jehovah (Yahweh): "Thus saith the Lord" or "What doth God require of thee?" In the early writings God is represented as a local deity who is interested in the military exploits of his people, as a god who speaks in a thunderstorm on Mount Sinai, or as one who walks and talks with men in the garden in the cool of the day. A man might see God, but to do so was highly dangerous; consequently Moses was permitted to see only His back (Exod. 33:20-23). Later, during the wanderings of the Israelites, God is represented as traveling in an ark, or holy chest. When the ark was with them, the Israelites believed, the presence of God was there with them; when they lost the ark, they lost the presence of God. At a later time God is represented as residing at Jerusalem, and still later as the God of Palestine. When the Israelites passed from his territory, they passed from the presence of their God.

In the earlier Hebrew writings of the preprophetic period, God is pictured as one who gives direction for the slaughter of the Amalekites —men, women, and children—without mercy, who encourages blood revenge, who hardens men's hearts and then punishes them for their deeds, and who sends evil spirits to confound men and permits deceit to gain desired ends. God's favor seems to depend to a considerable degree on the care with which men observe certain rituals and ceremonies.

The prophets of the eighth century (Amos, Hosea, Isaiah, and Micah) led the people more definitely in the direction of ethical monotheism. Amos told the people that they had no special claim on the favor of Jehovah, since He was the God of the nations and would punish the people for their sins. In their denunciation of the social evils of their day, Amos and Isaiah helped raise ethics to a central place, along with ritual, in the religion of the period. During the prophetic period, and especially as a result of the Babylonian exile when the people were asking, "How can we worship our God in a strange land?" the prophets assured the people that God was the God of all the nations and that, moreover, He loved righteousness and justice.

In some of the later passages of the Old Testament, and especially in the New Testament, the idea of God becomes spiritual and ethical. God is a loving father, and it is not His will that "one of these little ones should perish." He is interested in purity, truth, and sincerity of purpose. "No man hath seen God at any time," "God is a spirit" and "He that abideth in love abideth in God." This is a very different conception from the one presented in the early records of the Hebrews.

2. *Development from Group Morality to Personal Morality.* When the Hebrew people first came on the stage of history, they were nomadic tribes little different from the tribes about them. They entered Palestine (Canaan) with their flocks and herds. The tribe, family, or group was the important unit, and conflict with the earlier settlers tended to increase tribal clannishness and the solidarity of the group. The group morality or tribal customs made place for blood revenge, the sacrifice of the firstborn, polygamy, and other practices that later came to be forbidden.

The prophets of the eighth century and later had an important influence on three lines of ethical development: (1) The emergence of the individual and the transition to full individual responsibility. Instead of meting out punishment to an entire group, Ezekiel says, "The soul that sinneth, it shall die. The son shall not bear the iniquity of the father, neither shall the father bear the iniquity of the son." (2) The emphasis on personal purity and sincerity in place of ritual and outward conformity. "I hate, I despise your feast days." "What doth the Lord require of thee, but to do justly, and to love mercy, and to walk humbly with thy God?" (3) A growing social passion for justice and righteousness in the affairs of community and nation. Amos strongly condemns, in the name of God, those who "know not to do right" but "store up violence and robbery in their palaces"; those "which oppress the poor" and "swallow up the needy, even to make the poor of the land to fail"; and those who monopolize the corn and the wheat. Men are to look forward to a society in which goodwill and peace will be controlling principles.

3. *Treatment of Slaves and Foreigners.* The morality of a people is reflected in their attitude toward and treatment of foreigners and the weak. An examination of the earlier records of Hebrew history will make clear that the foreigner at first had few rights that the Israelites were bound to respect. Non-Hebrew peoples were ruthlessly slaughtered, reduced to a condition of servitude, or heavily taxed (I Sam. 15:3, I Kings 9:20–21, Judg. 1:28). There were really two ethical standards: one that applied to relations with other Hebrews, and another that applied to outsiders. While a Hebrew might not eat the flesh of an animal that had died "of itself," he could give it to a stranger within his gates or sell it to an alien (Deut. 14:21). A noteworthy exception, one which represents a more highly developed attitude toward the stranger, is reflected in Lev. 19:33–34. Here the stranger is not to be harmed, but he "shall be unto you as one born among you."

In parts of the Book of Isaiah and in later writings, the idea is set forth that God's sway was universal and that other nations might also be the servants of Jehovah (Isa. 19–25). These nations might even be used by God for the purpose of punishing Israel for her sins. According to Jeremiah, a little later, God had no favorites. He disliked unrighteousness and loved righteousness wherever these were found. The same sense of a growing international justice is found in the Books of Jonah and Ruth. Jonah wanted to see Nineveh destroyed, but God is represented as desiring that the people repent. The Book of Ruth is the story of a foreigner who became an ancestress of the kings of Judah.

The noblest ethical ideals of the Old Testament are carried over into the New Testament and expanded. Forgiveness of enemies, even those who are foreigners, is definitely taught. Jesus appears to go out of his way to place certain despised foreigners in an admirable light, as he did in the parable of the Good Samaritan. The doctrine of the fatherhood of God and the brotherhood of man is inimical to race prejudice.

When it arose, slavery was a moral advance, in many cases at least; it was an act of mercy to spare defeated peoples from the sword. Most slaves were obtained through warfare. If cities surrendered peaceably, the early Israelites were to take the inhabitants into their service, but if they resisted and fought, the males at least were to be put to the sword (Deut. 20:10–14). The foreign slave was the property of his owner, who could do with him as he wished. As time went on a more humane attitude developed, and the rights of the owner were restricted. As a human being, the slave was felt to have some rights.

In the New Testament, slavery is accepted as one of the institutions of the day. Christians, however, were to treat their slaves with consideration. While Paul sends Onesimus back to his owner Philemon, he exhorts the master to receive the slave as a Christian brother.

SUMMARY

The development of morality is one important phase of the growth of man as a person and of his culture as a whole; it does not take place in isolation from other elements of life and society. We have given a mere sketch of some of the steps and conditions that have led to the emancipation of the individual from exclusive control by the group. The growth of self-consciousness, knowledge, and intelligence, and such external factors as the growth of individual property ownership, the division of labor, and the need to combine against many hazards of nature, have played important parts in this development. The emancipation of the individual from subjection to the group has sometimes led to an extreme and selfish individualism; it has also made possible new areas of cooperation and mutual aid. Language, agriculture, industry, religion, and the arts and sciences have been socializing as well as individualizing agencies.

Among all groups of people, past and present, we find problems of conduct; we also find that human life is in some sense organized and directed. Agreements, regulations, or directives of some sort are supported by the approval of the group. The actual beginnings of morality are lost in the past. Among primitive groups the individual was almost completely submerged in the life and customs of the group. Man's rights and duties were fixed by the group, and there was a strong sense of social solidarity. While the average man was held in line, the exceptional man was retarded. Customary morality was and is ill adapted to changing conditions.

With the growth of society, regulations expressed themselves outwardly in law and inwardly in conscience. As conflicts arose, men searched for standards of judgment, and reflective criticism was born. Morality appears to have taken the form of such a redirection of impulses as would make for the development of the individual and the preservation and welfare of the group. Moral standards depend upon man's knowledge and intellectual and cultural development. As men become increasingly liberated from blind custom, they tend to direct their conduct more and more on the basis of a conscious philosophy of life.

We see, then, that morals are not something distinct and separate from the actual personal and social lives of men and women. Moral standards grow out of life and are related to human feeling and intelligence. As intelligence and experience grow and expand, the requirements of personal and social welfare are more and more taken into account.

This sketch of the development of morality from rigidly fixed customs and group morality to a more personal, reflective morality on the part of some members of society throws much light on groups in our society. Today we find men and women living at all stages of moral development. Primitive men, or our "contemporary ancestors," are with us still. The development depicted above is a very uneven one and the earlier stages have not been completely left behind. This explains in part the moral confusion found in society today. To use a simple, descriptive classification, we find at least three groups in present-day society when we ask what moral standards are actually followed by the general public.

First, a large group in our society live under *code morality* where some external authority is accepted as final. The authority may be custom, law, an individual or an institution, scripture, or what is declared to be the decree or will of God. The emphasis is on obedience to some norm. This legalistic approach may work well in a simple and fairly static society. In a rapidly changing social order with a host of new problems not recognized by the traditional codes, many people and especially the young rebel and refuse to give allegiance to the older rules and institutions. Second some of those who have given up the older authorities go to the opposite extreme and assert that there is nothing right or wrong but thinking, emotion, desire, or attitude makes it so. This can mean a ban on the attempt to develop rationality in moral judgments. In its extreme form this is *moral relativism,* the view that there are no objective standards beyond opinion, attitudes, and feeling. In more critical and reflective treatments of the place of desire, emotion, and attitudes—individual or group—in moral judgments, this outlook expresses itself as emotivism and as various forms of linguistic analysis. We shall consider both relativism and linguistic analysis in chapter 6. There is, however, a third position, which in our opinion, is more adequate. It consists of a *normative and reflective morality* which we have pointed out briefly in this chapter and will discuss in the following chapters of part 1, especially in chapters 5 and 11. While there can be different viewpoints on the basis of a reflective morality, there is no significant disagreement with the idea that mankind will do better to bring the resources of thinking and reason to the effort to realize the best possible life in the situation in which men find themselves.

QUESTIONS AND PROJECTS

1. Can you relate some instances in which custom makes an act approved or at least accepted in one area and disapproved, called wrong, or even made illegal in another area? For example, the *San Juan Star* (Puerto Rico), 24 February 1965, relates an incident in which a New York woman and her husband, meeting after a short separation, were arrested for kissing and embracing on the street. The kiss cost the couple $136.75. Would this have happened in New York or San Francisco?
2. The code of dueling was a binding code among large classes of European society a century or two ago. In American social life it was not until the 1860s that the duel was finally abolished. In its heydey, the duel was held under an inexorable Code of Honor. For example, if a man fired before the signal, his life was forfeit to his opponent's second. Insults or supposed insults, differences of opinion, love affairs, questions of politics or of business—any of an untold number of things—might lead to the dueling field for "settlement." The more skillful duelist won, even though he was often wrong. Outline what you think were or may have been the steps that led from the acceptance of dueling as an honorable custom to its rejection by society and its present illegal status.
3. Robert M., returning home unexpectedly one night, finds his wife with

a lover. He opens fire with a revolver and kills the man. In the state in which this happened, such actions do not ordinarily lead to any indictment, or at least are not severely condemned because such action is expected. Since public justice has replaced private revenge in nearly all antisocial acts, how do you explain the attitude depicted above? Is this merely a survival of a primitive practice?
4. What survivals of earlier moral standards are found in America today? You ought to be able to name half a dozen without much difficulty.
5. A student makes what he calls a confession, as follows: "I read a headline in a newspaper about the sinking of a ship in which 2,000 people were feared drowned. A shudder went through me and I recalled the *Titanic* and other sea disasters. When I picked up the paper and read on, I discovered that the incident had occurred in the Far East and that the victims were Oriental refugees. Before realizing the moral implications of my reactions, I recognized a sense of relief and remarked, 'Oh, they were only Orientals.' " Is this evidence of a lingering tribal morality? Where there are ties of blood, affection, friendship, or congeniality of interests, our feelings are touched and our judgments are likely to be influenced. To what extent is the reaction above, the good of the nearer, a common one? Is the reaction evidence of maturity or immaturity?
6. In China a businessman lives up to the moral standard if he starts to make payments on a debt at the time it becomes due. In America such a person would be considered in default, and a creditor could take action against him if he wished to do so. Among the Dakota Indian tribes, it is reported that courtesy is highly esteemed and that "they would rather lose double any day than profit double at another's expense." They cannot understand the sharp dealing of many white men. How are such differences as the above to be explained?
7. A considerable number of years after he had been graduated, a man returned his diploma to the president of his college, explaining that he did not want it because he had not earned it fairly; he had cheated while in college. Removing the name, the president posted the letter and the diploma on the bulletin board. From time to time the newspapers print stories about the return of stolen money or articles. Can you relate similar incidents? How do you explain such power of conscience even after a considerable lapse of time?
8. Is the statement of some writers that custom can make anything right or make anything wrong strictly true? Does it have more truth at some periods of moral evolution than at others?
9. Make a list of the groups of which you are a member, indicating ways in which they influence your conduct. Are you conscious of any changes in attitude or in conduct as you go from group to group?
10. Go over the main steps in the administration of justice and indicate how many of these steps have appeared in American history.
11. Are we in danger, in our drive for security, of moving back to the stage of group morality? There have been a number of widely publicized cases of what is sometimes called *guilt by association*. See Henry Steele

Commager, "Guilt—and Innocence—by Association," *New York Times Magazine,* 8 November 1953.

12. Certain tribes living in Borneo were reported to consider it an act of merit to slay and behead a member of an enemy tribe; yet they considered it a heinous offense to slay a fellow tribesman. Men of various primitive tribes have been willing to lend their wives to honored guests; yet they were as shocked as modern men if their wives did the lending themselves. The wives of some Fijian chiefs consider it a duty to suffer strangulation on the death of their husbands. Among the Eskimos it is a capital crime to steal from the common supply of blubber on which the life of the community is dependent. One writer reports that the women of certain primitive tribes seemed shocked to hear that in England a man had only one wife. How do you explain such attitudes and practices and such apparent inconsistencies?

13. Can you see any justification at all for the practice in an early hunting age of killing the aged and infirm?

14. There is an old tradition of the sea, at least in some Western countries, that the captain of a sinking ship, after doing everything he can to save the ship and ordering all others to leave in the lifeboats, goes down with the ship. This was supposed to show courage and loyalty to a naval and marine code of the seas. This traditional practice has been condemned by a number of groups, and on occasion even in war the captains of naval vessels have been ordered by their governments to abandon ship. Discuss this tradition. Would you agree that the only thing that can justly be expected of the captain is to do what he can do to ensure the safety of the passengers and crew? See *Time,* 11 August 1961, p. 41.

15. Another tradition of the sea is that when a ship is going to sink and the order is given to abandon ship, the cry goes up: "Women and children first!" Is this code of the sea in need of some revision? Two psychiatrists, after studying the experience of people when the ship *Stockholm* collided with the *Andrea Doria* in 1956 and consulting studies of the experience of children when separated from parents during bombings and disasters, point out that this often leads to "disastrous psychological consequences." Children, the study revealed, could go through trying and tragic experiences "psychologically intact so long as a parent was with them, but quickly collapsed when alone." As a result of this study the psychiatrists assert that the old rule should be modified and that "a parent should accompany the child, even if the only parent available be the father." See Paul Friedman and Louis Linn, "Some Psychiatric Notes on the *Andrea Doria* Disaster," *The American Journal of Psychiatry* 114 (November 1957): 426–432; and *Time,* 25 November 1957, p. 76.

16. Write a brief statement concerning your own moral development, including answers to the following questions: Where did you get your ideas of right and wrong when you were very young? Did the source of your ideas change any as you went through high school? Have parents, the social groups, and so on always had the same influence in framing your standards? At the present time, why do you think right is right?

SUGGESTED READINGS

Albert, Ethel M. "Social Science Facts and Philosophical Values," *The Antioch Review*, 17 (Winter 1957-58): 406-420.
Benedict, Ruth. *Patterns of Culture*. Boston: Houghton Mifflin Co., 1934.
Breasted, J. H. *The Dawn of Conscience*. New York: Charles Scribner's Sons, 1934.
Brinton, Crane. *A History of Western Morals*. New York: Harcourt, Brace, & Co., 1959.
Burlingame, Roger. *The American Conscience*. New York: Alfred A. Knopf, 1957.
Dewey, J., and Tufts, J. H. *Ethics*. Rev. ed., pt. 1. New York: Henry Holt & Co., 1932.
Edel, Abraham and Edel, May. *Anthropology and Ethics: The Quest for Moral Understanding*. Rev. ed. Cleveland, O.: Case Western Reserve, 1968.
Frankfort, H., et al. *The Intellectual Adventure of Ancient Man*. Chicago: University of Chicago Press, 1946.
Fromm, Erich. "Conscience." In *Moral Principles of Action*, edited by Ruth Nanda Anshen. New York: Harper & Brothers, 1952.
Ginsberg, Morris. *On the Diversity of Morals*. Essays in Sociology and Social Philosophy, vol. 1. London: William Heinemann, 1956.
Harkness, Georgia. *The Sources of Western Morality from Primitive Society through the Beginnings of Christianity*. New York: Charles Scribner's Sons, 1954.
Hunter, J. F. M. "Conscience," *Mind* 72 (July 1963): 309-334.
Macbeath, A. *Experiments in Living: A Study of the Nature and Foundation of Ethics or Morals in the Light of Recent Work in Social Anthropology*. The Gifford Lectures, 1948-1949. London: Macmillan & Co., 1952.
Mead, Margaret. *Continuities in Cultural Evolution*. New Haven: Yale University Press, 1964.
Roche, John P. and Gordon, Milton M. "Can Morality Be Legislated?" *New York Times Magazine*, 22 May 1955, p. 10 ff.
Smith, J. M. P. *The Moral Life of the Hebrews*. Chicago: University of Chicago Press, 1923.
Smith, T. V. *Beyond Conscience*, New York: McGraw-Hill Book Co., 1934.
Thompson, Samuel M. "The Authority of Law," *Ethics* 75 (October 1964): 16-24.
Warren, Austin. *The New England Conscience*. Ann Arbor: University of Michigan Press, 1966.

4
NATURE, HUMAN NATURE, AND FREEDOM OF CHOICE

In this chapter we shall make certain commitments—definite stands or common-sense declarations—in order to help clarify the point of view and the discussions in this and later chapters. These commitments grow out of human experience and are supported by an abundance of empirical or scientific evidence. It is not possible to present much of the evidence, however, and we ask the reader to consult the books listed. Paul Tillich reminds us of the importance of basing our ideas on the experience of mankind, for if we disregard it, we court tragedy. "Think before you leap," he says, "because a leap out of mankind is plainly neither reasonable nor sensible for one who pretends to be educated."

THE WORLD BEYOND US

There is a reality to which we have to relate and adjust our lives, a reality outside our minds that is not created by our wishes and desires. Alfred North Whitehead has called our attention to the fact that "we are in the world, not the world in us."[1] This means that the world has a determinate structure of its own, a structure to which we must make adjustment if we are to live. We can manipulate and to some extent control many natural processes but only by understanding their nature

---

[1] *Science and the Modern World* (New York: Macmillan Co., 1935), p. 125.

and obeying their laws. The view that there is a reality prior to our knowledge of it has sometimes been called the *postulate of antecedent reality.*

This structure of antecedent reality is intelligible and can be known, at least dimly or in part, by the man who seeks to discover its nature. We get almost daily evidence to this effect from the work of a multitude of scientists engaged in research in many special sciences. The affirmation that this reality is intelligible and discoverable has been called the *postulate of relevance to mind.* Because we cannot interpret or describe anything that is out of all relation to mind, these two postulates must logically be held together. Using them as a base, we reject panobjectivism or the view that only physical things exist, since this leaves no room for knowledge, truth or falsity, right or wrong, or a realm of values. We also reject the opposite, a pansubjectivism or extreme mentalism that rejects an external world and puts everything in mind.

This world which includes both objective and subjective elements is the world we seek to know and the area within which we live and act. The purpose and meaning of knowledge is to portray the nature of the world, the nature of man, and the values on which a person may base his well-being. The resolution of these issues is basic for our conception of morality. What man ought to be and do depends on what man is, the nature of the universe, and man's place in the universe. While the good life is valuable in and of itself, ethical questions cannot be separated from questions regarding the nature of the cosmos and the purpose and meaning we find or create in things in general. The answers to such questions affect man's outlook as well as his moral conduct and ethical theories.

The world which men experience contains creative and constructive processes of many kinds as well as destructive ones. There exists in the universe a creativity that makes for life, truth, beauty, goodness, and the development of persons. The creative urge within man is derived from the universe that produced him. Man's aspirations and ideals seem to be in part his half-conscious realization of his own inherent possibilities. If man is to grow and to have satisfaction, he must embody the creative processes of the universe. To do otherwise is to meet frustration and pain.

HUMAN NATURE

Our discussion of the origin and development of morality has shown that morality is dynamic and that moral codes have changed as men have sought to meet their basic needs under changing conditions. From ancient hunting, fishing, and pastoral eras to the modern industrial and scientific age, society has passed through various forms of organization embodying different types of behavior and forms of motivation. Medieval society, for example, was theologically minded and otherworldly in outlook; modern society is commercially minded, and the profit motive is prominent. At one time no gentleman would refuse a challenge to a duel, since his honor was at stake. Today we usually ignore insults and settle differences in other ways. In reply to a boy who said, "I can lick you," another boy was heard to say, "I suppose you can." Nothing happened! What has taken place in boy nature? Or was this boy just trained differently?

Today when men express the hope that persons or social conditions will continue to change and that we may look forward to better conditions in the future, someone is almost certain to remark, "You can't change human nature." Human nature has been the scapegoat on which the shortcomings, the failures, and the sins of the world have been placed. Once it was held responsible for slavery and dueling; today it is considered the cause of selfishness, prejudice, jealousy, crime, war, and poverty. This is a serious charge to direct against the nature of man. Is it a correct charge? Upon the answer to this question depends the approach we must make to numerous moral problems. If we cannot change human nature, the possibilities of moral progress, at least by means of education and social reform, are greatly restricted.

Three Views of Human Nature

The views of human nature that men have held in the past fall into three broad groups. First, there are those who say that human nature is essentially evil. Man, they insist, has been and always will be selfish, irrational, cruel, and destructive. Today such persons are likely to support their view by pointing to wars, revolutions, and the increase in delinquency, crime, and other social evils. This view has received support from at least three sources: (1) From some theologians, including Augustine (354–430), who emphasized the inability of sinful man to do any good through his own efforts. Man's nature was said to be corrupt and evil because of Adam's sin and fall. During the Protestant Reformation, Luther and Calvin reaffirmed many of the views set forth by Augustine, including his view of corrupted human nature. (2) The classical economists popularized the idea that, under economic incentives, man acts only in accord with his individual interest. The "economic man" is essentially selfish. For a time economics was called the "dismal science," since natural laws operating upon human nature were thought to be responsible for many human woes. (3) Nineteenth-century biological science set forth the view that man is an animal, and like other animals he inherits an array of drives or fixed instincts acquired in the struggle for existence; hence he can be expected to exhibit all the animal tendencies. Civilization is largely a veneer covering a bestial nature.

Second, the view that human nature is good has many ancient as well as modern supporters. A bit of Confucian lore taught to Chinese school boys states that "men at their birth are naturally good. Their natures are much the same; their habits become widely different." In the first chapter of Genesis we read "and God saw everything that he had made, and, behold, it was very good." Evil was to appear later and was not original.

In the eighteenth century, Rousseau (1712–1778) announced that nature is good and that, since man is a part of nature, he too is good. Man was good until advancing civilization brought corruption and vice. Let man return to nature and all will be well. Children should be permitted to grow up in a state of simplicity and without restrictions, so that their native tendencies for good may not be corrupted.

During the latter part of the nineteenth century, the view that human nature is good was supported by an interpretation of evolution as inevitable progress. For Herbert Spencer (1820–1903), a popularizer of the theory of evolution, the course of evolution meant change for the better. The chief duty of man, therefore, is to stand aside, keep hands off the cosmic process, and trust to evolution to bring changes in the human organism. The natural laws, without man's aid, will gradually bring about a harmonious adjustment of man's nature to the environment in which he lives.

From the many modern expressions of the view that man's nature is basically good, we select one for brief presentation.

The anthropologist Ashley Montagu in *On Being Human* contends that the cooperative forces in man's nature are biologically more important than the egotistical and destructive forces. The organism is born "with an innate need for love, with a need to respond to love, to be good, cooperative."[2] While the opposite view that life is a cruel struggle, handed down from the nineteenth century, does motivate the conduct of many people in the Western world, Montagu contends that it is completely false, and he marshals some of the evidence against it. He says that the principle of cooperation is the most important factor in the survival of animal groups and of men.

The third view of human nature maintains that man is born neither good nor evil but with great possibilities for both tendencies. Man's

---

[2](New York: Henry Schuman, 1950), p. 97.

original nature includes many unorganized responses that through maturation and learning take on a more definite social pattern. Man differs from the lower animals in, among other things, the flexible nature of his inherited tendencies. He has a long period of infancy during which learning capacity, rather than rigidity, is characteristic of his nature. Starting at birth, habit formation is so rapid that soon it is impossible to tell what is learned and what is unlearned, what is habitual and what inborn. Certainly we can understand the behavior of a man only as we understand the total situation in which he grew up. The child, like the plant or the animal, has an innate urge to grow, but the conditions necessary for growth must be present or the organism is stunted or dies. If unfavorable conditions persist, the child may become neurotic and antisocial.

Within man we find both constructive and destructive possibilities that do not appear to stem from the same level of man's life or from the same forces. Karen Horney, one-time Dean of the American Institute for Psychoanalysis, says that "briefly, our belief is that the constructive possibilities stem from man's essential nature, from the core of his being, from what we call his real self. . . . Man turns unconstructive or destructive only if he cannot fulfill himself—that it is an unfulfilled life which makes him barren or destructive."[3] In a somewhat similar way the theologian Paul Tillich distinguishes between "man's essential nature" and his "existentialist predicament." He says, "There is no existentialist description of the negativities of the human predicament without an underlying image of what man essentially is and therefore ought to be."[4]

Reinhold Niebuhr sees man as a curious blend of evil and good, of nature and spirit, and he includes both tendencies within man's essential nature. He contends that "there are resources in the Christian faith for an understanding of human nature which have been lost in modern culture." The various scientific studies of human nature are rooted in presuppositions, either idealistic or naturalistic, which fail to do justice to the full dimensions of that nature. The idealistic viewpoints interpret man too exclusively from the standpoint of his rational faculties, and the naturalists interpret man's nature as imbedded too completely within "nature." Man can be understood only as a "curious compound of 'nature' and 'spirit' which all human behavior manifests." Man is a child of nature, driven by its thrusts and impulses; yet he is a spirit who stands outside of nature. He is to be interpreted from the

---

[3] Quoted in *The Nature of Man,* ed. Simon Doniger (New York: Harper & Row, Publishers, 1962), p. 181.

[4] Paul Tillich, "Existentialism, Psychotherapy, and the Nature of Man," Ibid., p. 44.

standpoint of his relation to God, rather than that of his rational faculties or his relation to nature. If he believes himself to be good and attributes the evils of human history to social and historic causes, he fails to see that these evils cannot be explained apart from man's evil tendencies. If he judges himself to be evil, how can he be basically evil if he knows himself to be so? "To the essential nature of man belong, on the one hand, all his natural endowments and determinations, his physical and social impulses, his sexual and racial differentiations, in short, his character as a creature imbedded in the natural order. On the other hand, his essential nature also includes the freedom of his spirit, his transcendence over natural process and finally his self-transcendence."[5]

The notion that human nature is radically evil or essentially selfish appears to be untenable. The support for this position whether theological, economic, or biological has been weakened if not definitely undermined. In man we find plasticity and a long period of infancy during which the impulses to action may be directed in various ways. The opposite view that human nature is good may be less open to criticism than the opposite extreme, since there is much evidence that human beings reared in a home where love is ever-present and intelligently expressed exhibit a great capacity for love and cooperative living. Furthermore, to tell man that he is potentially good rather than evil has a great practical value, for man tends to live up to what is expected of him. At least he tends to do the things that the group he respects expects him to do.

Many human traits, such as generosity, sympathy, and sociability, are desirable; others, such as selfishness, combativeness, and jealousy, are undesirable. All these qualities and traits are found in man as we view him today. Human nature is many-sided and adjustable. Man may become good or evil according to the way in which his "original nature" is directed or conditioned by the total influence to which he is subjected and by his responses to these conditions. When every conditioning factor exerts a pressure in the direction of crude individualism, a person will become selfish and grasping. When conditioning factors emphasize constructive social motives, human nature reveals its possible nobility. Thus, the view that human nature is plastic and has great potentialities, for good and for evil, is the one we assume as a basis for further discussion. It is the one accepted today by most sociologists, psychologists, biologists, educators, and many religious leaders. Let us turn next to a brief sketch of the many conditions that, directly or indirectly, may influence human behavior.

---

[5]Reinhold Niebuhr, *The Nature and Destiny of Man,* vol. 1 (New York: Charles Scribner's Sons, 1943), p. 270.

HEREDITARY AND ENVIRONMENTAL CONDITIONS AFFECTING MAN

Man is sometimes said to be the product of heredity and environment. The two influences are not mutually exclusive. Let us turn to biology for two simple experiments on lower organisms. When the eggs of marine fish of the genus *Fundulus* develop in untreated sea water, they produce fish with two eyes. If certain magnesium salts and other substances are added to the sea water, marked differences result—notably, the development of fish with only one eye. Again, the axolotl is a creature (the larva of the Mexican salamander) that depends on its environment even to the extent of the parts or organs it develops. When it lives in the water, it develops gills and lacks lungs. When it lives out of the water, it develops lungs and lacks gills. Thyroid feeding will cause the water form of any age to change into the land salamander within a week or two. Apparently some abnormalities are normal developments under abnormal conditions. For the normal development of the organism, the proper materials or basic structure must be present, but it is equally important that the original nature mature in a favorable environment.

Some things a man is born with affect his conduct and character. While there is general agreement that we are born with the potential to do some things better than others, there is less agreement as to just what we inherit or how it should be defined. Heredity appears to be the important element in such things as: (1) physical makeup, including size, overdevelopment or underdevelopment (including a superior or inferior constitution), texture and color of hair, eye color, and the like; (2) mental inferiority and superiority; (3) temperamental or emotional tone, including reaction speed; (4) certain impulses, reflexes, and possibly "instincts." Some organic changes and physical defects also play an important part in human conduct and character. Antenatal conditions, the birth process, the conditions and experiences of early childhood, the adolescent period, pregnancy, overdevelopment and underdevelopment, physical defects and injuries, the glands, and diseases have a profound effect on emotional outlook and behavior.

The climate and geographical environment are other factors that may influence man. It is claimed by some students of the environment that mankind has always made the most rapid progress under essentially the same conditions, that is, mainly in the temperate zones with the stimulation of seasonal changes. The climate and geographical environment may influence man directly, as in the case of the sun's rays, which affect pigmentation, or indirectly, through their influence on the biological, psychological, and social conditions under which he lives. For good or bad, these climatic and geographical conditions have a direct and important bearing on man's health, energy, temperament, occupation, and general conduct. With the development of science and technology, including new means of travel and temperature control, modern man has numerous ways not available to earlier man of overcoming the limitations and checking the influences that the natural environment has on him.

The psychological and social conditions that surround the developing child are of crucial importance in influencing his outlook and behavior. The infant at birth possesses a wide and diffuse array of needs and many general reflexes and responses. His activity appears to rise out of the excess energy of the organism, as well as from specific stimuli; and many of his movements are random and unorganized. These diffused and unorganized responses soon begin to take on a more definite and meaningful social pattern partly because of development and maturation within the organism, and partly because of the learning process that goes on all the time. The more complex responses and patterns of social behavior are built up by a process of conditioning or by means of experience. Successful or satisfactory responses tend to be repeated and to become habits. On the basis of numerous experiments, most psychologists contend that our adult patterns of behavior and our complex social activities may be explained as the result of habit or "cultural conditioning."

Human behavior is never the result of environmental factors alone or of inborn traits alone; it is always the result of the interaction of the individual and his environment. In the satisfaction of needs and the attempt to avoid pain and gain pleasure, groups of men have come to adopt the same ways of fulfilling their desires, and their ways of acting become customs. These ways of acting, the folkways, produce habits in the individual and customs in the group, and become powerful forces in society. Our behavior ordinarily conforms to the standards approved by the group we trust and admire, and our traditional moral ideals tend to sanction these ways. Custom tends to make almost anything appear right or wrong. Just as an individual acquires the language and the ways of thinking, feeling, and acting of his group, so he tends to acquire its moral standards.

The institutions of society, such as the home, the neighborhood and the economic, political, and religious institutions exert strong pressures on the individual within the society. The home environment is of crucial importance. Fortunate is the young person brought up in a home where his basic needs are satisfied and where there is love and affection and an intelligent concern for his welfare. Along with the home the neighborhood has a strong influence over the standards and conduct of people, especially the young. Certain types of communities produce an unduly large proportion of offenders. In some districts with a reputation for antisocial behavior, the status of the individual is proportionate to his offense—the greater his offenses, the higher his standing.

Changeable and Enduring Elements in Man's Nature

The views that nothing changes in human nature and that all is flux are equally extreme and unacceptable. We would not recognize or be conscious of changes in man's nature if there were not some persistent or unchangeable elements in it. To create an analogy with nature, the banks of a stream must remain relatively stationary if we are to observe the flow of the water. So in man there must be a persistent self, subject, or knower as the center of personal identity and the integrator of experiences. The self includes those qualities of uniqueness and duration through change that enable the individual to say "I" or "me" in connection with experiences that happened years ago, yesterday, and today. There are certain basic characteristics of people—like self-consciousness, and the ability to communicate, to deliberate and evaluate, to love and be loved—which may be lessened or increased but which cannot be eliminated without destroying man's basic identity.

While conditioning will not abolish hunger or thirst or the tendency of life to defend and to propagate itself, conditioning does determine the ways in which these urges are organized and express themselves. Man's better potentialities may at times triumph over feelings and passions and unfavorable conditions. At times we see hungry men refuse to take food, tired men refuse to give up and rest, and men in extreme pain refuse to compromise with their ideals and take some easy way to lessen the pain.

Thus, while there are certain basic characteristics of man's nature, there is justification for regarding it as plastic in the sense that it is possible to change man's emotional reactions, his ideas and thinking, and his behavior or conduct. The view that human nature can be changed receives additional support from a number of directions. First, both education and religion assume that human nature can be changed. While the nature of a man's biological inheritance sets the limits of his educational achievement, the possibilities are great under normal conditions. The chief task of moral education is to train man's impulses and desires so that they express themselves in wholesome social activity. To be educated means to be changed to some extent. Religious insight and conversion also mean reshaping life around new goals or values. To be genuinely religious means to integrate one's life around some supreme loyalty.

Second, case studies of delinquents, clinical experiences, and psychoanalytic therapy have given us a great mass of evidence not only regarding the causative factors in human behavior but also on the ways in which conduct may be changed. For example, the removal of irritations in his environment or changes in his physical and mental condition may lead almost at once to a change in the attitude of the delinquent boy. The reconstructed situation and attitude may in turn affect his entire behavior pattern.

Finally, studies of feral (wild) men and children and other cases of isolation from human society have thrown much light on the changeable nature of man. Children born with normal potentials who have been lost and reared by animals or in some way deprived of the usual human contacts develop neither a language nor other elements of a normal personality or of culture and civilization.

Man appears to be the most plastic part of the living world. He is the most adaptable and educable. His infancy is longest, his drives least fixed, and his brain less finished at birth. Nature has largely finished other creatures; man, within broad limits, can choose the direction in which he wishes to develop.

Misconceptions Regarding Selfishness and Altruism

There is a duality in man's life which may be expressed as a conflict between his animal nature and his human nature, between his physical cravings and his rational and social behavior. Man's animal nature reaches back over a long period of time, whereas his human nature is a later acquisition. But even if the self-regarding impulses were the dominant ones, the human problem which we face would be essentially the same. Man's present problem is to modify these desires so that they will harmonize with the welfare of the group.

Two popular misconceptions have helped confuse the issue between selfishness and altruism. The first is that selfishness is original in man's nature, while altruism is something artificial or added. This fails to take account of the fact that some of man's impulses are concerned with the safety and welfare of offspring or other members of his group. Some unselfishness is as natural as selfishness. While feeling is personal, it is not true that feeling is always self-regarding.

If some unselfishness is as natural as selfishness to our original nature, then what we are in later life—unselfish or selfish—depends on the way we have been trained. According to our personal and social contacts and our reactions to them, we may develop our self-seeking or our social tendencies. If society in general were so organized as to emphasize cooperation between men, as some societies are organized, human nature might display quite different characteristics.

A second misconception is that self-interest is always evil and self-sacrifice or altruism always good. Actually, self-love may be morally good or morally evil, and the same is true of altruism. There are situations in which it is our duty to look after ourselves. Under ordinary circumstances, our first duty may be to guard our health and our reputations. There are cases where self-sacrifice may be morally wrong, as when a mother is so oversolicitious in her care of a child that she spoils the child and ruins her own health. To make a rigid separation between self-interest and altruism raises a false issue. Rather, we must inquire into the consequences of both. An act is not right merely because it aids someone else, nor wrong because it advances one's personal well-being. It is right or wrong according to whether it is fair or unfair, beneficial or harmful to those affected, directly and indirectly.

The important issue is whether as persons we are growing into narrow, small selves or selves that are broad in their interests and outlook. The really selfish person needs an expansion of interests and the intelligence to see that his life is bound up with the welfare of other people. He needs to cultivate the kind of self that gains happiness from common social values. Personality is a social product, and man's true self is a social self. The good in life is not exclusively either that of the self or that of others. It is a common good which includes the self and others. In chapter 12 we consider the selfishness of groups.

Someone is likely to reply that when men sacrifice themselves for others, they do so because this brings them joy or at least enables them to avoid dissatisfaction; therefore it is selfishness just the same. Two things need to be pointed out in reply. The first is that if all seemingly different motives are only partial manifestations of self-interest—if love, friendship, and self-sacrifice are only disguised examples of selfishness and man can act in no other way—then the notion of selfishness becomes meaningless. The "I ought" vanishes into a mere "It is." This attempt to meet the problem by denying its existence runs counter to our human moral consciousness. The second is the fact that, if every act does satisfy the doer, there is a great difference between finding satisfaction in an act that pleases only oneself and finding satisfaction in an act that considers the welfare of others. The latter kind of satisfaction is what may be called altruism. To say that all actions are motivated by self-interest and therefore are essentially selfish begs the question by assuming that all forms of self-interest are the same. If I satisfy my self-interest by "appreciating beauty because it is beautiful, pursuing truth because truth inspires and draws me to it, and cultivating virtue because I want and, further, *will* to be a better man, or because I feel the pull of moral obligation,"[6] these motives may not appropriately be classed with the exclusive gratification of personal advantage that we normally call selfishness.[7]

FREEDOM OF CHOICE

In discussing human nature we have assumed that man, at least at times, can make things happen that would not happen otherwise, and that to some extent he can deliberate, decide, and direct his own life and the course of events. Some degree of freedom of action is assumed by nearly all people in the course of their daily lives. They praise and blame, make plans for the future, and hold themselves and other people responsible for their actions. Unless men are free to act on moral principles, it is absurd to talk about duty, or what men ought to do, or to pursue studies in the area of ethics and morality.

On the other hand, in the light of the numerous factors influencing conduct—physical, biological, psychological, and social—it is evident that conduct is determined at least to some extent and is not to be explained merely as the product of an isolated or completely free will. Numerous scientific studies make it clear that human activity as well as the events of nonhuman nature are determined in some way by cause-and-effect sequences. We are naturally led, therefore, to ask to what extent man's life is determined, how free he is. Some men, impressed with the "reign of natural law," have claimed that man, like objects in nature, is caught in the grip of cause-and-effect relationships and that his every act is rigidly determined, so that he is not free to choose. The problem arises when man is interpreted both as a self-conscious, thinking being and as a part of physical nature, conditioned by his environment. Though this is one of the more difficult questions, the student of ethics needs to clarify his thinking and to be able to meet critical questions in this area when they arise.

Moral freedom, the subject of this discussion, means the capacity to choose and act on one's choice. It involves the power to choose between alternative courses of action and the power of the individual's deliberation to act as a causal agent in the process of behavior.

In the past, moral freedom has usually been called *freedom of the will*. Today the latter term is less used, since men do not think of *will*

---

[6]C. E. M. Joad, *Decadence* (New York: Philosophical Library, 1949), p. 157.

[7]For a discussion of selfish desire or attachment versus nonattachment in Buddhism and Christianity, see Morris Keeton, *Values Men Live By* (New York: Abingdon, 1960), ch. 2.

as naming a separate entity or faculty but as denoting the activity or motor tendencies of the organism. In a more restricted and personal sense, *will* refers to a person's ability to perform voluntary acts. The will is the person expressing himself in action.

Moral freedom—freedom of choice or self-determinism—stands in contrast to two other positions. *Indeterminism,* the more extreme view of freedom, is the idea that there are events in the mental and moral life of man that are uncaused in the sense that the mind may work without any motivation. Man may make choices, it is said, that are independent of his past actions including his heredity and environment.

In contrast to indeterminism, *determinism* as a postulate in scientific inquiry maintains the belief that the realm of nature, including man, is to be treated as an unbroken chain of cause and effect, so that human behavior is dependent on natural law and is conditioned by antecedent events. All events, including decisions of man's will, are to be explained by preceding events. What is called the *act of choice* is determined either by external pressures or by desires and tendencies within the agent's character.

Determinism needs to be distinguished from both fatalism and predestination. *Fatalism* is the view that at least certain events in man's life are determined independently of his own choices and acts, so that the future is removed from his personal control. It holds to the inevitable appearance of an event at a specific time and insists that "what is to be will be." Fatalism seems to have its origin or basis in human weakness or helplessness in the face of specific evils, especially death. This outlook is most prevalent in areas without advanced means of scientific and social control. It is also a convenient alibi for people who wish to shift responsibility and to blame outside forces for the conditions that exist, thus tending to undermine vigorous human effort to improve these conditions.[8] *Predestination* is the view that the events of our lives, including our eternal destiny, have been decreed by God. Based on a theological and a supernatural element, this doctrine, at least in its extreme form, has always aroused protests and opposition, since it seems to make God responsible for evil as well as good.

Let us begin our attempt to answer this question of seeming contradiction between a rigid determinism and a degree of freedom of choice by pointing out some different types of behavior that we observe in our everyday experience. Take, for example, the differences that exist between a stone, a tree, a dog, and a man. A stone stands in one place unless it is moved by some outside force. Although it is affected by weathering and certain slow changes that take place in its chemical or

---

[8]For a discussion of fatalism, see Richard Taylor, "Fatalism," *The Philosophical Review* 71 (January 1962): 56–66.

physical properties, it sets up no goals and exerts no effort. It has its existence in the realm of physical and chemical action and reaction. The tree, in contrast to the stone, is alive and grows. Its leaves and branches grow toward the sunlight, and its roots reach toward water and minerals in the soil. While it is alive, it is anchored to the earth, however, and has little or no power of movement or choice.

The dog, in contrast to the stone and the tree, moves about freely. He can learn from experience and can adapt himself to new conditions. He is very much alive, with appetites and desires and heightened sensitivity. He grows, reproduces, and develops his five senses to aid him in his many activities. Yet, though the dog can form percepts, he is quite limited in his ability to grasp concepts or to live by their aid.

When we come to human life, we find a wide range of new characteristics or powers. On the physical plane, man has erect posture and a larger brain. On the cultural level, he develops symbols, inventions, and institutions. Man has unique powers. Other animals are conscious; only man is self-conscious. He is conscious of the fact that it is he who is conscious. The growth of self-consciousness, memory, and imagination make possible a new creativeness and enable man, a child of nature, to rise to some extent above nature. Through reflective thinking and abstract thought, man is able to carry on the trial-and-error process internally and to live in a new world of meanings. He can manipulate nature to some extent to satisfy his desires. In the light of what is, he says that such-and-such *ought to be*. Ethical discrimination and aesthetic appreciation open up a new world to him. As a self-conscious being, man formulates ideals and strives to attain them. To hereditary and environmental factors must now be added man's capacity for personal response.

Our problem is essentially this: On every side man seems to be surrounded by conditions that affect his life and determine his conduct. From this point of view he is merely one event in a chain of events. On the other hand, man is not like the objects of inanimate nature and he is not a mere animal organism. He has powers and characteristics that seem to set him apart and make him to some extent a controller of nature rather than a thing controlled. How is this seeming contradiction to be resolved?

We see, then, that we must reject the views of those who hold that there are just the two clear-cut alternatives: You accept freedom of choice or you accept a rigid determinism, and there are no other positions. Here is a pair of incompatible presuppositions, and each point of view has been ably defended by outstanding thinkers in the history of thought. We cannot accept this rigid division; actually, the truth is not all on one side or the other.

If environmental or external determinism is complete and final, then values, thinking, and even truth are meaningless. It is absurd to appeal to ideas, ideals, and logical reasons. Everything is an equally necessary outcome of what has gone before. Reason is meaningless unless there is enough freedom to enable the person to discriminate and choose between two or more alternatives. We say that men are prejudiced when their decisions or judgments rest only on the basis of their own desires or emotions. Real knowledge depends on our ability to rise above such impulsive reactions.

Explanations that assume a complete determinism arise, we are told, when the methods of the physical sciences are taken as the only methods. In the physical sciences, investigators attempt to exclude all personal and nonquantitative factors. This approach is a legitimate one, but the investigator needs to realize that his conclusions or results must be confined to these fields of investigation and not be extended to human experience as a whole.

The interpretation of universal causation links determinism and freedom and stresses the significance and effectiveness of man's participation in the processes of nature. In any particular situation, man may be a passive effect or an active causal factor. He makes a selection among several alternatives, and the fact that the alternatives have antecedent causal connections does not destroy the element of freedom of selection. Man can make effective choices because of the causal connections that exist between events and between himself and nature's processes. This fact does not preclude the possibility that causal processes exist. Indeed, all social legislation is based on the assumption that human behavior can be controlled if the right technique is used. Without reliable cause-and-effect relationships, we would be frustrated at every turn. Freedom does not mean freedom from causes. It is reflection and choice that make the fundamental difference in the part man plays in his world. Frequently in the past men have not been able to carry out their purposes because they have not known how to accomplish what they wanted to do. Science, or man's special knowledge, is valuable because it may be the instrument of an enlarging freedom. Science thus may help set us free.

To be free is to be intelligent, informed, and responsible. Men need to develop a power of judgment and discrimination so that they will direct their lives and the affairs about them in intelligent ways.

An adequate determinism must include man's intelligence as an effective element in the causal series. We have already spoken of moral conduct as the voluntary action of human beings. A study of moral conduct implies the existence of a self-conscious personality. If there is any problem of human conduct, there must be a self, or a person, capable of conscious and deliberate discrimination between values. The organism man belongs not only to a physical and an organic world, but also to a rational and an ethical order. As a rational and an ethical being, man is free from some of the limitations of the laws of lower organisms and inanimate things. Unlike the stone, the tree, or the dog, he is able to carry on experiments that are mental. As a result of this mental trial-error process, he can to some extent select his future behavior. Man is a personality, a unit, with qualities and characteristics quite different from the parts of which he is composed. The human self is a center of energy that may mold the original materials given it by heredity and environment into a pattern of moral character distinctly its own. Ethical and rational discrimination, however, do not eliminate the influence of biological inheritance or of environmental pressure.

When we are considering the laws of nature, we should remember that it is man who has formulated these laws. If man were nothing more than a link in the chain of events, he would not even know that he is such a link.

FREEDOM AS SELF-DETERMINISM

In our opinion, neither indeterminism nor determinism, in any of the extreme forms that deny to men some freedom to choose between alternatives, gives a satisfactory answer to the problem of human freedom and responsibility. Indeterminism makes human conduct too capricious. It fails to take sufficient account of the conditions surrounding our actions. An interpretation of determinism that denies real freedom of choice does not permit an adequate account of many of the most significant elements in human experience. Determinism, as it applies to man, needs to permit recognition of degrees of self-determinism. Moral judgments are applied to the actions of human beings and in particular to the voluntary acts of persons. Let us sum up the reasons for claiming that men have some freedom of choice, some power of self-determination.

The Consciousness of Freedom

Practically all men have an immediate consciousness of freedom and believe that they choose between alternative courses of action. After many decisions, although not always, they feel that they could have acted otherwise. This strong conviction on the part of most people is difficult to explain if it has no basis in fact. Benedict Spinoza (1632–1677), in his defense of determinism, suggested that we feel free merely because we are ignorant of the causes that have influenced us. Sometimes, however, we know just why we are acting as we do and still we feel free. The development of self-consciousness, intelligence, and knowledge gives us a greater rather than a lesser sense of freedom.

The Sense of Personal Responsibility

Man is a creature who distinguishes between what *is* and what *ought to be*. At times he feels a personal sense of responsibility to exert himself on behalf of what ought to be. The development of this sense of moral obligation is quite meaningless apart from some power of alternative choice. The consciousness of freedom expresses itself forcibly in the sense of "ought." For Kant, "I ought implies I can." This is a central fact in the moral life. After some choices men have a keen feeling of blame or even of guilt because they did not act differently.

Moral Judgments on the Conduct and Character of Others

All judgments on conduct and character presuppose that men are free moral agents. We hold children responsible for their acts in proportion to their age and experience. At a very early age we do not hold them responsible, but as they come to an age of understanding and are able to grasp clearly the significance of an act and its rightfulness or wrongfulness, we do hold them accountable. In our courts we do not hold people responsible unless we think that they could have done otherwise than they did—that is, that their own deliberation made, or could have made, the difference. Our whole system of reward and punishment, praise and blame, approval and disapproval assumes freedom and responsibility.

With the growth of intelligence and hence of freedom, there is increased responsibility. Responsibility has a future bearing as well as a retrospective one. We hold persons liable in order to make their future conduct different. As Dewey and Tufts say, "It would be absurd to hold a stone responsible when it falls from a cliff and injures a person, or to blame the falling tree which crushes a passer-by. The reason for the absurdity is that such treatment would have and could have no conceivable influence on the future behavior of stone or tree. They do not interact with conditions about them so as to learn, so as to modify their attitudes and dispositions."[9] We dare not treat human beings as we would treat stones or even trees; people represent a different order of existence.

Society holds people responsible in order that they may learn or that

---

[9]John Dewey and James H. Tufts, *Ethics*, rev. ed. (New York: Henry Holt & Co., 1932), p. 337.

their growth may be directed. The fact that human beings are able to refashion or redirect old tendencies as well as to acquire new and additional information is another argument against a too narrow conception of the principle of causality.

The Fact of Deliberation or Reflective Thinking

Sometimes when men are confronted with a choice of alternatives, they stop to deliberate on the nature of the alternatives presented and weigh carefully the reasons for and against each possible choice. A football when kicked does not stop to deliberate whether or not it shall go, nor does a baseball reflect when hit by a bat. Their action is immediate and in the direction determined by the force of the blow. In human deliberation, something different takes place. After sensory or ideational stimulation, there may be a prolonged delay while further thought is given to the situation and many relevant factors are recalled and evaluated. Reflective consideration may change the relative strength of motives or desires, so that a motive that was strong before deliberation may lose its force and another motive may come to take its place.

In defending a type of determinism that accepts both universal causation and freedom of choice, Brand Blanshard says that in the realm of reflective thinking "there operates a different kind of causality from any we know in the realm of bodies," that "even within the psychical realm there are different causal levels," and that "a causality of a higher level may supervene on one of lower level."[10]

If I act in a certain manner because of a particular set of conditions of which I am unaware, my action takes one form. If, however, I become aware of these conditions that have influenced me, I may react to them in an entirely different way from then on. When I know what reaction a certain stimulus is supposed to produce in me, I have a new motive for deciding which way I shall act. Men can be managed through stimuli only as long as they do not know that they are being managed. When men become conscious of the fact that they are being influenced by other people or things, they may modify their reactions or even react negatively. Freedom thus means, in part, the ability to stop to think before committing oneself to a particular line of activity. It means the ability to place before oneself other satisfactions or courses of action than the one suggested by the immediate environmental situation.

When a man stops to deliberate before making a choice, he brings

---

[10]Brand Blanshard, "The Case for Determinism" in *Determinism and Freedom in the Age of Modern Science,* ed. Sidney Hook (New York: New York University Press, 1958), p. 26.

before himself, as far as he can, the consequences that would follow from the different possible courses of action. Deliberation would seem to be of little value if his final choice were not to be determined by this process of thinking. The foreseen advantages of one course of action and the disadvantages of another determine his choice. While every choice may be motivated by some desire, the desire may be the expression of a self-formed character. With the growth of the power to control the forces of nature, many of the older fears that haunted primitive man have disappeared, and man believes that in some measure he is master of his destiny.

HOW FREE IS MAN?

Primitive man was so pressed by his immediate need of food, clothing, shelter, rest, and protection that he had little opportunity for reflection on the aims of life or for choice as to means of attaining these ends. For modern man, these needs are only slightly less pressing. Consequently, the times when conscious choice and reflection are present are also likely to be few and fleeting. A free man, we are told, "must have knowledge of himself, his character, his attitudes and desires, as well as of the situations in which he decides and acts. The more these things are unconscious, the less free he is."[11] Men gain freedom with the development of self-consciousness, with the growth of intelligence and knowledge, and with the aid of leisure hours and the released energy that civilization usually makes possible, at least for some. Whereas consciousness is the awareness of one's environment, self-consciousness is the awareness of the contents and activity of one's own mind or self. It is the kind of consciousness that distinguishes the self from its environment and makes possible language, reasoning, and the sense of right and wrong. In the development of the child and of the race, consciousness precedes self-consciousness. The latter is a prerequisite of freedom.

With the growth of intelligence and knowledge, there is an increase in freedom. If in a crisis a man knows or can think of only one thing to do, he is not free. With an increase in reasoning power and in knowledge come additional choices. New ways of performing necessary tasks suggest themselves, and choices and moral problems arise where they have not been before. Not only physical and mental health but also a fertile imagination, a broad range of interests, and a capacity for intelligent valuation are necessary conditions of freedom.

---

[11] Harold Ofstad, *An Inquiry into the Freedom of Decision* (Oslo: Norwegian University Press, 1961), p. 306.

When a man is confronted with a perplexing situation, there is uncertainty, and a conflict arises in the organism between the principle of organization and the forces making for disorganization. At such times emotions arise as disorganized responses. As organization and control become less and less, the person's behavior tends to revert to the deep-rooted primitive responses of the race. Under these conditions a man has little or no freedom. In this sense we could avoid the word *freedom,* if we wished, and talk about unintelligent behavior versus intelligent behavior.

Some students of this problem tell us that a belief in freedom of choice has an effect not only on one's sense of responsibility but also on the degree of freedom one actually has or at least exercises; that is, a man who genuinely believes in freedom of choice tends to be more active and aggressive in his relation to the world in that he approaches nature as something to be understood, manipulated, and controlled. The man who denies or minimizes his freedom of choice is likely to take a more passive, fatalistic attitude and accept the world and events as they come, without making a strenuous effort to shape things so that they become better adapted to the promotion of human welfare.[12]

With the development of self-consciousness, intelligence, and knowledge, there is opened up for a man the possibility of self-control or self-determination that was not possible before. The important question is not "Is man free?" but "How free is man?" Some men have little freedom; others apparently have a considerable amount. Moral freedom means that people are genuine sources of action and can bring to pass events that otherwise would not occur. In the universe there are definite causal sequences or mechanical causation; there is also a capacity for personal response or personal causation. Our everyday lives and the work of the scientists are examples of the intimate interplay of purpose and mechanism. Man studies the laws of nature and learns the ways of nature so that he can make nature work for him. The more he knows, the greater his freedom may become. Freedom is in part the ability to make plans and then, within limits, to carry them out. We say that a person is free when he is able to initiate action toward ends that he foresees.

QUESTIONS AND PROJECTS

1. An Ohio newspaper carried an account of a man in a small community who bet on the honesty of his fellowmen and found that it worked.

---

[12]Allan M. Munn, *Free-Will and Determinism* (Toronto: University of Toronto Press, 1960), pp. 314–315.

Near his home he operated a serve-yourself roadside stand, where he sold fruit and vegetables from his own garden and some produce purchased from his neighbors. The prices of produce for sale were marked on a blackboard, and a tin can contained change. The purchaser selected what he wanted and made the change himself. The owner was often away from home at work. In four years he lost only forty cents. He said, "If you make people think you believe them to be honest, they will be honest." Is this typical or not? Does it indicate anything about human nature?

2. Some persons apparently do not hesitate to "gyp" their fellowmen even in the name of charity. Quite a number of cases have been described in which large amounts of money were raised and little or nothing given to charity. Discuss these incidents in the light of question 1 above.

3. A boy who lived on the outskirts of a large city was arrested for setting fire to haystacks. He was known as the bad boy, the scamp of the community, and the school authorities were unable to deal with him successfully. When he was brought before the juvenile court, the members of the staff noticed that he had a harelip which affected his appearance and speech and which they suspected might be related to his misbehavior. They sent the boy to a hospital, where the harelip was corrected. A short time later they returned the boy to his community and asked that he be given another chance. The boy gave no more trouble. To what extent do you think that loss of status among the boys had anything to do with the earlier abnormal behavior? What do you think would have been the outcome had the boy been whipped, sent to a reformatory or a jail, or reprimanded?

4. John Brown, a bank clerk, forged a check for one hundred dollars and was caught. Investigation showed that he was not a habitual criminal but had acted in a moment of weakness. He was a good father and husband, and he wanted to provide for his family some things they needed but had not been able to afford. The criminal court sentenced John Brown to from five to ten years in prison. The family, faced with the loss of support, was forced to move to a poor residential district. The mother was compelled to accept work which kept her from home all day, while the children shifted for themselves. Was this case adequately handled, or did society force all the members of the family to undergo a psychic and physical crippling? Considering the total situation, the man, and his family, which would have been the best solution: a prison term, probation, or guidance by some social agency?

5. The following incident is from World War II, but it is duplicated many times in the experiences of war and in disasters of many types. A convoy of thirty-eight merchant ships was crossing the Atlantic. The ships were unarmed except for the 14,000-ton merchant ship *Jervis Bay*, which had six six-inch guns and no armor plate. One evening an enemy raider appeared and opened fire with eleven-inch shells. Without an instant's hesitation the *Jervis Bay* headed for the raider, laying down a smoke screen behind which the rest of the convoy escaped. The captain and every member of the crew knew that the action was suicidal. With the

captain wounded and the bridges shot away, the *Jervis Bay* kept firing until the last active gun was being submerged and the captain gave orders to abandon ship. Sixty-eight men out of two hundred and fifty reached the lifeboat and two rafts remained floatable. The captain was not among them. No one protested, or complained that any other action might or should have been taken. (See *Time*, 25 November 1940, p. 22.) Can the action of the men on this ship be explained by theories of selfish human nature or social conditioning? If not, how can it be explained?

6. Imagine that you are defending the view that self-preservation is the first law of life. How will you account for the conduct of firemen, policemen, soldiers in time of war, or the mother and nurse who stay by a child with a contagious disease? Indicate how successful you believe you are in reconciling such facts with your theory, and what difficulties, if any, you find in applying such an account of human nature to the making of choices.

7. Primitive man crouched in fear when his community experienced an electrical storm. He knew nothing of the nature of the great natural forces. Modern man may enjoy the storm. He understands its vast forces, and he even controls similar forces to light his home, cook his meals, communicate with his friends. Give other illustrations of the freedom that comes through intelligence.

8. List the conditions you think are necessary for the largest degree of freedom. Do health, fatigue, intense pain, disease, mental habits, range of interests, and ability to reflect influence the degree of freedom we have at any one time?

9. Is it true that when we discover the part that heredity and environment play in our lives, their character and influence are thereby altered? Explain, and give reasons for your answer.

10. When the soldier in the army is commanded to perform an act that he feels is immoral, is he a free moral being? To what extent should he be held responsible?

11. What does it mean to say that people are responsible for their actions? Under what conditions can we justly hold people responsible, and when are they not responsible for their conduct? You may wish to consult Austin Farrer, "Responsibility and Freedom," *The Freedom of the Will* ch. 13, (London: Adam and Charles Black, 1958); and P. H. Nowell-Smith, "Freedom and Responsibility," *Ethics*, chs. 19 and 20 (Oxford: Basil Blackwell, 1957).

12. Mr. A accepts the position of complete determinism. He tries to convince his friend Mr. B, who accepts a degree of freedom of choice, that B's position is wrong. Mr. A says that B's conduct really is determined, although he does not know it and will not admit it. Mr. B replies that A cannot be a consistent determinist and say that he is wrong, since if he does, A assumes that he is a really rational agent who is able to change the course of events from what they would be otherwise. Mr. B contends that A assumes that a man may go counter to his past and accept a new position. Comment on this argument and the issues raised.

13. If all events in nature and all human action, including thought processes,

are rigidly determined by preceding events, why do we call some actions right and others wrong? If everything is rigidly determined, how can we educate people to detect errors of fact or errors of reasoning? While we may need to accept the notion of universal causality, do we also need to affirm that man is a center of creativity and that he is able at times to select from among various possible causal sequences?
14. Discuss and give your reaction to the following statements:
    (1) "Man is nature's rebel."
    (2) "Man is not only a creature of his environment, he is also a critic of his environment."
    (3) "We can no more blame people for their actions than for the color of their eyes."
    (4) "Science comes to the facts of experience with certain assumptions or postulates, one of which is that everything is determined."
    (5) "We do not know what is really inherited even in mice and dogs, to say nothing of men."

SUGGESTED READINGS

HUMAN NATURE

Adler, Mortimer J. *The Difference of Man and the Difference It Makes.* New York: Holt, Rinehart & Winston, 1967; also Meridian Books, 1968.

Barker, Roger G., ed. *The Stream of Behavior: Exploration of Its Structure and Content.* New York: Appleton-Century-Crofts, 1963.

Cassirer, Ernst. *Essay on Man: An Introduction to a Philosophy of Human Culture.* New York: Bantam Books, 1970.

Doniger, Simon, ed. *The Nature of Man in Theological and Psychological Perspective.* New York: Harper & Row, Publishers, 1962.

Krutch, Joseph Wood. *Human Nature and the Human Condition.* New York: Random House, 1959.

Passmore, John. *The Perfectibility of Man.* London: Gerald Duckworth, 1970.

Ramsey, Paul. *Fabricated Man.* New Haven: Yale University Press, 1970.

Rostand, Jean. *Can Man Be Modified?* Translated by Jonathan Griffin. New York: Basic Books, 1959.

Ulich, Robert. *The Human Career: A Philosophy of Self-Transcendence.* New York: Harper & Brothers, 1955.

FREEDOM OF CHOICE

Ayers, Michael Richard. *The Refutation of Determinism.* London: Methuen & Co., 1968.

Edwards, Rem Blanshard. *Freedom, Responsibility, and Obligation.* The Hague: Martinus Nijhoff, 1969.

Franklin, Richard L. *Freedom and Determinism: A Study of Rival Conceptions of Man.* New York: Humanities Press, 1969.

Hampshire, Stuart. *Freedom of the Individual.* New York: Harper & Row, Publishers, 1965.

Hook, Sidney, ed. *Determinism and Freedom in the Age of Modern Science.* New York: New York University Press, 1958. Also no. BS 37. New York: Collier Books, 1961.

Hume, David. "Of Liberty and Necessity." In *An Inquiry Concerning Human Understanding.* Sec. 8. 1748.

James, William. *The Will to Believe and Other Essays in Popular Philosophy.* Essay 5. New York: Longmans, Green & Co., 1912.

Lamont, Corless. *Freedom of Choice Affirmed.* New York: Horizon Press, 1967.

Pears, D. F., ed. *Freedom and the Will.* New York: St. Martins Press, 1963.

Skinner, B. F. *Beyond Freedom and Dignity.* New York: Alfred A. Knopf, 1971.

5
WHY RIGHT IS RIGHT

The question "Why right is right?" takes us to the center of the moral problem. Let us see where we have arrived in our discussion up to this point. We asked, first, what is happening in our time and why there is growing concern about the future. Among the many causes of our disorders we noted a neglect of our moral standards and values, or a conflict and confusion among them, so that we find it difficult to apply any generally accepted standards to the new conditions we face in today's world. Second, in considering many possible methods of approach to the study of ethics we said that our approach would be comprehensive or synthetic with the emphasis on a common-sense normative outlook. In this period of unusually rapid social change and baffling problems of human conduct, we saw in chapter 3 that traditional moral standards that guided men effectively in a less complex society seem unable to settle many current issues and to lead men on to clear convictions as to what is right and what is wrong. Moral standards grow out of life situations and moral codes have changed to meet human needs under changing conditions. This was illustrated in the changing stages of the administration of justice. As intelligence and experience grow and expand, the requirements of personal and social welfare need to be taken more and more into account. There are times, however, when our knowledge and use of means grow at a rapid pace while our knowledge of ends remains stationary or even becomes dim. When this happens society is in danger. In the preceding chapter we pointed out that human nature is adaptive and that a wide range of conditions influence human conduct. With the growth of self-consciousness, intelligence, and knowledge, man's conduct can be brought more and more under his own conscious control. Within limits man has freedom of choice and is master of his destiny.

In this chapter we seek to clarify the basic moral postulate, and the reason why we call some actions right and others wrong. We answer the question broadly, leaving for later chapters the discussion of more specific points that appear in various classical and contemporary theories of morality. Here we state what ethics as a study of right and wrong is about and give our overall viewpoint.

THE BASIC MORAL POSTULATE

In all fields of investigation we begin with certain assumptions, postulates, axioms, or value judgments. Something must be accepted as true for thought and reasoning to proceed. Some facts, ideas, or principles must be taken for granted. They act as the point of beginning or as our major premises. This is true whether we consider science, philosophy, or religion, although for most people these basic presuppositions may be largely unconscious or subconscious. We do not always see them, but we tend to view other things through them or by means of them. They are considered part of the nature of things and therefore are seldom made explicit for critical discussion and examination.

In the field of logic men take for granted the principles of identity (all A is A), noncontradiction (not both A and not A), and excluded middle (either A or not A). Men working in the various sciences proceed on the basis of a number of postulates, or axioms, such as the principles of causality, predictive uniformity, objectivity, empiricism, parsimony, and the like. These cannot be proven with any certainty, but they enable thought and action to proceed, and they are justified through use and experience.

Not only special disciplines or areas of study, but every society or civilization rests on a number of presuppositions about the world, man, and human values. A man's interpretation of his observations and experiences, and his generalizations from them, depend on these beliefs and value systems. One problem in today's world is that specialization has been carried so far that it has narrowed man's vision and goals. Specialization has brought many benefits, but it has led man to see life as compartmentalized and fragmented to an extreme and sometimes alarming degree.

In moral philosophy or the field of ethics, the basic moral postulate is the worth of persons—of men and women. This fundamental value judgment may be stated in many different ways including the dignity of man, reverence for life, respect for persons, and the like. The postulate of the worth of persons is as basic in morality as the postulate of predictive uniformity in the realm of science. When we accept this moral postulate we have a basis not only for distinguishing between right and wrong, good and evil, but a basis for defending a doctrine of human rights and a free and democratic society, as we shall see later.

We call something right and good, in the moral sense, if it promotes what is good for or has value for persons. Right is thus person affirming; wrong is person denying or degrading. Evil is that which denies the good, or impairs or destroys persons or human welfare. Some things are good by nature in the sense that they are based on natural human needs which must be met or acknowledged in any society if human beings are to be healthy and survive. For example, there must be opportunity and time for sleeping, eating, drinking, and preserving one's health and vigor. Some things are evil by nature such as pain, injury, and death. Some other things are good or evil by convention and may differ in different societies just as beliefs and conditions vary concerning such things as marriage customs, the training of children, and dietary regulations.

The common experience of mankind reinforces the conviction that some things are better than others, that some are good and others are bad (evil). For example: health is better than illness; knowledge and understanding are better than ignorance; love and goodwill are better than hate and ill will; friendship (having friends and companions) is better than loneliness; freedom is better than slavery; some wealth is better than deprivation and poverty; living a rich life is better than merely living; making a good life for self and others is better than having a good time from moment to moment.

Why do we take persons or selves as the basic value around which other values revolve? While we cannot conclusively prove this postulate any more than we can prove with any finality the scientific postulate of causal order or predictive uniformity in the universe, we can give good reasons or evidence for its acceptability.

In the first place, the concept of the worth of persons has its source in man's normal psychological reactions. If man's growth is stifled, his expression hampered, or if something brings dissatisfaction and pain, he resists. There is an almost universal indignation and resistance against injury. This is true not only if the injury is to ourselves as individuals but also if it is injury to our fellowmen. This resistance against injury and the presence of human sympathy for one's fellowmen are closely related to the principles of liberty, justice, equality, and well-being as seen in the drive to remove exploitation, discrimination, and all conditions that mar life in any way.

In the second place, this resistance against injury and destruction is found not only in man, for it runs through all living forms in the ever-present, persistent *will to live*. Every living creature, sub-human as well as human, strives toward the fulfillment of its functions. The fact that living things not only consent to live but also seek fulfillment and resist things that impair life is an indication that it is deeply rooted in biological nature.

In the third place, the concept of the worth and dignity of man is based on the unique and distinctive qualities of selfhood. Only in persons do we find in developed form these qualities which are universally recognized as valuable. Because of them man is said to be an end in himself. Following is a provisional list of the unique characteristics of the person: (1) *Self-consciousness*. Whereas all animals are conscious, man is self-conscious. He is not only conscious, but he is conscious of the fact that it is *he* who is conscious. (2) *Abstract thought or the power of reflective thinking*. Man can search for truth, and he has some ability to distinguish between truth and falsity. (3) *Ethical discrimination and some freedom of choice*. Man is conscious of a distinction between what is and what ought to be. He distinguishes between right and wrong and feels responsible for his actions. (4) *Aesthetic appreciation*. Man searches for aesthetic good and can distinguish between beauty and ugliness. (5) *Religious aspiration and commitment*. Man is a being who worships, prays, repents, and asks forgiveness. Most men have faith that they live in a meaningful universe and believe that there is a Spirit akin to their own with whom they may have fellowship or communion. (6) *Transcendence of particular conditions of space and time*. Man experiences himself as a unity and as a being who transcends the particular conditions in the midst of which he lives. He is not a mere thing of nature. He reaches out from the present to keep the past alive and to deal with the future. He transcends space and lives in a world of rich meaning. (7) *Development fulfilled through community living*. Man has a sense of community, and his unique powers as a person develop fully only as his life is cooperatively related to the lives of his fellows. People can meet their basic needs and develop their potentialities only through fellowship in a community or through cooperative living. (8) *Unique powers of creativity*. On the level of personality there is a creation of a new order that expresses itself in the search for truth, beauty, goodness, and God—in science, art, philosophy, and religion.

These qualiites or unique characteristics of the person need to be kept clearly in mind when we talk about the good life, the greater good, or the development of human personality. To be moral is to observe the facts and the principles of personal and social welfare as they are progressively discovered through man's search for a more satisfying life. To deny the criterion of the welfare of persons would seem to lead eventually to the elimination of both life and reason.

The fourth reason for accepting the concept of the worth of human beings is the result of an examination of the actual moral codes found around the world, in the world religions, and in the great philosophic systems of thought. They all indicate that, subject to the intelligence and stage of culture, men approve that which they think enriches life and condemn that which they think is detrimental or injurious. With new knowledge these judgments tend to change to conform to new outlooks even though at times the changes are long delayed. The virtues or those traits of human character that men value and approve, and the vices or those traits that are disapproved, are much the same in the different cultures. The differences are found mainly in the ranking of values at various times and places.

The view that man is a creature of great worth is central in the Judaeo-Christian tradition. Man is to be understood primarily from the standpoint of his divine origin. He stands at the point where nature and spirit meet. The former explains his weakness, the latter explains his uniqueness, worth, and great possibilities. Christians stress love or social-mindedness as the supreme virtue. In Judaism justice and righteousness are emphasized. The Islamic or Moslem faith is a blend of Arabic, Jewish, and Christian elements and shows affinity with Judaism and Christianity in its view of man. In Hinduism, man is said to be "subject, not object," in the sense that his essential nature is spirit, not matter, and his consciousness reflects the nature of the Supreme Spirit. Buddhism stresses the Noble-Eight-Fold-Path that emphasizes: (1) right views or understanding, (2) right aspiration or purpose, (3) right speech (honesty, kindness, and the like), (4) right conduct (avoid killing, stealing, and the like), (5) right mode of livelihood, (6) right striving and self-control, (7) right mindfulness or meditation, and (8) right contemplation and concentration. Sir S. Radhakrishnan of India, scholar and statesman, has said that "the basic principle of the dignity and freedom of the individual is common to all religious faiths."[1]

In philosophy from Plato and Aristotle to Dewey and Whitehead, the fulfillment of the life of the person and social welfare have been stressed.

---

[1] S. Radhakrishman, and P. T. Raju, eds., *The Concept of Man: A Study in Comparative Philosophy* (London: George Allen & Unwin, 1960), p. 9.

With new knowledge and new conditions these judgments are remolded to serve the changing needs of life.

That life is good and that men and women—the highest creatures in the world as we know it—have worth and are ends in themselves are descriptive as well as value judgments that furnish the moral authority for many of the ethical choices we make from day to day. Morality grows out of life and reflects many different life conditions; it is wisdom (intelligence and insight) applied to the conduct of one's life.

SOME MORAL GUIDELINES

We have spoken above of right conduct as that which is conducive to good, or that which has value for persons and makes for social welfare. Let us state this approach to right conduct in a number of different ways and thus offer general guidelines that will be made clearer and will be elaborated more in later chapters.

1. Action is right if it leads to physical, intellectual, and spiritual development or to a more harmonious personal and social life. Action is wrong—that is, neither morally permissible nor obligatory—if its net effect is detrimental to the individuals and society affected. The effect of action on personality—one's total physical, mental, and spiritual nature—is the key measure here. Morality, it should be noted, in addition to demanding good motives and certain conditions regarding the means used, as we shall see later, seeks effects that are beneficial to all the people affected by the action. Even the private act has public as well as purely individual effects. Some acts benefit individuals but harm society—we still call these acts wrong. Social well-being, conceived as embracing the effects on all persons involved, is the test. If we had a term other than *greatest good* that meant personality development in the direction of goodness, truthfulness, and capacity for aesthetic fulfillments and also included social integration and welfare—that would be the term to use. *The greatest happiness of the greatest number* is sometimes used with this meaning. Here *happiness* means the good life as a whole; it is not a synonym for *pleasure*.

Morality is observance of the laws of wholesome living. To be moral is to be, within one's capacities, intelligent and social-minded in the process of living. An act that is right enriches and strengthens the life of the group. An act that is wrong is one that has proved to be socially harmful or less beneficial than its alternatives. This standard was in operation before men became conscious of it. Men learned long ago through bitter experience that there are certain types of actions and ways of living that are detrimental to the larger community. These socially harmful actions were called *wrong*. Men also discovered that there are other ways of acting and living that are, on the whole, socially beneficial. These actions received group approval and were called *right*.

2. The same standard of judging between right and wrong may be stated a little differently. *The right choice is the selection of the greater or greatest value. The wrong choice is the selection of some lesser good or value.* While some choices in life are those between good and evil, in a great many cases we must choose between a good and a better. In such cases, right conduct is action in the direction of the better.

To the degree that a group of people accept a certain value as a norm, it becomes a matter of evidence as to whether a particular act leads in the direction of that norm. For example, good health is one norm that practically all people accept. The conditions under which we are most likely to maintain our health is a matter of evidence that can be tested. To the person who is morally mature, an act that is beneficial is a good act and an act that is harmful is a bad act, regardless of whether the community approves or disapproves. The growing knowledge of the specific elements that enter into human behavior and the way in which these factors affect our welfare will enable us to direct our lives more intelligently. The purpose of a study of moral problems and of standards of judgment is to lead men to consider more consciously what is most worthwhile in life, to recognize and approve conduct that has beneficial results, and to disapprove conduct that is harmful. Without some such scrutiny, their views of the worthwhile things in life may be superficial, and their knowledge of the personal and social effects of conduct may be warped or fallacious.

3. What factors affect the nature of a morally good life? The good life must be lived in the midst of changing conditions. It depends on the nature of man, as well as on the nature of the world in which man lives. Man must live in harmonious adjustment with the basic structure and processes of the universe or he will court disaster.

We have stated that running through all life is the ever-present, persistent *will to live*. Every living creature, subhuman as well as human, strives toward the fulfillment of its functions. Everywhere there are conditions that must be met. In the animal realm, what is good for the animal is not a capricious matter. How it ought to act or live is settled by its nature. The amount or conditions of food, shelter, exercise, and temperature are determined in considerable part by its anatomical and physiological structure. Some birds eat seeds; others eat worms. Some animals need flesh; others eat nuts; still others thrive on grass and herbs. The rules of living for the animal depend on its nature and on its habitat.

Man's conduct is prescribed for him within certain broad limits set by his nature and his environment. If he lives one way, he grows and continues to live; if he lives another way, he may become diseased or die. Consider first the physical level of man's life. In order to live, man must eat, sleep, and have available certain conditions of air, temperature, sunshine, and the like. In all these areas some things are good for life and others are detrimental. These are demands he will do well to obey. Again, anger, fear, and jealousy produce poisons in the human system and disrupt social relations, whereas love, contentment, and mutual trust make for health of body and mind. The physical and biological demands are not merely emotional and subjective. They impose duties on man that are both objective and universal in the sense that all men must recognize them in order to live well.

Man must associate with his fellows if he is to get the most out of life. In order to live together harmoniously, men must have regard for the feelings, desires, and needs of one another. Cooperation is necessary in order to obtain food, shelter, and protection. There are right and wrong ways of treating children, husband or wife, parents, and friends, just as there are right and wrong ways of playing games and running a business. There are basic needs and desires that express themselves in similar ways wherever human beings are together. Friendship, good will, honesty, courage, and self-control are respected and approved almost universally. Murder, treachery, selfishness, stealing, lying, and cowardice are condemned almost universally. While men do hold opinions about such matters, our judgments regarding these traits are not mere matters of opinion. Everywhere the demand is to live so that life is enhanced, and this is a matter of evidence.

When we come to the area of mind and spirit, there are important demands that man must meet. This area, let us acknowledge, cannot be separated sharply from the social and the physical. For many centuries, and especially since the time of the classical Greeks, men have recognized reason as one feature that distinguishes man from all other animals. Because of its power to guide action to preferred ends and to distinguish between better and worse ends, reason ought to be in control over the emotions and appetites. Plato said that just as it is the proper function of the heart to pump blood, so it is the proper function of reason to rule in the life of man. To think or to be reasonable saves time, energy, and life itself. The great religious and ethical systems have been united in the view that the satisfactions of the mind and the spirit are more noble than the pleasures that pertain to the body alone.

The good life involves more than knowledge and intelligence. Clever men may be vicious. Man is a being with feelings and emotions that need to be developed and expressed if life is not to be impoverished.

Love, hatred, fear, and anger are contagious and tend to produce their kind. The psychological fact of sympathy is the basis of the altruistic virtues and the Judaeo-Christian emphasis on love and social-mindedness.

THE GENERALIZATION AND OTHER PRINCIPLES

There are some principles, called by various names and given strong emphasis in different outlooks, to which men almost everywhere appeal. We come across them under such names as: the generalization principle; the principles of justice, impartiality, and fairness; the law of moral equality; the law of compassion; the Golden Rule; the principle of universality. Almost everywhere we find people appealing to some standard of conduct that they expect other people to know and to follow. We hear people asking what would be the consequences of extending some proposed individual action to the society at large. We are asked, "What would happen if everyone did that?" or "Is that fair?" At other times we hear them say, "Don't hurt him, he isn't hurting you." or "You promised to do so and so." Men do appeal to a standard of conduct that is more than passing emotion or opinion, and they believe in some right and wrong based on the nature of life and the structure of things. If the consequences of an action would be undesirable or harmful, a person ought not to take the proposed action. What is right or wrong for one man must be considered right or wrong for any similar men under similar circumstances. This is felt to be the very center of moral reasoning.

The principles set forth here do not mean that everyone under all circumstances must act in the same way. Circumstances do alter cases, and some persons depending on age, sex, state of health, position, special responsibilities, and the like, have obligations or duties that do not rest on other persons under different conditions. Some may be excused from obligations which most others are expected to meet.

Even those who reject the principles of living mentioned above usually do affirm them when they are adversely affected by the actions of others. While some men break promises, steal, and injure others, they will protest vigorously as a rule if someone else breaks promises, steals, or injures them. When we do not follow the practices we expect from others, we are usually quick to make excuses, shift the blame, or point out that there are extenuating circumstances. Then, too, people often make mistakes about what is fair, just, or right, but this is true also in arithmetic, medicine (what's good for one's health), and in scientific explanations. Most people recognize that some evil deeds are clearly worse than others. To murder a man is worse than stealing his car or failing to honor a promise. Furthermore, these moral judgments seem to be objective in the sense that they rest upon conditions outside or beyond the feelings, emotions, or personal opinions of the persons performing, or viewing, or judging the act.

The principle popularly known as the *Golden Rule* bears a close resemblance to the generalization principle. In at least eight different systems of religion and philosophy the principle of the Golden Rule appears in some form. In the literature of Hinduism we read, "Do naught to others which, if done to thee, would cause thee pain: this is the sum of duty." In Buddhism a clansman is to minister to friends and familiars "by treating them as he treats himself." Confucius is quoted as saying, "What you would not want done to yourself, do not do unto others." Jesus said, "As ye would that men should do to you, do ye also to them likewise."[2]

Some critics have pointed out that the Golden Rule needs qualification since an individual might wish for another's cooperation and assistance in performing an evil deed and be willing to reciprocate or return the favor. Stated precisely by men of goodwill, however, the Golden Rule is an example of the generalization principle.

Another example is Kant's moral philosophy, which we shall consider in a later chapter. The reader will note that one form of Kant's categorical imperative, or the direct command of the moral ought, is stated as the *principle of universality*. "Act only on that maxim whereby thou canst at the same time will that it should become a universal law." Another formulation is: "So act as to treat humanity, whether in thine own person or in that of any other, in every case as an end withal, never as means only." While stated in an abstract and formal setting, Kant's outlook is an outstanding example of the generalization principle. His use of the principle has been praised and criticized.

These different principles while in general harmony may, by difrent individuals or in different cultures at different times, be given a slightly different emphasis. The law of moral equality may emphasize that there shall be no law for one person which is not the law for all, unless there are circumstances which clearly justify different treatment. The law of compassion extends sympathy and concern to other persons including the weak, the sick, and the immature, and ideally to other conscious creatures to the degree that we can attribute feeling to them.

---

[2]For similar quotations from other religions, see Robert Ernest Hume, *The World's Living Religions* (New York: Charles Scribner's Sons, 1924), pp. 265–267.

MOTIVES, MEANS, AND CONSEQUENCES

Our understanding of the problems of morality can be amplified if we consider some of the practical questions that commonly arise when people are trying to decide what is right.

In the appraisal of conduct we talk about motives, means, and consequences. A motive is a dominant desire, a desire that causes a person to act. The means are the steps or ways by which he plans to arrive at some end or goal. The consequences are the results that flow from any specific action. These may be foreseen effects that are in line with the original motive; they may be unforeseen effects. Shall we judge conduct by the motive a person has in mind? Shall we judge conduct by the consequences (end result) of the act? Does the end justify the use of any means? Must we consider the entire act—motive, means, and consequences—in judging the moral quality of the act? Let us consider these questions by using examples to help clarify the questions involved, which will then be more fully treated as we study historic answers to them.

Motive Versus Consequences

A man driving in his car, going to an appointment, comes on the scene of an accident. He takes one man who needs medical care and speeds up to find a doctor. His extra speed is the cause of another accident. How are we to judge his conduct? Was his act right because his motive was good, or was his act wrong because the consequences were bad?

Notice the elements to be weighed in answering these questions. The results of the act of mercy were of several types. Some were foreseen and sought. Helping a man to receive needed medical care was one of these. Some were foreseen and accepted, though not desired. The delay in the driver's getting to his appointment was such a result. So was the possibility that he might have to testify in court about the extent of the injuries when the victim was picked up. But some of the results were unforeseen, and of these some were quite unwelcome (the second accident, for instance). The driver also intended some results that did not occur (reaching a doctor sooner than he did).

In appraising a person's act we also consider what he had in mind. In the incident above the rescuer applied the principles of assisting people in distress and treating others as he would himself be treated. The accident victim might have been a close friend. The rescue would then exemplify the principle of being helpful to those we hold in affection, though in stopping at the scene the driver had no such plan in mind.

The rescuer, in increasing his speed, was taking risks that are normally unlawful, though he intended no carelessness and did not foresee the accident his excessive speed would cause.

Should we judge the rescuer or his act only by those results and principles for the sake of which he acted? Should we, besides his explicit purpose, consider also what he anticipated and accepted as likely, but not the unexpected outcomes? Or should the actual outcomes be the test of him and his act?

For almost any act we can list a number of possible motives. Three persons go to college. For one, the primary motive is to get adequate preparation for a particular career. For another the motive is for wider social contacts and a good time. A third goes because it is the "thing to do" in his social set; without it he would lose prestige.

The motive for an act is basic for morality. On this point we can agree with Kant, whom we shall discuss in chapter 7, that an act which we wholeheartedly approve must satisfy certain conditions in regard to motive. If a good motive is absent, the act, even though it proves beneficial, is not approved without qualification. We know that the doer meant otherwise and that the good consequences were caused by his error of judgment or by conditions that he could not foresee. For example, a businessman, hoping to ruin his competition and gain a monopoly for himself, cuts his prices below cost for a time. His competitors meet his prices, increase their efficiency by the adoption of newer methods, and soon everyone except the would-be monopolist is benefited. On the other hand, if a good motive is present but the act turns out to be harmful, we tend to condemn less severely and partially to excuse the person by saying, "Anyway, he meant well." However, it must be noted that our condemnation or lack of condemnation will depend on whether we think he should have foreseen the consequences of his act or could have done otherwise than he did.

While a good motive is a prerequisite to an act that we approve without qualification, motive does not give us a sufficient clue to what is right. When a man asks, "What is right?" we assume that he wants to do the right thing but is unable to decide what it is. A. C. Ewing states this issue clearly:

> But when we ask whether an act was right we do not usually mean: Was the agent morally to blame or not? We are more likely to mean: Did he choose rightly in deciding what to do? And this is much the more important question in practice despite the fact that motives are more important for morality than outward acts. For in order to act rightly we must find out what is right, and in order to do that it is in general futile to ask about our motives, since the very question what is right, if and insofar as it is to be relevant to our action at all, assumes

that our motive is to do what is right. But we have still to find out what the right act is before we can express our motive in action, and we cannot therefore find this out by asking again what our motive is or even what it ought to be.[3]

There are thus two important questions that must be clearly distinguished. First, in performing a deed, has a man acted in a morally responsible way? Here we are considering what he intends to do, or his purpose. What is his motive? Does he genuinely endeavor to carry it out in action? Second, is the act right? Does the man choose correctly in relation to that motive in deciding what to do? In order to act rightly, a man must find out what is right. Here we ask, "Granted that this man wishes to act for the best, what ought he to do in this situation?" An answer to this second question demands evidence and reflection.

Means Versus the End

Just as there may be a number of motives for an act, there are often various ways by which we can arrive at some end or goal. We must employ some means or we cannot carry out our intent. To keep an appointment, I may drive my own car, go by bus, or take a train. To give myself relaxation from mental labor or from some trying experience, I may use any one of a large number of means including, perhaps, sleep, a theatrical performance, baseball, tennis, a walk, or getting drunk. Thus the same end may be gained by one of several means. Once chosen however, the means becomes part of the intended act.

The means used may be the reason why we approve or condemn some action. A businessman wishes to give a large amount of money for a hospital in his city. His motive may be good, and we may approve his achievement of this purpose. But the money he gives has resulted from unscrupulous practices in his business. In such a case our judgment of the man's action depends not on the purpose alone, but also on the means employed.

The means employed in action may be morally neutral, morally good, or evil. Provided I can keep my appointment, it will probably be morally neutral whether I go by bus or by airplane. In the illustration above, where a man is seeking relaxation, a walk or tennis match may be considered a good means, while getting drunk would be considered a bad means, because there are better ways of accomplishing the same results. If it is the only means of saving her life, the cashier is justified in

---

[3]A. C. Ewing, "Rightness and Consequences," *The Hibbert Journal* 29 (January 1931): 329. (Used by permission of the publishers, Constable & Co., London.)

giving up her keys to the cash box, even though under ordinary conditions this act would be wrong.

The question "Does the end justify the means?" is often asked and discussed. This question refers to cases in which the means is wrong by itself. The question continues to be debated because it is one of those questions that cannot be answered categorically yes or no. The answer depends on the net good to be anticipated, which in turn is a function of the circumstances. In the case of the surgeon who risks the death of his patient in the hope of saving or of prolonging life, we would answer in the affirmative if due care is used, because there seems to be no other good alternative. In the case of the man who sells drugs illicitly as a means of supporting his family, we would answer in the negative.

Cases in which the end does *justify*[4] the means are situations in which the goodness of the whole overbalances certain evil means that seem unavoidable. The morally mature persons, however, will use the best means available. We must not permit a means that of itself has previously appeared evil to prevent us from seeing the greater good of the act in its entirety. However, this cannot be interpreted to mean that any and every means may be used provided it can be shown that the end is in some sense good. In cases in which the end does not justify the means, the evil of the means is such that it outweighs any value gained from the act as a whole, or the good results might have been obtained by better means than the one used. As stated above, the question cannot be answered until we know the circumstances or total situation. Thus each case has to be judged on its merits. The principle might be stated thus: Use that combination of end and means that is the most beneficial possible to those affected directly or indirectly.

Another popular saying is "Do right, whatever the consequences." This is similar in substance to the question we have just considered. If it is interpreted to connote that men ought to consider only the motive or the motive and the means for an act and to ignore the consequences, then it omits a crucial element in the recognition of obligations. If it connotes that men should act for purposes they consider right regardless of what inconvenience or unpleasantness to themselves may result, then it is an acceptable principle. Here again the problem is one demanding reflection on the facts in the total situation. Ewing has pointed out that

> On the one hand, we cannot make the rightness of an act depend entirely on the character of the act itself in abstraction from its consequences, for if we take away the consequences nothing is left that we

---

[4]This is really an imprecise use of the term *justify*. What actually justifies the choice is its meeting the conditions outlined on pages 98–101.

can call an act or, at least, a reasonable act, and, on the other, we cannot make its rightness or obligatoriness depend entirely on its consequences, for it is unreasonable to suppose that what value there is always belongs to these and never to the act itself, which is after all only the initial part of one and the same process.[5]

AN EXAMPLE OF REFLECTIVE MORALITY

The problem stated. John is an art student about to be graduated from college. He is offered a position with a daily newspaper. The position pays well and he is interested in that type of employment, but in order to work on the staff of the newspaper, he must draw cartoons that express the sentiments of the owners and managers of the paper, not his own sentiments or convictions. The paper is jingoistic and isolationist, whereas John wishes to promote international machinery for the peaceful settlement of disputes; the paper stresses property rights, while John wishes to emphasize human rights. Should he accept the position?

How the problem is handled. John is very much pleased at first with the offer of the position. He feels that it is an honor and a compliment. Yet he does not accept at once. There are some questions in his mind, and he wants to think them over. He begins to weigh all the pros and cons. During this process he talks with some of his fellow students and consults a number of older persons whose judgment he respects.

In favor of accepting the position, John reasons with himself that it is a good position that pays well and that he may not be able to get another offer that is as good—in fact, no other position of this nature may be open in the near future. Furthermore, the position will give him experience and contacts, and he would like to take up this type of work as a profession. His roommate, Dick, when he hears about the offer, says, "Heck, you're in luck. Grab it while the getting's good. Why in the world would you even hesitate?" Another friend adds, "What if you don't agree with this point of view? If you don't accept this position, someone else will, so what's the difference?"

The older persons with whom he talks are less simplistic in their advice. They suggest that he think the problem through carefully. While they are not in complete agreement in the advice they offer, they do bring to light some aspects of the problem that John has not considered. John asks for an interview with the manager of the newspaper in order to gain more information about the position and what would be expected of him.

---

[5]"Rightness and Consequences," p. 337.

By this time some of the arguments against accepting the offer are beginning to take shape in John's mind; most important is the fact that when working for the newspaper he must express and promote sentiments opposed to his own. This means that he will be promoting social attitudes and movements in which he does not believe. He asks, "What will this position do to me? Can I be successful in work that is promoting causes in which I do not believe? Do I want my reputation and my influence to count on behalf of the issues I shall be asked to promote?" As he weighs the relative merits or values of the two courses of action, certain convictions emerge. First, if he accepts the position, he may not be able to throw his whole energy, mind, and heart into the work. Consequently, he is not likely to become as creative as he would be if he were promoting causes in which he believed. Second, if he does manage to throw his whole energy into the work, he will soon become a different type of person, with different sentiments or convictions. As his name becomes identified with causes, as he forms friendships in these circles, the possibility of breaking away will be increasingly difficult. Wouldn't it be better, he reasons, to accept a position with lower salary, if need be, and retain his personal freedom and self-respect?

After a few days of uncertainty, he declines the offer and asks the college placement bureau to keep his name on the active list for new openings.

A brief analysis. John's motive is undoubtedly good. He wants to do the right thing if he can discover it. That is evident in his procedure and in his attitude during the interviews as he seeks advice. His desire to get a good position so that he may be able to earn his living and become established professionally is commendable. The problem here centers around the means to be chosen and the general consequences to himself and to society of the use of these means.

The problem is handled by John in an intelligent, mature way for the following reasons: (1) He stops to think about the problem before making a decision. He could have decided to accept or reject the offer on impulse. (2) He makes a genuine and intelligent attempt to discover all the relevant factors in the situation. As a result, his decision is made with more facts in mind than would have been the case otherwise. (3) He weighs the relative merits of the alternative possibilities. (4) He judges the case on the basis of long-time considerations and not just on the basis of immediate interests. (5) He takes into account the social effects of his decision, not merely his personal interests. (6) He seeks advice from people who he thinks may throw additional light on the problem. (7) The final decision is his own. It is made on the basis of principle, on the basis of a scale of values.

The essence of reflective morality is the ability and willingness to weigh all relevant facts in moral conduct and to base choices on the results of such reflection. Thus in moral judgments it is conduct that we judge; therefore, we cannot disregard the motive, the means, or the consequences. Any ethical theories that stress motives alone or consequences alone are inadequate. There is no part of the entire process—motive, means, and consequences—the good or evil of which we can ignore except at great risk. Conduct is right if it proceeds from a high motive through the use of good means to effects that are beneficial. Let any one of these conditions be violated and men will approve the conduct only with reservations, or they will condemn it as immoral.

Reflective morality consists not only of forming judgments but of setting forth the reasons for one's moral judgments. When a moral problem confronts him, the morally mature person will examine and carefully consider the motives, means, and consequences involved in the selection of each of the possible lines of action. In the light of his comparison of the values involved, he will make his decision. Reflection will bring to one's attention values and considerations that would have been overlooked had he merely followed impulse or blind custom. The cases presented in *Questions and Projects* at the end of each chapter furnish material for practice in seeing what is involved in ethical decisions.

THREE VIEWPOINTS IN CONTEMPORARY ETHICAL THEORY

In this chapter we have given, in rather broad outlines, some central points in our own moral philosophy. This is done not to imply that our way of thinking is to be taken as authoritative; we want the readers to work out their own personal moral philosophies in a way that will enable them to meet the changing problems of contemporary society and make decisions that are their own. However, our viewpoint necessarily enters into the way we present issues and arguments. The reader is now forewarned of the point of view at work in the presentation.

The following chapters present as clearly and fairly as possible the three different viewpoints that are found in twentieth-century ethical theory. The next chapter treats the revolution in ethical theory that has taken place in recent decades which attacks the more traditional theories and goes under names such as metaethics, emotive theories, and linguistic analysis. Chapter 7 discusses the intuitionists, sometimes called *deontologists*, elaborating the views of Immanuel Kant and some more recent intuitionists who do not believe that empirical factual judgments alone give the basis for the sense of ought or duty that men experience. Chapters 8 to 10 present the three more traditional types of teleological theory. These theories contend that right conduct confers some benefit (good) on persons and that wrong conduct involves some injury. The end considered good may be evolutionary development, pleasure, happiness, or fulfillment of the self as a thinking, feeling, and acting person living in a community of persons. These views have been defended by many thinkers, ancient and modern.

We have learned much from the keen criticism and analysis of those who support the metaethics of this century. We cannot, however, agree with the more extreme analysts who reject normative ethics or refuse to become involved in the crucial decisions of today. In emphasizing the basic postulate of the worth of persons, we draw to some degree on the insight of the deontologists that empirical factual statements alone do not impose a moral demand or an ought. In order to form a moral conclusion we need a value judgment in a premise. On the whole, our views are within the framework of normative and teleological ethics.

QUESTIONS AND PROJECTS

1. What are some of the marks of right conduct as given by the authors? State in your own language why these or some alternative characteristics seem to you most appropriate in defining right conduct.
2. Suppose you believed that the end justifies the means. State the case for this position as well as you can. Now offer the best refutation of this position you can. Can you reconcile the claims and counterclaims in this argument with the aid of the distinctions we have offered? If so, how? If not, why not?
3. In the problem about John's decision as to whether to accept the newspaper position, in what respects can it be said that he decided the problem in a mature way? What refinements, if any, can you suggest on his method?
4. In the spring of 1971 the state of Michigan had a problem with "billboard bandits"—a group of youths that cut down billboards along freeways and highways. The billboards were not only garish and unsightly, but illegal because they were too close to the highway or to another sign. The incidents (one hundred sixty-seven signs were said to have been cut down) infuriated the state's billboard industry and some police departments, but led the Attorney General to propose a legislative crackdown on outdoor advertisers. Discuss the action of the youths in terms of motives, means, and consequences and give your own reactions.
5. A lighthouse keeper is located on a small and sparsely settled island that is visited once each month by a supply ship. When the ship stops, he is allotted enough oil to keep the beacon lighted for the following month. During one especially cold month, a mother comes and asks for oil to keep her children from freezing. A father asks for oil so that his son may

read and continue his studies. Both are given some oil. Near the end of the month the beacon goes out for lack of oil, and there is a wreck on the reef near the island. Are we to approve the actions of the lighthouse keeper because his motives were good? Are we to condemn his actions because of the consequences? Is the lighthouse keeper morally responsible?

6. Two college students, Ruth M. and Fred B., were leading their class and were in line for an important scholarship that would pay expenses for the following year. Ruth came from a large family in only moderate circumstances, and the scholarship would be a real help. Fred did not need the financial aid but wanted the scholarship for the honor. Ruth's standing was slightly better than Fred's. However, about a month before the final examinations, an epidemic of chicken pox broke out in the college. Though the disease was not serious, the doctor ordered a period of quarantine in the college hospital for each person affected, in order to check the spread of the disease. One morning Ruth discovered that her body was spotted with a fine rash. Since it was not conspicuous on her face, and since she felt fairly well, she put on a dress with a high neck, used extra face powder, and went to class. She felt that absence from class for a few days would mean that she would lose the scholarship. Since she avoided contacts and the light, no one discovered her condition. Give your reasons for thinking she was or was not justified in her action.

7. An advertisement in a city newspaper read: "Men Wanted, Good Pay." The men were merely asked to report at a specified place. Men came to report and were surprised to find that it was a recruiting station for a branch of the armed services. The officers responsible for the notice attempted to justify their action by the fact that some men were signing up. Give your reasons for thinking that this method of bringing men to the recruiting station was justified or unjustified.

8. One of the states, wishing to increase the consumption of milk, carried on an advertising campaign under the direction of the state department of health. The campaign was a model of dignity and accuracy of statement, but milk consumption did not rise materially. A year later another department took charge and hired a professional advertising agency, which made many extreme appeals. A picture showing an amorous couple declared that you should drink milk in order to have a glamorous complexion; testimonials from famous athletes stressed milk's athletic potency; and movie stars emphasized the value of milk for reducing. This campaign boosted milk consumption, as the state officials desired. Did the end justify the means? Discuss.

9. What part do agreements, explicit (spoken or written) and implicit (tacit or assumed), play in our views of what is right and wrong? May they ever be broken? If so, when? See Richard C. Cabot, *The Meaning of Right and Wrong* (New York: Macmillan Co., 1933), chs. 1 and 2.

10. A student asks, "If a person thinks hateful thoughts but does not express these thoughts verbally or in overt action, is he doing any harm either to himself or to society?" Outline the answer you would make to such a question.

11. An experiment on human beings started in 1932 has recently come to public attention and is causing considerable discussion. The United States Public Health Service officers induced four hundred poor black men with syphilis to go untreated so that science would know the effect of the disease on the human body. The experiment continued even after it was discovered twenty-five years ago that penicillin was an almost totally effective cure. Protests have come from many sources, and a United States senator has called the study "a moral and ethical nightmare." What moral issues and principles are involved? See Jane E. Brody, "Morality: All in the Name of Science," *New York Times*, 30 July 1972, p. E2; "A Matter of Morality," *Time* 100 (August 7, 1972): 54.

SUGGESTED READINGS

Anshen, Ruth Nanda, ed. *Moral Principles of Action: Man's Ethical Imperative.* New York: Harper & Brothers, 1952. See especially Weiss, Paul. "Some Neglected Ethical Questions."

Garnett, A. Campbell. "What Ought We to Do?" In *The Moral Nature of Man.* Ch. 5. New York: Ronald Press Co., 1952.

Johnson, Oliver A. *Rightness and Goodness.* The Hague: Martinus Nijhoff, 1959.

Lewis, Clarence Irving. *The Ground and Nature of the Right.* New York: Columbia University Press, 1955.

Mandelbaum, Maurice. *The Phenomenology of Moral Experience.* Baltimore: John Hopkins Press, 1969.

Maslow, Abraham H., ed. *New Knowledge in Human Values*, pp. 119–136. New York: Harper & Brothers, 1959.

Means, Richard L. *The Ethical Imperative: The Crisis in American Values.* Garden City. N.Y.: Doubleday & Co., 1969.

Moore, G. E. *Principia Ethica.* New York: Macmillan Co., 1903.

Ross, Sir W. David. *Foundations of Ethics.* London: Oxford University Press, 1930.

Shirk, Evelyn Urban. *The Ethical Dimension: An Approach to the Philosophy of Values and Valuing.* New York: Appleton-Century-Crofts, 1965.

Spock, Benjamin. *Decent and Indecent: Our Personal and Political Behavior.* New York: McCall Publishing Co., 1970.

Stace, Walter T. *The Concept of Morals.* Chs. 10, 11, 12. New York: Macmillan Co., 1937.

Ward, Leo. *Ethics.* New York: Harper & Row, Publishers, 1965.

Weiss, Paul and Weiss, Jonathan. *Right and Wrong: A Philosophical Dialogue Between Father and Son.* New York: Basic Books, 1967.

6
DO MORAL JUDGMENTS EXPRESS KNOWLEDGE OR FEELING?

We have said that in the past the appeal to external authorities was widespread. These authorities included customs, laws, political and religious leaders, and institutions of many kinds. The development toward a reflective morality has been slow even among the educated leaders of modern society. While authoritarianism is an extreme position moving in the direction of rigidity and a sterile legalism, the rejection of the older authorities in a rapidly changing world has led some persons to go to the opposite extreme and to claim that there are no objectively valid moral standards. They have not had the time or the background to work out or to discover new guidelines for conduct. Some have even become indifferent to all moral standards; others have become cynical and skeptical and have ridiculed them.

In this chapter, after examining the elements in a judgment and the nature of moral judgments, we shall consider the criticism of the more traditional systems of ethics, first from the point of view of historical relativism, and second from the approach of linguistic analysis. We shall then raise some critical questions for the reader's consideration.

THREE ELEMENTS IN A JUDGMENT

Human beings are continually expressing their thoughts, beliefs, or opinions about many topics, and we say that they are making judgments. A judgment written out in sentence form as a statement is called a *proposition* by some logicians. There are three elements that can be distinguished in any judgment. There is, first, the person who makes the judgment and who can be called the *subject* or *agent*. There is, second, the judgment passed, the opinion or pronouncement. The judgment may take many forms; it may be positive or negative, or it may attempt to compare things. There is, third, the object about which the judgment is made. The object may be a number, an idea, a flower, the quality of something, a person or persons, an institution, or a civilization. To simplify our discussion, let us call the thing which the judgment is about, regardless of its nature, the *object*. The purpose of a judgment is to say something about some object.

While in analytic philosophy, especially in logic and semantics, the nature of judgment can be made a highly complicated and technical question, we are staying close to common-sense meanings and use. A man may say, "My watch is gold," when he attempts to say something about the nature of the watch. He may of course be mistaken because a judgment may be true or false. A judgment may be made by a subject about himself, as when a man says, "I feel cold." Here the subject and object of the judgment coalesce. He can make a judgment about a judgment when he says, "That judgment was carelessly made or was mistaken."

Some judgments, especially those about physical objects, can usually be checked. If I say, "This stone weighs two pounds," this can be verified. Other judgments that are more abstract, however, cannot be verified so easily. When I say that kindness is good or that murder is wrong, such judgments cannot be verified by the objective measurements of science. While most aesthetic and moral judgments are stated in objective form, such as "This statue is beautiful," or "That action is right," they can be stated as subjective reactions. For example, we can say, "I feel pleasure in seeing this statue," or "I approve of that action." There are those who assert that when we make aesthetic and moral judgments, we merely express our attitudes and do not say anything about the aesthetic or moral qualities of the object. From this it is easy to take another step and assert that aesthetic and moral judgments express feelings, attitudes, and emotions, but that they do not describe qualities that are independent of the judgments. An easy next step is to assert that there is nothing right or wrong, beautiful or ugly, but thinking, attitudes and emotions make it so. There are no ideals, purposes, and goals other than those our minds fabricate. This process has been called by some *the dropping of the object*. The rejection of objective moral standards has led to moral relativity, skepticism, and a decline in moral standards so characteristic of the twentieth century. The assertion that a judgment of value is never true but is only an expression of the maker's feeling, taste, or bias has come to be known as *relativism*.

Subjectivism versus Objectivism in Ethics

The term *subjective* refers to that which pertains to the subject, knower, or the self. In contrast the *objective* is external rather than internal in that its existence is unaffected by one's thoughts, feelings, and emotions. Subjectivism, in ethical theory, is the view that value statements are about feelings and attitudes, and that moral values have no independent status outside of or beyond the self. Objectivism holds that an ethical theory is independent of the person who makes the judgment and usually of when and where the statement is made. There are many variations of these views which we cannot expound here.[1]

When men say that injury, cruelty, and murder are wrong, what are they saying? Are they merely giving vent to a feeling of dislike? Are they making a plea or issuing a command in an effort to influence conduct? Or are they making a statement that is true or false? If moral judgments do not express insights or truths, but only our feelings at the moment, a large part of the moral philosophy of the past is meaningless as some logical positivists and various analysts have asserted. If there are no good reasons and no genuine evidence for saying that one act is better or worse than another, and if feelings and attitudes vary from one person to another and from time to time even apart from different circumstances that justify changes, the very basis of morality is undermined. We shall see later that, even from the approach of the objectivist, many different standards are accepted and observed, and differences in attitudes and conduct may not only be accepted but required by a single moral standard. For example, under primitive hunting conditions the killing of the aged may be the humane thing when starvation threatens and when the aged are thought to go to the "happy hunting ground." Under modern conditions support for welfare legislation providing medical care and social security benefits may be the right way to show respect for the aged.

We pointed out in the previous chapter that there are three move-

---

[1] See Jonathan Harrison, "Ethical Subjectivism," and "Ethical Objectivism" in *The Encyclopedia of Philosophy*, ed. Paul Edwards (New York: Macmillan Co., 1967).

ments in ethical theory. The first and most recent we present in this chapter, setting forth two lines of development that help to explain its origin and appeal. One group of anthropologists and other social scientists using a historical and descriptive method became impressed with one trend in the recent movement—the historical relativity of morals. Another group whose interests were largely in mathematical logic, linguistic analysis, and scientific method, rather than in a broad study of human experience, defended the other trend—an emotive theory of ethics. The two lines of development reinforced or supported each other at various points.

THE HISTORICAL RELATIVITY OF MORALS

The fact that moral codes have varied from time to time and from place to place has led some persons to believe that morality is merely a matter of opinion. Values, they claim, are entirely subjective. One man's opinion is as good as another's. If you differ with this view, its proponent may reply, "Who are you to say?" or "That's only what *you* think!" This person does not stop with the assertion that what some men *think* is right at one time or place is *thought* by others to be wrong at some time or place. All of us would agree with that; ethical relativism so defined is simply a fact of anthropology. But some ethical relativists further assert that what *is* right at one time or place *is* wrong at another. Even this claim, if intended for only some cases, will not be disputed, for the pertinent conditions of life differ, knowledge of both physical and social relationships grows, and resources for acting to gain desired ends alter.

For example, it would be wrong for a person with a certain coronary ailment to indulge in a diet or in exercise that would be satisfactory for a person in good health. It would be right for a manager with extensive capital to take risks in his purchasing and selling that would be quite wrong for a manager with less means. The answer to the question as to whether children should be in a parade for civil rights will depend on particular local circumstances that determine the risks of the venture. Thus the principle that one should serve the welfare of his fellows not only permits, but even requires, different behavior in different circumstances. To the ideas that men differ in what they think is right and that circumstances affect what is right, ethical relativists add a further claim: there are, they say, no standards beyond human thinking and feeling to which we can appeal.

The moral relativists often appeal to the wide variety of standards and practices found among ancient and modern peoples. The writings of Frazer, Sumner, Westermarck, Benedict, Herskovits, and Margaret Mead are especially well known. Frazer set forth evidence of the great variety of practices and beliefs among different peoples. Sumner claimed not only that moral ideas come from customs but also that *mores,* the folkways which are considered right, can make anything appear right or wrong. Westermarck asserted that moral ideas are based upon emotions or feelings of approval and disapproval.

The moral relativists and the moral skeptics find it hard to reconcile the historical relativity of morals with the claim to any objective validity. They appear to assume that moral codes must be universal in order to have genuine worth. Such a position, it seems, rests upon a misunderstanding of the nature and function of morality. If the conditions of life change, and if there is progress both in man's knowledge and in his insight into the meaning of his life and his social relationships, then there must also be change and progress in his moral code. A growing knowledge of the effect of certain forms of behavior on life is especially likely to cause changes in moral ideas. Consequently, actions which we once approved we may come to condemn because we have discovered that they have some harmful effects. Things which we once condemned we may later approve because we have discovered that they are not harmful.

Today we find people living at all stages of moral development, from a primitive type of group morality to an intelligent, conscious type. Between the primitive man acting half consciously in keeping with the welfare of his tribe and the modern man thinking of the welfare of humanity, there is much in common even though there are at the same time wide differences in practice.

The descriptive level of the relativity of moral standards has been known by philosophers, at least from the time of Socrates, but this has never been a problem. Socrates and Aristotle drew from such facts the conclusion that many people do not know what is really good. From a variety of beliefs among people, they also concluded that many do not know what is right. This is no reason, they felt, to relax in the quest for the good, the true, the beautiful, and other values. Thinking or opinion alone does not make anything real, including right and good.

Man's thinking and opinions do tend to be swayed by his interests and run of attention. These in turn are aroused by the different and unusual so that he may overemphasize these features of another society. After discussing the diversity of behavior found among the many tribes and peoples of the world, Morris Ginsberg tells us that this diversity gives no more basis for moral relativity than the diversity of factual judgments gives for casting doubt on valid scientific judgments about questions of fact.[2] He says that "human needs and impulses are much the same everywhere" and that "in essentials the moral systems of the world show striking similarities."[3] For example, the codes drawn up by Buddhists, Christians, Confucianists, Jews, and Moslems do not differ greatly in the virtues that are approved and the vices that are condemned. The diversities are mainly in emphasis and in ways of attaining the desirable goals.

The apparent diversity of customs, then, may hide uniformities that are more important than the differences. Abraham Edel in *Ethical Judgment: The Use of Science in Ethics*[4] reports some outcomes of the anthropologists' search for common ground among cultures. We must grant, he says, the complexity of human affairs, the variety of their detail, the constancy of change in cultures, and the undeveloped state of social science. There are vast differences among "success-bent," "competitive," "cooperative," and "fear-ridden" cultures; among authoritarian theocratic, mystic individualistic, and "rationalistic" ones. Still, bases can be found for comparative evaluation of cultures and of elements within them. Witchcraft in some primitive cultures functions much like scapegoating in "advanced" cultures. Knowledge of physics withstands relativization by cultures, in spite of varied language and concepts to express this knowledge. Analyses of language and thought show a considerable all-human recognition of a common world.

Edel argues that the search for values shared by all cultures is meeting some success. The joys of bodily movement, of reflective processes, of elementary aesthetic response, and of increasing mastery over nature are not, he claims, culture-bound. Similarly, pain, frustration, killing within the in-group, and incest are viewed as bad in every culture. Certain more complex objectives seem to be shared, though not always identically conceived—for example, physical health and the satisfaction of emotional needs. The accomplishment of certain tasks or functions is attempted in every society: control over nature to provide food and shelter, organization of work and distribution of goods, insuring society's continuity by reproduction, protection from attacks from outside and disruption from within, pooling knowledge and skill and belief, transmitting customs, providing for emotional security in individuals, and standardizing communication.

---

[2]Moral relativity is the view that of the same action or situation, X, both "X is good" and "X is bad" may be asserted, since the meaning of *good* depends on who is making the statement.
[3]Morris Ginsberg, *On the Diversity of Morals* (London: William Heinemann, 1956), pp. x, 106.
[4](Glencoe, Ill.: Free Press, 1955).

That men think and do alike, however, no more proves that they *should* than their thinking and doing differently proves that "anything goes." The discovery of regularities such as Edel describes tends to show that if we seek certain objectives, then under given conditions certain ways of acting have been found useful for those objectives. The "if" remains. What of those who do not share the objectives? Even if there were agreement on the objectives, the agreeing parties might be mistaken. After all, men have been universally mistaken about their ideas in physics, geography, and psychology. They are even more likely, even when they can agree, to be mistaken in ethical matters that rest on knowledge of all of these disciplines plus further ideas about values. Would universal agreement to employ capital punishment against thieves make the practice right? Would universal agreement that one should never tell the truth make this principle right? The usefulness of seeking agreement on ethical questions is that the chances of eliminating errors are improved when many minds have examined a proposal. In that case, the agreement is a procedure for removing some mistaken ideas, but not a sufficient test for the soundness of a standard.

LANGUAGE AND EMOTIVE MEANINGS

We have seen that the argument of moral relativity based on a variety of beliefs and practices does not imply the impossibility of effective and meaningful ethical inquiry. Philosophers from ancient times including Socrates, Plato, and Aristotle have been aware of such differences. They sought to clarify the language and thinking of men and to help them distinguish between the apparent good, based on their immediate desires, and the real good, beneficial to the individual and society whether or not he is aware of its lasting worth.

In addition to the failure of traditional morality to give sufficient recognition to the various physical, biological, psychological, and social forces that influence human behavior, or to recognize the historical relativity of morals at the descriptive level, there is a second type of criticism of traditional moral philosophy that raises serious questions about the meaningfulness of moral judgments. It centers attention on language and on the differences between factual and scientific judgments on the one hand and value judgments on the other hand. There was a shift in ethical outlook on the part of some philosophers from normative to metaethical questions, from first-order questions about what men should do and seek to second-order questions about the language we use to answer the first-order questions. The questions and controversies about this procedure are involved and often highly technical, with many shifts of emphasis during the last one hundred years. We shall give a mere sketch of this development including some of the main points of view. We suggest that the interested reader turn to one or more of the books that trace this development in some detail.[5]

The nineteenth century was a time of great activity in the fields of moral philosophy and the theory of value in general. The evolutionists (e.g. Charles Darwin, Herbert Spencer) were directing attention to nature, the utilitarians (Jeremy Bentham and John Stuart Mill) were stressing the greatest happiness theory, and the supporters of self-realization (Bernard Bosanquet, F. H. Bradley, Josiah Royce, Borden Parker Bowne, and later John Dewey) were emphasizing personal fulfillment and social welfare. There were, however, various outspoken critics of the more popular trends, such as Sören Kierkegaard, Frederick Nietzsche, and Karl Marx, whose voices did not attract much attention until the twentieth century.

During the nineteenth century the task of the moral philosophers was seen as a practical as well as a theoretical one, that is, to set forth principles which would help men in making decisions and in influencing them to live more satisfactory lives. From the time of Plato and Aristotle in early Greece to John Dewey in the twentieth century, philosophers as well as religious thinkers sought to help men discern right from wrong, the greater good from the lesser good, and to guide them in actual everyday moral judgments.

In the late nineteenth century, idealism in one of its many forms was a dominant influence in the field of moral philosophy. Certain monistic idealists viewed the world as a single whole in which the only self-contained entity was reality itself, the Absolute, or God. These men looked for a metaphysical foundation to support their value judgments. Man's moral consciousness made sense and was adequately grounded, they thought, only if it could be viewed as an integral part of one organic whole.

Since the turn of the century, philosophy, at least in the English-speaking world, has undergone a profound change, and there has been a new type of confusion and conflict in ethical theory. Emphasis shifted from the world, man's daily activities, and value judgments to language, highly technical questions of meaning, and arguments about arguments. The shift is easier to understand if one has some knowledge of the fact that rationalism, the view that the mind has the ability to discover truth by itself, and empiricism, the view that factual knowledge

---

[5]For example, see Mary Warnock, *Ethics Since 1900* (New York: Oxford University Press, 1960), and George C. Kernes, *The Revolution in Ethical Theory* (New York: Oxford University Press, 1966).

must be based on sense experience, were in conflict. Four movements favored empiricism over rationalism: French positivism, logical positivism and the Vienna Circle, behaviorism as a philosophy, and various schools of philosophical analysis.[6] To many positivists and empiricists, it is a mistake to base ethics on metaphysical or theological assumptions. They feel that however certain these might have appeared while we were ignorant of other points of view, they now offer no secure point of departure in a quest for moral standards. Reliance must be placed on the data of experience as processed by the methods of science.

Early in this century certain philosophers including G. E. Moore, Bertrand Russell, and Ludwig Wittgenstein became interested in linguistic study and the logical analysis of terms, concepts, and propositions. Wittgenstein, born and educated in Austria, came under the influence of Russell and Moore and later succeeded Moore and taught at Cambridge. Alfred Jules Ayer acknowledged his debt to Russell and Wittgenstein. Many brilliant men and women have participated in the debates of the last seven or eight decades. We shall limit our presentation mainly to G. E. Moore, Alfred Jules Ayer, and Charles L. Stevenson, and conclude with a general evaluation of emotivism.

In 1903 G. E. Moore published *Principia Ethica*,[7] an exceedingly influential book in which the problem of the meaning of *good* and *right* became central issues. *Good*, Moore insisted, must stand for a non-natural, intuitive, or directly apprehended quality, property, or thing. Like *yellow* it cannot be adequately defined and analyzed because it has no parts. "Good is good and that is the end of the matter." It is the name of a discernible property of things and has an intrinsic quality of its own that men need to recognize. To define good in terms of any natural property, such as health, pleasure, happiness, is to commit what Moore called the *naturalistic fallacy*. Naturalism in ethics seeks to define good in terms of certain natural objects or qualities. While we cannot prove that certain things like health are good, it is evident that people do recognize them as worthy to be desired and know that they are good. An act is a duty or an ought if it produces more good than harm or evil, but since good is not definable it cannot be supported by reasons or empirical evidence. There is really no such thing as ethical argument. Moore considered the love of what is ugly or bad, the hatred of what is beautiful or good, and the consciousness of pain as great universal evils. We can see that in Moore the emphasis in ethics shifted from

---

[6]For a brief explanation of these movements see Harold H. Titus, *Living Issues in Philosophy*, 5th ed. (New York: Van Nostrand Reinhold Co., 1970), pp. 282–286.
[7](Cambridge: Cambridge University Press).

human activity to the issue of the meaning of terms like *good, right, duty,* and *ought.*

A number of influences led to what came to be known as the *emotive theory of ethics*—a point of view that went the furthest in making moral judgments the expression of feeling. David Hume in the eighteenth century said that reason is the slave of the passions and that moral judgments are a report on what people in general feel. Westermarck had gone a step further in stressing not feeling in general but how the agent felt. Emotivism contends that the function of moral judgment is to express emotion, not just to report it.

Moore's view that good is indefinable and that it cannot be located in any direct empirical fashion led, by various steps, to the position of the logical positivists and other empiricists that ethical terms like good have no cognitive meaning and can have only emotive meaning. "X is good," means they said, "I like or approve of X; do so likewise." The fact that Bertrand Russell and Ludwig Wittgenstein have come to philosophy by way of symbolic logic and mathematics was partly responsible for the strong emphasis on language and analysis. Disagreements, it was suggested, may be rooted in the ambiguities of ordinary language rather than in the complicated nature of the world that is studied by the sciences.

Another direct influence in the development of emotivism was the work of Alfred Jules Ayer (b. 1910). After graduating from Oxford University in England Ayer spent some time in Vienna studying logical positivism or logical empiricism, a school of thought that limits meaningful propositions to those that are based on sense experience or to those that are analyses of definitions and relations among terms. After returning to Oxford to teach he published *Language, Truth and Logic*[8] that elaborated and sought to defend logical empiricism. Ayer acknowledges his debt to Bertrand Russell, Ludwig Wittgenstein, and the logical positivists and does not claim originality for his views.

In discussing the function of philosophy, Ayer says that the philosopher must not attempt to formulate and set forth speculative truths, to look for first principles, or to make *a priori* (prior to experience) judgments about the validity or truth and falsity of empirical beliefs. He must confine himself to the function of clarification and analysis. The propositions of logic are linguistic, and philosophy, he asserts, is a branch of logic. From this point of view much of traditional philosophy is rejected and, not only metaphysical and theological questions, but also normative ethics drops out of the picture.

According to Ayer, there are only two kinds of truth or two forms of

---

[8](New York: Oxford University Press, 1936).

knowledge: Any statement which has meaning must be either analytic or empirical. Analytic statements are like those we find in logic and mathematics. They are statements in which the predicate is contained in the subject. For example, three times five is equal to fifteen; or all bachelors are males. These statements depend on the meaning and use of words and are not descriptive of the world; they are validated by an appeal to meanings and by deductive reasoning. An empirical statement, on the other hand, asserts in the predicate something that cannot be deduced from a knowledge of the meaning of the subject term. Such matter-of-fact statements are verified by checking with sense experience and by means of the methods used in the sciences. They may be true or false by virtue of some condition in the world. For example, Socrates taught in Athens, or water tends to seek its own level.

From the above it will be seen that Ayer excludes value judgments or ought statements from the area of propositions that are true or false. Statements of value are merely expressions of emotion and can be neither true nor false. He says that "the exhortations to moral virtue are not propositions at all, but ejaculations or commands which are designed to provoke the reader to action of a certain sort."[9] Since ethical statements, such as "Injury is wrong," do not come under either of the two classifications—analytic or empirical, matter-of-fact statements—they are not true or false, but mere expressions of feeling or emotion. Value, it is asserted, is not a part of the real world, and the task of philosophy is to clarify the terms and propositions of science.

While Ayer agrees with G. E. Moore and with various intuitionists and absolutists that the term good is unanalyzable, he does so for quite different reasons. We can state this view in two ways: first, as an observation on inferences in ethics, and then as a view of the meaning of language. Clearly, as some twentieth century philosophers have thought, to say that an act ought to be does not say anything about it that can be tested in sense experience. We can experience what *is*, but we cannot experience what *ought to be*. Experience has to be of what occurs or has occurred. To talk of what ought to be is to refer to what does not exist, but only *might* exist. To talk correctly of what ought to have been is to talk of what did not and cannot exist. At the time this conceivable or desired state of affairs has not been and cannot be experienced by the people talking. A valid inference states nothing that is not contained in the union of its premises. If we restrict ourselves to premises stating what we have observed, then we can never get a valid conclusion stating

---

[9]*Language, Truth and Logic*, 2nd ed. (New York: Dover Publications, 1946), p. 103.

what ought to be or has to be done. From the fact alone that men do seek pleasure, we may not conclude that they ought to seek pleasure.

A word purporting to stand for something whose elements we cannot find in sense experience is meaningless, a mere word and nothing else. Words, Ayer said, can also convey rules of language—rules for putting terms together in meaningful ways. Some words that we think refer to experienced things actually do not, as in many sentences about the Absolute. Thus "ought to be" is also without meaning, for it refers to neither a rule of language nor to anything experienceable. Such words convey no information about the actual world. So ethical statements are not false; they are rather without meaning at all. The statement "you ought to tell the truth" is an example of a meaningless statement.

The importance of this argument by Ayer and others for our search for moral standards is this: It would imply, not that personal perference, custom, or some other standard is right, but that no grounds exist for thinking one standard better than another. In fact, it implies that this notion of superiority itself makes no sense. Out of the controversy provoked by this idea of the literal meaninglessness of ethical statements there has come a new clarity on some aspects of ethical language and inquiry.

There are many usages of such ethical terms as *ought*. What appears in the form of an *ought* statement is actually in many cases an *is* statement. For example, "You ought not to drink poison" can be restated as "To abstain from poison is a condition of health and life." The statement that "you ought not to engage in civil disobedience" may be meant by the speaker as an expression of his opinion or of the prevailing view in the community: "X thinks that you ought not to take this action." While this translation does not get rid of the troublesome word *ought*, it is now a subordinate verb. Sometimes even this difficulty is not present if the speaker meant simply "I or my circle prefer that you not engage in civil disobedience."

There are also different kinds of meaning for ethical terms. They can express emotion. "He ought to be run out of town" may but serve to show depth of feeling rather than to suggest a specific action. Words express wishes, but not always literally. "This day should last forever" is clearly not meant as literally as "We ought to buy a new car," and the latter statement may not be meant to state a duty. Ethical terms are used to command, commend, plead, persuade, celebrate, or exclaim, or to do these things in combination. Thus "You shouldn't lie!" may mean, "My group and I disapprove of your lying. We feel strongly on the subject. We enjoin you to feel likewise." If we attend carefully to the variety of possible meanings of ethical words and to their specific meanings in particular situations, many misunderstandings and mistakes can be avoided.

Emotivism was modified by Charles L. Stevenson in a series of articles and later in two books, *Ethics and Language* and *Facts and Values*.[10] He is one of the more influential writers in the field of metaethics and agrees with Ayer that the function of philosophy is to analyze and clarify the meaning of ethical terms. He is, however, less extreme than Ayer and moves away from logical positivism. Philosophy, according to Stevenson, has the task of telling people what good means, but not of saying what things are good. Metaethics is a purely theoretical and ethically neutral discipline to be distinguished from everyday morality.

The early logical positivists and empiricists had made a sharp distinction between cognitive (pertaining to the knowing activity of the mind or knowledge) and emotive meanings. Stevenson recognized more fully that cognitive elements are present in the meaning of ethical expressions. There are often dual meanings that are partly descriptive. Disagreements can often be resolved by rational means if they are based on disagreements of belief, but not if they are deeply rooted in differing attitudes.

In discussing the statement "This is good," Stevenson points out two patterns of analysis. In the first pattern, the statement involves emotive meanings in the main and implies "I approve this; do so as well." Here the speaker's attitude is central: an attitude of approval or disapproval of some idea, act, person, or thing. In this sense the term *good* is not used to name a property. Ethical statements are not amenable to demonstrations, nor can they be tested by observation or experience.

In the second pattern some descriptive meanings are present or are added. "This is good" has now the meaning of "This has qualities or relations XYZ" in addition to laudatory emotive meanings. Emotive meaning in some instances parallels cognitive meaning, and reflective elements are present with appeals to reason. Here ethical statements may carry information about what the world is like or may be like.

Stevenson has stimulated extensive study of the ways in which we use terms laden with emotional import to redirect attiudes. For example, two men argue as to whether a mutual friend has true culture, each attaching a different descriptive meaning to the term *culture* but linking this meaning with the favorable attitudes attached to being a person of culture. Apparently descriptive terms such as *unproductive labor* carry a stigma that in turn affects our ethical judgments if we read an emotive meaning where none was intended. Thus Adam Smith meant

---

[10]Respectively (New Haven: Yale University Press, 1945); paperback ed. 1960; (New Haven: Yale University Press, 1963).

by unproductive labor merely that which did not turn out material things, but others read the term to mean that such labor was useless in a wider, more familiar sense of the term *unproductive*.[11] The effects of this usage in debates on social theory have been momentous. The fact that ethical terms bear emotive meaning and that persuasive usage of such terms can move men in their moral convictions does not, however, imply that ethical terms have only emotive significance. As Stevenson emphasized, the association of emotive with descriptive meanings is the secret of much of their importance. But also the fact that this association of meanings is used often to further personal preferences or group propaganda does not imply that the notions of moral obligation and worth can be reduced to nothing more than expressions of individual or group approval linked with persuasive phrasing. These facts suggest rather that the relations between fact, feeling, and evaluation have great variety and complexity. The emotivists such as Stevenson have contributed much to the understanding of this complexity.

The same word or phrase can be used for various purposes, for example to create an interest, to arouse sympathy, to inform, to make suggestions. Through wide use, words gather affective attachments so that they influence the feelings of those who hear them. In defining a word with emotive meaning such as *good*, the emotive element may be forgotten or left out of consideration and people may be deceived and think that the word is being used descriptively.

Central to the emotive theory is the claim that an ethical expression—for example, "to inflict injury is wrong"—cannot be stated in nonethical, matter-of-fact language, such as A hurt B, and that it is deceptive to do so. One must guard, it is asserted, against the error of making the meaning of a normative term a property of the object when it needs to be viewed as a property of the word or the person who is using the word. While reasons and arguments can be stated which call the attention of the hearer to aspects of the situation which may evoke in him the desired attitude, they do not thereby verify the original judgment. Stevenson does not set forth an ethical theory for the guidance of conduct, nor does he furnish "any conclusions about what is right or wrong"; he gives a "semantic of moral rhetoric" only.

In his essay "Retrospective Comments" Stevenson, while stressing the importance of linguistic analysis in clarifying meanings, says that the statement "ethical judgments are neither true nor false" is absurd in the light of examples he has been discussing. "Those who have insisted on the remark have spoken with an insensitivity to the ways of our language." He says that "the general sort of analysis that I am defending

---

[11]*Ethics and Language*, pp. 211, 215.

remains intact when 'true' and 'false' are restored to their proper place in ethics."[12]

Space does not permit a discussion of the contribution of other able thinkers who have written books on ethics in the general analytic tradition. The reader may wish to consult some of these and to note the points at which they agree and disagree with the points discussed above. For example, see books by K. Baier, Max Black, R. M. Hare, P. H. Nowell-Smith, Stephen Toulmin, and others.

Critical Evaluation

The emotivists and linguistic analysts of the last half century have cleared away much of the dead wood and exposed many of the confusions that have hindered the development and the appeal of moral philosophy of the traditional type. That philosophy was frequently tied to some particular metaphysical or theological system of belief. The clarification of terms, attention to the problem of meaning, and distinguishing between scientific and value judgments have been real contributions. We do need a clear understanding of the part that emotions play not only in moral judgments but in all areas of our lives. We may feel strongly and express our emotions in exhortations, exclamations, and a wide range of attitudes. Everyone wishes to influence others morally, to get them to do certain things, and to refrain from doing other things. Emotions do play a large part in human behavior, in our own conduct, and in our efforts to influence others, but emotions, attitudes, and expressions of opinion by themselves do not make an act right or wrong. A belief that some acts are objectively good and therefore right and others objectively bad and therefore wrong is normally present when people express their reactions about them. An act is right only when it enhances life rather than weakens or destroys it.

When people ask others for guidance in the business of living, they are not asking just to be made comfortable about some particular line of action or to have their emotions confirmed or changed. They are concerned with a factual or cognitive element also; otherwise there would be no way in which they could reasonably justify one ethical action rather than another. Murder, for example, is wrong because it is destructive of people and human relations, not merely because people have an aversion to it. For a group of people to say "hurrah for murder" would not make it right.

The search for goodness in the realm of morality is not entirely different from the search for truth in the realm of science. The search for

---

[12]*Facts and Values*, pp. 219, 220.

truth in science is often inspired by emotions and desires, as is the quest for goodness in the realm of morality. In science people seek to increase human knowledge; in morality they seek to advance human welfare. There is, we need to keep in mind, an area where human beliefs, desires, and agreements are important and have to be recognized and respected. There is also an order of things in the world unaffected by human beliefs and desires—an order that must be discovered and respected if we are to have health, happiness, and human fulfillment.

The recognition of different kinds of meaning in ethical terms and the awareness of the persuasive use of ethical language have encouraged a study of reasons given for ethical assertions. Reasons, to be fitting, must differ as the meaning of the assertion supported differs. Thus Carl Wellman has concluded that the claim to rationality for ethical statements does not mean that the evidence in their support is of the same kind as that in support of statements in physics or psychology. Wellman has distinguished five types of meaning: descriptive meaning (abstaining from poison is a condition of health and life), emotive meaning ("He's a beast!"), evaluative meaning ("This is a good book."), directive meaning ("Report at 15:00 o'clock today."), and critical meaning ("For the reasons cited, this painting is better than that." or "You ought to choose this method.").[13] Value judgments generally contain elements of all of the first three of these types of meaning, and judgments of obligation may contain all five. Thus the reasons that appropriately support such statements will necessarily be very complex, but not on that account impossible to discover. As Wellman says:

> There appears to be nothing in the nature of either value judgments or judgments of obligation to force one to deny their objective validity. Quite the contrary. That such sentences *claim* to be objectively valid can be seen by reflecting upon what is involved in asserting them. It seems unlikely that this claim to rationality is always mistaken. . . . The crux of the matter is whether or not it is possible to give genuine reasons for and against judgments of value and obligations. I think that it is.[14]

Underlying many of the challenges to the possibility of rationality in ethical judgments has been the idea that these judgments eventually rest on individual feelings and attitudes, thus on arbitrary likes and dislikes that have no further justification. There is a certain truth in this idea, and this truth must be acknowledged if its compatibility with the notion of an objective right and wrong is to be understood. It is true

---

[13]Carl Wellman, *The Language of Ethics* (Cambridge: Harvard University Press, 1961), ch. 6–10.
[14]Ibid., p. 299.

that the worth of things traces back in the end to their effects on human fulfillment, to which effects our individual feelings and tastes and interests give clues. The fact that individual wants, needs, and satisfactions differ and may be quite nonrational does not imply, however, that the acts and ways of life that will maximize their fulfillment can be capriciously chosen. If we postulate that one man's fulfillment has as much initial claim as another's, and if we grant that more rather than less fulfillment for each man is to be preferred, these and like postulates provide a basis for discovery that some ways of life are better than others. Moreover, this discovery accords with human experience that men who pursue personal preference in disregard of the interests of others or of the causal relations in man's interaction with his environment tend to find this pursuit self-defeating.

To the person who asserts that questions of right and wrong are matters of private preference or opinion and who asks, "Why may I not do as I please?" we may reply, "Within certain limits you may do as you please." A man can disregard social obligations and pay no attention to the rules of health. He cannot, however, avoid the penalty of such action. If a man wishes to travel, to advance in social life or in business, or to engage in any cooperative enterprise, he must adjust his action to the lives of others and to the demands of the situation. Society is an organization of persons who are cooperating in innumerable ways, whether at work or at play. A complete realization of individual preferences is out of the question in the kind of world in which we live, unless the person is highly intelligent and socially minded in his preferences.

In every department of life we have developed ways which are taken for granted. This is true whether it is business, science, law, or amusement that we are considering. Even in the less serious activities of life we need standards of procedure. Every game has its rules, which must be followed if one is to participate. Imagine eleven football players rushing to the field with one or more of them exclaiming, "Never mind the rules; I am going to express my individuality in this game!" Persons who take the attitude that everyone should be allowed to make his own rules usually do so because they resent some particular restriction or restrictions that are irksome to them.

While it is to be admitted that we cannot give the skeptic absolute or conclusive proof in the realm of morals any more than we can in the realm of truth, nevertheless men must act, and some ways of acting are better than other ways. Consequently, the intelligent person attempts to find some basis of selection or discrimination. In the last analysis, both the moral philosopher and the skeptic must appeal to intelligence. Both demand a reasonable explanation.

The historical development of morality does not necessarily imply relativity for the individual living under a code that is functioning effectively and that he recognizes as binding. Furthermore, it does not mean that there are no valid principles that apply to the lives of all persons. These principles may be progressively discovered.

In *The House of the Dead*, Dostoevski tells about stories he heard in a Siberian prison camp. He heard prisoners tell with spontaneous, merry laughter about the most hideous murders. Blanshard, in referring to these stories, says:

> Most of us would say that in this delight at the killing of others or the causing of suffering there is something very unfitting. If we were asked why we thought so, we should say that these things involve great evil and are wrong, and that to take delight in what is evil or wrong is plainly unfitting. Now on the subjectivist view, this answer is ruled out. For before someone takes up an attitude toward death, suffering, or their infliction, they have no moral quality at all. There is therefore nothing about them to which an attitude of approval or condemnation could be fitting. They are in themselves neutral, and, so far as they get a moral quality, they get it only through being invested with it by the attitude of the onlooker. But if that is true, why is any attitude more fitting than any other? Would applause, for example, be fitting if, apart from the applause, there was nothing good to applaud? Would condemnation be fitting if, independently of the condemnation, there were nothing bad to condemn? In such a case, any attitude would be as fitting or unfitting as any other, which means that the notion of fitness has lost all point.
>
> Indeed we are forced to go much farther. If goodness and badness lie in attitudes only and hence are brought into being by them, those men who greeted death and misery with childishly merry laughter are taking the only sensible line. If there is nothing evil in these things, if they get their moral complexion only from our feeling about them, why shouldn't they be greeted with a cheer? To greet them with repulsion would turn what before was neutral into something bad; it would needlessly bring badness into the world; and even on subjectivist assumptions that does not seem very bright. On the other hand, to greet them with delight would convert what before was neutral into something good; it would bring goodness into the world. If I have murdered a man and wish to remove the stain, the way is clear. It is to cry, "Hurrah for murder."[15]

The notion of an objectively right or wrong act is one that moral philosophers have used for centuries. This notion is the basis for our conception of duty—to find and to do the act which in the light of all the evidence would be the most beneficial for long-run human welfare.

---

[15] Brand Blanshard, "The New Subjectivism in Ethics," *Philosophy and Phenomenological Research* (March 1949): 507–508.

"The enterprise of human living can prosper," says C. I. Lewis, "only if there are value-judgments which are true." He says that one of the strangest aberrations of human thinking is the denial of truth or falsity in the field of value perceptions. If such denials are carried out consistently, they would invalidate all knowledge. "Believing . . . would have no point if it were not better to be right than wrong in what one believes."[16] The testimony of human experience is that one belief or one value judgment is not always as good as another.

If the more extreme contentions of some ethical relativists and emotivists are true, then no act can ever really be justified or condemned in moral terms, and there can be no genuine disputes about morals. Critical standards would appear to be ruled out, and almost all the moral philosophers from ancient to modern times have been mistaken and have tended to lead men astray. This is not only hard to believe but seems absurd. After describing the development of ethics since 1900, Mary Warnock says that "one of the consequences of treating ethics as the analysis of ethical language has been the increasing triviality of the subject" and the refusal of many moral philosophers to commit themselves to any moral opinions. One consequence is that "ethics as a serious subject has been left further and further behind."[17]

BASING CRITICISM AND ACTIONS ON WORKING CONVICTIONS

We have been considering the diversity of opinion about what is right, the effect of different circumstances on what is right and wrong, the effect of confusions of language upon ethical statements and reasoning, and the role of emotions in ethical judgments. None of these issues implies that ethical knowledge is impossible or that a universal ethics cannot be discovered or devised. They are conditions with which such knowledge and such an ethic must comply. Another condition of this kind is the fact that ethical decision and action often cannot wait for agreement on ethical fundamentals among the cooperators. We are highly interdependent in today's world. Catholics and Protestants, communists and parliamentary democrats, Chinese and Russian communists, economic liberals and economic conservatives, and other pairs of opponents must live together helpfully even though they cannot agree on crucial issues of ethics. If the hope for a universal ethic is not to be divisive, it must be seen as compatible with mutual respect among ethical adversaries.

---

[16]Clarence Irving Lewis, *An Analysis of Knowledge and Valuation* (La Salle, Ill.: Open Court Publishing Co., 1946), pp. 366, 373.
[17]*Ethics Since 1900*, pp. 202–204.

We are rarely in complete ethical agreement with our partners in action. Fortunately, however, joint action in a context of mutual respect often facilitates both clarification of our disagreements and removal of some causes of disagreement. Let us consider some cases in which there are (1) agreements among two parties on some objectives and principles and (2) a readiness to work together in spite of conflicts on some interests and disagreement on other principles.

Suppose that the United States government wishes to aid the Brazilian government in the development of its economy. Not all of the two governments' major interests are shared, but they do agree to seek a growth in Brazil's gross national product, a less uneven distribution of income among the people of Brazil, including means of at least minimum subsistence level for all Brazilians, and greater trust and cooperation between the two governments. Each views their joint action as contributing to the general welfare of humankind, but they are aware of disagreements among themselves as to just what this general welfare would be. They know that other governments disagree with their entire plan and its aims. Can they, starting from this measure of agreement in aims, make a reasonable case for policies in accordance with which the aid to Brazil should be granted and administered? They work under the handicaps that their ultimate ideals for human society are not clear and may not be in harmony, their political traditions and philosophies differ, and some of their interests are in conflict. They have certain common fears (for example, the fear of outside interference), common interests (in increased trade), and perhaps common ideals (as for a growth in freedom among both peoples). To cooperate effectively, they will have to devise plans with enough promise in the view of each government for its own interests and ideals so that the risks arising out of their differences seem tolerable.

Imagine the case of two people of differing but not conflicting interests who disagree about important ethical principles. Consider a teenage brother and sister, one of whom wants an expensive gun and hunting outfit, and the other a hi-fi setup with many dance records. The boy thinks the girl's way of using wiles on parents and boyfriends is downright unethical, while she regards his ways of dealing with people as ineffective and thus, as the wrong way to get even something he ought to get. They can nevertheless cooperate to persuade the parents to give each what he wants, whereas bickering with each other about their tastes would defeat both. Similarly, one can imagine two civic groups, one bent on desegregation, the other on economic betterment, and each initially disapproving of the methods of the other, yet finally agreeing that they *ought* (each on the basis of its own principles) to cooperate. The cooperating teenagers, like some cooperating congressmen, may seem to us immoral in that they team up to bilk third parties. We regard their loyalties as narrow and their logrolling as damaging to more important interests. But this judgment simply points up the further conflict between our ethic and theirs, and the question of whether we in turn can find grounds for respect and cooperation. If our ethic is better than theirs, it should suggest either ways of meeting the concerns of the teenagers and the parochial congressmen that are compatible with wider social interests, or ways to convince our antagonists of their error.

Consider, finally, the case of two parties who disagree about both main objective and means but who decide they ought to cooperate in an activity that each can approve. The limited nuclear test ban signed by the United States and the Soviet Union in 1963 appears to be an agreement of this type: each side, on the basis of its own values (different as they are) and a limited objective on which the two agree, agrees with the other as to the ban that ought to be undertaken and the terms under which this can rightly be done.

One danger of cooperation with a person of opposing goals or means is that the cooperation will help his cause to defeat one's own in the long run. He may have calculated the consequences more accurately. He may have other steps in mind that counteract the benefit of the cooperation to his opponent's interest. On the other hand, joint action by antagonists on behalf of a common interest may lead them to revise their basic disagreement. One or both may learn. One of the things they may learn is on what terms to trust each other. Their attitudes toward each other may be altered by the cooperation. Each may learn to appreciate the "good cause" of the other, or the circumstances that make the other's point of view reasonable. They may discover a still more fundamental common goal that removes the previous fundamental disagreement. Thus joint action by moral antagonists can be the occasion for fair criticism and refinement of their ethical positions.

Some ethical theorists who have stressed the common needs and interests of men of different cultures or of conflicting groups have had this practical approach to ethical conduct in view. In effect they say: We do not need to settle once and for all whether there are or are not any ultimate, unconditional ethical principles. It is sufficient to proceed with working convictions. These can be in the form either of agreement about basic values or of enough common interest at a more specific level that the basic disagreements can be left in the background for the time being. What is needed, then, they urge, is a theory of the proper conduct of ethical reasoning and decision-making in such a context. This kind of theory would help us decide how to deal with our conflict with the communist powers. It would provide a basis for cooperative ventures between such contenders as Protestant and Catholic, Christian and Jew, Confucian and Buddhist, fraternity man and independent, Black Muslim and integrationist NAACP-member, influencers of public policy with opposed conceptions of economic theory, adolescents and parents, and the like.

In defense of the objective of developing such a theory of ethics, it might be argued by analogy that the progress of physical science does not depend on agreement about the ultimate postulates of scientific inquiry. Soviet theory of these assumptions has differed from American. It is not true that the foundations of science are universally accepted. Yet by working on whatever agreement can be tacitly or explicitly used for the cases in hand (for example, the International Geophysical Year), scientists contribute to scientific progress as defined by all of the conflicting schools of thought.

If worst comes to worst, then, we can make justifiable ethical judgments merely on the basis of working agreements and each party's separate moral convictions. But this fact does not imply that there is no basis for moral judgment that transcends these social agreements. They still stand in need of critical evaluation. Think, for instance, of the four-year-old child who misunderstands his own interests. His parents may understand his wants and needs better than he does. It is conceivable, however, that their picture of the child is also imperfect. A child psychologist might understand still better. We can also imagine that a conception of the child's potentialities and interests that no one has in mind yet might be the most accurate of all. The views of the child, the parents, and the psychologist would be increasingly good approximations of a view as to how the child might best be encouraged to live and act. The thing that ought to be done is that action, among the possible actions discernible to the parties, which best approximates this accurate view. The standards to be used in making moral judgments would be ones most conducive to getting this accurate approximation. While in practice working agreements are often essential to taking a needed step, the working agreement itself is subject to criticism in the light of the standard that relates the fullest knowledge of the people and the situation to future possibilities. The recognition of the legitimate observations of moral relativists is entirely consistent with the agelong insistence that criticism of existing practices and standards must appeal beyond present agreements, judgments, and insights to a source not subject to their limitations.

SUMMARY CONCLUSIONS

1. The fact that moral judgments are complex and often difficult to support with good reasons has led some men in the past and the

present to regard these judgments as mere matters of feelings, attitudes, opinions, or cultural mores. The arguments centering around these questions, however, have led to important insights about the nature of morality.

2. The fact of the relativity of morals at the descriptive level has been recognized by philosophers since the days of the early Greeks and has not been a serious problem. The attempt by logical positivists and some emotivists and analysts to exclude value judgments from the area of propositions that are true or false has led to decades of debate and to many shifts in outlook some of which we have considered. A few analysts have been heard to say that they have gained a new insight into the need for a greater emphasis on normative ethics.

3. Ethical terms are used with a wide variety of meanings that must be recognized if misunderstanding and error are to be minimized in ethical discourse. To discover the appropriate methods and standards for criticism of ethical statements, we must take account of a variety of types of meaning: descriptive, emotive, directive, evaluative, and critical, as one classification suggests. Judgments of right and wrong involve elements of all of these types of meaning and thus require canons of criticism that consider each of them.

4. The ultimate locus of moral responsibility is the individual person, and each person capable of making moral decisions is responsible for making his own decisions. There are moral issues in which the personal preferences or convictions of the individual deciding should be a crucial factor in determining what is right.

5. A tempering of inclinations by the sense of duty in an individual is more likely to produce good than granting full rein to the inclinations. Men must act and it is evident that some ways of acting are better than others. We need to discover these better ways.

6. There are situations in which an authoritatively derived canon or custom or policy may be a better guide to choice than a newly formed judgment made under pressure of time and partisan influences. In this sense an "intuitive" judgment is sometimes sounder than a newly calculated one.

7. Specific conditions under which action is proposed, the availability of knowledge of physical and social conditions and relations, and the availability of resources for action are all relevant considerations in determining what is right choice or action; the content of the right will thus vary at times with variations in these factors. On the other hand, the question of whether the differences between situations or their likenesses are pertinent to specific choices has to be answered by using guidelines other than the circumstances, knowledge, and resources themselves.

8. Even where parties to a joint decision and action differ in moral

convictions, responsible choice and action may be possible without agreement on fundamental principles, aims, or standards.

9. The preceding points do not imply that one should exempt from criticism the bases for ethical choice and action used by individuals in the exercise of conscience, personal preference, reflective evaluation, or working agreements with others. These findings are also compatible with the effort to achieve objectivity and rationality in ethical judgment. We continue this search in the discussions that follow.

QUESTIONS AND PROJECTS

1. State in your own words what is meant by "the historical relativity of morals." Indicate the evidence used in support of this outlook and then state why many think it is inadequate as an explanation of much human conduct and especially as an adequate moral philosophy. Morris Ginsberg (see *Suggested Readings*) may be of help.
2. Give as many different types and uses of language as you can think of or find. Wellman, as we have seen, distinguishes five types of meaning. How many of these types do you find yourself using quite frequently?
3. What is meant by "the revolution in ethical theory" that took place in English-speaking countries in the twentieth century? The books by Warnock and Kernes (see *Suggested Readings*) will be helpful. See also Peter Caws, "The Contemporary Crisis of Value," *Science and the Theory of Value* (New York: Random House, Inc., 1967), ch. 2, paperback. Caws believes that the change of outlook and emphasis has had very unfortunate consequences.
4. State as clearly as you can the meaning and outlook of the emotive theory in ethics and then state the case for and against this outlook. What contributions has it made and what are its shortcomings or dangers as a moral outlook by which to live?
5. In *Decadence* (New York: Philosophical Library, Inc., 1949), C. E. M. Joad argues against the "dropping of the object" and the subjectivism in modern culture. Many philosophers stress ways of experiencing and neglect what is experienced. In *A Critique of Logical Positivism* (Chicago: University of Chicago Press, 1950), p. 148, Joad asks, "Can a man continue to feel indignant at cruelty if he is convinced that the statement, 'Cruelty is wrong' is meaningless?" If logical positivism is correct you can say "one atom bomb can destroy 50,000 people" (statement of fact), but not "it is a bad thing to destroy 50,000 people" (statement of evaluation); or if you say it, the word *bad* adds nothing to the factual content! Indicate the extent to which you agree or disagree with Joad.
6. Discuss the following quotations:
    1. "An ethical code is only an expression of an attitude."
    2. "We do not need ethical theories to tell us how to act."
    3. "Always prefer the greater good to the lesser good when either can be chosen but not both."

7. Review a book by one of the following authors as listed in the *Suggested Readings*: Brand Blanshard, Paul Edwards, R. M. Hare, D. H. Monro, Shia Moser, Carl Wellman.

SUGGESTED READINGS

Abelson, Raziel. *Ethics and Metaethics: Readings in Ethical Philosophy*. New York: St. Martin's Press, 1963.
Adams, E. M. "Classical Moral Philosophy and Metaethics." *Ethics* 74 (January 1964): 97–110.
Blanshard, Brand. *Reason and Analysis*. LaSalle, Ill.: Open Court Publishing Co., 1962.
Castaneda, Calderon; Neri, Hector; and Nakhnikian, George; eds. *Morality and the Language of Conduct*. Detroit: Wayne State University Press, 1963.
Edwards, Paul. *The Logic of Moral Discourse*. Glencoe, Ill.: Free Press, 1955.
Gellner, Ernest. *Words and Things: A Critical Account of Linguistic Philosophy and a Study of Ideology*. London: Victor Gollancz, 1959.
Ginsberg, Morris. *On the Diversity of Morals*. New York: Macmillan Co., 1957.
Hare, R. M. *The Language of Morals*. Oxford: Clarendon Press, 1961.
Hume, David. *An Inquiry Concerning the Principles of Morals*. Edited by Charles W. Hendel, Jr. Indianapolis: Bobbs-Merrill Co., 1955.
Kerner, George C. *The Revolution in Ethical Theory*. New York: Oxford University Press, 1966.
MacIntyre, Alasdair. *A Short History of Ethics*. New York: Macmillan Co., 1966.
Monro, David Heston. *Empiricism and Ethics*. Cambridge: Cambridge University Press, 1967.
Moser, Shia. *Absolutism and Relativism in Ethics*. Springfield, Ill.: Charles C. Thomas, Publishers, 1968.
Nielson, K. "Ethical Relativism and the Facts of Cultural Relativity." *Social Research* 33 (Winter 1966):531–551.
Sellars, Roy Wood. "In What Sense Do Value Judgments and Moral Judgments Have Objective Import." *Philosophy and Phenomenological Research* 28 (September 1967):1–16.
Stevenson, Charles Leslie. *Facts and Value: Studies in Ethical Analysis*. New Haven: Yale University Press, 1963.
Sumner, L. W. "Normative Ethics and Metaethics." *Ethics* 77 (January 1967):95–106.
Taylor, Paul W. *Normative Discourse*. Englewood Cliffs, N.J.: Prentice-Hall, 1961.
Veatch, Henry. "Non-Cognitivism in Ethics: A Modest Proposal for Its Diagnosis and Cure." *Ethics* 76 (January 1966):102–116.
Wellman, Carl. *The Language of Ethics*. Cambridge: Harvard University Press, 1961.

7
KANT AND SOME LATER INTUITIONISTS

For centuries there have been men who have believed that some actions are right or wrong in themselves, apart from circumstances, and that some things are good or bad in themselves. Among primitive peoples the tribal way, or the customary morality, was absolute and unquestioned. Later, when codes of law were formed, the same conviction of inherent right or wrong attached itself to the law. Still later, when morality became more inward and reflective, it was perhaps reasonable for men to think that right and wrong were parts of the very constitution of certain types of acts or that there was a special moral faculty within man by means of which the moral quality of acts was clearly and immediately recognized.

The theory of the nature of morality which views some acts as intrinsically right or wrong has been described under various captions according to the way in which it is set forth or which aspect of the outlook is given chief emphasis. These captions have included such terms as *formalism, rigorism, intuitionism, deontological ethics,* and the *ethics of duty*. *Formalism* is the view that the standard of conduct is found in moral rules which are inherently right or wrong quite apart from any particular results which flow from them. There are formulas in mathematics: If equals be added to equals, the results are equal. There are formal truths in logic: Of two contradictory propositions, both cannot be true. The formalist asserts that there are similar formulas in the field of ethics: Veracity is right. There is nothing good but a good will. Humanity must never be considered merely as a means, but always as an end. *Rigorism* is a closely related term that expresses an outlook of undeviating respect for the moral law which is not concerned with the particular circumstances or field of application. There is a universal and eternal right and wrong.

Intuitionism maintains that there is a kind of mental perception within man by which he may discern the intrinsic moral quality of certain judgments. Some would identify this moral sense with conscience; others say that reason is able to discern abstract moral truth. Human beings have special sense organs to apprehend the qualities of objects—color, taste, temperature, and the like. Do they have a special faculty of some kind which apprehends the moral quality of acts?

The term *deontology* comes from two Greek words: *deon* (duty) and *logos* (reason, science). A deontological theory of ethics holds that some acts are morally obligatory regardless of their effects on human welfare. For the ethics of duty right consists of a certain quality of the will, the rectitude of one's inner disposition, or loyalty to an unconditional command.

Immanuel Kant treated key themes in ethics so powerfully that his ideas have been the point of departure for many subsequent studies. His writings, still widely read, are the best elaborations of the ideas stated above. After a brief consideration of his life and work we shall state his central themes relative to the content or standards or moral judgments.

IMMANUEL KANT, 1724–1804

Kant, a professor of philosophy at the University of Königsberg, stated his ethical theory in extensive writings, principally his *Critique of Practical Reason* (1788) and *Fundamental Principles of the Metaphysics of Morals* (1785). They were a response to David Hume's forcefully presented skepticism about human knowledge of both nature and morals.

Kant was reared in a home which was deeply religious and moral. His parents, especially his mother, were devout pietists for whom a vital religion, strong moral convictions, and a sense of duty were ever-present realities. With this background he entered the University of Königsberg, where he came into contact with the rationalistic spirit and the methods of critical analysis prevalent in the German universities of his day. Kant became acquainted with the writings of Newton, Rousseau, Wolff, Hume, and others. He was startled by the conclusions Hume drew from Locke's suggestion that all knowledge is derived from sense impressions. Hume confessed himself unable to find anything in these impressions to warrant causal inferences as usually understood or to sustain the idea of physical or mental substances. Thus all support for supernatural explanations or theories drawn from the ideas of substance in the writings of Descartes and Locke was gone. Similar findings applied to ethics. Virtue Hume saw as merely what gives us the pleasing sentiment of approval. Moral judgments have only such sanction as derives from individual commitment and social agreement to these experiences of approval. Kant, however, had also been deeply impressed by both the advancement of scientific knowledge (in astronomy he shared honors with Laplace for proposing the nebular hypothesis) and by his religious and moral upbringing. Neither seemed to rest on so shaky a foundation as Hume had provided. The fault must lie in the assumptions with which Hume began.

Kant began, therefore, not with the skeptical finding of no knowledge, but with the opposite assumption: that we do indeed have genuine knowledge in both science and morality. He asked, in the case of science, what the necessary preconditions of such knowledge are. If these could be found, we would know that they surely pertain, since we unquestionably do have knowledge. This knowledge, his studies suggested, is not a knowledge of things in themselves (*noumena*), for they cannot be "known as they are" but are accessible only through the ordinary processes of sense perception. It is rather knowledge of the objects of experience (*phenomena*). When the knower receives the data of the senses, he orders these data in space and time. Apart even from deliberate interpretation, the mind shapes or orders data and so permits the functioning of our notions of quality and quantity, identity of objects, causal relations, and the like. Without these modes of receptivity and interpretation, knowledge as we know it could not be. We should not be surprised, therefore, that our experiences are orderable in space, time, identity and difference relations among objects, causal sequences, and the like. These possibilities exist by reason of the nature of the knowing consciousness, not because of the objects themselves.

The Essential Role of Reason in Ethics

Kant believed that there are also preconditions of moral endeavor. First among these is conformity to reason. A number of ideas were involved in Kant's conception of the role of reason in ethics. He thought of reason as objective and impartial, as requiring logical consistency, as producing truths that are necessary and universal in applicability, and as being that part of man that is both distinctive of his best nature and common to all men. Without objectivity ethical demands would carry neither authority nor the claim to represent knowledge. Without impartiality we would have partisanship, caprice, and whim but certainly not guides to conduct that would control passion, interest, and inclinations, in which men differ. In logic and mathematics, in which Kant saw the model of knowledge at its best, truths follow by necessity from unchallengeable starting points. A similarly solid foundation, he thought, was needed in matters of right and wrong. Given such principles, it seemed clear that they would apply to all men everywhere, just as the key principles of science and mathematics apply everywhere. This idea of the place of reason in ethics accords also with a view of all nature as capable of being understood as rationally orderable. Kant was impressed with the observation that all phenomena can be seen as if arranged according to some purpose. "Two things," he says, "fill the mind with ever-new and increasing admiration and awe the oftener and the longer we reflect upon them: the starry heavens above and the moral law within." The demand for reason in ethics is but a way of seeing the moral as an integral part of the larger framework of nature.

The moral law, which is the good will governed by reason, expresses itself, to use Kant's famous term, in the *categorical imperative*. A categorical imperative is an unconditional command. A hypothetical imperative or command depends upon an *if* and is conditional. It is not an expression of the moral law. The categorical imperative, however, is the voice of duty, the sense of "ought," or the positive command which arises within the morally sensitive person. It is *a priori*, or derived from the reason itself, and it is applicable to experience everywhere. This voice of duty has reference not to what *is* but to what *ought* to be. The categorical imperative may be stated in three different ways: as the principle of universality, the principle of humanity as an end in itself, and the principle of autonomy. We shall consider these next.

Action for the Sake of Universal Principles

For Kant, reason in morality requires that one act always in accordance with, and for the sake of, universally applicable principles. "Act only on that maxim whereby thou canst at the same time will that it should become a universal law." Expressed in another form, this principle appears thus: "Act as if the maxim of thy action were to become by thy will a universal law of nature."[1]

In the second section of his *Fundamental Principles*, Kant gives four examples to make clear the principle of universality. (1) A man after a succession of misfortunes feels wearied of life and is contemplating

---

[1] Immanuel Kant, *Critique of Practical Reason, and Other Works on the Theory of Ethics*, 6th ed., trans. T. K. Abbot (New York: Longmans, Green & Co., 1909), pp. 38–39.

suicide. Can such an act be justified? When he tries to universalize such behavior, he cannot because "his maxim is: From self-love I adopt it as a principle to shorten my life when its longer duration is likely to bring more evil than satisfaction. It is asked then simply whether this principle founded on self-love can become a universal law of nature. Now we see at once that a system of nature of which it should be a law to destroy life by means of the very feeling whose special nature it is to impel to the improvement of life would contradict itself, and therefore could not exist as a system of nature...."[2] (2) Another man finds himself in a position in which he needs to borrow money. In order to get the money he must promise to repay it within a definite time. He knows that he will not be able to repay it then. May he get out of his difficulty by making a promise that he knows he will be unable to keep? When this suggestion, which has arisen out of self-love and convenience, is changed into a universal law, he realizes how contradictory it is. Honesty in making and keeping promises is thus one of the duties of man. (3) A third man has in himself a talent that, if cultivated, would make him a more useful member of the community. He is in comfortable circumstances and prefers a life of ease and pleasure; yet he is concerned about his duty. As a rational being, he cannot will that it become a universal practice not to cultivate one's talents. He must will, therefore, that his own faculties be developed. (4) Finally, a man who is prosperous sees other persons in extreme poverty. He could easily help these persons, but he is not inclined to do so. While such a society in which each man would be left to his own devices might continue to exist, the attitude is wrong "for a will which resolved this [neither to take from nor to contribute to the welfare of others] would contradict itself, inasmuch as many cases might occur in which one would have need of the love and sympathy of others, and in which, by such a law of nature, sprung from his own will, he would deprive himself of all hope of the aid he desires."[3] In referring to the type of situation presented in the second example above, Kant says that the question is not whether it is expedient under the circumstances to follow the maxims considered but whether it is morally right. In order to answer the question conclusively, one needs to ask whether the maxim in each case can be willed without contradiction to become a universal law. Such a law would apply to others as well as to oneself. When the matter is stated in this way, we see at once that, while we may be able to will some particular lie, for example, we cannot will that lying should be a universal law. If lying were universal then "no one would consider that

---

[2] Ibid., p. 39.
[3] Ibid., p. 41.

anything was promised to him, but would ridicule all such statements as vain pretenses."[4] The principle thus proves itself to be self-contradictory when it is taken as a universal law. To tell a lie, even to shield oneself or others from serious disaster, is wrong regardless of the consequences of the specific act.

The Principle of Treating Men as Ends in Themselves

From his fundamental principle of morality, Kant derived two others. We have just considered the principle itself: "Act as if the maxim of thy action were to become by thy will a universal law of nature." When we reflect on the meaning of "what we can will to become a universal law of nature," we find that a moral community is a community of persons. These persons, Kant thought, are moral beings by virtue of their acting as rational beings, subordinating inclination to reason. From this view of persons Kant obtained this supreme practical imperative: "So act as to treat humanity, whether in thine own person or in that of any other, in every case as an end withal, never as means only."[5] Rational beings or persons are ends in themselves and cannot rightly be used simply as means. We may use physical things as means to our human purposes; but when we use another person as a means to an end or to our advantage, we degrade him and violate his very being as a person. Reverence for personality is a central principle of Kantian ethics.

In speaking of the above formulation of Kant's moral law, Professor W. K. Wright says:

> In this modified form it is one of the most fruitful that has ever been advanced in ethics. It is capable of endless illustration. The college student, the business and professional man and woman, the husband, wife, parent—each may properly ask himself or herself: "Am I respecting my own personality and making the most of it? Or am I allowing myself through idleness, selfish enjoyment, and irrelevant distractions to become less of a real person than I owe it to myself and those dearest to me to become? Am I respecting the personalities of those about me, contributing to their happiness when I can, and making it easier for them to make the best of their lives? Or am I selfishly exploiting those about me for my own advantage and at their real cost? Am I treating them as mere means, or as ends in themselves?"

> The principle has been applied since Kant's time to many social problems. Slavery was wrong, because the slave was exploited for the profit of others, and he was not treated as an end in himself. Prostitution is wrong, because in it a woman is treated as a mere means to man's

---

[4]Ibid., p. 40.
[5]Ibid., p. 46.

pleasure at the cost of the degradation of her own personality. Free Love is wrong, because the man and woman in such a relation do not truly respect themselves, and they refuse to develop their own characters in a manner best in the long run for themselves and for society Drinking and gambling are wrong for similar reasons. Mere idleness in college, or absorption in extra-curricular activities to the extent that the student cannot get a real liberal or professional education, are cases of lack of self-respect.[6]

This sense of the value and dignity of every person gives rise, according to Kant, to a kingdom or realm of ends. There is a rational system of duties to which men should be loyal and with which they should identify themselves. Whereas objects have only instrumental value, man is of worth in himself. This is the basis of human dignity and self-respect. By virtue of their latent rationality and their moral capacity, men have a claim on each other that such worth and dignity imply. These obligations or duties are principles that apply to all men everywhere.

The Principle of Autonomy

If man is to be treated always as an end, then he cannot be viewed as a mere means even to other men's fulfillment. Since reason, Kant held, distinguishes man among animals and is universal to all men, each man's own reason will dictate the same truths and demand the same respect as will that of all others. Thus both the will to act by universal principle and the respect for men as ends amount to imposing as a duty only those demands that a man's own reason puts on him. Thus Kant derived the principle of the moral autonomy of the rational individual from the imperative to act only on maxims that one can will to be universal. The rational man governs himself; he is his own lawmaker. He is not governed from without, but from within.

The moral law appears within man as a sense of obligation or conscience. In Kant's view, conscience applies the imperatives of reason to the testing of maxims that we consider practicing, and this test suffices to distinguish right from wrong. For Kant thought of every sane man as having the capacity to use this test. Thus, in obeying moral principle man is not deferring to any outside legislator but is obeying a law imposed by his own reason.

Kant did not view his principle of moral autonomy as incompatible with the concern for social order and law. Although each person im-

---

[6]William K. Wright, *General Introduction to Ethics* (New York: Macmillan Co., 1929), p. 306.

poses the moral law on himself, it is nonetheless universal and binding on all rational beings, for moral reason legislates alike in all men. Were it not for this last assumption, moral autonomy might produce moral anarchy. As Kant put it, although a person "is only under obligation to act in conformity with his own will," it is "a will which by the purpose of nature prescribes universal laws" and must be a good will at work in all men who are true to their own nature.

The principle of autonomy does imply, at the same time, that man has the freedom to choose. "I ought implies I can." While the world of natural phenomena is governed throughout by causal connections, morality loses its significance if we deny the capacity to choose. We cannot be responsible if we cannot respond of our own will to the call of duty. Freedom is the self-determination of reason rather than the direction of life by uncontrollable internal impulses and desires and external forces. Freedom is moral compulsion overcoming physical compulsion.

The Primacy of Duty Over Inclinations

Our remarks about universal principle have stressed the demand for action *in accordance with* universal principle. Kant also held, as we noted, that our action should be *for the sake of* principle. If the principle alone will not move us to a good act unless inclination or selfish advantage also call for that act, the action has no moral worth.

Inclinations and pleasures are capricious. They vary from time to time and from place to place. What pleases one person may displease another. The man who, simply because he likes me, tells me the truth even at cost to his own interests cannot be trusted to be so truthful with those he dislikes. The man who contributes to the community chest because he likes recognition for generosity to good causes cannot be counted on to be so generous to such causes as civil liberties, racial equality, and world peace if they happen to be unpopular in his community.

Kant was not saying, as some have supposed, that an action is wrong if we have an inclination to do it, or if we derive pleasure from it. He was saying that unless our concern for the principle for which it should be done is sufficient to evoke the action from us, our act is not morally right. If we do the act either solely from inclination or desire for some pleasure, or because our devotion to duty is reinforced by personal interest, our motive is not the one it should be. If devotion to duty brings us pleasure, that is a sign of virtue. We are to follow the line of duty, however, even if it runs counter to inclination and interferes with our pleasure. Consider an example.

It is a duty to maintain one's life; and, in addition, everyone has also a direct inclination to do so. But on this account the often anxious care which most men take for it has not intrinsic worth, and their maxim has no moral import. They preserve their life *as duty requires,* no doubt, but not *because duty requires.* On the other hand, if adversity and hopeless sorrow have completely taken away the relish for life; if the unfortunate one, strong in mind, indignant at his fate rather than desponding or dejected, wishes for death, and yet preserves his life without loving it— not from inclination or fear, but from duty—then his maxim has a moral worth.[7]

The Centrality of Motive to Morality

The idea that hypothetical imperatives are not moral imperatives and the demand to follow duty rather than inclination suggest that the actual consequences of an act are irrelevant to its moral quality. Not the results, but the motive determines whether the act is right. Kant insisted on this point. The view that moral acts are inherently right or wrong, apart from any results that may flow from them, has been subsequently labeled *formalism.* Kant insisted on a formalism in which it is the nature of the motive that is inherently right or wrong—and, as already indicated, that motive is right which is for the sake of universal principle. Although good results ordinarily follow from good actions and evil results from evil actions, right and wrong are inherent in the nature of the motive and do not derive from their fruits.

For Kant, then, a good motive or good will is central. While there are many things that men call good, a good motive is the only thing that is good without qualification. "Nothing can possibly be conceived in the world, or even out of it, which can be called good without qualification, except a Good Will." Goodness is to be found in an inner quality of will, motive, or attitude and not in an outward performance or the consequences of one's act. The true object of reason is to produce a will that is good in itself, since nothing else is always and necessarily good. Other things, like intelligence, courage, and happiness, are usually good, but they may be used to promote evil. Intelligence or courage, when used to carry out an evil purpose, may increase the evil. Happiness may be gained in ignoble ways, and one person may gain happiness from an act that would bring unhappiness to another person of higher ideals. A good will, "though not indeed the sole and complete good, must be the supreme good and the condition of every other, even of the desire of happiness."[8]

---

[7] Ibid., pp. 13–14.
[8] Ibid., p. 12.

Two men may contribute money to a good cause. One may give the money because he wants publicity, because he lacks the courage to say "no" when the appeal is made, or because he does not know what else to do with his money. For the other man, these considerations do not enter. He is genuinely devoted to the cause of humanity, and ulterior considerations play no part in his generosity. The second man is the generous man, whom we admire and approve. Virtue and vice thus go deeper than the act itself. Disinterested loyalty to the moral demand is the essence of goodness.

If a man acts from a good motive or out of a sense of duty, then the act is good, Kant thought, even though the intended consequences do not come about. If a man seeks to aid a sick friend but, because of some unforeseen factor, leaves him in a worse condition, the man's motive is nevertheless praiseworthy. On the other hand, if he seeks to injure the sick man but inadvertently helps him, his motive is still vicious. Kant did not say that results are unimportant. He said that the *moral quality* of the act is not determined by its results. A good will is therefore the indispensable condition of the moral life.

SUMMARY AND EVALUATION OF KANT'S ETHICS

In our brief elaboration of Kant's ethics we have set forth six theses. Some of them are peculiarly Kantian whereas others will be accepted, as we shall see, by other types of moral philosophy. To recapitulate, these theses are:

1. In ethical demands there is an implicit appeal to reason. This appeal to reason involves a claim to impartiality, objectivity, and consistency, and an attempt to eliminate caprice, passion, and mere inclinations from moral judgments.
2. The rationality thus claimed applies to all men to whom the demand is relevant; in this sense moral principles are universal.
3. Mankind, whether in our own person or in others, should be treated always as an end, and never merely as a means. Whereas objects have only instrumental value, man is of worth in himself.
4. The moral man must be viewed as his own lawgiver, freely recognizing and choosing his obligations. Man is responsible for his actions since he can respond of his own will to the call of duty.
5. For the moral man, duty has priority over inclinations, and the moral act is one in which the response to duty is sufficient to induce the act.
6. The moral quality of an act is a matter primarily of its motive and intent. A good motive or good will is central and the only thing that is

good without qualification. Goodness is thus found in an inner quality of will, not in outward performance or in the consequences of the act.

Kant's ethical theory is one of the ablest presentations of the formalist approach. During the latter half of the eighteenth century, when men were questioning the very foundation of things and especially all external authority, Kant impressed upon men the fact that order and consistency may be found within. Moral distinctions are not matters of mere expediency nor expressions of personal inclinations, nor are they caused by the blind pressure of social customs. Moral distinctions are real and intelligence is central. The sense of obligation is of critical importance in our moral consciousness, and there is an obligation to live according to some norm.

Because of Kant, men have come to realize more fully that there must be something of intrinsic value, that a good motive is essential to conduct which we wholeheartedly approve, and that human personality is an end in itself. No act is good without qualification unless it originates from a good motive or a good will. To live by reason and to be consistent, rather than to be creatures of impulse, and to respect the worth of persons—these are sound principles in line with the experience of the race. Formal ethics is properly a *part* of any satisfactory system of ethics. It is often called the *ethics of the right* in contrast to the *ethics of the good*, which we consider in the next three chapters.

Kant is to be commended for stressing rationality and the use of reason in the formulation of moral judgments. To live by reason, to be consistent, and to respect the worth of persons are sound principles. Desires, inclinations, and sense impressions by themselves are not reliable guides to conduct, and unless supplemented from other sources of knowledge may lead to an unbalanced and sensate type of society. On the other hand, some critics of Kant claim that he went too far in the opposite direction and either underrated or ignored the empirical and experiental elements in human existence.

In addition to points of strength and grandeur in Kant's outlook there are weaknesses which are pointed out by the critics of formalism and which need to be considered. Let us state some of these and raise questions for further discussion.

Because of the formal and abstract nature of his ethics, Kant is said to lack interest in the historical and empirical nature of ethics. Man's sense of duty is often very confused and is evidently culturally conditioned. A survey of the development of morality indicates that it grows out of life situations. The moral judgments of men have varied from age to age and from place to place. Ways of thinking, feeling, and acting are handed down by our ancestors through the process of cultural conditioning. Men frequently forget the way by which they have come to feel that one act is right and another wrong; consequently, they may insist that the rightness or the wrongness of the act is a result of some quality inherent in the act itself. Questions of right and wrong are likely to be presented to the child as commandments of some sort. When morality becomes more conscious and reflective and when external authority is laid aside, it is an easy step to the view that moral principles are absolute enactments which express themselves within the individual as a sense of duty. Men may fail to realize that the moral principles which have become a part of themselves in this way are the principles which make a wholesome life possible under existing conditions.

This lack of interest in the facts of human nature and human behavior has led Kant to rule out the importance of such facts and to maintain that particular circumstances are irrelevant to the determination of what is good and bad, right and wrong. We do our duty, according to Kant, simply for duty's sake, thus the ethics of the right has primacy over the ethics of the good. Most moral philosophers have given primacy to the term *good*. While a good motive is a prerequisite to an act that we approve, it does not give us a clue to what is actually right. As pointed out in chapter 5, there are two questions that need to be distinguished. First, in performing this action what does the man intend to do? What is his motive or intention, and is he morally responsible in this sense? Second, does the man choose correctly in deciding what to do? Is the act right? An answer to this question calls for reflection and evidence.

A person may act with a good motive and intent (rightly) and yet create undesirable effects or great harm in the world (bad results). On another occasion he may act in malice (wrongly) and unintentionally benefit all concerned (a good outcome). Where there is not the expected close correlation between rightness of motive on the one hand, and benefit of outcome on the other, we need to ask what conditions may have caused the correlation to fail at times. Among those that come to mind are failure to use due care to assure that the intent will be fulfilled, ignorance (not necessarily out of negligence to inquire) as to the type of consequences likely to flow from an act, intervention by others with opposing intent, and intrusion of unpredictable new circumstances of other kinds. Ethics has a proper concern with the reliable production of good as well as with the quality of motive and intent. We need to emphasize again that it is conduct we judge and this includes motives, means, and general consequences to all concerned.

Kant's principle of universality has been subject to much debate. This principle has the wholesome effect of encouraging men to consider the larger implications of their actions: What would be the effect if everyone proposed to act as I am now thinking of acting? This is a good question to ask, especially when the effects of the proposed action are reasonably clear. When, however, we ask what we should do in new and unique situations, this formal principle may not be satisfactory. Here we need evidence and an appeal to the facts so far as they can be known. Kant does not deal adequately with the possibility that two duties may come into conflict with each other. He speaks of the duty to relieve persons in distress and the duty always to tell the truth. But what if telling the truth is incompatible with relieving someone in distress? Kant does not provide a clear basis for deciding in such cases what one should do. The moral choice becomes one between competing ends or conflicting values. To universalize these principles may only add to the embarrassment. When a situation presents a choice between loyalty and disloyalty to family or to country, the issue may be decided on the basis of Kant's principles. We can universalize loyalty, but not disloyalty. When, however, a conflict arises between loyalty to family and loyalty to country, this principle appears inadequate.

The principle of universality may be interpreted in two very different ways. It may refer to particular acts under particular circumstances, so that a man could argue that if anyone else were in exactly this situation he would be willing to have anyone else do the same thing, such as steal or lie, if some good would result. If we judge an action from the point of view of the particular situation, it may lead to extreme laxity. However, there is another interpretation, and this is apparently the one which Kant means to establish. The principle of universality refers to general types or principles of conduct. If a man is tempted to steal or to lie, he should ask himself whether he is able to will that stealing and lying become universal. Since such action would not only make social life impossible but also would be contrary to reason, he cannot will that they be universalized. Consequently, these types of conduct are wrong without exception. Likewise, there are apparently some good actions which cannot be universalized without running into inconsistencies. For example, Kant believes that the principle of relief may be universalized, but if everyone were engaged in the relief of distress, it would not be *necessary* for anyone to engage in the activity. On the other hand celibacy, as Kant states, could not be universalized as a principle; yet we can see some cases in which celibacy is not only right but a duty to future generations.

The principle of universality might be stated in such a way that it would apply alike to all to whom it is relevant. A duty could apply universally (that is, to all relevant cases) without applying to all men. For example, it might be a duty for men of certain persuasions, responsibilities, and circumstances to remain celibate, without its being a duty that all men do so.

Kant's use of the term *happiness* is unsatisfactory since he thinks of happiness as consisting of the complete satisfaction of all one's desires and fails to distinguish clearly between actual and conscious desires of men and what ought to be desired by all men, and between what men mistakenly think is good and what is really good for one's self and society.

LATER INTUITIONISM AND THE ETHICS OF DUTY

Another form of the ethics of duty and intuitionism came to some prominence in the twentieth century. In 1912 H. A. Pritchard wrote an article entitled "Does Moral Philosophy Rest on a Mistake?"[9] His answer was affirmative. Since early Greek times it has been assumed by most students of moral philosophy that a moral judgment called for a defense of the good of the individual or society. From this point of view moral judgments sought to show that the act being considered was conducive to human welfare. This is the mistake, Pritchard asserted, since no justification is necessary or possible. What is right is not necessarily contributory to good. The reason most men keep a promise is that it is self-evidently right and obligatory. The act may be right even though there is no discernible good, or even if, at times, some evil may be the result.

Sir David Ross is an outstanding proponent of the influential school of twentieth-century British intuitionists. Whereas Kant took a more extreme position and pushed the principle of duty to the point where there were no exceptions, Ross said that, in practice, there may be exceptions where duties conflict or where an act or event has a diversity of obligations. The good act is self-evident, just as a mathematical axiom or the validity of a form of inference is self-evident. Certain *prima facie* duties have a direct claim on us and they grow out of the situation we are facing. Ross named seven of these duties: promise keeping, reparation for injuries, duties of gratitude, duties of justice, beneficence, self-improvement, and not injuring others.[10] A *prima facie* duty is an obligation or claim resting on us because of some circumstance of the situation, or because of the type of action which it is. It has a claim on us

---

[9]*Mind* 21 (1912): 121–152.
[10]Sir David Ross, *The Right and the Good* (Oxford: Clarendon Press, 1930) p. 21.

quite apart from any good or goods that appear to follow from our adherence to its demands. The man who does not realize that a solemn promise lays him under an obligation to respect it is morally blind. When two or more *prima facie* obligations are in conflict, one's duty lies with the claim that is more "stringent."

Our estimate of the comparative claims of these duties is a function of intelligence and reason. We compare, says Ross, two lines of action, then select the one whose claims have greater weight. In the abstract the keeping of promises is always right; in actual practice some other duty, higher under the particular circumstances, may intervene. Which of the claims is stronger must be settled from case to case, since no rule of thumb can be given for all cases.

While recognizing that such things as happiness, virtue, and knowledge are good, the deontologists reject the central principle of utilitarianism, that is, that one should act or choose so as to produce the greatest good or the best consequences. For example, a judge or jury should not convict an innocent though dangerous man for a crime he did not commit even though failure to do so would be likely to touch off riots and have evil consequences for a community that believes that he is guilty. The deontologists do not ordinarily make right actions independent of consequences. They recognize that the production of good consequences is one of the *prima facie* duties. They do, however, deny that consequences *alone* are sufficient. Some kinds of acts are obligations quite apart from consequences. Some kinds of actions have a rightness of their own which comes from the type of action which they are. Even before knowing what the consequences are likely to be, men feel quite certain that some actions are clearly wrong. They draw this conclusion with no consideration of consequences.

Over the years moral philosophers have sought some unifying principles that underlie acts that are right and obligatory. Those thinkers who emphasize the primacy of good have such a unifying principle. Some intuitionists seem to say that there is no such principle. Others suggest that a quality called *fittingness* may serve this purpose and that all acts that we can call right have this quality. That is, it is fitting that we keep promises, make reparation for injustices, and the like. It is fitting to add to the sum total of human good. The right will still be irreducible to good, for the fittingness of the act is distinct from its goodness. Thus fittingness is intuited as a quality of a moral act in a particular situation. A man of insight immediately senses by what we might call an intuitive induction what is the appropriate action for the occasion. He is able to choose not only between right and wrong in simple cases, but between one *prima facie* duty and another when duties are in conflict.

The critics are quick to point out that the *prima facie* duties are all things that the teleologists would call good, and also that in the total situation what is called fittingness is the result of the fact that the consequences are seen to be beneficial to all concerned. When two *prima facie* duties come into conflict, as they frequently do in actual life, we make the selection in terms of the greater good. In some cases what appears on the surface to lead to good social consequences, such as the punishing of an innocent man who is believed by the general public to be guilty to avoid riots and social conflict, may seem right. Yet here the long-range consequences and the general pattern of life that men wish to maintain puts the act in a new light and calls for devotion to justice. If the total and long-range good is taken into account, the right and the good may come together.

Some actions, such as promise keeping, have a rightness of their own, because of their very nature. This rightness is to be denied only under rather exceptional conditions. We cannot always predict the future or the consequences of our actions. In some cases there may be no one right thing to do. There are disagreements and conflicts among intelligent men of good will who are intuitionists or deontologists as well as among those who are teleologists. The intuitionist G. E. Moore said, "It seems to me self-evident that knowingly to do an action which would make the world, on the whole, really and truly *worse* than if we had acted differently, must always be wrong."[11] The majority of the outstanding students of ethics in the past have stressed good as the basic concept. A duty that would leave the world no better for doing it appears meaningless. In concluding his book *Rightness and Goodness*, Oliver A. Johnson says, "If it be true that rightness and goodness are so independent of each other that a person may have fulfilled his duty even though his action leaves the world a worse place than it would have been had he not acted, then, I should say, moral action becomes irrational and ethics, as an attempt to provide a theoretical interpretation of moral life, impossible."[12]

QUESTIONS AND PROJECTS

1. Explain Kant's view of the moral law and the three formulations which may be given to this law.
2. An impulsive and dangerous man is in a great rage because he erroneously thinks that your friend has injured him. He will seriously injure and

---

[11] G. E. Moore, *Ethics* (New York: Henry Holt & Co., 1912), p. 181.
[12] (The Hague: Martinus Nijhoff, 1959), p. 158.

perhaps kill your friend if he finds him before his anger has subsided. Do you think it right or wrong for you to tell him a lie so that he will not find your friend? How would Kant answer this question?
3. If a friend had threatened to commit suicide and you felt you could save him by stealing his revolver, would you feel justified in doing so? Why or why not?
4. The legal case *Regina v. Dudley* involved a group of shipwrecked sailors without food, who, thinking they were acting to protect the greatest good of the greatest number, killed and ate one of their group. The rest survived. The court which tried the case condemned their action on the basis of a principle of common law that condemns the killing of any man except in self-defense. What is your opinion of the action of the group? Would ethical formalism help you decide the merits of (1) the action of the sailors and (2) the decision of the court? See W. E. Hocking, *Present Status of the Philosophy of Law and of Rights* (New Haven: Yale University Press, 1926), pp. 52–53.
5. What do you think of the statement "To tell the truth is a duty, but only towards one who has a right to the truth"? Can it be defended? The French philosopher B. Constant argued that the idea of duty is inseparable from the idea of right. To tell the truth is a duty towards one who has a right to the truth, but a man does not have a right to the truth if it means injury to others. See T. K. Abbott's translation of Kant's *Critique of Practical Reason and Other Works on the Theory of Ethics*, 6th ed. (New York: Longmans, Green & Co., 1909), appendix, pp. 361–365.
6. In *Les Misérables*, Victor Hugo tells how Jean Valjean, an escaped convict living under the name of M. Madeleine, builds up a successful business and becomes the popular mayor of his town and a public benefactor. While he is mayor, Valjean learns that another man, a feebleminded old beggar, has been arrested as Jean Valjean and is about to be sent to the galleys. Since the welfare of many persons depends on the true Valjean, what is it his duty to do?
7. According to newspaper reports, a storekeeper was confronted by three gunmen, who ordered him to open the store safe. He immediatly pretended to faint and dropped to the floor. A customer screamed, "Call a doctor," and the robbers fled without the money—a considerable sum— that was in the safe. Could a Kantian approve the storekeeper's action? Explain your answer.
8. Some people consider that an excellent presentation of formalism is found in Josiah Royce, *The Philosophy of Loyalty* (New York: Macmillan Co., 1908). See also Peter Fuss, *The Moral Philosophy of Josiah Royce* (Cambridge: Harvard University Press, 1965); and James Harry Cotton, *Royce on the Human Self* (Cambridge: Harvard University Press, 1954), ch. 7. Study Royce's view, especially as found in chapter 3 of *The Philosophy of Loyalty*, and be ready to discuss his position. Does the injunction to be "loyal to loyalty" give us sufficient guidance in the world of everyday affairs?

SUGGESTED READINGS

Bradley, Francis H. *Ethical Studies*. Essay IV. 2nd ed. London: Oxford University Press, 1927.
Broad, Charlie D. *Five Types of Ethical Theory*. Ch. 5. New York: Harcourt, Brace & Co., 1930.
Caird, Edward. *Critical Account of the Philosophy of Kant*. 2 vols. New York: Macmillan Co., 1911.
Hartmann, Nicolai. *Ethics*. Translated by Stanton Coit. Vol. 1, pt. 1, sec. 4. New York: Macmillan Co., 1932.
Jensen, O. C. "Kant's Ethical Formalism." *Philosophy* 9 (April 1934): 195-208.
Johnson, Oliver A. *Rightness and Goodness, A Study in Contemporary Ethical Theory*. The Hague: Martinus Nijhoff, 1959.
Jones, Hardy E. *Kant's Principle of Personality*. Madison: University of Wisconsin Press, 1971.
Kant, Immanuel. *Critique of Practical Reason and Other Writings in Moral Philosophy*. Translated and edited with Introduction by Lewis White Beck. Chicago: University of Chicago Press, 1950.
———. *The Moral Law; or Groundwork for the Metaphysic of Morals*. Analysis and notes by H. J. Paton. London: Hutchinson's University Library, 1948.
Paton, H. J. *The Categorical Imperative: A Study in Kant's Moral Philosophy*. Chicago: University of Chicago Press, 1948.
Pratt, James Bissett. *Reason in the Art of Living*. Chs. 4-5. New York: Macmillan Co., 1950.
Schilpp, Paul Arthur. *Kant's Pre-Critical Ethics*. Evanston, Ill.: Northwestern University Press, 1938.
Singer, Marcus George. *Generalization in Ethics*. New York: Alfred A. Knopf, 1961.
Taylor, Richard. *Good and Evil: A New Direction*. Ch. 8. New York: Macmillan Co., 1970.
Wood, Allen W. *Kant's Moral Religion*. Ithaca: Cornell University Press, 1970.

8
PLEASURE AND HAPPINESS AS THE END OF LIFE

A century ago, before some of the distinctions in ethical theory we are making today had been widely employed, teleologists, as we have seen, held that it is the consequences of an act which determine its value. They opposed the formalists who thought that the motive providing the form of an act alone determines its moral value. Among teleologists, in turn, there were different opinions about the decisive feature of consequences. Hedonists thought pleasure or happiness the defining mark of values. Those who advocated what is called *evolutionary ethics* considered the survival value of behavior as crucial. Self-realizationists treated the end as the fullest actualization of the individual's potentialities.

PROPONENTS AND TYPES OF HEDONISM

Hedonism dates back at least to Aristippus (c. 435 B.C.–c. 356 B.C.) and Democritus (c. 460 B.C.–c. 362 B.C.). Aristippus, a pupil of Socrates, named pleasure the one and only good. The most intense pleasure, he said, is the highest good and the aim of life; one need seek only his own pleasure, and the pleasure of the moment should not be subordinated to the uncertain pleasures of the future. Because Aristippus' home was at Cyrene on the northern coast of Africa, his view is known as *Cyrenaicism*. It fits the popular conception of hedonism—take the cash and let the credit go—mistakenly attributed to Epicurus and called *Epicure-*

anism. Epicurus himself (c. 342 B.C.–270 B.C.) sharply modified the views of Aristippus. In genuine Epicureanism, men are counseled to seek, not the most intense pleasures, but those most likely to produce long-run satisfaction. Epicurus identifies these, on the basis of experience, as pleasures of the mind and spirit rather than physical pleasures. Self-control, friendship, and wisdom are recommended as the avenues to the greatest personal happiness.

Hedonism was revived during the Renaissance and was propounded in England during the seventeenth century by Thomas Hobbes (1588–1679) and John Locke (1632–1704). Later exponents of a pleasure standard were Jeremy Bentham (1748–1832) and John Stuart Mill (1806–1873).

Hedonism takes a number of forms. We shall distinguish first between psychological hedonism and ethical hedonism, then between egoistic and altruistic ethical hedonism, and finally among meanings of the term *pleasure* or *happiness* that give different content to each of these statements.

Psychological hedonism is the view that every person does as a matter of fact seek his own pleasure in life. The only motive that is effective in conduct is the desire to get pleasure and to avoid pain. Just as it is natural for water to seek its own level, so it is natural for men to seek pleasure. This position, defended by Epicurus, Hobbes, and Bentham, is a hypothesis in psychology. It purports to say not what men should do, but what they in fact do. If true, it states a condition with which any reasonable theory as to what men should do must be compatible.

Ethical hedonism, in contrast, does not claim that we do always seek to gain pleasure and avoid pain, but that we *ought* to do so. Men should choose their actions so as to bring about the most happiness or the least unhappiness. Pleasure or happiness is not simply the sign or accompaniment of some other value, but is itself the important value.

Those who accept pleasure as a standard differ in emphasizing self-interest or the common good. The first is called *egoistic hedonism,* the second, *altruistic hedonism.* Aristippus, Epicurus, and Hobbes reduced morality to enlightened self-interest on a pleasure-pain criterion. If there is conflict between our own interests and those of others, our sole duty is to ourselves, regardless of the cost to others. Bentham and Mill stressed, on the contrary, "the greatest happiness for the greatest number." This last phrase leaves room for a range of opinions as to the way the standard of the social or common good should be taken. For example, if the largest sum of pleasures is possible only where some men enjoy much more than others, which is better: the largest sum of pleasure or the greatest pleasure which is evenly distributed?

Thus far we have spoken indifferently of pleasure, the absence of pain, and happiness; and even the term *interest* has crept into our statements. Closely considered, these are not equivalent expressions, though only in the past century have the distinctions among them been closely studied. An adequate ethical theory must explore their interrelationships. We begin with a review of the hedonism of two distinguished nineteenth-century proponents as they themselves stated that view.

THE UTILITARIANISM OF JEREMY BENTHAM

The Utilitarian Movement, the revival of hedonism in the late eighteenth and the nineteenth centuries, grew out of the wretched conditions that existed in England as a result of revolutions and wars. Jeremy Bentham lived through the period of the American Revolution, the French Revolution, the Napoleonic Wars, and the early stages of the industrial revolution. Conscious of serious political, economic, and social abuses in the world of his day, he became interested in reform. This interest influenced him to seek a basis for morality that was practical and that was social in its nature. He was especially interested in honest government and the correction of administrative abuses, in better laws, and in prison reform for the sake of the general happiness. He used the phrase "the greatest happiness of the greatest number," and he felt that in it men have a yardstick that can be applied both to individual conduct and to social behavior.

In *An Introduction to the Principles of Morals and Legislation* (1789), Bentham says that nature has placed man under the guidance of two masters, pleasure and pain. It is for these masters to indicate what man ought to do or leave undone. "Man is a pleasure-seeking, pain-avoiding animal." Pleasure and pain "govern us in all we do, in all we say, in all we think." Psychological hedonism is thus set forth and defended as a true account of man as he actually is. Bentham adds that whatever brings pleasure is good, whatever brings pain is evil; our duty is to maximize the balance of pleasure over pain in life. All men need to do is to make their choices intelligently.

This position Bentham called the *principle of utility*, and his position is traditionally called *utilitarianism*. An action conforms to the principle of utility when it tends to increase the happiness of the individual concerned and the community. Utility is that property of any act or object that tends to produce an advantage, a benefit, pleasure, or happiness— that is, that makes the act or object good or useful for something or for someone. When Bentham mentions the community, he is not thinking about some fictitious body; he has in mind "the sum of the interests of the several members who compose it."

Since pleasure is good and pain is evil, Bentham reasons, the consequences rather than the motives are the important parts of actions. While in everyday speech we may refer to actions as proceeding from good or evil motives, the expression is not an accurate one. If motives are good or evil, it is only because of their effects.[1] Acts are good when they tend to produce pleasure, evil when they lead to pain. The proper ethical attitude is to calculate carefully the amount of pleasure and the amount of pain any act will bring, then to subtract the pain from the pleasure and find the balance. If there is a balance in favor of pleasure, the act is a good act. Since men naturally tend to seek pleasure and to avoid pain, there is no need to use the word *ought* in connection with this choice, but only in connection with how it is exercised.

Bentham's utilitarianism was established on a roughly quantitative basis, that is, in accordance with the strength or the amount of pleasure and the number of people involved. These are the only relevant differences that need to be considered; the quality of the pleasure may be disregarded. Bentham lived in an age that had just passed through great development in the mathematical sciences. Qualitative differences of such things as heat and sound were being treated with numerical expressions. What was more natural than to seek to apply exact measurements to pleasure and pain? This leads us to Bentham's famous *hedonistic calculus,* according to which there are seven elements or dimensions of value in a pleasure or a pain. The first six are sufficient when an individual is considering his own happiness. When the act has social implications, the seventh is important. The legislator must always keep the seventh clearly in mind. Pleasures vary in: (1) *intensity,* whether they are strong or weak; (2) *duration,* whether they are long or short; (3) *certainty,* or the degree of probability that they will occur; (4) *propinquity,* or nearness in time; (5) *fecundity,* or the chance that they will be followed by more of the same kind of sensations; (6) *purity,* or the likelihood that they will not be mixed with or followed by pain; (7) *extent,* or the number of people who will be affected. Bentham assumed that a man's personal happiness will harmonize with the happiness of all.

Bentham hoped that ethics could be put on a strictly scientific basis and that these seven elements could be measured. Ethics would then be able to give exact guidance in specific problems of conduct and of legislation. A person could add the pleasures, subtract the pains, strike a balance, and decide.

---

[1] See Jeremy Bentham, *An Introduction to the Principles of Morals and Legislation* (London: Oxford University Press, 1879), ch. 10.

THE UTILITARIANISM OF JOHN STUART MILL

John Stuart Mill, an ardent and able disciple of Bentham, defended utilitarianism against numerous attacks and modified it. Mill defines utilitarianism thusly: "the creed which accepts as the foundation of morals, Utility, or the Greatest Happiness Principle, holds that actions are right in proportion as they tend to promote happiness, wrong as they tend to produce the reverse of happiness. By happiness is intended pleasure and the absence of pain; by unhappiness, pain and the privation of pleasure."[2] Pleasure and the absence of pain are the only things desirable as ends. All desirable things are so because of the pleasure they give or because they are a means to the attainment of pleasure and the prevention of pain.

Of the many criticisms that Mill answers, we consider only two here. First is the charge that utilitarianism promotes sensuousness, or that it is a doctrine "worthy only of swine." Mill points out that it is not the utilitarians but the critics themselves who would debase human nature, since they assume that human beings are capable of enjoying only those pleasures of which swine are capable. Human beings with refined faculties are not satisfied with the pleasures of beasts, but seek the higher pleasures of the intellect, of the feelings and imagination, and of the moral sentiments. Those who are equally acquainted with and equally able to enjoy both the higher and the lower pleasures definitely prefer those pleasures that engage the higher faculties of man. Mill also denies the charge that utilitarianism encourages selfishness. He points out that not the person's own happiness but the good of all men is the standard of what is right in conduct. As long as we live in an imperfect and unjust society, Mill continues, the sacrifice of one's own happiness for the happiness of others is the highest virtue. Such sacrifice, however, is never an end in itself; it is a means to some greater happiness for mankind.

The most important change that Mill made in utilitarianism was to add a qualitative standard to Bentham's quantitative standard: "It is quite compatible with the principle of utility to recognize the fact that some *kinds* of pleasure are more desirable and more valuable than others. It would be absurd that while, in estimating all other things, quality is considered as well as quantity, the estimation of pleasures should be supposed to depend on quantity alone."[3] As we have seen, Mill felt forced into this position in his defense of the happiness princi-

---

[2]John Stuart Mill, *Utilitarianism*. Everyman's Library. New York: E. P. Dutton & Co., 1910), p. 6.
[3]Ibid., p. 7.

ple. A person whose faculties are more highly developed is capable of higher pleasures and also of more acute suffering. The mental pleasures are superior to bodily pleasures; and once a man has lived on a higher level, he can never really wish to sink to a lower level of existence. This may be because of a human sense of dignity, man's realization of the desirability of the higher pleasures, or some other factor. "It is better to be a human being dissatisfied than a pig satisfied; better to be Socrates dissatisfied than a fool satisfied."

What evidence or proof is there that men actually do desire pleasure? Can they be sure that happiness is the greatest good in life? Mill warns us that questions of ultimate ends cannot be proved in any final sense. This is true of all first principles, those of knowledge as well as those of conduct. Consciousness is immediate or direct, and knowledge grows out of such experience. The only evidence we have that an object is visible is that people do see it. In the realms of sight and sound, our perceptions are our undeniable evidence. In like manner, says Mill, the only evidence that anything is desirable is that men do actually desire it.[4]

The utilitarians believe that the best evidence of a good character is good actions—hence they stress the consequences of conduct. An action is not to be called right or wrong because it is performed by a good or a bad man or because the man is courageous or amiable. Such considerations are relevant to our estimation of persons but not of actions. On the other hand, a right action does not necessarily mean that the person has a virtuous character; it means that the act in question leads to desirable results. The morality of an act depends not on the motive that prompts it but on the effects of the act on society as a whole. In some instances, however, where unforeseen circumstances prevent good consequences, we recognize the act as praiseworthy because of the intended effects. In other instances, where a vicious intention miscarries and some good effect ensues, we condemn the man because of the intended consequences.

Whereas Bentham depended on the person's enlightened self-interest to explain consideration for the welfare of other men, Mill felt that, since the social state is natural and habitual to human beings, there is no clear line of separation between the interests of the individual and those of society. The social feeling of mankind is a powerful force, which tends to grow stronger as men advance in civilization. A society of equals can exist only when "the interests of all are to be regarded

---

[4]On Mill's meaning in this famous argument, see H. D. Aiken's *Reason and Conduct* (New York: Alfred A. Knopf, 1962), pp. 48–59.

equally." When men cooperate as they must in society, their interests tend to be the same. They realize that the interests of others are in essential harmony with their own interests. To promote, not individual happiness, but the greatest total happiness, is the burden of Mill's position.

AN EVALUATION OF HEDONISMS

It is not easy to identify correctly the contributions and limitations of the work of hedonists, particularly since many of the issues they raise are still unsettled. Nevertheless, we will express an opinion on four main points, so that the issues may at least be easier to identify.

Do Men Always Seek Pleasure?

Men's motives are more complex than psychological hedonism suggests. Yet the roles of pleasure seeking, pain avoidance, and interest satisfaction are undoubtedly very important in motivation and warrant careful and extensive study. The stress by hedonists on pleasure as an actual object of choice has helped these investigations to get under way.

C. E. M. Joad, though not himself a psychological hedonist, has shown that for every motivation one can propose an explanation based on the idea that a person seeks only his own pleasure. Thus Joad shows that the child who appears better behaved simply recognizes that he will get more pleasure from social approval than from eating more than his share. The mother who subordinates her own interests constantly to those of her family enjoys more seeing others happy than having direct satisfaction of her other wants. Even the martyr may see his eternal glory as a greater pleasure than life or may take more pleasure in stubbornly sticking to his point than in avoiding the fire. Critics who have thought to refute psychological hedonism by reference to such cases have thus failed.[5] It would be extremely difficult, however, to demonstrate that the suppositions necessary to save the theory are warranted; and even if some men seek pleasure all the time, and all men are motivated by it part of the time, the theory may not be true. Its adequacy requires that every act of every man be so explained—a virtual impossibility. Does every man who rushes to save the life of another person first weigh the pleasure and pain involved for himself? Are ordinary choices about the

---

[5] C. E. M. Joad, *Guide to the Philosophy of Morals and Politics* (New York: Random House, n.d.), pp. 396–412.

order of tasks we do or the response we make to unexpected problems best explained by reference to our calculating the prospective pleasures involved? We can support the theory by treating some patterns of choice as derived from earlier experience of what pleased us and so viewing unconscious preferences as really based on what we think will produce our own pleasure. But if we wish to predict others' conduct or to explain conduct of the past, there are more economical and reliable ways of doing so.

To defend psychological hedonism, we would have to refute the common claim by men that they act for objectives other than pleasure. They say they desire certain concrete things that usually meet some particular needs. The fact that these things give pleasure does not prove that they were sought for the sake of pleasure. Indeed, it may be that they give pleasure because they are desired rather than the other way around. While we sometimes are surprised to find something pleasing, we ordinarily get pleasure because we have obtained what we preferred or sought.

A further defect of psychological hedonism is a confusion, sometimes typical of its defense, between every desire's being selfish and the fact that a man's every desire is his own. It is a tautology that every one of my desires is my own and that if I get it, I get something I wanted. It does not follow that each of these desires is for pleasure or is in disregard of the desires of others. To be selfish is not to have only one's own desires—an unavoidable condition—but to have predominantly desires that disregard or interfere with the fulfillment of others' desires.

Psychological hedonism was first advocated before the differences were as clear as now between happiness, pleasantness of experience (hedonic tone), nonpain, interest fulfillment, and desire. Early in the twentieth century, physiological psychologists identified specific pain receptors in the human organism. They disclosed in specific tests that positive hedonic tone is not fully correlated with nonpain. With the aid of this distinction it is possible to understand that some abnormal people derive great pleasure from excruciatingly painful experiences. With this distinction it becomes appropriate to ask under what conditions, from a hedonist viewpoint, we prefer a course of action that is predominantly painful even over the long run. Similarly, we are not always pleased when we get what we desired or had an interest in getting. "At least half of the world's avoidable troubles," said C. I. Lewis, "are created by those who do not know what they want and pursue what would not satisfy them if they had it."[6] Thus desires are not always for pleasure itself, nor does their satisfaction always give pleasure.

---

[6] Quoted in Aiken, *Reason in Conduct*, p. 29.

Is Pleasure the Only Intrinsic Good?

Hedonists' arguments have prompted recognition of important relations between pleasure and the good life. We have already noted that there are instances in which a personal preference may be decisive as to what ought to be done. Similarly, at times there is a place for doing whatever pleases oneself or someone else. Hedonists have nevertheless given an unduly restricted account of the things that are of intrinsic worth—that have traditionally been called "good in themselves" or "good for their own sake." The hedonistic view is that only pleasure is good in itself. Four confusions seem to have contributed to this conclusion. By reviewing them we can also see how controversy about the hedonist view has added to our understanding of the possibilities of the good life.

A first source of the too narrow view of intrinsic goods is psychological hedonism itself. If men did in fact prize only pleasure for its own sake, and if values are experienced only by conscious beings, then there may be no escape from limiting the intrinsic good to pleasure; but we have already discussed the defects of psychological hedonism and the questionable assumptions on which it is based. While pleasure is often a good, it is not the only good.

This thought leads to the second source of confusion, the idea that ethics should begin with a search for something that is always and everywhere good, something that is good in itself apart from its relations to time, place, circumstance, or any other matter. Most of the good things of life, however, are unpleasant and unwanted, if not morally out of place, in at least some contexts. Courting is a pleasure, but not at every time and place. Yet the fact that courting is no diet for the whole day and year does not render it less enjoyed for itself when the time and place are right. Once we lay aside this notion that to be of worth for itself a thing must be good at all times, we can see that the things found directly good by us are multitudinous. Of this variety of goods, C. I. Lewis says:

> If "pleasure" or any other name is to serve as synonym for the immediately and intrinsically valuable, then it must be adequate to the wide variety of what is found directly good in life. It must cover the active and self-forgetting satisfactions as well as the passive and self-conscious ones; the sense of integrity in firmly fronting the "unpleasant" as well as "pleasure"; the gratification in having one's own way, and also the benediction which may come to the defeated in having finished the faith. It must cover innocent satisfactions as well as those of cultivation; that which is found in consistency and also that of perversity and caprice; the enjoyment of sheer good fortune, and that which adds itself to dogged achievement. All this in addition to the whole range of the

sensuously pleasing and the emotionally gratifying. And the immediately disvaluable has its equal and corresponding variety.[7]

A third source of confusion about the intrinsically good was also mentioned in the discussion of psychological hedonism: the confusion of the by-product of a want's fulfillment with the thing sought and prized. As Joseph Butler noted long ago, the fact that we get satisfaction from something does not mean that we want it for the satisfaction. It is rather the other way around: it is because we want the thing that we get satisfaction from obtaining it. Hence, two distinct things may be true: (1) men prize a great variety of things for themselves, and (2) there is some experience of gratification or satisfaction common to the attainment of each of them. In fact, of course, we are not always gratified when we get what we seek: we may find that the trinket in hand feels cheap and the triumph achieved tastes bitter. Too, we experience pleasure in some things we did not set out to obtain, things that simply "fall into our lap." Yet at the moment of envisaging or experiencing a thing as valued for itself, there is a certain positive or pro attitude toward that thing, whatever it is. If this response was the thing for which hedonists were reaching in speaking of pleasure as the only intrinsic good, they may be said to have enunciated these important ideas: All values relate eventually to the good experienced by conscious beings. Unless a thing is in some sense "enjoyed" in prospect or in hand, it has no meaning for human choice, and hence for ethics. In this sense the intrinsic goods are the data of ethics out of which we derive, with the aid of other knowledge, our judgments about what is useful, what is obligatory, and what is best as a way of life.

A fourth source of confusion has been the equating of intrinsic value with immediately experienced value, and the failure to distinguish between what we actually desire and what we ought to desire for its own sake. Men do at times attribute intrinsic worth to the wrong things. They may erroneously prize an organization for its own sake, letting its preservation outweigh the values it was set up to make possible.

While we cannot go all the way with the hedonists who say that pleasure is the highest good, they may nevertheless be correct in the claim that we ought to strive for a happy life for ourselves and others. Both Kant and Aristotle acknowledged that in the complete good, pleasure and virtue are both present.

---

[7]C.I. Lewis, *An Analysis of Knowledge and Valuation* (LaSalle, Ill.: Open Court Publishing Co., 1946), p. 405.

Can the Worth of an Act Be Calculated?

To choose right is to choose the comparatively better. But comparison implies, in some sense, calculations of relative magnitude. Thus the utilitarians insisted that a sound ethic requires a calculus of pleasures. While, as we have seen, the effort to provide such a calculus runs into great difficulties, the demand for a reasoned system of comparison of the worth of effects is a significant contribution to ethical thinking. If we are to reject the hedonists' specific suggestions for such a system, then we must at least be ready with a better alternative. To grasp this point, we need notice only a few of the many questions that have been raised about this problem.

Mill himself proposed, as we saw, the introduction of qualitative as well as quantitative standards for the measurement of pleasure. Socrates dissatisfied is better off than a pig satisfied, Mill said. He thus spoke of different *kinds* of pleasure, some higher and better than others. If he meant merely that the pleasure of truth-telling is so great compared with that of spectator sports that they may best be viewed as of different kinds, he would have simply been introducing a shorthand device into the task of estimating quantity of pleasure. But he seems to have meant rather that, though no greater in its product of intensity, duration, and so on, the pleasure of truth-telling is to be given priority because people of greater experience and character will prefer it. Thus he appears to introduce another standard than quantity of pleasure.

Even if we were to view Mill's amendment as convenient shorthand calculation, we see how difficult it would be to calculate by the utilitarian formula. We can see that each new truth may enhance the earlier ones, whereas each additional bite of food after a certain quota becomes less appetizing and more hazardous to health. We can see that in eating more we compete with others for scarce means and thus raise the specter of countermeasures, whereas truth-telling—with all its hazards—is not so inescapably self-limiting. Yet how to add these intangibles is baffling indeed. They are rightly called incommensurable.

To these difficulties we must add a further one: Bentham and Mill did not think through adequately the fact that the distribution of pleasures as well as their total quantity on balance might have a bearing on the fulfillment of the good life. Suppose, for example, that in a community of twenty people we could produce the greatest net total of pleasures by giving four persons one thousand units of pleasure each, and everyone else only one hundred units each, while the next greatest amount of pleasure producible would be one obtained by either distributing three hundred units to each of ten persons and two hundred units to each of the remaining ten, or by providing two hundred and fifty units to every one of the twenty citizens. Bentham's calculus is open to different interpretations. One of these (choosing the greatest net pleasure) dictates choice of the first alternative, but this choice is offensive to both his and our sense of the equal rights of citizens in an ideally democratic society. Moreover, as between the second and third cases, this interpretation provides no grounds for a choice, whereas it would seem that such grounds should surely be provided by an adequate ethic.[8] Various answers have been offered for this dilemma: that the condition of equal treatment is itself a source of great pleasure and thus tips the balance, that in actual life the hypothetical conditions described above could not be met (preferential distribution of goods always eventually leading to great strife, pain, and suffering), and so on.

Consider a quite specific problem of estimating the worth of two complex objects of choice. Suppose that I want a new house for my family. I list many good things that this house might have. They can not all be put in the same house, especially in view of my limited means. How can I compare the net prospective worth of the various combinations that I can afford? Difficult as this problem is, we do not simply give up and make a guess. Typically we call in an architect to provide the best professional design in the light of our own preferences and his knowledge of means, costs, and the arts of combining and serving the desired functions. In this process he shows us various possible designs. In reacting, we do not simply add so many pleasure-units for a shower in the bathroom and so many more for a fireplace in the sitting room. The way parts of the house are related to one another will affect not only their cost, but also our pleasure in their use. But in the end the architect provides the contractor a very complex, even geometrically sketched account of his idea of the best house for our purposes. While there could be dispute as between alternative plans that this architect or others might supply, one or several of these plans will seem to me and my family superior to schemes we might have considered as we began to think of a new house.

Bentham spoke of a calculus of pleasures in arithmetical terms. Arithmetic, algebra, and even calculus are structured sstems. Baffling as they are to some people, they are relatively simple systems compared with one which would reflect all the interrelations involved even in choosing a house, to say nothing of an even more complex moral problem. Yet it is a sound idea that moral judgment can be improved by analysis of the factors affecting the outcome and by effort to estimate the effect of their interplay in the actual world.

---

[8]Walter T. Stace, in his *Concept of Morals* (New York: Macmillan Co., 1937), pp. 161–166, states this argument with different examples.

Ought We Always to Seek Happiness or Pleasure?

The crowning thesis of hedonism is not one about human motivation or about the intrinsic good. It is rather a moral theory that we *ought to seek* the maximum pleasure or happiness, either each for himself, as Epicurus held, or each for the greatest number, as the utilitarians said. Though defenses against all objections to this view are possible, we shall conclude that pleasure is an essential component of the life we ought to seek—one often underplayed by moralists, but by no means all that we ought to seek. To enable you to weigh the reasons for this view and reach your own conclusions, we shall review some major criticisms of ethical hedonism.

A first criticism is that the equating of happiness, pleasure, and absence of pain cannot be accepted. The day after a serious operation, when considerable pain is being felt but when assurance of recovery is possible, a patient may be happier and have more pleasure by far than before the painful experience. While this type of example does not show that one ought not to seek pleasure, it does suggest that pleasure and absence of pain are not the same. The bodily mechanisms that affect pleasure and pain are not the same. Tests have shown, as we stated earlier, that positive hedonic tone (feeling of pleasure) does not fully correlate with non-pain. Some pleasure apparently is compatible with the presence of some pain.

Regarding the relationship between pleasure and happiness, William Frankena has written:

> "Pleasure" suggests rather specific feelings whereas "happiness" does not. We can speak of "pleasures" but hardly of "happinesses." Pleasure" also suggests physical or "lower" pleasures more than "happiness" does. Again, it suggests short run and superficial enjoyment rather than the longer span and more profound satisfaction connoted by "happiness." Finally, phrases like "the pleasant life" and "a life of pleasure" call to mind something rather different from the phrase "the happy life." In fact, in ordinary discourse, we must and do distinguish a whole family of kinds of satisfactoriness which experiences and lives may have. Pleasantness is only one of them. Happiness, contentment, and beatitude are others. In this sense, the hedonist's thesis is a mistake, though he is right in thinking that happiness is a kind of satisfactoriness. He could, of course, redefine the terms "pleasure" and "pleasant" to cover all of these good-making qualities of experience, but doing this is like trying to redefine the word "red" to cover all of the colors.[9]

---

[9] William Frankena, *Ethics* (Englewood Cliffs, N.J.: Prentice-Hall, 1963), p. 73.

Even if we assigned the same meaning to the terms *pleasure, happiness,* and *absence of pain,* we would still need other terms to refer to the genuinely different experiences to which these terms ordinarily refer.

A second criticism of ethical hedonism was put by John Dewey in this way: The statement that all good has enjoyment as an ingredient is not equivalent to the statement that all pleasure is a good. Dewey's point is confirmed by the way we assess character. We do not call the man of the most pleasant life thereby the most virtuous or best. We may judge character adversely by what gives a man pleasure. The dishonest or stingy man will obtain pleasure from acts that would trouble and pain the honest or generous one. A hedonist reply has been that in such cases the unvirtuous make a false estimate of the long-run way to maximize pleasure or that they mistakenly put personal pleasure above the net pleasure of all. In view of the problems of the calculus of pleasure, however, it is difficult to make this claim convincing. In this sense the hedonist view is, though useful, not an adequate instrument in guiding our day-to-day decisions and even our choices as to major features of our way of life.

Ethical hedonism has been criticized for putting exclusive emphasis on feeling, to the neglect of the intellectual, aesthetic, and religious side of man's nature. Of transitory feelings, Bradley wrote:

> Pleasures, we saw, were a perishing series. This one comes, and the intense self-feeling proclaims satisfaction. It is gone, and *we* are not satisfied. It was not that one, then, but this one now; and this one now is gone. It was not that one, then, but another and another; but another and another do not give us what we want; we are still left eager and confident, till the flush of feeling dies down, and when that is gone there is nothing left. We are where we began, so far as the getting of happiness goes; and we have not found ourselves, and we are not satisfied.[10]

Kierkegaard attempted in various ways to imagine a life of immediate feeling as pleasant as possible and wrote accounts of the possibilities of such life. He was unable, however, to imagine such a life as successful in satisfying the whole individual. To abstract the feeling side of life and to stress it alone, he held to be self-defeating. Man is an intellectual as well as a feeling being, and his fulfillment requires the greatest possible satisfaction of all of his capacities, not merely his ability to feel pleasure.

It is further argued against the emphasis on pleasure as the sole good that a feeling of pleasure may arise as the result of a pathological per-

---

[10]F. H. Bradley, *Ethical Studies,* 2nd ed. (London: Oxford University Press, 1927), p. 96.

version. Pleasure can be associated with the inflicting of pain or with cruelty (for example, in masochism and sadism). Pleasure may also be felt in malice. In these instances it is not merely not good; it is positively evil. Just as the sweet taste of a poison does not prove that it is good for the bodily organism, so the feeling of pleasure does not prove that an action is morally good.

A hedonist may reply that these arguments are plausible because they neglect the distinction between the immediate or short-run pleasurable effects of an act and the over-all effect. Bentham or Mill would thus share our dismay about the sadist and the masochist and the man who aims to fulfill himself by a succession of pleasant episodes. In the long run, they would say, man gains the greatest pleasure only if he exercises his full capabilities. The way we know that these capabilities are good is that their exercise in right proportion does in the long run provide the most pleasant life for all.

Pleasure, it is finally argued, is a by-product and not an end in itself. To seek it directly is to miss it. This hedonistic paradox—that it is self-defeating to seek pleasure directly—applies both to specific choices and to the larger aims of life. The man who goes to the concert to hear good music may gain great pleasure from hearing it; the man who goes to get pleasure has no assured basis for coming away rewarded. The man who sets out to meet significant and feasible goals needs only to progress toward them in order to be happy; the man whose aim is a life of positive hedonic tone is in no such happy circumstance. We should not confuse the seeking of specific objectives (a pluralism of ends) with the seeking of pleasure for its own sake. Thus hedonism is an awkward guide in that (1) it does not give clues as to how its goal can be attained, and (2) its explicit and deliberate pursuit may even hinder its accomplishment.

To this argument also the hedonist has answers. If it is self-defeating to seek pleasure directly, one may do so indirectly. It can still be, and rightly be, our main goal. We may also prize many specific objectives because they share the characteristic of yielding pleasure, which is good on its own account.

We have stated four criticisms of ethical hedonism and have noted some of the arguments they evoke. The replies and rebuttals could be further extended. But where do they lead? Bentham and Mill acknowledged that one cannot prove by deduction from indubitable premises that pleasure is *the* intrinsic good. Bentham sought to make the principle of utility plausible by showing that our best judgments do derive or could be derived from it. We shall see, however, that evolutionary ethics and the theory of self-realization make similar claims. Which of the standards provides the combination of clarity, consistency, impartiality, efficiency in application, and adequacy to the guidance of ethical choice and action that best serves that guiding function? We cannot answer this question without first examining the claims of still other standards.

We do well to observe, in the meantime, that the teleologists, who propose that the consequences of an act determine its worth, try to meet the need for a practically usable test for choice. Teleological theories instruct us: (1) to forecast the outcomes of the proposed action, and (2) to evaluate them by a measure of pleasure or some other end that is good for its own sake.

We do, in fact, often obtain light on the merits of a course of action by asking whether it leads to unwanted outcomes. Unhappiness and pain indicate that something in ourselves or in our environment is wrong and needs to be changed. Even Kant thought it would not be right for the virtuous to be deprived of happiness. A parent who construes his own and his children's duties in such a way as to cause the children constant unhappiness is probably in error himself. In England, where utilitarianism arose, the antislavery movement, the new missionary program, and the Reform Bill of 1832 were to a considerable extent expressions of a new urge to bring greater happiness to all mankind. Asking the question "Are these members of society happy?" points quickly toward trouble spots in society where duty is somehow being misconstrued or poorly performed, where injustice or cruelty survives under the guise of legality, customary rights, or even religious sanction.

CONCLUSION

That pleasure is a good and pain an evil under most circumstances appears to be undisputed. The desire to have pleasant experiences is a normal human desire which appears to be widespread if not universal. Unhappiness and pain indicate that something in ourselves, in our relationship with others, or in our environment is wrong and needs to be changed. Within very broad limits the happiness standard is a fairly accurate guide to conduct, especially if the higher or intellectual pleasures are kept to the fore. The utilitarian movement, the revival of hedonism in the nineteenth century in England under the leadership of such men as Jeremy Bentham and John Stuart Mill led to many practical, social, economic, and political reforms as students of history well know.

While many persons will acknowledge that pleasure is a good, a great many will reject the notion that it is the only good or the highest good. Many persons also say that it is a mistake to equate pleasure and happiness, as if the two terms were synonymous in the way that Bentham and Mill seem to take for granted. Whereas pleasures are of many types, suggest short-run enjoyment, and put the emphasis largely on feeling, happiness seems to imply and include the good life as a whole. There is a vast difference between having a good time (pleasant experience) from day to day and leading a good life that is unlimited in its variety and richness.

According to Mill, one person living on a higher cultural level and another on a lower cultural level will require different *kinds* of pleasure. But if some pleasures are higher or better than others, there must be some standard other than pleasure by which they are judged. If pleasure were our only standard of moral value, how could pleasures be evaluated or graded and some of them praised and others condemned? Furthermore, the pleasure and pain which come to a person depend to a considerable extent on his character and cultural development, and they may change in a few years or during a man's lifetime.

Pleasure, and even happiness, are evidently by-products rather than ends in themselves. At least the direct pursuit of pleasure by itself often leads to its defeat. The person who says, "I am going out to find happiness" is not likely to find it. Life is not made happy by getting what we happen to desire impulsively, but by learning to desire the objectively best things. Happiness seems to come as a by-product of achievement, of creativeness, and of the fulfillment of function. Happiness is closely connected with some worthwhile work into which a person can put forth his best efforts, with a loyalty or devotion to something beyond oneself, and with an expanding and friendly interest in other persons and things. While external circumstances are important, happiness is largely a state within. The cultivation of a rich inner life and a well-integrated self are among the important elements in a happy life.

QUESTIONS AND PROJECTS

1. How do you explain the fact that many creative artists appear to have done some of their best work when in ill health, depression, or strain? Among the many examples are Mozart, Robert Louis Stevenson, Goethe, Milton, Beethoven, Michelangelo, and Charles Dickens.
2. After a few decades of successful farming, a farmer decides to retire. He purchases a new home in the town nearby. This home is equipped with many modern conveniences that he has not had in the country. However, the long-looked-for leisure and comforts that he thought would bring him happiness do not give him the contentment and peace he expected. Is this typical? How might a hedonist explain it? How do you explain it?
3. A young woman from Central Europe relates this account of her experiences and those of her family during the years of extreme inflation

and then the destruction of war. Her parents had been quite wealthy, and during this early period of prosperity she scarcely knew them, her time being spent mainly with governesses, tutors, and chauffeurs. When misfortune came, the family went to live in a cottage in the country. They then used to go off as a family on long walks through the fields and over the hills. She looks back to that period as the most enjoyable time of her life. For the first time she had two interested and amusing parents, and comradeship within the family. As money returned, her parents, apparently with some regrets, dropped back into the routine of fashionable society. She says that the "real goods of life again diminished." How do you explain her experiences? How might a hedonist explain them?

4. A sales executive, in speaking to a group of fashion experts, warned that utility cannot be the basis for a prosperous clothing industry. Your task, he said, is to make women unhappy with their apparel as soon as possible. "You might call us 'merchants of unhappiness.' . . . We must make these women so unhappy that their husbands can find no happiness or peace in their excessive saving." [H. H. Wilson, "Cynics and Feeble Good Men," *The Nation* 173 (November 24, 1951):440.] Comment on this statement and the social outlook implied.

5. One student writes: "Last summer I worked on a farm in a Mennonite community. On very warm afternoons I wanted to take off my shirt, but I did not do so because it would be against the religious convictions of the sect of the Mennonites among whom I was working. I might have made some agitation over the situation but concluded that my personal comfort was not as important as living in harmony with my associates. The latter, I felt, was of greater value than the former." To what extent should we deny ourselves the gratification of a pleasure that we consider harmless if our indulgence offends the moral or religious sentiments of those with whom we are associated?

6. What is the meaning of suffering? Is there any value at all in pain? Can your view of the good of pain and suffering be reconciled with hedonism?

7. What part does a sense of humor play in helping us to be happy? What part does laughter play?

8. What are John Stuart Mill's answers to the charges that utilitarianism is (1) too lofty an ideal for humanity, (2) a view that renders man cold and unsympatheic, a "godless" doctrine, (3) mere expediency? (See Mill, *Utilitarianism*, ch. 2.)

9. The *Rubaiyat* of Omar Khayyam voices a preference for taking immediate pleasures and not worrying about the longer term risks to health, to others, and to other values. How would you, on hedonist grounds, rebut this plea?

10. It has been said that preoccupation with immediate pleasures is a mark of decadence in a society. On this basis how do you appraise our own culture?

11. Is it possible that people in general might be happier with a simpler style of life than most people experience today? You might be interested to

read "Experimenting with a Simpler Life Style: An Interview with Harvey Cox," by Charles Fager in *The Christian Century* 88 (January 6, 1971):9–13.

SUGGESTED READINGS

Aiken, Henry David. *Reason and Conduct.* Ch. 3. New York: Alfred A. Knopf, 1962.
Baumgardt, David. *Bentham and the Ethics of Today; With Bentham Manuscripts Hitherto Unpublished.* New York: Octagon Books, 1967.
Bentham, Jeremy. *An Introduction to the Principles of Morals and Legislation.* Hafner Library of Classics, no. 6. New York: Hafner Publishing Co., 1948.
Binkley, Luther J. *Conflict of Ideals: Changing Values in Western Society.* New York: Van Nostrand Reinhold Co., 1969.
Broad, Charlie D. *Five Types of Ethical Theory,* Chs. 3, 4, and 5. New York: Humanities Press, 1930.
Frankena, William K. *Ethics.* Pp. 19–21 and 67–73. Englewood Cliffs, N.J.: Prentice-Hall, 1963.
Hill, Thomas English. *Contemporary Ethical Theories.* Ch. 12. New York: Macmillan Co., 1950.
Hyde, William De Witt. *The Five Great Philosophies of Life.* Ch. 1. New York: Collier Books, 1962.
Jones, Howard Mumford. *The Pursuit of Happiness.* Ithaca: Cornell University Press, 1953.
Lucretius, Carus T. *Of the Nature of Things.* New York: E. P. Dutton & Co., 1935.
McGill, V. J. *The Idea of Happiness.* New York: Frederick A. Praeger, 1968.
Mill, John Stuart. *Mill on Bentham and Coleridge.* Introduction by F. R. Leavis. London: Chatto & Windus, 1950.
———. *Utilitarianism.* Everyman's Library. New York: E. P. Dutton & Co., 1910.
Moore, G. E. *Ethics.* Chs. 1 and 2. New York: Henry Holt & Co., Home University Library of Modern Knowledge, 1912.
———. *Principia Ethica.* London: Cambridge University Press, 1959.
Pratt, James B. *Reason in the Art of Living.* Chs. 10, 11, and 12. New York: Macmillan Co., 1950.
Schilpp, Paul Arthur. "The Place of Pleasure in the Good Life" in *The Student Seeks an Answer.* Edited by John A. Clark. Waterville, Me.: Colby College Press, 1960.
Taylor, Richard. *Good and Evil: A New Direction.* Chs. 6 and 7. New York: Macmillan Co., 1970.
Werkmeister, W. H. *Theories of Ethics.* Chs. 3, 4, and 5. Lincoln, Neb.: Johnsen Publishing Co., 1961.

9
NATURE AS THE STANDARD

In this chapter we shall consider the ethical theories that emphasize the individual as an organism competing for survival in an evolving natural order, and as one exerting his will in an environment where there are many obstacles to overcome. The system of ethics which emphasizes nature, biological development, and adaptation to environment is often referred to as the *ethics of evolution*. Traditionally, evolutionary ethics and the theory of self-realization have been viewed as sharply opposed schools of thought. Yet Darwin in his conception of the good life for man is closer to some contemporary self-realizationists than he is to other evolutionists such as Herbert Spencer. This situation arises because a theory is only a vehicle through which a person expresses a smaller or larger part of what he himself understands. Men of very different insights may thus employ the same abstract framework with quite contrasting effects, while advocates of different theories may hang on those contrasting frames of reference much the same body of insights. We cannot then fairly attribute to a type of theory all the defects found in its various expressions or all the understanding reflected in its best presentation. We stress the contributions made by each school through one or another of its spokesmen and the limitations that nevertheless generally characterize it as an account of the good for man.

Evolutionary ethics has given needed emphasis to the following facets of morality: (1) Survival and adaptation to environment are essential in the achievement of good. (2) To lead a good life, men must accept and cooperate with the physical and biological forces that shape the possibilities for good. (3) Just as life is a precondition of other values, so social group survival is a precondition of peculiarly human values. (4) Cooperation and social concern improve the chances of group survival; hence, a merely egoistic or prudential ethics is inadequate for the best life available to men. (5) Even so, self-assertion, will, and the exercise of power in the interest of the self may also be important means to the greatest good. Spokesmen of evolutionary ethics have generally acknowledged that self-sacrifice, rationality, human freedom and initiative, and commitment to a good more inclusive than himself and his tribe are crucial to a man's achievement of his greatest fulfillment. However, attempts to derive the warrant for all virtues, obligations, and ideals from their utility for survival have not succeeded.

DARWIN'S ETHICS

Obviously, there can be no good life unless the living organism survives. In an age when other values are subject to constant challenge, it is still plausible to suggest that life and its multiplication may be a universally accepted good. Men have also wanted their values to be permanent, outlasting the evil and the wrong. With Darwin's work on the evolution of species, the goal of fitness for survival of one's kind on this earth became attractive. Moreover, by comparison with the greatest sum of pleasures, the survival or viability of a species or individual seems much more reliably measurable. Thus the publication in 1859 of Darwin's *The Origin of Species* and, a few years later, of his *The Descent of Man* sparked active interest in survival power as the criterion of the good life.

Darwin's contribution was, in part, to assemble by long and careful investigations a mass of evidence from which he concluded that present-day species have evolved from earlier forms of life. He drew his evidence from comparative anatomy, embryology, vestigial remains, and data on geographical distribution of life forms. His resulting theory of natural selection focused attention on four points:

1. *Heredity.* Parents produce offspring more or less like themselves. Like tends to beget like.
2. *Variations.* No two offspring are exactly alike. There are always small differences.
3. *The struggle for existence.* Food supply increases by simple addition of more production, but population increases by compounding, each generation producing larger numbers than the preceding one. There thus

arises, as Malthus had argued fifty years earlier,[1] a competition for scarce food, a struggle both within each species and against enemies in other species. Other factors also affect survival, but the most important is competition for food.

4. *The survival of the fittest.* In the struggle for existence, only those best adapted to the environment survive. We are familiar with the work of animal breeders who select only the best animals for breeding and thus improve the stock by preserving the most desirable combinations of traits. Nature may be viewed as getting a similar effect by normal agencies of cause and effect. Progress occurs by elimination of the less fit and propagation of the abler.

Not all of the early supporters of Darwin's theory of evolution of species by natural selection were ready to accept natural selection as an agent of morality. Thomas Huxley, for example, acknowledged that nature is "red with tooth and claw" and therefore argued that it is our duty to prevent the operation of such selection in human affairs. Darwin, however, did not agree that natural selection occurs only by brutal struggle. He argued that, even among animals, sociability as expressed in sympathy, fidelity, and courage has proved to have survival value.

Such social qualities, whose paramount importance to the lower animals is disputed by no one, were no doubt acquired by the progenitors of man in a similar manner—through natural selection. When two tribes of primeval man, living in the same country, came into competition, if (other circumstances being equal) the one tribe included a great number of courageous, sympathetic, and faithful members who were always ready to warn one another of danger, to aid and defend one another, this tribe would fare better and would conquer the other.[2]

Darwin avoided two further inferences that some evolutionists have made from his theory: (1) that the later emerging forms in evolution are higher and therefore, in an evolutionary ethic, better than the earlier, and thus that man occupies a position of high value, and (2) that inevitable and continuous progress is assured by the process of evolution. Of these points Darwin wrote:

> On our theory the continued existence of lowly organisms offers no difficulty: for natural selection or the survival of the fittest, does not necessarily include progressive development—it only takes advantage of such variations as arise and are beneficial to each creature under its complex relations of life. And it may be asked what advantage, as far

---

[1]See Thomas Robert Malthus, *An Essay on the Principle of Population* (1798).

[2]Charles Darwin, *The Descent of Man*, (1859) ch. 5.

as we can see, would it be to an infusorian animalcule—to an intestinal worm—or even an earthworm, to be highly organized?[3]

It does not follow that human traits may not prove to have uniquely great value on survival grounds alone, or that no improvements in a species can be shown to occur purely on grounds of survival value. The survival criterion alone, however, leaves the case for man's preeminent worth a more open question than many men would like. As a criterion of worth, the survival criterion requires clarification if it is to be useful in guiding men as they make choices.

On this last point several questions arise: If merely being the current survivor does not prove the particular value of a form of life, what does? Being the longest surviving type? Then man surely is one of the less valuable types of beings. Having the prospect of long survival? The population explosion and atomic bombs and germ warfare leave man's worth still a matter of great doubt. Moreover, how are the prospects of survival to be assessed? Being the survivor in the type of conditions predicted to prevail in the future? Since man himself can affect these conditions, and his choice as to which conditions to establish can affect who survives and for how long, some criterion is needed by which to decide which conditions ought to be created. A proposed answer to this problem, a proposal in the spirit of an evolutionary ethic, is that some modes of survival and environments are mutually supportive, while others are self-defeating. This proposal is that man's best prospects for survival involve maximizing conditions for co-survival with other species of many varieties. In a recent book,[4] for instance, Rachel Carson's pleas against poison sprays to control pests are based on two lines of argument: (1) she prizes different varieties of life for their own sake and thus argues against careless killing or killing not required for some urgent human need; (2) she argues, for those who do not accept her premise of the value of life other than human, that we damage ourselves and the prospects of human life when we interfere with the balance of nature. Thus, by killing certain insects inadvertently as we spray a crop for other pests, we shorten food supply for birds and other beneficial animals. At the very least this argument shows that there is much to learn about the interacting relations among animals and plants if we would maximize our own survival, not to speak of that of other forms of living beings.

Darwin argued that man owes his strength as a social animal to his weakness in the struggle for existence as a solitary physical animal. To make up for his weakness, man had to develop intelligence (the

---

[3]Charles Darwin, *The Origin of Species* (New York: Modern Library, 1937), pp. 94–95.

[4]Rachel Carson, *Silent Spring* (Boston: Houghton Mifflin Co., 1962).

stronger gorilla had less need of sharp wits to escape his enemies and get his food) and cooperative habits (the weak must band together to survive). Lacking natural weapons, man had to invent tools and learn to use group strategies. Intelligence, cooperation, and tool-making at the same time made man able to move from climate to climate and environment to environment. With the increase of these adaptive powers, the improvement of man's physical capacities became less needed for survival. When men competed with other bands of men, said Darwin, the tribes with the greatest supply of resourceful men would supply themselves better, win the conflicts, and propagate more rapidly. Similarly, the virtues, as we know them, can be seen to have had adaptive value. Darwin went so far as to say:

> I fully subscribe to the judgment of those writers who maintain that of all the differences between man and the lower animals, the moral sense or conscience is by far the most important. . . . It is summed up in that short but imperious word *ought*, so full of high significance. It is the most noble of all the attributes of man, leading him without a moment's hesitation to risk his life for that of a fellow creature; or after due deliberation, impelled simply by the deep feeling of right or duty, to sacrifice it in some great cause.[5]

Darwin went on briefly to show that religion can act either to strengthen man's capacity to survive in a society or to rigidify the culture and render it unresponsive to the needs of adaptation.

The evidence in hand about survival value is, of course, most abundant concerning what has been of survival value under past conditions. Thus mores tend to reflect these data insofar as they are known and understood. The evidence as to what *will* or could have greater survival value is more difficult to get. Thus the argument for a world community, as opposed to fighting tribes or nations or states, is harder to provide than the argument for in-group loyalty, be it to tribe, to family, to state and nation, or to alliances of nations. Similarly, for a standard such as survival value, the argument for individual freedom has an uphill battle. These are reasons, even admitting that the forward-looking concerns can be reconciled with an evolutionary ethic, that this ethic is not a sufficient moral guide.

At the same time, an evolutionary ethic points to one fact about the scope of human responsibility that is generally overlooked in other ethical theories. This has to do with the inherent worth of other life. On an evolutionary ethic it would be arbitrary to recognize only human life as of value. Why should man use other life as a mere means to his own interests?

---

[5]*The Origin of Species*, p. 471.

As man advances in civilisation, and small tribes are united into larger communities, the simplest reason would tell each individual that he ought to extend his social instincts and sympathies to all the members of the same nation, though personally unknown to him. This point being once reached, there is only an artificial barrier to prevent his sympathies extending to the men of all nations and races. If, indeed, such men are separated from him by great differences in appearance or habits, experience unfortunately shows us how long it is, before we look at them as our fellow-creatures. Sympathy beyond the confines of man, that is, humanity to the lower animals, seems to be one of the latest moral acquisitions.... This virtue, one of the noblest with which man is endowed, seems to arise incidentally from our sympathies becoming more tender and more widely diffused, until they are extended to all sentient beings.[6]

It is the fashion nowadays to make fun of anthropomorphic religions —religions that shape their gods after the model of man or of particular kinds of man. Yet most ethical theories are highly man-centered. It is even argued at times that the very nature of ethics is to be concerned only with man. Thus the human good is said by stipulation to be the sole area of ethical concern. A few, such as Schweitzer, have raised their voices to the contrary. An evolutionary ethic makes it clear that this limitation, if accepted, is an arbitrary stipulation unless reasons are given for restricting our primary concern to human life. As far as we know, Darwin himself did not draw this implication out and elaborate it, though he was aware, in the passage cited, that man is not alone a center of worth. Kenneth Hunt recently proposed a "biocentric community" as the object of intrinsic concern in ethics—a concept whose implications and ethical utility bear further exploration.[7]

SPENCER AND LATER EVOLUTIONISTS

Herbert Spencer (1820–1903) gave one of the most elaborate and influential interpretations of evolutionary ethics in the nineteenth century. The idea of evolution became, in his philosophy, a cosmic principle, not simply one affecting species of living beings. Though we cannot discover the nature of ultimate reality, he said, we can know that there is a Cosmic Unity, a World Energy or Power behind the realm of appearances. Spencer linked the survival principle to pleasure in order to make clear the relevance and applicability of the principle to specific decisions. While, he said, pleasure is not what makes an action good

---

[6]*The Descent of Man*, pp. 491–492.
[7]Kenneth Hunt, "A Biocentric Concept," *Unity* 146 (March 1960): 13–16.

or pain what makes it evil, pleasure tends to accompany acts that lead toward human welfare and survival, and pain accompanies actions with the opposite effect. Thus, where the connection of survival with the sanction for moral conduct is difficult to see, it may be grasped by way of its connection with pleasure or pain.

Some of Spencer's amendments to evolutionary ethics amount to partial abandonment of the position. Two such amendments are his redefinition of life and his faith in evolution as progressive. Life, he suggested, is "the continuous adjustment of internal relations to external relations." The greatest good is harmonious adaptation to the environment. Not only a long life but the richness or fullness or "breadth" of life must be sought, and not merely the individual life but all life. The central mechanism for the preservation and enhancement of life is still seen as adaptation to the environment; but the adaptation is a mechanism rather than the criterion of good.

Spencer had an unshakable conviction that the natural laws of the evolutionary process itself lead in the direction of the good. As the individual improves physically, he is also passing from a crude gregariousness to conscious sympathy and intelligent cooperation. The laws of nature gradually bring harmony, so that acts that bring pleasure, acts that bring personal adaptation, and acts that preserve the group and the race tend to coincide in one grand harmony. There are occasions, however, when the sacrifice of an individual for the preservation of the species is necessary. This opposition between individual good and social good was becoming less, Spencer felt, and will eventually disappear.

Spencer's view of the social and political implications of evolutionary ethics reflected dominant ideas of his culture and social class. The chief duty of man is to stand aside and avoid interference with the processes of nature. Let man trust in nature, since it is gradually bringing about a more harmonious adjustment of man's nature to the environment in which he lives. Biological changes in the constitution of man tend to eliminate evils and to bring happiness and progress. A system of morality should be founded on the laws of the evolution of life.

The duties of society or of the state with respect to individuals are also clear, Spencer thought. Apart from artificial devices or manipulation, the strongest members of society will achieve the greatest success and will propagate their kind. The desirable qualities will be handed on to future generations and will increase. The individuals with defects or weaker strains will naturally fail to survive. In this way society will be purged of its weaklings, and the race will be strengthened. Thus, apart from protecting men from foreign aggression and preventing crime within the group, the state has few, if any, duties. Individuals must be as free as possible from all interference by the state, so that the laws of nature will work without hindrance in their own lives and in social relationships. Spencer regarded even education, the postal service, and the making of roads as outside the proper jurisdiction of government. Individuals may assist others, since charity is good, at least for the giver. Such benevolence, however, is outside the function of government.

THE SELF AS POWER AND WILL: NIETZSCHE

At the outset of this chapter we indicated our intention to discuss the ideal of the individual as an organism competing for survival or exerting its will in a resistant environment. This latter facet of the self is exemplified, in one of its influential forms, in the thought of Friedrich Nietzsche (1844–1900). We emphasize here one view of what Nietzsche thought.[8] In this interpretation there is less said of man's adapting himself to the environment than of his shaping the environment. The good is viewed as the enforcement of the individual will. Yet in the end the criterion as to the individual will that is best is that it survive in a struggle in which other wills and group efforts compete for domination.

Since Thrasymachus debated with Socrates, and even before, there have been those who have thought that we are often so sentimental about goodness as to miss its relationship to the vigorous exercise of power. Plato reported, though not sympathetically, that Thrasymachus championed the idea that morality is determined by the will of those in power. Machiavelli, Hobbes, and Nietzsche echoed this theme in more refined forms. In elaborating this idea, Nietzsche built on two other major elements in the thought of the nineteenth century: the idea of the will as the essence of the self (Schopenhauer, 1788–1860), and the idea that in the evolution of the human species the superhuman is within man's grasp. Schopenhauer thought, unlike Kant, that we can know the ultimate reality, things in themselves, for this reality expresses itself in us in that we are part of the universe. The inner essence of both man's nature and the universe is will. The energy, power, or striving that is seen in plants, in animals, and in human nature is the same energy or will that underlies all existence—the will to live. Combining these influences with the lesser influence of the musician and composer Richard Wagner, Nietzsche proposed a robust morality in which the strongest succeed and might is defended as right. Studies in the ancient classics evoked in Nietzsche a sense of the importance of

---

[8]Students of Nietzsche sometimes disagree in their interpretation of aspects of his thinking. For example see Walter Kaufman, *Nietzsche: Philosopher, Psychologist, Antichrist* (Princeton: Princeton University Press, 1950).

the individual, a notion that became central in his thinking. He was impressed also by the desire of the Greeks to live to the fullest, and by their physical prowess and courage.

In the hands of Nietzsche, the will to live became the will to power.[9] He wrote, "A living thing seeks above all to discharge its strength—life itself is *Will to Power;* self-preservation is only one of the indirect and most frequent results thereof."[10] This will to power explains why living creatures struggle. The struggle for existence is meaningless unless there is a will to exist or a will to dominate. The will to power thus becomes a fundamental principle in nature, one that is essential to the evolutionary development of the race. It is a cosmic law, a fundamental metaphysical reality.

Nietzsche recognized goodness only as it is an expression of the will to power. He branded all other motives as morally unsound. " 'Exploitation' does not belong to a depraved or imperfect and primitive society: it belongs to the *nature* of the living being as a primary organic function; it is a consequence of the intrinsic Will to Power, which is precisely the Will to Life."[11] A passive submission to the environment is the opposite of life. Those survive who *will* to survive. Nietzsche set the will above all other parts of human personality. Reason, for example, is a mere instrument of the will, and the will is narrowed to a single purpose—the will to power.

Based on the doctrine of the will to power is Nietzsche's belief in an aristocratic cult of the elite, a race of supermen who have power and genius. These superior men determine or create values; they are not subject to obligations, except to the duty of living according to their natures. Nietzsche said, "I teach you the Superman. Man is something that is to be surpassed. What have ye done to surpass man?" "The Superman is the meaning of the earth." "In real life it is only a question of strong and weak wills." "All that proceeds from power is good, all that springs from weakness is bad."[12]

Virtues are those traits of character which enable one to survive in the struggle for existence. They reflect the position and the point of view of those individuals and groups which entertain them. The basis of all values is the superior man's sense of his own nobility. Based largely on natural physiological differences in men, there is a master-morality and a slave-morality. Master-morality is a morality of the ruling class, or of

---

[9]See especially Friedrich Nietzsche, *The Will to Power*, I and II.
[10]Friedrich Nietzsche, *Beyond Good and Evil*, ch. 1, sec. 13.
[11]Ibid., ch. 9, sec. 259.
[12]Friedrich Nietzche, *Thus Spake Zarathustra*, trans. Thomas Common (New York: Modern Library, 1917), prologue, no. 3.

the supermen. Morality for them is an affirmation of their own demands. Men who are strong and virile, who have strong wills, need to build a system of morals appropriate to their natures. Such men value courage, self-reliance, high-mindedness, candor, mastery, and creative leadership. They scorn cowardice, humility, sympathy, and weakness. The masters emphasize the Dionysian ideal of strength and abundant life expressed in "the feeling of plentitude, of power," and by physical "healthiness." Severity, conquest of the weak, and violence may serve the elevation of the species. Nietzsche held it the "right of masters to create values," to transvalue the old "herd" values, and to pass "beyond good and evil." The race is to the swift and the battle to the strong.[13]

An ethics that exalts humility, sympathy, self-denial, and the sacrifice of the stronger for the weaker is slave-morality. It is a perverted morality for which the Judaeo-Christian tradition is responsible. It is based on a denial of "life" and upon principles of dissolution and decay. Suppose, wrote Nietzsche, that the oppressed, the suffering, the unemancipated, and those who are uncertain of themselves should establish moral codes; what would they do? They would oppose the virtues of the powerful and stress those qualities and traits that make life easier for themselves. "Slave-morality is essentially the morality of utility." In the masses the will to power takes the form of resentment against the strong and magnificent men who abound in creative energy. The traditional Western or Christian values lead toward nihilism.[14]

Real progress will come, according to Nietzsche, not by raising the weak and emancipating the masses, but through the cultivation of a superior race of men. The superman must rise above the masses, not sympathize with them. Gradations of rank, not equality and equal rights, are among the decrees of nature. The inferior groups may retain their illusions; they are needed as a foundation on which the superior man can build. The masses may continue to follow their slave-morality. However, the superior man, in whom the will to power has come to fruition in courage, beauty, and culture, may "reject the categorical imperative" and live beyond good and evil.

In concluding this brief statement of the moral philosophy of Nietzsche, it may be well to reject two fairly popular though false impressions. One is that Nietzsche was the enemy of all moral values whatsoever. The other is that Nietzsche's position justifies anyone's doing anything at any time that will make him happy or satisfy immediate desire. Nietzsche was setting forth a very unconventional code, it is true, and one that most people will be unable to accept. He insisted, however,

---

[13]*Beyond Good and Evil*, ch. 2, sec. 44.
[14]*The Will to Power*, I, bk. 1.

that man is born not to be happy but to perform his duty according to the demands of his nature. He insisted also that man cannot evade natural law (the will to power), which he interpreted as a certain simple type of animal behavior. He was opposed to conventional morality, democracy, and intellectualism.

LATER EVOLUTIONISTS

More recent biologists have stressed the struggle in natural selection even less than did Darwin. Thus G. G. Simpson writes:

> Struggle is sometimes involved, but it usually is not. . . . Advantage in differential reproduction is usually a peaceful process in which the concept of struggle is really irrelevant. It more often involves such things as better integration into the ecological situation, maintenance of a balance of nature, more efficient utilization of available food, better care of the young, elimination of intra-group discords (struggles) that might hamper reproduction, exploitation of environmental possibilities that are not the objects of competition or are less effectively exploited by others. . . . In intra-group selection . . . struggle is not necessarily or even usually of the essence. Precisely the opposite, selection in favor of harmonious or cooperative association is certainly common.[15]

Later evolutionists amended the ideas of Darwin and Spencer on the mechanisms of evolution and on the implications of evolutionary ethics for practice. Edmund Montgomery in America and Henri Bergson in France questioned the idea that the development of higher forms of life and values occurs simply by natural selection among chance variations. They held that the creation of new values occurs in evolution, not by mere aggregation of matter in new arrangements, but by the emergence of novel forms and behavior out of inherent potentials not previously exhibited. Some evolutionists, such as C. Lloyd Morgan and S. Alexander, viewed this creation of values as the work of an inherent purposiveness in nature.

Spencer had drawn from his view of evolution a model of society in which free competition should reign and the ablest and best should emerge as rightful victors. The good of humanity would be served best by this struggle. Edmund Montgomery and Marius Deshumbert, on the contrary, stress cooperation, sympathy, and mutual aid through social and political organization as the means to a better life. It was Henri Bergson (1859–1941), however, who gave evolutionary ethics its most

---

[15] G. G. Simpson, *The Meaning of Evolution* (New Haven: Yale University Press, 1949), pp. 222–223.

influential expression in the half century after Darwin and Spencer. "All morality . . . is in essence biological," Bergson said. The biological roots of morality generate both intellectual and nonintellectual manifestations. The nonintellectual are of two kinds: instinct and impetus. Obligation takes two forms, corresponding to these two roots. In a closed society or in an individual bound by his culture, obligation arises as pressure to conform. It is a mistake, Bergson insisted, to think that moral pressure finds its final explanation "in social life considered merely as a fact." We say that the constraint of society on its members is obligation, Bergson noted. But for society to exist at all "the individual must bring into it a whole group of inborn tendencies." So, Bergson argued, we must search below the social accretions to "get down to Life, of which human societies, as indeed the human species altogether, are but manifestations."[16]

There is a second morality, according to Bergson, the morality of the open individual and the open society. This is the morality of aspiration, and it too wells up from within a nonintellective part of man's nature that is also a product of evolution. This part of human nature is the impetus, manifest in aspiration.

If society is self-sufficient, it is the supreme authority, he pointed out. But since it is only one of the aspects of life, we can see that life outreaches present societies through exceptional individuals who have immersed themselves anew in the vital impetus itself.

Individuals who are open to new insight and new impulsions in morality become so, according to Bergson, not so much by an overtly intellectual grasp of new understanding as by a welling up of a deep drive to something better that is not fully understood at its inception. It is not that intelligence plays no role in this creativity. Intelligence is the critic and rationalizer. It can ferret out what is wrong with custom and the obligations of pressure. It can explain to us, after the fact, what is better about the prophet's insight and the new modes of life of moral genius. In both ways it interacts with the instinctual to free man from the limitations of the insect society, the closed society. But most great reforms appear at first sight impractical, just as the first explanations of the differential calculus and the physical theories of Newton and Einstein seemed illogical in the framework of thought of their times. The moral creators, Bergson continued, see in their mind's eye a new social atmosphere, an environment in which life will be more worth living, a society such that, if men once tried it, would make them refuse to go

---

[16]Henri Bergson, *The Two Sources of Morality and Religion*, trans. R. Ashley Audra and Cloudesley Brereton, with the assistance of W. Horsfall Carter (New York: Henry Holt & Co., 1935), p. 91.

back to the old state of things. Thus only is moral progress to be defined; but only in retrospect can it be defined. Like works of genius in art and science, moral inventions are at first disconcerting in their society. Then little by little, by the simple fact of their presence and influence, conceptions develop that enrich the idea of justice, the conception of good taste, and the content of men's aspirations. This dynamic of moral genius unites responsiveness to obligation of both pressure and aspiration with intelligent criticism of old ways and rationalization of new insights. The dynamic is that of the vital impetus underlying evolution, the *élan vital*.

There is an increasing recognition that mankind is involved at one and the same time in two kinds of evolutionary development: the biological which through the genes sets broad possibilities as well as imposes some limitations; and the cultural which to a considerable extent has freed man from being a slave of his genetic heritage. During a period in which man's biological nature has changed only slightly if at all, he has gone through great changes. All normal healthy individuals can learn a language, but this can be any language; they can acquire a culture, but again this may be the culture of any group of people anywhere. Biological evolution has not been suspended, but man is not closely tied to his biological past. Recent research in this field points to the most radical possibilities for the future as the secrets of the structure, synthesis, and function of some DNA and RNA molecules are gradually becoming known. Is man to become the master rather than the slave of his genes?

Theodosius Dobzhansky in a number of books[17] has pointed out that while biologists are not in agreement about the forces at work in evolution, most of them reject three views held by some minority groups: (1) *Finalism* or the view that all evolution was directed for the purpose of producing man, and that this development was guided by some supernatural power or powers. (2) The view that the variations of organisms in successive generations proceed along some predestined line independent of external conditions. According to this interpretation, sometimes called the *theory of orthogenesis*, the process is directed by drives inside the organism and moves in straight-line fashion toward a fixed goal. The billions of years involved, the false starts, the extinctions, and the disasters make these views hard to accept, and they also fail to allow for the effects of human freedom and creativity that appear evident in

---

[17]*Mankind Evolving* (New York: Bantam Books, 1962); *Heredity and the Nature of Man* (New York: New American Library of World Literature, 1966); *The Biology of Ultimate Concern* (New York: New American Library of World Literature, 1967).

evolution. (3) *Social Darwinism,* a view that Darwin himself would probably have rejected. This outlook assumes that human progress requires a fierce struggle, a cut-throat competition and rivalry, not only between individuals but also between social and economic classes, nations, and races. Racists, past and present, have claimed that qualities set by the genes determine that some people are inferior, warlike, or both, and that education and culture can do little about it.

Dobzhansky insists that the "struggle" involved in natural selection is frequently misunderstood. It does not necessarily mean strife, war, or combat. (Except in a limited sense plants do not struggle against each other.) Animals resist cold by developing warmer fur, seeking warmer living places, and by similar means. Success is often achieved by cooperation and mutual aid. According to Dobzhansky, the idea that nature sanctions ruthless competition, laissez-faire economics, power politics, and the exploitation of the weak by the strong is a misreading of natural selection and a travesty on science. The failure of some peoples and races to evolve a high culture at some historical epoch is no evidence of genetic incapacity. An unfavorable environment and cultural handicaps of many kinds may be responsible.

While some biologists have assumed that man is "nothing but" an animal, many modern biologists insist that men have evolved properties so unique and unprecedented that in man biology has transcended itself. Dobzhansky speaks of "turning points," "levels," or "dimensions of existence." Two fateful turning points were the origin of life and the appearance of man, both of which marked the emergence of new evolutionary eras. Man is the only creature to discover the fact of evolution, to know that he knows, and to have the ability to think in terms of symbols and abstractions. He can choose to control his own life and to control and dominate nature. He even has the power to destroy himself if he so desires.

Whereas the older evolution was essentially amoral, the new outlook recognizes the central place of knowledge, including the knowledge of good and evil and man's responsibility for the choices he makes. Darwin's "fitness" was reproductive fitness or the ability to produce offspring that could survive under existing conditions. While organisms other than man have a "wisdom of the body," according to Dobzhansky, man has the "wisdom of humanity" so that he can raise the big questions not derived from science alone. Man who is conscious of himself and of the environment is challenged to direct and channel changes in the direction he thinks desirable and good.

The management and direction of the development of the human species and attention to nature's processes are among man's most urgent problems. Genetic defects can be detected and where possible eliminated. Some people have a duty not to produce offspring. Remedial measures, such as eugenical artificial selection are possible. For persons who are mentally incompetent, segregation or sterilization may be justified. Man has acquired the ability to distinguish between what is and what ought to be. He is the only ethical creature, and the evolutionary process has implanted in him "extraordinary strivings for self-realization and self-transcendence, for beauty, and for rectitude."[18]

SUMMARY

The application of the principle of natural selection to morals was seized upon by many people because it seemed to put ethics on a scientific and naturalistic basis. Standards for human conduct were now to be found in the very nature of things. But as we have seen, the derivation of standards from the ideal of natural selection is not easy. What then is to be learned from the efforts to state an ethics of nature in a tenable form? We find six principal contributions to this effort.

1. To achieve the best of which we are capable invariably involves attention to the specific environment in which we live and act. It thus involves in some sense "adaptation to environment" and the survival, in that environment, of what we cherish. The phrase "adaptation to environment" is ambiguous on two questions: (a) To what extent is the right or best act one that shapes the environment, and to what extent is the right act one that yields to the environment? (b) Which of the many possible environments is most important in determining the right: the past, the present, or the future? the local or the universal? this place or that place? In different versions of evolutionary ethics different elections are made among these possibilities, from Nietzsche's stress on conquering to Darwin's on cooperating, from Spencer's acceptance of the political and social *status quo* to Bergson's on moral invention. Some of these difficulties in applying the ideal of survival can be met by the use of growing knowledge about what is conducive to group and individual survival. Some may be overcome only by the genius of the moral innovator, whose insight becomes clear only after he has put a new mode of conduct into practice. But any ethic, evolutionary or not, will be obliged to take into account the organism's interaction with environment in the creation of good and the performance of right.

2. In attending to an environment to which we adapt, there are things that need changing. However, there are other things which

---

[18]*Mankind Evolving*, p. 356.

should be accepted as unalterable or not worth altering in the given act or lifetime. For a complete ethic we would need a comprehensive theory of the things unalterable or best not attacked. Evolutionary ethicists emphasized given environmental physical and biological forces and ways of developing that we would do well to accept. Subsequent studies have added to our fund of knowledge of these matters and have underlined the importance of this component of an ethical outlook.

3. In speaking of "survival" we write an incomplete statement until we specify what we want to survive. Darwin had in mind the living organism as the key value, and his research convinced him that among men the social group is crucial to the individual's survival. If life alone is the concern, the individual's survival then becomes secondary to the survival of the species or group. The continued life of at least some sentient individuals is a precondition of all other values. For peculiarly human values, social group survival is similarly a necessary starting point. This idea both explains some of our common moral priorities and can help us avoid disastrously individualistic or self-willed choices that would put in jeopardy all life and society. Morally mature men recognize the necessity of subordinating prudential or egoistic concerns to a more inclusive good. Prudential concerns may—even on prudential grounds—be wisely pursued only within bounds that support a viable society. Perhaps, as Bergson thought, some openness about what we want to survive is necessary if there is to be progress in morality.

4. Too timid an appraisal of one's own convictions and aspirations can cut off the wellsprings of social reform and of heroic service to values higher than contemporary society recognizes. For many persons the sheer exercise of one's own powers is a source of enjoyment. Nietzsche's insistence on the will to power and the individual's forcing through his own way as the greatest good points up the need for individual determination, self-assertion, and free expression as part of the good life, but Nietzsche carries the position to an extreme point. This outlook has its frightening aspects, as reflected in German nazism.

5. In considering the relation of man to nature there are two extreme positions we wish to identify and reject. The first is the attempt to separate man rather completely from nature and to stress only his special and unique qualities and powers. In the past ethics has been concerned almost exclusively with man's relations with his fellowmen and it has tended to ignore his relation to the external world of nature. Nature is seen, from this point of view, as an area independent of man, whose purpose is to serve human desires and needs. It is regarded as a region to be used and exploited without any questions asked. Thus men with an easy conscience have exhausted the soil, permitted strip mining, cut down the forests, and killed animals at will—for food, for sport,

or in war. Chemicals and insecticides have been spread over the physical environment; the earth, water, and air have been polluted; and the balance of nature has been upset.

The second extreme position is found when man is submerged so completely in nature that there is nothing distinctive or unique about him, nothing that cannot be explained adequately by physics and chemistry. Such reductionism neglects, if it does not actually deny man's freedom, responsibility, and the other characteristics that distinguish him from the rest of nature. These views undermine the sense of the worth and dignity of man.

Until the last decade or two there has been no widespread understanding of the relation of man to nature in general or of the interaction between biophysical facts and conditions and sociocultural systems. The comparatively new science of ecology deals with the mutual relationships between living things, including men, and their environment. The term *ecology,* which comes from a Greek word meaning "house" or "habitat," has come into prominence because of widespread concern over the serious threats to human welfare and animal life in general that have come from man's ignoring and abusing the nature around him. If he is to live well, man cannot dismiss the environment from consideration any more than he can dismiss the facts of eugenics. Man's food, drink, and the air he breathes are part of the world of nature of which he, too, is a part. Next to the threat of atomic destruction, human fertility leading to overpopulation and the polluting of the environment are among the most serious dangers man is facing.

The situation today calls for considerable revision of traditional values and ethical standards. Greater attention to nature may lead us to question the exploitation of the environment by science and technology in the interest of financial gain apart from considerations of human welfare. Such use of nature in the interest of profit alone is not merely bad economics in the long run, it is also basically immoral. We may need to question the demand for a constantly expanding economy and the right of people to have large families. There is a need for simplifying our lives, for eliminating needless waste, and for planning in the interest of long-range human welfare.

6. Finally, the emphasis of the evolutionists on life as the highest good discloses a limited outlook that has characterized other ethical theories. We cannot put life (or evolution, nature, adaptation, survival) on a pedestal as the sole arbiter of worth. A less arbitrary ethic will embody a more inclusive reverence for life. Thus the theory that life or survival is the highest good presents, in spite of contributions, difficulties that seem best met by other theories. In the next chapter we turn to a group of interpretations of the self wherein reason, love, and

the harmonious development of diverse potentialities are taken as the marks of the greatest good.

QUESTIONS AND PROJECTS

1. Our understanding of the mechanisms of genetics is growing rapidly. There is now a possibility of selecting the human traits that should survive and be propagated. Devices such as sterilization of the mentally unfit and artificial insemination could be used in a program of eugenics to better the human species. Does the ideal of survival of the fittest justify the adoption of a program of eugenic control? Why or why not?
2. A dentist is working to save a tooth of Mr. A which is considerably decayed. The dentist protests against government regulation in our economic life. He thinks we should not interfere with natural laws. Our economic disorders will right themselves if we keep our hands off. Mr. A replies that, just as the dentist manipulates certain processes so that men will have healthy teeth, the government must manipulate so that economic disorders will be eliminated and conditions will be more conducive to healthy living. Is the trend in present-day society to "let nature take its course" or to "bend nature so that it will serve human desires and aspirations"? Give evidence for your answer.
3. Does the fact that a connection can be established between animal and human behavior necessarily mean that no new principle or element is present in human behavior? State as clearly as you can the difference between inorganic nature, animal nature, and human nature.
4. In *On Being Human* (New York: Henry Schuman, 1950), Ashley Montagu discusses, among other things, the nature of life and human nature. He gives cases and cites other evidence that indicates the need for mother love in the development of children. While aggressiveness and a healthy, nonruthless competition do exist in nature, he believes that "the principle of co-operation is the most dominant and biologically the most important" among the various drives in nature. Discuss some of these cases which Montagu presents, especially those on pages 57 to 71. Have we tended to overemphasize competition and misrepresent nature as "red in tooth and claw"?
5. If man is considered a part of nature, then intelligence is a part of nature. Is it possible, then, to call intelligent control a natural thing?
6. Do you think that the test of an institution should be its survival value or its social desirability? Can the two be equated? Give reasons for your answer.
7. In *Man For Himself* (New York: Holt, Rinehart & Winston, 1947), pp. 22–23, Erich Fromm has written: "Man can adapt himself to slavery, but he reacts to it by lowering his intellectual and moral qualities; he can adapt himself to a culture permeated by mutual distrust and hostility, but he reacts to this adaptation by becoming weak and sterile. Man can adapt himself to cultural conditions which demand the repression of sexual

strivings, but in achieving this adaptation he develops, as Freud has shown, neurotic symptoms. He can adapt himself to almost any cultural pattern but in so far as they are contradictory to his nature he develops mental and emotional disturbances which force him eventually to change these conditions since he cannot change his nature." In what sense, then, is nature the determiner of the right?

8. Compare and contrast the views of a theologian, a philosopher, and a biologist on nature and ethics. For the first see Jacques Maritain, "Natural Law and Moral Law" in *Moral Principles in Action,* ed. Ruth Nanda Anshen (New York: Harper & Brothers, 1952), ch. 3. For the second see Karl Jaspers, "Nature and Ethics," Ibid., ch. 4. For the third see Theodosius Dobzhansky, "Human Nature As a Product of Evolution," in *New Knowledge in Human Values,* ed. Abraham Maslow (New York: Harper & Brothers, 1959), pp. 75–85. This last selection is reprinted in *The Range of Ethics,* eds. Harold H. Titus and Morris T. Keeton (New York: Van Nostrand Reinhold Co., 1966), pp. 123–132.

9. There are philosophies that stress nature that have not been discussed in this chapter. Look up and report on the following in encyclopedias and in other library sources: (1) Stoicism and what Stoics mean by living according to nature, (2) Pantheism and the divine as identical with nature, (3) Theistic naturalism and the conviction that values are continuous with the natural world.

SUGGESTED READINGS

Adams, E. M. *Ethical Naturalism and the Modern World View.* Chapel Hill: University of North Carolina Press, 1960.

Bergson, Henri. *The Two Sources of Morality and Religion.* Translated by R. Ashley Audra and Cloudesley Brereton with the assistance of W. Horsfall Carter. New York: Henry Holt & Co., 1935.

Darlington, C. D. *The Evolution of Man and Society.* New York: Simon & Schuster, 1970.

Darwin, Charles. *The Descent of Man.* Thinkers Library, no. 12. New York: Frederick Warne & Co., 1930.

———. *Origin of Species by Means of Natural Selection.* Everyman's Library. New York: E. P. Dutton & Co., 1928.

Deshumbert, Marius. *An Ethical System Based on the Laws of Nature.* La Salle, Ill.: Open Court Publishing Co., 1917.

Dewey, John. *Influence of Darwin on Philosophy and Other Essays in Contemporary Thought.* New York: Henry Holt & Co., 1910.

Dobzhansky, Theodosius. *Mankind Evolving.* New York: Bantam Books, Matrix Edition, 1970.

Flew, Antony G. N. *Evolutionary Ethics.* New York: St. Martin's Press, 1968.

Handler, Philip, ed. *Biology and the Future of Man.* New York: Oxford University Press, 1970.

Hill, Thomas English. "Evolutionary Theories" in *Contemporary Ethical Theories*. Ch. 8. New York: Macmillan Co., 1950.
Huxley, Julian S. *Evolutionary Ethics*. London: Oxford University Press, 1943.
Keeton, Morris. *The Philosophy of Edmund Montgomery*. Dallas: Southern Methodist University Press, 1950.
Kropotkin, Petr. *Ethics*. Translated by Louis S. Friedland and Joseph R. Piroshnikoff. New York: Dial Press, 1924.
———. *Mutual Aid: A Factor in Evolution*. New York: Doubleday, Page & Co., 1902.
Marnell, William H. *Man-Made Morals: Four Philosophies That Changed America*. Garden City, N.Y.: Doubleday & Co., Anchor Books, 1968.
Montagu, Ashley. *Darwin, Competition and Co-operation*. New York: Henry Schuman, 1952.
Nietzsche, Friedrich. *The Philosophy of Nietzsche. Beyond Good and Evil* Translated by Helen Zimmern. *The Genealogy of Morals* Translated by Horace B. Samuel. *Thus Spake Zarathustra* Translated by Thomas Common. New York: Modern Library, 1937.
———. *The Will to Power* Translated by Anthony M. Ludovici. 2 vols. London: Allen & Unwin, 1909.
Ross, Herbert H. *A Synthesis of Evolutionary Theory*. Englewood Cliffs, N.J.: Prentice-Hall, 1962.
Spencer, Herbert, *Principles of Ethics*. New York: Daniel Appleton & Co., 1900.
Waddington, C. H. *The Ethical Animal*. New York: Atheneum Publishers, 1961.
Willey, Basil. *The Eighteenth Century Background: Studies on the Idea of Nature in the Thought of the Period*. London: Chatto & Windus, 1953.

10
THE FULFILLMENT OF THE INDIVIDUAL IN SOCIETY

We turn now from viewpoints that seem to emphasize some single segment of man's life—reason, duty, pleasure, happiness, nature—to one that claims to include all aspects of human nature in a well-rounded development in accordance with man's basic needs and potentialities. This outlook calls for the integrated development of many elements under the control of reason and love. Different advocates call this doctrine *self-realization, idealistic perfectionism, eudaemonism* (from Aristotle), and *energism*. Proponents say that this outlook accommodates the values summarized by the discussions in preceding chapters. They claim to offer complementary insights as to the nature of man's complete or highest good.

For the realization of man's needs and potentialities, he cannot be egoistic but must exhibit an impartial concern for all persons or for human welfare. While the self needs fulfillment, this fulfillment comes only in a society of persons, and something beyond the self must be stronger than interest in the self.

ANCIENT GREEK CONTRIBUTIONS

Two early and notable contributions to the understanding of man's good were made by Plato (c. 427 B.C.–347 B.C.) and Aristotle (384 B.C.–322 B.C.). Each concerned man's ideal good as centered in the control of reason over other "parts of the soul." Though there is disagreement as to which of his *Dialogues* represent Plato's most mature views, the account of justice in *The Republic* has been given the most extensive study and was the source of much of Plato's influence on subsequent thinking.

Plato

The universe, Plato believed, is an order in which the real, the true, and the good are closely related. There are, however, two realms within this universe. There is (1) the world of perceptions or the realm of appearances. This is the world of nature, the phenomenal world of sights, sounds, individual things, and change. It is not the real world. Then there is (2) the realm of eternal forms or ideas. This is the supersensible world of abiding realities. We recognize individual cases of justice because of our grasp of the eternal form of justice. The same is true for all other things. The soul of man, because of its previous existence in the realm of ideas, grasps the innate or inborn forms which enable man to recognize things through "recollection." Perceptions are copies of the real things, and they remind the soul of what it formerly knew. The goal of the world process is the expression of the idea of the good. The goal of life is to be guided by the true vision of the form of good.

Man is composed of three parts: (1) A rational soul, whose true function is to rule the body. This is the seat of wisdom. (2) A feeling part, the seat of man's sensations and the basis of the heroic virtues, especially courage. (3) A desiring part, the seat of man's passions and appetites. There is no principle of order here, and this part of man needs to be brought under the control of reason. Reason is the basis of self-control or temperance. When these three parts operate in harmony, each carrying out its own function, there are peace, order, and justice in the individual.

The well-ordered state is also made up of three parts, corresponding to the three parts of the soul of man: (1) The rulers, or philosophers, whose function it is to rule the state by the use of their training and insight. These men are devoted to the common good and the ideal of perfection, and their chief virtue is wisdom. (2) The officials, or warriors, who execute the laws and guard the state. Their chief virtue is courage. (3) The workers, or the artisans and peasants, who furnish the material foundations of the state. With officials they share the obligation to be temperate and to exercise self-control.

Justice or righteousness was, for Plato, the all-inclusive virtue, implying harmony within a man's life and harmony between the individual's life and the ordered life of the state. When each part of the individual and each part of the state fulfills its function, there is justice. Man's life and the organization of society should be patterns of the harmony and the moral order of the universe. The greatest good is for each particular thing to fulfill its purpose—perform its function—and for all to be in harmonious relation to one another.

Aristotle

In Aristotle's *The Nicomachean Ethics* we have the first systematic treatise on ethics as a separate study and one of the most influential books in this field. Aristotle differed from Plato chiefly in method and emphasis rather than in fundamental point of view. Whereas Plato attempted to explain particulars as copies of eternal forms, Aristotle began his study with an examination of the facts of human experience. For Aristotle there was one world of reality—the visible world of nature. Forms exist, but they exist in things. Reality is found in things; it is an unfolding process. Ideas and things, or form and matter, are united, and there is a continuous development from potentiality to actuality. The moral ideal is found in the structure of man's own nature.

What is the goal of human life? What do men seek? Men apparently are seeking many different things. Men engaged in medical pursuits seek health; the military man seeks victory or proficiency in military tactics; the bridlemaker aims to make good equipment for horses; the businessman wants to acquire wealth. But these are not ends in themselves; they are means to still other ends, and there is apparently a hierarchy of ends. Is there any final end, or highest good (*summum bonum*) that is an end in itself and not a means to another end? The good is "that at which all things aim." The highest good, according to Aristotle, is *eudaemonia*, sometimes translated as "happiness," but better taken as "well-being." It includes the complete development of the functions that make a man a human being and a member of a society. It is not a passive achievement but the active exercise of functions. Wellbeing is activity in accordance with virtue. It does not come from wealth or from pleasure. According to Aristotle, only the vulgar man would identify the good with pleasure. Pleasure is *a* good; it is not *the* ultimate good. "The pleasures of creatures different in kind differ in kind."[1] One man's pleasure is another man's pain. The pleasures follow activities, and so we have to ask what activities (hence what pleasures) are proper to man. Just as the excellence of the sculptor lies in the skill with which he practices the principles of his art, so the excellence of man lies in the proper performance of his function. The function pecul-

---

[1] Aristotle, *The Nicomachean Ethics*, book 10, ch. 5.

iar to man is his life of reason. Consequently, he should exercise this function and live in the light of reason.

Like Plato, Aristotle viewed the soul or human nature as complex, comprising a vegetative part shared with all living things, a sensitive or appetitive part shared with lower animals, and a rational part distinctive of man. Reason can contemplate reflectively the nature of things. It can control the impulses of the sensitive soul and the vegetative soul. Its doing so is essential to man's highest welfare.

Whenever reason achieves the mastery and the direction of life, human excellence and happiness are attained. While the intellectual virtues rank among the highest, knowledge alone is not sufficient. Reason must become a functional reality to the extent that it moves the will and expresses itself in habitual activity. The virtues are acquired by practicing them. "For the things we have to learn before we can do them, we learn by doing them; e.g., men become builders by building and lyreplayers by playing the lyre; so too we become just by doing just acts, temperate by doing temperate acts, brave by doing brave acts."[2] Unless he does these things, a man does not have "even a prospect of becoming good." The habit of right thinking, right willing, and right acting is a virtue. This brings us to another important principle.

The doctrine of the golden mean, or of moderation, is central in the ethics of Aristotle. Reason seeks the balanced course between too much and too little. "Nothing overmuch" is the counsel of sanity. That conduct is virtuous which avoids the extremes either of excess or of deficiency. The good life is characterized by neither extreme repression nor excessive indulgence, but rather by the harmonious development of all normal functions of the organism.

> Virtue, then, is a state of character concerned with choice, lying in a mean, i.e., the mean relative to us, this being determined by a rational principle, and by that principle by which the man of practical wisdom would determine it. Now it is a mean between two vices, that which depends on excess and that which depends on defect; and again it is a mean because the vices respectively fall short of or exceed what is right in both passions and actions, while virtue both finds and chooses that which is intermediate.[3]

For example, courage is the middle position between rashness and cowardice; liberality is the mean between prodigality and stinginess; self-control is the mean between overindulgence and repression. For any virtue, the point between the extremes that is moral action will depend on the circumstances. More courage is expected of the soldier than of

---

[2]Ibid., book 2, ch. 1.
[3]Ibid., book 2, ch. 6.

the artist. Circumstances and reason together enter into the determination of what conduct is virtuous.

Aristotle made it clear that this doctrine of the mean must not be carried too far. Even here reason is the balancing agent. "[N]ot every action nor every passion admits of a mean; for some have names that already imply badness, e.g., spite, shamelessness, envy, and in the case of actions adultery, theft, murder; for all of these and suchlike things imply by their names that they are themselves bad, and not the excesses or deficiencies of them. It is not possible, then, ever to be right with regard to them; one must always be wrong."[4]

The intellectual or contemplative virtues come in the main through teaching; the moral virtues that discipline the passions come chiefly through the formation of habit. Both require experience and time for their fruition. Education should teach us to find happiness in worthwhile things and to feel discomfort in seeking wrong things.

MEDIEVAL AND MODERN CONTRIBUTIONS

The extent to which the early Judaeo-Christian ethical ideals are forms of the ethics of fulfillment or of self-realization will be considered in the next chapter. Here we examine briefly the emphasis made by certain medieval and modern philosophers.

Aristotle's view of the good for man was restated within a Christian framework by Thomas Aquinas (1224–1274), whose thought has become the basis for the official philosophy of the Roman Catholic Church. As reformulated by neo-Thomists of this century, the view has exerted widespread influence.

Aristotle, though generally interpreted today as sketched in the preceding pages, left open another interpretation of his meaning as to man's *highest* good. This version, as stated by Thomas Aquinas, is that man should actualize his reason to the exclusion of all other elements of his nature. Why? Reason is both the best of man's potentialities and the distinctive one, the one he shares with God or the Good, which is pure reason. Aquinas distinguished between man's good in this life and his ultimate good, amended the position described already as an account of the good for this life, and identified the love and contemplation of truth (that is, of God) as the ultimate fulfillment of man. In the *Summa contra Gentiles,* after reviewing other possible goods and showing why each fails to fulfill man's highest possibilities, Aquinas wrote:

---

[4]Ibid., book 2, ch. 6.

Accordingly, if man's ultimate happiness does not consist in external things which are called goods of fortune; nor in goods of the body, nor in goods of the soul, as regards the sensitive part; nor as regards the intellective part, in terms of the life of moral virtue; nor in terms of the intellectual virtues which are concerned with action, namely, art and prudence:—it remains for us to conclude that man's ultimate happiness consists in the contemplation of truth.

For, this operation alone is proper to man, and it is in it that none of the other animals communicates.

This is not directed to anything further as to its end, since the contemplation of the truth is sought for its own sake. . . .

Now, it is not possible that man's ultimate happiness consist in contemplation based on the understanding of first principles; for that is most imperfect, as being most universal, containing potentially the knowledge of things. Moreover, it is the beginning and not the end of human inquiry, and comes to us from nature, and not through the pursuit of the truth. Nor does it consist in contemplation based on the sciences that have the lowest things for their object, since happiness must consist in an operation of the intellect in relation to the most noble intelligible objects. It follows then that man's ultimate happiness consists in wisdom, based on the consideration of divine things.[5]

This highest good cannot be attained in this life, and thus requires, in the Catholic view, the supplementation of the endeavors of conceptual reason by contemplative reason and faith and the ministrations of the Church to assure man's sojourn with God.

The idea of union with the divine as the ultimate in man's fulfillment of his own nature is not unique to Roman Catholic thought nor to Christianity. We find it in other forms in the ancient Lao-Tzu, in the Hindu goal of union with Brahman, in Christian and Jewish mystics of many periods, and in the twentieth-century naturalistic theists of various religious traditions. In some of the latter, the objective is viewed as achievable in this life. Identity with the divine is here taken, not as complete absorption into the infinite nor as attainment of divine perfection, but as a matter of alignment with that which makes for the increase of good or with "the creative." Many religious humanists—some of whom eschew the use of the term *divine*—similarly adhere to this last type of view.

There is a reason for this congeniality of religious perspectives to the ideal of self-realization. Religions are attempts to align man's loyalties with those powers for good that control human destinies. As understanding of the universe develops, man comes to see it as a thoroughly inter-

---

[5]Thomas Aquinas, *Summa contra Gentiles*, III, ch. 37 in *Basic Writings of Saint Thomas Aquinas*, vol. 2, ed. and annotator Anton C. Pegis (New York: Random House, 1945), pp. 59–60.

related order of things in which everything has possibilities for good or, if misused or improperly adjusted to, for evil. Too, in the perspective of the whole universe, it is clear that no one tribe or individual should have preferred status. Thus man's religions have on the whole evolved in the direction of universality of concern and in the direction of seeing the good of the individual as inextricably interrelated with the most inclusive good.

Many philosophers reach a similar view from the examination of man's relation to nature, whether or not viewed in the perspective of religious loyalties. Stoics such as Marcus Aurelius viewed nature as a rational whole and man as realizing his own true nature only when he acted "according to nature." Spinoza similarly viewed nature as a rational order: Man attains his essential good when he grasps clearly the whole of things and the causes and nature of his own desires and emotions, and when he brings his emotions under the control of reason. Spinoza equated God with nature (God is nature active; nature is nature passive). He did not rule out the possibility of man's achieving "the intellectual love of God" in this life. This end is not unlike the contemplation of truth that Aquinas posited as the ideal.

During the nineteenth and early twentieth centuries this point of view was held particularly by philosophical idealists, from Hegel and his German followers to T. H. Green, Bernard Bosanquet, F. H. Bradley, and James Seth of England. In America, idealists such as Josiah Royce and George Herbert Palmer were followed by personalists such as Borden Parker Bowne, and even by the pragmatist John Dewey, in enunciating the view. Nor has the theory had currency only among the technical philosophers. Supporters of the Ethical Culture movement and of Christian Socialism stand for the development of persons and social welfare, the former with more individualistic and the latter with social emphasis. Each of these schools brought added emphasis to the general theory. The idealists stressed man's inherent interrelatedness with the society and the universe as a whole and reaffirmed the ancient emphasis on reason as the essence of man. The personalists stressed personhood as the culmination of the evolution of capacity for worth in living beings. Dewey stressed growth and the use of intelligence in problem-solving, directed toward satisfaction of those purposes that are envisaged as best. He joined earlier voices in emphasizing man's dependence for his best on the creation of a good society, one permitting a broad scope for personal freedom.[6]

---

[6] A recent expression of the ideal of self-realization by a pragmatist is found in Stephen C. Pepper, *Ethics* (New York: Appleton-Century-Crofts, 1960), pp. 181, 190–193.

DISTINCTIVE POINTS OF EMPHASIS IN SELF-REALIZATION

Now that we have considered various representatives, let us briefly present, in summary fashion, five contributions that proponents of the theory of self-realization can add to our understanding of the good life.

The Distinctiveness of Human Potentialities

Man is both present actuality and present and future potentiality. As a person he has a wide range of characteristics and powers—self-consciousness; power of reflective thought; ability to make ethical and aesthetic judgments, to worship, to transcend particular conditions of space and time; unique powers of creativity; and the like. Man's capacities for reason, love, and sociability permit a choice among more alternatives than if he lacked these distinctive potentialities.

The self is the perceiving, conceiving, thinking, feeling, willing, and deciding entity that persists through the changing experience of a person's existence. People experience the world as a realm of objects open to observation; they experience themselves as an inner and immediate awareness of being alive. Thus the nature and content of the self is not completely within the reach of any, or even all, of the special sciences. While men seek survival, pleasure, and happiness, they seek and need other things too. One of the merits of the ideal of self-realization is its explicit recognition of the distinctiveness of human beings and of the more worthwhile possibilities of life that are open to man.

The Social Nature of Man

Since the choice of a future is a choice among many possibilities not all of which can be jointly realized, it is a selection of harmonizable possibilities. This harmony is one not simply of logical compatibility, but of possibilities that can be brought about in the specific circumstances of life. On the question of what is jointly possible under actual conditions, we have evidence from the physical and social sciences. Though these sciences do not tell us all we would like to know on this question, they do tell us much of what has been realized and of what has been unsuccessfully attempted. Among the key findings are those summed up in the statement that man is a social being. The social nature of man means not only that by cooperation he is able to achieve more of what he wants, but also that he experiences greater worth in social relations than do other animals. Now the very notion of ethical effort means the effort to achieve the greatest possible good. So, in whatever way man defines the greatest good, he must seek it in ways compatible with the survival and development of social relations.

The critic of the ideal of self-realization says that the ideal alone does not tell us why we should not be cruel, selfish, and inhumane. Taken with the facts about man's social nature and with the objective of maximizing the good, however, it does exclude antisocial conduct as not harmonizable with man's best possibilities. Even those who disagree as to what is best can recognize this fact. Man can hardly live at all, much less live the best life, apart from his fellows. This fact results in part from man's psychological need for his fellows. In part it derives from the advantages of division of labor and specialization of function in society. Though occasionally an individual may "get away with" an antisocial act, and though an occasional highly selfish individual may live a long while with relative success, the odds are against his doing so; and the odds are that the individual would experience greater fulfillment through a mode of life more congenial to the well-being of others. Darwin the evolutionist and Mill the utilitarian concurred on this point: Even the sacrifice of high honors or life may yield a reward of self-fulfillment that a man could not have had if his concern were only for his potentialities apart from other men.

Man As a Complex, Active, and Integrated Person

Selfish and socially harmful conduct is not the only kind that cannot be harmonized with man's maximum fulfillment. It is possible to overemphasize reason and concern for others. In doing so, we can neglect the part played in the good life by immediately consummatory experiences of pleasure, enjoyment, and satisfaction of individual wants. Hedonists stress the intrinsic worth of pleasures and the development of a character that takes pleasure in the social good. This stress on the individual and the consummatory good is an important complement to the emphasis just given to the social and the deferred good. In Plato's ideal city-state and Hegel's ideal nation-state there is a subordination of individual freedom that would not, in our judgment, make for the greatest fulfillment of contemporary American society. Such a judgment, however, rests not only on the ideal of a growth in realized good but also on forecasting what values are possible in our particular culture and circumstances. Too, the ideal of a highly interdependent society implies division of labor. One man governs; another teaches; a third is a doctor; others build and farm and manufacture. This specialization leads to the cherishing of persons with different talents and interests. Unique and diverse types of persons may thus be prized within the ideal of self-realization in a complex culture. Insofar as men are distinct in their personalities and in their contributions to society, individuality is a keystone of human worth, as Kierkegaard, Nietzsche, and some modern existentialists and naturalists have said. The capacity of the human species to develop and harmonize distinctive kinds of personality is one aspect of its ethical advantage over other species. At the same time, insofar as men are alike in their nature, the different ways of life that are ideal will be limited to those that give expression and satisfaction to this common humanity. Since men are growing persons and live in a dynamic and changing world, even their goals tend to alter with new knowledge and new insight. Yet not all of the diversity of opinion among self-realizationists can be attributed to these causes. Some of the disagreement arises out of incompatible views about what is common to all men or about what is likely to be jointly possible under the conditions we will confront in the future.

The many facets of man's nature have been variously described in different ages and cultures: vegetative, sensitive, and rational; passionate and rational; purposive, consummatory, and rational; and the like. Integration or harmony of values means the avoidance of frustration in the fulfillment of these various facets of the individual and the human group. This harmony implies the limitation of each human potentiality to what is possible in conjunction with the realization of the others. If man were merely or even predominantly a feeling being, his highest good might consist in so living as to secure the maximum of pleasurable feelings. If he were merely a biological organism seeking adjustment to its physical environment, adaptation and survival would be a sufficient ideal. In opposition to such overemphasis on one or another of the sides of human nature, the proponent of self-realization maintains that it is the optimum harmony of man's complex potentialities that should be sought.

The Need to Study Man and Society

We have discussed man's distinctiveness, his social nature, and his complex and dynamic being. Studies in biology, psychology, sociology, and anthropology have greatly enhanced our knowledge of man in each of these respects. This knowledge does not, by itself, tell us what is good or right. Our possession of the knowledge does not guarantee us a better life than that of men of the past. That knowledge, however, is crucial to our achieving as much of human possibility as we can in our time. If there is meaning in the idea of our achieving a higher level of morality and fulfillment than before, growth in knowledge will be one of the essential means.

As understanding of men and societies grows, the specific applications suitable to the ideal of self-realization change. This fact is both an advantage and a limitation. It is an advantage in that the ideal can remain relevant and useful as a guide to choice-making. This utility is retained by the continuous replacement of outdated information by knowledge linking the ideal to the present. The limitation is that from the ideal alone one cannot infer anything about what is or is not good action, right choice, or the best life. This limitation, however, is inherent in the nature of abstract ideals. Such ideals, as Wayne Leys has said,[7] should be read, not as a set of questionable answers from the past about present duties and rights, but as a set of answerable questions that can elicit the information needed to apply ideals to practice. The question "What choice among those open to me will best fulfill my potentialities and those of my fellow men?" invites a consideration of available knowledge about other men, about me, and about the things we can jointly accomplish. This question will evoke different answers from men with different knowledge, culture, physical environment, and maturity. The repeated asking of the question is a way to bring out all the knowledge men have that might assist them in their ethical decisions.

Religion and Self-Realization

There is no single science of all that man knows about himself and his universe. Philosophy is a study in which we try to integrate whatever man understands from all the sources he has. Religion, as we here view it, is a man's application of his philosophic understanding and his energies and resources in a living commitment to his ideals and to that in the universe which supports and sustains them. Historically philosophers, prophets, and seers have insisted on three further points not yet adequately treated in our discussion of the search for moral standards: (1) The best life requires commitment to something other than oneself. (2) If this object of commitment is to yield man his highest fulfillment (variously called heaven, Nirvana, salvation, union with God or Brahman, and so on), it must be greater than the individual, his tribe, or his nation. (3) The ideal commitment will provide a man a sense of purpose, meaning, and worth for his life as a whole, even in the face of death, human sinfulness, and all the other limitations to which man may be subject.

The commitment to something other than oneself seems, on the face of the matter, to be a direct contradiction of the ideal of self-realization. Proponents of the ideal use several arguments to show that no contra-

---

[7]Wayne Leys, *Ethics for Policy Decisions* (New York: Greenwood Press, 1968), ch. 1.

diction is involved. One is that concentration on oneself is self-defeating, whereas in serving the nation or mankind or God one can succeed in fulfilling himself. Thus the ideal of self-realization is not lost by focus on another loyalty; rather, the other loyalty is the best means to self-realization. "He that findeth his life shall lose it: and he had loseth his life for my sake shall find it."[8]

One student of moral philosophy, discussing this seeming conflict between devotion to the self and devotion to that which is beyond the self, says:

> The tragedy of the moral life, whereby a concern for the best in oneself becomes the very root of evil, is unavoidable if the goal of the moral life is the cultivation of virtue in the self. It can be averted only if attention is turned outward from the moral and intellectual properties of the self to goals beyond the self. If there is to be an object of supreme devotion, it must be something other than self, other than one's own "salvation," other than one's own virtue, or "dignity", or integrity, or perfection, or holiness. The moral salvation of a man lies in his having objectives beyond himself in pursuit of which he can forget himself, objectives which will keep the inner structure of the self wholesome without making inner wholesomeness itself the goal.[9]

It is not enough, however, that a man be devoted to just anything other than himself. It must be something he can regard as worthy of the risk of his own destruction, thus something of greater worth even than he regards himself as having. It should, indeed, be that which is most worth his full loyalty. Human experience of those who have given this place to the tribe or race (like Nazis) has indicated the dangers of such circumscribed loyalties. The difficulty of an adequate choice is the point of a famous remark by a Russian writer: "A friend once wrote to Turgenev: 'It seems to me that to put one's self in the second place is the whole significance of life.' To which Turgenev replied: 'It seems to me that to discover what to put before one's self, in the first place, is the whole problem of life.' "[10]

Loyalty to something greater than oneself can be seen, not merely as a superior means to self-realization, but as also giving a new and more rewarding meaning to self-realization. Man's intelligence and his capacity for identification of his own concerns with things other than his present self enable him to equate his own fulfillment with that of the

---

[8] Matt. 10:39.
[9] A. Campbell Garnett, *Religion and the Moral Life* (New York: Ronald Press, 1955), p. 36.
[10] John C. Schroeder, "A Deeper Social Gospel," *The Christian Century* 56, pt. 2 (July 26, 1939): 925.

most worthwhile object of loyalty. Whether that object is mankind, the whole of nature, creativity, God, or whatever name it is called, man is able to see in his participation in it or his loyalty to it the means of his own realization. These divinities do not die, and they are not bound by other human limitations. By serving them, men sense that they transcend in worth and power the limitations they would suffer but for this relationship to the divine. It is not our purpose here to consider arguments about the existence or merits of different gods. Our point is simply that the ideal of self-realization is one that is suited to the recognition and application of whatever insights these religious perspectives have yielded.

AN EVALUATION OF THE IDEAL OF SELF-REALIZATION

The ideal or the moral standard of the fulfillment of the individual in society has had able supporters as well as keen critics. Self-realization has been interpreted differently by different proponents, yet there are a number of common convictions which are stressed. The approach appeals to many thinkers since it recognizes those qualities which are distinctive of human beings and which common sense regards as higher or more valuable.

Rather than concentrating on some limited or even single element in man's nature, self-realization is comprehensive and broad. It is congenial to the recognition of man's personal distinctiveness as well as his social nature and the unique and complex integration of which the individual personality is capable. The ideal invites, as an aid to its application, the search for and use of the growing knowledge about man and his environment. It also permits ready use of the insight that scientific, religious, and philosophical orientations provide about the meaning and possibilities of human fulfillment.

The ideal of fulfillment recognizes and includes the elements of truth in other moral standards. Pleasure, happiness, and survival under normal conditions are good, but they are not exclusive goals or sufficient in themselves.

Some critics of the theory of self-realization or fulfillment say that the self may find its satisfaction in ways that are morally bad as well as in ways that are of ethical value. Some men inherit capacities which would be undesirable if developed in modern society. To tell them to develop themselves does not give them instruction or wisdom as to which aspect of the self should be realized, if they are in doubt. In moral action men may have a choice between realizing one or another element of the self.

In answer to these critics, the supporter of the theory of self-realization will reply that a distinction must be made between the part self and the harmonious development of the whole self. To develop antisocial traits would be at variance with the rational and ethical sides of man's nature or with the development of the distinctive characteristic of man as compared with mere animal nature. If the all-comprehensive demand is to grow, then growth presupposes life and survival and recognizes pain as a warning and happiness as one sign of harmony.

The man of character needs to make commitments. This is an insight or truth which may not be neglected when the idea of well-rounded development is stressed. Since a man cannot be all things to all men, there is need for self-discipline and singleness of purpose. The ideal of the development of all of one's potentialities does not prevent a man from saying at times, "This one thing I do." The theory of self-realization makes adequate room for the specialist, the man committed to some special service, the martyr, or the hero who may sacrifice his life for causes beyond himself.

From the time of the early Greeks until the present, we have been told that the way to get happiness is to forget about happiness. The way to develop the self is to forget the self in objects and causes beyond the self. For the realization of the highest qualities of personality one must not be egoistic; one must have an impartial concern for others or for human welfare. To forget oneself through loyalty to some great task may be the way to attain fullness of life. The full realization of the person is to be found in the development of the social and enduring values, in sense of community, and in what is often called man's larger self.

If some critics say that the terms *self-realization* and *fulfillment* are vague and lack preciseness, the proponent of the theory may reply that any vagueness is in part the result of the fact that we are considering ends and not concrete means for the attainment of these goals. Since men are growing persons who live in a dynamic and changing world, even their goals tend to expand and require restatement with new knowledge and new insight.

In previous chapters we have considered various answers to the question "What is the greatest good?" Each approach has tended to select and emphasize some aspect of human conduct and to use it as a standard of evaluation. We have been told to follow the line of duty. Unless an act expresses a person's genuine convictions and comes from a good motive, it is not entitled to the highest moral approval. Again with another approach we are asked to seek happiness. Pleasure and happiness are elements in the good life; unhappiness is an indication that something is wrong. If the happiness theory stresses merely the feeling side of life or emphasizes personal pleasure and happiness, it appears inadequate. If by happiness is meant the continual quest for the greatest good, there is little objection to the approach.

Evolutionary ethics is inadequate if its emphasis is mainly biological; it is satisfactory to the extent that it recognizes all aspects of man's nature. Man is tied to the physical and organic world in innumerable ways, yet he is not completely submerged in the natural order. To some extent he interprets, controls, and transcends nature. He has been called nature's rebel. While we do need to recognize the relevance of empirical facts given to us by the many special sciences, we need at the same time to recognize the distinction between facts and values. Normative conclusions may not be validly drawn from premises that are exclusively factual.

Linguistic analysis and the emotive theory of ethics have made clear that moral judgments are sometimes mere expressions of inclinations, attitudes, and emotions. Among these are the cases in which lesser values are mistaken for greater values. The acceptance of these emotivist insights does not require us to claim that all normative or value judgments lack objective truth. We would, also, reject the outlook of those intuitionists and deontologists who insist that analysis must derive the good from the right and who include as intuitively known a wide range of duties and obligations that seem to us to be open to question.

Considered in a narrow sense, each of these approaches is inadequate. Each of the teleological theories may be so explained that it includes the values stressed by the other views. In this situation there are probably few objections to be offered. For any of these theories, and even for formalism, most problems will be decided in the same way. Their differences are most likely to be noticed in the unique, exceptional, or borderline cases.

All of these views have had able supporters who, in spite of differences, agree in certain respects. They agree that there is a higher and a lower standard with respect to human conduct. The problem for them is to identify the higher and to attain it. They agree that there is an obligation to follow the good or to do the right if the way can be found. They agree, with few exceptions, that men must think—that the intelligent life is more desirable than any life devoid of intelligence.

The theory of fulfillment or self-realization accepts the fundamental postulate of the worth of persons and aims to rectify some of the deficiencies it claims to find in other approaches. It may fail to give sufficient recognition to the place of self-denial in the development of selfhood. Self-realization and self-denial, however, may not be the opposites that some persons imply. He who loses his life in some great devotion may truly find it. If the self-realization approach is narrowly construed, it may lack something on the social side. If it is stated so that the social as well as the personal implications of personality are kept clearly in mind, it is then in our opinion the most satisfactory philosophical statement of the goal to be sought.

QUESTIONS AND PROJECTS

1. Make a list of the human qualities, potentialities, and needs that must be met if man is to gain fulfillment, self-realization, or the abundant life. Then see if you can arrange the items in some sort of hiearchical order with the most essential at the top. It would be a stimulating exercise if others would do the same and you could compare and discuss your lists.
2. Consider the following cases and discuss them with care, indicating principles you think are involved. There are many examples of "the right to die" and "mercy killings" (euthanasia). What terms—*murder, manslaughter, mercy killing, suicide, self-sacrifice*—would you apply to each of the following cases?
   (1) One doctor says that he has taken life five times and justifies his actions because some patients suffering from incurable diseases have pleaded to be relieved from pain by death. In certain cases doctors with or without the consent of the families have taken positive action to end life.
   (2) In the late sixties a Florida legislator introduced a bill that would give a person "the right to die with dignity." His bill was prompted by a letter from a woman who said her mother after two strokes "has not recognized any of her family for four years, and lies in a rest-home covered with bed sores. In short, she is a vegetable." The proposed bill does not permit a physician to induce death but gives him the right, with consent of relatives, to do nothing and permit death to come naturally.
   (3) In Chicago in 1967, an 84-year-old man said he strangled his 78-year-old ailing wife because she pleaded with him to end her pain. The judge who reduced the charge from murder to voluntary manslaughter placed the man on three years' probation. The judge is quoted as saying, "It is not the province of this court to condone what you have done, but you were attempting to be merciful to someone you loved."
   (4) There are many cases on record, from all over the world, of what is sometimes called *suicide for a cause* or *holy suicide*. From Buddhist monks in Vietnam and protesters in Japan to anti-war persons in America, different methods have been used, including burning and starving to death. One man who has written his approval said it is inappropriate to view these as suicides since they sought to convince us of evils that were obscured by the cultural screen of propaganda, advertising, and a superficial public opinion. The courageous self-sacrifice was said to deserve the utmost public respect. Opponents

of the act were strong in condemnation and said a rational being should devote his life to attempts to correct wrongs.

(5) When Scott's expedition was returning from its ill-fated dash to the South Pole one man, who was exhausted and knew he was a burden to the other members of the group, walked out into a storm and never returned.

(6) A narrow-gauge railway transported men with their tools and explosives from a town in Mexico to a mine six miles away and brought back the newly mined copper ore. One day when the train was loaded with high explosives for the mine, the engineer stopped to talk with people at the station. Suddenly one man shouted, "Your train is on fire." The engineer said to a friend, "Tell the Father to say Mass for me." He went to the train alone, made a quick start, and was well out of the town before the explosion rocked the air. The town was saved but the train and engineer were blown to pieces.

(7) The case of Charlotte Perkins Gilman led to much discussion. Mrs. Gilman, suffering from cancer, ended her life. She left a note indicating her belief that, while there is no excuse for ending one's life while any possibility of service remains, when all usefulness is past and death is unavoidable and near, one is justified in choosing a quick and easy death in place of a slow and horrible one. Give your own reaction to the conduct of Mrs. Gilman. What relation do such cases have to the subject of this chapter? For a discussion of the argument for and against "mercy killing," see "Shall We Legalize 'Mercy Killing'?" in *Reader's Rigest* (November 1938):94–98; Joseph Fletcher, "Euthanasia: Our Right to Die," *Morals and Medicine* (Princeton: Princeton University Press, 1954), ch. 6, pp. 172–210. Where legal action is brought against people who are involved or responsible for such action, it appears difficult to get juries to indict or convict them. Can you explain why?

(8) The following problem has been vigorously debated by naval personnel. When a submarine is on the surface of the water and must submerge immediately because of some danger, it is submerged a certain number of seconds after the order is given to go below. If anyone on deck fails to get down in time, the hatch is closed and the submarine is submerged. These questions are asked: Does anyone have the right to send any man to a certain death? On the other hand, does anyone have the right to risk the lives of many for only one or two?

3. A man (age 28) was slowly dying of a kidney disease. According to the doctors the only therapy that could save him was a kidney transplant. The best donor would be his younger brother (age 27) who idolizes his older brother, but who at the time was in a state mental hospital. The mother of the boys asked a court to authorize the transplant operation, but the guardian appointed by the state to represent the younger brother objected. The court approved the surgery on the ground that the loss of his older brother would jeopardize the well-being of the younger man more severely

than the removal of a kidney. According to reports both boys were recuperating and there was a community of feeling and understanding. Do you approve the court's decision and the action taken?
4. Consider the cases presented in chapter 7, pages 148–149. From the point of view of the theory of self-realization, how would these problems be faced? If you think that the outcomes would be the same, would the reasoning be the same? Explain.
5. In present-day society, which of our potentialities tend to be overdeveloped and which of them underdeveloped?
6. What are some evidences of man's need to grow, and what forms may his growth take? See Richard C. Cabot, *The Meaning of Right and Wrong* (New York: Macmillan Co., 1933), ch. 5 and 6; Harry Emerson Fosdick, *On Being a Real Person* (New York: Harper & Brothers, 1943); John W. Gardner, *Self-Renewal* (New York: Harper & Row, 1971), Paperback; H. A. Overstreet, *The Mature Mind* (New York: W. W. Norton & Co., 1949).

SUGGESTED READINGS

Aristotle. *The Nicomachean Ethics*. Book 1. Translated by H. Rackham. Loeb Classical Library. Cambridge: Harvard University Press, 1926. Also in *The Works of Aristotle*. Vol. 9. Translated under the editorship of W. D. Ross. New York: Oxford University Press, 1925.

Ewing, A. C. *Ethics*. New York: Free Press, 1965.

Flewelling, Ralph Tyler. *The Person; or, The Significance of Man*. Los Angeles: Anderson & Ritchie, 1952.

Foss, Martin. *The Idea of Perfection in the Western World*. Princeton: Princeton University Press, 1946.

Gardner, John W. *The Recovery of Excellence*. New York: W. W. Norton & Co., Publishers, 1970.

Garnett, A. Campbell. *The Moral Nature of Man*. New York: Ronald Press, 1952.

Hardie, W. F. R. "The Final Good in Aristotle's Ethics." *Philosophy* 40 (October 1965):277–295.

Hill, Thomas English. "Self-Realization Theories." Ch. 16. *Contemporary Ethical Theories*. New York: Macmillan Co., 1950.

Joachim, Harold H. *Aristotle: The Nicomachean Ethics; A Commentary*. Edited by D. A. Rees. Oxford: Clarendon Press, 1951.

Joseph, H. W. B. *Knowledge and the Good in Plato's* Republic. London: Oxford University Press, 1948.

Montague, William P. "The Good As the Abundant Life" in *Moral Principles of Action*. Edited by Ruth Nanda Anshen. New York: Harper & Brothers. 1952.

Otto, Herbert A. *Human Potentialities: The Challenge and the Promise.* St. Louis, Mo.: Warren H. Green, 1970.
Plato. *The Republic.* Translated with Introduction and Notes by Francis Macdonald Cornford. New York: Oxford University Press, 1945.
Royce, Josiah. *The Philosophy of Loyalty.* New York: Macmillan Co., 1908.
Ulich, Robert. *The Human Career: A Philosophy of Self-Transcendence.* New York: Harper & Brothers, 1955.
Veatch, Henry B. *Rational Man: A Modern Interpretation of Aristotelian Ethics.* Bloomington: Indiana University Press, 1962.

11
ADDITIONAL TYPES OF ETHICS

Up to this point our discussion has not included several types of ethics, and indeed we will not treat all the various types that appear in the literature. In fact it is sometimes hard to tell whether an outlook reflects a new point of view or merely a new name for an older one. In this chapter we shall consider Marxism and ethics, existential ethics, and some features of the Judaeo-Christian ethics. For Marxism the distinction is clear, but it is not so for others. Kierkegaard, for example, who is sometimes referred to as the founder of modern existentialism, is also a Christian. Some Christian and Jewish thinkers could be classified under the ethical systems previously considered, but others need to be discussed in much greater detail.

MARXISM AND ETHICS

A considerable portion of mankind holds as an ideal the Marxian, Marxist-Leninist, or Communist ethics. The persons most directly responsible for this outlook are Karl Marx (1818–1883), Friedrich Engels (1820–1895), and Vladimir Lenin (1870–1924). Marx was influenced by many persons and movements including Rousseau, Kant, and German Romanticism, and more directly by Georg Hegel (1770–1831). This way of thinking has been interpreted and expanded by Stalin, Khrushchev, Mao Tse-tung, and others. Marx himself wrote nothing systematic on moral philosophy, and there is no agreement among scholars regarding various points of emphasis. For example, shall we stress his earlier writings that are humanistic in outlook and leave room for freedom of choice by the rational man, or his later writings that are more materialistic and deterministic and stress social engineering? How are we to interpret the development that took place under Lenin and later Communists?

We have said that Marx was influenced by Hegel, a German idealistic philosopher. Hegel held that the universe is an unfolding process of thought whose changes are dialectic, that is, they proceed through an affirmation or thesis to a denial or antithesis to an integration or synthesis. Development takes place through the overcoming of contradictions, for example, being, nonbeing, becoming; individualism, collectivism, a society that reconciles the two poles. Marx and Engels reject Hegel's idealism and claim that matter, not mind, is basic. They accept, however, the principle of the dialectic. The mode of production determines the social and political institutions of society, and these in turn influence the ethical, religious, and philosophical notions that prevail in the society. Marx and Engels said that the dialectic is a pattern that exists in nature. While the early Greeks discovered it, Hegel was the first to explain it adequately.

Marxian ethics also reflects the economic and social conditions in Europe, especially in England, in the nineteenth century. The industrial revolution during the early stages led men to expect great gains in general human welfare, but as men were driven off the land and into the mines and factories, great masses of men, women, and children faced poverty, drudgery, and misery. Marx was convinced that the workers were being cruelly exploited by small groups of owners and others in positions of power. The reasons for the tragic conditions, according to Marx, were the class structure of society and the private ownership of the natural resources and the means of production, distribution, and exchange. He viewed history as a long record of class conflict in which the moral standards grow out of these class relationships and conditions. Some students of Marx, especially those who emphasize his earlier writings, think of Marx as a humanitarian who might be classified as a supporter of the theory of self-realization. Marx was insistent that human beings should be treated as persons and not as commodities. He believed that the industrial system of his day enslaved men to machines and money and led to their dehumanization.

According to Marx the five main historical types of productive systems are: primitive communism based on the communal ownership of property; the aristocratic-slave system marked by the rise of private property; the military-feudal era in which serfs replace the slaves; capitalism that appears with the factory system; and finally, after a transitional period during which capitalism is to be destroyed, communism is expected

Additional Types of Ethics / 211

to bring the end of conflict and the beginning of freedom, equality, and abundance.

How is the transition from capitalism to communism to be brought about? Since the owning class, the bourgeoisie, controls the key institutions of society and will permit no thoroughgoing changes by peaceful means, the way out is "the forceful overthrow of all existing social conditions." After the revolution, according to Marx, there is a transitional stage, the dictatorship of the proletariat or working class, necessary to eliminate classes and the private ownership of the instruments of production. The final or fifth stage of society is the classless society when exploitation will have ended and all men can be assured of the means of a good life. The formula to be achieved is: From each according to his ability, to each according to his need.

Marxists tell us that, up to the present era, philosophers have explained the world in a great many different ways. What is needed now is a group that will change the world for the better. This is the ethical mission of the Communists. In this mission they will take direct action if it is necessary to eradicate the evils in society, since they say that the power structure in capitalist society does not hesitate to use violence to resist thoroughgoing changes.

The dialectic, when stripped of its mystical and idealistic forms, throws light on social change and gives theoretical and ethical justification for abrupt changes and revolutionary action when the conditions are ripe for change. Communists are often charged with accepting and following what various Western moralists have termed the unethical principle that the end justifies the means. For Communists, norms grow out of the social conditions men face at the time. While truth and honor are respected and falsehood and dishonor condemned, circumstances do alter cases. If he holds to the ideal a Communist would not betray his comrades or his cause to the enemy. However, Lenin adopted a hard line, since he had to assume leadership in a revolutionary struggle. There are, he said, no morals in politics, only expediency, and he sanctioned deception and violence to gain what he considered were noble ends. Under Lenin and later Communists the views of Marx were adapted to the conditions and fortunes of war and the cause of Russia in the world struggle. After the new regime was firmly established in Russia, revolutionary tactics became counterrevolutionary at least in countries under Communist control.

In 1961 a moral code was authorized, approved, and publicized by the Communist party of the Soviet Union. It viewed morality as a supplement to law and force as a means of social control and a basis for social stability. The code includes twelve basic principles which citizens are expected to cultivate:

212 / Chapter Eleven

Moral Code of the Builder of Communism

The party holds that *the moral code of the builder of communism* should comprise the following principles:

Devotion to the communist cause; love of the socialist motherland and of other socialist countries;

conscientious labor for the good of society—he who does not work, neither shall he eat;

concern on the part of everyone for the preservation and growth of public wealth;

a high degree of public duty; intolerance of actions harmful to the public interest;

collectivism and comradely mutual assistance; one for all and all for one;

human relations and mutual respect between individuals—man is to man a friend, comrade and brother;

honesty and truthfulness, moral purity, modesty, and unpretentiousness in social and private life;

mutual respect in the family, and concern for the upbringing of children;

an uncompromising attitude to injustice, parasitism, dishonesty, careerism and money-grubbing;

friendship and brotherhood among all peoples of the USSR; intolerance of national and racial hatred;

an uncompromising attitude to the enemies of communism, peace and the freedom of nations;

fraternal solidarity with the working people of all countries, and with all peoples.[1]

In this code the emphasis is placed on the party and the Communist cause, on work as a moral obligation, and on society (public wealth, public duty, and public interest). The court of appeal is society's decision, not one's conscience or a reflective personal morality. Some values have a lasting social significance, such as special duties toward children, parents, friends, and the community. There are other acts which are condemned, as among practically all peoples, such as killing, stealing, lying, and the like. In Marxian theory ethics is a social phenomenon and there are no absolutes in the traditional sense. Ethics is a reflection in consciousness of the social situations men are facing and of the continuing desires, needs, and aspirations of men. Since acts are judged by the goodness or badness of the consequences, the ethics is teleological. It is also naturalistic and objective and denies any sharp distinction between fact and value, theory and practice, and form and content. Faith is placed in science and the scientific method. The approach, how-

---

[1] *The Road to Communism*, Documents of the 22nd Congress of the CPSU (Moscow: 1961), pp. 566–567.

ever, is from the point of view of the organic and the social sciences, as well as from history and politics.

Marxian ethics denies the ideal of universal love and seems closer to the injunction to "love your friends and hate your enemies." It also differs from traditional Western morality in its view of the relation between the individual and society. The codes of Judaism and Christianity place primary emphasis on the individual. Instead of stressing the worth of the individual and personal morality, Marxian ethics derives its moral standards from society or from the collective. This difference at times has led to confusion and to a dangerous polarization of social and political action. The extreme right in the West, often without realizing it, may give support to the Communist cause by asserting that any change or reforms looking toward a greater social good is "communistic" and by opposing any social planning and many welfare measures. Communists can then pose, although falsely, as the only party of protest and the only group working for a better world. In reality, of course, reforms and social welfare measures may be supported for the purpose of defending individual rights and values and the cause of freedom and democracy.

EXISTENTIAL ETHICS

Existentialism is a reaction against some features of traditional philosophy and some trends in modern society. It is more specifically a protest in the name of individuality against the classical tradition and the concepts of reason and nature that men strongly emphasized during the eighteenth-century Enlightenment. It is a revolt against the impersonal nature of the modern technological age and against scientism, positivism, and the mass movements of our time. It is also a protest against totalitarian movements, whether Fascist, Communist, or other, which tend to crush or submerge the individual in the collective or the mass.

More positively, existentialism emphasizes the uniqueness and primacy of human existence—the inner, immediate experience of self-awareness. Reality or being is existence that is found in the "I" rather than the "it." Thus the center of thought and meaning is the existing individual thinker. The fundamental drive or urge within man is to exist and be recognized as an individual in his own right. If man is so recognized, he is likely to gain a sense of meaning and significance in life.

The meaning of the term *existentialism* will become clearer if we understand the distinction between *existence* and *essence* in philosophy. The term *essence* is that which distinguishes a thing from other types of objects. The essence is common to many individuals, and we may speak meaningfully of an essence even though no instances of the thing actually exist at the time. For Plato and many classical thinkers, the concept of *man*, for example, had more reality than the percept or the individual human being, John Smith. They thought that the participation in the idea, or essence *man-ness* is what makes a person, any person, what he is. Existentialists reject this classical or Platonic view and insist that there is something which cannot be conceptualized and this is the personal act of existing. Personal existence has to be experienced or lived through to be actually known; it cannot be described in its fullness by propositions alone. Existence means the state of being actual, of occurring within space and time—something given here and now.

From a slightly different point of view existentialism is a movement concerned with describing and diagnosing the human predicament. Paul Tillich has said that "wherever man's predicament is described either poetically or artistically, there we have existential elements."[2] To the extent that existentialism emphasizes the human situation and man's prospects in the world, it is found in ancient Judaism, among the early Christians, and in the outlook of philosophers like Socrates. Thus it reaches far back in history. As a modern movement, it gained prominence in the twentieth century. During the nineteenth century, however, certain "lonely prophets"—Kierkegaard, Nietzsche, Dostoevsky, and others—were expressing their protests and concern about the condition of man. During the twentieth century, the expression of concern over man's sense of alienation and meaninglessness has grown into a strong chorus.

Existentialism, while not setting forth any system of moral philosophy, has clear implications in the area of ethics. We have seen that it is a protest against many of the movements and things that neglect or threaten the person in his most private, separate, individual existence. On this basis it can approve of some actions and condemn others. Objectivity, as expressed in modern science and technology, as well as in some philosophical and psychological outlooks, has tended to stress the physical and quantitative. This emphasis has made the person and his uniqueness and individuality of secondary importance to things, if it has not actually denied them. When this outlook is carried to extremes, man's life becomes hollow and meaningless. Existentialism represents man's rebellion against all attempts to ignore or suppress the uniqueness of his subjective experience.

---

[2]Paul Tillich, "Existentialist Aspects of Modern Art," in *Christianity and the Existentialists*, ed. Carl Michalson (New York: Charles Scribner's Sons, 1956), pp. 129–130.

This movement has led to a new emphasis on man's freedom—on moral freedom or freedom of choice as well as on the civil liberties including freedom of speech, press, religion, and the like. The various determinisms, whether hereditary or environmental, biological or psychological in emphasis, do not tell the whole story; at best they are half-truths. In existentialism attention is directed not to the impersonal world of nature, to man in the abstract, or to man's institutions, but to the individual person and his choices and decisions. Freedom does not need to be proved or argued about as it is a reality to be experienced.

Closely allied with the emphases on subjectivity and personal freedom is the recognition of man's responsibility for his own life and actions. Existentialists are usually quick to deny, first, thought systems that stress the mechanical nature of all processes, organic as well as inorganic; second, all views of predestination that make God responsible for all events in man's life, the evil as well as the good; and third, the fatalisms that interpret events as so definitely fixed that human effort cannot alter them. These outlooks that deny freedom and personal responsibility for the course of human events and for man's decisions may be comforting to some persons who wish to evade responsibility and concern over problems of ethics and morality.

Apart from a few affirmations and a few common denials, as set forth above, there are widespread differences among the views of the people who have been influential in the development of existentialism. Support in some form has come from philosophers, theologians, writers, and artists; from Protestant, Roman Catholic, and Jewish thinkers; from theists, agnostics, and atheists. Space permits little more than brief statements regarding a few of these.

Among theologians, the Danish thinker Sören Kierkegaard (1813–1855) is often considered to be the founder of existentialism. He was not a systematic thinker and he is difficult to interpret. He glories in paradoxes and devotes much space to his own moods, anxieties, and "existential introspection." His main concern is what it means to be a Christian or to become a whole man. The two great enemies, according to Kierkegaard, are the Hegelian philosophy with its abstract speculation that depersonalizes man, and the unreflective church member who depersonalizes religion and who thinks he is a Christian because he is a good citizen and performs some good works. There is, he says, an "unbridgeable gulf" between God and the world. Only when man is in anguish, abandons reason, and takes the "leap of faith" is man's salvation in sight. Faith and obedience to God are essential. Kierkegaard believed that there are three "stages on life's road." The first is the aesthetic stage which is the life of sensuous enjoyment. This stage, if one stops here, is the "path of perdition." The second is the ethical stage where man reaches the level of the universal human. At this point man begins to have some awareness of his vocation as a human being. At the third or highest stage, the religious man discovers the meaning of existence and realizes that as an individual he stands alone before God. At times man may rise above ethics and do what appears to be "immoral" in the sight of man. This is "the teleological suspension of the ethical" in response to what he thinks is the will of God.

Ethics for Kierkegaard is not a matter of discovering the good; it is a matter of obedience and the making of a decision. Kierkegaard has strongly influenced certain Protestant theologians such as Karl Barth, Emil Brunner, and neo-orthodox groups in Europe and America. The French Roman Catholic philosopher and lay theologian Gabriel Marcel and the Jewish thinker Martin Buber are often included among the existentialists, but they both dislike being typed and reject the label.

Among philosophers Friedrich Nietzsche (1844–1900) has exerted a strong influence on such existentialist philosophers as Karl Jaspers, Martin Heidegger, Gabriel Marcel, and Jean-Paul Sartre. Both Nietzsche and Kierkegaard lived lonely and unhappy lives and concerned themselves with the human predicament. Both of them found much that was wrong with human nature, and they opposed what they considered the shallowness of conventional middle-class morality. Whereas Kierkegaard's main problem was how to become a Christian, Nietzsche opposed Christianity as the enemy of reason and a robust culture. His problem was how to live as an atheist. His emphasis was on life, instinct, and power. He stressed the "Will to Power" and wanted to clear the way for the "higher man," the Lords of the Earth, or the supermen who are "beyond good and evil." He wanted a transvaluation of all values that would leave behind the virtues of mediocrity as exhibited in Christianity, democracy, and socialism. We have considered Nietzsche's viewpoint in chapter 9.

Karl Jaspers (1883–1968) was a German existentialist who rejected the trends in Anglo-American philosophy that stress rigorous analysis of terms, logic, and objective science as the way to understanding and truth. Jaspers was interested in the good life and in the self that makes decisions. He felt that philosophy is a perpetual quest in which living, feeling, deciding, acting, and risking are facts of life, and man is always more than he thinks or knows. An examination of personal existence indicates that at least three areas need to be considered: man's direct consciousness of selfhood, man's communication with his fellowman in social activities, and the various structures of community life—morals, law, family, the state, and the like. In these areas man has duties and responsibilities. In addition to the self studied in sciences like psychology, there is the intimate human experience of love and hate, joy and tragedy, aspiration and anxiety. We can be guided in part at least by love, faith, and insight. This discovery of the authentic self makes choice and freedom possible. Only through life in society and through communication can individual existence be developed and fulfilled.

In the areas of literature and art, existentialism has made its widest appeal. The sense of the human predicament and the spirit of revolt have been expressed in the novels and plays of Kafka, Sartre, and Camus; in the poetry of Eliot and Auden; in the paintings of Cezanne, Van Gogh, Picasso, Chagall, de Chirico; also in confessions, memoirs, personal diaries and journals, as well as in autobiographies. Many sensitive men and women have used these literary and artistic forms to symbolize what they experience in the depths of their lives. We shall limit our presentation to a brief statement on Jean-Paul Sartre (b. 1905), a leader of existentialism in mid-twentieth-century France. While he is most widely known for his novels, plays, and essays, his *Being and Nothingness* brought him some attention as a philosopher.

Man, says Sartre, is not born ready-made; he has to make himself and to choose and create the conditions under which he is to live. Man is what he wills. He has no external support but must rely on his own resources. There is no God and no meaning or purpose apart from that which man in his freedom creates. In this sense "everything is permissible" and man is really "beyond good and evil." Though man's condition may appear absurd, meaningless, and tragic, he can still live by the rules of integrity, nobility, and valor, and he can create a human community. Since man's destiny is in his own hands, his hope is in choosing and acting so that he may live reasonably well. While the goal of human striving is a more ideal self that may be achieved by free and responsible men, Sartre acknowledges that this is an endless quest. Freedom, in the last analysis, is deceptive and futile, but even in failure man can retain his integrity and dignity.

What is the appeal of Sartre for many persons, especially the young? The suggestion has been made that there is a thrill in saying the world is absurd since a person may thus gain a sense of superiority over the established order and a sense of mastery over his own life. The existentialist is dissatisfied with philosophers and others who spend their time on highly technical questions of analysis and refuse to take a stand on the life and death issues of our time. But if existentialists minimize the importance of reason, science, and the external world, and if there are no external standards of truth and goodness, how can we settle disputes except by force? If existentialism is an attempt to restore the person and his inner strivings to a place of respect and dignity, that is one thing; but if it is a retreat from reason into the world of metaphor where objective standards do not apply, that is something quite different. Existentialists, however, have moved in many directions so that no one point of criticism applies to all.

TYPES OF RELIGIOUS ETHICS

Religious persons might wish to state their moral philosophy in terms of one or another of the outlooks we have already set forth. They are likely, however, to add some distinctive points of emphasis. In the history of the race, morality and religion have been closely associated. Morality has been concerned with human values, the right, the good, and the desirable in respect to conduct. Religion has been concerned not only with the ordinary values of human life, but also with what is highest in spirit and deepest in nature. Ethical questions, it is asserted, cannot be separated from questions about the nature of man, the nature of the universe, and man's place in the universe.

The ethical theories that are related to philosophical systems are known and consciously followed by a comparatively small proportion of the human race, whereas the religions number their adherents by the tens and hundreds of millions. If we would know the ideals that have influenced the conduct of great masses of men and women, we need to study the ethical ideals of these world religions. We shall need, however, to limit our attention to a brief consideration of Judaism and Christianity and to some comments about religion in general.

The Ethics of Judaism

In Judaism, morality and religion are united, not separate or distinct. The one God who created the world and made man in His image is also the author of the moral law, which applies to all men everywhere. The Decalogue and later codes proclaim man's duty to man, as well as his duty to God. While morality and religion may have grown out of different roots in human nature, they are both parts of man's quest for wholeness, and both assume that man cannot live by and for himself alone. Judaism links morality and religion as inseparable aspects of the spiritual life.

The Prophets delivered their moral insights and warnings as supernatural dicta: "Thus said the Lord." Though the law was the product of centuries of social and moral experience, the observance of it was presented as a matter of obedience to God's will. Morality here is in part the way in which religion—that is, man's relation to God—expresses itself in life and character.

In Judaism there is emphasis on the worth of human personality and on man as a free moral agent, one endowed with the capacity to distinguish between right and wrong. Man needs to avoid the extremes of sensuality and asceticism. His powers and appetites lead to good or evil depending on the ends toward which they are directed. While the prophets call attention to the divine commands, it is clear that acceptance is voluntary and not forced. Man has the power to choose between genuine alternatives. The people are asked by Moses to choose life. "I have set before you life and death, blessing and curse; therefore choose life. . . ."[3]

Central in the ethics of Judaism are the virtues of righteousness or justice and love or loving kindness. When the question is asked, "What doth the Lord require of thee?" the Prophet answers, "To do justly, and to love mercy, and to walk humbly with thy God." Justice is mentioned first because love ought not to disregard the demands of justice. In answer to the question "Who shall stand in His holy place?" the Psalmist replies, "He that hath clean hands and a pure heart." Faith is a good thing, but it is incomplete without action. It needs to express itself in the deed. The law is expressed in two forms. There is the ceremonial law, symbolizing the duties that man owes to God. With these external forms the priest was especially concerned. And there is the moral law, demanding justice and loving kindness toward one's fellowmen. The Prophets were especially concerned with this law.

Another feature of the ethics of Judaism is emphasis on community- and social-mindedness. The individual life is bound up with the life of the community, and responsibility is social as well as individual. God's will affects all the people and applies to the home, the family, and larger communities. Throughout the Old Testament and other rabbinical literature, the personal and social virtues stressed include justice, love, truth and wisdom, charity, peace, labor, and friendship. The Prophets warn against injustice, oppression, and exploitation. They commend concern for the needy, the poor, the orphan, the widow, and the stranger.

Modern Judaism has three main divisions. Orthodox Judaism maintains in principle the authority of the revealed law and places relatively greater emphasis on ritualistic observances. Conservative Judaism, while continuing rabbinical Judaism, claims the right to adapt the traditions to today's world. Reform Judaism emphasizes the Prophets and the ethical teachings of Judaism. For the Reform group, Judaism is an evolving religious experience, which has been and is subject to change.

---

[3] Deut. 30: 15, 19.

Christian Ethics

Jesus took the rich legacy of morality inherited from Jewish history and gave it new form and emphasis. He came, he said, "not to destroy but to fulfill." Parts of the legacy he brushed aside; other parts he reemphasized and expanded. He took the nationalistic morality of the Jews of his day and, drawing on the later prophetic antecedents, gave it universal application.

Our knowledge of Jesus of Nazareth derives from the New Testament, chiefly from four interpretations called the Gospels—Matthew, Mark, Luke, and John. Jesus did not set forth a complete system of ethics; his teaching was directed to the particular problem he was facing. Frequently it took the form of the parable, or illustrative story. Though he accepted much of what had been worked out or discovered by the race up to his time, his message came to men with such freshness, directness, and ring of reality that men said he spoke with authority and in truth was the Son of God. He brought together the central truths of religion and morality and embodied them in his own life in a unique way.

In Western civilization, Christianity, with its emphasis on both the Old Testament and the New Testament teachings, has given form to the moral ideal and has exerted a strong influence on the development of moral codes. There is an outlook on life and an ethics that is distinctively Christian. This way of life, however, is not to be identified with Western civilization. There is much in the folkways and mores of Western societies that is indifferent or even antagonistic to the Christian ideal.

A study of the history of the Christian Church shows that Christian ethics has varied from age to age and from group to group. Yet the golden thread running through all these systems has been certain key teachings of Jesus as recorded in the New Testament and a certain spirit embodied there. Paul the Apostle also played a significant role in the development of Christian thought and practice. The Epistles of Paul are concerned with ethical issues. Origen, Augustine, Thomas Aquinas, Martin Luther, John Calvin, and many others have either systematized Christian ethics in accordance with the outlook of their age or have emphasized certain aspects of it.

Let us consider some of the central points of emphasis, or distinguishing characteristics, in Christian ethics:

First, Christian ethics places emphasis on the inner character of a man—on his motives, will, and desires. It is an ethics of the spirit that is inner, free, and responsible. Such an ethics is the very opposite of legalism, externalism, and static authoritarianism, even though, as we shall see, some have attempted to make it the latter. The inner quality of a man's life is of supreme importance: "From within, from the heart, flow evil deeds."

Second, Christian ethics is an ethics of love. Such an ethics is non-reciprocal—that is, the person does not bargain, or ask what he is to receive for what he gives. For Jesus, morality was positive. Men are to take the initiative in applying the principles of the good life in their relations with others. Each man is under obligation to promote the interests of those with whom he comes in contact. Men are to love even their enemies. Love must go beyond self and neighbor and include God. When asked regarding the great commandments, Jesus said, "Thou shalt love the Lord thy God with all thy heart, and with all thy soul, and with all thy mind, and with all thy strength: this is the first commandment. And the second is like, namely this, Thou shalt love they neighbor as thyself. There is none other commandment greater than these." The Ten Commandments of the Hebrew Old Testament and the classical virtues of the Greeks were accepted by the Christians. Love, however, was made the supreme virtue. Love is the fulfillment of the law and goes beyond justice. Other virtues emphasized were faith, hope, loyalty, patient endurance, and conquest over the flesh.

Third, Christian ethics, like Judaism from which it developed, interprets man's duties as duties to God, and thus gives cosmic significance to the moral life. In this respect, Christian ethics differs from some types of philosophic ethics. In Christian ethics, the highest morality springs out of a new relationship with God and is thus based on a distinctive view of man and of the universe. Man is not a mere animal organism. There is in man a creative urge that is part of or related to the creative processes of the universe—the good life is life lived not only in harmony with other lives but also in harmony with God.

Fourth, in Christian ethics the good life has been personalized as loyalty to Jesus. The ideals of the moral philosophers lack "the appeal that comes from the *incarnation* of a way of life in a living person and the inspiration that is derived from *imitation* of him."[4] The Christian life is a quest for the good under the inspiration of devotion to the ideals of Jesus. Jesus so impressed his spirit on the Christian movement that it continues to be expressed as loyalty to him even as new insights and truths are added.

Loyalty to Jesus Christ has produced a fellowship known as the Chris-

---

[4]George F. Thomas, *Christian Ethics and Moral Philosophy*, (New York: Charles Scribner's Sons, 1955), p. 372.

tian Church. Christian ethics is an ethics that has been formulated by this living fellowship, through which it has become a way of life that has affected many millions of people.

Two Contrasting Types of Religious Ethics

There are many kinds or varieties of religious ethics, just as there are of philosophical ethics. We shall limit our attention to two broadly contrasting types of religious interpretation of moral problems. Before stating these two approaches, we wish to remind the reader of two questions, mentioned earlier in the text, that need to be kept in mind to avoid confusion. First, what is the motive or the spirit in which an action is performed? What is the man's intention or purpose? This question has to do with the person's moral character, with his will and commitment. Both Christianity and Judaism have said that "the Lord looketh on the heart." Second, there is another important question —that is, is the act right? Granted that a man has a good will, a good motive, and that he wants to do the will of God, does he actually choose rightly in deciding what to do? In order to act rightly a man must choose what is right. This second question demands knowledge of the relevant factors in the situation; it demands evidence and reflection. Let us now examine two types of religious interpretation of moral problems.

The Ethics of Duty or the Right. This first type of religious interpretation requires obedience apart from the goodness of the act and is sometimes called deontological ethics (from *deon*-duty and *logos*-science). It stresses obligation or duty, as opposed to teleological or axiological ethics, which stresses some end or goal considered good.

The ethics of duty asks what is required by the moral law, or by the Great Lawgiver, God. What is right is obedience to some authority— conscience, the Bible, the church, or the will of God. This type of religious ethics attempts to keep ethics strictly theological by refusing to seek or by minimizing other reasons as a justification for right acts. Ethical duties stand out by themselves with no reason or justification except that they follow the authority or the code. One form of this approach is a Biblical or a creedal literalism characteristic of the movement known as *fundamentalism* where the Bible or some creed is taken as a rule of faith and practice.

Another movement within this general approach, one that was more prevalent during the middle decades of the twentieth century among educated religious leaders, is known as *neo-orthodoxy*. It accepts the historical approach to Biblical literature and the results of modern historical scholarship but seeks revelation in the events it relates. The content of ethics becomes a matter of ascertaining what God expects us to do and then obeying his commands.

In Protestant Christianity this type of ethics appealed to the Reformation leaders, especially Luther, and is now sometimes called the *ethics of faith*, the *ethics of revelation*, or the *ethics of obedient love*. In the twentieth century Emil Brunner, Karl Barth, and Paul L. Lehmann have been among its defenders. The right or the good, we are told, is not to be found in some moral system or set of principles or in some intrinsic value. "Reason sees what is human but not what is divine" is a typical claim of those who stress the ethics of faith. Ethics involves reflection upon life and upon morality from the standpoint of certain theological presuppositions. For example, Lehmann speaks of this ethics as *koinonia* (the fellowship or body of believers) ethics in that it emerges from a fellowship, although the ethical content cannot be stated as rational generalization or general principle.

This approach has sometimes been called the *ethics of self-renunciation* in contrast to the *ethics of the good* or the *ethics* of *self-fulfillment*. It is antinomian (*anti*–against, *nomos*–law or norm) because it stresses freedom from law and all external regulation of human life. The emphasis is on faith and on the inner man. The approach is often, but not always, individualistic, emphasizing the individual and ignoring group relationships.

The Ethics of the Good or the Ethics of Fulfillment. This second type of religious ethics is a form of teleological ethics. The ethics of fulfillment is person-affirming. Right conduct confers benefit on people; wrong conduct brings harm or injury.

In religious language it is said we should obey God because He is good and has concern for all His creatures. Love and an outgoing concern for all men constitute the heart of goodness. People have an obligation to care for their own lives, but equally for the lives and welfare of people everywhere. This outlook is found in both the Old Testament and the New Testament. "If thou meet thine enemy's ox or his ass going astray, thou shalt surely bring it back to him again"; "If thine enemy hunger, feed him, if he thirst, give him drink"; "I came that they might have life and have it more abundantly"; "Whatsoever ye would that men should do to you, do ye even so to them." The two "great commandments" of Jesus—love of God and love for neighbor—though they were not original with him, express the very center of his thought. In the parable of the Good Samaritan he showed that the neighbor is any one in need. In the parable of the Last Judgment he placed service to one's fellowmen as the test of devotion to God. According to this ethical outlook, one cannot love God or one's neighbor and fail to be concerned with the social, economic, political, and racial conditions that affect him.

The ethics of both Judaism and Christianity emphasize the worth of the person. Man is of greater value than things. Things, programs, and institutions derive their worth from their relation to or their effect on human welfare. When asked a question regarding the use of the Sabbath, Jesus said, "The Sabbath was made for man, not man for the Sabbath." People are ends in themselves; other things are means.

Closely related to this emphasis on man is the principle of the progressive growth of personality. Life is not a static achievement; it does not stand still. Men must grow or they deteriorate. From this point of view man was a part of the creative process, and there is something in him that responds to the appeal of the higher life.

According to the Christian form of the ethics of the good or fulfillment, men are inspired by their Christian view of man and of God and by their love of God to discover the right and to live according to it. For many Christians, loyalty to Christ means loyalty to the best life possible in the situation in which people find themselves. The spirit of Jesus is best expressed as a supreme concern for people. The Christian life is a quest for the good under the inspiration of devotion to the ideals of Jesus. Men discover through experience the tasks that need to be done, and these tasks then are viewed as a part of their duty to God. Religion is thus a powerful motivation directing men's lives in the way they should go rather than indicating the particular acts they should perform. This throws on man himself the responsibility for the decision as to what is right in any particular situation. There is a tendency in both Christianity and Judaism to interpret morality as growing or as empirical and functional.

Many Christian theologians have regarded Christian ethics and moral philosophy not as completely separate but as complementary or supplementary. For example Thomas Aquinas (1225–1274), whose ethics is still dominant in Roman Catholicism, recognizes the validity of both philosophy and theology, reason and faith, as he brings together Aristotelian naturalism and the Christian faith.

Virtue is, according to Aquinas, natural to man, whereas sin is unnatural and contrary to man's truest nature. Man may discover and follow the natural virtues, such as justice, wisdom, courage, and self-control. These are within the grasp of reason and they are attainable in the natural life. In addition to these virtues man needs the theological and Christian virtues, such as faith, hope, and love, which are given by the grace of God.

Many Protestant moral philosophers and religious leaders also regard moral philosophy and Christian ethics as complementary even though the two fields are distinctive in emphasis.

Christian moralists, says Georgia Harkness, need to "familiarize themselves as thoroughly as possible with the history of philosophy" and become acquainted with other world views in their best forms, since "God has found many channels for the disclosure of truth to men." Christian ethics, she says, should neither sell its "birthright by accommodation to secular standards," nor refuse to "respect and learn from the moral wisdom of the ages."[5]

Through the ages men have heard God speak to them through the events recorded in the Scriptures and also in conscience, reason, history, and in nature. Both religious and philosophical ethics grow out of the same problems of human living. The ethics of Judaism reflects the insights included in the Old Testament and the Rabbinical literature. In Christian ethics the good life has been personalized as devotion to Jesus, while associating itself with the forward movement of mankind.

Along with the above ethical systems let us very briefly present a form of Christian ethics that might be described as a variant of the ethics of fulfillment. Recently in the United States and Great Britain, there has been discussion of what is called *situation ethics* or *contextual ethics*. Its proponents see it, on the one hand, as a middle ground between a legalism or authoritarianism that stresses a fixed code permitting few if any exceptions, and on the other hand, a freedom from all norms other than the "existential moment" where decisions are made spontaneously. Situation ethics, while respecting the moral maxims and wisdom that have come down to us from previous generations, is willing to make exceptions when love (*agape* or self-giving love) demands some relaxation of the standard. Only love, it is claimed, is universally good and can be directed only toward a person and not toward some abstract good. In "Love Justifies Its Means" Joseph Fletcher says, "The new morality, situation ethics, declares that everything is right or wrong, according to the situation."[6] This approach is said to give freedom in a rapidly changing society. Critics point out that man is always acting in a community and that love alone can be blind and uninformed. They also contend that knowledge and reason must be added to love.

Concluding Comments

Both of the positions stated above—the ethics of obedience and the ethics of fulfillment—can find support in biblical literature. The attempt, however, to keep ethics closely tied to conventional theological

---

[5]*Christian Ethics* (New York: Abingdon Press, 1957), pp. 18, 19.
[6]*Situation Ethics: The New Morality* (Philadelphia: Westminster Press, 1966), p. 124. See also *The Situation Ethics Debate,* ed. Harvey Cox (Philadelphia: Westminster Press, 1968).

systems has meant that it has not been sufficiently responsive to the demands of a new and rapidly changing world. Simply telling a man to do the will of God when he is perplexed and seeks advice does not fully answer his questions. Almost all people have attributed their moral standards to their gods or to God. Yet these standards have been most diverse and have changed with the development of the group and with changed conditions. Why not seek to discover that which promotes human welfare and then view this as God's will for you, or as your duty, until you gain some additional evidence or some larger insight calling for revision?

In our opinion the aim of maximizing the good experienced by man is basic in ethics; and the right, whether in moral philosophy or religion, must reflect this aim. To view the right and the good as so independent of each other that a man may fulfill his moral obligation and his religious duty through actions that leave more evil than good in the world is to make the moral life irrational and ethics as a sensible interpretation of it exceedingly difficult. The development of morality in response to man's growing knowledge of the effects of actions on human welfare, and man's everyday responses to acts that affect his life appear to give support to these contentions.[7]

In what ways may a reflective morality and an enlightened religion support each other? In addition to clarifying the terms and concepts used in ethical discussions, moral philosophy serves religion and theology by the purifying effect of its criticisms. Moral standards may advance beyond those implied by the prevailing religious outlook. When this happens much harm is done to the growth of religion and the respect with which it is regarded. Ethics may also aid religion in recognizing and promoting worthy social ends. Religion apart from moral insight may become narrow and divisive and may reinforce prejudices and hatreds. Ethical religion, however, will tend to unite men and stimulate a respect for human personality, regardless of barriers of tribe, class, nationality, or race.

Religion has usually given support to the moral standards recognized by the group. It tends to give meaning to life and to strengthen morale by tapping and releasing new levels of energy with which men are able to meet the crises of life. Morality tends to gain in warmth and vigor when associated with religion. The masses of men are not deeply stirred by the appeal of abstract ideas but are more easily moved by loyalty to

---

[7] See Oliver A. Johnson, *Rightness and Goodness, A Study in Contemporary Ethical Theory* (The Hague: Martinus Nijhoff, 1959). Ch. 6 discusses these questions. The author says we have "only one actual duty. That is, maximize goodness" (p. 159).

a dynamic and courageous personality. By combining and harmonizing their more mature moral and religious insights, men have increased their normal powers and have more effectively promoted their chosen ends.

QUESTIONS AND PROJECTS

1. Marxists and many Communists have asserted that their approach is strictly scientific. Critics have claimed that communism is an ideology, a philosophy, or even a theology. Comment on these assertions.
2. Arnold Toynbee, the historian, and others have said that Marxism is a Christian heresy since it carries over the Judaeo-Christian passion for a better world while rejecting theism and other religious tenets. Comment on this interpretation.
3. Compare and contrast Christianity and communism. See John C. Bennett, *Christianity and Communism Today*, rev. ed. (New York: Association Press, 1970).
4. Existentialists have stressed alienation and the human predicament. To what extent do you think ethical or moral issues are responsible for this attitude and outlook?
5. Do you find any common elements in Marxism, existentialism, Judaism, and Christianity? If so what are they?
6. How can a personally founded religion and ethical ideal remain true to the principles of the founder and at the same time keep up with changing conditions and knowledge?
7. According to reports, a "praying textile manufacturer" shocked the members of a Senate-House labor committee. When pressed with the question about what he thought was a fair and reasonable minimum wage, he is said to have replied that he never thought of paying men on the basis of what they need. Those things about which the members of the committee were asking had to do, he said, with the emotional side of living. "I attend to them in my church connections." Comment on the attitude expressed here.
8. Discuss the use of the expression "the will of God" in relation to moral problems. In your discussion consider the following quotations or incidents:
   (1) When Benjamin Franklin invented the lightning rod to protect buildings, many members of the clergy in England and America, with the support of King George III, condemned the device as an impious effort to defeat the will of God. Similar protests were voiced when anesthetics were first used to ease the pain of childbirth.
   (2) In *The Will of God* (Nashville: Abingdon-Cokesbury, 1944) Leslie D. Weatherhead, discussing the loose and confused way in which many people use the phrase "the will of God," relates an incident which took place while he was a military chaplain.

The matter came to me most poignantly when I was in India. I was standing on the veranda of an Indian home darkened by bereavement. My Indian friend had lost his little son, the light of his eyes, in a cholera epidemic. At the far end of the veranda his little daughter, the only remaining child, slept in a cot covered over with a mosquito net. We paced up and down, and I tried in my clumsy way to comfort and console him. But he said, "Well, padre, it is the will of God. That's all there is to it. It is the will of God."

Fortunately I knew him well enough to be able to reply without being misunderstood, and I said something like this: "Supposing someone crept up the steps onto the veranda tonight, while you all slept, and deliberately put a wad of cotton soaked in cholera germ culture over your little girl's mouth as she lay in that cot there on the veranda, what would you think about that?"

"My God," he said, "what would I think about that? Nobody would do such a damnable thing. If he attempted it and I caught him, I would kill him with as little compunction as I would a snake, and throw him over the veranda. What do you mean by suggesting such a thing?"

"But, John," I said quietly, "isn't that just what you have accused God of doing when you said it was His Will? Call your little boy's death the result of mass ignorance, call it mass folly, call it mass sin, if you like, call it bad drains or communal carelessness, but don't call it the will of God." Surely we cannot identify as the will of God something for which a man would be locked up in jail, or put in a criminal lunatic asylum.

9. Is it true that when religion and ethics break down or are separated from everyday affairs, politics tends to be governed by the self-interest of pressure groups rather than on the basis of any conceptions of right and wrong? Explain your answer.
10. State the case for and against the view that the main ethical truths do not depend directly on religion. If you feel able to do so, state your own position on this issue.
11. What things seem to be worshipped most enthusiastically in our age? The following have been suggested: physical strength, personal beauty, pleasure, material things (homes, autos, and the like), financial success, political power, human progress, some traditional concept of God, God as a living reality.
12. How do you explain the fact that while some religious leaders are in the forefront of the struggle for social justice, many church groups are used to support some old injustices? You may wish to consult Kyle Haselden, "11 A.M. Sunday Is Our Most Segregated Hour," in the *New York Times Magazine*, 2 August 1964, p. 9.

SUGGESTED READINGS

MARXISM AND ETHICS

Ash, William F. *Marxism and Moral Concepts.* New York: Monthly Review Press, 1964.
———. "Marxist Ethics and the European Tradition." *Science and Society* 30 (Summer 1966):326–334.
Drechkovitch, Milorad M., ed. *Marxism in the Modern World.* Stanford: Stanford University Press, 1965. Published for The Hoover Institute on War, Revolution, and Peace.
Kamenka, Eugene. *The Ethical Foundations of Marxism.* New York: Frederick A. Praeger, Inc., Publishers, 1962.
———. *Marxism and Ethics.* New York: St. Martins Press, 1969.
Parsons, H. L. *Ethics in the Soviet Union Today.* New York: American Institute for Marxist Studies, 1965.
———. *Humanism and Marx's Thought.* Springfield, Ill.: Charles C. Thomas, 1971.
Somerville, John. "Marxist Ethics, Determinism, and Freedom." *Philosophy and Phenomenological Research* 28 (September 1967):17–23.

EXISTENTIALIST ETHICS

Aron, Raymond. *Marxism and the Existentialist.* New York: Harper & Row, Publishers, 1969.
Barnes, Hazel Estelle. *An Existentialist Ethics.* New York: Alfred A. Knopf, 1967.
Cavell, Stanley. "Existentialism and Analytic Philosophy." *Daedalus* 93, no. 3 (Summer 1964):946–974.
Dufrenne, Mikel. "Existentialism and Existentialisms." *Philosophy and Phenomenological Research* 26 (September 1965):51–62.
Warnock, Mary. *Existentialist Ethics.* New York: Oxford University Press, 1970.
Wild, John. "Authentic Existence." *Ethics* 75 (July 1965):227–239.

JUDAEO-CHRISTIAN ETHICS

Barr, O. Sydney. *The Christian New Morality: A Biblical Study of Situation Ethics.* New York: Oxford University Press, 1969.
Brown, Robert McAfee, and Weigel, Gustave, S. J. *An American Dialogue.* Pt. 2. Garden City: Doubleday & Co., 1960.
Cohon, Beryl D. *Judaism in Theory and Practice.* Rev. ed. New York: Bloch Publishing Co., 1954.

Corkey, R. *A Philosophy of Christian Morals for Today.* London: George Allen & Unwin, 1961.
Finkelstein, Louis, et al. *The Religions of Democracy.* New York: Devin-Adair Co., 1949.
Gordon, Robert. *A Faith for Moderns.* Ch. 13. New York: Bloch Publishing Co., 1960.
Herberg, Will. *Protestant, Catholic, Jew: An Essay in Religious Sociology.* New York: Doubleday & Co., 1955.
Johnson, F. Ernest, ed. *Patterns of Ethics in America Today.* Chs. 1–3. New York: Collier Books, 1962.
Lehmann, Paul L. *Ethics in a Christian Context.* New York: Harper & Row, Publishers, 1963.
Lewis, H. D. *Morals and the New Theology.* New York: Harper & Brothers, 1947.
Thomas, George F. *Christian Ethics and Moral Philosophy.* New York: Charles Scribner's Sons, 1955.
Tillich, Paul. *Morality and Beyond.* New York: Harper & Row, Publishers, 1963.
Trueblood, Elton. *The New Man for Our Time.* New York: Harper & Row, Publishers, 1970.

12
REFLECTIVE MORALITY IN A CHANGING WORLD

Modern man faces many problems that men in the past have not faced—problems not covered in the traditional codes, problems on which even contemporary man has had little time to reflect. The conventional morality knew nothing, for example, about

Heart and organ transplants—From whom should they be taken and to whom given?

Kidney machines—Since they are limited in number and very expensive, who shall live and who shall be left to die?

Artificial insemination—Should we build up sperm and ova banks?

Biological engineering to control heredity—What danger is there in the manipulation of the DNA molecule and man's probable control of his future development?

Population control—Should we require the limitation of the size of families?

Use and control of outer space and the oceans—Who should own or control what?

Automation, cybernation, and computers—Shall we guarantee an income for those who cannot find work because machines have replaced them?

There are many more such problems.

In a rapidly changing world there is the continuous need of bringing our morals up to date and of closing the gap between principles and practices. As knowledge and understanding have increased men have shifted more and more from external to internal guidance, from smaller to more inclusive circles of the in-group, and from external forms to a consideration of the present and long-range effects of acts on persons. In short, there is need for an adventurous, inquiring morality that is concerned with both principles and all the available facts or evidence relating to the questions under consideration.

When controversies arise over what is good for health, the best type of marriage regulation, the effect of television programs on children, fair trade laws in industry, and the like, ethics by itself does not provide all the answers or all the evidence on the basis of which decisions should be made. People who wish to come to reasonable conclusions about what is right and what is wrong in human conduct need to consult the moral experience of the past as well as the findings of sciences and other disciplines that throw light on such problems.

When the external authorities are supported by valid evidence, people prefer to go directly to the evidence. When the authorities make pronouncements unsupported by evidence, people feel that the claims ought to be open to question and to examination. They are convinced, however, that it is possible to discover what is right and what is wrong.

As men decided to break away from the traditions of an earlier past and to face the facts of nature with open minds, a new day dawned. The great scientific advances of recent centuries have not come from authority or any infallible organization; they have come in great part from human intelligence applied in what is known as the scientific method. The essentials of this method include careful observation, analysis and classification, setting forth hypotheses, and testing those hypotheses.

In a somewhat similar way, when there has been evidence that some ancient moral practice or code has tended to injure rather than to advance human life, men have sought new ways of acting and have appealed to the evidence in justification for accepting the change. The steps in thinking in science and morality may be similar, but the purpose to be achieved is different. Whereas a scientific hypothesis is a new principle of organization or a tentative solution designed for the purpose of gaining knowledge, the revised moral code is designed for the purpose of guiding human conduct. In the next section we shall examine more fully this way of proceeding as we attempt to bring our moral standards up to date.

IS EXPERIMENTATION POSSIBLE IN THE REALM OF MORALITY?

Can one apply the method of revision, which is open-minded and stresses evidence, to the field of morals? As we look back over the record of how codes of conduct arose and we observe the moral development of the race, we are impressed by the slow adaptation of moral ideas and practices to the needs of life. Apparently there has been much experimentation, even though it has been often ill directed and only partly conscious. We are lead to the question of whether it is possible for us to do consciously and more intelligently what has been going on in a rather haphazard and confused way.

In the broadest sense of the term *experiment,* man is a born experimenter. He has always experimented to some extent, and today he can do so more consciously and intelligently. It is not a question of experimenting or not experimenting; it is only a question of either experimenting intelligently toward better methods of living or unintelligently toward practices that impair growth and development. Individuals can and do experiment with the amount and kinds of food, drink, and exercise they need for most effective living. Professional groups experiment to find the codes and standards they need to enforce. Athletic directors and coaches keep records and test the rules by which games are played in order that there may be fewer injuries. Governmental bodies, educational institutions, and other organizations conduct many experiments with better principles and greater human welfare the conscious aim. Experiments are possible; which of them we call *scientific* is in part a matter of definition and in part a matter of the refinement of methods used. New statistical and other devices now enable people to observe and record things that could not be observed and recorded even a few generations ago. Thus new modes of confirmation are possible. This is not to say than an ethical statement or a moral code is susceptible of the same kind of confirmation or verification as a statement in a natural science; human affairs are much more complex and have more variables than most of the subject matter treated by the sciences. It is to say, though, that it makes sense to speak of "evidence" for and against such a statement or code, and that some factual basis exists for arriving at a justifiable decision.

In his essay "Science and People" Warren Weaver attempts to dispel certain misconceptions about science, including the views that it is a thing apart and that scientists are not like other men. He says that science is a "very human enterprise"; it is a "common part of the lives of all men." Its methods "involve only improvement—great, to be sure —of procedures of observation and analysis that the human race has always used." He says further that the methods of modern science improve on and "make it possible to crystallize our experience rapidly and reliably." Science is a "friendly companion" of moral philosophy, since the sciences and the arts are "partners in the business of life."[1]

---

[1] Paul C. Obler and Herman A. Estrin, eds., *The New Scientist: Essays on the Methods and Values of Modern Science* (New York: Doubleday & Co., 1962), pp. 95–111.

We should be careful, of course, not to expect too much from experimentation or to jump to conclusions from too little evidence. It is wrong to represent a hypothesis as proved when the facts support only a claim to its probability. But it is equally wrong to refuse to consider available evidence and not to search for new knowledge and better ways of doing things.

WHY WE NEED TO EXPERIMENT IN MORALITY

An experimental approach to morality seems essential today for a number of reasons. First, we live in a social order that is rapidly changing and that is a mixture of good and bad. We face new situations on which the ancient authorities could not declare themselves. From the past we have customs, traditions, laws, and other standards of conduct. Some have arisen in response to particular needs, some by accident or chance, others out of peculiar geographic or political or economic conditions, and still others form the conscious work of teachers and religious seers. Customs that arose in an agricultural or a feudal civilization are intermingled with conventions and laws applicable only to a complex mechanized civilization. Under these conditions it is not surprising to find many tensions and conflicts. It seems clear that codes should be adapted and amended to meet the needs of life under present conditions. This task cannot be accomplished at once; it is a continuous task, one that necessitates a conscious reflective morality.

Second, we need an experimental approach because we desire intelligently directed change. Violent revolutions occur in political states controlled by groups that endeavor to keep society static and unchanging. Authority and supression work for a time, but the social life becomes stagnant in acquiescence and eventually the expanding forces break forth in a more or less violent upheaval. The absolutism of political authorities in France and in Russia was responsible for much of the destructiveness of the French and Russian Revolutions. There seems to be little hope of orderly progress in the future unless society adopts a form of control that permits progress by evolution or by experimentation —rather than by revolution. We need intelligent reconstruction rather than destruction.

A third reason for the current need for experimentation in morals is our growing awareness not only of the part that geographic, biological, psychological, and social forces play in human behavior, but also of the possibility of inventing better specific combinations of these conditions. Man's moral conduct and other personal traits are influenced by the physical conditions under which he lives, by his organic makeup and level of energy, by his intelligence, and by his emotional balance as well as by the intellectual and social climate in which he is reared. What is right for men living in the North Temperate Zone may not be right for men of the same aspirations living in the tropics. Once it is known, as it now is, that a child's apparent intellectual ability can be increased or decreased by environmental conditions and once some of these conditions are identified, new moral opportunities and new obligations arise.

Finally, we need to develop an intelligent experimental morality because we need to grow as persons, and experimentation contributes to personal growth itself. There is a vast difference between the young person who is brought up to think of all moral precepts as resting on some external authority and the person who is taught to view morality, not as a fixed system of rules and commands, but as principles and ideals which he comes to understand, accept, and follow. In the latter case when the person discovers that some teachings have been mistaken or need revision, he does not rebel at all restraints or feel at liberty to gratify every impulse. A reflective approach to ethics challenges the person to think for himself and develop a sense of personal responsibility, not only for doing the right thing, but also for discovering what *is* right in the situation.

Guidelines for Moral Experimentation

Granted the possibility of meaningful moral experiment, especially through the current need for it and the use of "trial and error" or "trial and success" methods, under what conditions, by whom, and on what topics should it be conducted?

Four conditions need to be kept clearly in mind if we are to profit by experimentation. The first is that a genuine moral experiment is conducted for the purpose of adding to moral knowledge and improving human conduct. One does not just happen into an experiment. Merely doing something contrary to tradition with the aim of "seeing how I like it" is no experiment and is not a moral adventure. There is an intent in moral experimentation to compare outcomes with those of earlier ways of acting so as to be able to say with good reason that a given way is better or is not better than the earlier way.

A moral problem, as we have seen, is never just a moral problem; it is also a problem of personal growth, domestic affairs, sport, economic and political concern, or international relations. In some cases, the question of whether an experiment is a genuinely moral one, as distinct from an experiment that may merely have some moral uses, is a matter of purpose and intent. Consider a medical experiment made to determine the effects of systematic starvation (dietary deficiency) over a period of six months. A risk of permanent injury to the health of participants is present. There is thus a moral issue as to whether the risk should be taken or under what conditions it is morally justified. If the experiment is one simply to determine the effects of such deficiency of diet on specified types of organisms and the effects of given diets designed to recoup the effects of starvation during the rehabilitation period, the experiment is not a genuine moral experiment. If the results are intended to develop better plans for feeding starving populations, the experiment takes on the form of a moral experiment. To be a moral experiment, it is essential that the problem being investigated be itself a moral one.

It may be argued that on such a definition of moral experimentation, it should never be performed, since it is better always to experiment with more manageable parts of a problem than with the whole of it. Is this limitation incompatible with an overall moral evaluation of outcomes? We think not. Much institutional or industrial research is really moral inquiry, for the organization involved wants to know not just whether a given change in working conditions will yield greater efficiency of production but whether the company ought to institute this new condition, all things considered. The desire is to observe all of the interacting forces at work in different ways. Thus the study of the new practice may involve close observation of its use, observation not only of the bearing on production and costs but also on the attitudes of the people involved. When the concern is with the welfare of the people involved, the experiment becomes a moral experiment.

The second criterion of a warranted moral experiment is that it give promise of a gain in human good sufficiently large to warrant the cost and risks involved. In the physical or social sciences an experiment is performed in the hope that it will add to knowledge. In a moral experiment there should be a reasonable prospect that it will advance human welfare.

No responsible investigator will proceed with an experiment unless, on the basis of available knowledge, the probability of success makes the costs and risks worthwhile. In conduct affecting people, we need to be even more cautious than with costly materials. This is no argument against trying out new ways, however, because the continuation of destructive practices when they might be replaced is itself dangerous and costly. When an existing system has become obsolete and is generating ill will and injuring people, an experiment that has reasonable probability of success ought to be tried even if there is risk involved.

A third requirement for a moral experiment is that it be devised by people well informed and competent in the field in which the experiment is to be made and that, when others are affected, they also accept and agree to the purpose and conditions of the venture. When moral codes are themselves in question, the determination as to who is competent or has exercised due care may be a controversial one. The experimenters need to know the history of this type of endeavor. An uninformed and inexperienced person is as likely to blow up a chemistry or physics laboratory as to make valuable contributions to the knowledge of those fields. In moral experimentation an uninformed and inexperienced person can create frustration for himself and others by repeating ventures that have already been proved futile. Waste is also often involved in experimentation by the incompetent, for a perfectly sound moral venture can be conducted in an inconclusive way because of the inadequacy of the plans for its testing and evaluation. In view of the many moral questions on which we need greater understanding, we have no resources to waste on ill-considered experiments. To try some things even once makes a man irrevocably a different kind of person. In increasingly large areas of human experience, there is quite clear knowledge of consequences to be expected and of the appraisals by men who have experienced them. In medicine, law, social work, or even such a field as sports there are those like the doctor, the judge, the caseworker, or the Olympic coach who have expert knowledge of these facts. The opportunity to improve the laws of the land, to add to the quality of community life, or to advance the rules of the game will be wasted unless we draw on this expertness in devising and conducting our experiments.

The standard of due care in planning moral experiments touches on the question of who is competent to decide what experiments should be made and under what conditions. As we have said, the experimenter should be thoroughly informed about past practices and ideas in the area under study. Of the available people, he should also be of relatively outstanding character, because the scope of his concern for people, the capacity he has for good will, and his sensitivity to elements of moral relevance in a complex situation will bear on his ability to define a sound experiment, to observe what needs seeing, and to evaluate the outcomes. He will also need competence in the experimental method, for no amount of good will or high character will compensate for lack of know-how. It is probably desirable also that an experimenter have a degree of disinterestedness in the subject of his inquiry, though historically some of the most creative scientists have been men of decided opinions on the very issues on which they were experimenting. Objectivity is a *sine qua non* here, as in all experimentation, in the sense that the experimenter must perform his experimentation in ways that may be repeated. He must also permit others to check and evaluate his findings.

The experimental approach we suggest places a premium on the thoughtful use of intelligence in morality. Morality is not a mere matter of opinion. An act is right if it makes for optimum development of personal and social well-being; it is wrong if it fails to do so. Whether it does is a question of fact—a peculiar kind of fact involving in its certification the values men will find in its outcomes. Intelligence is as applicable to this kind of fact as to the other kinds.

If experiments are to be made in the field of morality, it must be kept in mind that, like experiments in other areas, they are performed within a frame of reference or within a structure of beliefs and agreements. These beliefs and agreements, which are usually taken for granted, rest on past experience, on both explicit and implicit commitments of various kinds, and on faith in certain principles and assumptions. That life is worth living, that there is some meaning in the universe, that it is better to be rational than irrational, and that the world can be made better, are principles for which there is much evidence. If people believe that the world can be made better and if they put forth effort to make it so, they may not reach their goals completely, but they are likely to live in a better world than if they had not held these beliefs and tried to fulfill them. To remain always in a critical mood may mean failure where success is possible. In making experiments we need to respect the agreements and commitments into which we have entered, since the deepest and richest experiences of life arise only when there are trust and confidence. The bonds of matrimony and professional and business commitments are of this nature.

IS IT EVER RIGHT TO COMPROMISE?

There is often a considerable gap between our ideal, the choice or way we believe to be best, and the action that seems possible under the circumstances we face. Since this is true, is there any place for compromise? May an agreement or a promise ever be broken? Are there exceptions that may be made to what is ordinarily considered the line of duty?

The term *compromise* is used when, by means of partial concessions, we make a practical adjustment of two rival positions or courses of action. Compromise involves concessions, adjustments, or the waiving of some claim or right. Compromise may also involve mutual concessions involving some issue that has arisen between two individuals or groups. It may connote the contrast between the agreement, standard, or ideal of an individual and the course of action he selects.

Men of intelligence and good will often disagree as to what is best. Traditionally, where an irresolvable disagreement of this kind has arisen, either there has been a compromise or one side has overpowered the other, and the basis for the disagreement has continued unresolved. Politics has been called the art of effective compromise. The leaders of two parties may come together and work out some compromise to which both parties can agree, or one party which has a majority may force its will and pass the legislative measure strictly along party lines. There is another possibility that should increasingly be used. It is one in which a temporary arrangement is made that reflects as fairly as possible the highest priority concerns of the disagreeing parties. It further provides, however, for some experimentation that would resolve at least the most crucial of the sources of the disagreement. Some political measures are passed with the understanding that they are experimental in nature and will be reviewed within a specified time. In exploring these possibilities, let us first consider types of compromise.

There are three generalizations that can be made about compromise. First, there are some types that are clearly wrong. In fact, the term *compromise* itself has an unpleasant connotation for many people. Here it means laxity or indifference toward some agreement, standard, or principle, or doing what one ought not do because of fear, avarice, or some other inadequate reason. To indulge some personal desire at the expense of our principles, whether we give way completely or "split the difference" between a line of duty and some vice, is immoral. Our repugnance for the person who cannot stand against social pressure makes it easy for us to condemn all compromise of this type.

The man who is true to his convictions and who lives consistently is admired. For some people this statement may seem to be all that is needed. But such is not the case in the realm of reflective morality. We do admire the man who is true to his convictions, but we also dislike the fanatic who is legalistic and intolerant and who wrecks good causes by refusing to make concessions. Right action is positive and personal rather than merely formal and negative. In an imperfect and changing society conflicts of obligations and loyalties often present themselves to individuals and groups. Compromises sometimes may be required if peaceful adjustments are to be made. This leads to our next generalization.

Second, in some situations compromise is the way to the achievement of higher values and to social progress. Here compromise means acceptance of a solution less than what he considers ideal but as good as he can get when agreement or accommodation is essential to the best outcome. Life requires that we make continuous adjustment to the ideas and convictions of other members of society. Any orderly, peaceful society requires such interaction, accommodation, and adjustment. In small groups of like-minded people, where relationships and contacts are on a personal basis and conflicts are few, there is little need of compromise. The same is true of small organizations and societies that people may join and leave by choice or desire. As groups become larger and more impersonal and as we pass to larger groups like the state, where choice of membership is restricted or even nonexistent, the situation is different. In government and the fields of law and politics, in industrial relationships, and in the relations between states or nations, adjustment can be secured only by give-and-take, by compromise. In some of these relationships the way of adjustment and compromise may be essential if open conflict is to be avoided. As long as partisan groups insist on getting their own way, and as long as nations insist on their right of absolute sovereignty and refuse to consider any interests but their own, progress toward a better world will be impeded.

Those who have wide experience serving on committees and commissions or attending conferences where action is to be taken know that the final report seldom embodies the complete wish or will of any single member of the group. It is typically a compromise that all members accept because it gives harmony, or an adjustment that enables action to continue and progress to be made.

Third, it is essential to keep moving in the right direction. Compromise may be upward or downward. We do not usually need to lower our ideals. They are to be maintained as guides to action. Some of them can be achieved practically; others tend to recede into the future, or they change their form. In any case, we get our direction from them. An intelligent philosophy of compromise will keep men from becoming either disloyal or hypocritical in the presence of ideals, will enable them to take action, and will guide them to an ever higher level of living.

The stand a man should take in specific circumstances cannot be determined in advance by rules. When competing loyalties or duties are involved and when the two sides in a dispute are balanced fairly evenly, two or more equally intelligent, conscientious persons may decide on different courses of action. This arises in part out of different experiences and backgrounds and in part from man's inability to predict the future. The essence of a reflective morality is willingness to weigh the factors involved and to decide on the basis of one's judgment of the relative values.

BRINGING OUR MORALS UP TO DATE

Our great-grandfathers lived in a society that was predominantly rural, agricultural, individualistic, and self-sufficient. We live in a society that is predominantly urban, industrial, complex, and interdependent. Recent generations have seen the end of free land and pioneer conditions, the spread of the industrial and scientific revolutions, increasing control by private individuals of many of our great natural resources, the growth of great corporations, and the growing dependence of both farmer and businessman on world markets. These changes have come on us so rapidly that we have found it difficult to adjust our thinking and our moral codes to them.

In the early nineteenth century if a gentleman or his wife were insulted, he would challenge the insulter to a duel to maintain his "honor." The duel itself was held under a rigid set of rules. Today dueling is considered not only immoral, but, in most parts of the world, illegal. Once men took breathing of fresh air pretty much for granted. Today with gas fumes and smog in some cities and with radioactive dust in the air at times, the availability of pure air takes on moral significance. Once nations declared war over issues that today merely lead to protests, if they are not actually ignored. Some things once called right, we now call wrong; some things once called wrong, we now call right. New occasions and new knowledge teach new duties in many areas of life.

A simple illustration from the field of milk distribution shows our modern problem. About a hundred and fifty years ago there were scattered farms where the city of Chicago now stands. One farmer with a surplus might sell one or two quarts of milk to a neighbor. The farmer's boy, or his neighbor's, ordinarily made the delivery. In this simple transaction there were few problems and little likehood of injustice. Today there are perhaps eighteen thousand farmers, some of whom have large herds, who supply the Chicago area with milk. The task of the small boy is now handled by more than one hundred corporations with fifteen thousand men in a milk-distributors' union. The neighbors, the purchasers of milk, have grown to considerably more than four million people. The possibility of manipulation, of control, and of injustice is much greater. Think of this changed condition as applying to a great number of commodities, then magnify it so as to include national and world trade, and you can see the magnitude of our modern problem.

Morality and Secondary Group Relations

The changes mentioned above have brought a host of new moral problems and have led to the development of many secondary group relations distinct from those of the primary group. Primary groups, where contacts between persons are of the intimate, face-to-face type (home, play groups, companions), are the groups most important in the development of personality including the formation of habits and early ideas and ideals. In the modern world, because of the increasing complexity of society, life is becoming dominated more and more by secondary and institutional groups where people meet only for a particular purpose or only in one segment of life. Increased specialization and division of labor have altered in numerous ways the forms of human relationship.

Our traditional moral codes were formulated under simple primary group relationships and are often silent or give little guidance to men who live under the new institutions and ways of doing things. Modern society is characterized by interdependence. More than ever before, men's lives are at the mercy of their fellowmen, not only on the highway but also in the matters of the food they eat, the water they drink, and the air they breathe. This interdependence has created numerous new forms of wrongdoing. Long-range immorality is possible since our acts may injure people who live at a distance and whom we do not see. Men need virtues such as honesty and kindness, but they also need insight and social consciousness. Some of the great wrongs of our time are perpetrated by men who are honest and kind in their personal relations but lack the vision and the knowledge to foresee clearly the social effects of their acts.

The rise of corporations—with the separation of ownership and management, limited liability of shareholders, and other financial, industrial, and political devices—has greatly lengthened the range of human contacts. It has made possible great concentration of wealth and power and has tended to make human relationships more and more impersonal and to conceal from man the effects of his actions. While the corporation has made real contributions to human welfare, it has also brought new opportunities for doing wrong.

Also during the last hundred years, new forms of property have come into being. In the area of business activity, in place of actual mills or factories over which the owner had direct supervision and for which he felt personally responsible, the predominant type of ownership is now one in which the owner holds "shares" or pieces of paper representing his ownership in the enterprise. The owner, in this latter sense, has little control and may feel little if any responsibility for the operation of the property. These mobile shares of stock or other tokens pass from people to people and require little or no attention. The owner merely expects the management or "control" to show a profit.[2]

While most business and professional men are honest and law-abiding they are frequently placed in a difficult position because of a conflict of interest between their personal convictions and interests and the interests of the groups they represent, or between either of these and the

---

[2]This point of view, widely defended by early capitalists, is still supported by some businessmen and economists. See Milton Friedman, "The Social Responsibility of Businss Is to Increase Its Profits," *New York Times Magazine*, 13 September 1970, pp. 32–33, 122–126.

larger interests of the community or nation. This problem may be a very real and pressing one for the corporation official, the lawyer, the journalist, or the banker. The power to hire, to fire, to evict, to grant or withhold credit, to enter into price-fixing and market-dividing deals has far-reaching consequences for individuals and communities.

The Supreme Court of the United States has ruled that an official may be held liable for violations of law by a corporation of which he is an officer. Therefore, it is now possible to hold officials responsible, individually as well as collectively, for any illegal and immoral acts in which they are participants. No man should carry out orders that he knows are opposed to both law and social welfare. Today we urgently need to apply our accepted principles of morality to our new group and institutional relationships.

PRINCIPLES THAT NEED WIDER APPLICATION

Let us consider a few moral precepts that are almost universally recognized but that call for more general application in today's world.

Thou Shalt Not Kill. Respect for human life is basic if civilization is to survive. If one man kills another man, we call it murder or manslaughter and it is strongly condemned as immoral. Today there are many ways of killing, some of which have not sufficiently come under public condemnation. Consider the following: the group that gains monopoly control of some needed food or drug supply and sets exorbitant prices and thus limits use; food adulteration; dilapidated tenement houses; defective construction of buildings; quack doctoring; ignoring regulations of the health department or mine inspector; farmers who refuse to have cows tuberculin tested or who, after they know there is infection, continue to sell the milk; the pollution of air, water, or earth; the reckless operation of vehicles. The reader will probably be able to extend this listing. Life in society will be increasingly precarious unless we all become more aware of, and sensitive to, these modern forms of injury and killing.

Thou Shalt Not Lie. We cannot develop a good society and carry on our normal relations with people except on the basis of mutual trust and confidence. Yet the widespread practice of lying in wholesale form, as in some types of journalism, advertising, and propaganda, is frequently passed over with a shrug of the shoulders. Some newspapers print only one side of certain issues or print statements out of context so that they give false impressions. Advertisers often say what they think will sell merchandise regardless of the truth of the claim. We severely condemn misrepresentation on the part of individuals, but our moral principles and our practices have not been brought up to date in their application to our group relationships.

Thou Shalt Not Steal. Respect for the possessions of others is also essential for an orderly, peaceful society. If a man takes a dollar from a person's pocket, the latter is rightfully indignant. What is strange is that he is not equally indignant when a group takes many dollars from his pocket. Are corporations or the members of some other groups justified in charging excessively high prices for an article simply by reason of the fact that they have been able to gain a near-monopoly of some needed commodity or by reason of their superior strength and bargaining power? Holding up prices is merely a modern form of piracy. Shall we call it stealing when an organization refuses to pay workers what they earn or when it forces wages down below what is a reasonable level? Such practices may be more harmful to personality and social welfare than taking a dollar occasionally from men's pockets. They need to be branded as the immoral acts they are.

Individuals and groups may steal by means of fraudulent promotion, monopolies, watered stock, tax-dodging, manipulating an election, using "pull" to get a franchise unfairly, and so on. If it is wrong for me to steal from you, is it not equally wrong for one nation to seize a hundred thousand square miles of territory from another nation? If we are to bring our morals up to date, then the accepted principles of living must be applied also to our group relationships.

New Traits of Character Needing Emphasis

Under changing social conditions the virtues that are emphasized may vary from age to age, as we have seen. The medieval age, with its other-worldly ideal, stressed humility; feudal leaders stressed honor and courage; a capitalist society stresses initiative, self-reliance, and material success. As society seeks to protect itself from abuses arising from excessive emphasis on self-interest, the concept of social welfare has come more and more to the forefront of attention. While we continue to respect the old virtues like justice, courage, and self-control, we will need to cultivate qualities of character less evident in the past. These will include cooperation and a willingness to share, tolerance, open-mindedness, reliability and a sense of responsibility, international-mindedness or the cosmopolitan spirit, a concern for all people as persons, and a desire to conserve the resources and beauties of nature.

A greater concern for all people as persons would express itself in more adequate support for measures such as public health, recreation, housing, and education. Our affluent society is marked by a sharp contrast between the way money is spent so lavishly on personal and family possessions and so grudgingly on projects for the welfare of the entire community or for the care of its less priviledged members. Many sections of many of our cities are not fit for human habitation and consequently breed disease, crime, and delinquency. Unless we are willing to share the benefits of our civilization with all members of society and the world at large, we may not be able to retain them indefinitely for ourselves.

Man's concern for other people and for the world needs to include a new ethical attitude toward nature. "The golden rule," says Julian Huxley, the biologist, "applies to man's relations with nature as well as to relations between human beings." He points out that "plants, animals, soil, water, man—all are parts of one seamless garment. You cannot tear it anywhere without destroying it."[3] The wanton disfiguring of nature and the careless and wasteful exploitation of its resources are immoral. There is a moral obligation to conserve the life-giving bounties and the beauties of nature.

INDIVIDUAL VERSUS GROUP MORALITY

There are those who claim that a distinction must be made between individual moral standards and conduct, on the one hand, and the behavior of professional and social groups and organizations on the other hand. There are elements, they say, in man's collective behavior that cannot readily be brought under the guidance of reason and conscience. Relations between groups will be more ruthless than relations between individuals, especially where self-preservation is at stake.

Group selfishness is an exceedingly dangerous kind of selfishness. While masquerading under the cloak of loyalty to one's group, one may do much harm to other groups and to social welfare in general. Sociologists make a distinction between the *in-group* or *we-group* and the *out-group* or *other-group*. Toward members of our in-group we may have sympathy and affection and show attitudes of cooperation, loyalty, and mutual aid, while harboring an attitude of avoidance, suspicion, hatred, or even in extreme cases actual warfare toward the out-group. During World War II the allies were an in-group. Other in-groups may be one's race, gang, club, church, or a faction within any of these groups.

---

[3] Julian Huxley, *The Human Crisis* (Seattle: University of Washington Press, 1963), p. 24.

The family is usually a strong in-group, but men urgently need the insight to see that the highest loyalty to the family does not ordinarily conflict with loyalty to one's city or nation, and that our duty is not to further the interests of one group at the expense of another but to further the interests of mankind as a whole. We have not grown up morally and spiritually until the in-group becomes the human family as a whole.

The relations between groups is a field into which the moral consciousness and the thoughts of men have not penetrated deeply. The clashes between classes, between business groups, and between nations have been bitter and difficult to eradicate. The loyal attitudes of individuals toward groups may blind them to the antagonistic attitudes of groups toward one another. A laborer's loyal support of his union may give him a sense of exalted satisfaction while he is supporting a labor program that may be detrimental to the interests of the community. A businessman's devotion to his company or to his trade association may blind him to the immoral nature of his activities. Part of the problem of ethics is to help men free themselves from the bias of narrow self-interest and the pressure of group opinion and to develop a concern for the welfare of the larger communities of which they are a part. "No man is an island," and the same may be said of any group.

Before closing the discussion of bringing our morals up to date let us ask, as a number of students of our age have done, if we have probed deeply enough in examining our moral standards. Is it possible that our morality is itself immoral? Kyle Haselden points out that men tend to isolate their sense of morality from specific areas of life and asks, "Do we not judge what is right and what is wrong in racial relationships by a righteousness which is itself unrighteousness, by codes and creeds which are themselves immoral?"[4] Erich Fromm calls our attention to conditions such as outbursts of destructiveness and paranoid suspicion; the high degree of mental illness and mental disturbances that lead to suicide, homicide, and alcoholism; and an economic system in which a big crop is often a disaster to many people. He then asks, "Are we sane?"[5] Is it possible that society as a whole is maladjusted and lacking in sanity? James Warburg in a chapter titled "How Civilized Is Our Civilization?" sees a danger of decline in the condition of Western morality. He says, "Our civilization has for centuries practiced neither the Jewish teaching of justice under moral law nor the Greek teaching

---

[4] *The Racial Problem* (New York: Harper & Row, Publishers, Torchbook, 1964), p. 48.
[5] *The Sane Society* (New York: Rinehart & Co., 1955), ch. 1.

of rational thought and behavior, and least of all the Christian teaching of love, compassion, and human brotherhood."[6]

Many of our ideals and principles—treat persons as ends, not as means, for example—appear to be unimpeachable. The real problems seem to be the gap between principles and practice, and our "double morality" which limits the application of our principles when it comes to certain areas of human life and relationships. In previous chapters we have pointed out many of these inconsistencies between principles and practices, and we shall not repeat them here.

Improvement in public morality as distinct from private morality must wait, first, until a proportionately larger number of persons attain the level of reflective morality and, second, until individuals are made to feel a sense of individual responsibility for the acts of the groups of which they are a part.

The problem of bringing our morals up to date is a continuous one. Should we do this now and then forget about them, they would soon be out of date again and there would be new maladjustments. That is because growth is a law of life—of individual life and of social life. A keen moral sense, imagination, and intelligence are continuously needed. The progress we have made in the past gives us hope for the future.

QUESTIONS AND PROJECTS

1. Infants tend to put their hands out to touch fire, a hot stove, or some other object of danger. One mother pulls her child back and says, "Don't go near. If you do, I'll slap you." The child stays away from the danger because of the threat and the authority of the mother. Another mother, in such a situation, takes the child's hand holding it near the heat so that his own mechanism of withdrawal will be stimulated as she explains the danger involved. She helps the child do some experimenting of his own in order to know the real nature of heat. Which approach is likely to lead the child to moral maturity?
2. Discuss the following examples of adventurous action, indicating whether you think the term *experiment* may properly be applied to them, and whether or not you consider them experiments in the area of moral conduct.
    (1) In 1971 the President of the United States declared a freeze on wages and prices for a period, because of the fear of runaway inflation and the unfortunate state of the economy.
    (2) Many bills passed by Congress are said to be experimental and are supported to see if their effects are beneficial to the country as a whole.

---

[6]*The West in Crisis* (Garden City: Doubleday & Co., 1959), pp. 16–17.

(3) A group of young churchmen volunteer and train for a summer's effort to register black voters in parts of the country where there is strong local resistance to such efforts. The churchmen enter into commitments to one another, to their churches, and to the nation that involve considerable personal risk.

(4) A group of experimental colleges was formed in 1964 to encourage experimentation in higher education and to engage in it themselves.

(5) During the 1930s, Judge Ben Lindsey of Colorado gained notoriety for advocating companionate marriage to permit young people to test their compatibility before lifelong commitment.

3. A student who has been working long and conscientiously at his studies has been getting only mediocre grades. He is eager to make good grades because he wants to repay his parents for the sacrifice they are making to keep him in college. He realizes that he is getting lower grades because many of the other members of his class are copying or receiving illegitimate help, thus forcing down the grades of those who are not cheating. Shall he accept the lower grades and say nothing? Shall he report to the professor that the others are cheating? Shall he himself cheat?

4. A jeweler is shown a ring by a young woman, who asks a question about the setting and quality of the stone. On examination he discovers that the stone is not a genuine diamond. If he discloses this fact it may break up a romance. If he tells her that it is real, he will be false to his professional ideal. What is his duty?

5. A student has built a personal library of considerable size by joining book clubs, getting the bonus books offered, and then withdrawing from the clubs without buying more books. He argues that in making the offer the clubs admit that this can happen and that they make no effort to stop the practice. Is it ethical to join such clubs with the intention of buying only the initial bargain? Do the conditions set by the clubs or the explicit or implicit agreements play a part in your decision?

6. While working for a large company, a man makes many trips out of town in order to make business contacts. The company allows him travel expenses. Every now and then his friends invite him to stay at their homes, and thus occasionally he gets a room and meals without charge. His friends are doing this favor for him and not to assist the company. Is it morally right for him to add to his expense account the amount he would normally pay if he stayed at hotels and ate all his meals at restaurants?

7. A minister of a church in a fairly wealthy residential district occasionally speaks out against racial prejudice and discrimination. He has suggested a number of specific ways in which the members of the congregation may cooperate with other racial groups in the vicinity. A prospective donor who may make it possible for the group to build a new educational building to increase the effectiveness of the church program is opposed to the minister's views on racial equality. In a conversation, the prospective donor tells the minister that he disagrees with the latter's views on racial issues. The minister has been planning for the new addition for many years, and he agrees to preach on different subjects in the

future. The church gets its new building. Is the minister's change of emphasis right or wrong?

8. The directors of a railway company reject the recommendation of one of their managers that they provide a certain safety device for their trains at a total cost of several thousand dollars. Soon after this an accident occurs in which a number of men are killed. This accident probably could have been prevented had the safety device been provided. To what extent were the directors responsible for the deaths of the men because of their refusal to provide the safety appliances?

9. A young man was confined to the college hospital for three days. Since he was pressed for funds, he asked and was permitted to go to his own room for further recuperation. His fraternity was participating in a swimming meet and needed his swimming ability, and members of the group urged him to take part. After some hesitation, he went. The result was that he was forced to return to the hospital and remain there until it was safe for him to travel to his home in another city. The student paper on the campus suggested that the following inscription be engraved on the trophy: "This two-dollar cup cost one of our boys a semester." Discuss this case and be ready to give similar examples. Is this a case of an injustice growing out of group loyalty?

10. A federal judge sentenced the manager and owner of a restaurant to four months in jail because he had forced a waitress in his employ to pass a counterfeit ten-dollar note she had accepted by mistake during the manager's absence. Do you agree with the decision of the judge?

11. Incidents involving conflict of loyalty between one's personal convictions and what is required of employees in a profession or a business occur frequently. For example, a man on a newspaper staff supports the United States Supreme Court decision on integration but is asked by his editor-in-chief to write a stinging article against that decision; or a man who is a lover and advocate of classical music is asked by the advertising director of his company to take charge of a television program featuring rock 'n' roll. Can you give other examples?

12. What major trends are taking place in our society? State how many of the following you would be willing to include in your list: toward world government, toward a social-service view of the state, toward use of noneconomic motives (such as the creative urge, the desire for public approval, loyalty to family or group), toward racial understanding, toward reflective morality.

SUGGESTED READINGS

Adler, Mortimer J. *The Time of Our Lives: The Ethics of Common Sense.* New York: Holt, Rinehart & Winston, 1970.

Allen, Frederick Lewis. *The Big Change: America Transforms Itself, 1900—1950.* New York: Harper & Brothers, 1952.
Blanshard, Brand. *Reason and Goodness.* New York: Macmillan Co., 1961.
Conover, C. Eugene. *Personal Ethics in an Impersonal World.* Philadelphia: Westminster Press, 1967.
Hart, Samuel L. *Ethics: The Quest for the Good Life.* New York: Philosophical Library, 1963.
Hocking, William Ernest. *Strength of Man and Nations.* New York: Harper & Brothers, 1959.
Huxley, Julian. *The Human Crisis.* Essay 1. Seattle: University of Washington Press, 1963.
Johnson, A. H. *Whitehead's Philosophy of Civilization.* Boston: Beacon Press, 1958.
Johnson, F. Ernest. *Patterns of Ethics in America Today.* New York: Collier Books, 1962.
Lepp, Ignace. *The Authentic Morality.* Translated by Bernard Murchland. New York: Macmillan Co., 1965.
Macbeath, Alexander. *Experiments in Living.* London: Macmillan Co., 1952.
McKeon, R. "Mankind: The Relation of Reason to Action." *Ethics* 74 (April 1964):174–185.
"New Morality: What, Why—and Why Not?" Symposium in *Religion in Life* 35 (Spring 1966):170–229.
Toulmin, Stephen E. *An Examination of the Place of Reason in Ethics.* Cambridge: Cambridge University Press, 1950.
Wilson, John. *Reason and Morals.* Cambridge: Cambridge University Press, 1961.

13
VALUES, RIGHTS, AND OBLIGATIONS

Before we make the transition in part 2 to the application of our principles of morality to specific problems of personal and social living, we need an overview of the various rights and responsibilities that human experience has demonstrated to be of worth as men and women seek fulfillment. This examination of the relationship among values, rights, and obligations will throw light on the specific problems we face as we live in today's world.

Life forces us, both as individuals and as groups, to make value judgments. Valuing occurs whenever anything—a physical object, a way of acting, an idea or ideal, a person—is preferred or chosen. We rate things as better or worse and act on these decisions and ratings. The issue is not whether we are going to have loyalties and ideals around which our lives are organized, but what kind they will be. Will they be consistent or inconsistent? Will they be mutually supporting or mutually interfering and lead to conflicts? Will they further self-development or hinder it? To assist in making specific moral inferences from abstract standards such as "Seek the fulfillment of the individual in a community" or "Seek the greatest happiness," we need guidelines of intermediate-level abstraction. Such guidelines can state our priorities among the available choices and modes of action for the betterment of life. Thus help can be given in determining which of several alternatives might best be conducive to the richest fulfillment or greatest happiness in a specific situation.

THE GROUNDING AND SELECTION OF VALUES

Most men and women are anxious to see the increase of decency, justice, freedom, love, beauty, and devotion to truth, and to see the decrease of brutality, tyranny, bondage, hate, ugliness, and falsehood. Some values are embedded in habits, customs and traditions, and in the legal enactments that we find in practically all societies. But do values have any more secure grounding in the scheme of things? Are they more than ephemeral elements in the "passing show"? Apart from some groups like the extreme skeptics, nihilists, and subjectivists on the one hand, and the positivists and materialists on the other hand, values have been justified from a number of points of view including the following two.

During the past twenty-five hundred years, Western philosophy with its origin in Greece and the Judaeo-Christian outlook with its source in Palestine furnished Western thinkers with a world view, a life view, and a scale of values by which to live. This outlook was accepted by most thinkers in Western Europe and spread to those parts of the world where Western civilization came to prevail. According to this view, there are certain basic or persistent values. They are given to men by God or they are grounded in the very nature of the universe. They transcend the phenomenal world which we contact by means of our senses and which is studied by the various sciences. Beyond this world of the senses and the sciences is a more permanent order of reality about which such disciplines as metaphysics or speculative philosophy, theology, ethics, aesthetics, and logic seek to tell us something. Because there is a moral order we have justification for calling some things right and others wrong, some things good and others evil. In a similar way, because there is an aesthetic order, some things are beautiful and others ugly; and because there is an order of truth, some things are true and others false. Some people say that alongside of the good, the true, and the beautiful, they would add the holy. Some have suggested that happiness (bliss) should also be added to the list of the eternal values.

During the last century or two this so-called Great Tradition has been under attack by men in different fields who have left behind absolute and authoritative systems. They are critical of metaphysics in general and claim that knowledge comes from experience or mainly through the senses and is organized by the mind or the self. We see here the influence of such philosophies as pragmatism or instrumentalism, personalism, and the various process philosophies. In this approach the ground of values is found in the nature of man. Just as in science the quest is for knowledge and truth, so in moral philosophy the quest is for the fulfillment of the human person or the good life in a community of persons. This quest is a continuous one since conditions change and knowledge is accumulating at a rapid rate.

We shall make no attempt to set forth any rigid classification of values (moral, aesthetic, intellectual, religious, scientific, economic, and so on). The reader may wish to consult the more specialized studies of value and value theory, a field known as *axiology*—from the Greek *axios* meaning "value." In considering the ranking of values as higher or lower there are certain widely accepted principles which it is well to keep clearly in mind. We briefly mention four. First, of two values that we can achieve, the greater ought to be chosen or sought. Where we are forced to choose between two evils, we should choose the lesser evil. This principle is implicit in the notion of comparative worth. The terms *greater* and *lesser* should sometimes be taken figuratively, referring to settled social preference rather than to quantities that we can add and subtract. The idea of comparative worth requires that there be some sense in which some values are ranked above others.

Second, an intrinsic value, that is, one which has worth in its own right, is ordinarily to be sought in preference to one that is extrinsic or has instrumental worth only. An intrinsic value is an end in itself. For example, beauty, truth, love, and strength of character would be considered intrinsic values by most persons. Money and most other possessions as well as position and fame would be placed on a lower level. Intrinsic and extrinsic values are not always either mutually exclusive or fixed. What is valued by one person for its own sake may be valued by another person merely as a means to an end—for example, a work of art.

We need to avoid two extremes. One is to seek immediate enjoyment or pleasure at all times. This is the weakness of most immature persons. The other danger is always to be postponing enjoyment and failing to enjoy things for what they are. The habit of looking at things only as instruments to later enjoyment can cause a withering away of much of our capacity to enjoy.

Third, the productive values are to be sought rather than the unproductive. Some relations and activities, such as friendship and learning, increase in productiveness as they are cultivated. To share these values with others is not to lessen the value for oneself. The more widespread they are the more productive they are. In this respect they are in marked contrast to material values which diminish in quantity as they are shared and used.

Finally, lasting values ought to be chosen rather than transient ones. By "lasting" values we mean those that, once created or achieved, continue to be valued. Thus, while a car is relatively durable, it will wear out, whereas a quality of patience or truthfulness developed in one's character will not. Human experience has shown that the values called social, intellectual, aesthetic, and religious tend not only to be productive but also to be more lasting than those called economic or material.

To sum up, in every society men accumulate experience concerning the ways of living that best apply these four principles in their situation: (1) Seek the greater of two alternative values. (2) Select a value that has worth in itself over one that has instrumental worth only, and a present good to a future one that has no greater intrinsic worth. (3) Choose the more productive of two otherwise equivalent values. (4) Choose the more permanent or lasting values, other things being equal.

VALUES AND RIGHTS

Recognition of the ranking of values leads to recognition of certain human rights. A right is a claim to an achievable condition that the individual and his society need for a better life. If there is something available and indispensable to a good life, it is man's right to have it. Man also has a right to some things if their absence will impoverish him or their presence will enrich him, provided it is within the means of society justly to supply them with appropriate effort on his own part. Rights thus have meaning only within a society. The rights of an individual are not constant; they are relative to time and to place and they depend on social conditions. A right is not usually created by law —it is recognized and protected by law.

Since rights are based on other values, the recognition of a value greater than those already achieved should lead to the recognition of the right to share in it insofar as the means are available. Two centuries ago, for example, a free education was not claimed as a right. The recognition of the value of education, however, led people to see that every child should be given, first an elementary, then a secondary, education. Now the talk is of adding whatever college and post-graduate education the youth is capable of best using.

In political discussions as well as in most of our industrial disputes we hear much about rights. The employer talks about the rights of business—the conditions he feels valuable from the point of view of his success in business. The laborer talks about the rights of labor—the conditions he feels are necessary for the wholesome life of workers. Other groups voice their claims with equal vigor. When the discussions have been more specific, we have heard about the right of private property, the right of contract, the right to work, the right to organize, and so on. To say that life is an essential value or that a person has a right to live is to recognize that he has a right to those things essential to life insofar as his culture, with his appropriate effort, can provide them. Are there rights today that our society does not but should recognize? Should the list of human rights change with changing times? For thousands of years men have appealed to certain rights that they felt were theirs in a special sense. These rights, they have felt, are based on nature. The doctrine of "natural rights" goes back at least to the great thinkers of ancient Greece. It played an important part in the great struggles of the eighteenth century. The colonies, in the Declaration of Independence, based their claim to independence on "certain unalienable rights," among which were "life, liberty, and the pursuit of happiness." While neither the Articles of Confederation nor the Constitution of the United States, as originally ratified, contained a list of rights, there were those who desired such a declaration. The first ten amendments to the Constitution, added in 1791, were regarded by Jefferson and others as such a declaration. Many of the states starting with Virginia in 1776 included such a declaration or bill of rights in their constitutions.

Stripped of features peculiar to different times and places, the doctrine of natural rights expresses three claims: (1) that a person has some rights which apply no matter what the circumstances or the culture, (2) that these rights are due him whether or not his society or government recognizes them, and (3) that these rights are inalienable —the person may not surrender them nor the society take them away for any cause. In the seventeenth and eighteenth centuries a typical advocate of natural rights based these claims on two further ideas: (4) that all men share the same essential nature and needs, and (5) that by divine ordering or simply in the nature of things, certain rights such as those to life, liberty, and property are implied by the very idea of treating a man according to his essential nature.

Today most advocates of human rights disagree with at least one of these five ideas, and they talk about "human rights" rather than "natural rights." In this changing world, notions of a fixed natural order such as were held in earlier times are hard to defend. The theory of natural rights, held as part of the doctrine of individualism in the eighteenth century, was used to defend a kind of property and social arrangement quite different from that which exists today. At least in the field of the social studies, leaders are in considerable agreement that the test of any program or institution must be its social desirability. Not some supposed natural right but present value for human life is the test which must be applied. There must be evidence that the claim will add to the total realization of life. Any theory of rights must be in harmony with this principle.

In previous chapters we have pointed out ways in which the culture and circumstances affect what is good and what is right, even though they do not provide a sufficient standard of good and right. They similarly affect rights. For example, consider monopolies. If circumstances prevent any person or group from obtaining a monopoly of a product, price-fixing by government is unnecessary interference with freedom to use one's own labor to profit in the market. Circumstances today do not prevent monopolies unless a government intervenes. Does such a change of circumstances affect not only the ways private property may rightly be used but, in some situations, the very right to property itself?

It is not our purpose here to review the arguments for competing theories of human rights. We shall, instead, discuss some rights and obligations that arise from values that rank high among human concerns. As we do so, we shall consider in what respects these rights and duties pertain to peculiar conditions or customs, and in what respects they are of more general relevance.

HUMAN RIGHTS

In the struggles of the past, certain values and hence certain rights were considered fundamental. Further rights are claimed in recent discussions that have grown out of new legislation, industrial disputes, and conferences and groups, such as the White House conferences on social issues. Anyone who talks to his neighbor and to the man in the street will find that they claim still further rights which they believe should be recognized and protected.

Three recent documents are of special significance in the discussion of rights. The first, a study of civil rights in the United States, is titled *To Secure These Rights*.[1] This study shows that the struggle for human rights is far from won, even in democratic countries.

In 1960 there appeared a report of the President's Commission on National Goals entitled *Goals for Americans*.[2] It defines aspirations—recognized values that we can provide if we will organize and commit ourselves appropriately—that can be expected to generate further revisions in our view of our rights in American society. The third document, *The Universal Declaration of Human Rights*,[3] is worldwide in its significance and scope. After discussions lasting some years, it was pre-

---

[1] President's Committee on Civil Rights (New York: Simon & Schuster, 1947).

[2] *The Report of the President's Commission on National Goals* (Englewood Cliffs, N.J.: Prentice-Hall, 1960).

[3] Department of State, International Organization and Conference Series, III, 20 (1949).

sented to the United Nations Assembly and adopted in 1948. Representatives of forty-eight nations signed the declaration, which was then submitted to the member nations. By the 1970s, standards set by the declaration have been written into a considerable number of national constitutions; many nations have ratified conventions to outlaw genocide, abolish slavery, and promote equal rights for women; and between forty and fifty former colonial territories, with a total population of two hundred fifty million, have gained self-government. The nations of the world, however, still have a long way to go to implement the declaration in spirit and in practice.

The fundamental rights which all men today demand are the claims made by the individual on the state or the social group of which he is a part. In some cases they are the claims made by minorities or small groups on the majority or the group in power. Call them natural rights, God-given rights, or just social or human rights that are instrumental and functional, they are based on the nature of man and on the conditions necessary for the development of his potentialities as a person. They are the conditions of life without which a person cannot live at his best.

For those who accept a totalitarian view of the state, rights tend to disappear entirely. From this "statist" point of view, the formula "society for individuals" must be revised to read "individuals for society." In this case, the state has rights and individuals have only duties, or at least only those rights that the state wishes to grant them. For those who reject the above approach, as we do, the state is not an end in itself but a means for the promotion of justice and social well-being. Institutions are good or bad in proportion as they promote or fail to promote these conditions. Human rights grow out of the mutuality of individual and social relations, and they express a position that is neither extreme individualism nor extreme statism.

The Rights of Man

Any list of human rights will need to be restated from time to time as conditions of life change. The following ten rights, however, are among the most basic today, and they are coming to be so recognized by society. They appear to be necessary conditions for human development. The fact that they are relative and functional makes it difficult to state their exact nature and scope apart from the specific conditions in which they are to function. If pressed to an extreme, some of them may seem to overlap or to conflict with other rights—for example, the right to freedom and the right to security. It is part of the task of each age to determine the point at which one right must yield to another.

The human rights may be tentatively stated thus:

1. *The Right to Health.* Health is so important that without it life may be hardly worth living. Recognition of the right to health would mean that society would see that every person needing medical care received it. The importance of health is treated in the next chapter.

2. *The Right to Education.* This right is now recognized by our society and many other societies. We feel that every child has the right to an education, regardless of the ability of his parents to pay for it. Education and knowledge appear to be almost indispensable to the realization of other rights. Knowledge is essential for self-preservation as well as for creative achievement. Young people face a world of bewildering complexities. Such conditions call for a wide range of knowledge if coming generations are to meet the world's changing problems with resourcefulness and vision.

3. *The Right to Freedom.* The advantages of education and of democracy mean little if freedom of expression, such as freedom of opinion, of speech, and of the press, is denied.[4] The problems of intellectual freedom and the right to considerable privacy are discussed in a later chapter.

4. *The Right to Work and Receive a Living Wage.* Emphasis on this right was not so necessary in an agricultural civilization. With the development of a complex, industrial civilization, however, access to the means of livelihood is often beyond the control of the individual. Since the forces affecting a man's opportunity to earn are social, society must assume a responsibility and must recognize the human right to a means of livelihood. Because under ordinary conditions man can live only by means of work, to refuse him work is to deprive him of the opportunity to develop his personality. When work cannot be provided, it would appear that society is obligated to share with the individual the goods and services produced. In the numerous forms of relief and in the principles of unemployment insurance, society is coming to recognize this fact.

The mere right to work does not meet the needs of civilized society; we must stipulate the right to work at a wage sufficient for health and decency. Every man needs food, clothing, and shelter as a bare minimum

---

[4]President Franklin D. Roosevelt, in his State of the Union message to Congress on January 6, 1941, spoke about "The Four Freedoms: freedom of speech and expression, freedom to worship, freedom from want, and freedom from fear." See Walter Yust, ed. *10 Eventful Years: 1937 through 1946* (Chicago: Encyclopaedia Britannica, 1947), vol. 2, pp. 401–405.

for subsistence; and unless his personality is to be stunted, he needs a wide range of things that lift life above the level of the merely organic. Increasingly, men are beginning to question the right of a few to luxury before others have even a bare sufficiency.

5. *The Right to Security.* This right includes not only protection of life and property but also security against unemployment and economic provision for old age, sickness, and accident. Insecurity today affects the officials of industrial comporations, professional groups, and small businessmen as well as wage earners. Fear of the future has become one of the dominant fears. Since the age limit set by many private industries for hiring new employees is forty-five or even thirty-five, many workers over these ages find it impossible to secure positions. Perhaps the most tragic results of insecurity are found in the lives of the children of the unemployed. A feeling of insecurity is exceedingly destructive of human happiness.

6. *The Right to Love and a Home.* Love is here interpreted to include friends and companions. Because of the importance of intimate social contacts and a normal home life in the development of personality, each person has a right to the conditions that make the establishment of a family and a home possible. Care for the children during the long period of infancy is best provided by the family in the home. Every child has a right to be well born—to have a sound heredity—and to be reared in conditions that will make the development of a wholesome personality possible. Parents have a right to such information as will enable them to have children when they want them and when they are able to care for them properly.

7. *The Right to Recreation and to Leisure.* Under a machine system of production, the development of personality must come, for many people, in the hours of leisure. If the labor has any element of drudgery, probably a seven-hour or eight-hour day is the most man can work and still expect to understand and enjoy the complex life about him. Technical advance is making possible more leisure for all.

8. *The Right to a Share in Controlling the Conditions of Life.* This right includes the privilege of assisting in choosing the people by whom one is to be governed or of being chosen as a leader, if one can persuade others to choose him. This right to share in controlling the conditions of life has been accepted in principle in our political thinking. Today, however, men's lives are controlled almost completely by the industrial conditions under which they live. The power to hire and fire, to evict, to give or withhold credit, to produce goods or not to produce them may mean the power to give or to take away life. The claim to a share in

the control of the economic order may be as valid as the right to share in the control of the political order.

9. *The Right to Share in the Cultural Heritage of the Race, Including Art and Literature.* If rights are based on values, this claim appears to be valid. Man has aspirations toward the good, the beautiful, and the true. Unless he can fulfill and express these aspirations, he falls short of self-realization and lasting happiness. The values expressed in goodness, beauty, and truth are creations or discoveries of the race and belong to all individuals and classes. They belong to humanity, and if they are shared, all men will be the richer.

10. *The Right to Worship.* Every person should have the right to worship according to the dictates of his conscience. This includes the right to worship God or not to worship God. It includes the right of any person to change his religion or belief and to express his religious convictions, not only in private and public worship but through teaching and by means of religious organizations and activities.

Human Rights and the Social Order

Taking the above list of rights as tentative objectives, the reader will do well to consider each right separately, and to ask whether or not it is adequately recognized and safeguarded in the present social order. Are we subordinating life to the means of livelihood? Is it a fact, as some people assert, that human values and human welfare are often forgotten in our drive for wealth or power? Are these human rights usually placed first in politics, in business, the professions, and in human relations in general? What relation do such rights as health, work, and security have to discussions regarding minimum-wage legislation, social security, fair-employment-practices acts, the guaranteed annual wage, and the like? Does the doctrine of sovereignty ever interfere with the protection of human rights? Is the idea of government as an instrument of social welfare now being substituted for the concept of government known as *laissez faire*, or individualism? Can you give examples of conflict between property rights and human rights, between the right to security and the right to freedom, or between the right of adults to love and a home and the right of their offspring to be well born? How does one proceed when rights appear to be in conflict?

In later chapters we shall consider certain social problems in relation to human rights. War, racial hatred, power, unemployment, pollution and crime are among the major enemies of human values. Probably all of them could be eliminated or at least reduced if society would use the knowledge and the means available. Most of our problems are tied together and must be faced jointly. However, an emphasis on human rights may enable us to face them more intelligently.

As a nation we have been eager to progress, but we have not always been greatly concerned about the direction in which we are going. We have sought more and more money and more and more power, but we have not seriously inquired about the objects for which money and power should be used. We may have thought at times that money and power were good in themselves. Today we are beginning to realize that they have only instrumental value. We cannot move ahead intelligently until we have some clear, even though tentative, objectives. Clarity as to the ends that are desirable may be conducive to efficiency in the selection of means. It is even more important to reach correct conclusions about what we want than it is to reach correct conclusions about what to do in order to attain what we want, though the latter is also very important. If we gain a clear idea of human values and of the rights based on them and set them before us as our goals, we may be more willing to take the steps that will make their achievement possible.

OBLIGATIONS

For anyone to have a right, there must be someone—an individual, a group, society or its governing representatives—who has an obligation or duty to see that he is protected in this right. For example, while a child as a person has rights, his parents, who have brought him into the world or who have adopted him, have a special responsibility for his care while he is dependent. Society holds the parents accountable for such care and may, in extreme cases, place the child in the care of others. If all men have the right to life, liberty, and the pursuit of happiness, then we all have corresponding duties to respect the lives of others, to refrain from infringing on their liberties, and to refrain from placing avoidable obstacles in the way of their happiness. Thus for every right there is an obligation in some quarter or other. The one who has the right may under some circumstances forego the enjoyment of his right, as, for example, when he owns a piece of property and lets a neighbor use it in ways usually reserved to the owner only. There are circumstances, however, in which one should insist, if he can, on his rights. For example, if a student's acceding to improper invasion of his academic freedom would encourage a pattern of suppression of inquiry in the university, he should not voluntarily surrender the right. In such circumstances the right carries obligations for its beneficiary. In any case, he is obligated in another way: to use his rights for their intended purpose to the best of his ability. Thus if there is a right to work and to receive a living wage, those who enjoy these rights have the responsibility of giving a fair day's work for that wage. The right to security carries with it the duty of assisting in the defense of the group. The right to be well born implies corresponding obligations on the part of parents and of society toward future generations of children.

Obligations, like rights, are relative to the situation in which they are incurred, and they function to foster the betterment of life. Obligations arise from the nature of the relations of people to one another under a particular set of conditions. When conflicts between rights or between duties or even between rights and duties arise, the conflicts should be decided in the interest of the greater of the achievable net values. The values at stake, the needs of the persons involved, and other circumstances will bear on the decision as to what ought to be done in such conflicts. There is thus an overarching obligation to do, of all the things we can do, what serves the greatest good.

In deciding how we ought to act when duties and rights conflict, one of the critical circumstances is, often, that we have specific obligations growing out of the past. As a result, our decisions should differ from those we ought to make if we attended only to present circumstances. For example, there may be unmet promises, contracts, pledges, or an unmet need to make reparation for injuries. These specific obligations give some other party a right to expect something of us, even if the right is not an absolute one. When a greater evil or loss of good would result from fulfillment of the promise than from its nonfulfillment, there may be an obligation to set it aside, though the consequences of breaking a promise are themselves so extensive that they normally outweigh any social advantage that might accrue from making an exception. The fact that the discernment of obligation requires us to consider and weigh conflicting duties and rights has led many authors to distinguish between our obligations and what they call *prima facie* duties—that is, duties that stand unless in conflict with another *prima facie* duty or with a higher priority obligation.[5]

The Obligation to Exercise Due Care

Society expects each person to meet his obligations to other persons with diligence. This is the principle of *due care*, a term used fairly widely in legal cases. It refers to the care which the moral sense of society demands with respect to the effects of actions that may reasonably be anticipated. If a person did not plan nor foresee some ill effect

---

[5]See R. M. Hare, *The Language of Morals* (Oxford: Clarendon Press, 1952) and William D. Ross, *Foundations of Ethics* (New York: Oxford University Press, 1939).

of his action, can he be held responsible for the consequences? The man who "thought the revolver wasn't loaded" but did not stop to make sure killed a friend as surely as if he had planned to do so. A doctor who does not keep up with the latest developments in medicine may thereby cause a patient's death. In these cases we may not hold the person legally responsible, but there is a clear implication of moral responsibility. In the case of an engineer who fails to check details and use available information in the construction of a bridge and so becomes the cause of its collapse, we are likely to charge legal responsibility as well as moral. We hold a bus driver or a railroad engineer responsible for exercising due care and for being intelligent as well as good in the sense of well-meaning. While we cannot blame a person for unforeseeable effects of an act or for conditions beyond his power to control, and while we have to realize in assigning responsibility that we are all human and all make mistakes, it is clear that our obligation goes beyond merely meaning well and following the principles we think right.

The Obligation to Be Well Informed

The obligation of due care can be thought of as involving care about both knowing and doing. To do right we must first know right, and understanding the right has many facets. Among these are awareness of the law, understanding of the general demands of good conduct, self-knowledge that gives insight into one's motives and intentions, a grasp of the alternatives that should be considered, and awareness of the consequences of each alternative. In none of these matters can one be expected to have complete knowledge, so that the judgment of the scope of the obligation to know and understand is itself one that requires consideration of the circumstances, the capacities of the individual, the time at his disposal to learn, and the like.

In primitive times the things to be known concerning good action were less complex than now. Direct and intentional wrongs were the chief, if not the only, forms of antisocial behavior recognized as moral issues (though in some societies individuals were condemned for housing evil spirits). In modern society, where men wield great power and where their actions affect the lives of many people in both obvious and subtle ways, public well-being can be imperiled or injured quite as much by ignorance and carelessness as by willful aggression. That "ignorance of the law is no excuse" has long been recognized. An intelligent, morally sensitive person is expected to know the law of the community in which he lives. If he drives a car on the highway, he has a responsibility to know the rules of the road and the types of hazards for which to watch. If he manages an enterprise, he must know and consider potentially large effects on the welfare of others. When the danger to public welfare from ignorance is obvious, as in the case of ships' captains and airline pilots, society may set up rigid standards that are enforced by law.

When a man professes some special knowledge or skill and, on the basis of such claims, offers a service to society, those who accept the service assume ordinary care and diligence within the context of specialized knowledge and competence. If such a person shows gross neglect leading to injury, the courts will support a claim against him.

There is also an obligation to understand the general demands of good conduct. A person who cannot have this degree of understanding, one who does not know right from wrong, may be excused by the court and sent to a mental hospital if he has committed a crime arising out of this incapacity. It is obvious that to do our duty, we must first know what is involved in duty.

There is a further obligation to understand the specific implications or consequences involved in right conduct insofar as one can reasonably know these things. If we are to do to others as we would have them do to us, we must understand them well enough to know what would fulfill this intent. Otherwise, emphasis on the Golden Rule becomes pious sentiment. If the road to hell is indeed paved with good intentions, the paving stones in that road can be labeled "carelessness about understanding." Simple illustrations will occur to the reader:

> I didn't think.
> I didn't think you'd mind.
> I didn't know it was against the law.
> I didn't know you were there.
> I didn't think we needed to be quarantined for so light a case.
> Your letter was mislaid.

These expressions, when genuine, are not expressions of bad intent, but of inadequate care in knowing the demands of good conduct.

A much-neglected aspect of due care in knowing is that of being aware of the alternatives one should consider in choosing. Alternatives are possibilities rather than actualities—hence knowing them is in part a matter of imaginative attention. Many a disastrous choice has been made for want of attention to better alternatives. Arthur E. Morgan, the first chief engineer of the Tennessee Valley Authority, has often emphasized this point. After describing an interview with Thomas A. Edison on his approach to inventing—one that involved an exhaustive exploration of different hunches for a solution—Morgan said:

> I was pleased with his account because it was just the method which I had deliberately adopted on important engineering jobs. Working as a consulting engineer, I once went onto a job on which an able staff of engineers had spent several years and $150,000 in preparation of plans.

With my limited schooling, I dreaded to meet these highly trained men. Their trouble was that, having found a good answer, they were satisfied, and did not exhaust the possibilities. By letting my mind rove over all possibilities I was able to find a way to do for $5,000,000 two or three times as much as they would accomplish for $10,000,000.

On another job, where a staff of engineers and lawyers had spent ten years and a lot of money in preparing plans, there was early in the proceeding a similar satisfaction with a fairly good plan, and after that everyone was giving attention to the details, and not to the over-all picture. For that reason they remained unaware that their plans would provide only about a third of the necessary capacity. By that same process I was able to point out a way by which three times the degree of flood protection could be secured, and at a total cost of half a million dollars less than the plan that had been worked out. The works were successfully built by the amended plan. Simple as is this policy of trying to look into every possibility, where the issues justify such a search, it has not been too generally followed in the past. We followed that policy in planning the Miami River flood control system, and arrived at a program by a method which nearly all engineers in the country considered impracticable, but which they accepted when it was presented in detail.[6]

A final example of the facets of due care in understanding what is right can be taken from the need to understand oneself. Now that we know of the operation of subconscious drives in the determination of our choices, sometimes toward results incompatible with our ostensible aims, it is open to us to remove or reduce these effects by deliberate effort. To do so, however, we must have enough self-understanding to be on guard for these built-in tendencies that normally escape our awareness and deliberation. The teacher who is careful may recognize in his reaction to a foreign student's thinking that the teacher's own culture has conditioned him to make an unfair appraisal of certain behavior. The college student who has learned to watch for such drives in himself may recognize rebellion against parental figures in his way of interpreting the remarks of a teacher or college administrator. To these more difficult aspects of knowing himself, a student can add the tasks of getting an accurate picture of his own talents and persistent interests. He can then make sound choices about his vocation and his education.

The Obligation to Act Diligently on One's Knowledge

To know well, however, is only half of acting with due care. The other half is applying that knowledge diligently. We spoke earlier of the

---

[6]Arthur E. Morgan, "Some Types of Creative Thinking," March 1956; a mimeographed essay originally given as a lecture to Professor Morris Keeton's class in Reflective Thinking.

specialist with particular knowledge and competence. If he does not apply his expertness well, however, he may do greater harm than the person of less knowledge. The psychiatrist, the teacher, the lawyer, the engineer, the airplane mechanic, and the executive—all hold in their hands a heavy responsibility for care in performing to the best of their understanding.

On the morning of September 8, 1934, the *Morro Castle,* a ship steaming between New York and Havana, burned at sea with a loss of more than a hundred lives. Did the officers, the company that owned and operated the ship, and those responsible for the inspection and the policy of the merchant marine exercise due care, or were some or all of these groups morally to blame? The inquiry conducted by the United States Department of Commerce concluded with charges of negligence against the master of the ship and four of his staff. A few of the facts brought out by the inquiry were the following. The officers delayed the sending of SOS signals for thirty minutes or more, hoping to save salvage fees for the company. The officers failed to stop the ship soon enough and neglected the usual routine of fire fighting. Of the first ninety-eight persons to leave in lifeboats, ninety-two were members of the crew, in violation of a rigid law of the sea requiring that passengers be taken off first. Responsibility rested on a number of groups: on the officers and the crew, who did not conduct themselves in the way the public has a right to expect; on the company, which had an unfair labor policy, paying low wages and exacting long hours; and on a merchant marine that permitted low standards and a spirit of "every man for himself" to dominate its operations.

The law sometimes makes heavier and sometimes lesser demands in its definition of due care than might at first be expected. In part its demands are geared to protecting society from fear and worry about untoward effects of the carelessness of others; in part it seeks to provide assurances that minimize adjudication over unwanted and unexpected outcomes of acts. In the field of transportation the concept of common-carrier liability illustrates these concerns. A common carrier undertakes to carry goods or persons and deliver them for hire. People who offer such services to the public have explicit obligations, including willingness to serve all people equally and to be responsible for safe delivery. With some exceptions, there is a presumption of carrier's fault in case of injury or loss. Liability irrespective of negligence is usually enforced by the courts. This can hardly be done on the basis of blame in the usual sense unless the carrier is held responsible for incurring the risk of such loss even where he has not been negligent. The question thus arises whether a principle other than that of due care is actually at work in the assessment of liability—perhaps the principle of convenient allocation of social costs, a principle that setting responsibility in this way avoids litigation that would be costlier than the direct damages, or the like.

In other cases, however, the law will exact a requirement of only such care as the ordinary man could reasonably be expected to have exercised, even though the man in the case may be extraordinarily able. In defining the limits of due care, Richard C. Cabot says:

> One is responsible morally as well as legally for blunders: (1) up to the limits of average intelligence, or of the intelligence to be expected in the individual concerned; and (2) except in situations which one could not reasonably have been expected to foresee and prepare for.[7]

CONCLUDING QUESTIONS

In our rapidly changing society are there emerging ethical demands involving new rights and duties? Consider the following issues being discussed in the 1970s.

1. Should society, through its official agencies at some level, compensate the victims of criminal violence? Since government has failed to provide protection for its citizens, does it incur a liability and obligation to compensate for the injury or loss?

2. Since all members of the population are not needed to help produce the goods and services required, does an enlightened moral outlook call for a guaranteed annual wage? Does the ethical principle of respect for persons call for society to provide at least a minimum income for physical fitness, health, and decency?[8]

3. Have we as a society sufficiently recognized the people's right to know what their government is doing that affects their lives, their fortunes, and their future? This question has come to widespread public discussion in connection with the publication of *The Pentagon Papers* (1971) about the war in Southeast Asia.

Specific moral decisions and actions occur in the context of certain overarching rights and obligations. They are relative to the culture, the people involved, and the circumstances. Due care or moral concern implies the union of moral earnestness and intelligence. It calls for sincerity, attentiveness, a willingness to learn from experience and to profit by previous mistakes. We shall have occasion for further examples and elaboration on issues of personal and public policy and action as we consider the field of applied ethics in part 2 of this book.

---

[7]*The Meaning of Right and Wrong* (New York: Macmillan Co., 1933), p. 222.

[8]See Philip Wagamen, *Guaranteed Annual Income: The Moral Issues* (Nashville: Abingdon Press, 1968).

QUESTIONS AND PROJECTS

1. Going beyond the discussion in this chapter, discuss the extent to which human rights are respected or ignored in the society in which you now live.
2. Read the Constitution of the United States and its Amendments, and list the rights they guarantee. How well are these constitutional rights recognized and followed? Give particular attention to Amendments I, V, XIV, and XV.
3. Go over the ten rights listed in this chapter and indicate by specific instances whether you think these rights are or are not coming to be increasingly recognized and respected.
4. A Chicago surgeon, contrary to accepted medical practice, refused to operate to save the life of a baby boy a few days old. He explained that the baby was extremely defective and that he believed it would remain so throughout life. Without an operation the infant would die; its life would be prolonged or saved if an operation were performed. With the consent of the parents, nature was allowed to take its course, and the infant died. Comment on this case and the issues involved.
5. List any cases of negligence or carelessness like the following that have come to your attention. Indicate what moral issues are involved in each case.

    A false fire alarm, sent in as a prank in a Pennsylvania city, led to the wreck of a fire engine, heavy damage to a streetcar, and injury to twelve persons.

    A thoughtless hunter in Idaho, for want of a better target, shot the insulator at the top of a rural electric pole and blithely went on his way. The pole was soon on fire, and the surrounding farm country suffered the following damage: seventy-five farms were without light until the next morning: one hundred twenty-five other farms were without power for eleven hours; the eggs in many chicken and turkey incubators were spoiled; twelve dairymen were unable to use their milking machines; the stock for miles around went without water; and a school and two grain elevators were without power all day.
6. In recent years the papers have reported manslaughter charges and convictions in some cases of lack of due care. For example, a druggist misread a prescription as "sodium nitrate" instead of "sodium citrate," and this error led to the death of an infant. In another case, a driver of a truck said to the owner, "You need to have those brakes fixed or you will get into trouble." Some time later, the owner ordered another driver to make a delivery in the truck. The driver could not stop until after he had killed one person. How far should society go in penalizing such lack of due care?
7. Compare the case of the *Morro Castle* with the sinking of the *Andrea Doria* after a collision with the *Stockholm* on the night of July 25, 1956 and the loss of the *Yarmouth Castle* in November 1965. Along with the loss of the *Titanic* in 1912, these are famous disasters at sea where ques-

tions of negligence and due care are involved. The *Reader's Guide to Periodical Literature* will furnish many references. Discuss the issues of due care in at least one of the disasters.

8. "If I discover that ten years ago my neighbor served a term in prison, during which his wife had a child by another man, [have I] the right to pass that knowledge to the general public?" In commenting on this question, Gilbert Highet says that no such right exists unless it is clear "that the public interest would be injured by concealing it." [*Man's Unconquerable Mind* (New York: Columbia University Press, 1954), p. 79.] Do you agree with the answer? State in your own words the principles involved and indicate whether or not you think people usually follow these principles.

9. In recent investigations or hearings involving governmental officials and agencies, the question of wiretapping has led to much discussion. Along with such inventions as the telephone have come a number of devices which make it possible to record a conversation. One of the parties may not know that the conversation is being tapped. The record may be made by a third person or by a mechanical recording machine. What rights are involved? Should monitoring by public officials conducting public business be illegal unless both parties are informed that the conversation is being monitored?

10. A man and his wife collect antique furniture and glassware for their home. They have fairly accurate knowledge of the market value of many items sought by collectors. Occasionally they find valuable articles offered for sale by individuals who need the money but have no knowledge of their value. When such articles are offered at prices far below their actual value, should they be purchased at the prices offered?

11. The customs inspectors hold a person responsible for what is in his baggage, even if he claims that he did not know a certain article was there. If he fails, even unintentionally, to declare a dutiable article, he is liable for the penalty. Do you think that this is fair? Give your reasons.

12. Why is our society so backward in holding persons guilty of civic indifference and of failure to report crimes? Misprision is the crime of omission—the concealment of a felony by one not guilty. Misprision is a 176-year-old federal crime (U. S. Code, Title 18, Section 4) punishable by a five hundred dollar fine and up to three years' imprisonment. It is a common-law charge in Vermont and a statutory offense in Maine. We do charge persons for assent or assistance in a felony and require them to report serious traffic accidents to the police. Aren't violent assaults on persons as important as automobile damage? Discuss this question from the point of view of a mature morality. For some cases see *Time*, 4 March 1966, p. 45.

13. A little more than a decade ago a young singer with some fame as a sex idol was released from the army and returned from overseas. He received, according to reports, one hundred twenty-five thousand dollars for one night's appearance on a network television program. That is, for two dances and two songs he received more than the yearly salary

of many school teachers or ministers, or an amount sufficient to feed a few thousand refugee children for the same period. What does this indicate about the state of our scale of values?

SUGGESTED READINGS

Albert, Ethel M. "Social Science Facts and Philosophical Values." *The Antioch Review* 17 (Winter 1957–58):406–420. Reprinted in *The Range of Philosophy*, eds. Harold H. Titus and Maylon H. Hepp. 2nd ed. (New York: Van Nostrand Reinhold Co., 1970), pp. 250–263.
Bell, Daniel, ed. *Toward the Year 2000*. Boston: Houghton Mifflin Co., 1968. Book version of special issue of *Daedalus*. Journal of American Academy of Arts of Sciences. (Summer 1967).
Bird, Otto A. *The Idea of Justice*. New York: Frederick A. Praeger, 1968.
Brickman, William W. and Lehrer, Stanley, eds. *Automation, Education and Human Values*. New York: School & Society Books, 1966.
Bronowski, J. *Science and Human Values*, rev. ed. New York: Harper & Row, Publishers, Torchbook, 1965.
Dorsen, Norman, ed. *The Rights of Americans: What They Are—What They Should Be*. New York: Pantheon Books, 1971.
Douglas, William O. "The Bill of Rights Is Not Enough," in *The Great Rights*, ed. Edmond Cahn. New York: Macmillan Co., 1963.
Edwards, Rem Blanchard. *Freedom, Responsibility, and Obligation*. The Hague: Martinus Nijhoff, 1969.
Hart, H. L. A. "Are There Any Natural Rights?" *Philosophical Review* 64 (April 1955):175–191.
"Human Rights." *The Monist* 52 (October 1968). LaSalle, Ill.: Open Court Publishing Co. Published for the Edward C. Hegeler Foundation.
Institute for Religious and Social Studies. *Great Expressions of Human Rights*, ed. R. M. MacIver. New York: Harper & Brothers, 1950.
Jonsen, Albert R. *Responsibility in Modern Religious Ethics*. Washington, D.C.: Corpus Books, 1968.
Keeton, Morris T. *Values Men Live By*. New York: Abingdon Press, 1960.
Melden, A. I. *Human Rights*. Belmont, Calif.: Wadsworth Publishing Co., 1970.
Schiller, Marvin. "Are There Any Inalienable Rights?" *Ethics* 79 (July 1969):309–315.
United Nations Educational, Scientific, and Cultural Organization. *Human Rights: A Symposium*. New York: Columbia University Press, 1949.
Vickers, Geoffrey. *Value Systems and Social Process*. New York: Basic Books, 1968.

part 2
SPECIFIC PROBLEMS OF PERSONAL AND SOCIAL MORALITY

14
PHYSICAL AND MENTAL HEALTH

In the last chapter "Values, Rights, and Obligations" we began the transition from moral principles and guidelines to their application to the society in which we now live. We are now in part 2 about to give our attention to specific problems of personal and social morality. We live in a world with tremendous potentialities for good as well as for evil, and many are asking "Does mankind have a future?" We are hoping for a better future, yet in many areas of today's world we witness deterioration. "Our air, water, and food are all becoming increasingly polluted from by-products of technology; our forests and wildlife are steadily being encroached upon by the relentless growth of cities and population; our limited mineral wealth is rapidly being depleted; and over all looms the shadow of possible nuclear annihilation."[1]

We have said that what is right is that which is person affirming or person fulfilling, and we have stressed the worth of human beings as a basic moral postulate. Anything that mars men's bodies, stunts their minds, or blights their spirits is to be condemned as wrong, except where some greater value, under very special or unusual conditions, intervenes. The first right set forth in the United States Declaration of Independence was the right to life. For many centuries in one form or another the great philosophical and religious systems have been saying:

> You shall not kill.
> You shall not injure or maim.
> You shall develop your capabilities and talents.
> You shall seek the good of your own life and the life of the community.

---

[1] Judd Marmor, "Psychiatry and the Survival of Man," *Saturday Review* 54 (May 22, 1971): 18.

Let us concern ourselves in this chapter with our own bodies and minds. To live well we need to have sound minds in healthy bodies and to be a part of a just or good society. Good health is a value in itself, and it is the basis for the realization of many other values. The man of abundant energy has a sense of the joy of merely living. He has open to him experiences and opportunities for growth not open to others. Those who experience good health often fail to realize its central place until misfortune or lack of health calls their attention to its value. Then they realize that health is more important than all the wealth or fame they might achieve. There is this paradox, though: of itself, good health means little; but without it, nothing else means much!

THE IMPORTANCE OF PHYSICAL HEALTH

At various times and places during the history of society, men have regarded the human body as something to be distrusted or scourged. The disparagement of the body and of bodily activities was suggested to the consciousness of men by the intense inner struggles men occasionally experience. These moral conflicts were interpreted as evidence of the sinfulness of man's natural passions rather than as a part of man's upward struggle. Repressive methods, however, were not always successful. Suppression rather than control and direction of the natural impulses tended to intensify the struggle and to give rise to lurid imagery and other abnormal physical conditions. Such phenomena tended to convince men still further of the wickedness of their natures.

Much Sickness and Pain Unnecessary

In the modern world there are few people who regard the body as evil, yet multitudes neglect the care of their bodies and fail to realize the important place physical well-being plays in effective living. From various independent studies as well as from the United States Health Service, the investigations of insurance companies, and army medical tests, there is available a body of facts that is somewhat alarming. If malnutrition, defective sight and hearing, and defective teeth are included with the more serious ailments, probably a large majority of school children have some kind of physical defect that is either potentially or actually injurious to health. All but a small fraction of these abnormal conditions can be corrected; yet many of them receive no attention. Apparently many persons are ignorant of small ailments that in some way affect their lives. This fact clearly indicates the advisability of periodic health inspection. Perhaps, indeed, such examinations are a *duty* of all people.

Other studies indicate that the average person is ill nine days a year. At any one time between two and three percent of the population are incapacitated because of sickness, and at times the percentage is considerably higher. Also at any one time the members of another large group of people feel ill but are not too ill to work. Members of this latter group remain at work with impaired efficiency.

In the light of the above facts, it is encouraging to know that there is growing interest in and emphasis on health and physical development. In part, this emphasis has come from a realization of the military and economic importance of health. In the wars of history, down to recent times, more men have been lost through disease than from wounds. The economic loss from disease is tremendous. The direct costs include doctors, hospitals, medicine, and loss of wages. The indirect costs include decreased efficiency caused by minor ailments and the cost to society of preventable or premature deaths.

Pain and suffering are facts of life and are likely to be present on occasion from birth until death. While there is a struggle to escape from pain and suffering, they come at times from calamities or acts of nature; from sickness, disease, and accidents; and from human folly, ignorance, selfishness, and moral evil. Much pain arises from "man's inhumanity to man." We are tied together in a social order, and we pay the penalty as well as reap the rewards. Pain, in one sense, is nature's danger signal; it is a warning that something is wrong and needs to be changed.

Probably the most important factors in the present emphasis on health have been new knowledge about health, a growing realization of the fact that much pain and misery are unnecessary and can be eliminated, and a sense of the paramount value of health as an element of the good life. Because of the vital importance of good health, the existence of so much ill health and suffering should give us great concern.

A Moral Obligation to Maintain Health

Let us now consider more fully why care of the body is essential from the point of view of morality. As noted earlier, a human being is not a series of independent parts but a unified structure in which the malfunctioning of any one part may affect the whole. For example, a headache, a toothache, a case of indigestion, or any major disturbance may seriously affect emotions and thoughts. In turn, memory, imagination, or reason may influence digestion or cause other body changes. Man is a delicate mechanism, and the happy life is one in which the physical and mental capacities all function in one harmonious whole. Fatigue, backaches, and nervousness mean a depressed vitality and a lowered resistance to impulses and passions. Much irritability, nagging, and anger result from such conditions. At least one case is on record where a child's delinquency appeared to be closely related to his mother's irritation, which was caused by a dental condition. The delinquency ceased after the mother was provided with a comfortable set of false teeth. Man's higher powers and his comfort depend to a large extent on a sound body.

Good health is essential for community welfare as well as for personal happiness and growth. There is a moral obligation to be as healthy as we can, and to live so that others may be as healthy as possible. Of course, we can all think of people who have been able to achieve wonderful things in spite of poor health and physical disability. The list is long and includes such persons as John Keats, Robert Louis Stevenson, Charles Darwin, and Helen Keller. Everyone honors these people. Nevertheless, it is probably fair to say that it is the unusual person who accomplishes things in spite of such handicaps. The handicap itself does not contribute to creativity. A tubercular genius may compose a beautiful poem or song, but he does so because he has genius rather than because he has poor health. Many men of genius have gone to an early grave when good health would have enabled them to continue their contributions to art or literature for many years. For the average person, poor health is one of the worst hindrances not only to success but also to harmonious living. Therefore, it becomes a moral duty to guard one's health and strength. Such a thing is not wholly within our control, but we can do a good deal about it. To lower one's usefulness deliberately by unhealthful practices is a vice. Morality demands both physical and mental hygiene. We should endeavor to know all we can about our bodies, our individual needs and demands, and the conditions under which we function most adequately. If our bodies are to operate harmoniously and efficiently, there are certain conditions which must be met.

Basic Bodily Needs

In order to function well and not be a source of disturbance and pain, our bodies need fresh air, sunshine, sleep, food, and exercise. For most persons who do not live under congested urban conditions, fresh air and sunshine come as a matter of course. We are more likely to violate the principles of healthful living in connection with the last three.

Sleep is one of our greatest needs. We may go longer without food than without sleep and yet continue to live. Infants need to sleep nearly all the time, children of four or five years of age need to sleep about half the time, and most adults need eight hours of sleep or more. The proper amount of sleep at regular intervals is necessary for sound nerves and for growth. Insufficient sleep is responsible for the dull, irritable lives of millions, for numerous family quarrels, for many accidents, and for the crowding out of our finer emotions and thoughts. Of course, people vary considerably as to the amount of sleep needed. It is each one's duty to get the sleep essential for his personal efficiency.

Food is another bodily demand that must be satisfied. Both lack of sufficient nourishment and overeating cause numerous warped lives. While from a fifth to a third of all preschool children suffer from a greater or lesser degree of malnutrition, others in our population go prematurely to their graves because of overeating. A vast amount of peevishness and anger may be traced to indigestion from overeating or from an unbalanced diet.

Exercise and recreation, which may take the form of play, amusements, or sports and competitive athletics, are fundamental needs of the human body. The play impulse grows normally and spontaneously out of life. Play means doing things for the sheer joy and satisfaction the activity itself brings. For a child, play is preparation for adult life. For an adult, it is the renewing of life. It is one method of recreating body and mind and avoiding nervous exhaustion. A proper balance between work and play or recreation is an essential condition of health and efficiency. As the adage puts it, "all work and no play makes Jack a dull boy." Recreation through play in one form or another may save many persons for high moral purposes.

Amusements have great potentialities both for good and for evil. Among their values are the joy they add to living, the zest they give to life. There is probably a definite place in life for pleasures or amusements that have no immediate relation to the duties of life but contribute to one's capacity for enjoyment. The modern moral consciousness rejects the Puritan view that amusements, because they add to mere bodily enjoyment and "waste" time, are therefore evil and should be rejected. The Puritan attitude was too severe and one-sided, and it failed to do justice to the needs of both children and adults for play and recreation. Happiness is normal and desirable. Unhappiness is an indication that something is wrong. The desire for enjoyment needs to be satisfied wisely.

There is social value in many forms of recreation and amusement. There is nothing like play to break down reserve and artificial barriers, for instance, and to aid in the formation of friendships. With both children and adults, amusements, especially in the form of group games, help stimulate sociability and foster a spirit of cooperation and teamwork. Laughter and mirth tend to draw people together. They also act as a means of release for emotional pressures which otherwise may express themselves in irritation or in anger.

Some of the most serious evils in connection with amusements have come with the growth of commercialism and professionalism. With the development of an industrial order, it was inevitable that the recreational habits of men should undergo some changes. Men and women who work for long hours at hard and monotonous tasks and who come out tired prefer emotional excitement to vigorous physical exercise. Industrialization and urbanization create conditions conducive to the growth of commercialism and professionalism in amusements. Since people are inclined to spend more freely when their emotions are stirred, such commercialized pleasure resorts tend to work on the passions and the weaknesses of men. Professionalism, one form of commercialism, substitutes "the love of being played upon" for the desire to play. From being active participants in games, it encourages people to sit as idle spectators and pay to be amused.

Any amusement, however innocent in itself, may become a means of self-indulgence. If excessive participation in it impairs our health or efficiency or if its untimely pursuit leads us to neglect the performance of duty, an amusement may become harmful and morally reprehensible. Amusements cease to be ethically valuable and become forms of dissipation when they sap our strength, lead us to neglect social obligations, or cause us to lose interest in the serious tasks of life. Each individual will have to find the line of demarcation between amusements that are ethically defensible for him and those which are unethical.

A considerable part of the above discussion applies also to athletic competitions as found on most college campuses. In favor of such sports as football, baseball, basketball, hockey, and track may be mentioned the training and the discipline such games require. The good athlete must be alert of mind and sound in body. He must develop coordination of sense and muscle, persistence, and self-control. Such socially desirable qualities as cooperation or teamwork, loyalty to and willingness to sacrifice for the group, and a spirit of fair play may be cultivated. The athlete may also gain a sense of personal worth in performing an activity well.

On the other hand, competitive athletics may require so much time and energy that health is impaired and studies are neglected. On some campuses some students overexercise, while others do not exercise sufficiently. The overemphasis on athletics on some campuses was the basis for the jocular remark that colleges are athletic clubs in which opportunity for study is provided for the physically unfit. Here, as elsewhere, a virtue may become a vice. A program of intramural sports in which practically all students participate is to be desired over a system which permits a few good athletes to carry on the athletic program of the school. Another danger is that the spirit of rivalry and the temptation to win at any cost may undermine good sportsmanship and character.

Since intercollegiate and intramural sports are among the most powerful influences on student life, it is important that they contribute to the development of sound bodies and strong characters. The responsibility rests both with members of the student body and with the faculty and administration to see that the recreational life of the college leads to the growth of worthy standards of conduct.

THE USE OF ALCOHOL, TOBACCO, AND DRUGS

A discussion of physical and mental health would be incomplete without a consideration of the use of alcohol, tobacco, and narcotics. In this field we need clear thinking, since in the past the issues have frequently been clouded by high emotion or confused by propaganda. When we ask, "Does the use of certain substances affect life beneficially or adversely?" we need scientific evidence in order to answer the question adequately. If the results of the use of narcotics, for example, are in the long run destructive of health and happiness, their use is unquestionably wrong. If there is no detrimental effect or if the effects are beneficial, then they can be justified. Because of their importance and widespread use, we give considerable space to a discussion of alcohol when used as a drink, of nicotine as inhaled in smoking, and of some drugs that are being used by more and more people today.

Alcohol and Human Welfare

Alcohol is used for a number of purposes. Besides certain commercial uses, it has definite uses as a medicine. When recommended by members of the medical profession to fill a need of the organism, it naturally should be taken. There are situations in which to refuse to take alcohol causes more injury than to take it.

In addition to the medical and commercial uses of alcohol, other seemingly beneficial effects have been noted. Up to a certain point, alcohol may give a release from tension and a sense of well-being. It helps some overinhibited or diffident persons remove inhibitions and become "better mixers." Thus it is said to be conducive to good fellowship.[2] Some musicians and other artists have thought they do better work when slightly under the influence of alcohol.

---

[2]Chauncey D. Leake, "Good-Willed Judgment on Alcohol," in *Alcohol and Civilization*, ed. Salvatore Pablo Lucia (New York: McGraw-Hill Book Co., 1963), pp. 3–22.

Let us dispose at once of a few false impressions. The thirst for alcohol is not hereditary. It is acquired, learned through experience. Alcohol does not affect the germ cells. A woman who is a habitual drinker may injure her health and vitality, however, and so affect her unborn child adversely and give it a handicap in life. Alcohol is not a stimulant, as many persons assume; it is a depressant. It acts first on the higher centers of the brain and the nervous system and, by loosening the inhibitions, may cause increased activity and give the false impression that it has acted as a stimulant.

It is the excessive use of alcohol as a drink that creates a special problem. The common effect is known as intoxication. According to the amount imbibed, three stages of intoxication have been noted. In the first stage, the higher functions of the brain, including reasoning power and self-control, are weakened or inhibited. Impulses are freed from their habitual control, and critical self-awareness is dulled. This leaves the lower centers comparatively free to act and, if there is added stimulus under social conditions, hilarious behavior, contentiousness, or combativeness may result. Much of our education consists of building up useful inhibitions and developing our judgment and critical powers. Alcohol tends to reverse this process. In the second stage, movements and sense perceptions are disturbed and confused. Clumsiness of action, ill-adjusted movements, and a narrowing of observation or attention are in evidence. The intoxicated person may see double. He may also give way to violent outbursts of emotion. In the third stage, all his functions are depressed, and he sinks into a deep sleep or into unconsciousness. He will probably remain in this condition until oxidation has disposed of the alcohol in his system.

In the light of recent evidence, it appears that alcohol in one way or another may affect the action of every organ of the body. When taken as a drink, it is readily absorbed by the body and enters the bloodstream. Since its absorption is much more rapid than its elimination, the largest amount of alcohol in the bloodstream is found between one-half hour to two hours after ingestion. The severity of the symptoms of intoxication varies according to the person and the amount consumed. The habitual drinker tends to be less affected than the neophyte, and for both the effects are greater if the alcohol is taken on an empty stomach.

The chief effect of alcohol is on the central nervous system, consisting of the brain and spinal cord. A sense of freedom and relief is experienced through the deadening of the powers of reason, memory, self-control, and discretion. The person is less keenly aware. Even moderate amounts of alcohol affect very definitely the response of sight, hearing, and touch sensation. There is delay in reaction to stimuli and often inaccurate interpretation of the sensation. The danger of such delays in an age which depends so largely on the use of speed and power is evident. It explains the insistence of industrial and transportation firms that their employees refrain from the use of alcoholic beverages while on the job. We have been told that a moderate amount of alcohol is sufficient to cause a difference of a quarter mile in the location of a swiftly moving airplane between a signal of danger and the pilot's effective response, and of fifteen to thirty feet in the position of a motor car traveling at thirty-five to fifty miles an hour. During the past decade, evidence reported by the National Safety Council indicates that alcohol is a leading factor in at least fifty percent of fatal auto accidents.[3]

In a special report to Congress on alcohol and health in February 1972, the United States Department of Health, Education, and Welfare called alcohol the nation's most abused drug that afflicts more than nine million persons and drains the economy of billions of dollars a year. The report said that drinking is linked to one third of all homicides, one half of all traffic deaths, and that one half of all arrests reported each year relate to public intoxication, drunken driving, disorderly conduct, and vagrancy. Furthermore, the report said that alcoholism can cut ten to twelve years off an imbiber's life.[4]

The personal and social effects of the use of alcohol cannot be separated completely. The social effects are serious, since the disturbance of the higher functions of the brain leads to a marked lack of self-control. As a result, the intoxicated person is likely to offend the public sense of decency and to exhibit unbecoming conduct.

One of the chief counts against alcohol is that it is a habituating substance. Alcoholism has become, indeed, one of the four or five most serious public health problems in the country. No one seems to know in advance whether or not he will be able to remain an occasional and moderate drinker.

While there are many persons who do not fully realize the harm that comes from drinking, there are others who do know the effects of alcohol and yet continue to drink. Why? Alcohol is used for a number of reasons. For many it is a means of temporary escape from the worries and burdens of life, from social conventions and self-criticism. The drinker often experiences a sense of well-being and power. After the monotony and the fatigue of the day's work, an alcoholic drink may give a feeling of comfort and relaxation. The danger is that

---

[3]See Charles R. Carroll, *Alcohol: Use, Nonuse, and Abuse* (Dubuque, Ia.: W. C. Brown Co., 1970), p. 39.
[4]*New York Times*, 19 February 1972, p. 1.

release from small difficulties may lead to habits of evasion and eventually to escape from reality. When problems arise, we may face them with intelligence and energy or we may escape from them into a world of fantasy. Then, too, the habit of indulging in alcohol may be formed from the enjoyment of an occasional drink. For many people a considerable degree of self-control is required to keep from passing from light drinking to moderate drinking and then to heavy drinking.

Another reason for the prevalence of drinking is group pressure. If others are imbibing, there is strong pressure to join the group, to be a good sport. To be sociable and to give in to group suggestion is often easier than to resist or to seek another group with different conventions. Finally, there is the legend of the romance of alcohol, propagated by advertisements and played up by the mass media. Alcohol, it is said or implied, will relax you, make you a "man of distinction," or do almost anything else you want done.

Morality demands that we live at our best and bring our lower natures under the control of reason or of our higher natures. Inasmuch as alcohol acts as a depressant, it tends to deaden the higher centers first. The higher faculties are stupefied, and the impulses and emotions are less restrained. Man has no justification for impairing his health and efficiency. The excessive use of alcohol, in dulling the functions of critical self-awareness, perception, and thought, takes us back toward infantile consciousness and conduct. Duty demands that we preserve our health and strength of body and that we exercise diligence in respecting the rights of others. Whether drinking is to be approved or disapproved depends on the evidence of its effect on human welfare. The evidence of the harmful effects of excessive alcohol is most conclusive.

Tobacco: Smoking and Human Welfare

Since the beginning of the century the average consumption of chewing and pipe tobacco and cigars fell but cigarette smoking increased rapidly until the early sixties. This is in spite of the fact that for some decades there have been studies and reports by various agencies that causally linked cigarette smoking to several diseases. In June 1961 the heads of the American Cancer Society, the American Public Health Association, the American Heart Association, and the National Tuberculosis Association sent a letter to President Kennedy urging the formation of a presidential commission to study the widespread implications of the smoking of tobacco. Evidence from various sources indicated that cigarette smoking was associated with increased deaths from lung cancer, coronary artery disease, chronic bronchitis, and emphysema.

The rate of deaths from some of these diseases has been increasing with great rapidity for some decades.

In 1962 the Surgeon General of the United States selected a committee of ten from a list of one hundred fifty outstanding scientists and physicians competent to review the evidence. The list was sent to nine organizations, including the Tobacco Institute, with permission to "blackball" any person to whom there was any objection. Men who had previously taken a stand on the issue were eliminated. The aim was to select men who were uncommitted at the time of their appointment. Those selected were asked to examine the evidence, which included more than nine thousand scientific reports and documents. After this examination they reached the conclusion that smoking is a major health hazard. In January 1964 they released a 387-page report, *Smoking and Health: Report of the Advisory Committee to the Surgeon General of the Public Health Service*.[5] The reader is referred to this document and to various later reports released by the American Cancer Society and other health, research, and medical agencies, since the studies are too extensive to be presented here in more than brief summary conclusions.

The Surgeon General's committee evaluated three main kinds of scientific evidence: (1) animal experiments, (2) clinical and autopsy studies of both smokers and nonsmokers, and (3) population studies of a variety of types. They found that "the mortality rate of cigarette smokers over nonsmokers was particularly high for a number of diseases": cancer of the lung (nearly one thousand percent higher than for nonsmokers), bronchitis and emphysema (five hundred percent higher), cancer of the larynx, oral cancer, cancer of the esophagus, peptic ulcer, a group of other circulatory diseases, and coronary artery disease. In general, the more cigarettes smoked daily, the higher the death rate. "Men who began smoking before age 20 have a substantially higher death rate than those who began after age 25." The danger increases with the number of years during which a person smokes and is "greater for inhalers than noninhalers." Cigarette smoking is a health hazard of sufficient importance in the United States to warrant appropriate remedial action."[6]

For pipe smokers and cigar smokers, the danger of developing lung cancer, for example, is greater than for nonsmokers, but much less than for cigarette smokers. Pipe smoking also appears to be related to some extent to lip cancer.

---

[5] U. S. Department of Health, Education, and Welfare, Public Health Service Publication No. 1103 (Washington: U. S. Government Printing Office, 1964).
[6] Ibid., p. 33.

Some independent research centers have told us that smoking by pregnant women affects the weight of their babies and that there is a relation between heavy smoking and premature birth. For years athletic coaches, observing that wind and endurance are affected by smoking, have asked athletes not to use tobacco, at least during the training season. The Commissioner of Health of the State of New York says that "no other single factor kills so many Americans as cigarette smoking." The Director of Health of California believes that "cigarette smoking is one of the greatest threats to well being in modern times."[7]

Some persons say that smoking brings relaxation and that they do their best work while smoking. They claim that it aids rather than hinders their efficiency. The habitual use of tobacco is related to psychological and social factors. Its beginning, habituation, and occasional discontinuation are psychologically and socially conditioned. After smoking has become a habit, it is difficult to stop, and nervousness or tension may result when one tries to do so. We see that the beneficial effects of smoking occur mainly in the search for contentment.

Because of increasing evidence that smoking, especially cigarette smoking, is hazardous to health, the Federal Communications Commission cited the "fairness doctrine" which requires broadcasters to present all sides of controversial subjects and on June 2, 1967 ordered significant free air time for anticigarette announcements. After April 1, 1970 a health warning was required on each package of cigarettes. The United States Congress outlawed all cigarette advertising on television and radio effective January 2, 1971. The public has been warned that the effects of smoking are far more widespread than previously supposed. Consequently, the person who wishes to make the most of his life needs to ask himself whether the formation of such a habit is conducive to health and happiness.

The Use and Abuse of Drugs

From a medical point of view, drugs are chemicals which have an effect on the human body. They have both beneficial and harmful uses. Most drugs have beneficial uses and when prescribed by physicians they may help to ward off disease, relieve pain, and maintain good health. The abuse of drugs, however, has become one of the major social problems of contemporary America. Some decades ago drug

---

[7]Harold S. Diehl, *Tobacco and Your Health* (New York: McGraw-Hill Book Co., 1969). For these and statements by other health officials, here and abroad, see pp. 2–4. See also Walter S. Ross, "Do You Know What Happens When You Smoke?" *Reader's Digest* 101 (July 1972): 121–125.

addiction of a serious nature affected chiefly the poor, mainly racial or ethnic minorities in ports or border cities. Today drug abuse has spread throughout the country, and young people from junior high schools through university graduate departments are the growth market for drugs.

In this discussion we wish to present well-established, scientific evidence and avoid the current misconceptions and myths[8] which have sometimes led to a disrespect for law. Drugs will continue to be used by many people who seek stimulation, sedation, or escape from frustration, boredom, anger, and despair, especially if they do not know the consequences of addiction.

Let us, first, clarify some terms that are found in the literature and in discussions of the drug problem. Drug *dependence* is a state of psychological or physical attachment, or both, which results from chronic or continuous use. The term *addiction* is also used where there is an inner compulsion to use the drug: the basis may be physiological or the result of conditioning. If increasing use leads to greater tolerance the tendency is to increase the dosage and the dependence may become both physiological and psychological. The term *habituation* is often used when the desire for a drug is prompted by its psychological effects without the element of physical compulsion.[9] *Hallucinogens* or *psychedelics* are drugs that are capable of bringing about changes of sensation, self-awareness, thinking, and emotion. While marihuana is medically classified as a hallucinogen, the most potent of the hallucinogens is LSD (lysergic acid diethylamide). The *stimulants,* most usually *amphetamines,* increase alertness, provide a feeling of euphoria (well-being), and reduce hunger. The *sedatives,* especially the *barbiturates,* induce sleep and are used to relieve daytime tension and anxiety. The *narcotics* are pain-killing drugs made from opium obtained from the juice of the poppy. They include heroin, morphine, paregoric, and codine. Heroin is the drug used by most addicts today.

We shall limit our discussions to brief statements about marihuana, LSD, amphetamines, barbiturates, and heroin and then draw some general conclusions about the moral and legal aspects of the problem.

Marihuana is a drug found in the flowering tops and to a lesser extent in the leaves of the Indian hemp plant *cannabis sativa.* In the United States, it is called by various names including pot, grass, tea, and weed. The green substance is usually rolled and smoked in cigarettes

---

[8]*A Federal Source Book: Answers to the Most Frequently Asked Questions about Drugs.* (Washington, D. C.: U. S. Government Printing Office, 1971).

[9]See Robert Kaplan, *Drug Abuse: Perspectives on Drugs* (Dubuque, Ia: W. C. Brown Co., 1970), pp. 2–3.

(reefers, joints, sticks) or in pipes, but it may be taken in food. A dark brown resin from the tops of the plant is about five times stronger than marihuana and is called *hashish* or *hash*. As in the case of other drugs the effect varies with the strength of the drug, the person, and the conditions under which it is taken. Marihuana is not addicting, but continuous users become psychologically dependent. It affects the person's self-control and in different persons may be a stimulant or a depressant. The immediate physical effects are likely to be an increased heartbeat, a redness in the whites of the eyes, and a cough from the effect of the smoke on the lungs. Psychological effects, while variable, include distortions of perception including vision, hearing, and sense of time and space. Thought tends to become dreamlike. The most frequent effects are euphoria ("high") and withdrawal, although anxiety and delusions of suspicion may result. Users may get talkative, unsteady, or drowsy. While stopping the use of the drug does not produce physical sickness, the long-term effects are not known and more research and knowledge are needed.

LSD is the most potent of the hallucinogens (psychedelics) or the consciousness-expanding, mind-affecting drugs. It comes from the fungus (ergot) that grows as a rust on rye. Taken in a sugar cube or a cookie, it is noted for producing strong and unusual mental reactions and fantastic distortions in what people see, hear, touch, or smell. Strong emotions may vary from bliss to horror. Sensations are said to "crossover" if music is seen or color heard. Under strong doses the person may lose his ability to discriminate or to evaluate his experience. The emotional state may be a "good trip" or a "bad trip" ("bummer"). The responses to LSD cannot be predicted, and how it works in the body is not definitely known except that it appears to affect the levels of certain chemicals of the brain and produce changes in the electrical activity.

While LSD is not physically addicting as are the narcotics yet to be considered, reports from medical authorities warn of serious dangers including panic when the person fears he is losing his mind, suspicion that someone is attempting to control and harm him, the recurrence of trips after the individual has stopped using the drug, and accidental death when the user feels he can fly from a high window or drive or walk in front of moving vehicles. The relation between the use of LSD and mental derangement and also the possibility that the drug may cause chromosomal damage affecting offspring of LSD users are not clear and call for more research.

Amphetamines such as benzedrine, dexedrine, and methedrine are sometimes called *pep pills, bennies,* or *speed* since they stimulate the central nervous system and combat fatigue and sleepiness. Doctors may use them to curb appetite in supervised weight reduction programs.

Stimulants speed up the action of the heart and metabolism, raise blood pressure, and cause sweating, headache, diarrhea. They may drive a person to do things beyond his normal physical endurance and leave him exhausted. Sport associations have banned their use. While the stimulants mentioned above do not lead to physical dependence, there often does develop psychological dependence when the person becomes accustomed to using the drug for mental and emotional reasons. Injections may lead to hepatitis and abscesses, and unaccustomed high dosages may cause death.

Barbiturates stand in contrast to amphetamines because they are sedatives that relax the central nervous system. They induce sleep and calm daytime tension and anxiety. Often called *goof balls, sleepers, downies,* or *barbs,* they include pentobarbital, phenobarbital, butabarbital, and the like. Doctors use these drugs to treat high blood pressure, epilepsy, insomnia, and some other disorders since, in supervised doses, they depress the action of the nerves, and skeletal and heart muscles. In higher doses the effects resemble alcohol drunkenness. Barbiturates distort vision and slow down reactions and are important causes of automobile accidents, especially when combined with alcohol. They are a leading cause of accidental poison deaths and one of the main methods used to commit suicide.

Barbiturates are physically addicting and the user needs increasingly larger doses to feel their effects. When the drug is withdrawn or not attainable the user experiences withdrawal sickness that is likely to include nausea, cramps, delirium, convulsions and, in extreme cases, death. These drugs can be obtained legally only through a physician's prescription.

Heroin, as stated above, is the narcotic or pain-killing drug that is used by many addicts today. When mixed with a liquid solution and injected into a vein, the first reaction is relief from tension and worry. The user becomes "high" and feelings of pain disappear as the drug dulls certain areas of the brain. It may reduce hunger, thirst, and sex urges. In 1970 President Nixon said, "More than 100,000 . . . lead totally unproductive lives because of their addiction to narcotics." While addiction does not directly lead to crime, once the user is "hooked," his body demands larger and larger doses, and a continuous supply of the drug becomes the main object of his life. Because heroin cannot be obtained legally and because it costs so much to support the heroin habit (sometimes twenty-five to a hundred dollars for a day's supply), crime is often the only way to get that much money. The user's crimes, apart from possession of the drug, are nearly always thefts or crimes against property, seldom crimes of passion or violence. The more common crimes are shoplifting, car theft, selling heroin, pimping, and prostitution.

Attempts to stop the use of heroin lead to serious withdrawal sickness that may include nausea, diarrhea, sharp abdominal and leg cramps, shaking, sweating, and chills. While the assertion "Once an addict, always an addict" is not true, a long period of medical treatment and rehabilitation is needed. Since there are no medical, social, or legal uses of heroin, great effort is being made to prevent its human consumption.

What can be done about drug use and addiction? The impulse of some uninformed people is to condemn all drug use and to demand more severe laws. In spite of very heavy penalties, however, the use of drugs has grown rapidly. Federal penalties for illegal narcotics usage were set under the Harrison Act of 1914 which provided heavy fines and imprisonment (from two to ten years for the first offense and heavier penalties for later offenses) for possession, usage, or sale of dangerous drugs such as heroin, LSD, and marihuana. Conviction for a felony and a police record can close the door to some professions and even require special conditions to obtain or renew a driver's license. While marihuana has its real dangers, the evidence makes clear that it is less harmful than heroin, amphetamines, barbiturates, LSD, alcohol, and possibly tobacco. Many young persons as well as various specialists are critical of what they consider the unjust and perhaps hypocritical difference in treatment between marihuana and alcohol. The former is not physically addictive and does not incite individuals to violence, crime, and sex, whereas the latter is implicated in perhaps half of the convictions for robbery, rape, and murder, and a considerable number of automobile accidents. What is the justification for the government's enforcing severe penalties against the use of marihuana and not only condoning but profiting from the use of alcohol and tobacco, the two most damaging narcotics, from the point of view of the numbers affected and the general social effects?

The victims of drug abuse need to be considered as sick persons needing medical attention. The Narcotics Addict Rehabilitation Act of 1966 gives addicts a choice of treatment instead of imprisonment if no other crime is involved. The newer forms of treatment include civil commitment to a hospital for several months for treatment and rehabilitation, the methadone treatment—this drug blocks the euphoria-producing effects of heroin and other opiates—and group therapy in a community of addicts carried on by ex-addicts who understand and help in rehabilitation.[10]

---

[10]See National Education Association, *Drug Abuse: Escape to Nowhere* (Philadelphia: Smith, Kline & French Laboratories, 1967), part 2 "The Drug Abuser and Methods of Therapy" and appendix C "Where to Get Help"; James B. Shuman, "An Anti-Drug Program That Works," *Reader's Digest* 98 (March 1971): 139–142.

THE CULTIVATION OF MENTAL HEALTH

Mental health is as important as physical health. In fact, the two cannot be separated in any clear-cut way. The attempt to cultivate mental health is often called *mental hygiene*. On the negative side, its purpose is the prevention of mental diseases and disorders; on its positive side, it teaches people to live normal lives in the actual world. It attempts, therefore, to keep people from escaping into a world of unreality or wishful thinking and to help them get the most from their own lives, their social contacts, and the world around them. This brief discussion does not consider mental diseases, but only the normal or near-normal individual.

Our mental condition may affect the physical functions of the body for good or for ill. It can weaken our resistance to infection and disease, cause changes in vital organs, and upset the normal functions of the body. For example, anger and other emotional disturbances can speed up the action of the heart, increase the blood pressure, and affect the flow of hydrochloric acid, which aggravates stomach ulcers. A knowledge of a patient's frustrations, anxieties, worries, or fears is often as important as a chemical analysis of his blood in discovering the causes of his illness. Some doctors say that a knowledge of the type of patient who has the disease is as important as a knowledge of what disease the patient has. The desire of the patient to get well may be a critical factor in his recovery of normal health.

There is a physical fatigue from physical overexertion that quickly passes away with proper sleep and food. There is also a mental fatigue or nervous exhaustion that is frequently the result of emotional tension, lack of interest in what one is doing, or other psychological phenomena. Much fatigue results from boredom and monotony or from such things as fear, worry, resentment, and a sense of frustration. Mental fatigue is not so likely to come from mental effort as it is from attitude. Consequently, it is more difficult to relieve. Armies in retreat lose more soldiers from exhaustion psychoses than do armies that are driving ahead. A clerk in a store may come home completely exhausted, but when her friends call and ask her to go out for an evening of fun, she perks up and goes off for hours of strenuous exercise.

Some Principles of Mental Health

If we are to escape undue fatigue, fear, worry, mental conflicts, and other disturbances, what are some of the conditions we must meet? What are some of the principles of mental health?

First, *we must accept ourselves*. We must accept ourselves as ourselves and not as someone else. This means accepting our handicaps or limitations as well as our abilities and talents. The advice of Socrates to his countrymen was "Know thyself." In a somewhat different sense, return to normal living was possible for the Prodigal Son in the New Testament when he "came to himself." Of course, to accept oneself and the conditions of one's existence does not mean resignation or passive submission to conditions as they exist. It is, rather, a first step toward growth and improvement.

A frank acceptance of our handicaps and limitations may be a positive stimulus to future achivement. Sometimes, through the principle of compensation, we can make our handicaps spur us to success. Demosthenes, the orator, once stammered; Helen Keller was blind and deaf; Darwin, Stevenson, and Keats were sick men who mastered their handicaps through great effort. Civilization has moved forward most rapidly in the temperates zones, where men cannot continue to live without forethought and effort—not in the tropics, where life is comparatively easy.

Second, *we must accept other persons and the world in which we live.* The acceptance of other persons means that we must adjust our lives to the demands of the group in which we live. Social life involves give-and-take and a friendly, cooperative attitude. Always to have one's own way is not good for mental development. Normal persons are cooperating members of families and other groups. Furthermore, a person needs to give and receive recognition, praise, and affection. Ridicule, shaming, and excessive criticism tend to destroy personality.

Normal persons also accept the order of nature in the midst of which they live. They adjust themselves to it and try to improve it where they can. When told that Margaret Fuller had said, "I accept the universe," Carlyle remarked, "Gad, she'd better!" We need to accept the causal relations and the orderliness of the world in which we live. We need to be consistent persons in an orderly society.

Third, *we need to control and to sublimate some of our desires or drives.* Some of our desires such as the generous, loving, helpful impulses need to be expressed and others redirected or sublimated. Sublimation is the substitution of some ethical or socially approved outlet for energy when the original or natural outlet is blocked or undesirable. Self-discipline, or the control of our passions by intelligence or forethought, is the essence of mature living. An important part of maturity is the ability to discern what is fitting in the situation at hand. For example, the sex urge and maternal desires may be fulfilled best within marriage; but where marriage is not feasible, the urge may be expressed through child welfare or some form of social service or through artistic creativity. Neither repression on the one hand nor indulgence on the other hand is a desirable solution. To permit any appetite or urge to run rampant squanders energy and leads to conflicts within the individual and between the individual and society. A person who is emotionally mature is able to delay his responses. The child, on the other hand, wants to satisfy each desire the moment it arises. He cannot wait, since he lacks foresight and endurance. The adult is restrained and reflective and is willing to forego immediate desires for more remote ends that will be more beneficial in the long run.

Fourth, *we need an interest in some work or in a worthy cause that calls forth our latent energy and enables us to forget ourselves.* Interest in some worthwhile task is an important element in human happiness, as we saw earlier. Without joy in work there is only boredom and fatigue. Unless a man finds some creative work for which he is fitted, he is likely to work under strain and to become a maladjusted person in society. Fortunate indeed is the person who finds early in life where his interests and his aptitudes lie. Some find their niche through the hard process of trial and error; some never find it. Today, however, through numerous interest, aptitude, personality, and character tests, it is possible for a person to get fairly reliable help. Some schools and colleges as well as numerous child guidance clinics and psychological clinics are rendering valuable service in this area.

Interest in a cause to which we can be loyal and give our best service lifts us out of ourselves, helps us maintain our self-respect, and makes us feel that we are part of a larger and meaningful whole. Without self-respect, an important task to be done, and a sense of mission, human life loses its sense of direction. Some men find interest and satisfaction in their work; others must depend on their avocations and hobbies. Hobbies of many kinds have helped many people to find more joy in living and to maintain mental health.

Fifth, *we need to seek to live a balanced life.* We have spoken of the need to find worthwhile work. Few persons respect a playboy, yet some recreation or play is essential for most people. Life can be out of balance in any one of a number of directions. A man can have physical health, comforts, and work and still be frustrated and miserable. Without food an individual can live sometimes for a month; without water he can survive only a few days; without air he dies in a few minutes. Yet with these, but without faith, hope, love, and a sense of meaning in life, he may destroy himself. Some decades ago Richard C. Cabot wrote the book *What Men Live By* in which he dealt with four central ingredients of life: work, play, love, and worship.

Many of us have to be specialists in one area, or at most a few areas, but we can keep linkages open to, and some interest in, areas other than our specialties. One of the arguments for a liberal arts education is that, in addition to preparing men for specialties and graduate studies, it gives some attention to the four great areas of human interest and aspiration: science, philosophy, the arts, and religion.

Sixth, for growth and continuing mental health *we need a faith, a set of consistent ideals, or a philosophy of life that is life-affirming.* "As a man thinketh in his heart so is he."[11] "There is a deep tendency in human nature to *become like* that which we imagine ourselves to be."[12] If you believe you are a victim of circumstances, you may be just that. If you earnestly believe that life and the world can be made better, you may not attain everything you desire, but you are likely to live in a better world than you otherwise would.

The life of a person who is mentally mature is integrated around a philosophy of life. A realistic attitude toward one's personal problems, toward one's relationships with other people, and toward the world is a condition of mental health. Intelligence is important, and there is a moral obligation to be well informed, but intelligence does not guarantee purpose and is not a substitute for it. "We cannot insist too much nor too often," says a popular treatise on mental hygiene, "that a sound mind means sound morals much more than it means sound reasoning, and that normality is a matter of character rather than of intelligence."[13]

THE NEED FOR A NATIONAL HEALTH PLAN AND PROGRAM

While the United States is spending more of its gross national product for health and medical care than is any other country and while American medicine has achieved many outstanding successes, the country as a whole has fallen behind a number of others in various areas of health care. During the last two decades the country has dropped from seventh to sixteenth in the prevention of infant mortality, in female life expectancy from sixth to eighth, in male life expectancy from tenth to twenty-fourth. We read about many disturbing situations: a shortage of doctors although thousands of well-qualified students are turned down by medical schools, some medical schools facing a possible closure for lack of funds, a maldistribution of doctors between urban and rural areas, a system that places too great an emphasis on hospital care of the sick with too little emphasis on prevention, that only about two-thirds of the doctors in the United States are actually treating patients, that one-sixth of the active physicians consist of

---

[11]Prov. 23:7.
[12]Marie Beynon Ray, *How Never to Be Tired*, rev. ed. (Indianapolis: Bobbs-Merrill Co., 1944).
[13]Ibid.

graduates of foreign medical schools, that the percentage of men rejected for medical reasons by the armed forces is increasing every year while individual health care costs and hospital charges (up fifty percent in the last three years) have increased much faster than the Consumer Price Index.

At present many types of medical service are provided. Some groups, notably the rich, receive the best medical care that can be provided, while some others are very inadequately covered. The types of medical practice offered to the public include: (1) The individual fee system where the patient or the members of his family select a physician and pay his fee for each item of service. The fee may be fairly standardized or according to the doctor's estimate of what the patient is able to pay. (2) State medicine, such as one finds in the armed services or in Veterans Administration facilities. Federal, state, and local governments work in various ways to improve public health. (3) Medical services provided by industries for their employees where the cost of these is an operating cost. (4) Medical groups controlled and operated by physicians. (5) Insurance programs of many types to help cover the cost of medical care. Since we insure against fire, theft, accidents, and death, the idea of health insurance is far from unique. Insurance by Blue Cross, Blue Shield, private insurance companies, benevolent societies, and the like, cover about half the people of the United States. Medicare provides a form of protection for older people through the social security system. More than forty countries of the world have some form of health or sickness insurance programs operated on a compulsory, semicompulsory, or voluntary basis.

While we do not have any one plan to recommend, we do feel that the crisis in health care is such that there is an urgent need for a comprehensive nationwide or national health plan that will eliminate the fragmentation and give order, direction, and more complete health care for those who are physically or mentally in need of care. In 1949 President Truman urged consideration of a national health system. The discussion has continued and many proposals have been made. Some action in the 1970s is a probability and would appear to be an urgent moral demand.

QUESTIONS AND PROJECTS

1. Getting material from any source that is available, outline what you consider a sensible national program or programs to:
   (1) Improve the general physical health of the nation.
   (2) Meet the problem of increasing mental illness.
   (3) Help solve the problem of drug use and addiction.

2. Speaking about a certain habit, a young lady remarked, "I think it is injurious, but I don't think a moral issue is at stake." Is this attitude prevalent? What is your criticism of it?
3. Do college students as a whole maintain healthful habits? At what points or in what areas are they most likely to ignore the principles of good health?
4. What is meant by good sportsmanship (1) in games or sports? (2) in life? Give some illustrations. What is good sportsmanship in the following situation?

    A centerfielder grabbed a fly ball just on the surface of the ground. He had really not caught the ball. However, nobody else knew whether he had caught the ball in his hands or trapped it as it hit the ground. The umpire called the batter out and the batter's team lost the game, which was a critical game in the pennant race. Should the centerfielder let it be known that the ball was not caught? Should he accept the umpire's decision, whether it is favorable or unfavorable to his team, and remain silent?
5. To what extent is there (1) professionalism, (2) commercialism, (3) evasion of rules in the athletic life of your school and athletic conference? To what extent do you think it possible to eliminate such conditions?
6. A coach is usually judged, and the tenure of his position determined, by the number of games his team wins. Is this as it should be?
7. A football coach is having difficulty getting all his squad to abide by the rule against smoking during the season. He finally announces that he will remove from the team any player he catches smoking. Soon afterwards he finds one of his star players smoking a cigarette. If he drops him from the team, he will undoubtedly lose some games his team would otherwise win. Should the coach drop the player, lose the games, and incur the hostility of the various groups that want the team to win, or should he overlook the infraction? Give reasons for your answer.
8. Do you agree with the statement that "a gracious hostess, if she is serving drinks, provides for those who don't want alcoholic drinks"? One student who very much prefers not to drink asked if, when others are drinking, he should drink too and be a good sport, or refuse and perhaps be thought a social misfit or an embarrassment to his hostess. How would you answer his question?
9. How does each of the following approach the problem of alcohol?
    (1) The Rutgers University Center of Alcohol Studies, New Brunswick, New Jersey. See *Quarterly Journal of Studies on Alcohol* and *Alcohol Treatment Digest*.
    (2) Alcoholics Anonymous, P. O. Box 459, Grand Central Station, New York, N.Y. 10017. Various publications are available.
    (3) Intercollegiate Association for the Study of the Alcohol Problem. c/o Dr. Lawrence Riggs, 1715 Morgan St., Wooster, O. 44681. Publications include *International Student Journal of Alcohol Studies* (5 issues annually).

10. Since the publication of the Report of the Advisory Committee to the Surgeon General, *Smoking and Health,* various measures have been taken by the United States Federal Government or by various state governments to reduce the sale and use of cigarettes. For example, each package of cigarettes contains the statement: "Warning: The Surgeon General Has Determined That Cigarette Smoking Is Dangerous to Your Health." There are restrictions on cigarette advertising and bans on cigarette sales to minors. Federal and state taxes on cigarttes have been raised until, in most states, the total is well in the teens per pack. Other measures, actual or proposed, include: a requirement that nicotine and tar content be given on the pack; prohibition of sales through unattended vending machines; an educational campaign in the public schools to discourage young persons from starting to smoke; a poster campaign against smoking on the part of the general public; a search for tobacco substitutes for those who need psychological props of this kind. Find what measures are in force in your area. Critically evaluate these measures as well as the proposals suggested above. Do you have other measures to suggest?
11. Comment on the following reactions to the report *Smoking and Health.*
    "I love cigarettes—and if they kill me, I'll die happy."
    "I don't plan to stop smoking. That's my bread and butter." (tobacco company employee)
    "An asinine report; a smear on the tobacco industry."
12. In discussions of health in the modern world, questions often arise as to the proper division of responsibility for health care—for the young, the aged, and people in general. Can you formulate any principles, or make practical suggestions, as to what you think are the proper responsibilities of the individual, his family, the local community, the state, and the federal government?

SUGGESTED READINGS

PHYSICAL HEALTH

Diehl, Harold S. *Healthful Living.* New York: McGraw-Hill Book Co., 1955.
Diehl, Harold S. and Dalrymple, Willard. *Healthful Living: A Textbook of Personal and Community Health.* 8th ed. New York: McGraw-Hill Book Co., 1968.
Duncan, Margaret M., and Johnson, Ralph H. *Introduction to Physical Education, Health Education, and Recreation.* New York: Prentice-Hall, 1954.
Jones, B., ed., *Health of Americans.* Englewood Cliffs, N.J.: Prentice-Hall, 1970.
Jones, Kenneth L., et al. *Health Science.* New York: Harper & Row, Publishers, 1971.

Jones, Kenneth L.; Shainberg, Louis W.; and Byer, Curtis O. *Age of Aquarius: Contemporary Bio-Social Issues.* Pacific Palisades, Calif.: Goodyear Publishing Co., 1971.
Rice, Thurman B., and Hein, Fred V. *Living.* Rev ed. Chicago: Scott, Foresman & Co., 1954.
Schifferes, Justus J. *Healthier Living Highlights.* New York: John Wiley & Sons, 1971.

ALCOHOL, TOBACCO, AND DRUGS

Carroll, Charles R. *Alcohol: Use, Nonuse and Abuse.* Dubuque, Ia.: W. C. Brown Co., 1970.
Cohen, Sidney. *The Drug Dilemma.* New York: McGraw-Hill Book Co., 1969.
Diehl, Harold S. *Tobacco and Your Health: The Smoking Controversy.* New York: McGraw-Hill Book Co., 1969.
Duster, Troy. *The Legislation of Morality: Law, Drugs, and Moral Judgment.* New York: Free Press, 1970.
Federal Source Book, A: Answers to the Most Frequently Asked Questions About Drugs. Washington, D.C.: U. S. Government Printing Office, 1972.
Grinspoon, Lester. *Marihuana Reconsidered.* Cambridge: Harvard University Press, 1971.
Jones, Kenneth L.; Shainberg, Louis W.; and Byer, Curtis O. *Drugs, Alcohol and Tobacco.* New York: Harper & Row, Publishers, 1970.
Kaplan, Robert. *Drug Abuse: Perspective on Drugs.* Dubuque, Ia.: W. C. Brown Co., 1970.
Laurie, Peter. *Drugs: Medical, Psychological, and Social Facts.* Baltimore: Pelican Publishing House, 1969.
Marihuana and Health. A Report to the Congress from the Secretary of Health, Education, and Welfare. Washington, D.C.: U. S. Government Printing Office, 1971.
National Education Association. *Drug Abuse: Escape to Nowhere.* Philadelphia: Smith, Kline & French Laboratories, 1967.
Whitney, Elizabeth D., ed. *World Dialogue on Alcohol and Drug Dependence.* Boston: Beacon Press, 1970. See Appendix 389–390, for sources of information on alcohol and drugs.
Wolk, Donald J., ed. *Drugs and Youth.* Washington, D.C.: National Council for the Social Studies, 1971.

MENTAL HEALTH

Arieti, Silvano. *The Intrapsychic Self: Feeling, Cognition, and Creativity in Health and Mental Illness.* New York: Basic Books, 1967.
Barron, Frank, *Creativity and Psychological Health.* New York: D. Van Nostrand Co., 1963.
Delgado, Jose M. R. *Physical Control of the Mind.* New York: Harper & Row, Publishers, 1969.
Mental Hygiene. Journal of the National Association for Mental Health, Inc., Albany, New York. (See this journal for up-to-date articles.)

Mowrer, A. H. *Morality and Mental Health.* Chicago: Rand McNally & Co., 1967.

National Clearing House for Mental Health Information. *Resource Book for Drug Abuse Education.* Chevy Chase, Md.: National Institute of Mental Health, 1969.

15
FREEDOM OF THOUGHT AND EXPRESSION

Aristotle defined man as a thinking being, and reflective thinking or critical intelligence has usually been listed among the unique qualities of persons. In every age, however, there have been attempts by influential persons or established institutions to limit or to control man's thinking and the expression of his opinion. Today the struggle for freedom continues all over the world.

FAITH IN CRITICAL THINKING

Freedom of Expression As a Right

In an earlier chapter we noted that a human right is a just claim to a condition that an individual needs in order to live at his best. In modern societies men have certain rights established by the laws of their community. These rights vary from state to state and from nation to nation. There are some rights, however, that are said to belong to man as a human being. These are said to be human, natural, or God-given rights grounded in man's nature as a person. They are rights that all men may claim. Men may on occasion appeal from some legal enactment to the "law behind the law," to man's basic rights as a human being. Since rights and duties are correlative, if a man has rights, then other men are duty bound to respect those rights.

From a wide range of civil rights and civil liberties, which include freedom from arbitrary arrest, the right of *habeas corpus,* the right to a fair trial, the right to vote, and the like, we shall limit our discussion to freedom of thought and expression. While moral philosophers have been concerned with a wide range of rights, freedom of thought and expression is central in the development of a reflective and mature morality. If a man is to develop his distinctively human qualities and if he is to experience mental health and growth, he must be free to express himself: to think, speak, write, or assemble without threat of coercion or undue restrictions by the state or by groups and individuals in the community or nation.

Man's struggle for freedom goes back for some thousands of years, but widespread belief in the right to express one's ideas freely and faith in intelligence as a means of bettering man's condition are comparatively recent. The ancient Greeks, it is true, prized both freedom and intelligence. Reflection, however, was regarded largely as a means of knowing reality and disciplining one's self and not as an instrument for controlling the fortunes of life. From the close of the Greek era until modern times, faith in intellectual freedom was eclipsed by faith in revelation and emphasis on obedience to some established order. Thinking was kept within narrow limits.

Since Francis Bacon, faith in critical thinking has been increasing. There has been a growing belief that many of the evils of man's personal and social life can be eliminated through creative intelligence. This conviction has expressed itself in the rise of public education, the growth of democracy, and many types of voluntary associations that are characteristic of free societies. Education has an important ethical function to fulfill. It must teach youths and adults to think and then to apply intelligence to social purposes. Yet this by itself is not enough. Education without a determining center or apart from some commitment may lead to confusion. People need a scale of values and a comprehensive view of the world in which they live in order to be able to meet that world's changing problems with resourcefulness and vision. Education and democracy mean little unless they are accompanied by freedom of the mind and the right to give expression to the best that every man has in him. Each person has an obligation to use his freedom and his intelligence in ways which further his own development and the welfare of the group.

Some Obstacles to Critical Thinking

If man is a thinking being, and if there is an obligation to be significantly informed and to exercise "due care," why is it that few persons live truly intelligent lives? Why is it that even in a society that praises freedom, there are obstacles within the lives of individuals and in society to the free exercise of intelligence? Part of the answer lies in the fact that we are largely creatures of habit. And while habits are valuable in taking care of the routine details of life, they not only do not help but actually hinder in new or unfamiliar situations. Habits are emotional and intellectual as well as physical; they form a mass of notions that are accepted uncritically and used to interpret the world.

Another obstacle to thinking is prejudice. A prejudice is a judgment in advance without adequate examination of the evidence, or one influenced by emotional considerations. In the first case, it may be made without examination of evidence, or after examination of the evidence, but in disregard of or inadequate regard for significant portions thereof. Thus the conclusions that are reached are likely to be false. When people are confronted with their prejudices, they tend to rationalize them—that is, they seek arguments for continuing to believe what they wish to believe. Prejudice is often a product of wishful thinking.

The third obstacle to thinking is propaganda. The word *propaganda* was once a perfectly good term referring to the spread of any belief or doctrine, not necessarily by methods that were not open and honest. In the twentieth century, however, the term is used to refer to attempts to create public opinion by the spread of misinformation, with indirect methods and selfish motives. Whereas education at its best extends knowledge by encouraging an examination of the facts and by teaching men to think, propaganda stifles thinking by attempting to indoctrinate one point of view. Since the propagandist wants action, he does two things. First, he arouses some strong desire or emotion; second, he suggests a program that appears to be a satisfactory way of satisfying the desire or emotion. There need be no logical connection whatever between the desire aroused and the line of action suggested as a way of satisfying it. For example, the clever advertiser knows that the emotion of love may be aroused and then connected with the idea of flowers, an insurance policy or any other thing. Propaganda is a subtle means of making up the other man's mind for him while he believes he is thinking independently.

The pressure of public opinion is a fourth obstacle to thinking. A public is any group of persons who are joined by some common interest. Thus a person may belong at one and the same time to many publics, with one standing for regulation of the currency, another advocating lower tariffs, and so on. Public opinion is the aggregate of the views held by people in a given community regarding issues that interest them or the community. Public opinion tends to align itself for or against proposals about how to meet public problems. It is easily swayed by emotion and tends to thrive on stereotypes or slogans and the opinions of people who have prestige. The mass media, which we shall consider in a later chapter, play a large part in the formation of public opinion.

While public opinion exerts a strong pressure on the individual, its dictates are not necessarily intelligent or moral. Indeed, since it tends to represent the average or mediocre mind, public opinion is often unenlightened. At its worst it is the result of manipulation by special-interest groups.

If we want to learn to face life in an intelligent manner, we must recognize these obstacles to thinking and try to eliminate them, as far as possible, from our own thinking. The task is not easy, but it is part of our obligation to think intelligently.

HISTORIC DEFENSES OF FREEDOM OF EXPRESSION

The struggle for freedom goes back many centuries and embraces many peoples in different parts of the world. To discuss all the great defenders of freedom and the significant documents of freedom would take more space than we have available. We shall mention only a few Anglo-Saxon champions of freedom of expression since the seventeenth century.

In 1643 the two Houses of the English Parliament drew up a law which provided that no book or other publication should "from henceforth be printed or put to sale, unless the same be first approved of and licensed by such person or persons as both or either of the said Houses shall appoint for the licensing of the same." This measure prompted John Milton, one of the outstanding figures of English literature, to write one of the great defenses of free speech entitled *Areopagitica*, which states the intellectual and moral case against censorship and for freedom of expression. "Who kills a man," Milton says, "kills a reasonable creature, God's image; but he who destroys a good book, kills reason itself. . . ." We cannot know what is good unless we know what is evil, or recognize truth except as we can distinguish it from falsehood. Milton asserts that free discussion of all social problems, the good and the evil as well as the abuse of governmental power is needed. We cannot, he says, improve human nature and morals by repressive measures.

Another historic defense of freedom of expression was made by John Stuart Mill (1806–1873) in his essay *On Liberty*. There Mill contends that attempts to limit freedom of speech are, with very rare exceptions, to be condemned. To suppress the views even of very small minorities, even of single individuals, is harmful to the society and the discovery of truth. "If all mankind minus one were of one opinion, and only one person were of the contrary opinion, mankind would be no more justified in silencing that one person, than he, if he had the power, would be justified in silencing mankind." The one opinion may be right, but even if it is clearly wrong society gains by "the clearer perception and livelier impression of truth produced by its collision with error."[1]

The first ten amendments to the United States Constitution are often called the "Bill of Rights." No one may be restrained, we read in the First Amendment, from merely talking and expressing a point of view: "Congress shall make no law respecting an establishment of religion, or prohibiting the free exercise thereof; or abridging the freedom of speech, or of the press; or the right of the people peaceably to assemble, and to petition the government for a redress of grievances." In the Fifth Amendment, which deals with prosecution and imprisonment and private property taken for public use, there is a due process clause. Certain things are not to be done "without due process of law." The First Amendment, however, contains no such clause; it simply says "no law." When it comes to thoughts, ideas, and opinions, a man is free to express himself. The opinions of others are not to be forced on him, and there is to be no coercion or repression by state, church, or other group on the mere expression of his opinions. His freedom to speak does not depend on what he says being true or right as others view it. According to this tradition of freedom the "only opinion established . . . by the Constitution is the opinion that a man is free to hold any opinion." There is to be no official party line or demand for conformity. The principle here seems to be that the important thing is the man, his worth, his uniqueness, his individuality, and that this uniqueness will be damaged or lost if attempts are made to enforce uniformity.

In many statements and actions Thomas Jefferson reinforced this tradition of freedom. He said, "It is time enough for the rightful purposes of civil government for its officers to interfere when principles break out into overt acts against peace and good order."

Early in 1947 Harry S. Truman, addressing a newly appointed Committee on Civil Rights, said, "I want our Bill of Rights implemented in fact. We have been trying to do this for 150 years." The Committee report *To Secure These Rights*[2] is one of the outstanding documents of our free society. This report dealt with a wide range of civil liberties, pointed out various flaws in the nation's record, emphasized the heritage and the dream not fully attained, and made recommendations for action.

The civil rights acts of 1957–1965, a series of Supreme Court decisions, and various executive orders and legislative enactments too nu-

---

[1]Stuart Mill, *Utilitarianism, Liberty, and Representative Government*. Everyman's Library. (New York: E. P. Dutton & Co., 1910), p. 79.
[2](Washington, D. C.: President's Committee on Civil Rights, 1947).

merous to mention in detail indicate that some progress is being made in the age-long struggle for freedom of expression, especially on the part of minority groups that have felt the main force of repressive measures in the past. Scores of excellent books and articles dealing with these issues have appeared in recent years. The public is now more sensitive and more concerned about them. Opponents of greater freedom are active but are on the defensive, and notable changes are in the offing. The American Civil Liberties Union states that

> The civil rights issues are among the "great issues" of our times, not because of their novelty—the century since the Emancipation Proclamation belies that possibility—nor because of their complexity, but because of their relationship to our national purpose. It is in this sense that they differ from the host of lesser but important questions that have prior to 1963 occupied the forums of national debate. But the 1960's promise to pose for us other "great issues"—issues which will "test whether [our] nation, or any nation so conceived and so dedicated can long endure"—and many of these issues will in addition be both novel and complex. The world-wide revolution of rising expectations will test the premises of our conduct of foreign affairs. The accelerating growth of the world's populations, and of our own, will test that and much more. The technology of production will test the premises of our economic order. And the technology of destruction will test the premises of both foreign policy and national defense. Today's civil rights test has become the proving ground on which to demonstrate whether we can use our rights and our machinery of self-government to resolve the first of these great issues to which the nation has turned its attention[3]

INTELLECTUAL FREEDOM UNDER ATTACK

During recent years the restrictions placed on freedom of speech have caused much concern, especially on the part of many intellectual leaders and student groups. In the mid-fifties the president of a distinguished university, while recognizing that the climate of opinion may change from time to time, said that "the predominant pressures in our culture" have been moving for some decades with increasing force in the direction of conformity, so that as a people we are coming more and more to think, talk, act, and even dress alike. "Since World War II," he said, "there has been a rather violent shift in public opinion which has resulted in increased pressure in the direction of conformity."[4]

---

[3] *To Secure: To Use: These Rights;* 43rd Annual Report, July 1, 1962 to June 30, 1963 (New York: American Civil Liberties Union, 1964), pp. 4–5.
[4] Nathan M. Pusey, "The Vision of the Liberal Education," *Harvard Alumni Bulletin,* 20 February 1954, p. 389.

304 / Chapter Fifteen

Writing in the early sixties, a member of the Supreme Court of the United States expressed a similar view: "The trend to conformity has possessed us since World War II. The causes are numerous, some of them reflecting no more than a conservative outlook that is usually reflected in an affluent society."[5] The same judge writing a few years earlier said, "We have witnessed in this country a virtual witch hunt that has had a paralyzing effect on students, teachers, scientists, and writers."[6] When men fear that mere mistakes and differences of opinion may be called disloyalty or subversion, they hesitate to speak out and make decisions. Loyalty oaths and other restrictions have an intimidating effect on the expression of new and different ideas and have tended to prevent free discussion of controversial issues.

Recently various keen observers have asked if we are moving towards something like Aldous Huxley's *Brave New World* or George Orwell's *1984*, where some "Big Brother" will attempt to control our thoughts and actions. Certainly a great struggle is being waged for the minds and loyalties of men and women, and some defenders of our heritage of freedom have expressed dismay at the intolerance, arrogance, and dogmatism of large sections of the population.

During the sixties and early seventies the struggle for freedom of thought and expression continued unabated in many areas. We shall deal briefly with five such areas.

1. In the field of education, teachers have been dismissed for discussing such topics as civil liberties, race relations, labor relations, the war in Southeast Asia, the United Nations and other international organizations. In some localities teachers fear to discuss such questions and so free inquiry and free discussion become impossible. A teacher at a junior college was dismissed for writing a letter to a local newspaper in which he was critical of the educational standards of the county public school system.[7] The American Association of University Professors reported that in the academic year 1970–1971 the number of complaints alleging violations of academic freedom and tenure increased significantly over previous years.[8]

In the early seventies young people, and especially the students in some high schools, were protesting against the tendency of some school

---

[5]William O. Douglas, *Freedom of the Mind* (Chicago: American Library Association in cooperation with the Public Affairs Committee, 1962), p. 2.

[6]*The Right of the People* (New York: Doubleday & Co., 1958), p. 83.

[7]For this and other freedom issues see *Freedom through Dissent*, 42nd Annual Report, July 1, 1961 to June 30, 1962 (New York: American Civil Liberties Union, 1963), pp. v, 16, 30.

[8]Bertram H. Davis, General Secretary of the Washington Office, April 1971: personal communication to association members. See also recent issues of the *AAUP Bulletin*.

officials to ignore the United States Constitution as well as recent court decisions that made clear that neither the Bill of Rights nor the Fourteenth Amendment were for adults only. If young people are to be prepared for enlightened citizenship and the free mind is not to be strangled at its source, basic rights must be protected in the schools. Among the reported limitations of freedom are the following: student speakers in school assembly warned not to say anything about the war, censorship of school papers, refusal to permit students to wear armbands or buttons while in school, removal of a student from the ballot for a school office because he had written an article critical of the administration, arbitrary suspensions, and refusal to admit students because of a dress code that said that hair must not touch the ears of men students.

The United States Supreme Court, or Courts of Appeal, have handed down decisions declaring, among other things, that a student has a right to express his opinions in the classroom or on the campus if he does not interfere with appropriate discipline or interfere with the rights of others; that the wearing of an armband is "symbolic speech" and is protected under the First Amendment; that students could not be suspended for wearing buttons saying, for example, "Freedom Now"; that school officials could not claim that the wearing of long hair was "inherently distracting" to other students; and that students may publish and distribute their views.[9]

2. Freedom of thought and expression has been violated by the banning of speakers. Private vigilante groups have been active in this area, and there have been reports about various "black lists" and "gray lists" being circulated. These lists have included not only "dangerous radicals" but persons whose views were not approved by the groups circulating the lists. Sometimes the pressure from some self-appointed vigilante group or even some individual has led a timid group to cancel a meeting or a proprietor to refuse to rent a hall for a meeting. Sometimes the banning is effected by city ordinances that require police permits for any special gatherings. If the speaker, topic, or sponsoring organization is not in favor or is "controversial," the permit may be refused.

3. The issue of censorship has been a persistent one in recent decades. In some areas a police officer has the right under state law to enter and check the books in a bookstore if a complaint has been filed charging that the store was offering obscene or offensive material

---

[9]For a discussion of these topics and the court decisions, see Nat Hentoff "Why Students Want Their Constitutional Rights," *Saturday Review* 54 (May 22, 1971): pp. 60–63, 73–74.

for sale. While in some instances the concern is about the obscene, in others the concern is also with material that is antiestablishment or politically inflammatory.[10]

A disturbing wave of text and reading-list censorship in recent decades has threatened not only to ban the writings of some revolutionaries who advocate direct action but also to eliminate many controversial issues and some important classics from public school teaching. Some of the lists of banned books include works by Plato, Shakespeare, Hawthorne, Thoreau, and Mark Twain and read like a who's who of outstanding literary figures. Many groups of scholars have spoken out in protest. The following statement is somewhat typical.

> Across America today increasing pressures are exerted on schools to restrict the access of students to important and worthwhile books. In many communities attempts have been made to remove literary works from classrooms and school libraries. . . . Merely from fear of such attacks, schools have removed enduring books from libraries and classrooms. Many students continue their "education" in a climate hostile to free inquiry, with limited access to important literary documents. . . . In the National Council of Teachers of English, the National Education Association, the American Library Association, as well as in the publishing industry and among writers themselves, informed observers agree: the pressures are great; the danger is increasing.[11]

A statement by President Eisenhower should be kept alive and remembered because it is as applicable today as when uttered. Expressing his concern about various cases or instances of repression of reading matter in the news at the time, he said:

> Don't join the book burners. Don't think you are going to conceal faults by concealing evidence that they ever existed. Don't be afraid to go in your library and read every book as long as any document does not offend our own ideas of decency. That should be the only censorship.[12]

In a censorship case, a Superior Court judge in Illinois declared:

> Let the parents control the reading matter of their children; let the tastes of the readers determine what they may or may not read; let each reader be his own censor; but let not the government or the courts

---

[10]See Nina Sydney Ladof, "Censorship—The Tip and the Iceberg," *American Libraries* (March 1971): 309–310.

[11]*The Students' Right to Read* (Champaign Ill.: The National Council of Teachers of English, 1962), pp. 5, 6.

[12]From President Dwight D. Eisenhower's address at Dartmouth College, June 14, 1953, quoted in "The Freedom to Read," (Chicago: American Library Association, 1953).

dictate the reading matter of a free people. The constitutional right to freedom of speech and press should be jealously guarded by the courts.[13]

4. Freedom of thought and expression in the area of security clearance has presented many problems in recent decades because of cold and hot wars. Security regulations are set up for those who serve or wish to serve the nation in either a civil or a military capacity. No thoughtful or loyal person will deny the need for protecting the national security, and this protection may call at times for some limitation to our traditional liberties. We do not want disloyal people or poor security risks in sensitive positions. A special problem, however, has been created by reason of the fact that security proceedings have been extended to include companions, friends, and the personal beliefs, real or imputed, of the person under consideration. The progress that produced our technological advances (civilian and military) has depended on the free exchange and cross-fertilization of ideas and on criticism. Excessive pressure for orthodoxy and conformity is not likely to give us the security we seek.

The situation in this area today is not as serious as it was a decade or two ago. The improvement is encouraging, but if some scientists have been discouraged from working for the government because of "fear of smear," or if some government workers have to be in constant fear about what they read and with whom they talk, the situation is by no means ideal.

5. The investigating committees of various governmental agencies have tended to ignore the important principle of the separation of powers and functions and to act as prosecutors, juries, and judges as well as investigators. This statement implies no criticism of the legitimate and useful investigative functions of Congress. There are many areas in which we need more facts, and we do want to expose disloyal, illegal, and subversive activities. But in so doing we do not want to undermine our own way of life and ignore the constitutional rights we have built up over the years. During the late sixties and early seventies, leaders in various branches of government, including congressmen, have complained that their telephones have been tapped, their offices bugged, and their activities kept under surveillance.[14]

Among the safeguards for our freedoms are the following: that a man is innocent until proven guilty; that he has a right to know the charges made against him; that he should be confronted by his accusers and have a right to cross-examine them; that he has a right to a speedy

---

[13]*Freedom through Dissent*, p. 6.
[14]See the books by Myron Brenton, Omar V. Garrison, Arthur R. Miller, and Jerry M. Rosenberg listed in the *Suggested Readings*.

and public trial, with counsel. Recently we have heard much about "trial by publicity," "guilt by association," "character assassination," and the like. We had believed that, over the years, we had gained the right to think freely and to declare our convictions openly on all issues, to read what we wish to read, or to publish our views. Now many fear to express themselves on issues that are in any way controversial.

These five fields by no means exhaust the types of attack on the principles of a free society. In religion there appears to be an attempt to break down the traditional separation of church and state and to spread abroad the false notion that any concern for social justice or a better world is the sign of communism. In art, a work should not be banned or suppressed merely because some groups do not like the artist or his political and social views, or because he portrays something in his art we do not approve or something that is of a controversial nature.

The problems above are set forth not in any negative attitude but with the confidence that when the people know the facts and recall their heritage, the trends will be reversed. We can have confidence that the sober second judgment of the great majority of the people will assert itself.

The attempts to deny freedom of expression, as seen in some of the incidents above, are somewhat typical in three respects. First, some special-interest group is usually attempting to guard its privileges by keeping certain facts or ideas from the public. Second, suppression takes place regardless of the truth or falsity of the ideas. Usually there is no attempt to discover the truth or the effect of the ideas on public welfare. Third, there is frequently an attempt to divert attention to some other issue by introducing some term of reproach, such as communist, fascist, subversive, or dangerous person.

When asked, "Do you believe in freedom of speech?" many people will answer something like this: "Yes, I believe in free spech, but of course I would limit it to what is right and true." That, however, is not free speech. The worst tyrant would permit others to express the ideas *he* favors or thinks right and true. Freedom of speech means the right of a person to think honestly and to speak on any public issue without fear of interference. It means your right to criticize the other fellow, and it means his right to criticize you.

There is, of course, a difference between the right to voice opinions on all sides of any public question and defamation. While citizens should be free to criticize public officials and to expose immoral acts, laws against slander and libel are necessary for the protection of innocent people. There is also a difference between advocating a change in laws or in institutions and inciting people to break those laws while they are in force. Slander, libel, inciting people to break actual laws, and indecent speech in public places are probably the only "restrictions" that we need to make in the field of freedom of expression. And these are not really restrictions, but ground rules which must be observed if we are all to be free.

Ask yourself these three questions: Would I permit other people to express views that are apparently true but that are unpleasant or opposed to my interests? Would I permit others to say what I consider false but more or less harmless? Would I permit others to express views that I believe to be both false and harmful? If you cannot say "yes" to the above questions, you do not really believe in freedom of speech. Punishment for mere opinion expressed on questions of public concern makes for violence and disorder instead of orderly progress.

THE INVASION OF PRIVACY

The Constitution of the United States, especially as stated in the Fourth Amendment, recognizes the right of privacy: "The right of the people to be secure in their persons, houses, papers, and effects, against unreasonable searches and seizures, shall not be violated, and no Warrant shall issue, but upon probable cause, supported by Oath or affirmation, and particularly describing the place to be searched, and the persons or things to be seized."

On the basis of past experience and present expectations, for example, we think that we should not be subject to search and seizure of our property on the basis of mere suspicion. Suppose that I suspect someone of having stolen something and I think the evidence can be found in his house. I may not simply slip in and collect the evidence. He has, in our society, a right to protection from unreasonable search and seizure. To be sure that this right is not violated, I must obtain a search warrant and have the search conducted by a qualified officer of the law. So important to the well-being of the community is the protection of privacy that my right to recovery of stolen property may have to go unfulfilled if it would require tapping his telephone. With the rapid development of the new technology and the manufacture and sale of a great variety of electronic and other instruments of surveillance (spying, bugging, tapping telephone lines, and the like) the issue of privacy has become a matter of great concern.

While the problem has been with us for some decades, during the late sixties and early seventies discussions of wiretapping, secret files, and computerized national data banks have taken on a new urgency. Some people mainly interested in "law and order" favor wiretapping and the use of other means of surveillance, since they believe that only known criminals and subversives will have their conversations recorded. They also assert that they have nothing to hide and ask, "What is the danger to law-abiding citizens?" Others are vigorously opposed on moral, legal, and practical grounds. Once started and legally permitted the practice tends to expand and to reach into more and more areas and include eventually the whole country as witnessed in the totalitarian states. Investigating bodies, civilian or military, easily move from the area of known criminals to agitators, protestors, and persons who might become dangerous. During urban disorders the police and the army want to know who are radicals and dissatisfied persons. Officials become overzealous and a practice started by honorable men for worthy ends soon becomes a far-reaching apparatus extending into the homes and offices of many people. During the early seventies congressmen and national and state officials were charging that their phones had been tapped.

The issue of privacy has become an important matter as governmental agencies are reported to be compiling data books on individuals who file income tax returns, receive Social Security benefits, apply for a passport, are arrested, or participate in a demonstration even though it is legal. Some private agencies, such as credit associations, hope to have the record of every man and woman in the country included in their computerized data bank in the very near future. Our privacy appears to be "up for sale" as an ever-growing group of private "investigators" seek out and record even intimate information that can be gleaned from neighbors and acquaintances, police court records, internal revenue and social security systems, income tax payments, banks and credit card transactions, insurance purchases, employment background, telephone calls, flying trips, and the like. Many junior and senior high schools give personality tests to students that reveal the most secret recesses of their personalities. "Problem checklists" may disclose data on the young person's fears, dates, sex life, the family finances, and on his parents and home life. These tests have a legitimate use in helping counselors give advice and aid to students; they can also be abused.

There are reported to be between twenty and forty makers of eavesdropping or electronic devices for penetrating otherwise private or secret areas of our lives. Representatives of some large suppliers of eavesdropping devices have testified under oath before congressional investigating committees that their biggest customers are governmental agencies, both security and nonsecurity units. Private agencies are also large users of bugging equipment. Sales are reported to amount to twenty million dollars a year. Private detective organizations have been growing and some large states have many hundreds of licensed private detective agencies collecting and selling information of some value to its clients.

Suggestions have been made for a National Data Bank in which there will be dossiers or files on all citizens as well as aliens. This step has been made possible by giant computers and the sharing or exchange of information by the many separate data-processing systems. When this takes place "Big Brother" and "1984" will be near. The loss of privacy will mean the loss of individuality, the marks of the police state, and the death of freedom and democracy as men fear to take stands on controversial issues, to think for themselves, or to struggle for reform. This is one of the central moral issues of our time.

We do not believe that in a complex society privacy can be an absolute condition. The central question is how to maintain effective law enforcement and to retain our human and constitutional liberties at the same time. Fear and suspicion tend to destroy the human personality and disrupt the intercommunication that is the basis of a free society. We have been warned that the growing espionage and the invasions of privacy are threatening to undermine the mental health of the country.

WHY FREEDOM IS IN JEOPARDY

What has been happening in our world? Have we as a people forgotten that "eternal vigilance is the price of liberty"?

1. We are in danger of losing our traditional liberties through ignorance—what might be called neglect or default. A few years ago a research agency asked the public what it knew about the Bill of Rights. One in four had not heard of it, and two out of three could not identify it. An enterprising newspaper reporter went out on a recent Fourth of July with a copy of the Declaration of Independence. He sought the signatures of persons who would endorse its principles. Some thought it too radical, others said it was communist propaganda, and only one out of one hundred twelve persons was willing to sign his name to this document of freedom. Popular ignorance of the principles of our rights and freedoms is endangering free discussion and intellectual freedom. It is threatening to make us morally timid and to turn us into frightened conformists.

2. We have been through periods of war and social change. Such periods are times of frustration and irritation that are likely to lead to fear and aggression. As we have noted, our society changed physically and economically from one predominantly rural and agricultural to a

highly complex industrial civilization becoming increasingly interdependent and impersonal. Psychologically and spiritually, the change has been equally great. The optimism, faith, and confidence of the beginning of the century have given way to disillusionment and anxiety. Immature, insecure individuals, therefore, fall back on what is safe or orthodox.

3. The growth of the mass media of communication, such as radio, television, motion pictures, and newspapers, has given us powerful new instruments for creating public opinion. Today it is easy to stir the emotions of large groups, even of whole nations, for or against persons and programs. Through personal and group contacts, these effects may be further heightened and may "snowball" into a "mental epidemic." Individuals have stopped doing their own thinking, and they tend to react for or against certain stereotypes. Public relations groups, special interest groups, the propagandists, and advertisers manipulate us. In response to appeals for group loyalty and group conformity, people have been adhering to hard and fast lines, which means that fewer of us are in the area of maneuverability.

4. Psychologists tell us that "what gets our attention tends to get us," and we move in that direction. Recently we have been giving our attention to things we fear or hate. Two or three decades ago it was fascism; more recently it has been communism. We have centered our attention on these rather than on our ethical ideals and our free way of living. Consequently, we stand in danger of what has been called "imitative disaster"—of acting more like totalitarians than like free men and women.

The contemporary world is in a state of crisis over the question of the direction in which we should move, if at all, and the presence of extremist groups has made the preservation of freedom more difficult. While these extremists are often separated into two antagonistic groups, called the Far Right (reactionaries, ultra-conservatives, and fascists) and the Far Left (those who seek radical changes in social institutions, the Communists, and the like), actually the two groups have much in common, especially in type of thinking and methodology. They are both dogmatic and intolerant of those who disagree with them. They line up in hard and fast lines, resort to name calling, and exhibit what is often called "black-and-white" thinking; they assume things are all good or all evil, with no middle ground. They think they have all the truth and virtue; other groups all the error and evil. Any mistakes or failure by a public official is likely to be called betrayal or disloyalty. They have a strong distrust of democratic processes and tend to be authoritarian and to support some minority, elite group, or leader. They want to control the institutions in our society and suppress criticism, at least of their program and tactics.

WHY INTELLECTUAL FREEDOM IS IMPORTANT

While freedom of thought is not an absolute—there are other rights to be considered—it is one of the fundamental human rights. First, freedom of expression is a basic condition for the development of mature persons and the creation and enjoyment of human values. If people cannot think and express their thoughts freely, they give up, relax, or go stale and become something less than well-developed persons. Such repression, if prolonged, tends to damage or destroy a part of their selfhood or personality. They feel stifled, and it will not be long before they cease to have thoughts worthy of expression. They tend either to become docile "yes men" with slave minds and habits, or to become aggressive and rebellious. The distinctive qualities of persons, such as self-consciousness, reflective thinking, ethical discrimination, and aesthetic appreciation develop most adequately in a society where men and women can think and express themselves freely.

Second, intellectual freedom is a necessary condition for the discovery of truth and new ideas, and for creativity. If men and women cannot think and express themselves on controversial issues, how can they discover what is true? If they cannot discover what is true and right, how can they live wholesome moral lives? We need freedom because we need new ideas that are essential to progress. Almost every idea and ideal that we prize today, including those of public education and democracy, were at one time considered false and dangerous. Most of our cherished institutions arose as a protest against some way of doing things. In the second quarter of the nineteenth century, a man was chased out of a section of New England with the warning that he would be shot if he ever came back advocating the heresy of taxing one man's property to educate another man's child. He was proposing taxation for free public schools. Most of the founders of the nation were denounced as radicals and heretics. In fact, as we look back through history, we find that most of the great benefactors of the race were misunderstood, and that frequently they were persecuted.

None of our institutions is perfect. Each needs the free play of criticism if there is to be normal and healthy growth. If we suppress the critics, we cut ourselves off from criticism. If we avoid criticism, we are almost certain to make unnecessary mistakes. Uncriticized groups and institutions tend sooner or later to become dictatorial and to deteriorate. They cease to remain efficient and responsive to popular demands. If we attempt to enforce conformity, we must have some standard of conformity or orthodoxy. Who or what is to set this standard? Shall it be the government or some party or agency within the government? Shall it be some church or ecclesiastical organization? Shall it be the mass media of communication?

Who today is sufficiently intelligent and sufficiently good to set himself up as a judge of what ideas are true? If an idea is false, the way to destroy it is to expose it. To prevent our opponents from expressing themselves is to admit the weakness of our own position. Let reason, discussion, and experimentation combat error. An attempt to suppress an idea or a doctrine is frequently the way to cause it to grow.

Third, freedom of expression is the basis of democracy. We cannot have a genuine democracy unless we recognize the right of a minority to become the majority if it is able to do so by persuasion and orderly change. When rulers are cut off from criticism and opposition, they fail to see things from the citizens' point of view, so that before very long they are likely to rule in their own interests or in those of a narrower group than the community. Irresponsible power tends to be used in the interest of the group that wields the power.

The democratic ideal involves talking things out rather than fighting them out. Repression is dangerous in individual lives; it is equally dangerous in society. When we drive opinion underground and permit no peaceful expression, we are likely to sow the seeds of violence and revolution.

The police power established for the purpose of protecting us against physical evils and maintaining law and order has come, in the course of time, to take as its duty the task of maintaining the established order. Too often, preserving the peace has come to mean preserving the peace of mind of those in favored positions, who want no criticism and no tampering with things as they are. Orderly progress can be achieved only in an atmosphere of tolerance and freedom. If this is true, our duty is to stand for freedom of thought and freedom of speech and to protest any denial of those rights.

Fourth, to defend freedom of the mind is to defend a way of life that is rooted not only in human experience but in our constitutional and religious heritage. To defend the free way of life is to defend a tradition that goes far back in Anglo-Saxon history to great landmarks like the Magna Charta. This tradition has been reinforced by petitions and bills of rights and is firmly established in English common law and in American constitutional law and practice. To defend freedom of expression is also to defend a religious heritage that goes back to the Hebrew prophets, to the teachings of Jesus, and to numerous leaders, events, and documents in the Western religious heritage. It has been further strengthened by insights from Greek thought and practice.

Man's freedom or need for freedom is grounded in his very nature and in the nature of the relationships in the midst of which he lives. While man is part of the flux of nature and subject to its laws, he is conscious of the fact that he is so involved. He is not, therefore, totally involved. He seems to live at the point where nature and spirit somehow meet. Freedom of thought and speech are not privileges granted by the state or by any group in society. We may call them "natural rights" or "God-given rights." At least they are based on the nature of man and the conditions necessary for his moral, intellectual, and spiritual development. If the state had the power to grant these rights, then the state could take them away. To admit that would be to admit the very core of totalitarianism—that the state can dictate in all these areas. And that is something no lover of freedom and no open-minded student of history can admit. Science, art, philosophy, and religion develop most adequately when there is a free individual in a relatively free society.

QUESTIONS AND PROJECTS

1. Why do many persons think freedom is in jeopardy in the late twentieth century? Can you relate some incidents (events, laws, pronouncements, and the like) that have taken place in the early seventies that indicate gains or losses in the area of freedom of expression?
2. Read the twenty statements on civil liberties listed below. They have been prepared by the American Civil Liberties Union (156 Fifth Avenue, New York, N. Y. 10010). You probably accept the Constitution and the Bill of Rights, but problems arise when men attempt to interpret and apply them in specific instances. As you read and think about each question, write a "yes" or "no" on paper to record your judgment. Play fair and do not look for the answers until you have completed your record.
    (1) Any private individual should have the right to criticize any government or government official anywhere in the world.
    (2) Congressional investigations into "un-American activities" are essential to our nation's security.
    (3) Segregation in public schools violates the equal protection of the laws guaranteed to all Americans by the Constitution.
    (4) A trade union member should be permitted to advocate "right-to-work" laws without jeopardizing his union membership.
    (5) Belonging to the Communist party should be punishable by fine or imprisonment.
    (6) Everyone who invokes the privilege against self-incrimination must be guilty as suspected.
    (7) Religious exercises, such as the Lord's Prayer and Bible reading, should be barred from public schools.
    (8) Books like *Tropic of Cancer* should be banned from newsstands and libraries.
    (9) States' rights clauses in the Constitution justify efforts by certain states to prevent Negroes from voting.
    (10) Communist leader Benjamin Davis and Birch Society head Robert Welch are both entitled to make public speeches.

316 / Chapter Fifteen

(11) Movies, books and plays presenting an offensive characterization of a particular racial or religious group should be suppressed.
(12) Everyone should have the right to leave any country, including his own, and to return to his country.
(13) In their war against crime policemen are entitled to listen in on private phone conversations.
(14) Parochial school pupils are entitled to free bus service, paid for from public funds.
(15) Laws against the use and sale of birth control devices violate rights of privacy guaranteed by the United States Constitution.
(16) Those accused as security risks under the federal security program should have the right to confront and cross-examine their accusers.
(17) Students receiving financial aid from the government should be required to swear that they are not members of the Communist party.
(18) Racial discrimination in housing, public and private, should be prohibited by law.
(19) Police are entitled to hold and interrogate arrested persons as long as twenty-four hours before arraigning them in front of a magistrate.
(20) To "emancipate the American Indian," reservations should be closed and federal services terminated—regardless of the tribes' wishes.

According to the American Civil Liberties Union, you get five points each for answering "yes" to statements 1, 3, 4, 7, 10, 12, 15, 16, and 18; and five points each for answering "no" to statements 2, 5, 6, 8, 9, 11, 13, 14, 17, 19, and 20. If your score is 75 or more you are in substantial agreement with the ACLU. Do not hesitate to criticize the ACLU's position on any statements, and be ready to give reasons for all your answers.

3. Discuss the following statements made by members of the United States Supreme Court:
   (1) ". . . the ultimate good desired is better reached by free trade in ideas . . . the best test of truth is the power of the thought to get itself accepted in the competition of the market. . . . That, at any rate, is the theory of our Constitution." (Oliver Wendell Holmes, Jr.)
   (2) "Fear of serious injury cannot alone justify suppression of free speech and assembly. Men feared witches and burnt women. It is the function of free speech to free men from the bondage of irrational fears." (Louis Brandeis)
   (3) "If there is any fixed star in our constitutional constellation, it is that no official, high or low, can prescribe what shall be orthodox in politics, nationalism, religion, or other matters of opinion, or force citizens to confess by word or act their faith therein." (Robert H. Jackson)
   (4) ". . . [A] function of free speech under our system of government is to invite dispute. It may indeed best serve its high purpose when it endures a condition of unrest, creates dissatisfaction with conditions as they are, or even stirs people to anger." (William O. Douglas)

(5) "I have always believed that the First Amendment is the keystone of our government, that the freedom it guarantees provides the best insurance against the destruction of all freedom." (Hugo Black)
4. Are loyalty oaths a danger or a safeguard for our freedom and security? What are the personal and social effects of requiring such oaths from teachers, lawyers, or churches (to secure tax exemption, as in one state)? Do you think that a teacher should be required to take the loyalty oath to hold his position if he feels that such oaths are wrong? For example, when Massachusetts passed a law requiring all teachers in the state to take the oath of allegiance that is required of officials of the state, certain professors at Harvard University and other institutions protested vigorously. They objected because teachers were singled out from the other groups and because such loyalty oaths seemed to be veiled attempts to control teachers and to transfer to officials appointed by partisan governors a responsibility which has constitutionally resided in nonpolitical quarters. See Alan Barth, *The Loyalty of Free Man* (New York: Viking Press, 1951), pp. 208–215; Zechariah Chafee, Jr., "The Freedom to Think," *The Atlantic Monthly* 195 (January 1955); pp. 27–33; Harold M. Hyman, *To Try Men's Souls: Loyalty Tests in American History* (Berkeley: University of California Press, 1960), ch. 13; John W. Caughey, "Farewell to California's Loyalty Oath,' " *Pacific Historical Review* 38 (May 1969): pp. 123–128.
5. Does silence imply guilt? To what extent may a witness be justified in refusing to testify on the ground of self-incrimination? Discuss the use of the Fifth Amendment. See Laurent B. Franz and Norman Redlich, "Does Silence Mean Guilt?" *The Nation* 176 (June 6, 1953): 471 ff.; Sidney Hook, "The Fifth Amendment Today—A Moral Issue," *New York Times Magazine*, 1 November 1953; Erwin N. Griswold, *The 5th Amendment Today* (Cambridge: Harvard University Press, 1955); "The Fifth Amendment," *Time* 62, pt. 1, (September 5, 1953): 16–17; C. Dickerman Williams, "The Founders and the Fifth," *National Review* 21 (March 11, 1969): 235–236; Alan Dershowitz, "Stretch Points of Liberty," *The Nation* 212 (March 15, 1971): pp. 329–334.
6. There have been attempts by states and communities to ban or censor motion pictures, reading material, and the like. There are also vigorous protests against any and all attempts at censorship. What issues, moral and otherwise, are involved? See William Dix and Paul Bixler, eds., *Freedom of Communication* (Chicago: American Library Association, 1954), pp. 125 ff.; Walter M. Daniels, ed., *The Censorship of Books*, The Reference Shelf, xxvi, no. 5 (New York: H. W. Wilson Co., 1954); Richard S. Randall, *Censorship of the Movies: The Social and Political Control of the Mass Medium* (Madison: University of Wisconsin Press, 1968).
7. On various occasions teachers have been dismissed for wearing symbols (e.g. black armbands and the like) that indicated opposition to the war in Vietnam. If you were a member of the school board, how would you vote on this issue and why?

8. Many persons in our society are concerned about the increasing invasion of privacy (electronic data banks, wiretapping and eavesdropping of various kinds, spying on individuals, "no-knock" laws that permit police to enter private homes without knocking if they think a warning would allow suspects to destroy evidence). What do you think should be permitted or banned? You may wish to consult the books dealing with privacy listed in the *Suggested Readings*.
9. What do you think the founding fathers who wrote the United States Constitution and later added the Bill of Rights would say to the following:
    (1) An attorney general who asserts his authority to tap a telephone or electronically invade a home or office without a court order?
    (2) A Federal Bureau of Investigation that assigns secret agents to monitor meetings—even a conservation meeting on Earth Day?
    (3) The compiling of millions of dossiers on its citizens?
    (4) A high executive official who uses the prestige of his office to attempt to silence television and press criticism of officials and policies and to vilify private citizens whose opinions vary from his own?
    Some keen observers of the Congress and the mood of today assert that the Bill of Rights, if presented as new legislation today, would be defeated. Comment on the questions above and on this observation.
10. A report of the official Commission on the Bicentennial of the American Revolution (1976) recommends a year-long, countrywide "Festival of Freedom." The dictionary defines a festival as a time for feasting and celebration. How do you think freedom should be celebrated? Indicate, in some detail, items in the program you would advocate if you were an official of the Festival of Freedom.

SUGGESTED READINGS

Brenton, Myron. *The Privacy Invaders*. New York: Coward-McCann, 1964.

Capaldi, Nicholas. *Clear and Present Danger: The Free Speech Controversy* New York: Pegasus, 1969.

Cohen, Carl. *Civil Disobedience: Conscience, Tactics, and the Law*. New York: Columbia University Press, 1971.

Commager, Henry Steele. *Freedom, Loyalty, Dissent*. New York: Oxford University Press, 1954.

Dewey, Robert E. and Gould, James A. *Freedom: Its History, Nature, and Varieties*. New York: Macmillan Co., 1970.

Douglas, William O. *Points of Rebellion*. New York: Random House, Vintage Books, 1970.

Ford, Leighton. *One Way to Change the World*. New York: Harper & Row, Publishers, 1970.

Garrison, Omar V. *Spy Government: The Emerging Police State in America.* New York: Lyle Stuart, Publishers, 1967.
Harris, Richard. *Justice: The Crisis of Law, Order, and Freedom in America.* New York: E. P. Dutton & Co., 1970.
Hofstadter, Richard. *Anti-Intellectualism in American Life.* New York: Alfred A. Knopf, 1963.
Hook, Sidney. *Political Power and Personal Freedom.* New York: Criterion Books, 1959.
Knight, Harold V. *With Liberty and Justice for All: The Meaning of the Bill of Rights Today.* Rev. ed., with Introduction by Roger Baldwin. Dobbs Ferry, N. Y.: Oceana Publications, 1968.
Lewis, Anthony and the New York Times. *Portrait of a Decade, The Second American Revolution.* New York: Bantam Books, 1965.
Mill, John Stuart. *On Liberty* (1859). Edited by Alburey Castell. New York: Appleton-Century-Crofts, 1947.
Miller, Arthur R. *Assault on Privacy: Computers, Data Banks, and Dossiers.* Ann Arbor: University of Michigan Press, 1971.
Muller, Herbert J. *Issues of Freedom.* New York: Harper & Brothers 1960.
Plato. *Apology.* Many editions are available and this treatise is found in many collections of philosophical writings.
Rosenberg, Jerry M. *The Death of Privacy.* New York: Random House, 1969.
Stokes, Anson Phelps, and Pfeffer, Leo. *Church and State in the United States.* New York: Harper & Row, Publishers, 1964.

16
MORAL EXCELLENCE IN EVERYDAY LIFE

What are the specific traits that men have cultivated and prized as they have reflected on human life and conduct? *Character* is the word frequently used to describe the sum total of an individual's motives, attitudes, dispositions, habits, and moral values. The moral qualities included in character are judged apart from the individual's knowledge and intelligence, competence in particular fields, and special talents. The organization of these traits of character in any one individual is not fixed and complete; it is always in process of formation—for better or worse. While certain traits of character have been prized or approved by nearly all men everywhere, the emphasis has varied from age to age, and one society may differ from another in the attitudes and habits most highly prized. A large part of the behavior of most people depends on the rules, regulations, customs, laws, principles, and the like that have grown out of the experiences of generations of men as they have observed the effects of attitudes and actions on the welfare of the group under particular conditions. Some of the ways of acting passed on from one generation to another are taken for granted or seldom made explicit; others are clearly stated in commandments and laws and in precepts taught in the home and school.

The "good" traits of character are often called *virtues;* the "bad" traits are called *vices*. The virtues are those qualities or traits of human character that men value or that merit moral approval. They are considered necessary or desirable for the survival or welfare of the group and are therefore deliberately cultivated. A vice, on the other hand, is a trait of human character or a habit that is considered to run counter to the welfare of the individual or the group. Vices, like other habits, may develop unconsciously and so establish themselves that the individual later finds them difficult to control. For example, a drug taken on the advice of a physician to relieve pain may gain such a hold on the person that its use is continued after the original need has ceased.

Any classification of the traits of character is arbitrary and artificial since they overlap and the social order in which men live is continuously undergoing change. Virtues and vices are too numerous to receive separate and extended treatment. In this chapter we shall consider briefly the moral traits stressed in the West from the time of the early Greeks and Hebrews to the present, and we shall then turn to the ethical ideals followed by different peoples in the East. Next we shall select one virtue, truthfulness, for special emphasis. While truthfulness has been prized and deception condemned by nearly all peoples, it has not always received major emphasis. It does, however, present special problems in today's world. We shall conclude the chapter with an evaluation of the conventional approach to the virtues and a brief summary statement.

MORAL EXCELLENCE AS EMPHASIZED IN THE WEST

The Greeks sought excellence of character and stressed justice, wisdom, courage, and self-control or temperance as the fundamental virtues. For Plato these are the four cardinal virtues. Self-control means the rational and harmonious control of all the impulses and desires of the individual in the interests of the whole self and of society. Wise self-control avoids the evils of extreme indulgence as well as the dangers of excessive repression. Our energies need to be harnessed to great ideals and loyalties and to worthwhile tasks. Happiness and health spring from a well-balanced and disciplined life. Courage is the ability to sacrifice safety and comfort and to endure hardship for the sake of some noble cause. It may be physical courage, the willingness to endure physical pain or risk for some worthy end, or moral courage, the readiness to endure ridicule and unpopularity for one's moral convictions. The man with moral courage stands for what he believes to be right even though it means personal loss. Wisdom as a virtue goes beyond knowledge and intelligence and involves conscientiousness, discrimination, and insight into the values related to personality. Wisdom is not something easily attained. The wise men of different ages, from the Psalmists, Socrates, and Plato to the present, have stressed the value of meditation and reflection, and then of action on the basis of these moral insights, so that moral discrimination becomes part of our very nature. For Plato, justice is the harmony of all the virtues; it is "giving every man his due," the satisfaction of all rightful claims, and an attitude of respect for human personality and the welfare of the community. Problems of ethical justice based on the needs of man as a moral being, of social justice or the nature of the good society, and of legal or political justice will be discussed at various points throughout this book.

Aristotle (384 B.C.–322 B.C.) wrote the first systematic treatise on ethics, *The Nicomachean Ethics,* in which he added to the list of virtues and indicated that the virtuous man is one in whom a right relation exists between reason, feeling, and desire. The reasonable man avoids the dangerous extremes; he follows the golden mean and does "nothing overmuch." For example, courage is the mean between foolhardiness and cowardice, liberality the mean between extravagance and avarice. Justice is the practice of virtue toward all persons. Truthfulness, friendliness, and other virtues are also given considerable attention.

Among the Hebrew prophets of the eighth century B.C., we see the development of ethical monotheism and a passion for righteousness and justice. The virtues and ideals of the Old Testament are carried over into the New Testament and expanded. With the rise of Christianity there emerged a new group of moral values. To the virtues inherited from Judaism and from the Greeks the early Christians added faith, hope, and love. The supreme virtue became love—not in the sense of romantic love or the mere love of a friend, but brotherly love of one's neighbor, meaning any needy person. The Hebrew-Christian conception of sin and salvation and a Kingdom of God into which men could enter by means of divine grace was in marked contrast to the intellectual and naturalistic conception of the Greeks.

The Greek virtues had to do mainly with one's own person and interests. Virtues such as self-control, courage, and wisdom are largely personal. Even justice was concerned merely with the claims and rights of other people and with the relationships between men. Love, on the other hand, surpasses justice and is more positive. It is the transference of interest from the I to the Thou. Love involves consideration for the other man as a person and for whatever affects him. It does not stop at mere rights but is concerned with the person for his own sake. Love is the fulfillment of the law; it is the whole law. Love strives for the well-being of others. This emphasis on the supreme worth of each personality is central in Christianity.

Besides faith, hope, and love, the early Christians emphasized loyalty and obedience to the church, martyrdom or the willingness to suffer, patient endurance, alms-giving, conquest over the flesh, stewardship (care for and use of one's talents and resources in service), work, and avoidance of avarice. For Augustine the life on earth is but a pilgrimage to God, and it is the love of God which makes the "pagan" virtues genuine virtues.

During the medieval period, as a result of the growth of the ascetic ideal, humility, abnegation, and self-mortification came to be prized virtues. Lists of vices included pride, avarice, anger, gluttony, unchastity, envy, vainglory, gloominess, and indifference. There was no universal system of ethics applicable alike to all men. The standard of conduct expected from the clergy and the ecclesiastical orders was different from that expected from the ordinary layman or the people in general. The ideals of poverty, chasity, and obedience were stressed in some religious orders. The layman was permitted to engage in worldly activities and to compromise to some extent with the desire of the flesh. But all activities were expected to be carried on for the glory of God. "To glorify God and to enjoy Him forever" was the chief end of man.

With the growth of Protestantism there was a tendency to elevate the virtues related to the natural relations and associations of men and to reject the dual standard. The rise of Puritanism and of a middle class interested in commerce and industry led to emphasis on certain virtues, sometimes known as the Puritan virtues. The Puritan stood for a purification of the forms of worship, the authority of the Scriptures as opposed to an established church system, and an austere and rather ascetic code of morality. The Puritan frowned on spontaneous enjoyment of life in this world. Life was a serious affair, and every man had a calling, whether he was a laborer or an employer of labor. Unwillingness to work or lack of success in business was an indication of lack of grace. To make money, to save it, and to contribute to worthy causes would help men grow in grace and lay up treasure in heaven. Thus industry, individuality, personal initiative, thrift, and benevolence came to be the new virtues stressed by the growing commercial and business groups in capitalist societies in the West. They are the virtues of a laissez-faire economy.

The twentieth century has witnessed rapid scientific, technological, social, and economic changes. As we pass from an economy of scarcity to one of abundance, due in part to automation, the virtues we stress seem again to change in emphasis. When all men had to work hard to gain a living, the virtues of industry and thrift were readily accepted. In recent years, with unemployment a serious problem, men are thinking more and more about the intelligent use of leisure time, sharing, cooperation, and group action. Many people no longer believe that if each individual thinks only of himself and vigorously seeks his own interest, general social well-being will automatically result.

For years the leaders of our business society encouraged men to save, to be thrifty. In periods of business recession and depression, however, men have been encouraged to spend as a duty—to put money in circulation in order to stimulate the economy. Over the years, benevolence has been praised as a virtue. Generosity, of course, is praiseworthy, unless it leads to the injury of the recipient or is a substitute for much needed reforms and becomes a salve for the conscience of the contributor. The need for benevolence may have arisen because of injustices in society.

MORAL EXCELLENCE AS STRESSED IN THE EAST

When we turn to the ethical systems and ideals of the peoples of the East we find striking differences in the metaphysical and religious backgrounds but remarkable similarities in the traits of character that are approved and disapproved. Because of this educated and cultured men, East and West, can associate with and respect each other. The chief differences come in the ranking of values, not in disputes over the desirable and undesirable traits of character.

The Ethics of Hinduism

Hinduism, found mainly in India, includes widely different beliefs and types of conduct moving from the superstitions of the masses to the lofty idealism of many Indian leaders. Lists of virtues and vices are frequently found in Hindu literature. According to the *Laws of Manu* there are ten great virtues. From the failure to live according to these virtues come all the vices of man. The ten virtues are contentment, truthfulness, purity, self-control, suppression of sensual appetite, respect for the property of others, wisdom, knowledge of the supreme soul, avoidance of anger, and forgiveness, or returning good for evil. Among the more lofty sentiments are some like the following: "Let not any man do unto another any act which he wisheth not done to himself, knowing it to be painful to himself. And let him also purpose for another all that he wisheth for himself." The ideal life means, in part, "A virtuous son, a loving wife, a kind master, a devoted friend, an affectionate kinsman, and a mind free from care, a handsome figure, lasting riches, and lips that speak wisdom."

The moral code of Hinduism contains those elements common to the human race. For example, it condemns lying, stealing, murder, injury, adultery, slander, gambling, and drunkenness. There is emphasis on self-control and moderation. The Hindu philosophers seem to agree that overcoming selfishness is necessary in order to realize one's true self. As in other societies, the dominant social, religious, and political forces have compromised these high principles to forward their own narrower interests and understanding. However, many new movements of reform are in existence today, and the caste system and untouchablity are now illegal.

The Ethics of Buddhism

Buddhism is based on the life and teachings of Siddhartha Gautama (born about 563 B.C.). Gautama, reared in luxury, renounced wealth and ease and lived a life of self-denial and meditation. In the religion he founded the ethical way, which will give release from suffering, sorrow, pain, disease, loneliness, old age, and death is found in the Four Noble Truths and the Noble Eightfold Path. The Four Noble Truths which Gautama discovered by means of his Enlightenment under the Bo Tree are as follows: (1) All individual personal existence leads to misery. (2) The cause of this misery is thirst, or desire. (3) Release is possible through passionlessness. (4) The way to remove desire is through the Noble Eightfold Path.

The Noble Eightfold Path consists of (1) Right views. This involves the knowledge that the destruction of suffering comes through the elimination of craving, desire, and thirst. (2) Right aspirations. Man needs to aspire to love, to serve all things, and to attain the state of bliss. (3) Right speech. The individual is to be truthful, kind, humble, and encouraging, and never harsh, gossiping, slanderous, backbiting, or frivolous. (4) Right action. This does not depend on ritual, sacrifice, prayer, or magic. Man must avoid killing, stealing, unchastity, lying and other abuses of language, intoxicating liquor, envy, anger, devotion to money, and a soft and easy life. (5) Right mode of livelihood. In order to live, one is to do nothing that will harm or endanger any living creature. (6) Right striving. Self-control is a step in the attainment of an upright character. (7) Right mindfulness or meditation. Our thoughts are all-important. (8) Right contemplation or absorption. This leads to the mystic illumination, or nirvana.

When the Noble Eightfold Path is followed, the ten fetters that bind man are broken. These fetters are the delusion of self, doubt, trust in the efficacy of good works, bodily passion, ill will, love of life on earth, desire for a happy future life in heaven, pride, self-righteousness, and ignorance.

In Buddhism the common virtues are stressed, especially those that tend in the direction of self-renunciation and denial. The inner attitudes, the desires and motives of the person, are all-important. The idea of the brotherhood of man and respect for all living things has taken the form of abhorrence for the taking of life in war and the prevention of cruelty to animals. Envy, malice, and uncharitableness are condemned. Prohibitions are set before the Buddhist: "Do not kill, steal, commit adultery, lie, or drink intoxicants." Self-control and self-purification are stressed. Caste and all superficial distinctions have been broken down. The same appeals are made to all men, and the same goals are set before them. Whereas Theravada Buddhism was, on the whole, individualistic with an emphasis on rugged self-reliance, Mahayana Buddhism that included the Zen sect stressed the sense of loving unity with all men and women.

The Ethics of Confucianism

Confucianism shows a remarkable unity from the days of Lao-tze and Confucius in the sixth century B.C. to the twentieth century. In Confucian ethics the central concept is community or "right relationships" with the family as central. The "duties of universal obligation" are spelled out in some detail.[1]

To the question of what things are considered right, the answer given in *Li ki* is as follows: "Kindness in a father, filial piety in a son; gentleness in an elder brother, obedience in a younger; righteousness in a husband, submission in a wife; kindness in elders, deference in juniors; benevolence in a ruler, loyalty in a minister."[2] On the other hand, to quarrel, plunder, and murder are things that are disastrous to men everywhere. Thus the good of society is an ordered harmony reaching from the humblest tiller of the soil to the ruler and even to the limits of the cosmic order. Justice arises when each man plays his part in society and when there is harmony and excellence in the various relations and duties of men to one another. Consideration and reciprocity are central concepts.

According to Confucius the normal person aspires to become a superior man, a courteous gentleman who strives for his own development. He renounces worldly lusts and is on guard against avarice and quarrelsomeness. The doctrine of moderation reminds one of Aristotle's doctrine of the Golden Mean. The prevailing emphasis is humanistic and practical.

A few Chinese seers stressed love. For example, Mo Tse (about 400

---

[1]See *Analects*, book 9, in *The Four Books* trans. and annotated by James Legge (China: The Commercial Press, n.d.). See also the *Book of Filial Piety*, trans. Mary Lelia Makra (New York: St. John's University Press, 1961).

[2]*The Sacred Books of the East*, rev. ed., vol. 28, bk. 7, sec. 2 (New York: Wiley Book Co., 1945).

B.C.) believed in a personal divinity animated by love toward all creatures, but this movement lasted only a few generations. Mencius (378–289 B.C.) believed that evil could be overcome by love for the evildoer, but he said that one must be realistic in this approach.

The Ethics of Islam

The term *Islam* which means "submission" is the outlook of Moslems and denotes both a creed and an ethical system or way of life. The tribal morality of the early inhabitants of the Arabian peninsula emphasized honor, courage, loyalty, hospitality, generosity, and pride of race. To this was added the personal experience and leadership of Mohammed (570–632) along with Jewish and Christian elements. The ethical code of the Moslem is inseparable from this religious background. For the good man there are certain practical duties that must be carried out. Called the Five Pillars of the Faith, they include repetition of the simple creed, "There is no God but Allah, and Mohammed is the Prophet of Allah"; prayer five times a day; the thirty-day fast of Ramadan; alms-giving; and the pilgrimage to Mecca.

Moslem morality based on the Koran encourages alms-giving, hospitality, truthfulness, humanity to slaves, justice for orphans, and abstinence from the use of alcoholic beverages. There is legislation against suicide, inhumanity, robbery, gambling, slander, perjury, usury, and the sale and consumption of intoxicating drink. Mohammed accepted slavery and polygyny found in the society in which he was reared but set limitations and made reforms.

The statement sometimes heard that Islam tends to confuse the ceremonial and the moral and to make its ethics a legal code must be qualified. Development has taken place in the past under new conditions and reform movements are in existence today. The development of law, of reason and knowledge, and of new climates of opinion are having their influence, especially in progressive communities. Some modern leaders have said that right is what is conducive to human welfare.

THE IMPORTANCE OF TRUTHFULNESS

We have said that truthfulness presents special problems in today's world. This is caused in considerable part by the rise of a complex industrial society, the mass media and competitive advertising, hot and cold wars, and the desire of the military-industrial-scientific complex to maintain secrecy. For some the lie that increases profits is permissible or at least tolerated with the excuse that others are doing it.

How can four pain-relieving remedies each claim to be stronger than the other three? How can a considerable number of soaps and detergents each give a cheaper, whiter wash than any of the others? For some years we have heard discussions about a "credibility gap" and the deterioration of confidence in the integrity of various public officials. Have some leaders sought to deceive not only the enemy but citizens in general? These are just a few of the many questions people have in mind when they ask what is happening to truth and truthfulness.

A truthful person is free from duplicity or fraud; he is characterized by sincerity, genuineness, and straightforwardness in conduct, thought, and speech. Truth and truthfulness are not the same. Truth may mean conformity to fact or reality or the agreement between one's thought and objective conditions. Truthfulness is the agreement of one's word with one's thought; it involves the intention and the responsibility of the person. The truthful man may say what is untrue or false, and the liar may speak the truth by mistake. The essence of the lie or the deceit is not the presenting of what is untrue but the presenting of what one believes to be untrue.

Truthfulness means representing accurately one's thoughts and intentions and keeping one's agreements, stated or implied, until they cease to be valid agreements. It calls for faithfulness in action and a sense of responsibility. The term *veracity* is usually used to mean verbal truthfulness. A lie is an intentional statement of an untruth designed to mislead another. It is usually uttered or acted with the intention of affecting wrongfully the opinions, emotions, or acts of another. An unintentional misstatement or a slip of the tongue is not a lie, nor are the deceptions used in games and performances when these are an understood part of the action.

What is the value of truthfulness? First, to be true to ourselves contributes to psychical self-preservation. To be dishonest is to destroy a portion of our own personality and to lower our self-respect. Trustworthiness is the main element in a man's integrity. The man of integrity is undivided and free from corrupting practices. "In truthfulness and uprightness there is an element of purity. A lie is a kind of stain; . . . it is a degradation of one's own personality. . . . In it there is always a certain breach of trust. And there is also in it an element of cowardice."[3] Deceit is usually an indication of weakness or of selfishness or of some other undesirable attitude. The secrecy and evasion that tend to accompany deceit are detrimental to the development of the finest human qualities.

---

[3]Nicolai Hartmann, *Ethics*, vol. 2, trans. Stanton Coit (New York: Macmillan Co., 1932), p. 282.

Second, dishonesty is the betrayal of another person. It is the misuse of faith and confidence. The deceived person is injured and led astray. We assume the truthfulness of statements that are made to us unless we have reason for doubting them. The lie or other deception takes advantage of this trust and thus tends to create suspicion.

Third, deception tends to undermine social life itself. The present organization of society is based on mutual confidence. Friedrich Paulsen illustrates the influence of falsehood by an example of counterfeiting. The counterfeiter injures the person who receives the spurious money and is unable to pass it; he also brings sound money under suspicion and injures society. Lying does the same thing; it tends to invalidate the truth and to cast doubt and suspicion on the "intellectual medium of exchange." The man who deceives, suspects others of deceit. This distrust tends to break down human fellowship. Hence it is evident that falsehood casts suspicion on statements, undermines confidence, and makes any cooperative social life extremely difficult.

Finally, there is a practical value in truthfulness. Since a lie is likely to be discovered, it keeps the liar constantly on guard. If one tells the truth, he has no problem of remembering what he has said. A truthful person simply recalls the events as they were; a dishonest person must remember the lies he previously told or run the risk of detection. The liar is thus in an embarrassing and difficult position. Since dishonesty as a means of avoiding some present embarrassment easily becomes a habit or a permanent character trait, and since the habitual liar is almost universally despised and loses status among men, lying tends to shut one off from many of life's richest values.

Is Truthfulness Absolute or Relative?

Are there exceptions, or is the duty of truthfulness absolute? Real problems arise in answer to this question. Let us present views on both sides of the issue.

On one side we find certain rigorists who claim that truthfulness is an absolute obligation and that a lie is never justifiable under any circumstances. R. C. Cabot, who argues for absolute honesty, calls attention to the fact that "no one wants to be called a liar." And if we permit exceptions to our rule, it is difficult to localize the area of permissible exceptions; it tends to grow. He states that

> A single lie spreads. It is difficult to draw the line around it. It spreads in the habits of him who tells it and it spreads in the community as soon as it is openly defended. Self-permitted lying tends to spread beyond the limits allowed. Pious frauds are easier the second time; found convenient here, they are temptingly handy elsewhere. If one lies

to the insane, shall one lie to the neurasthenic, to the irritated, to the prejudiced, to the unbalanced? But who is unprejudiced? Who is perfectly balanced"[4]

While it may appear easy to defend a certain lie on a special occasion, we are told that it is hard to get a satisfactory principle to justify it. Moreover, we assume that the people to whom we lie are either enemies of society or weaklings. If one falsehood is admitted, justification can easily be found for others.

The best argument for absolute honesty, according to Cabot, is the one first stated by Augustine—that we are put on our guard against a man's attempts to lie, and confidence is impaired. As soon as a man avows his belief that lies may be told occasionally, we must suspect him of lying whenever it suits his purpose. Moreover, if a man admits that a lie may be permitted under special circumstances, how can anyone be sure that he is not conscientiously lying when he defines the conditions under which a lie may be justified? In other words, we can never be sure just where such a person is going to draw the line.

In arguing that no lie is ever justifiable, Robert E. Speer says that those who allow exceptions in their principle of honesty do so from an erroneous standard of value. They consider life the greatest value when in reality it is not. Life is not the one thing for which everything else is to be sacrificed. "Men die for their honor, for their country; why should men not die for the truth? The truth is more than any man's honor."[5]

On the other hand, probably a considerable majority of present-day moral philosophers agree that in the concrete situations of life, men occasionally face the alternative of sacrificing one value or another and that in some cases the selection of the greater value may mean the temporary denial of the obligation of truthfulness. Nicolai Hartmann states this position very effectively. After pointing out the injury that follows untruthfulness and making it clear that truthfulness never ceases to be a value, and deception a moral wrong, he says:

> Still we are confronted here with a very serious moral problem, which is by no means solved by the simple rejection of each and every lie. There are situations which place before a man the unescapable alternative either of sinning against truthfulness or against some other equally high, or even some higher, value. A physician violates his professional duty if he tells a patient who is dangerously ill the critical state of his

---

[4] R. C. Cabot, *The Meaning of Right and Wrong* (New York: Macmillan Co., 1933), p. 165; see also Cabot's *Honesty* (New York: Macmillan Co., 1938).

[5] Robert E. Speer, *The Marks of a Man* (New York: Methodist Book Concern, 1907), p. 34.

health; the imprisoned soldier, who, when questioned by the enemy, allows the truth about his country's tactics to be extorted from him, is guilty of high treason; a friend who does not try to conceal information given to him in strictest personal confidence is guilty of breach of confidence. In all such cases the mere virtue of silence is not adequate. If the physician, the prisoner, the possessor of confidential information will do their duty of warding off a calamity that threatens, they must resort to a lie. But if they do, they make themselves guilty on the side of truthfulness.

It is a portentous error to believe that such questions may be solved theoretically. Every attempt of the kind leads to a one-sided and inflexible rigorism concerning one value at the expense of the rest, or to a fruitless casuistry devoid of all significance—not to mention the danger of opportunism.... It is the morally mature and seriously minded person who is here inclined to decide in favor of the other value and to take upon himself the responsibility for the lie. But such situations do not permit of being universalized.... For it is inherent in the essence of such moral conflicts that in them value stands against value and that it is not possible to escape from them without being guilty.[5]

Hartmann makes it clear that the problem arises from a conflict caused by the structure of the particular situation. To refuse to decide might mean the violation of two values: moral cowardice, or the unwillingness to assume one's responsibility. A man in this situation is not denying the value of truthfulness if he feels that he should select the other value; he is merely choosing the lesser of two evils or the greater of two values, according to the way we view it.

The morally mature man, when confronted with such situations, will weigh all relevant factors and decide according to his best judgment. In making his decision he will take upon himself the consequences (and guilt, if any) for the violation of what he considers to be, in this case, the lesser value. Out of such a conflict a man may emerge stronger. In the words of Hartmann, "Real moral life is not such that one can stand guiltless in it," but "it is only unavoidable guilt which can preserve a man from moral decay."

The position of the liberal, as opposed to that of the absolutist, is that while the virtues and our everyday standards of conduct are good, there are situations where exceptions must be made. In such cases there is a vast difference between recognizing a particular exception to a standard and making the exception a new standard.

Again, virtues, like rights and duties, are instrumental and functional. Certain types of conduct are considered virtuous because they are the kinds of action favorable to the welfare of the group. Absolute rules fail to recognize the unique character of some life situations, and they do

---

[6]*Ethics*, vol. 2, pp. 283–284.

not permit the creative adjustment of a person in a changing social order. A type of conduct that is moral in one situation may not be moral in a different situation.

The teleologist or liberal, who may allow some exceptions to the duty of truthfulness, challenges the arguments of the absolutist that it is not possible to draw the line or to state a satisfactory principle. He thinks that he has the only satisfactory principle in that it requires him to analyze the conduct situation and to act in the direction he believes will lead to the greater good. Instead of breaking down human confidence, he believes that men can have greater trust in one another when each is dedicated to serve the greatest good. In his opinion the absolutist makes the mistake of giving an abstract principle a value greater than anything else in life or perhaps than life itself.

If exceptions are to be allowed, it is generally agreed that it should be when some greater value is at stake or when some great harm can thereby be avoided. Among the examples found in the literature on the subject are the following:

1. A theater manager discovers a fire in his theater while a play is in progress. Realizing that word of the fire would lead to a panic and serious injuries, perhaps even to loss of life, he goes before the audience and gives a false reason for stopping the play. As a result, the audience leaves calmly, and no injuries result. Did he do right?
2. A mother has lost a son whom she believes to be pure and noble. His companions know that he was otherwise. Will they add to her grief if they tell her the truth? Should they do so?
3. A mob is intent on lynching a man. You know his hiding place. When the leaders of the mob ask you if you know where the man is, will you feel obligated to tell the truth?

In such cases as these, few people will feel remorse if they deviate from the truth. Probably few would not feel remorse if their insistence on the truth caused a tragedy they could have prevented.

Again, there are the deviations from literal truthfulness known as "conventional lies," "white lies," and "polite lies," where no one is seriously misled and where embarrassment and perhaps even loss of a friend is avoided. To thank a gracious but dull hostess for the pleasure she has not given is "loving one's neighbor as one's self." If a guest, though still hungry, sees that the food is running short, is it wrong for him to say, "No thank you," when his hostess asks him if he cares for more? When a man returns home sad and bitter after some trying experience and puts on a cheerful front for his wife and children, is his deceit justifiable? Should you tell the truth to an easily disheartened beginner if your frank comment on his work will in all likelihood lead to his discouragement and failure? These are questions that every morally sensitive and mature person must decide for himself. Solutions to such problems cannot be written down in fixed rules covering all occasions.

Degrees of Concern for the Truth

The character of a man may be judged to some extent by the answer to the question. "How much concern does he have for the truth?" The degrees of concern may be stated as follows:

At the lowest level, there is the man who lacks any evident concern for the truth. He has no scruples against lying and often lies when he has nothing much to gain. He lies to gain recognition or even "just for the fun of it." He may be a compulsive liar.

After him, there is the man who prefers the truth and usually speaks it, but has no aversion to lying if he can gain something by doing so. Lying is not a matter of honor and principle with him. He might be called the occasional liar; one should not put much trust in him.

Then, there is the man who will never deviate under any circumstances from what he thinks is the truth—"though the heavens fall and the earth is destroyed." This man is the absolutist, who genuinely believes that truthfulness is the supreme value and must always have right of way.

Next, there is the man who is a truthful person devoted to the truth, who stands near to the absolutist, but cannot go all the way with the absolutist. He will not say what is untrue just to promote his own interests, but his dedication and concern is for the greatest good. The exceptions he makes, if any, will be few, and only in those unusual situations where he genuinely believes that some greater value than strict adherence to the truth is at stake.

Finally, we come to the man who is not only personally honest but who is willing to spend time and energy to discover the truth. Much falsehood is disguised as truth and is widely propagated. Men who check reports and rumors and seek the truth in public life, in the professions and business, are positively and actively honest. They read widely, try to think clearly, and form opinions on the basis of evidence. These men are benefactors of civilization.

The Nature of Deception

The investigations of the Character Education Inquiry[7] have thrown

---

[7]*Studies in the Nature of Character*, 3 vols. Character Education Inquiry, Columbia University Teachers College, in cooperation with the Institute of Social and Religious Research (New York: Macmillan Co., 1928–1930).

considerable light on the nature of honesty and dishonesty. Hartshorne and May in their *Studies in Deceit* set forth the *doctrine of specificity,* which maintains that traits such as honesty and dishonesty are achievements, like ability in arithmetic, and consist of skills and attitudes found to be successful. They are not qualities or unified traits that are either definitely present or entirely lacking. After pointing out that there is no inherent capacity for figures that will enable children to subtract when they have been taught only to add, they say:

> Honest and dishonest acts are specialized in the same way. Even after the principle of honesty is understood, the deceptive aspect of certain acts may not be noticed until one's attention is drawn to them. One may be meticulously honorable in his relations with the neighbors but steal a ride on the streetcar without thinking himself a thief. Acts are not accurately labeled because they are not completely analyzed. Consequently, an otherwise entirely honest man may be shocked and insulted when his sharp business practices are called stealing or his purchase of votes, political corruption.
>
> Our conclusion, then, is that an individual's honesty or dishonesty consists of a series of acts and attitudes to which these descriptive terms apply. The consistency with which he is honest or dishonest is a function of the situations in which he is placed in so far as (1) these situations have common elements, (2) he has learned to be honest or dishonest in them, and (3) he has become aware of their honest or dishonest implications or consequences.[8]

In this study, deception was associated with such things as dullness, emotional instability, personal limitations, social and economic handicaps, cultural limitation, and parental discord in the home. Thus the amount and the character of the deception appear to be largely functions of particular situations. Deception is especially likely to arise when a conflict exists between a person and some element in his environment. Subterfuge is then used to gain the desired end. In such circumstances, discussing the virtues or merely urging the person to be honest is not likely to be effective.

The study adds that

> When deception is found to be the way in which an individual usually adapts himself to a situation, we can be fairly certain, then,
> 1. that what he wants to get or to do is disapproved and must be concealed; or
> 2. that when the thing he wants is legitimate, straightforward ways of getting it are either more onerous or less adequate or have never been learned; and

---

[8]Ibid., vol. 1, p. 380.

3. that even if deception is disapproved by the group within which the behavior occurs, it is approved by some other group to which the individual belongs in fact or fancy; or
4. that the individual is mentally disordered and must resort to self-deception of some kind to maintain his self-respect—such as the adoption of ingenious excuses, or telling himself that it won't count this time or finding justification in other ways.[9]

The removal of personal and social handicaps should accompany attempts to reconstruct attitudes and habits.

Self-Deceit

Besides the various ways by which men attempt to deceive others, there are ways in which they deceive themselves or blind themselves to the full implications of their acts.[10] Self-deceit differs from simple ignorance in that we know what is right but refuse to face the facts. Let us examine briefly some forms self-deceit may take.

Rationalization. One way we can deceive ourselves is by rationalization. This should not be confused with rationality or reasonableness. Rationalization is finding arguments or excuses for doing what we want to do because of impulse, emotion, or self-interest. It is a way to make unreasonable conduct appear reasonable and proper.

Projection. A second means of self-deceit, one closely related to rationalization, is projection. In projection, when we cannot get what we want or when we fail in some task, we blame others. We contend that other persons are the weak or immoral persons that we know we are. Projection is the act of shifting responsibility for one's deeds to some other person or thing. Most of us have known someone who got excited, insulted another person, and then went off maintaining that the other had deliberately insulted him and that he was quite innocent.

Compensation. A third form of self-deceit is compensation. A man who is immoral in some personal conduct or unscrupulous in business may attempt to gain prestige and self-respect by unusual devotion elsewhere, instead of eliminating the lapses from acceptable standards. The man who is guilty of sharp dealing may show exceptional devotion to his club, his church, or his family. Criminals are often very sentimental

---

[9]Ibid., p. 22.
[10]Henry Clay Lindgren, *Psychology of Personal Development* (New York: American Book Co., 1964), pp. 118–125, 146–173.

about their mothers. There is an old story of a man who went home one evening with a large bunch of roses and was met by his wife at the door with the exclamation, "John, what have you been up to today!" This was a case of attempted compensation that did not work.

Exception-making. A fourth form of self-deception is exception-making. This operates in at least two ways. When we attempt to maintain an indefensible or extreme position and our opponent points out a valid exception, we reply, "This is the exception that proves the rule." The use of such tactics to attempt to side-step the refutation of an extreme position is a frequently used device that should be exposed as false and perhaps occasionally dishonest.

Self-deceit is especially dangerous because it grows upon us so rapidly that we are not fully aware of its presence. In fact, we may become quite unconscious of it. It stunts our moral and intellectual growth and leads us toward unreality instead of reality. When we cannot satisfy our desires and our life energy is blocked, the only sane thing for us to do is to face the facts and make a rational decision. The boy who is failing in college may sit down and analyze the situation. After arriving at his conclusions, he would be wise to submit them to someone whose judgment he trusts. Then he may outline a campaign of attack on the causes of failure. This may involve changes in his daily schedule or the choice of a new boarding house. If he finds that the causes of failure cannot be removed, he should face the facts and turn to some activity in which he can be successful. Frankness and honesty in dealing with oneself as well as with others are important for growth and for happiness.

EVALUATION AND CONCLUSIONS

A number of students of human nature and conduct have criticized the conventional approach to character as consisting of a list of formal virtues. We need, they say, a more dynamic and functional approach, one which stresses the needs of the growing individual and of human well-being in a changing society. Some critical comments follow.

The term *virtue* is indefinite and vague. It may refer to the results of an action. Virtues like neatness and accuracy obviously refer to some object, such as a neat letter or an accurate account. A virtue like sincerity, on the other hand, has reference not to some object or to a result of one's act but to one's inner purpose or intention. When we speak of *courtesy,* we think of a process, such as a manner of speaking or acting. As distinct from these, *reliability* refers to the person himself quite apart from any particular situation. To put all of these into one category is somewhat confusing.

Even more confusing is the fact that these virtues show little consistency. A boy who is courteous at a party for girls and boys may be a bully on the recreation grounds. A person who is neat in his written work may leave his desk untidy. One who is loyal in one situation may be disloyal in another. Furthermore, when we talk about certain virtues, there is a tendency to imply that some quality or trait is either wholly present or wholly absent. As a matter of fact, there are all degrees between the two extremes. Virtues have the property of "continuous variation." The ignorant and the wise are not sharply separated. It might be possible to make a continuum of people who are progressively less wise or less courageous, and so on, but, while there are real differences between people in respect to the virtues, there are no sharp dividing lines.

On occasions at least, the virtues conflict with one another and with themselves. If they are taken as absolutes, dilemmas may arise. In time of war, loyalty to one's country may conflict with loyalty to one's religious convictions. Loyalty to a man's family may conflict with loyalty to his employer. At other times the demands of loyalty may conflict with the demands of honesty. It is one thing to evaluate conduct in the light of some abstract ideal; it is quite another thing to evaluate it in the light of its effect on human personality or of the consequences that follow the action.

A man's fundamental outlook on life, his central ethical purpose, is the important thing, rather than certain abstract qualities. To say that a man has self-control does not tell us much about his central purpose in life. A man may have courage in executing any plan, praiseworthy or not. His view of justice depends on his general philosophy of life. Slavery and infanticide were once thought to be just. Whether industry and initiative are good or not depends on what a man intends doing. Patience is frequently good, but men may well be impatient about some things.

Courage, loyalty, and intelligence by themselves do not make a good man. These must be considered in the light of the motives and the consequences to which they are related. A successful criminal may possess qualities similar to those of a successful corporation executive. The criminal may have courage, patience, persistence, and perhaps other desirable traits. What he lacks is an ethical goal.

Two men may exhibit courage. From the point of view of the physical organism, they may be the same; yet ethically they may be far apart when their actions are related to the total conduct situations of which they are a part. The courage displayed may be the means to the attainment of a worthy goal or an unworthy goal. Ethics cannot ignore that goal.

Of course, criticism of the traditional view of the virtues must not blind us to the value of the types of conduct they represent. Self-control, courage, wisdom, justice, brotherly love, and other virtues are as valuable as ever. In any wholesome society the dispositions and behavior represented by these virtues will be present in no small degree. We have tried to make clear, however, that virtues, like other moral principles, are valuable only to the extent that they promote the good life. The virtues are instrumental and relative to the function of society and to the need of the human personality to grow.

We have emphasized truthfulness and used this virtue to illustrate the conflicts that occasionally occur among the virtues. Such conflicts raise the perplexing question of exceptions to the universal application of a particular virtue. Respect for the truth is essential for both personal and social well-being. A few moral philosophers believe that the duty of truthfulness is absolute, admitting no exceptions. Others believe that in the concrete situations of life the virtues occasionally conflict, and that in exceptional cases some other value may take precedence over truthfulness. In these cases the value of truthfulness is not denied. Right action is action leading to the greatest good in the situation presented.

A list of virtues may point out to us the general direction in which conduct should move. Such virtues, however, do not furnish us with all the knowledge we often need in order to act wisely in any specific situation. The knowledge can be gained only from a study of the characteristics of the situation we face. How a man acts in any situation will depend in part on what he has learned from his actions in similar situations and on his awareness of the implications of his conduct. There also tends to be a close relation between group standards and the conduct of a member of the group. For example, as a boy changes from one group to another, his attitudes and conduct tend to change accordingly. A boy may even have three or more vocabularies and types of conduct: one for church or synagogue, one for the home, and one for his life with a gang. A trait may be evident when he is in one group and entirely lacking when he is with another group. The virtues thus appear to be in part the function of particular situations rather than completely unified traits. As people gain understanding and maturity, they tend to be less swayed by the passing external pressures and to exhibit more consistent traits of character. While knowledge does not guarantee right conduct, it does bring to a person's attention the way in which acts affect his own future as well as the lives of other people. This enables a man to distinguish between social and antisocial ends.

QUESTIONS AND PROJECTS

1. State in your own words the traditional approach to the virtues or the approved traits of character, and then indicate what criticisms have been directed toward this approach. In concluding your presentation make clear your own convictions or the position you consider most reasonable.
2. A committee of three students arranging for a dance given by their class is allowed one hundred fifty dollars for a band. When the three find that they can get a satisfactory band for one hundred twenty dollars, they feel justified in keeping the remaining thirty dollars for themselves. Comment on this action.
3. A fraternity-house steward, in charge of ordering the food and other supplies for his group, receives an offer from an agent of a food company. He is told that if he gives the orders to that particular company, he will receive a cash rebate on each order. This will be done without any increase in the usual prices paid by the group. The steward is being paid by the fraternity for his services. Is it ethical for him to accept this remuneration?
4. A club is sending one of its members as a delegate to a convention, and is paying all his expenses, including carfare. When ready to leave for the convention, the delegate discovers that his uncle happens to be driving to the same city and is glad to take him along free of charge. The delegate keeps the carfare and says nothing. Should he keep the money or return it to the club? Why?
5. Read the following selection and tell whether you think the firm should return the check and call attention to the mistake.

    We are engaged in the wholesale linoleum business. A short time ago a customer owing us approximately one thousand dollars suffered a severe fire loss. Although he was covered amply by insurance and although he is a man of considerable means, he took advantage of his accident to request a settlement from all his creditors on a 75 percent basis. In order to keep the future patronage of this man, with whom we had been dealing for a long time, we decided to accept the offer. When, however, we received his check, instead of the 75 percent, he sent us by mistake the full amount owing to us. [From *Golden Book* (October 1928), p. 509. Reprinted by permission of *Review of Reviews*.]
6. A bank president, alone in his bank, is confronted by a pair of bandits. He tells them that he has sounded an alarm and that they are in immediate danger of capture, although this is contrary to fact. The bandits leave without robbing the bank. Did the bank president do right or wrong? Why?
7. Comment on the conduct in each of the following incidents.
    (1) A watchman who was on duty at a railway crossing when an accident occurred in which several people were killed testified at the

inquest that he swung his lantern when the automobile approached the track. What he omitted to disclose was that through negligence he had neglected to light the lantern.

(2) A woman repeated in good faith some very uncomplimentary gossip about her neighbor. Later she discovered that the report was completely without foundation. Because of her dislike for her neighbor, however, she did not relay this discovery to her auditor, who continued to believe the false report.

(3) A young woman was given permission to go to a dance on condition that she return home not later than twelve o'clock. She returned home at about three in the morning, but when asked by her father, she said she had returned at "a quarter of twelve." Since three is a quarter of twelve, she considered that she had made an honest statement.

(4) "A manufacturer selling candy in small packages uses an 'extension box'—a box with a piece of cardboard under the outer surface extending over the edges nearly half an inch, thus increasing its apparent size and capacity, although the content is gauged by weight."

[Incidents (1), (2), and (3) are from Frank Chapman Sharp and Philip G. Fox, *Business Ethics; Studies in Fair Competition* (New York: Appleton-Century, 1937). Incident (4) is from Everett W. Lord, *The Fundamentals of Business Ethics* (New York: Ronald Press, 1926), p. 184.]

8. One frequently hears respected speakers tell stories as if the events related had happened to them personally. In some instances identical stories have been found in books which these people must have read. The stories may have been more effective by being told in the first person, but is the misrepresentation justified?

9. A man was convicted and sent to prison. After two years, new evidence showed clearly that he was not guilty, and he was released. He moved to a part of the country in which he was unknown. He believed, and there was some evidence to support his views, that a knowledge of his prison sentence would prevent him from getting as good a position as he would otherwise get. Was he morally right in giving false information about his activities during the two years he was in prison?

10. Should a deathbed promise ever be broken? A man's father, on his deathbed, exacted from his son a promise never to marry anyone outside his own faith. When he made the promise, the man thought it would be an easy one to keep. Now he is miserable, torn between the promise and the one thing that he thinks can bring him happiness, for he has met and fallen in love with a young woman of another faith. Do you think he would be justified in breaking his promise?

11. Comment on the following: "In a discussion on the subject of military morale, an officer of much experience and of large responsibility maintained that, if he knew an accused man to be innocent and if he also knew he was so generally believed guilty in his regiment that an acquittal

would lower the morale at a critical time, he would order sentence to be carried out. 'Justice to individuals,' he said, "is never more than approximate, at best; the interest of the cause is supreme.'" From William E. Hocking, *Philosophy of Law and of Rights* (New Haven: Yale University Press, 1926), pp. 47–48.

12. A man paid his life insurance premiums diligently for many years but allowed the policy to lapse and died on the day the policy expired. The agent who had sold the insurance policy was a good friend of the insured man. He paid the premium himself and dated it the day the policy lapsed. As a result, the widow had an income sufficient to keep her comfortable for the rest of her life. Should the insurance man have taken this action?

13. Do you agree with the person who said that patriotism is an oldtime virtue that we must "extinguish in ourselves before it extinguishes us"? What are the values and what are the dangers of patriotism?

14. On December 7, 1941 the Japanese attack on Pearl Harbor disabled the battleships and many aircraft in the Hawaiian area. Nearly a score of naval vessels were sunk or damaged, so that they were not available for immediate duty at sea. The facts about the damage were not given out and the success of the raid was minimized. There was fear that disclosure of the facts might encourage Japan to attack the rest of the Pacific fleet or to attempt an invasion of Hawaii. Were officials justified in misleading the public?

15. During the last few decades in the United States there have been many incidents that have led to much publicity and discussions of honesty and related traits of character in general. Since the Pearl Harbor disaster mentioned above, the following are among the more recent examples:

    (1) The television quiz-show scandals. See *New York Times,* 3 November 1959, pp. 1, 22; *Time* 74, pt. 2 (October 19, 1959): 67.

    (2) The U-2 case of 1960. See David Wise and Thomas B. Rose, *The U-2 Affair* (New York: Random House, 1962).

    (3) Cases of college cheating. See Jerome Ellison, "American Disgrace: College Cheating," *The Saturday Evening Post* 232 (January 9, 1960): 13 ff.; Samuel Middlebrook, "No Panacea for College Cheating," *New York Times Magazine,* 9 April 1961, pp. 17 ff; "Sales of Term Papers Are Flourishing," *New York Times,* 30 January 1972, p. 59.

    (4) The Pueblo case. In December 1968 United States officials signed a phony statement in order to secure the release of the crew of the Pueblo, a ship seized by North Korea. See "Pueblo Captain Tells His Story of Capture—and Captivity," *U. S. News and World Report* 66 (January 6, 1969): 30–31; 66 (January 20, 1969): 40–41.

    (5) The Pentagon Papers and their release to the press. Were the American people given a distorted view of the war in Southeast Asia? See *The New Republic* 165 (July 3, 1971): 5–7, 11–12; "The Government vs. the Press," *Newsweek* 78 (July 5, 1971): 17–19.

16. From time to time there are reports in the newspapers and in magazine

articles about the considerable number of rich Americans who accumulate large sums of money in secret Swiss bank accounts. This is hard to investigate since bank secrecy is protected in Swiss laws. The number of persons involved and the total amounts of money are known to be large. Some say it has become a national scandal as an illegal way of avoiding taxes in the United States. Comment on this practice and the traits of character revealed. See Neil Sheehan, "More Rich Americans Find Haven for Funds in Secret Bank Accounts," *New York Times*, 30 November 1969, pp. 1, 62.

SUGGESTED READINGS

Aristotle. *The Nicomachean Ethics.* Translated by H. Rackham. Cambridge: Harvard University Press, Loeb Classical Library, 1926.

Burlingame, Roger. *The American Conscience.* New York: Alfred A. Knopf, 1957.

Cabot, Richard C. *Honesty.* New York: Macmillan Co., 1933.

———. *The Meaning of Right and Wrong.* New York: Macmillan Co., 1933.

Demos, Ralph. "Lying to Oneself." *Journal of Philosophy* 57 (September 1, 1960): 588–595.

Faber, Frederick. *Self-Deceit.* Pendle Hill pamphlet no. 50. Wallingford, Pa.: Pendle Hill, 1949.

Fingarette, Herbert. *Self-Deception.* London: Routledge & Kegan Paul, 1969.

Hartmann, Nicolai. *Ethics.* Translated by Stanton Coit. New York: Macmillan Co., 1932. See vol. 2, sec. 4 and 7.

Hartshorne, H. and May, M. A. *Studies in Deceit.* Studies in the Nature of Character, vol. 1. Columbia University Teachers College. New York: Macmillan Co., 1930.

Leonard, Henry S. "Interrogatives, Imperatives, Truth, Falsity, and Lies." *Philosophy of Science* 26 (July 1959): 172–186.

Mumford, Lewis. *The Conduct of Life.* New York: Harcourt, Brace & Co., 1951.

Peters, William, "American Morality." *Redbook* 116 (February 1961): 25–27, 94–101.

Riesman, David and Glazer, Nathan. *Faces in the Crowd: Individual Studies* New Haven: Yale University Press, 1950.

Riseman, David and Glazer, Nathan. *Faces in the Crowd: Individual Studies in Character and Politics.* New Haven: Yale University Press, 1952.

Taylor, Richard. *Good and Evil: A New Direction.* New York: Macmillan Co., 1970.

Trueblood, David Elton. *Foundations for Reconstruction.* New York: Harper & Brothers, 1946.

Ulich, Robert. *The Human Career: A Philosophy of Self-Transcendence.* New York: Harper & Brothers, 1955.

17
INSTITUTIONAL AND PROFESSIONAL ETHICS

In chapter 12 we pointed out that our traditional notions of morality and our commonly accepted moral standards have developed under what the sociologist calls "primary group relationships." The contacts between persons were of the intimate, informal, face-to-face type. The moral codes gave attention to the problems that arise within these fairly simple groups. Today, however, our lives are largely in contact with secondary groups, where there is social distance and where people meet for some particular purpose, or only in one segment of life. In these complex and more impersonal relationships there arise many problems to which older codes gave little or no attention.

THE IMPORTANCE AND DANGERS OF INSTITUTIONS

Whenever a group of people organize for some special purpose or function, they create an institution. We can do together what we cannot do alone, and so we get all sorts of groups-for-doing-things. In the modern world, institutions have multiplied rapidly, and many exist that are related to recreation, education, religion, science, the professions, business, government, and the like. Institutions influence mental development and moral outlook. Like the trellis that directs the growth of the vine, they may lead in one direction or another and thus help shape sentiments and standards of value. The child in the home, the boy in the gang, the pupil in school, the man in his professional association or in business are all influenced by the attitudes, ideas, and actions of the groups of which they are members.

Interdependence and Specialization

At one time, when society was less complex, people carried out most functions for themselves. When they needed clothes, they made them. They raised their own food, built their own homes, and educated their children at home. If someone became sick, he was treated at home, usually with homemade remedies. Any surplus supplies were stored or sold to someone nearby. If there were surplus earnings, they were hidden away in some relatively secure spot. It is said that if, in 1790, all the banks in the United States had failed, probably three-fourths of the population would not even have heard about it, much less have been greatly concerned. A few generations ago people did not need electricians, plumbers, and the host of other specialists we depend on today.

We all recognize the important advantages of the division of labor and specialization. Through specialization we can get much greater skill and a higher quality of service. Without it modern civilization would be impossible. While specialization brings benefits that we do not wish to minimize, it may also lead men to develop "blind spots" in their thinking and to tolerate actions that are harmful to society as a whole. The specialist may see life in segments or fragments. He may give his undivided attention to the technical side of his field but little or no thought to morals, social philosophy, and the application of his special knowledge to human welfare. He may come to think that his own small area of human experience is nearly the whole world. An attitude of detachment has sometimes led to an irresponsible attitude toward social relationships and social problems. The specialist also may come to see all issues and problems from the point of view of his own special interests. A profession may become commercialized, so that a desire for personal gain crowds out a sense of social responsibility.

This tendency for society to break up into parts or segments can have two unfortunate results. First, these parts may claim autonomy and independence from the rest of society. They may wish to operate according to rules or principles that, while promoting their own immediate interests, may be detrimental to the larger interests of society. Second, they may resent or at least resist criticism or interference by outside agencies, whether private or governmental. Teachers, for instance, are likely to think that, since they are specialists in educational methods and needs, educational policy should be left in their hands.

Organized medicine resists pressure from patients and from public health services for new systems of preventive medicine and new methods of payment. Lawyers may think that they alone ought to administer legal justice, and they often brand outside demands for change as misguided idealism. For example, trial lawyers have opposed no-fault automobile insurance. Professional people in general as well as businessmen, scientists, and artists may claim self-government in their special fields and resist all outside demands. No part of society can be a law unto itself and disregard the good of the whole; at least, it cannot do so without harm. At its worst, a profession may become a conspiracy against the public. At its best, it can promote human welfare and further the progress of civilization.

The more specialized the knowledge, the higher the skill, and the less the public knows about the quality and the technical aspects of the work, the greater the opportunity for abuses to arise. Consequently, the need for developing and maintaining high standards of conduct is greater. Such standards will need to be concerned not only with the relations of the professional man to other members of his profession but chiefly with his relation to the public interest and welfare.

The Danger of a Double or Multiple Morality

An institution set up for a specific purpose may change in its outlook as time goes on, or even lose its original purpose. Such an institution may continue and become an end in itself, and its members may see their main task as that of keeping the institution in existence even though its original purpose may have been accomplished or is no longer needed. The institution thus becomes an idol instead of a means for promoting some cause or the welfare of men and women.

Excessive loyalty to institutions has led some men to break the law and undermine the moral code they profess to follow. During recent years men who have been honorable and pillars of their local communities have been put in prison for practices carried on in connection with their professional and business activities. Such men have had double—possibly multiple—moralities and loyalties as they have moved from group to group or institution to institution. "One of the great moral dangers" in our complex and rapidly changing civilization is a "truly pious man with a conventional morality in the midst of a great crisis." Since religion tends to foster and support moral standards, it is interesting that one group of churchmen has charged that religious faiths may foster a double code of morality: "Not 'too little religion,' but double-minded religion, its divorce from practice, is our sickness.

This fact is a judgment upon the churches and the religion they have been content to foster."[1]

Arnold Toynbee, who has studied a score or more of civilizations which have existed in the past, tells us that over periods of time institutions tend to be captured by "collective self-centeredness" and thus often come to serve "anti-social and anti-human ends."[2] Another historian, Carroll Quigley, makes a distinction between "instruments" and "institutions." An instrument, he says, is a "social organization that fulfills some purpose for which it arose"; an institution, on the other hand, is "an instrument that has become an end in itself and taken on purposes of its own."[3] The institution then persists to keep itself alive and promote the interests of its leaders. It is easy for leaders to get in a rut and to believe that their private or group interests are the interests of society as a whole, and for institutions to harden in outworn channels.

While institutions are important and through them we carry on a large part of the work of the world, a man need not give up his individuality and become a slave to any institution. The mature man must transcend special interests and serve the larger society to which all men belong. This is not always easy, and the individual often needs the help and guidance of other more mature and conscientious men. If the professional man is an egotist interpreting his own interests narrowly, for example, his actions will be motivated by his desire for personal pleasure and self-interest. If such a person is a physician, he will give advice that increases his fees. He may even be opposed to preventive medicine that will reduce the amount of sickness in his community, and he will be willing to perform unnecessary operations. If he is a lawyer, he will use any tactics to win cases. He will sell his services to the highest bidder and help criminals go free if he is well paid for his work. If he is in business, he will be out to make money and will be likely to use any methods or tactics he can "get away with."

If, on the other hand, the professional man is interested primarily in the development of persons and in social welfare, and if he sincerely accepts and attempts to live by such moral standards as we have advocated in this text, he will plan to make a living in the service of mankind. As a doctor, he will render efficient service to and will aid the

---

[1] *Report of the Special Committee on National Purpose,* 173rd General Assembly of the United Presbyterian Church in the United States of America (Buffalo, N. Y.: May 17, 1961), p. 4.

[2] *A Study of History,* vol. 12, *Reconsiderations* (New York: Oxford University Press, 1961), p. 638. See also *An Historian's Approach to Religion* (New York: Oxford University Press, 1956), chs. 3, 10, and 17.

[3] *The Evolution of Civilizations* (New York: Macmillan Co., 1961), p. 49. See also chs. 4 and 5.

unfortunate as cheerfully as he attends the rich. As a lawyer, he will strive to see that justice is done and that crime is eliminated. As a businessman, he will be willing to make money only by methods that benefit society.

PROFESSIONS AND PROFESSIONAL STANDARDS

What Is a Profession?

A profession consists of a limited group of people who have acquired some special knowledge and skills and who are therefore able to perform some function in society better than the average person. What are the general characteristics of the professions?

Special Preparation or Training. This preparation includes an accurate knowledge of the fundamental facts on which the professional actions are based and the ability to apply this knowledge in a practical way. The nature and length of the period of preparation varies according to the nature of the different professions.

A Clearly Defined and Comparatively Permanent Membership. All professional groups attempt to keep out the amateur as well as the "quack" or the "shyster." Most countries or their states or subdivisions require members of most professions to obtain a certificate or a license in order to practice.

The Acceptance of the Service Motive. Acceptance of this motive, as distinct from the money-making motive, is characteristic of the professions as a whole. The purpose of the professions is not to make money but to promote health, knowledge, good laws, and so on. The profession is, of course, a means of livelihood, and the professional man needs and is justified in demanding compensation that will permit him to maintain a comfortable living, to dress well, to purchase such books, magazines, and equipment as will enable him to perform his work well, and to contribute to community enterprises. Without these, success will be difficult.

A number of years ago Professor Frederick G. Banting of the University of Toronto discovered insulin, used in treating diabetes. Had he chosen to keep the treatment a secret and cater to wealthy patients, he could have built a great fortune. Instead, he made the discovery available to medical men the world over. Some years ago the papers announced the development of an artificial heart-pacer for reviving persons whose hearts have stopped under certain conditions. Jacob Witkin, endower of the foundation that developed this device, announced that it would be put on the market on a nonprofit basis and be distributed free to hospitals. The discoverer of a method of producing vitamin D and introducing it into foods, Dr. Henry Steenbock, refused an offer of two million dollars from a breakfast food manufacturer for the exclusive right to control the discovery. He is reported to have said that he did not wish to pervert his lifework by commercializing its greatest achievement.

When a businessman is approached, the question that arises is whether the transaction will yield a reasonable profit. In business one is likely to be dealing with commodities that are more tangible and definite. The doctor, the teacher, or the clergyman is unable to stipulate the exact amount of service he will be able to render for a definite sum of money. Private interest is to be promoted only insofar as it also advances the public interest. This distinction between a profession and a business must not be drawn too sharply, however, for some businessmen appear to be adopting the professional ideal, and some professional men are excessively motivated by monetary gain and are in danger of losing the professional ideal.

While the professional man is usually dependent on fees or a salary in order to live, such considerations, ideally at least, are not uppermost in his mind. Actually, the extent to which the quality of the service depends on the remuneration expected varies from profession to profession and from individual to individual. The principles on which charges are based also vary in the different professions. In a few professions, like teaching and the ministry, a regular salary is agreed on before the work begins. Some fees have become more or less standardized, as in the case of the family physician. In other cases the professional man may consider his own standing or prestige and the financial standing of the patient or client and adjust his fee accordingly. This is a fairly common practice with medical specialists such as surgeons, and with fees for legal talent. In still other professions, fees may be figured as a percentage of the cost of the work, as for some architects, or on the basis of the time required, as for many accountants.

The fees that professionals charge and the form the fees take are largely traditional. Even where there are no published lists of fees, charges may be determined by custom, and the man who attempts to undercut the rate brings on himself the disapproval of his professional colleagues. Where the individual or the firm has gained considerable reputation for special skill or where the service is highly personal, fees and charges much above the average are common. Much dissatisfaction arises when fees are excessive and when the basis of calculation is not known by the person who is paying. The most satisfactory principle is probably to make the charges known beforehand and to base the charges on the time and the skill required for the work. The principle of "service as received" is that in which the professional man bases his charge on the real or supposed benefit of the service to the recipient. In this case the patient's or client's ability to pay is a major determining factor. Such a practice may lead to serious abuses. Whether good fortune or natural processes or skill led to success cannot always be determined. This procedure gives the unreasonable or the selfish man too much power over his fellows. The principle of "service as rendered" is found where the professional man bases his charges on the relative time and energy and skill that he finds it necessary to give. His training and overhead expense may be taken into account in such charges. On the whole, the latter principle appears to be more reasonable and to lead to fewer abuses.

MORALS, LAW, AND PROFESSIONAL ETHICS

What is the relation between morals, law, and professional ethics? The term *morals* is the broadest term; it includes any form of voluntary human activity where the judgment of right and wrong, as these are defined in chapter 5, may enter. Morality covers the extensive field of personal and social behavior. It includes many acts that are not of sufficient public concern or are not sufficiently amenable to social control to come within the sphere of the law.

The law, on the other hand, is a command of the state. It is usually set forth in some statutory provision; it applies to all individuals in a specific territory and generally provides penalties for disobedience. Today there is a considerable amount of administrative law that is not in statutory form. This law may be an attempt by some governmental agency to apply the law to objectives which are not specified in the statute but which, it is believed, derive from the statute. Morals are basic, and laws tend to follow the moral ideals of the community and to change with the development of the moral consciousness. Since obedience to the law is usually considered a part of moral behavior, however, all laws may be included in the moral realm.[4]

Professional ethics, as distinct from morals and from the law, gives attention to certain additional ideals and practices that grow out of a

---

[4]There may be times, however, when a man on moral grounds will refuse to obey some law. We shall consider this problem later in the text.

man's professional privileges and responsibilities. Professional ethics applies to certain groups and is the expression of the attempt to define situations that otherwise would remain indefinite or uncertain and to direct the moral consciousness of the members of the profession to its peculiar problems. The ethical codes crystallize moral opinion and define behavior in these specialized fields.

The fields of morals, law, and professional ethics are fairly distinct, yet they overlap in many ways. There are some acts which fall within one field only. Lying is considered immoral, although neither the law nor professional ethics takes cognizance of the ordinary lie. Unintentionally parking one's car longer than the specified time may be illegal only, for there are laws that deal with issues not involving morals and professional ethics except as the breaking of any law may be considered immoral. In some professions advertising oneself is considered unprofessional, though it can hardly be classed as either immoral or illegal in the usual sense.

Some types of conduct concern all three fields. For example, misappropriation of a client's funds by a lawyer would be immoral, unprofessional, and also illegal. Again, certain acts fall within two of the fields only. To steal is immoral and illegal, but it is conduct with which the professional code does not concern itself. Professional neglect of a client, a patient, or a pupil is immoral and unprofessional, but unless the situation is exceedingly grave, the law does not concern itself with it. Contempt of court is both illegal and unprofessional for the lawyer, but under some circumstances it is not immoral. Thus we see that, while there is a clear-cut distinction between morals, law, and professional ethics, many acts fall into two or even all three of these fields.

The Value and Function of Professional Codes

In the field of professional activities, written ethical codes have been in existence as guiding influences for many years.[5] Why are professional codes of ethics being written? First, as a means of social control. They define professional conduct for the new member and help keep the older members in line. Every profession has its own special or unique

---

[5] By 1924 about two hundrd codes had been drawn up. See Edgar L. Heermance, *Codes of Ethics: A Handbook* (Burlington, Vt.: Free Press Printing, 1924). More recent codes may be obtained from the various trade and professional associations. From time to time, codes are published in The Annals of the American Academy of Political and Social Science. See the volumes cited in the *Suggested Readings* at the end of this chapter.

problems, and a statement representing the mature judgment of leaders in the profession can be a great help. For example, should the teacher tutor his own pupils for pay? The dignity and standing of the profession is dependent on the confidence the public has in it.

Second, professional ethical codes if effective prevent control or interference by the government or by society through some of its agencies. If a degree of standardization is desirable, who is to determine the bounds of good behavior? Should the law attempt to regulate in detail the behavior of doctors in dealing with patients or with other doctors? Should it regulate the relationship between the lawyer and his client, the teacher and his pupil, or the engineer and his employer and the public? Such regulation is conceivable, but it would seem highly undesirable. Law tends to be negative, while ethics points to the goal desired. Although law is the most conspicious means of social control, it should be used only where other methods of safeguarding personal and social rights are not sufficient. Groups that maintain high standards are seldom interfered with by the government, which takes on regulative functions only where they seem to be necessary.

Third, ethical codes can be important in developing higher standards of conduct. The codes crystallize what is usually the best opinion and judgment of the profession; thus they tend to eliminate misunderstanding and conflicts. They enable the group to bring pressure to bear on those who would lower the standing of the group or cast reflection on its good name.

Professional ideals vary greatly from group to group. Some of them are open to criticism from the point of view of the larger ethical claims. In considering particular codes, we need to ask such questions as these: (1) Does the code attempt merely to protect certain selfish interests, to advance the profession economically, or is it concerned with the service the profession can render to society? Professional societies have gone through and are still going through various stages of liberation, from selfishness to a spirit of broad-minded public service. (2) Is the code sufficiently definite and clear or is it merely an expression of vague idealism that is subject to varied interpretations? (3) Does the code represent only a small conscientious minority within the profession, or do the rank and file members respect and attempt to follow it? (4) Are there effective means of enforcing the code? Are delinquent members of the profession called to account or penalized in some way? This has been the weakest point in the development of professional standards. (5) Is there some plan and effort to keep the code up to date as conditions change? If so, and if all the above questions and conditions can be met, professional codes may be forces in the right direction.

THREE PROFESSIONAL GROUPS

When a professional group, a business, or a trade association formulates a code or a set of standards, it deals, as a rule, not with the moral standards of society at large, but with the problems that are characteristic of or peculiar to that field of service. If the discussions that follow appear to stress problems and abuses, it needs to be kept in mind that ethics is concerned with *what ought to be* and with the improvement of persons and conditions. We select three professions—medicine, law, and education—for brief consideration not because these professions are any better or any worse than others, but because they are closely related to the lives of most people.

Medical Ethics

The physician's code embodies ideas that have been in the process of formation since ancient times. The laws of Hammurabi—written in Babylonia about 2500 B.C.—dealt with fees to be given a physician and with punishment when injury was done. Later, during the fifth century B.C. in Greece, the "Oath of Hippocrates"—an oath still taken, in revised form, by physicians—set forth the duty of the medical man.

Physicians generally have been men of character and integrity who have worked long hours and been respected members of their communities. The profession as a whole has made outstanding advances in medicine, especially in the last century. Yet after reading many of the current books and articles on health problems and medical ethics—many of which have been written by doctors or other health specialists—one is left with the impression that there are many problems and much to be done to maintain and improve the health of the people of the country as a whole. Controversies surround such matters as fees and charges, insurance and prepayment plans, fee-splitting, "ghost surgery," group practice, experimenting with patients, transplanting organs from healthy to diseased persons, and the like. There are a number of conditions responsible, in part at least, for the new problems: (1) The rapid increase of medical knowledge and new laboratory techniques, with the creation of numerous specialties and subspecialties. This has changed the nature of the doctor-patient relationship and has brought various forms of "multiple practice" or clinical and group practice into being. (2) The growing and insistent demand on the part of the public for some method of payment that distributes the cost of medical care more evenly over the years. Many patients want medical costs put on a prepayment or insurance basis. (3) The growing demand for more preventive medicine, which has led to health programs and research that involve the government and other third parties. (4) The fact that industrial concerns, labor unions, the armed services, and other groups are employing doctors on a salary basis to provide medical services for their members. Are these newer forms of medical practice that disturb the older "individual fee for individual service" basis to be approved or condemned as unethical? Is it possible that some of these new forms of practice may be models for the future?

The American Medical Association was organized in 1847 and immediately became concerned with a code of ethics and with setting minimum standards for medical education and practice. Amendments in and additions to the code have been made from time to time. Students should read the complete and latest form of the "Principles of Medical Ethics,"[6] since we have space here merely to point out some of the things that are approved and some of the things disapproved and called unethical. For example, the code states that "The principal objective of the medical profession is to render service to humanity with full respect for the dignity of man." It affirms the "patient's right to choose his physician"; the "physician's right to choose whom he will serve"; individualism in the practice of medicine and free competition among doctors; a "fee commensurate with the service rendered and the patient's ability to pay." The doctor is asked to expose incompetent or corrupt conduct on the part of other members of the profession and unlicensed quacks and charlatans, to be willing to discuss fees with his patients, and to keep confidences entrusted to him.

The "Principles of Medical Ethics" clearly condemns certain practices as unethical. These include fee-splitting, the secret division of fees among doctors for referring patients to them; "ghost surgery," in which one doctor passes his patient over to another in the operating room to perform the operation; advertising or the solicitation of patients; "acceptance of rebates on prescriptions and appliances or of commissions from those who aid in the care of patients"; taking a patent on a surgical or diagnostic instrument so as to retard research or restrict its use; association with or assistance of cultists, optometrists, and medical organizations controlled by groups of laymen; and criticism of other doctors in the presence of patients.

Since the practice of fee-splitting is an evil that, according to reliable reports, is fairly widespread, an additional comment on it is in order.

---

[6]Published by the American Medical Association, 535 North Dearborn, Chicago, Illinois 60610. In 1957 the 1955 edition of the Principles of Medical Ethics was reduced to a preamble and ten short sections. For a more detailed statement of the code, see the 79-page booklet *Judicial Council Opinions and Reports*, published by the Association in 1964.

Fee-splitting has grown with the development of specialization until today it is, in the words of a prominent medical man, "a menace to the public and a disgrace to the profession." Through it an incompetent man may build up a large practice, since the man who pays the largest commission may be the one recommended by the referring physician. Fee-splitting introduces an inducement which is likely to influence the professional judgment of the referring doctor. The result may be bad surgery and many unnecessary operations. The practice is said to lead to high fees, unmerited praise of incompetent men, and untimely deaths.

Medical Ethics and the Public Interest

Do the standards embodied in recent pronouncements by the American Medical Association express the highest ethical ideals, or do they in the main protect the self-interests of the physician? Much has been written to support each position. If all medical men were conscientious in living up to the ideals, as a large number of them are, much of the criticism of the profession would have less justification. A partial explanation of some loss in public esteem in recent decades appears to be the attempt of the profession to maintain the *status quo* of medical practice in the face of rapidly changing conditions, and its failure to discipline or expel the incompetent and the unscrupulous practitioner within the profession.

In behalf of the medical profession, it should be said that the code is being changed from time to time and is beginning to take account of some of the newer trends in medical practice. Furthermore, the medical profession has done more than most other professions to set up machinery for enforcing the code and dealing with offenders. Each county medical society is expected to set up a grievance committee or other body whose duty it is to hear complaints and investigate charges of unethical practice against members of the association. The member charged with unethical conduct must be notified of the charges and be given a full and fair hearing. The grievance committee may recommend acquittal, censure, suspension, or expulsion. A member who has been disciplined may appeal to the council of the State Medical Association. On questions pertaining to law and procedure, he may appeal to the Judicial Council of the American Medical Association.

Problems Facing the Medical Profession

1. *The uneven distribution of doctors.* The United States has about three hundred thirty thousand doctors, or about one for every six hun-

dred fifty people, and spends nearly seven percent of the gross national product on health care. This amount may be sufficient to provide adequate, efficient care for everyone. Yet among the major industrial nations, the United States is the only country that has failed to devise some kind of national health program. There is a surplus of medical personnel in some areas and not enough (or none) in others. For the country as a whole there is probably a shortage of doctors since many doctors are engaged in research and are not practicing physicians. A more even distribution of medical personnel and resources, and of the cost of care, would partially remedy the present unsatisfactory conditions.

2. *Experiments with patients.* To what extent and under what conditions may doctors experiment with patients? For years experiments have been carried on with animals, and undoubtedly much experimentation has been conducted on human patients. What risks may legitimately or ethically be taken? Transplanting organs from a healthy to a diseased person is a case in point that is disturbing some doctors today. There are real risks involved and who is to decide who is to live and who is to die?

3. *Can practices such as sterilization, abortion, and artificial insemination be morally justified?* If children have a right to be wanted and to have sound minds in sound bodies, and if the offspring is likely to be defective and diseased, is sterilization or abortion the answer? If the law will not permit diseased or defective people to adopt a child, why should we permit them to give birth to children? Abortion is a practice closely related to sterilization and raises some similar problems. More people, however, oppose abortion since it means the destruction of the already living fetus during the early months of gestation. The tendency today is for states to liberalize their abortion laws.

4. *May euthanasia ("mercy killing") ever be justified?* At present men sometimes consider killing in war and capital punishment the lesser evils. Legal euthanasia would also permit the ending of life, in this case for merciful release when all efforts to save life have failed. Those who oppose euthanasia under any condition say that it is the doctor's task to save life, that there are now effective pain-relieving drugs, that where there is life there is hope, and that *incurable* is a very tricky word. They point out that mercy killing can lead to grave abuses, and that to sanction such practice tends to weaken respect for life. Those who favor mercy killing point out that the law requires men to put seriously wounded animals to death, that doctors now on occasion decide to save

a mother and sacrifice the life of a baby, and that with proper safeguards abuses may be prevented.

5. *Does an individual have a right to know the truth about the condition of his health?* There are times when a patient is emotionally unable to cope with the full knowledge of his illness, and this knowledge could be detrimental to him. Yet without a knowledge of his condition and the freedom to choose on the basis of the known facts, patients are little more than puppets. If the patient is frank with the doctor and wishes to know the truth, should the doctor be equally frank, and does he then have an obligation to inform the patient of his actual condition? When people are denied available knowledge, a part of their moral nature is taken from them—they are treated like children or weaklings. Even if death is imminent, a man may wish to make preparations for his demise in his will and in discussions with his next of kin.

6. *What ethical issues arise in meeting medical costs?* In 1970 the people of the United States directly or indirectly spent over sixty-seven billion dollars for health care. This represents about three hundred twenty-four dollars annually for every person in the country. This is probably enough to finance a comprehensive national health program. During the early 1970s various plans were being submitted to Congress, and the reader should keep informed about the progress of these plans. Many doctors as represented by the American Medical Association are opposed to prepayment plans, but many patients favor them. The Student American Medical Association, which represents about eighteen thousand medical students and many younger doctors, supports the more liberal programs that stress prepayment, preventive medicine, and the like.

Physicians who oppose these newer schemes for medical care are likely to say that the doctors themselves should have charge of the practice of medicine and should control the quality of medical service; that they want to avoid bureaucracy and the political control of medical practice; and that they wish to retain the personal relationship between doctor and patient. That doctors should have *complete* charge of the practice of medicine and should determine the quality of medical service has been rejected by practically all modern societies that insist on certain standards and a license before a doctor can practice. Society has also made provision for legal punishment for improper pratice or injury. With these exceptions in mind, most of us will agree that doctors should have considerable freedom in determining the kind of medical service that patients receive. On the other hand, an increasingly large number of people are asking for some method of payment that distributes the cost of medical care more evenly and that does not increase costs at a time when people may be least able to meet them. There is also the desire for more emphasis on preventive medicine. These, too, are legitimate demands. If some people desire a different kind of payment scheme than the traditional one, and if some doctors wish to cooperate and feel that the new plans enable them to give better service, we have no right to call such plans and people "unethical," as some are doing.

In any event we appear to need a more adequate health program. The present system needs to be supplemented by medical groups of different types and by health insurance. For the lower income groups, we may need more tax-supported clinics, hospitals, and county nurses. Little harm and possibly great benefit may come from experimenting to find more adequate methods of handling our problems of health.

In considering all these problems facing the medical profession, the interests of the physician and his fellow practitioners as well as the larger interests of humanity have to be considered and adjusted. The harmonizing of practice and ideals in a changing society is an ever-present problem. Unfortunately few medical schools give any systematic attention to the subject of professional ethics.

Legal Ethics

Like the medical profession, the legal profession stands in close relation to the lives of all of us. There is some truth in the statement that "lawyers run our civilization for us." They are important in the running of our government, since most legislators are lawyers; they administer our laws. Most presidents, governors, and commissioners are also lawyers. The judges who interpret and enforce our laws are lawyers. Lawyers play an important part in the affairs of industry and business. Laws prescribe the details of business activities. Whenever a deal is made or property is transferred, the law is involved. Many lawyers sit as directors of corporations, and all large corporations retain legal advisers to watch over and guide their activities. We cannot get divorced, inherit property, or will it to our children without lawyers. Throughout our lives we must observe many rules and formalities that lawyers have created for us.

There are nearly four hundred thousand lawers in the United States. A considerable number of them, however, are not members of the American Bar Association. To practice law, a person must be admitted to the bar of some state. Admission is ordinarily by bar examinations, but in some states graduation from certain law schools exempts one from these examinations. Disbarment is possible through court action.

Sentiment for the creation of standards or canons of legal ethics did not make much headway until the first decade of the twentieth century, when the number of unscrupulous lawyers was increasing at an alarming rate and public indignation and criticism could no longer be disregarded. It became apparent that standards were essential in order to make clear what courts could require of lawyers, what lawyers could expect of their colleagues, and what the public could expect from members of the legal profession.

Standards Adopted by the American Bar Association

The American Bar Association was organized in 1878 with five objectives: to uphold the honor of the legal profession, to encourage cordial relations among lawyers, to promote the administration of justice, to advance the study of jurisprudence, and to work for uniform laws throughout the country. The original thirty-two Canons of Professional Ethics adopted in 1908 eventually grew to forty-seven. Efforts to revise the canons were made in 1928, 1933, 1937, and 1954 but came to nothing. Many persons felt that the older codes dealt too largely with questions of etiquette and were not sufficiently concerned with the more fundamental questions of standards and obligations. However, in 1964 a Special Committee on Evaluation of Ethical Standards was appointed and, after much work and consultation with groups and individuals, the Code of Professional Responsibility was adopted by the House of Delegates of the American Bar Association in 1969 to become effective on January 1, 1970.[7]

This code is composed of nine canons, each consisting of a general statement followed by more detailed "Ethical Considerations" and "Disciplinary Rules." The canons state that a lawyer should assist in maintaining the integrity and competence of the legal profession; assist the profession in fulfilling its duty to make legal counsel available; assist in preventing the unauthorized practice of law; preserve the confidences and secrets of a client; exercise independent professional judgment on behalf of a client; represent a client competently; represent a client jealously within the bounds of the law; assist in improving the legal system; and avoid even the appearance of professional impropriety.

The lawyer is to avoid many practices considered unethical. These include engaging in any conduct involving dishonesty, deceit, fraud, or misrepresentation, or in conduct that is "prejudicial to the administration of justice." The lawyer must also avoid and discourage litigation

---

[7]See the *Code of Professional Responsibility and Canons of Judicial Ethics* (Chicago: American Bar Association, 1970). The codes may be obtained from the ABA, 1155 East 60th St., Chicago, Illinois 60637.

that is brought merely to harass or injure another person. He is not to engage in competitive advertising, or to contact a nonclient, directly or indirectly, for the purpose of being retained to represent him for compensation. Stirring up strife and litigation is sometimes called "ambulance chasing." A lawyer may decline employment, but once a case is accepted, he should not withdraw except for good reasons. He should not accept employment on a case in which he has previously acted in a judicial capacity nor should he aid a nonlawyer in the practice of law. Fees should be reasonable in the light of the time and nature of the services. Money or other trust property should be reported promptly and should be kept separate from the lawyer's own funds or accounts.

Problems Facing the Legal Profession

There are at least five serious problems facing the legal profession.

1. *Too many lawyers.* This is one of the profession's most important problems. Low educational and other entrance requirements in some states are partly responsible for this condition. While about five thousand lawyers are needed each year to fill up the ranks, about twice that many are entering the profession annually.

High-quality professional service depends on knowledge as well as character. If either is deficient or missing, the service is likely to deteriorate. Today most states have set up examining boards by legislative enactment. These boards replace the earlier method of admitting men to the bar by a court order following what was usually a perfunctory examination by a committee of the bar. Only a few states require a college degree before admission to the bar, though most require at least two years of college or its equivalent. The American Bar Association recommends as a minimum preparation at least three years of study in college and three years in a law school. Today the better law schools require such preparation for a degree, and a few require the baccalaureate degree as part of the entrance requirements.

2. *The prevalence of abuses within the profession.* Abuses are caused in part by overcrowding and lack of strict disciplinary control. There is a marked contrast between a fairly lofty ethical ideal and practices that fall far below this ideal. No one wants to cast aspersions on the many lawyers who are thoroughly professional and who exhibit a spirit of unselfish service, but there are far too many who use the profession as a means of money making and political advancement.

In recent years the "ambulance chaser" has come into considerable prominence. A firm or a private practitioner may work up litigations and business in various ways. Agents and "runners"—policemen, nurses, reporters, and others—receive a commission for locating possible clients. Accidents and deaths are recorded. Some lawyers go over titles to property and other legal papers in the hope of finding flaws or errors that will afford the basis for suits. Others read the papers for slips that may lead to libel suits, or attempt to discover episodes in the lives of men or women from which divorce suits may develop. In its attempt to prevent these abuses, the canon of professional ethics prohibits the solicitation of clients either directly or indirectly.

The above practices are closely linked with the contingent fee. Here the client agrees to pay the lawyer a certain percentage, usually high, of the money gained in case of success in a pending suit. The lawyer thus becomes in effect a partner in a business enterprise, and there is strong incentive for him to win at all costs. Contingent fees are not absolutely condemned, since there are poor men who have valid cases and would be unable to pay except after a favorable verdict. If the lawyer loses, he pays the expenses of the suit. While not evil in itself, the contingent fee obviously can be abused.

Among the lawyers deserving condemnation are those who, in order to serve their clients, seek technicalities, delays, and use bribery and perjury. Such persons bring the law into disrepute and make a mockery of justice. In this connection we are likely to notice the "shyster" who frequents the police court, but we may overlook some corporation lawyers who do the same things for their wealthy employers or other lawyers who use every conceivable device to protect criminals.

3. *The tendency of the profession to develop into a trade.* This tendency is causing considerable concern to persons both within and without the profession. The lawyer is closely associated with the business life and activity of his community and readily adopts its outlook and sanctions its practices. Many men in the profession devote their time to pleading for special tax legislation or for tariffs or subsidies. Some lawers spend their time helping special business groups do what they want to do, regardless of the social consequences.

4. *Lack of social consciousness.* The almost total lack of a social consciousness on the part of a considerable number of the members of the profession is unfortunate. The conviction is left, not only after considering the unscrupulous lawyers but also after examining the careers of some of the most prominent lawyers of today and of recent years, that a great many members of the profession are ready to sell their services for almost any cause and to the highest bidder. Outside their

profession these men may be devoted to human welfare, yet in their professional activities they are the hired servants of their clients. Men eminent in the profession and in good standing in the bar associations may spend their time and talent advising individuals and corporations how to observe the letter of the law while conducting practices in opposition to the spirit and intent of the law. Consider the number of wealthy men who are able to evade income tax through the advice of their lawyers.

A keener social consciousness on the part of members of the profession would result in an interest in eliminating technicalities, in closing loopholes, and in preventing wrongdoing within the law. There is urgent need for more lawyers who will not only refuse to prey upon the misfortunes of others but help mold the law to meet the demands of present-day society.

5. *The continuation of an antiquated system.* Lawyers are not only a part of, but help to propagate, a system that is antiquated and that in too many cases leads to miscarriages of justice.[8] Why should the ordinary criminal trial consist of two partisan groups each trying to win a victory rather than a group of experts using every scientific means available to determine the facts of the case and the condition of the offender and to recommend a disposal of the case after consideration of the interests of society and of the offender? There are two theories of court procedure. The first is the prevalent "fight" or "adversary" theory, which comes from the past and which substitutes a court or legal battle for private brawls and feuds. The aim is to win, and the trial is a game in which the contestants are the lawyers rather than the litigants. Under this system lawyers want to win all (or most of) their cases and so build reputations for themselves. If they are prosecutors, they appeal to their record as a basis for reelection.

The second is the "truth" or "investigatory" theory of handling cases. Here the attempt is to discover the facts, to remove causes and occasions for error, to eliminate the tricks and questionable strategems.

Under present practice many guilty people go free and some innocent men are punished. An examination of works on criminology, reports of crime commissions, studies of police practices, and studies of the jury system will furnish much evidence of the need for reforms.

---

[8]Virgil W. Peterson, "Case Dismissed," *Atlantic Monthly* 175 (April 1945): 69–74; Ferdinand Lundberg, "The Law Factories," *Harper's Magazine* 179 (July 1939): 180–192; Fred Rodell, *Woe Unto You, Lawyers!* (New York: Reynal & Hitchcock, 1939); Arthur T. Vanderbilt, *The Challenge of Law Reform* (Princeton: Princeton University Press, 1955); David Dressler, "Trial by Combat in American Courts," *Harper's Magazine* 222 (April 1961): 31–36.

Attempts at Reform

Probably all of us can number among our friends and acquaintances several lawyers of high professional skill and personal honor and integrity. Such members of the profession deserve the highest esteem. Many of them spend time and energy, both within and without the bar associations, to raise the standards of practice.

Progress in the field of legal ethics during recent years is indicated by the fact that the Canons of Professional Ethics and the Canons of Judicial Ethics have been accepted by the bar associations and courts in most states. In those states which have bar associations established on an "integrated basis," membership in the State Bar is compulsory for those who wish to practice law. This means that the Canons have the force of law and that lawyers are subject to discipline for infractions of the code.

In addition to the American Bar Association, there are a number of other organizations for lawyers or societies which are working for legal reform. We can mention here the work of the American Law Institute, which works to clarify and simplify the law; the American Judicature Society, which sponsors conferences on judicial reform and works to combat court congestion and delay; the National Bar Association, primarily black with increasing white membership, which promotes fellowship among members of the bench and bar; the Association of American Law Schools; and the National Lawyers Guild.

In a period of rapid social change and steadily advancing science, law can be a barrier to reform as well as the mechanism through which reform may be effected. Some lawyers have regarded the legal profession as a game, a trade, or even a high-class racket to be used for personal advantage. Others have administered the law efficiently but in a conventional way. Some lawyers, fortunately, have been in the forefront of the struggle for human freedom and human progress.

The Ethics of Educators

When a problem arises in modern society, whether it concerns war and peace, labor troubles, racial conflict, or social organization, someone is almost certain to say that education is the cure. Such an assertion cannot be accepted without qualifications. The important thing is not just education, but the *kind of education*. Education can bind people to the past; it can be narrow and bigoted; it can lead people to be militaristic; it can make people extremely self-centered. On the other hand, education can train people to face the future with vision, to be broad and tolerant, to be seekers after peace, and to consider the rights of others. Mere education or mere teaching is not enough. Teachers are responsible, at least in part, for the kind of education that exists and for the individual and social attitudes that arise from the educative process.

In the past, formal education has been too limited in its objectives to serve these larger social interests. Teachers have been occupied almost exclusively with imparting a particular body of facts in a specialized field, and they have trained their pupils to be good competitors and to adjust to the *status quo*. Today it is increasingly evident that young persons being trained to live in society as it is now may graduate in a few years into a society changed enough to require a quite different kind of training. The rapidly changing social environment is making new demands on education and placing new responsibilities on the teacher.

Modern schools must see that students acquire an understanding of contemporary society and the changes through which it is passing as well as a keener sense of personal and social responsbility for helping establish an even better social order. Since the atmosphere and the attitudes prevalent throughout the school system are created mainly by the staff, the conduct and the ethical ideals of the teacher are exceedingly important.

Teachers are gradually becoming aware of the need for self-regulation. Certain standards of conduct that members of the profession can be expected to follow were in the past largely taken for granted. Education in the United States is administered largely by the various states, and the first codes of ethics for teachers were drawn up and adopted by the state teachers associations about the beginning of the century. In 1857 a National Teachers Association was organized, and in 1906 it was incorporated as the National Education Association (NEA). It is the chief professional organization for teachers and includes not only classroom teachers, but administrators and others concerned with education in the schools and colleges of the United States. In 1929 after some years of work, a committee on ethics of the NEA drew up a code of ethics which was approved by the association. This code is revised from time to time and the NEA has authorized a "national study of the code every five years for the purpose of keeping it up to date to meet the needs of a dynamic profession."[9]

The NEA Code as amended in July 1970 is too long to present in detail. It consists of a preamble and four principles or sections with from five to nine specific items under each principle. The preamble stresses the worth and dignity of man, the importance of the search for truth, and devotion to excellence and democratic citizenship. Principle

---

[9]*Opinions of the Committee on Professional Ethics* (Washington, D. C.: National Education Association of the United States, 1964), p. 7.

I—"Commitment to the Student" has eight subdivisions dealing with such subjects as independent study, the rejection of discriminatory action on the grounds of race, color, creed, or national origin. Principle II—"Commitment to the Public" includes the prohibition of gratuities, gifts, or favors that might influence professional judgment. Principle III—"Commitment to the Profession" calls for equitable treatment of all members of the profession. Principle IV—"Commitment to Professional Employment Practices" deals with a wide range (nine) of topics that include applying for a specific position, termination of service, contracts, and the quality of professional service. There are also bylaws and provisions for national enforcement of the code by the NEA. The code, if followed conscientiously by all members of the profession, would eliminate many unethical practices.

Those concerned with the implementation of the NEA code hope that educational associations will call for adherence as a condition of membership, and that the code will receive legal recognition and eventually become a condition for "maintaining a certificate and continuing on a contract." The educational associations of each state are urged to establish a committee on professional ethics if they have not already done so, to investigate reported violations of the code, and to crystallize sentiment in support of it. It is stipulated that any person accused of a violation should have an opportunity to defend himself.[10]

The American Federation of Teachers (AFT) was organized in 1916 as an affiliate to the American Federation of Labor (now AFL-CIO). Whereas the NEA had about a million members in the late sixties the AFT had less than two hundred thousand members. The AFT is a union of classroom teachers and some other educational workers (such as librarians, school nurses, and counselors) but is not open to administrators who are in the position of hiring and firing. The strength of the NEA is in rural and small-town areas, and especially in the South; the strength of the AFT is in the big cities and especially along the eastern seaboard.

The AFT supports collective bargaining, academic freedom, and civil rights and seeks to improve salary scales, working conditions, and fringe benefits. The Bill of Rights of the AFT (Twelve Declarations) includes such phrases as the following: "the right to think freely . . . and to hold views contrary to the majority"; "the free exercise of religion"; "the right to take part in social, civil, and political affairs . . . outside the classroom"; "the right to be secure in their jobs"; "in cases affecting

---

[10]*The Code of Ethics of the Education Profession* may be secured from the Committee on Professional Ethics, National Education Association, 1201 Sixteenth Street, N.W., Washington, D. C. 20036.

employment . . . the right to a full hearing and due process"; "the right to an adequate salary"; "the right to tenure terminable only for just cause"; "the teacher is entitled to good classrooms, adequate teaching materials, teachable class size and administrative protection"; "the right to be members of organizations of their own choosing."[11] The overall objective is stated as "democracy in education and education for democracy." The NEA and the AFT have much the same goals, but there is rivalry between them and the AFT is on the whole more aggressive in its outlook and tactics.

Problems Facing Educators

There are a number of problems facing educators in the second half of the twentieth century, problems needing solution if the schools are to keep up with the rapidly changing world and be ready to meet the challenge of a highly complex society. Here in brief are six areas calling for consideration:

1. *The need for freedom of investigation and discussion for both teachers and students.* Educators must insist on their right to freedom of research and freedom in the exposition of their subjects. But note that, while teachers are (or should be) the best judges of truth in the fields in which they have special training, they have no right to use the power inherent in their classroom position to pass judgment on controversial topics that have no relation to their fields of special competence. Outside the classroom, teachers have the same right of expression as other citizens.

The teacher should demand that pupils have freedom to grow and develop their personalities. The development of intelligent understanding and the power of self-direction are among the central aims in education. The person who must accept without question the ideas of another is not likely to develop the capacity to grow. The moral autonomy of each person is a basic value that should be cultivated, not warped, by the educational process.

2. *The demand or the right of students to some voice in educational policy and administration.* This is a question being widely debated in many schools and colleges during the 1970s. Some conservative educational leaders ask how competent students are to determine such issues.

---

[11]The Bill of Rights and literature stating the philosophy and objectives of the AFT may be secured from The American Federation of Teachers, AFL-CIO, 1012—14th St., N.W., Washington, D. C. 20005.

The more liberal leaders point out that students are the consumers and usually know the difference between effective and incompetent teaching, and that they should be heard. Some students supported by some teachers and administrators say that students should have the right to present their views on such matters as curricula, teaching methods, and even the hiring, firing, and the salaries of educators. In many colleges and in some high schools, students do have representatives on various committees and other educational bodies.

3. *A lack of adequate financial support.* This plus the lack of adequate facilities and supplies for an increasing student population are other areas for consideration. There is also a need for improved teacher training. The shortage of well-trained, highly competent teachers and administrators is due in part to low salaries in comparison with those of some other professions and the business world, and in part to the working conditions that do not enable them to perform their services in the most effective and professional manner.

The question of adequate financial support for schools is tied up with other issues, especially the question of federal aid to education. Some local communities and states have meager resources whereas other areas are well-to-do and can spend many times more per student than in the poorer school districts. The problem is primarily that of equalizing educational opportunity throughout the country.

4. *The problem of racial integration.* Integration has been a fact and has worked well in some communities for years. In other areas it has created strife and met resistance. Shall the method of integration, and possibly busing, be settled by the courts and the federal government or by local communities? Questions of race relations will be discussed in a later chapter.

5. *The right of teachers to strike.* During the 1960s and early seventies some teachers in the United States, Great Britain, Italy, and elsewhere have remained away from their classrooms on strike for long or short periods, and others have threatened to strike if unjust or unfair conditions are not remedied. Opponents of the right of teachers to strike have called such actions immoral and have attempted to prevent them by law or ordinances. Others contend that teachers, like other workers, have a moral right to strike when all other attempts to remedy grievances have been exhausted and they still are plagued by such obstacles to professional effort as overcrowded and obsolete buildings, low salaries, and inadequate equipment. In a free society may such tactics be used to arouse an indifferent public and governmental officials to the need to do something to save a deteriorating school system? A strike of edu-

cators is unfortunate, since it affects innocent persons who cannot do much to remedy the situation. On the other hand, it may show that some teachers have the courage to stand up and be counted for their convictions when the best interests of their students and the community as well as themselves are at stake.

6. *How to achieve a sense of direction and a moral purpose within which to direct our scientific and technological knowledge and skill.* Along with our quest for the truth must go a concern for individual fulfillment of character and the welfare of the community. Education all too frequently fails to instill in students any vital affirmations, convictions, and discipline. Science and research have often become detached from human values and loyalties.

The desire to win the cold war has led to a demand for greater emphasis on science in our educational program. But this by itself is not the key to victory. "A scientist," says James P. Warburg, "without an inner-directed philosophy, moral sensibility, and humane sympathy is a dangerous member of society. Science itself, without philosophy to direct the use of scientific discovery, is a menace."[12] A problem facing education is how to motivate people to strive for the true and the good as well as the useful and the entertaining.

A CONCLUDING QUESTION

Is the professional ideal a "way out" for society? Recent years have witnessed the growth of the professional ideal and a multiplication of professions. Will society continue to develop in this direction until all of the major functions are professionalized, or is this merely a minor back-eddy in a civilization that will continue to be dominated by a drive for material gain? Is it possible for us to increase the number and the extent of the activities motivated by the true professional ideal?

Material incentives have their place, and the enjoyment of material satisfaction will undoubtedly continue to be a spur to greater activity. This type of incentive must have as its purpose, however, social well-being rather than acquisitiveness or accumulation. The fact that most persons appear today to be dominated by the money-getting drive is no reason to believe that this is an inborn trait or that this condition must continue. The explanation may be merely that our business civilization has held before men the principle of getting as much as possible and giving as little as possible in return. Men may, however, be motivated

---

[12]James P. Warburg, *The West in Crisis* (Garden City: Doubleday & Co., 1959), p. 166.

by things other than the desire for personal profit or material gain. During both World Wars we took many workers for the army or set them to work producing war materials, yet the remaining workers enormously increased their production of the necessities of life. The money-getting motive was subordinated to the patriotic and service motive.

Public approval, recognition, group loyalty, the creative impulse, the desire for power, and rivalry are all powerful motives. With the development of an increasingly complex and interrelated social order, we need to stress motives that are social.

QUESTIONS AND PROJECTS

1. A businessman sends a letter of inquiry to a teacher. He wishes to learn the qualifications of a senior who is applying for a position. The young man in question has been known to cheat, but he possesses a number of admirable qualities. Should the teacher mention the cheating in his letter and perhaps lessen the young man's chances of getting the position; should he disregard the cheating and mention only the admirable qualities? Give reasons for your answer.
2. A teacher in a sociology class at a large university, when asked what he thought should be done about a certain social problem, replied: "Young man, I am not interested in betterment. I am a scientist interested in discovering and describing facts." Discuss the attitude represented here and give your reaction to it.
3. The statement has been made that specialists (professional people, scientists, research workers) tend to be progressive and even radical only in their special fields—that they welcome change and new ideas in the area of their specialty but tend to be conservative or even reactionary in nearly every other area. They are especially likely, it is claimed, to be conservative in social, economic, and political matters. Can you give any evidence for or against this attitude?
4. Make lists of acts or types of behavior and show their relation to these classifications: morals, law, professional ethics. Indicate whether each act is (1) included in all three of the classifications, (2) outside all three, (3) included in only one, or (4) included in only two of them.
5. In recent years there have been many important discoveries that have benefited humanity. In many cases the discovery or the knowledge was made available to society with no attempt on the part of the discoverer to use it as a means of creating a fortune. Do you think that these men did the right thing? If so, do you think that persons who do otherwise should be condemned? Does the type of the discovery or the invention make any difference?
6. Is there any justification for the practice of some professional men of overcharging the rich and undercharging the poor? On what basis can it be justified? What are its dangers? Does it make the professional

Institutional and Professional Ethics / 369

man a collector and a dispenser of taxes if he really does collect from the rich and pass such benefits on to the poor?
7. Are there any reasons why a surgeon or a lawyer should charge what the traffic will bear while the teacher or the social worker is paid a fixed amount regardless of the service rendered? If so, what are they?
8. If a doctor, lawyer, or minister gains information as to the identity or whereabouts of criminals who are sought by the police, what is his duty? Do members of the different professional groups have the same duties? One of the authors heard a body of churchmen in an Eastern European country debate the question of whether or under what circumstances a minister may hide a fugitive from a totalitarian government when the fugitive has acted in accord with his Christian duty and cannot expect a fair trial. How is a professional man to act when such conflicts between duties and codes arise?
9. May a clergyman properly refuse to testify in court to statements made to him in confidence and in his capacity as spiritual adviser, regardless of the law? This question was heatedly debated in a state where the law recognizes privileged communication only between lawyer and client. A minister refused to testify in a divorce court and was fined $50 and given a ten day suspended jail sentence for contempt of court. Though more than thirty states allow some degree of privileged communication to clergymen, the right is not clearly recognized as a rule of common law.
10. Doctors are licensed to practice by states, and the license does not extend beyond the borders of the state, except in some cases where states have agreed to recognize each other's licenses. There are a number of cases on record of doctors who stopped to treat emergency accident victims and have been charged as criminals because they treated patients in a state in which they were not licensed to practice. Many doctors now say they will not stop to aid injured persons in accidents that occur while they are traveling. This is often the case whether they are traveling in their own state or in states in which they are not licensed to practice because of the danger of malpractice suits. Discuss the problems involved. Note that some states have passed or are considering what are called "Good Samaritan Laws," which exempt doctors from criminal charges and from liability suits when they stop in good faith and do their best to aid accident victims.
11. A physician learns that a patient is afflicted with a venereal disease. Yet the patient is about to be married to a woman who does not know he has the disease. Is the doctor bound by professional duty to remain silent, or is it his duty to inform the woman or her family, provided the man refuses to inform them or to postpone the wedding until he has been cured?
12. Discuss the issues raised in the following criticisms of American medical practice. The first was made by a Chinese scholar.

> The more I study Americans, the more I am convinced that they are mentally diseased. Instead of doing everything in a commonsense manner, they try all they can to do it in the very opposite way. At

home, for example, you and the other members of your Mutual Health Association would pay Dr. Wun Lung and his assistants each a liberal salary to keep you all well, and pay nothing when you are sick. On this account he and his young men work very assiduously in calling regularly and examining every member of the union, and all of you enjoy comparative immunity from illness. Here in America a physician is paid by the amount of your sickness, and the less you are able to earn any money, the larger and more onerous is his bill. As a result some doctors, I am told, yield to temptation and keep their customers sick. The consequence is that those who have the largest number of sick and dying are the richest, most esteemed, and influential, while in China they would be ostracized and not allowed to practice. [Quoted by Harry H. Moore in *Public Health in the United States* (New York: Harper & Brothers, 1923), pp. 373-374.]

In speaking about the honor of doctors, George Bernard Shaw says:
They have as much as any other class of men, no more and no less. And what other men dare to pretend to be impartial where they have a strong pecuniary interest on one side? Nobody supposes the doctors are less virtuous than judges; but a judge whose salary and reputation depend on whether the verdict was for the plaintiff or defendant, prosecutor or prisoner, would be as little trusted as a general in the pay of the enemy. To offer me a doctor as my judge, and then weigh his decision with a bribe of a large sum of money and a virtual guarantee that if he makes a mistake it can never be proved against him, is to go wildly beyond the ascertained strain which human nature will bear. It is simply unscientific to allege or believe that doctors do not under existing circumstances perform unnecessary operations and manufacture and prolong lucrative illnesses. [From the Preface to *The Doctor's Dilemma* (New York: Brentano's, 1931). Used by permission of the author.]

13. How would you answer a student who argues that the American Medical Association is little different from some labor organizations in that it resists the expansion of medical school facilities for training more doctors? This is done, he asserts, in the interest of high fees. He asks whether many doctors are opposing this policy because in 1971, for the first time, less than half the doctors in the country belong to the AMA.

14. Discuss the following practices from the point of view of morality:
   (1) The practice of some doctors in protecting each other, even to the extent of failing to expose incompetence.
   (2) The practice of doctors in giving placebos to patients who have an imaginary illness.
   (3) The use of technicalities by lawyers to enable their clients to evade what is the clear intent and spirit of the law.

15. A doctor or clergyman can minister to or counsel a criminal or the worst villain without concern about taking on his guilt. Yet lawyers are often criticized because they defend the rights of such persons, and

politicians are frequently charged with being "soft on communism" if they talk to Communists. How do you explain the difference? For the story of a criminal trial lawyer, see Edward Bennett Williams, *One Man's Freedom* (New York: Atheneum Publishers, 1962).
16. In a Midwestern city it was discovered that some druggists were selling cocaine to schoolboys. Such a practice is illegal and led to court actions. The sale of other similar narcotics, such as eucaine, was not mentioned in the law. The druggists and their lawyers discovered and profited by this loophole. Members of the legal profession sat in judgment on the cases and decided them on the basis of the law, but did nothing to remedy the situation. To what extent is a lawyer who is conscious of loopholes and inconsistencies in the law under obligation to work for their elimination?
17. A district attorney in a criminal trial interviews a number of witnesses who appear to be about equally intelligent and honest. The testimony of two of them tends to prove guilt, while the testimony of the others tends to prove innocence. Since the district attorney is prosecuting the case, he puts the first two witnesses on the witness stand and tells the others to keep out of sight. The highest court in one state has declared that "a prosecuting officer is violating no canon of legal ethics in presenting evidence which tends to show guilt while failing to call witnesses in whom he has no confidence, or whose testimony contradicts what he is trying to prove." Comment on the above case and on the declaration of the court.
18. A client brings a contract to his lawyer and requests that it be broken. The lawyer discovers that there is a technical defect on the basis of which it may be possible to have the contract invalidated. However, the contract was signed by both parties in good faith, and its annulment at this time would result in a grave injustice to the other party. Is it the lawyer's duty to serve his client's interests or to consider the unfairness to the other party?
19. For a discussion of forty-four problem cases dealing with a wide variety of problems facing educators, see *Opinions of the Committee on Professional Ethics* (Washington, D.C.: National Education Association of the United States, 1964). Read a few of these cases and be ready to state the problem and to indicate whether and why you agree or disagree with the decisions of the committee.
20. By what yardsticks should a college teacher be judged? In 1964 a considerable discussion arose when a university notified a teacher that his contract would probably not be renewed. After seven years of teaching during which the administration acknowledged that he had been "effective in the classroom," the teacher was to be dropped because "the promise of scholarly contribution has not materialized." See "Education," *New York Times*, 19 April 1964, p. E7; Donald Adams, "Speaking of Books," *New York Times Book Review*, 19 April 1964, p. 2; and John G. Kemeny, "Once the Professor Was a Teacher," *New York Times Magazine*, 2 June 1963, pp. 14 ff.

SUGGESTED READINGS

For the Ethics of certain groups not considered in this text, including engineers, ministers, librarians, social workers, accountants, business groups, and public officials, see *Ethical Standards and Professional Conduct*, Vol. 297; *Ethics of Business Enterprise*, Vol. 343. The Annals of the American Academy of Political and Social Science (Philadelphia: The Academy, 1955, 1962).

GENERAL REFERENCES

Hall, Cameron P., ed. *On-The-Job Ethics*. New York: National Council of Churches, 1963.
Leys, Wayne A. R. *Ethics for Policy Decisions*. Westport, Conn.: Greenwood Press, 1962.
MacIver, Robert M. "The Social Significance of Professional Ethics." *Ethical Standards and Professional Conduct*. Vol. 297. The Annals of the American Academy of Political and Social Science. Philadelphia: The Academy, 1955, pp. 118-124.

MEDICINE

American Academy of Political and Social Science. *Medicine and Society*. Vol. 346. The Annals. Philadelphia: The Academy, 1963.
"The Crisis in American Medicine." *Harper's Magazine* 221 (October 1960): 124-168. (A special supplement.)
"Ethical Aspects of Experimentation with Human Subjects." *Daedalus* (Spring 1969): viii-xiv, 219-594.
Fletcher, Joseph. *Morals and Medicine*. Princeton: Princeton University Press, 1954.
Hawley, Paul R. "Too Much Unnecessary Surgery." *U. S. News and World Report* 34 (February 20, 1953): 47-55.
Opinions and Reports of the Judicial Council 1964. Chicago: American Medical Association, 1964.
Vaux, Kenneth. *Who Shall Live? Medicine, Technology, Ethics*. Philadelphia: Fortress Press, 1970.

LAW

Barkun, M., ed. *Law and the Social System*. Chicago: Aldine, 1972.
Dressler, David. "Trial by Combat in American Courts." *Harper's Magazine* 222 (April 1961): 31-36.
Drinker, Henry S. *Legal Ethics*. New York: Columbia University Press, 1953.
East, Sara Toll, ed. *Law in American Society*. The Reference Shelf, 23, no. 2. New York: H. W. Wilson Co., 1963.
Grossman, J. B. and May, M. H., eds. *Law and Change in Modern America*. Pacific Palisades, Calif.: Goodyear Publishing Co., 1971.
Hart, H. L. *Law, Liberty and Morality*. Stanford, Calif.: Stanford University Press, 1971.

Parkinson, C. N. *Law and the Profits.* New York: Ballantine Books, 1971.
Phillips, Orie L., and McCoy, Philbrick. *Conduct of Judges and Lawyers.* Los Angeles: Parker and Co., 1952.

EDUCATION

Bertocci, Peter A. *Education and the Vision of Excellence.* Boston: Boston University Press, 1960.
Blanshard, Brand. "Values: The Polestar of Education." In *The Goals of Higher Education.* Edited by Willis D. Weatherford, Jr. Cambridge: Harvard University Press, 1960.
Childs, J. L. *Education and Morals: An Experimental Philosophy of Education.* New York: Arno Press, 1971.
Hechinger, Grace and Fred M. "College Morals Mirror Our Society." *New York Times Magazine*, 14 April 1963, pp. 22 ff.
Kilpatrick, W. H. *Education for a Changing Civilization.* New York: Arno Press, 1971.
National Education Association of the United States. *Opinions of the Committee on Professional Ethics.* Washington, D.C.: The Association, 1964.
Silberman, Charles E. *Crisis in the Classroom: The Remaking of American Education.* New York: Random House, 1970.
Smith, Huston. "Values: Academic and Human." In *The Larger Learning.* Edited by Marjorie Carpenter. Dubuque, Ia.: W. C. Brown Co., 1960.
Weinberg, C. *Education and Social Problems.* New York: Free Press, 1971.

18
ETHICS OF BUSINESS AND THE INDUSTRIAL SYSTEM

May one put excessively high and fictitious prices on merchandise, with a reduction or sale price beside it, so that customers think they are getting a real bargain? Is it right to give costly presents to influence business deals? Is price-fixing among supposedly competing companies ever to be condoned? Does a corporation have social responsibilities apart from making a profit for investors? May an industry pour waste matter in the air, rivers, and lakes, if this is cheaper than other forms of disposal, and expect the public to pay the cost of pollution? These and similar questions are being asked. Some of the serious moral problems of our time are connected with business and industry.

An economy has as its main function the satisfaction of human wants. Some goods are obtained only by human effort. Others are not found in sufficient quantities to satisfy all human desires. How such goods are to be produced and distributed is one of the important problems of our time. Some methods of production are efficient, others wasteful. After goods are produced, they may be distributed to those who need them or to those who have the most power to command them. An economy must provide for the production of goods and services and for their distribution to the consuming public. Can we discover a system that will provide maximum satisfaction of human needs?

Dr. Leland J. Gordon, author of *Economics for Consumers* and other books, has read this chapter and made valuable suggestions.

A CHANGING INDUSTRIAL SYSTEM

One hundred and fifty years ago, the isolated homesteads and crossroad villages in most parts of America were, in the main, economically self-sufficient. Men gained their living chiefly by hunting, fishing, raising cattle, or tilling the soil. Industrial pursuits were carried on under what we know as the domestic or handicraft system. Work was performed in the home or in a nearby shop, and nearly every person had ready access to raw materials. There was an intimate, personal relationship among the workers, and each worker owned his tools, which were simple. When a man specialized in making a product, such as shoes, he did the whole job, and then usually sold the product of his labor to someone he knew.

With the spread of the industrial revolution and the growth of the factory system, these conditions changed. Men now worked in factories as hired labor; there was no ready access to raw materials; relations within industry became more and more impersonal; machines were expensive and complicated, and they were owned by the employer; articles were made for profit under conditions of increasing specialization; products were sold to distant buyers.

Since the middle of the nineteenth century, our social, economic, and political problems have been multiplied by the rapid development of banking and credit, the establishment of limited liability in joint-stock corporations, the separation of ownership and management, and ever-greater technological advances and industrial concentration. During recent decades atomic energy, automation, large mergers, electronic computers, and a host of new devices and methods have brought further changes. In contrast to the last century, the population is increasingly concentrated in large cities, and some degree of unemployment, perhaps as much as three to four percent, appears to be permanent.

Capitalism—In Theory and In Practice

In the twentieth century the changes within the industrial system have taken place so rapidly and have been so far-reaching that the older terms, such as *capitalism* and the *free enterprise system*, do not apply very accurately. Some have talked about first, second, and even third stages in the industrial revolution. Others have used terms like *orthodox capitalism, liberal capitalism, regulated capitalism,* and the *welfare state*. The curious thing is that while the system and its operation have changed drastically, the ideology or doctrine has remained relatively unchanged for many years.

The economic system that prevails in the United States, Canada, and some other parts of the world is called capitalism or the free enterprise system, although many people do question the use of the same terms for the nineteenth and the late twentieth century ways of producing goods and doing business. Capitalism is, in brief, the system that emphasizes the private ownership of the instruments of production, distribution, and exchange, and their operation under a plan of open competition and individual initiative, for private profit, with a minimum of governmental interference. Capitalism rests on four main doctrines.

1. *The Doctrine of Free Enterprise.* The doctrine of free enterprise, which arose during the seventeenth and eighteenth centuries, is sometimes called *individualism* or *classical liberalism*. It assumes minimum interference by the government in economic and social affairs. On its individual side, capitalism expresses the doctrine of self-interest. The individual should be free to pursue his own interests so long as he keeps the peace. He should be free to make as much money as he can and to spend it as he sees fit. Many capitalists today defend this attitude and claim that the pursuit of self-interest will promote the common good. On its economic side, this position is referred to as the *doctrine of the economic man*. The economic man of classical capitalist theory consults his own interest and is motivated by profit for himself. He is free to produce, to buy and to sell, or to refrain from such activities, depending on his own desires and interests. On its political side, the doctrine expresses itself as *laissez faire,* or noninterference on the part of government. Governmental activities, where necessary, should be kept to a minimum. There should be little if any regulation of business activities, since these should be left to "natural laws." Free enterprise, it is said, develops initiative, resourcefulness, and self-reliance, whereas government ownership and control create indolence, inefficiency, and bureaucracy.

In its origin, the doctrine of *laissez faire* was in part a reaction against the excessive and irritating restrictions placed on trade and business by the grasping monarchs of the seventeenth and eighteenth centuries. Some of these restrictions were relics of the guild system and even of feudal days. Not only business but the free movement of labor had been hindered. Another cause was the philosophical doctrine of natural law and natural rights, held so strongly during the eighteenth century. Men believed that there were natural laws which, if left to themselves, would work to the best interests of all, and that nature would regulate wages, prices, and supply and demand in the most equitable way. During the latter part of the nineteenth century this belief seemed to receive biological sanction in the doctrine of natural selection and the survival of the fittest. In the United States especially, individualism was fostered by pioneer conditions. As settlers moved westward and faced hostile Indians and the obstacles of nature, they could not be bound by plans or regulations. Rugged individualism was indispensable in conquering a continent. An increasing number of people, however, are now questioning its adequacy to deal with the problems of the intricate industrial mechanism of the later years of the twentieth century. The philosophy of the day of the oxcart may be inadequate for the day of automobiles, airplanes, atomic power, and spaceships.

2. *The Doctrine of Competition.* Capitalism rests on the assumption that competition is the life of trade. Capitalists believe that a system of free competition will bring the best results in the long run. Competition among buyers and sellers, it is said, will regulate the prices of goods, wages, and supply and demand in an equitable way. Ethical justification is sought in the view that if men seek their own self-interest through competition, the result will be social well-being and progress.

The student will need to ask whether or not competition is adequate, under modern conditions, to make a fair adjustment among wages, profits, and prices or to secure the interests alike of workmen, employers, investors, and the general public not included in any of these groups. Too, is free competition any longer a reality? One may be legally free to compete with some of our billion-dollar corporations, but is such freedom anything more than theoretical? There is a strong drive in modern industry toward the elimination of competition, and we are witnessing the truth of the statement that competition begets combination. The rise of trade associations, great corporations, and huge mergers or conglomerates is evidence of the tendency to eliminate or restrict competition.

3. *The Doctrine of the Profit Motive.* Capitalism stresses the profit motive as the most effective incentive in business activities. The incentive to effort that is given by the hope of personal gain in the form of profit is said to be the great driving force in modern industry. People will not work efficiently unless they are offered the possibility of unrestricted profit. As medieval society built cathedrals and stressed salvation, so our modern society builds factories and stresses profits.

Profit is the surplus earnings of a business after all costs—research, production, sales and distribution, salaries, depreciation, and so on—have been met. Thus the word *profit* should not be used as synonymous with *income*, since there are many forms of income, including wages, salary, rent, interest, dividends, gifts, commissions, and royalties.

4. *The Doctrine of the Right to Private Property.* Private property means not only the consumer's or user's property but rights in the instruments of production, distribution, and exchange. The assumption

prevails, at least in orthodox capitalist circles, that a man has a right to all the property to which he can gain legal title, irrespective of its nature or its quality.

Our present economic order takes for granted the institution of private property—the exclusive right to own, enjoy, and dispose of a thing. In early times such articles usually consisted of clothing, tools and weapons, ornaments, the family dwelling or shelter, and food in the dwelling. There was no common practice concerning land, which might be either communal or private. Private claim to the ownership of land probably arose with the development of settled agricultural pursuits and with the conquest of one tribe by another. Today the concept of property has come to include a wide range of claims.

The holding of private property appears to be justified where a man has contributed to its making and is capable of utilizing it, and where his possession of it does not interfere with the rights and welfare of other people. Consequently, the view that all private ownership is vicious must be rejected. During earlier days, ownership of land and tools was defended because such things were indispensable for providing food and clothing, and hence health and efficiency. The protection of property was therefore the protection of work. With the growth of society, property has come to be an instrument for the acquisition of wealth and the exercise of power. Thus ownership and use have often been divorced.

Private property is ethically indefensible where it is merely a form of private taxation that one man is permitted to levy on the industry of others. In recent times the claim of private property has been extended to include great areas of land and other natural resources, vast accumulations of capital, and even anticipated profits. Today a few men possess vast aggregates of property for which they have contributed little or no labor and which are more than is necessary for the development of their personalities. With the rise of the corporation, the concept of property has taken on new meanings. Property in the form of shares of stock becomes liquid or fluid. It passes from person to person. The owners become passive agents, with little or no sense of personal responsibility. The owner of property often does not even know the nature of the property he owns, and he therefore feels no personal responsibility for the effect on human welfare of the use of this property.

A Mixed Economy

Capitalism in its traditional forms has made great contributions to society. It is not either all good or all bad. It has given, with the aid of scientists and engineers, a high degree of technological efficiency and large organizations of men and machines that have bestowed on us a great variety of merchandise and services. It has stressed certain values and virtues such as individuality, initiative, self-reliance, and personal freedom. If we are honest, however, we have to acknowledge that there have been criticism, dissatisfaction, and even revolt against many features of capitalism. In the main the criticism has centered around moral issues and concern for persons.

In the United States at the present time the system under which we operate is a mixed system. The public has found it dangerous to leave all functions and great power in private hands, yet it fears too great a concentration of governmental functions and powers. The principle of private enterprise is deeply embedded in our thinking, habits, and customs. It arose under very different conditions from those that exist today and, almost unawares, private monopolies have developed alongside it. Where effective and free it will probably remain. The principle of public ownership and control of those functions that are really public in scope is also well established. In some cases the solution used to avoid a private or corporate monopoly has been a combination of corporate ownership and public regulation and inspection. Certain functions (e.g. the provision of money and credit, and the operation of utilities) are too monopolistic and too important for human welfare dependent upon them to be left completely in private hands.

Between these two areas—free enterprise and public ownership or control—a considerable amount of experimentation is going on of which the consumers and producers cooperative movements are perhaps the most important. In various ways voluntary groups are banding together to carry on services for themselves. Relative to industry and the state this third area is weak but has been growing. If the three areas are free to expand or contract in relation to each other, and no one area attempts to dominate the others, this could give progress and novelty as well as checks and balances in the area of economic affairs, such as we have in political life.

CRITICISM OF THE BUSINESS AND INDUSTRIAL ORDER

Let us acknowledge at once that in the capitalist countries living standards for most citizens are the highest in the world and are continuing to rise, and that in them suffrage has steadily broadened and there is considerable concern for the underprivileged and for human welfare. From a material point of view, "never have so many had so much." In spite of these advances, an examination of recent literature and reports on social conditions will convince one that there is considerable dissatisfaction with modern industrial society. In some parts of the world capitalism has been swept aside and has been replaced by other economic systems, such as communism, fascism, national socialism (nazism), democratic socialism, and the consumer's cooperative movement. Let us look briefly at some of the main criticisms.

General Criticisms

1. *Extreme and Unjust Inequality.* During recent centuries there has been a tremendous drive toward greater equality and toward the elimination of artificial and unfair inequalities. In the past we have seen this movement break down many barriers that had been erected on the basis of race and color, class distinctions, property qualifications, religion, and sex. Today men are complaining of inequalities in connection with wealth, power, risks, and work. For example, the ownership of the great wealth produced by industrial nations is highly concentrated, so that fabulous riches exist side by side with the most degrading poverty. In periods of high level employment and prosperity, when a majority has sufficient food, clothing, and shelter, the inequalities that exist cause less concern and criticism. In slack periods or serious economic depressions, the contrasts become more obvious and are frequently the occasion for bitterness and protest.

Unequal distribution of wealth means unequal distribution of power. Men with great wealth and property gain control over the lives, the thoughts, and the standard of living of many others. Today a comparatively few men control our natural resources (iron, coal, oil, gas, and the like), our industries, our public utilities.

Even more serious than control of material resources is control of the avenues of opinion made possible by the concentration of wealth. Newspapers, the radio, and television are not free from control. Our newspapers are business enterprises, whose policies are determined (at least in part) by monetary considerations.

Unequal distribution of wealth and power has led to unequal distribution of risks. While the risks to life, limb, and health are the most serious of all, we are here thinking of economic risks. Some persons and classes appear to bear an unfair proportion of the risks involved in our business organizations. Depletion, obsolescence, depreciation funds, and other reserves set aside to meet the risks of the depletion of mines, the replacement of factories and their equipment, and the payment of dividends during idle periods are recognized by our courts as legitimate charges against running expenses. Until recently much less provision was made for the care and security of workers in these enterprises.

The last inequality that we shall discuss here is the unequal distribution of work. Some people work hard all their lives, yet eke out only a bare subsistence, while others live their entire lives in luxury and do little work or none. Some people live on the income from their property, even though they may have secured their possessions through no social contribution whatever.

Men can amass fortunes through the exercise of great ability and through social inventions; they also amass them by such means as monopolies, adulteration, speculation, and financial manipulation. When men live without working or by work that is essentially parasitic, they place an extra burden on others.

2. *Waste and Lack of Planning from a Human Point of View.* Why is it that, in an age of machinery and power, not everyone has an abundance of food and clothing and the other good things of life? A part of the answer is that the purpose of the industrial system, to supply human needs, has often been obscured by the desire to make money. Another part of the answer is that the present system is wasteful.

Waste in methods of production accounts for a considerable loss in human effort. These wastes include excess plant capacity, which causes greater overhead expenses, and failure to standardize products and to take advantage of improvements. To productive inefficiency must be added waste due to the production of useless or even harmful commodities, which detract from rather than add to human welfare. This includes such things as many patent medicines, adulterated goods, and super-luxuries; and the abuse or misuse of drugs, liquor, and tobacco.

We hear protests against the exploitation of our natural resources—forests, mines, oil, natural gas, and soil. As a nation we have carelessly used or wasted what should have been the heritage of future generations. In the case of oil we have been told that, in the drive for immediate profits, methods have been used that have led to the loss of an amount equal to or greater than that which has been refined and used. Our natural resources are too limited to excuse the wasteful exploitation that has existed at times in the past.

We need to apply foresight, rationality, and organization to abolish human misery and economic maladjustment, and to raise the level of living for the people as a whole. Children and the aged must be cared for, and workers must be adequately insured against unemployment. A way must be found to bring about some redistribution of income, so that there will be an effective money demand for the goods our factories are able to produce.

An objection frequently raised against social planning is that men should not interfere with the natural laws that are said to operate in the field of economics. Three facts should be taken into account. (1) A failure to plan is probably in part responsible for depressions and for some forms of maladjustment. (2) We do not hesitate to control the action of natural laws in such fields as physics, chemistry, and physiology. We manipulate things and apply these laws so that they will produce health rather than disease and serve our interests in other ways. In like manner, we must control economic laws so that they will operate in the direction of abundance and a higher standard of living. If the use of intelligence is valuable, then it is an ethical demand. Moral action is intelligent action. (3) What we sometimes call economic laws may not really be laws at all; they may be merely tendencies toward a particular action under certain conditions. When these conditions are changed, other results are in evidence.

3. *Overemphasis on the Acquisitive Motive.* An industrial civilization that is capitalist tends to emphasize the profit motive and to neglect other values. The profit motive, its critics say, leads to the development of antisocial practices in that each man is encouraged to seek his own interests and to prize monetary values too highly. The profit motive is the foundation of an acquisitive society, in which men revere the possessors of wealth and admire those who get rather than those who give. Men who do not possess wealth may even be considered weak. A pressing ethical problem is to discover the conditions under which the profit motive may serve the enrichment of personality or to supplant this motive by some loftier appeal. As men grow in moral insight, they will increasingly emphasize and stimulate incentives that are social.

The profit motive appears to be merely one of a number of incentives to work. Along with it must be mentioned the creative urge, the desire for security, the desire for power and for public approval and recognition, loyalty to a family or group, rivalry, fear, love, and religion. There is probably no close relation between creative mental effort and monetary reward. In fact if a man is thinking primarily of money instead of his workmanship, he does not usually make as good a manager, laborer, doctor, or engineer as he would otherwise.

4. *A Lopsided Society.* Various students of Western society have warned that man has produced a lopsided culture with his emphasis on the fabrication of machines, the rapid exploitation of nature, and the drive for power and profits.[1] This technological mentality, created by the industrial-scientific-military complex is changing and perhaps de-

---

[1] See Lewis Mumford, *The Pentagon of Power,* vol. 2, *The Myth of the Machine* (New York: Harcourt Brace Jovanovich, 1970); Morton Mintz and Jerry S. Cohen, *America, Inc.: Who Owns and Operates the United States* (New York: Dial Press, 1971).

stroying the emotional and the collective life of the whole society because of its disregard of the unique. Human beings have some basic emotional and personal needs that must be expressed or met. These include control over their own lives, fellowship with those around them, a sense of the sacred, and a sense of mystery that escapes mechanization. When these needs are repressed and the drive for power, profit, speed, and standardization become dominant goals, the outcome is dehumanization, savage wars, revolutions and riots, and widespread mental disorders. The withdrawal of allegiance to the system or society is seen in indifference, resentment, alienation, defiance of authority, and an extension of the area of violence.

Some Specific Unethical Practices

Most businessmen are quite frankly motivated by the desire to make money. Consequently, they sometimes tolerate practices that exploit the public, the workers, and even investors. There is considerable agreement on the part of students of business ethics that the businessman has not applied his stated ethical ideals to business practices as fully as might be desired or expected. What are some of these unethical practices?

1. Adulteration, misbranding, and misrepresentation of merchandise. An examination of the *Notices of Judgment in the FDA Papers* published by the Food and Drug Administration will disclose the details and the wide variety of adulteration and misbranding or mislabeling. Misrepresentation may also take the form of dummy bottoms in boxes, bottles or boxes that look large but hold very little, and other gimmicks that deceive the unwary.

2. Advertising that is misleading or that creates false values. A comparatively small number (150 to 200) of United States corporations that represent the greatest concentration of economic power in history dominate the mass media and, by their advertising, influence the habits, desires, and values of the population. The assumption of those who prepare the advertising is that people in general are selfish and irrational and that the appeal should be, not to reason, but to their selfish desires.[2] In the face of clear evidence that cigarettes are a cause of lung cancer and other disorders, the tobacco industry has made great efforts in recent years to discredit the findings. With little regard for public

---

[2] See Ernest Dichter, *The Strategy of Desire* (Garden City, N. Y.: Doubleday, 1960); *Handbook of Consumer Motivation* (New York: McGraw-Hill Book Co., 1964); Martin Mayer, *Madison Avenue, U.S.A.* (New York: Harper & Brothers, 1958).

health the drug industry has spent a little less than a billion dollars a year—about three times the amount spent on medical education—in its effort to increase drug sales. Yet a panel of scientists testing drugs said that two-thirds of those tested bore misleading labels, and more than a hundred were "totally ineffective."[3]

3. Bribery has been called "the greatest curse of modern business." The bribe is often in the form of presents, commissions (often secret) to sales persons or clerks, checks in the mail, even trips abroad. Not only does this occur within business circles but occasionally it takes the form of the bribery of governmental officials in order to secure special favors. The disclosure of huge expense funds and elaborate entertainments that have included liquor, sex, and espionage to secure trade secrets are reported from time to time.

4. Price-fixing and market-rigging scandals or conspiracies have been frequently uncovered since the fifties. They included such fields as drugs, electrical equipment, oil and gasoline, hand tools, and various steel products. For example, in 1961, twenty-nine electrical equipment companies, including some of the largest and best known in the industry, and a group of their officials were fined nearly two million dollars for having "conspired to fix prices, rig bids, and divide markets." A few executives went to jail, but more than a score were given suspended jail sentences. The presiding judge of the United States District Court in which the case was tried said, "This is a shocking indictment of a vast section of our economy, for what is really at stake here is the survival of the kind of economy under which this country has grown great, the free-enterprise system."[4]

5. Planned obsolescence appears to be a device to increase profits since profit, not use, is a major aim of many businesses. Manufacturers and dealers do not want automobiles to last many years. One business executive has been quoted as saying, "Who would want a lifetime storage battery . . . muffler and exhaust pipe . . . double-lived shoe soles . . . ? We could make all of these but we don't."[5] When we add to planned depreciation the thousands of patents that are purchased and unused to forestall their use by competitors, the waste is great. The failure to install safety devices on automobiles has been tragic—a lack of due care and concern for persons. An energy-absorbing steering assembly was patented in the 1920s, yet until prodded by Senate Commit-

---

[3]Reported by Herbert J. Muller in *The Children of Frankenstein* (Bloomington: Indiana University Press, 1970), pp. 173–174.
[4]Richard Austin Smith, "The Incredible Electrical Conspiracy," *Fortune* 63, pt. 1 (April 1961): 133. See entire article pp. 132–180 and *Fortune* 63, pt. 2 (May 1961): 161–224.
[5]*Children of Frankenstein*, p. 172.

tee hearings and much publicity from various sources, manufacturers largely ignored it. New models of cars after December 31, 1967 were to install the new type steering equipment. The National Safety Bureau calculated that if all automobiles had had this device the annual traffic deaths could have been less than 40,000—a saving of 13,000 deaths on the highways.[6] Without a more conscious ethical ideal our dynamism may be only "expansion without design, growth without plan, the extension of power without an extension of responsibility . . . a momentum over which there is no adequate social control."[7] In that direction lies trouble.

6. Business has opposed effective legislation intended to protect the general public. This has included opposition to many pure food and drug measures, to truth-in-packaging and truth-in-lending laws, and a wide range of legislation meant to protect the health and safety of consumers. When such laws have been enacted and regulatory bodies set up, all too frequently business lobbyists in the nation's capital have used their great influence to see that the federal agencies are run by men congenial to their interests or are granted inadequate budgets and lack means for vigorous enforcement.

While opposing measures to protect consumers and low-income groups, private businesses have received large sums by way of subsidies. Corporations, while working under government contracts, have profited by guaranteed incomes. Large corporations such as those in the areas of aircraft, railroads, electronics, space, and atomic energy have been rescued from failure by the Pentagon, Congress, or some other branch of government. However, self-interest and a lack of an enlightened social consciousness is not limited to any one group; it is a deficiency found among people in all walks of life.

EFFORTS TOWARD IMPROVEMENT OF BUSINESS STANDARDS

In the light of the above criticisms of business and industry, it is encouraging to note that, on the whole, standards have improved during the last one hundred years, and that there are many businesses in which these abuses are not found. The majority of businessmen are honorable and want to do the right thing. Like other specialists in society, they are caught in a system and their vision or outlook is often very limited.

---

[6]*America, Inc.*, p. 3.
[7]Robert L. Heilbroner, "The Perils of American Economic Power," *Saturday Review* (August 10, 1968), p. 24.

The businessman of earlier days usually operated on the policy of *caveat emptor*—"let the buyer beware." Business was business, and a man was not in business for his health. He might have two ways of dealing—one for the people he knew and with whom he expected to conduct future business, and another for the stranger who would probably not come his way again. The merchant felt that he had a right to ask any price he pleased. Wasn't the business his own, and didn't he own the articles? He might ask a high price in the beginning, and then reduce it if there were a chance that he would lose the sale otherwise. Business proceeded on the theory that the man who was purchasing should take care of himself in the transaction.

With the nineteenth century began the era of the building of the railways, the exploitation and settling of the West, the amassing of great fortunes and, toward the end of the century, the growth of finance capitalism and the building of large corporations and financial structures such as trusts and holding companies. It was the "Gilded Age," with lavish entertainments and conspicuous wealth alongside widespread poverty. It was the age of the titan, the tycoon, the robber barons, of whom much has been written. Hard in a business deal, they were often mild-mannered and gracious at home, and sometimes even pious in their church connections. They were products of their time, not so much immoral as amoral. In the twentieth century and especially since the Great Depression that began in 1929, such people have lost some prestige and have had to cope with new standards and the restraints imposed by government, organized labor, and an enlightened conscience.

Since the beginning of the century, there has been a constant demand on the part of enlightened business leaders and the public for improvement in business standards. This movement has expressed itself in such diverse ways as Theodore Roosevelt's campaign against corruption, the emphasis on the "social gospel" in the churches, and the development of codes of ethics for business and professional groups.

Organizations Seeking to Set Standards

Various organizations have been active in promoting higher ethical standards and practices. These include business organizations like the trade associations and the Better Business Bureau, governmental agencies like the Federal Trade Commission, and some service clubs.

The trade association is an example of the regulation of an industry from within. It is an organization or union of businessmen or employers, and it is to be clearly distinguished from the labor union, which is an association of workers. Businessmen, through their trade associations, attempt to elevate and standardize their practices, just as they attempt to standardize terms, forms of contract, products, and the like. Hundreds of codes of ethics have been adopted by trade associations and other groups of businessmen. Business life today is exceedingly complex. Each new specialty and each new relationship adds to the difficulties of maintaining correct standards and of knowing which business practices are right and which wrong. If there is a clear-cut statement representing the best minds of the members of the group, it can help businessmen act honorably. The practices of conscientious men vary widely. The written code, if it is sufficiently specific and if it represents the mature judgment of the group, can replace the caprices of individual judgments with consistent ethical standards. The object of the code is to standardize business practice on a higher ethical plane.

The Better Business Bureau is an organization founded in 1911 and supported by "legitimate business to protect itself and the public against that which is unfair, misleading or fraudulent in the fields of advertising and selling." There is a National Better Business Bureau with bureaus in most of the principal cities of the United States and Canada.

The aims of the bureaus may be summarized as follows: to increase public confidence by the reduction of unfair and deceptive advertising; to reduce unfair competition through the establishment of ethical standards; to hear claims and complaints and settle disputes; to expose fraudulent promotions and easy-money schemes; to encourage the public to investigate before buying. The bureaus attempt to correct unethical trade practices by persuasion, but they often have to bring recalcitrant offenders to the attention of law-enforcing agencies.

In addition to courts and the regular machinery for the administration of justice and for the punishment of crimes, practically all countries of the world have established governmental agencies for the protection of the public and the upright businessman against unfair and harmful practices. One of the most important of many such agencies is the Federal Trade Commission, established in the United States in 1914. In 1938 its jurisdiction was broadened to cover additional unfair and deceptive practices. The commission is empowered to issue cease-and-desist orders. If these orders are not obeyed, it can apply to the courts for an injunction, for condemnation of merchandise, or for a review of the order. If the order is sustained, the people involved are subject to the jurisdiction of the court and can be disciplined by it.[8]

The membership of the *service clubs* is limited to a few leaders of

---

[8]In recent years the FTC has been criticized as ineffective and even on occasions as giving in to the interests of groups it was established to regulate See Edward F. Cox et al, *The Nader Report on the Federal Trade Commission* (New York: Richard W. Baron, 1969); Leland J. Gordon and Stewart M. Lee, *Economics for Consumers*, 6th ed. (New York: Van Nostrand Reinhold Co., 1972).

each business or professional group, but they have usually been active leaders in their groups and thus are able to influence them in the direction of a concern for promoting higher standards. In order to guide trade associations in the formation of more adequate codes, Rotary International prepared a specimen code that gives the framework and the topics to be considered. Rotarians have also developed "The Four-Way Test" as a simple measuring device that may be applied to find out whether any proposed plans, policies, statements, or actions are right or wrong. This test is stated in four questions: "1. Is it the *truth*? 2. Is it *fair* to all concerned? 3. Will it build *good will* and *better friendship*? 4. Will it be *beneficial* to all concerned?"[9]

Is Enforcement of Business Codes Possible?

The codes of ethics that have been accepted among business groups have given the most attention to the relations among competitors, and it is in this field that the greatest changes have taken place. If this does not mean merely getting together to make the public pay, it is a forward step. Undoubtedly there is room for a great improvement in relationships between business and labor groups, and in the development of a sense of social responsibility when the interests of the consumer are at stake. One weakness of this attempt to elevate the practices of businessmen is that there is no guarantee that trade associations will act in the public interest.

On the other hand, the growth and complexity of our modern industry, and especially of our financial and credit mechanism, is an indication of a fairly widespread standard of integrity. Businessmen have made considerable progress in raising standards of practice. Good will and confidence are essential elements in the whole scheme of business activity as conducted today.

In the past the only sanctions widely used have been the businessman's own desire or conscience and the pressure of public opinion. Yet if businessmen are not to be rigidly controlled by law, they must regulate their own business. When sufficiently aroused or motivated they, like other groups in society, show a great capacity for public service, loyalty to mankind, and even self-denial. Most codes of ethics are drawn up by those members of the group who are most conscious of evils and most sensitive to public demands. Other businessmen need to be made more conscious of their standards and of the gap between standards and practice.

Some trade associations have set up a standing committee on business ethics and practices. Such a committee receives complaints from both

---

[9]*Rotary Manual* (Chicago: Rotary International, 1946).

members and the customers of members, investigates these complaints, and recommends action. The collection of cases of actual problems, together with their analysis, explanation, and adjudication by a competent committee, provides a cumulative set of precedents. Such material can be an invaluable aid in dealing with new cases or problems. Today the business groups that make any effective effort at enforcement of their codes are in the minority.

To the force of the code must be added the weight of publicity, so that the public will know what to expect and will be led to protest against any evils that exist. The profiteer and the person who is guilty of the adulteration of goods must be identified, discredited, and ostracized. For those who are insensitive to appeals of moral idealism and the pressure of public opinion, the law may be the only remedy, and that is not always effective.

INDUSTRY AND LABOR

The traditional capitalism of a few generations ago assumed free competition among a large number of people. There was no need for public control because no one had complete power over supply and demand, prices, or wages. Thus no one could bring great harm to producers, consumers, or workers. As a result of changes brought about by modern technology, however, the later decades of the twentieth century are characterized by big business, big labor, big agriculture, and other pressure groups. These groups maintain considerable control over the economy and exert political pressure on federal, state, and local governments.

In the area of business and industry, the National Association of Manufacturers speaks for big business and the Chamber of Commerce represents the rank-and-file merchants. Together with a number of strong organizations that serve particular business interests, such as the metal trades, lumber, and investment banking, these larger associations seek to protect the interests of business. Concentration of output among a relatively few manufacturers or sellers is the dominant pattern in modern industrial society. Control of a commodity by a single corporation is rare, but oligopoly, control by a few companies, is fairly common. Under these conditions, supply can be controlled and prices manipulated.

The rise of big business led to the organization of labor in an attempt to protect the interests of workers. In the nineteenth century, before workers were organized, they often worked as many as sixteen hours a day, and wages were pitifully low. Women and children were drawn into the factories and mines to work under deplorable conditions. Workers and their families lived in poor dwellings without proper light, heat, water, or sewage disposal. In these slums, disease was prevalent.

When workers attempted to act as individuals, they found themselves helpless. Eventually they became dissatisfied with entrusting their welfare to the "automatic market mechanism" of supply and demand or to the benevolence of employers far removed from personal contact with them. Therefore they organized unions to deal more effectively with the organized capital that employed them. Various causes have operated to improve the conditions of labor, but workers have turned primarily to the unions as the means of improving their working conditions, raising their standards of living, and forcing recognition of themselves as persons.

Today in most communities there is a division between employers and laborers, often referred to as capital and labor. This condition exists not only in business and industry but also in large-scale farming. It is part of the age-old conflict between those who have and those who have not. Some of the conflicts of interest are the division of the earnings between wages and profits; the control of the conditions of labor, including security of position; and the question of relative bargaining power, since each party seeks to strengthen itself economically and politically. Let us briefly consider these three conflicts.

1. What is an equitable division of the earnings of a firm or a farm? Shall the employer pay as little as he can, a policy that is shortsighted, even from his own point of view, in the long run? Shall he pay the market scale of wages, a policy that will help him keep on good terms with his competitors? Or shall he pay what he considers to be a comfortable living wage or even more, if profits warrant doing so? To see that workers receive a proper share of the fruits of their endeavor is one duty of employers.

2. Should the worker have a voice in the control of the conditions under which he works and lives? In democracies it is assumed that each citizen has a right to share in the control of political conditions. This right has not been extended to industrial relations. We have inherited a tradition of legal and political equality, but economic inequality.

The employer regards the business as *his* business; if workers do not like the conditions they find, they may look elsewhere for work. The worker, on the other hand, has long felt that if the democratic ideal is good in political life, it should also apply to what for him is the more important realm of his economic relations. He wants to be considered a human being, not merely a commodity to be bought and sold. Until labor is put on a more participating basis, sharing in profits as well as in production, we are likely to have tension and conflict.

3. If employers have the right to organize into corporations, trade associations, and Chambers of Commerce, workers have an equal right to organize and to present a united front. In organization there is strength, and relative bargaining power may determine how much of the surplus shall go to the employer in profit, to the workers in wages, and to the consuming public in lower prices. Until recently the employers had a distinct advantage in bargaining power. This was made possible by the fact that the state traditionally had recognized and protected his property rights in his business, while it had not recognized or protected the rights of workmen to an adequate standard of living. In recent decades the bargaining power of capital and labor has been more evenly balanced in many sections of the economy.

If bargaining power is not kept fairly equal, the laborer fears he will get little or no consideration. Some of the most bitter labor struggles have centered around the recognition of labor unions and collective bargaining. The laborer reasons that if the employer may limit his output in order to increase prices and profits, why should the laborers not limit work and raise wages? He feels that he is treated unjustly when his employer and the public object to his methods. The right to life is meaningless unless it includes a right to the particular things that make life possible under existing conditions. The laborer feels that he has a right to work, to receive a living wage, and to be secure in his position.

Our recognition of the right of workers to organize should not blind us to the excesses to which such organizations may lead. Some unions have abused their power and privileges and have resorted to unethical practices. A powerful union may become a narrow, self-interested, pressure group that is unfair to workers outside the union, to workmen in other unions, to employers, and to the general public. Strikes may be called when peaceful methods of settling disputes are readily available, and such strikes may unnecessarily endanger the health and safety of large sections of society. Workers who are only union-minded or self-minded, like employers who are merely company-minded, not only are unethical in attitude and often in practice but also tend to create a bitter class struggle that may be disruptive of all human relations. In return for fair wages the worker owes his employer a fair and efficient day's work and aid in the elimination of waste. Likewise we should not be blind to the power and excesses of employer associations. Only as workers, managers, and owners cooperate as partners in the common task of satisfying human needs will there be industrial peace.

Businessmen and labor unions are not the only pressure groups in modern society. Any complete coverage would need to consider many other groups including professional associations, farmers' organizations, veterans, and certain church organizations. Big government is in part a response to the complexity of modern society and to the need for keeping the big pressure groups in check. The role of government in a democracy is to represent all the citizens and to prevent any special interest group from acting contrary to the good of society as a whole. As well as preventing any one pressure group from forcing its will and interests on the country, and maintaining some just balance of interests, the government at times must act positively to protect the interests of consumers who are not organized or able to protect themselves effectively.

FOR IMPROVEMENT OF INDUSTRIAL SOCIETY

Institutions do not exist as ends in themselves; they derive their value from their contribution to human welfare. A business or an industry is one form of public service whose function is the satisfaction of economic wants. Like any other institution, it is ethically justified only to the extent that it performs some social service better than or at least as well as some other institution that would take its place. So far, many business codes have failed to make clear the conditions and principles underlying ethical practices. For example, what is a fair deal or business exchange, a fair bargain or price? What are just relations between employers and employees? A fair exchange or business deal is one in which each party knows what he is giving and getting and can reasonably expect to feel satisfaction later with the exchange.

There has been, as we have seen, considerable improvement since the nineteenth century in business standards and practices. With increasing social complexity, however, new forms of wrongdoing appear. Beyond the area of what public opinion and the law at present term criminal or immoral there is an area of antisocial conduct of which the public moral consciousness is only beginning to become aware. To make the public and the businessman alike aware of the nature of these activities is part of the task of ethics.

Pressure for improvement in business ethics has come from at least four sources. First, it has come from within business itself. Most business and industrial leaders are men of integrity who desire to establish higher ethical standards and practices. The same can be said of most labor leaders. Sometimes, however, even these men are under heavy pressure from competitors and customers to use means they would prefer not to use if they could control the conditions themselves.

Second, it has come from governmental agencies and laws. Governmental action is necessary at times not only to protect the public and laborers but to protect the more honorable businessmen. Such pressure or even control is needed when standards are lacking, when codes are mere "fronts" that protect self-interest, or when there are actually "conspiracies against the public." Included in this general area are factory and antitrust laws, pure food and drug acts, and much recent social legislation.

Third, pressure for improvement has come from various religious groups. During recent decades, numerous statements of social ideals have been set forth by Protestant, Roman Catholic, and Jewish religious groups. Roman Catholic official declarations have been numerous, especially since Pope Leo XIII in 1891 issued the encyclical *Rerum Novarum*, often called *The Condition of Labor*. Jewish groups, particularly the National Conference of American Rabbis, have made similar declarations. Many Protestant denominations have issued pronouncements, and the World Council of Churches through its various Ecumenical Conferences has made reports on questions of social ethics. The National Council of the Churches of Christ in the United States of America has departments concerned with international affairs, social justice, and the like.

Fourth, the general public by its demands can do much to improve business standards and practices. Each citizen exerts not only political influence but some economic power. If he is careful to purchase merchandise made and sold under fair and honorable principles and conditions, he helps raise the ethical standards of business. The problem for the consumer is how to find out which merchandise is of high quality and made under fair conditions. Some information is available from such organizations as Consumers' Union of the United States, Consumers' Research Bulletin, and buyers' clubs. If the consumer is acquainted with the code of ethics of the businessmen with whom he is dealing, if he knows what he has a right to expect from them, he can aid in eliminating unethical practices. If he follows high standards himself and demands high standards from those with whom he trades, he can help build up the moral consciousness and community sentiment that is the foundation of all social ethics.

There are some principles that should be kept in mind during a period of social change.

1. Our problem is so to direct social changes that there will be a continuous readaptation of institutions to human needs. Our present industrial order is neither entirely good nor entirely evil. Social life tends to expand. This expansion is not always uniform in all phases of society; hence we have not only social change but also social mal-

adjustment. Our task is to recognize these disorders and work for their elimination.

2. Certain methods of meeting social problems lead to disaster, whether they are used by conservatives or by radicals. These include dogmatic appeals to authority, emotional outbursts or appeals to the mob mind, propaganda and trickery, and brute force. If social changes are more or less inevitable, we need an open-minded, experimental attitude toward the social order of which we are a part.

3. The democratic ideal, not the autocratic, is to be accepted. Democracy is an ethical ideal as well as a political program, a theory of character as well as a theory of social organization. It must rest on a free and educated electorate.

4. The attempt to succeed at the expense of others should give way to the realization that each succeeds in proportion as everyone else succeeds. Cooperation must replace the law of the jungle. We live in a social world of which each person is an integral part.

5. Finally, people are ends in themselves. Any institution, social class, or method that regards people as means instead of ends is to be condemned. Privilege or position that is gained or maintained at the expense of others or at the price of insecurity of others is unethical.

For a better society, we need transformed individuals. A change of systems or programs is not enough. Selfish, dishonest, narrow individuals can ruin any system. Yet the system may predispose men either to selfishness or to social service. A system that emphasizes cooperation, social welfare, and intelligent planning will make the development of more mature individuals possible.

QUESTIONS AND PROJECTS

1. What are the values which the doctrine of *laissez faire* and individualism sought to conserve? What are the values the supporters of the social-service view of the state and those who seek a greater degree of community or governmental control wish to protect? To what extent do you think these differences in outlook can be reconciled?
2. A businessman asks, "Why do we need ethical codes and all this discussion about ethics? Aren't the Ten Commandments, the Golden Rule, and the Sermon on the Mount all we need?" How would you answer such a man? You may wish to consult William A. Spurrier, *Ethics and Business* (New York: Charles Scribner's Sons, 1962), ch. 2.
3. In connection with business, is it right or ethical:
    (1) To restrict the output of certain commodities for which there is a need in order to increase prices and get larger profits?
    (2) To increase the prices on articles at special times and seasons when there is greater demand for the merchandise?

(3) To hold scarce articles for friends and old customers and refuse to offer them for sale to the general public?
4. Is there ethical justification for the action of corporations that purchase inventions in order to keep them off the market?
5. "'Mocha and Java' is a trade name of a high-grade coffee, presumably imported from the East Indies. A coffee importer sells a mixture of Santos and Colombian coffees—grades costing much less and usually considered less desirable—under the name 'M. and J. Coffee.' The price asked is less than that of Mocha and Java, but considerably above that for Santos and Colombian. Is this ethical?"
6. "The Primo Pen Company, manufacturers of fountain pens, puts out pens priced on the label at fictitious figures, far above cost, thus making possible apparent great reductions. A retailer handling these pens advertises 'Five-dollar pens at $1.25.' At $1.25 the pen is fair value. Can the transaction be defended?"

The cases quoted in Questions 5 and 6 are from E. W. Lord, *The Fundamentals of Business Ethics* (New York: Ronald Press, 1926), pp. 175, 181, 187.

7. A group of businessmen planning to build a shopping center was acquiring options on all the land and property in an area about the size of two city blocks. They obtained the options at or near the market price for all the property except one plot, whose owner held out for an excessive price. The market value of this piece of land was approximately $15,000. The owner was offered $20,000 but declined the offer, saying that his price was $50,000. He did this because he had heard that a shopping center was being planned and that the promoters needed his land. He did not think they would change their plans for a mere $50,000. Was the owner of the land justified in asking $50,000 for it? Why or why not?
8. List the restrictions or limitations on private property in modern society, and consider the justice of these restrictions. Is it ethical for a court to rule that a man cannot use his property so as to harm his neighbors? What are the implications of the doctrine of "property affected with a public interest"? For a discussion of the ethics of property, see Joseph F. Fletcher, ed., *Christianity and Property* (Philadelphia: Westminster Press, 1947); Richard Schlatter, *Private Property; The History of an Idea* (New Brunswick, N.J.: Rutgers University Press, 1951); Roland N. McKean, "Products Liability: Implications of Some Changing Property Rights," *Quarterly Journal of Economics* 84 (November 1970): 611–626; D. R. Denman, "Mine and Thine," *Twentieth Century* 176, no. 1035 (1967–1968): 18–20.
9. Society demands special training and proof of competence from the lawyer, the doctor, the sea captain, and the railway engineer. The businessman needs only to own property or secure credit. Again, society does not permit the lawyer, the doctor, the sea captain, or the railway engineer to hand over his trade to his son unless the son also has obtained the training and competence required. The son of a businessman, however, may inherit his father's business without regard to his training or his

mental qualities. Do you think evidence of competence or qualities of character should be demanded of an employer of men? Could any supervision be exercised to see that capital invested is directed into socially valuable production?

10. A large manufacturer of food is considerably perplexed. In order to secure certain large orders, he must give personal tips and favors (such as a trip to Europe) to the buying agent of a large concern. He needs the business to keep his plant going and his men working, yet he disapproves of these commissions or tips. Should he give the favors or let his competitors have the business?

11. Numerous cases are on record in which unions have objected to the use of labor-saving devices such as spray guns for painting and prefabricated materials for houses. When pipe of fitted lengths with threads already cut was delivered to one building, plumbers insisted on their right to cut off the thread and rethread the pipe on the job. Discuss the ethical issues involved. Is a labor union justified in picketing a theater because the star of the play does not employ a union chauffeur? Is the situation different when a theater is picketed because some beads and buttons have been sewed on one of the costumes by nonunion hands? Is a union justified in ruling that a particular play is a musical and that the theater presenting it must hire a sixteen-piece orchestra when the management was not planning to use an orchestra?

12. The expense account has created problems for business concerns and for salesmen. The issue is often more than just a simple matter of honesty. Can you formulate principles or rules that you think would help? You may wish to consult Thomas M. Garrett, S. J., *Ethics in Business* (New York: Sheed and Ward, 1963), ch. 6.

13. A few years ago the news services reported a conflict of interest between the oil companies and automobile manufacturers over the question about how often a car's oil needs to be changed. The oil companies were advising 1,000 miles, whereas the automobile manufacturers were suggesting 4,000 or 5,000 miles, according to driving conditions. Give your reaction to the oil companies' attempts to get their formula written into the owner's manuals. What do you think were the motives and reasons involved, and where do ethical principles enter the picture?

14. In New York in 1970 the City's Department of Consumer Affairs issued regulations that would require major food stores to put more specific price labels on packages. The purpose was to simplify the task of shoppers in comparing prices of similar items. Unspecific labels such as "giant," "king," "jumbo," or "economy size" meant little. A group of food retailers sought to strike down the regulation through legal action. What ethical questions are involved in your opinion?

15. Discuss the following from the point of view of ethics:
    (1) The practice of some wholesale or traveling salesmen to give cash or merchandise bonuses to clerks in retail stores for recommending one article and advising against competitive brands regardless of their real value.

(2) Since the passage of the Motor Vehicle Safety Act (1964) millions of vehicles have been recalled for repairs or a change of parts. The government has also had to bring pressure on manufacturers to speed up the installation of antipollution devices.

(3) In 1971 when the Penn Central railway was facing bankruptcy and appealing for governmental aid, top officials of the company were reported to have taken out a $10 million Lloyd's of London insurance policy to protect themselves—the cost borne by the company.

(4) The selling of drugs by brand names rather than generic names. Large sums were spent by drug companies on promotion to get doctors to prescribe brand names which druggists have to supply. Prices have sometimes varied from $17.00 to $.59 per hundred.

16. Suggest some things you think might well be included in a code of ethics for each of the following groups or relationships:

   (1) Business-Competition Relations. See Theodore N. Beckman, "Ethics in Business-Competition Relations" in *Ethics in Business*, ed. Robert Bartels, Bureau of Business Research Monograph no. 111. (Columbus: Ohio State University, 1963), ch. 11.

   (2) Management-Customer Relations. See W. Arthur Cullman, "Ethics in Management-Customer Relations," Ibid., ch. 7.

   (3) The business executive, banking, sales practice, chain store operation, labor organizations, insurance. See J. Whitney Bunting, ed., *Ethics for Modern Business Practice* (New York: Prentice-Hall, 1953).

   (4) Ethical problems in connection with advertising. See Leland J. Gordon and Stewart M. Lee, *Economics for Consumers*, 6th ed. (New York: Van Nostrand Reinhold Co., 1972), chs. 9 and 10.

17. The London department store of Selfridge and Company pays in cash an amount about equal to $50 for any mistake the public can find in its advertising. Since 1933, when the offer was first made, the equivalent of many thousands of dollars has been paid in claims. Even minor errors are recognized. For example, a dress did not have as many pleats as the sketch showed, and a cakestand advertised as china should have been called earthenware. When a claim is paid, the information is relayed to employees. Not only has the staff of the store been made more careful, so that claims have declined, but the plan has appealed to other stores, and a code of advertising has been published. Good will and better advertising have resulted. Comment on the method.

18. Some banks are reported to have a double standard in computing interest. When they borrow money, they pay interest on a 365-day year, but when they lend money, they collect on a 360-day year, thus increasing their profit. Most people who do business with these banks are not aware of the practice which is said to take $145 million a year from the general public. Discuss this practice of some banks from the point of view of the power of vested interests that often distorts judgment, and from the point of view of banking ethics. For more details see Richard L. Tobin, "What Can One Person Do? Interest: Compound Fracture," *World* 1, no. 2 (July 18, 1972):45.

SUGGESTED READINGS

Barbour, Ian G. *Science and Secularity: The Ethics of Technology.* New York: Harper & Row, Publishers, 1970.
Bartels, Robert, ed. *Ethics in Business.* Bureau of Business Research Monograph no. 111. Columbus: Ohio State University, 1963.
Baumhart, Raymond C. "How Ethical Are Businessmen." *Harvard Business Review* 39 (July-August 1961): 6–9, 156–176.
Boulding, Kenneth E. *Beyond Economics: Essays on Society, Religion, and Ethics.* Ann Arbor: University of Michigan Press, 1970.
———. *Organizational Revolution: A Study in the Ethics of Economic Organization.* Chicago: Quadrangle Books, 1968.
Braden, William. *The Age of Aquarius: Technology and the Cultural Revolution.* Chicago: Quadrangle Books, 1970.
Burke, John G., ed. *The New Technology and Human Values.* Belmont, California: Wadsworth Publishing Co., 1966.
Childs, Marquis W., and Cater, Douglass. *Ethics in a Business Society.* New York: New American Library of World Literature, Mentor Book, 1954.
Drucker, Peter F. *The Future of Industrial Man.* New York: New American Library of World Literature, 1969.
Ellul, Jacques. *The Technological Society.* New York: Vintage Books, 1967.
Ferkiss, Victor C. *Technological Man: The Myths and the Reality.* New York: New American Library of World Literature, 1970.
Galbraith, John Kenneth. *The New Industrial State.* 2nd ed. rev. Boston: Houghton Mifflin Co., 1971.
Garrett, Thomas M.; Baumhart, Raymond C.; Purcell, Theodore V.; and Roets, Perry, eds. *Cases in Business Ethics.* New York: Appleton-Century-Crofts, 1968.
Hall, Cameron, ed. *Human Values and Advancing Technology.* New York: Friendship Press, 1967.
Michelman, Irving S. *Business at Bay: Critics and Heretics of American Business.* New York: Augustus M. Kelley, 1969.
Miller, Arthur S., ed. *The Ethics of Business Enterprise.* Philadelphia: American Academy of Political & Social Science, 1962.
Mintz, Morton, and Cohen, Jerry S. *America, Inc.: Who Owns and Operates the United States.* New York: Dial Press, 1971.
Muller, Herbert J. *The Children of Frankenstein: A Primer on Modern Technology and Human Values.* Bloomington: Indiana University Press, 1970.
"Perspectives on Business." *Daedalus.* (Winter 1969): v–xx, 1–207.
Riesman, David. *Abundance for What? And Other Essays.* Garden City, N.Y.: Doubleday & Co., 1964.
Wogaman, Philip. *Guaranteed Annual Income, The Moral Issues.* Nashville-New York: Abingdon Press, 1968.

19
ETHICS AND THE MASS MEDIA

The ability to communicate occurs in all forms of animal life from the bees and ants, that signal to others when food is found, to man who can transmit not only facts but also thoughts and feelings. This capacity to share with others is crucial for man's survival and welfare. In recent decades man's capacity to communicate with his fellows has increased at a fantastic pace. While the printed page—books, newspapers, magazines—have been with us for a long time, a wide range of electronic devices, including the telephone, motion pictures, radio, television, and communication satellites are now or soon will be within the reach of all mankind. This development has brought great potentiality for good as well as for evil. Many ethical problems are involved because all instruments are vulnerable to abuse and corruption. The mass media have been called the great teachers of our society, more pervasive and persistent in their influence than the schools and churches. Mass media performers, officials, and advertisers are in one sense the unlicensed teachers of countless millions of people. Where are these new instruments leading us—toward a more mature culture, higher moral standards, and more critical thinking—or toward a heightening of the sensual and materialistic nature of man?

The word *mass* in "mass media" is used in this chapter to refer to a big audience or big circulation rather than to any social stratum in the population. The word *media* is used for certain instruments for transmitting words, pictures, and sound and thus for shaping opinion, belief, and taste. The term *mass communication* may be used, but communication usually implies a dialogue between people rather than a one-way transmission. In the big media, reader or audience response is likely to be slight, if it exists at all.

The opinions, attitude, and conduct of persons depend to a considerable degree on the information available to them and on the images and "feeling tones" impressed on them. Most of our knowledge of contemporary events comes to us from newspapers, radio, and television. Thus our attitudes, our perceptions of reality, and our actions, are formed in large measure by these mass media. Those who control the media not only report current events and the history of the world but, to some extent, help make that history.

We cannot think correctly and clearly about either domestic or world affairs unless we can obtain accurate information. If the sources or channels of information are tainted, distorted, or in any way slanted, we are in serious danger of being led astray, even though our logic may be faultless. The continuation of our democratic way of life depends on the existence of free agencies of mass communication, so that the public is kept informed and alert. A free society is in danger unless its citizens are able and willing to think for themselves. Let us consider in turn the newspaper, broadcasting, and motion-picture industries and then raise some questions of a general nature.

THE NEWSPAPER

The newspaper is one of the chief avenues of contact with the world. The relative influence of the press may be declining, as some people claim; nevertheless, newspapers still play a very important part in our daily lives. They are a basic means for the day-by-day dissemination of news. Many of us gain our impressions of the world and its events from newspaper accounts. They have some influence on all of us.

Newspapers vary widely in the type and quality of service they render. Most of them combine at least five functions: (1) They furnish news or information regarding the events of the contemporary world. (2) They editorialize or make comments on these events. This is not merely a matter of so-called editorials; the whole editorial policy decides what shall and shall not be stressed. Papers can headline some items of news or opinion and make them seem very important, or they can suppress items or omit them entirely. (3) They advertise for business and other establishments, acting as a sales medium. More than half the space of some newspapers is given to advertising. Approximately two-thirds of the revenue of newspapers comes from advertising. (4) They furnish entertainment of various types, from comic strips to puzzles.

(5) They provide miscellaneous information which it is difficult to classify under any of the above headings. This includes feature articles, historical information, helpful hints for housewives or other persons, and items of general education. In any newspaper, one or more of these five functions may be emphasized, and some items may be absent.

During the nineteenth century most newspapers were individually owned independent dailies. Since the beginning of this century this type has been disappearing. Many of them have been purchased to form great chains or newspaper syndicates. In the United States today there are fewer papers in proportion to the literate population than there were in 1787, when the Constitution was adopted. From 2,600 daily papers earlier in the century we have come down to about 1,750 papers. In more than one thousand cities there are no competing daily newspapers. A few years ago ten states were without a single city that had competing daily newspapers. Twenty-two states are without Sunday newspaper competition. In only about one hundred cities is there more than a single newspaper ownership. When we are told that in a majority of the cities of the United States the only newspaper owns or controls the local radio and television stations, we find the situation disturbing. Competition in the newspaper field, so essential in a democratic and free society, is slowly vanishing.[1]

Current literature dealing with the press in North America abounds in high praise and in bitter denunciations, in charges and in countercharges. The press in America is probably the best and the freest in the world today. There is minimal interference by the federal government. Newspapermen, on the whole, compare favorably with men in most businesses and in many professions. Many newspaper correspondents are men of keen intelligence and upright character, who give one a sense of the potential dignity of the journalist's profession. They have sometimes exposed graft and corruption at great personal risk. They have also encouraged and helped to bring about various much needed social reforms.

Before we consider some of the criticisms brought against the press and the efforts of some newspapermen to raise the standards, there are certain additional facts to be noted. First, many errors or distortions of the truth that appear in our papers are unintentional. Some of them are caused by ignorance or faulty observation. Even sincere, intelligent reporters often disagree widely about what they have seen. There is also carelessness in handling the material that is assembled. Errors in quoting and copying are frequent. In foreign news, there is the problem of

---

[1] Carl E. Lindstrom, *The Fading American Newspaper* (New York: Doubleday & Co., 1960).

translating and of coding and uncoding messages. Further, there may be unintentional slanting of the news in line with the reporter's predispositions and point of view.

Second, the evidence seems to indicate that many newspapers have a policy that is quite conscious. The owners of newspapers can eliminate, dilute, or distort items, or insinuate motives for actions that put a different light on them. Newspapers can play up some things and play down others, depending on the point of view and policy of the owners and editors. The attention of readers may be focused on certain events or on certain aspects of those events, thus making them appear more important than they actually are. The extreme form of playing down a news item is the silent treatment. Some newspapers, for example, seldom if ever print anything favorable to the United Nations and its subsidiary organizations. Labor unions and representatives of minority groups have complained that newspapers do not give their side of the case in industrial or other disputes. While acknowledging that some distortion of the news does take place, one well-known commentator says, "The news is played more fairly in this country than in any other and infinitely more fairly than it was a couple of generations ago."[2]

Third, there are many parts of the world where a strict censorship exists. Consequently, from these areas little or no real news is received. Censorship is the attempt on the part of officials to conceal the truth. The suppressed truth may be further concealed through propaganda, which is the attempt actually to manufacture news. All countries use censorship and propaganda during war times, and many countries do so in time of peace. All governments are engaged in the task of slanting the news so that it is favorable to their national interests. We know that this has been done vigorously in Fascist and Communist countries. Sometimes we fail to realize that the democracies are engaged in the same practice of building up good will and popularizing their way of life.

Let us state briefly the four main criticisms directed against newspapers today.

1. Perhaps the main criticism of newspapers is that they seek out and stress catastrophes and trivia because these stories or news items sell papers. The newspaper, it has been said, has a vested interest in catastrophe. Much foreign news as well as local political and industrial news is cast in the form of fights. Happenings that bring ill to someone—a murder or other crime, a quarrel involving prominent people, a scandal, a wreck, or a flood—tend to get the headlines. Individual reporters tend

---

[2]Eric Severeid, "The Big Truth," in *The Press in Perspective*, ed. Ralph D. Casey (Baton Rouge, La.: Louisiana State University Press, 1963), p. 83.

to exaggerate and some even make up stories since they themselves are often judged by the amount of sensational or paper-selling news they produce. While the above statements do not apply equally to all newspapers, the press as a whole tends to direct public attention to activities that are hostile and destructive and away from the constructive, peace-seeking activities of men. Where this is the case, men get a distorted view of life with a resulting personal and social loss.

2. The press, it is said, while claiming to be an objective agent for the dissemination of news, is in reality a group of business corporations run in the interest of profits for the owners or stockholders. Because of this, it is subject to financial pressure and is controlled by a small group to serve their social, political, and economic interests. For example, the power interests have spent millions of dollars to fill the newspapers with articles and editorials opposed to the public ownership of water power and utilities.

3. The newspapers, it is claimed, are subject to additional pressure from large advertisers. Since newspapers receive as much as two thirds or even three quarters of their revenue from advertisers, they are anxious to please them, or at least not to offend them. Distortion and improper slanting of the news may result. In the past, for example, most newspapers joined with the patent medicine interests in opposing the passage of an effective Pure Food and Drug Act.

4. The press, it is claimed, is an active participant—not a neutral or impartial reporter—in the social, economic, and political struggles of our time. Most newspapers are frankly partisan in politics. When economic issues are involved, newspapers, with few exceptions, serve the interests of the dominant groups. Various minority groups have claimed that they are misrepresented and that there is discrimination against them.

To understand the newspapers and their coverage of the news, we need to remember that reporters and correspondents as well as owners and editors have as a rule definite social, economic, and political viewpoints. These beliefs are the inarticulate major premises that necessarily color the reports they make. Then the editorial offices make further selections from these reports. Much news is gathered and dispatched by great news-gathering agencies or press associations, and these have points of view that further color the news. The Associated Press and United Press International have almost a monopoly of news services, a fact which makes it difficult to start new papers. Many papers regularly purchase ready-to-print material from news syndicates. Such material may come in a thin stereotype plate (known as "boiler plate") or in papier-mâché molds taken from such plates. Many weekly newspapers purchase an eight-page paper ready to be printed, having four blank pages to be filled by the local editor with local news and advertising. This is "block booking" of the worst type, especially when the public is not aware of the practice.

Newspapermen are conscious of the criticisms directed against their profession, and they have made some attempts to establish standards. The American Newspaper Publishers Association has no code of ethics of its own, but it has given some publicity to a code drawn up by the American Society of Newspaper Editors. The code includes many broad generalizations. While no efforts are made to enforce the code, a secretary of the American Society of Newspaper Editors feels that there are "extraordinarily few violations of it." He says that "every member of the Society is put upon his honor to observe the code of ethics."

The canons of journalism are stated under such headings as Responsibility, Freedom of the Press, Independence, Sincerity, Truthfulness, Accuracy, Impartiality, Fair Play, and Decency. A few sentences will indicate the general nature of the code: "The primary function of newspapers is to communicate to the human race what its members do, feel, and think. . . . The right of a newspaper to attract and hold readers is restricted by nothing but considerations of public welfare. . . . Promotion of any private interest contrary to the general welfare, for whatever reason, is not compatible with honest journalism. . . . A newspaper cannot escape conviction of insincerity if, while professing high moral purpose, it supplies incentives to base conduct, such as are to be found in details of crime and vice, publication of which is not demonstrably for the general good."[3]

Since little or nothing is done to enforce the code from within the profession, can anything be done to raise standards? From among the many suggestions that have as their object to keep free the channels of information and to raise standards in the newspaper world, we shall mention only four. (1) It is suggested that, through legislative action, we break up the monopolies and monopolistic practices in the handling of news. We might also require that editorials be signed and that information be made public regarding the business connections of newspapers. (2) As individuals, we should widen our range or variety of reading and check items or articles that arouse our suspicion. We should not rely on any one paper, and we should supplement our reading in newspapers with some of the better weeklies and news services. (3) Both public and private bureaus of information and investigation should

---

[3]Published in 1955, by the Board of Directors of the American Society of Newspaper Editors. This is the code first adopted by the society in 1922; in the early seventies there was no plan to add to it or amend it.

be developed and supported. Governmental agencies such as the Federal Trade Commission and private agencies such as organized consumer groups may be sources of information not fully obtainable otherwise. (4) We might establish a few endowed newspapers or community papers and broadcasting stations on a nonprofit basis, with different sections of the paper (or program) assigned to different interest groups. This innovation might stimulate thought and discussion to an extent that we do not have today.

BROADCASTING: RADIO AND TELEVISION

Broadcasting is a comparatively recent phenomenon. The development of radio and television has been rapid; their power is tremendous. Radio broadcasting began about 1920 and by 1925 it was already a large commercial enterprise. A few television stations were operating on an experimental basis in the thirties, but television developed rapidly on a regular commercial basis during the late forties. Listening and seeing are now among the important functions of our society.

During the twenties, there were no direct commercials, in the present sense of the term, and no price quotations, since only the name of the sponsor was given. About 1930, as a result of the depression and reduced incomes, radio standards were lowered. High-pressure advertising, even for questionable services like fortunetelling, was the result. Later the efforts to raise standards in broadcasting met with some success.

In a business in which growth has been so rapid, it is not surprising that excesses have existed. But there has been an attempt on the part of the industry itself and on the part of the government through the Federal Communications Commission to maintain or to raise standards and to protect the public interest. Let us consider, first, the main excesses, and, second, the efforts that are being made to meet the problems involved.

Certain facts need to be kept in mind if we are to understand the problems involved in broadcasting. The number of stations and the number of people who can broadcast at any one time are limited. Some persons or groups must select those who are to be favored with the privilege of using the available frequencies or channels. In many nations the government owns or operates the broadcasting stations. This is true even in lands where the newspaper and motion pictures are in private hands. In the United States the Communications Act of 1934 set up a Federal Communications Commission of seven men to license stations, assign wavelengths, and designate amounts of power. The FCC cannot interfere with or censor individual programs, but it can refuse to renew licenses.

A second fact of importance is the rapid and enormous growth of broadcasting networks, and the large profits that have been made. Stations themselves, or the licenses to operate stations, have sold for millions of dollars. A few networks have control of most of the radio stations and of a large portion of all nighttime broadcasting power.

A third fact is that, except for a few educational and listener-sponsored stations, advertising is the sole support for broadcasting. A few large advertisers account for about half the broadcasting income of the networks. If it is true that money talks and that he who pays the piper calls the tune, these facts have serious implications.

One immediate effect of these facts has been the great increase in commercial advertising to the diminution or elimination of discussion and educational programs. Most programs on the air are commercially sponsored. Some of the advertising has been of low-grade or of questionable nature.

The proportion of time devoted to advertising has become excessive. The FCC found that one station some years ago "broadcast 2,215 commercial announcements in 133 hours on the air." Conditions are not much improved today. Advertisements have been known to run as long as five minutes. Commercial "plugs" may pile up so that as many as five or six are made between programs. They interrupt newscasts, plays, or musical performances at frequent intervals.

Detrimental to the public interest is the use of commercials for social, political, or economic propaganda. Yet there is a considerable amount of such propaganda on the air. We all know commentators who have a "line" or who are cleverly plugging for or against certain issues of the day.

The air is closed by some stations and networks to some organizations and groups. Various minority groups have found it difficult or impossible to buy radio or television time. Some persons within the industry have argued that time should be kept exclusively for the sale of merchandise and services. One reason given for keeping some groups off the air is the ban imposed by some stations and networks on the sale of time for the discussion of controversial public issues. This policy is wholly out of line with our traditional policy of freedom of speech. We need more programs, rather than fewer, of the forum or round-table type.

During recent years television has been praised for the progress it has made and for many fine programs; it has also been attacked for putting earnings above public interest. Soon after a quiz show scandal that involved both performers and officials of the large networks, the editor of a popular magazine wrote that many people were concerned over a small fraud while failing to see the principal fraud.

The main fraud has to do with the predominant character of American television itself. It is made to appear that television deals primarily in entertainment. It does not. It deals primarily in the exploitation of crime and glamorizing of violence. What is most dangerous about this fraud is that those who are responsible for it profess to see no connection between what they are doing and the staggering prevalence of crime in America, especially among young people. The TV operators make all sorts of claims about the power of their medium to sell all sorts of goods. They boast about the ease with which they can dominate the fashions of teen-agers just by having TV stars dress in a certain way. Yet they see no cause-and-effect relationship between what they show on the screen and the increasing addiction of young people to cheap violence. . . . Of course there are good things on TV. In fact, the good things are getting better. But the bad things are getting worse, and there are many more of them. . . . Increasingly, the connection between the superabundance of glamorized violence programs and the mounting national bill for juvenile delinquency and crime in general will become manifest.[4]

In writing about television and our moral standards, the philosopher Charles Frankel asks, "Are we suffering from an outbreak of immorality?" Certain features of our society, he says, tend to lead toward moral disorientation. These include overemphasis on success and the market place, and the weakness of institutions that stress public purposes and exist to promote them. When the salesman's ethics is deplored and changes are suggested, those who defend present practices say that no one has a right to impose his own value-judgments on the public. This, however, is what the mass media as molders of our tastes and the educators of our minds have been doing. We have a right to ask "a degree of moral responsibility from them which they have not so far shown in their use of an instrument as powerful as television."[5]

The Chairman of the FCC, 1961–1963, speaking before the National Association of Broadcasters, after complimenting the promoters of television for some genuine achievements, invited his listeners to sit down and watch the programs on their stations from the time they go on the air until they sign off. "I can assure you," he said, that "you will observe a vast wasteland." In the procession of things they would see

---

[4]Norman Cousins, "The Real Fraud," *Saturday Review* 42 (November 21, 1959): 27.
[5]Charles Frankel, "Is It Just TV—Or Most of Us? *New York Times Magazine,* 15 November 1959, pp. 15, 105.

he listed game shows, violence, sadism, murder, Western badmen and goodmen, and "endlessly, commercials—many screaming, cajoling, and offending." They would see "a few things you will enjoy. But they will be very, very few. . . . I am not convinced that the people's taste is as low as some of you assume."[6]

Efforts to raise standards in broadcasting have come from both within and without the industry. Let us look first at the efforts to raise standards through voluntary self-regulation.

The National Association of Broadcasters is a trade association which represents a majority of the companies, including most of the larger ones, within the industry. As a result of criticism and the opening of public hearings, the association in 1937 formulated a code for radio broadcasting. This code has been revised from time to time. In 1952 "The Television Code" was promulgated and it has been revised from time to time. The two codes "The Radio Code" and "The Television Code"[7] have only slight differences which result from the nature of the two media. They deal with the same subjects. They are also similar in emphasis and on a considerable number of points are identical in wording, so that separate treatment is not necessary.

In both codes broadcasting is seen as a means of augmenting the educational and cultural institutions of society, and broadcasters have a responsibility for promoting the "common good of the whole people." The codes include such statements as the following: "News reporting should be factual and objective." Programs relating to controversial public issues are "to give fair representation to opposing sides of issues which materially affect the life or welfare of a substantial segment of the public." Respect is to be maintained for "the sanctity of marriage and the value of the home." "Law enforcement shall be upheld and, except where essential to the program plot, officers of the law portrayed with respect and dignity."

Both codes have sections dealing with "Responsibility toward Children." While the education of children involves "giving them a sense of the world at large," programs intended for viewing by children or broadcast during times when children may be expected to be a part of the audience "should be presented with due regard for their effect on children." Subjects such as violence and sex where required by plot

---

[6]Newton N. Minow, "Program Control: The Broadcasters Are Public Trustees," *Vital Speeches of the Day* 27 (June 15, 1961): 533-537.

[7]For the National Association of Broadcasters' Radio Code of Good Practices, see the *Broadcasting Yearbook*, 16th ed. (Washington, D. C.: Broadcasting Publications, Inc., 1971), pp. D6–8. For the Television Code, 15th ed. see Ibid., pp. D3–6. The codes can be secured from the National Association of Broadcasters, 1771 N Street, N.W., Washington, D. C., 20036.

development or character delineation shall be presented "without undue emphasis." "Crime should not be presented as attractive or as a solution to human problems, and the inevitable retribution should be made clear." "Material which is excessively violent or would create morbid suspense . . . should be avoided." Programs should reflect "respect for parents, for honorable behavior, and for the constituted authorities of the American community."

Both the radio and television codes specify things that are to be avoided or are forbidden. These include profanity, obscenity, smut, and vulgarity; attacks on religion and religious faiths; lewdness and impropriety; morbid, sensational or alarming details in connection with stories of crime or sex; the "use of television to transmit information of any kind by the use of the process called 'subliminal perception' " (transmitting messages below the threshold of normal awareness); programs presented for the purpose of fostering "fortune-telling, occultism, astrology, phrenology, palm reading, numerology, mind reading, or character reading; narcotic addiction, except as presented as a vicious habit." Cigarette smoking is not to be "depicted in a manner to impress the youth . . . as a desirable habit worthy of imitation."

Considerable attention is given in the codes to the presentation of advertising—what is permitted and what is to be avoided. The broadcaster is to exercise "great care . . . to prevent the presentation of false, misleading or deceptive advertising." Certain things are not to be advertised including hard liquor, "tip sheets" or other aids for betting or lotteries, firearms and ammunition by mail order, and so on. The time allowable for nonprogram material is specified. The Radio Code says that the amount of time to be used for advertising should "not exceed 18 minutes within any clock hour," except under special circumstances and with permission of the Code Authority. The Television Code says that "in prime time, non-program material shall not exceed 10 minutes in any 60 minute period." At other times the limit is 16 minutes for the hour.

The code points out that television makes available "the finest programs of information, education, culture, and entertainment" and that it is "a valuable means of augmenting the educational and cultural influence of schools, institutions of higher learning, the home, the church, museums, foundations, and other institutions devoted to education and culture." We can agree, can we not, that this is true? We all recall excellent programs in these areas. However, several recent studies have indicated that some parents complain of too much violence and a lack of educational, cultural, and religious programs. Western movies, watched widely by children, have averaged from ten to seventeen violent episodes in an hour. One student of violence on television reports that one station "showed in one week, mostly in children's viewing time, 334 completed or attempted killings."[8] Another states that "between the ages of 5 and 14 the average American child witnesses the destruction of 13,000 human beings on television."[9] After explaining a series of experiments set up to test the extent to which children copy aggressive patterns of behavior, Albert Bandura says, "The results leave little doubt that exposure to violence heightens aggressive tendencies in children." The experience, it is claimed, tends "to reduce the child's inhibitions against acting in a violent, aggressive manner" and tends "to shape the *form* of the child's aggressive behavior."[10] Some educators have warned of the possible dangers to health (physical, mental and emotional), character, and education if a child spends two or more hours a day before a television screen. Others contend that these dangers are being exaggerated.[11]

Efforts to regulate and improve broadcasting have been undertaken by the government as well as by the National Association of Broadcasters. In the United States the Radio Act of 1927 set up a Federal Radio Commission whose functions and records were transferred to the FCC by the Communications Act of 1934. Broadcasting stations are licensed "to serve the public and not for the purpose of furthering the private or group interest of individuals." Benefits derived by advertisers were to be incidental and entirely secondary. The broadcasting system was to be a kind of community mouthpiece for keeping the people informed, stimulating discussion, and presenting music, drama, and athletics for the entertainment of the public. In a speech replying to an attack made on the FCC, Judge Thurman Arnold said, "The public gets the maximum benefit only if an even chance at the best hours is given to education, public discussion, literature, and the best types of music in programs not controlled by any business interest."[12]

The ethical standards of the radio and television industries appear to be the generally accepted standards of society—that is, the industry tries to follow the folkways, mores, and law of the land. But the idealism

---

[8] Frederic Wertham, "School for Violence," in *Violence and the Mass Media*, ed. Otto N. Larsen (New York: Harper & Row, Publishers, 1968), p. 37.

[9] Eve Merriam, "We're Teaching Our Children That Violence Is Fun," *Violence and the Mass Media*, p. 41.

[10] Alfred Bandura, "What TV Violence Can Do to Your Child," *Violence and the Mass Media*, pp. 125, 126.

[11] For many articles representing different points of view, see William P. Lineberry, ed., *Mass Communications*, The Reference Shelf, vol. 41, no. 3 (New York: H. W. Wilson Co., 1969).

[12] Thurman Arnold, "Radio As a Form of Public Discussion and Education," *Congressional Record*, June 5, 1946.

of the codes is offset by the drive for profits and the desire to do the things that lead in this direction, regardless of public welfare.

Pressure for higher standards and for a closer approximation of standards and practices must be brought to bear on broadcasting stations and networks from a number of different sources. First, those within the industry who see the need for improvement, such as individual station owners and broadcasters, can press for higher standards and closer adherence to them. To be effective, this pressure will need to move the National Association of Broadcasters to more vigorous action in behalf of higher standards. Second, the FCC can do much to protect the public interest. Anyone who reads the reports of this commission will be convinced that it has already performed a useful function, but more remains to be done. Third, professional critics can do a great deal in this field, just as the critics and reviewers do for the theater and the concert halls. Since the radio or television audience is much greater, the need for criticism and reviews is also greater. Finally, the general public and especially listeners' councils can perform a useful service by making articulate or vocal the views of listeners and viewers and by aiding, through study and publicity, the promotion of better programs.

MOTION PICTURES

Like the newspaper, the radio, and television, the motion picture theater has great power for good or ill in the lives of people, in social relationships, and in the relations between nations. Numerous studies in recent decades have indicated the great influence of motion pictures, especially on the thinking and conduct of youth. Movies set the pattern for mannerisms, for ways of courtship and lovemaking, and for personal adornment. They stimulate emotions that express themselves in fantasy and daydreaming as well as in overt behavior. They help create ideas of right and wrong and mold desires and ambitions.

During the early development of the movie industry, there were some scandals, considerable criticism of the type of pictures shown, and a growing movement toward censorship. In 1922 the Motion Picture Producers and Distributors of America was incorporated as a trade association. At that time seven states had passed censorship legislation, and bills were being introduced in a score of other states. In 1927 the trade association published a list of "Don'ts" and "Be Carefuls." In 1930 these were replaced by a production code which, as amended, is still the self-imposed code of producers and distributors. Although a producer cannot be compelled to produce pictures in accordance with the code regulations, the code has had a beneficial effect.

In some of the larger cities the censorship boards have each year eliminated from the films brought before them several thousand scenes that they considered undesirable. The publication of a number of studies of motion pictures and some vigorous criticisms have brought some improvements and more high quality films. Many of these films were among the most popular, a fact that would seem to refute the claim of some people that better films do not draw crowds and make money.

Attempts have been made in as many as thirty states to impose official censorship, but only a small number of states have censorship laws. The United States Supreme Court has held that motion pictures come under the freedom-of-speech provisions of the United States Constitution. A number of notable decisions during the last decade or so have dealt a blow to censorship. But the federal Criminal Code prohibits obscene, lewd, and filthy films and forbids the importation of any film that is immoral or obscene. Motion pictures are included in the list of articles that may be prohibited on the grounds of immorality or indecency from the channels of interstate commerce or circulation through the mails.

The fairly widespread criticism naturally has been a matter of concern to the motion picture industry. Besides making some amendments in its code and adopting an advertising code, the industry has taken steps to clean house from within and to enforce the provisions of the code. Now many theaters will not show a film unless it has been given the seal of approval of the Motion Picture Association of America.

Since a considerable amount of criticism of motion pictures has been directed against the portrayal of violence and of vulgar forms of sexual passion, we shall limit our quotations from "The Production Code" to these items. Under General Principles, we read: "No picture shall be produced which will lower the moral standards of those who see it. Hence the sympathy of the audience shall never be thrown to the side of crime, wrongdoing, evil, or sin." Under "Crimes against the Law," subtitle "Murder," the code says: "a) The technique of murder must be presented in a way that will not inspire imitation. b) Brutal killings are not to be presented in detail. c) Revenge in modern times shall not be justified." Under "Sex," item 2, "Scenes of Passion," reads in part: "a) These should not be introduced except where they are definitely essential to the plot. b) Excessive and lustful kissing, lustful embraces, suggestive posture and gestures are not to be shown."[13]

The code itself is a fairly commendable statement of objectives. Unfortunately, it has not been effectively implemented or enforced. It has been used at times, furthermore, to bar criticism of our social order and to suppress a frank probing of the human predicament.

---

[13] Motion Picture Association of America, *A Code to Govern the Making of Motion Pictures* (1955).

During recent years the government has forced the separation of theater ownership from production and distribution and has prohibited "block booking," "blind selling," and various monopolistic tactics. Films may now be rented individually, and exhibitors cannot legally be forced to accept blocks or groups of films some of which they do not want. Higher standards of motion picture entertainment may be brought about by increased public demand that practice conform more closely to the standards set up. In this connection, as with broadcasting, we should encourage more critical reviews as well as the extension of the use of Film Estimate Services. Today there are a number of excellent Estimate Services carried by several magazines that give reviews and estimates of films and enable one to pick what he wishes to see.

In 1968 the Code and Rating Administration of the Motion Picture Association of America issued rating symbols to guide the public and assist parents in selecting motion pictures for their children. The four types of ratings are: G—general audiences or all ages admitted; PG—parental guidance suggested—some material may not be suitable for preteenagers; R—restricted, that is, persons under age seventeen must be accompanied by a parent or adult guardian; X—no one under seventeen admitted (the age limit varies in certain areas). The association engaged the Opinion Research Corporation of Princeton to study the film-rating system. The report indicated that among moviegoers, nearly two-thirds of the adults questioned and nearly three-fourths of the teenagers found that rating system to be "very or fairly useful." Efforts are now under way to "make the ratings more accurate and informative," to "tighten ratings enforcement at the boxoffice," and to "monitor trailers" (accompanying film) with more effectiveness.[14]

The motion picture industry can be a great force for raising standards and tastes or for lowering them. There is a moral obligation resting with everyone to see that the films to which they and their dependents are exposed are elevating, not degrading.

FREEDOM, CONTROL, AND THE MASS MEDIA

In our discussion of human rights in part 1 we included the right to freedom along with nine other rights; in the chapter "Freedom of Thought and Expression" we pointed out that freedom of expression is a basic condition for the development of mature persons. The distinctive qualities of persons including self-consciousness, abstract

---

[14]From speech by Jack Valenti, President, Motion Picture Association of America, delivered before the annual National Association of Theatre Owners Convention, November 3, 1970.

thought, ethical discrimination, and aesthetic appreciation develop most adequately in a society where men and women can express themselves freely. Only free men, it is said, can be genuine and creative persons. The struggle to achieve freedom is a long and honorable one.

While freedom is one of the basic human rights and values, it is not an absolute. There are other values and rights that need to be recognized and protected. My freedom ends where it brings injury to you. The oft repeated statement that no one has a right to shout "fire" in a crowded theater, still stands. Such principles as "the public interest" and the "common good" are basic in free democratic societies. This is an issue where there will always be some differences of opinion and opposing views. Some controls are dangerous and repressive; others are beneficial and needed.

Throughout the centuries censorship and other forms of control have been more harmful than beneficial and have retarded man's development as a moral creature. Some individuals and groups have been convinced that they alone know what is true and what is good, and they have used whatever power they have to control the rest of the population. This is most evident in nondemocratic and totalitarian societies, but is not limited to them. Even in the "free" societies, governments, churches, and extremist groups may move from keeping the peace to keeping everyone's peace of mind, and so they would ban what they do not like or what is new and different. A government may censor the news and keep from its citizens information about the nature and purpose of its international commitments and foreign adventures. Churches have frequently stood on the wrong side where questions of truth and welfare have been concerned.

The overwhelming majority of citizens in our so-called free and democratic societies demand and approve a wide range of controls. These include pure food and drug laws; laws against the false labeling and advertising of merchandise; banning of advertisements of some commodities and some ideas and organizations; regulations governing investments by the Securities and Exchange Commission; copyright laws to protect books and artistic and dramatic productions; the right of the editors of magazines and journals to accept or reject articles submitted to them. The public also approves of laws against libel and slander, and laws against a wide range of sexual activities considered harmful including adultery, prostitution, incest, and so on. Most parents feel that they need to control what their young children read, hear, and see, at least until the young person has the maturity and the time to develop some inner or self-control.

In the mass media the chief controversy has centered around books, films, and the movies. During the early years of the development of motion pictures, the family film was the predominant feature and advertising was lacking or minimal. During the 1950s, however, two events were largely responsible for a drastic change in the content and emphasis of movie films. First was the very rapid development of television which soon became the major supplier of family entertainment. As a result attendance at movie theaters dropped, often as much as fifty percent or more. The second event was the inclusion by the courts of movies within constitutional guarantees of freedom of speech of the first amendment. Up to that time motion pictures were censored and movie theaters, in the view of the law, were considered no different from any other profit business. Under the new freedom, coupled with the desire to make up for past losses and to increase box office receipts, there soon were "unprecedented excesses in the detailing of erotica, nudity, and violence."[15]

How much freedom or how much control is desirable in the interest of the common good? There will probably always be a tension between the sections of society that lean in opposing directions. Are there other things besides shouting "fire" that should not be said or done in a crowded theater or even in a democratic society? Opinion polls indicate that a majority of the people in the United States do want censorship of some sort applied against obscenity and probably the details of gruesome crimes and violence. There is something wrong with a society that refuses to protect its children and its own future development. The Supreme Court leaves adults free to read what they like, but leaves the states free to protect children from obscenity and to control the offensive display of such material in public.

The fact that some persons move further in the direction of freedom than others may feel is wise does not necessarily mean that these persons are libertines. Nor does the fact that other persons think some motion picture and television content may be harmful to viewers mean that their ideas can be dismissed as the product of a morbid imagination. Some intelligent men have set forth a reasonable case for censorship. Freedom and the public interest are both principles that need to be emphasized. At the end of a discussion in which he makes a case for freedom, but not as an absolute, Kyle Haselden says, "Freedom to receive and to utter ideas should not have to defend itself; censorship should.... The control and the censorship of human communication are highly questionable, potentially dangerous, and occasionally necessary human enterprises."[16]

---

[15] Richard S. Randall, "From 'Business' to 'Speech,'" *Censorship of the Movies: The Social and Political Control of a Mass Medium* (Madison: University of Wisconsin Press, 1968), ch. 2.

[16] Kyle Haselden, *Morality and the Mass Media* (Nashville, Tenn.: Broadman Press, 1968), pp. 93, 97.

SOME CONCLUSIONS AND SUGGESTIONS

Viewing the mass media from an overall point of view, there are certain things we need to keep in mind. First, the goods and services distributed by the press, radio, television, and the movies are probably the most important consumer commodities purchased. They are the food for the minds and the emotions of men and so affect their habits, customs, and their outlook on life as a whole. We have been told that the mass media hold the attention of the average person for about thirty-five hours a week and that television is the major attraction. In *Understanding Media*[17] Marshall McLuhan has insisted that "the medium is the message" and that the medium is more important than the content. While this may not be literally true, it is true that the electronic media have an influence that reaches beyond the content. Television, for example, as distinct from the printed page, gives us an all-at-once quality and impression so that in a new sense we become a part of the action.

Second, because of the importance of these means of communication and their power to change us and society, the control of the media of communication must not be left in the exclusive control of any small group. Mass advertising has available more money than the entire nation spends on its elementary and high school public education, and much more than the contributions to all the churches and synagogues. The Communications Editor of *Saturday Review* expresses his concern about a coming age of news monopoly in which "more than 95 percent of all the daily newspapers in the United States will have no local print competition, where only two national newsgathering organizations will supply virtually everything broadcast over the average radio or TV station, and where a tiny handful of executives and news operators in but three networks will pretty much determine what the American electronic audience is allowed to know about the world in which it is trying to exist."[18] Power to determine what the people read, hear, and see, or what they are led to desire must not be left entirely in the hands of a small group of men with a large financial interest in the decision. If any area is, this is surely an area affected with a public interest.

Third, censorship and rigid control are likely to be more harmful than beneficial. We want an open rather than a closed society, since only in a relatively free society and through the conflict of ideas can truth in the long run be found. We do, however, need regulating commissions, such as the FCC and the FTC responsible to the people's

---

[17] (New York: McGraw-Hill Book Co., 1964); paperback edition 1965.
[18] Richard L. Tobin, "The Coming Age of News Monopoly," *Saturday Review* 53 (October 10, 1970): 51.

representatives. We need these as we need pure food and drug laws to protect the public interest and guard against abuse. All too frequently these regulating commissions have seemed more concerned with pleasing the industries they are set up to regulate than with protecting the public interest. In the last few years because of public interest and concern, these commissions have issued new guidelines that point in the direction of protecting the public and the consumer.

Fourth, the concerned reader should watch for new developments in electronic media that are in the offing and think about their ethical implications. We hear discussions about new uses for computers, the expansion of cable television with many more channels, publishing by cathode ray tube, the video cartridge that will transform television and records, and cassette storage and retrieval libraries. Looking a short time into the future one student of this problem says that most of the homes will "have an electronic communication center connected to a national control for both entertainment and news. If you want television you press one button; if you want a fresh daily newspaper printed right in your home, you will press another."[19]

A crucial question is whether the new technology is to be controlled so as to reap the highest profits for the owners or operated so that the public interest will be foremost. Will monopoly be an ever-present danger or will we be able to continue to live as free men?

Finally in the last analysis the direction in which we are to move in the future will depend on alert and concerned individuals and on certain institutions that have the good of persons as a major goal. We have made some specific suggestions for possible safeguards and improvement. In the long run the solution may rest with the schools, colleges, universities, churches, and with men and women in many walks of life who have the genuine professional ideal. They can help to raise a generation of young people with higher tastes and expectations and a passion to close the gap between the ideal and the real. The general public must be taught to be more discriminating and more critical of what it reads, hears, and sees.

QUESTIONS AND PROJECTS

1. What are the characteristics of a good newspaper? After thinking about this yourself, consult the report of a committee of the Associated Press

---

[19]Richard L. Tobin, "Publishing by Cathode Ray Tube," *Saturday Review* 53 (October 10, 1970): 61. See also Fred W. Friendly, "Asleep at the Switch of the Wired City," *Ibid.*: 58; Dan Cordtz, "The Coming Shake-up in Telecommunication," *Fortune* 81 (April 19, 1970): 68–71, 158, 163–164.

Managing Editors' Association in 1962. See John H. Colburn, "What Makes a Good Newspaper?" *Saturday Review* 45 (June 9, 1962), pp. 50–52.
2. How should one read and use a newspaper? What principles or suggestions can you offer to help the average reader? See Edgar Dale, *How to Read a Newspaper* (Chicago: Scott, Foresman & Co., 1941).
3. Recently a boy, thirty-two days old, was kidnapped from his home in a fashionable suburb of a large city. His mother had left him sleeping in the yard while she went into the house for a few moments. She found a note demanding a two thousand dollar ransom to be placed at a particular spot. The kidnapper had written: "I'm scared stiff. Do not notify the police until noon tomorrow or I'll be forced to kill the baby."

The father, returning home soon afterwards, called the police headquarters and a group of detectives started an investigation. The news spread through the community and someone called the city newspapers. As newspaper men called police headquarters to check their tips, they were asked to withhold the story until after the ransom deadline next day in hope the kidnapper would collect the ransom and return the baby. All the news agencies except one withheld the story. One paper gave a brief bulletin in an early edition and then ran a headline on page one and a full account in a big second edition. The police then released the other papers from their pledges. Although the ransom was left, to no one's surprise the kidnapper did not return and the baby was never found.

Interviewed by three reporters, the mother cried out, "I could cut all your throats." The Chief of Detectives said, "We would have gotten a lot further if there had been no interference from the press."

Is it the first duty of the news media to print the news at any price, no matter what the injury, or should news agencies, in special circumstances, acknowledge a higher duty by withholding a story for a time? Was the newspaper partly responsible for the death of the child?
4. In the early 1960s an incident occurred in a midwestern city that raised various questions of ethics. A respected businessman, principal stockholder in a corporation, had given half a million dollars to a university in his city. While gathering biographical material for a story, a city paper discovered that years ago, between 1908 and 1925, the donor had served three prison terms. This fact was known by many of his friends and business associates, but not by his wife and son. The paper printed the story in detail. The common stock of the businessman's corporation took a drastic fall. The businessman said, "I have never asked anyone not to publish anything about me, but this is a vicious thing." Although he had attached no strings to his gift, the university had planned to name a building for him. After this incident the chancellor of the university said he knew all about the man's record and that the university would still name the building for him. Discuss the ethical aspects of this case.
5. A reporter learns of an affair in the life of a girl from a prominent

family. When the girl discovers that he knows the facts, she begs him not to print the story in his paper. If the story is published, it will undoubtedly harm the girl's reputation. For the reporter it would be a "scoop"; consequently, he would like to send it in. What is the reporter's duty?

6. A liberal columnist, a Pulitzer prize winner, has been described by one of the weekly news magazines as "a man with a merciless conscience." He speaks out courageously on many public issues. His column is carried by many newspapers some of which do not always print his column. On days when his opinions clash with the editorial policy of some of the papers, his material is not published. This practice has been quite general with the papers of one particular chain, and the columnist has requested that the chain drop his column altogether. Many members of the chain refuse to do this. Such a refusal prevents rival papers from carrying the column. Is such a practice fair to the columnist or to the general public?

7. Discuss the following questions relating to newspapers:
   (1) Is a single newspaper or a chain of newspapers justified in printing material on one side of an important issue and refusing to print or putting in an inconspicuous place all material on the other side?
   (2) In reporting speeches, is a newspaper justified in reporting only the remarks that happen to agree with its editorial positions? Is this fair to the speaker and to the public?
   (3) Is a newspaper doing its duty when it reports accurately what someone says is the truth, if members of the staff have information that clearly indicates the statements are false and they give no indication of this latter fact?

8. What is the relative influence of newspaper, radio, and television in today's world? What news does the public most readily accept? See John Tebbel, "What News Does the Public Believe," *Saturday Review* 45 (March 10, 1962), pp. 43–44.

9. Give your reaction to the statements by Norman Cousins, Charles Frankel, and Newton N. Minow in this chapter. Do you think they are fair or unfair in their criticisms of television? Why?

10. What is the effect of television on children? This has been a topic of controversy for some years. Two careful studies are now available, one made in the United States and one in Great Britain. Stanford University researchers found that "during the first sixteen years of life, the typical child now spends, in total, at least as much time with television as in school." The study in England showed that "gradually, almost imperceptibly, television entertainment brings about changes in children's outlook and values," even though this is not through any deliberate attempt on the part of the producers. See Wilbur A. Schramm, et al., *Television in the Lives of Our Children* (Stanford: Stanford University Press, 1961); Hilde T. Himmelweit, et al., *Television and the Child* (New York: Oxford University Press, 1958; reprint of chs. 1–4, 1961); "TV

Violence: 'Appalling,'" *U. S. News and World Report* 67 (October 6, 1969): 55–56 (Excepts from statement by National Commission on the Causes and Prevention of Violence).
11. Which criticisms of the mass media do you think are sound and which unsound? Ten indictments of the mass media are stated, then answered or discussed in Leo Rosten, "The Intellectual and the Mass Media: Some Rigorously Random Remarks," in *Culture for the Millions,* ed. Norman Jacobs (Princeton: D. Van Nostrand Co., 1961), pp. 71–84.
12. Do you agree or disagree with the statement that it is virtually impossible today, except from the religious rostrum, to teach that life means discipline and self-sacrifice?
13. In 1969 a news cameraman and occasional reporter covered many left-wing groups as an accredited newsman, but passed along items of news and pictures to the FBI. He soon found himself on the police payroll for continuing such activities. He had been in the army and felt that communism and radical groups should be stopped at home as well as abroad by any means. Most newsmen consider their relationship with informers as sacrosanct as those of a priest with a penitent confessor, a lawyer with his client, or a doctor with his patient. Comment on this case. What ethical questions are involved?
14. In 1970 a reporter who had reported on the Black Panther group and who apparently had the confidence of one or more of them, received a subpoena to testify about them before a grand jury. He refused, saying that he would be accused of betraying confidences, and that any future effort to gather information about radical groups would be useless. He was held in contempt, but later a Court of Appeals reversed the decision. Do you think journalists should be granted immunity in such cases? Give reasons for your answer. You may wish to see *Time*, 14 November 1969, p. 69.
15. In an article "Isn't Choosing a President As Important As a Moon Shot?" Newton N. Minow, Chairman, Twentieth Century Fund Commission on Campaign Costs in an Electronic Era, defends the recommendation of the commission that all radio and television stations be required to carry some prime time broadcasts to be used by candidates. Such a change is essential unless a candidate's access to the electorate is to depend on his access to big money. The United States is the only country where the candidate must purchase his time. The alternate system is that in which the broadcaster provides time as a public service (e.g. "Meet the Press"). In 1968 candidates had to spend more than forty million dollars for radio and television time. The proposal is that voters' time would be purchased with public funds by the federal government at half rates. See *New York Times*, 9 November 1969, p. D23. Discuss the above proposal and its possible influence on democracy in a free society.
16. Critically evaluate the following statements:
    (1) "Every war of aggression in modern times has been preceded by distrust, then fear, and finally hatred, all created by a systematic poisoning of the news."

(2) "Half the ills of modern society would be cured if it were ever possible to get the truth to the people."
(3) "It is up to the intelligent radio and television listeners . . . to see . . . that private advertising interests do not get the power to take over our great town meetinghouse of the air."
(4) If those who control our means of communication "continue to cater to the lowest tastes, the result will be more people with lower intelligence. You don't educate children by keeping them in kindergarten."
(5) *"All* television is educational television." "The mass media are the great teachers of our society . . . more pervasive in their influence than school or church."

SUGGESTED READINGS

Arons, Leon, and May, Mark A., eds. *Television and Human Behavior: Tomorrow's Research in Mass Communication.* New York: Appleton-Century-Crofts, 1963.

Casey, Ralph D., ed. *The Press in Perspective.* Baton Rouge, La.: State University Press, 1963.

Clor, Harry M. *Obscenity and Public Morality: Censorship in a Liberal Society.* Chicago: University of Chicago Press, 1969.

Elliott, William Y., ed. *Television's Impact on American Culture.* East Lansing: Michigan State University Press, 1956. See especially ch. 6, Eugene David Glynn, "Television and the American Character—A Psychiatrist Looks at Television."

Frank, Josette. *Children and TV.* Pamphlet no. 323. New York: Public Affairs Committee, 1962.

Haselden, Kyle. *Morality and the Mass Media.* Nashville, Tenn.: Broadman Press, 1968.

Himmelweit, Hilde T. et al. *Television and the Child.* New York: Oxford University Press, 1958; pamphlet reprint of chs. 1–4, 1961. A study sponsored by the Nuffield Foundation.

Jacobs, Norman, ed. *Culture for the Millions? Mass Media in Modern Society.* Intro. by Paul Lazarsfeld. Princeton: D. Van Nostrand Co., 1961.

Koenigil, Mark. *Movies in Society.* New York: Robert Speller & Sons, Publishers, 1962.

Larsen, Otto N., ed. *Violence and the Mass Media.* New York: Harper & Row, Publishers, 1968.

Lineberry, William P., ed. *Mass Communication.* The Reference Shelf, vol. 41, no. 3. New York: H. W. Wilson Co., 1969.

Mayer, Martin. *About Television.* New York: Harper & Row, Publishers, 1971.

McLuhan, Marshall. *Understanding Media.* New York: McGraw-Hill Book Co., 1965.

Randall, Richard S. *Censorship of the Movies: The Social and Political Control of a Mass Medium.* Madison, Wis.: University of Wisconsin Press, 1968.
Schramm, Wilbur, ed. *The Science of Human Communication.* New York: Basic Books, 1963.
Tyler, Poyntz, ed. *Television and Radio.* The Reference Shelf, vol. 33, no. 6. New York: H. W. Wilson Co., 1961.

20
NEW DESIGNS FOR FAMILY AND MARRIAGE

New designs for living are among our most urgent needs today. So Margaret Mead contended in 1970: "We need to ... plan for ways in which families can live that are more in accord with the changes emerging in our society. Above all, we must find ways of breaking out of the isolation in which each small family—parents and their children—still is expected to live."[1]

At one time the nuclear family helped to insure security and independence for its members and freed them for other things. Now, however, the task of maintaining a home "squanders an inordinate amount of energy" without serving these ends well. We need, concludes Margaret Mead, settings in which adults can experience a greater sense of community and in which children, as they grow up, can be close to other adults as well as to their own parents.[2]

Within the past decade there have surfaced with unprecedented force similar dissatisfactions with marriage, with the roles of women in our society, and with what once would have been called the patterns of courtship; that is, with the mores and laws surrounding roles and relationships among men and women in and out of wedlock. Altogether these complaints amount to a sweeping indictment of contemporary

---

[1] Margaret Mead, "New Designs for Family Living," *Redbook Magazine* 125 (October 1970): 22.
[2] Ibid.

institutions controlling primary relationships between men and women, adults and children.

We propose here to organize these doubts, the evidence bearing upon them, and suggestions about their resolution. We will not speak of the pros and cons of upholding existing ways of life, but of the evaluation of these ways in comparison with alternatives. Rather than try to be comprehensive, we will use a selection of options to illustrate the main types of choice about marriage and family which seem to be emerging amidst other social changes. These options have to do with alternative forms of family life, alternatives to or within marriage, new roles for women, and new patterns of sexual relationships among adults.

To assist in understanding and evaluating these options, we do well to recognize trends in contemporary attitudes and technology and in demographic and social conditions which will affect both what is possible and what is likely to be experienced as desirable. Among these trends the examples presented in the next section bear particularly upon the roles and relationships among men and women.

CHANGES IN THE PREVAILING VIEWS OF RIGHTS

Four trends seem to us to be strongly growing in American thinking about the rights and the respect to which people are entitled. Each of these trends is having effects, both helpful and disruptive, in family and marital relationships. To seek solutions to courtship, marital, and family problems while disregarding these trends will be self-defeating. We view these trends as ethically sound, but each of them can be misapplied or overemphasized relative to other equally valid ethical aspirations; and it is difficult to know where the golden mean among counterbalancing principles falls. The four trends are:

1. *A trend toward equal rights and respect for women.* The principle that all human beings should enjoy equal rights and respect is not new to American culture. What is novel is an awareness of the ways in which that principle has been wittingly or unwittingly violated with respect to women in the habits and institutions of our society. As these habits and institutional patterns are challenged, there are women and men who are offended, for they both have adapted to old forms and tailored their personal satisfactions and their moral codes to the maintenance of these forms. If a double standard in sexual morality violates the equality of women with men, it should be challenged. But the challenge may take either the form of a more puritan standard for men or a less puritan one for women; this has already happened. If the

dominant pattern of expecting a woman's work to be in the home is a violation of her equal rights, it should be altered. But it can be altered by methods that either get men more involved in work at home or take both men and women out of such work; the two ways are being tried. In these two examples, the ensuing effects change the conditions of competition for personal advantage—between the wife and the extramarital partner in sex relations when the double standard is discarded, and between women and men in the competition for high-salaried jobs in the career market. The examples also create novel problems concerning the greatest overall benefit to society. For example, what should be done about the care of children in the new definition of men's and women's work, the development of self-esteem, and the provision of security and love in the alternatives to monogamous marriage?

The fact that movement toward more pervasively equal rights among men and women creates this turmoil about what is desirable and right is no excuse for toning down the movement toward equality. It does, however, call for greater patience and sophistication than we have historically required in seeking the best.

2. *A trend toward equality and respect for younger adults.* This trend is another part of the awakening of people to the implications of a general egalitarian outlook. What is novel here are the questions as to whether young people have been denied the rights of adulthood long past the time of their arrival at maturity, and whether the patterns of parental and legal controls over youth have prolonged and entrenched infantilism and created problems of delinquency and nonproductivity. In 1971 the voting age for national elections was finally moved to eighteen by amendment of the Constitution of the United States. In part, the change was a response to the anomaly of laws drafting youths into war service while denying them a voice in the election of the officials who create such legislation. Because of the large proportion of the population which youths form today and the large numbers between the ages of eighteen and twenty-one who are in college, this amendment raises the prospect of domination of elections in college communities by the students, provoking sharply different reactions in different communities.

This trend toward granting earlier recognition of youths as adults is actually a turn back toward earlier conceptions of the time of maturation. In primitive societies puberty rites occur at ages nearer thirteen to fifteen, and in frontier America the young person of twelve to sixteen had to assume adult roles. The trend runs counter to the prolongation of adolescence caused by prolonged economic dependence and by linking the image of youth to continued enrollment in school and college. However, if youths who may drive at sixteen or vote at eighteen are adults, then the traditions of a college's acting *in loco parentis* and of parents' controlling the courtship and marital patterns of their children are doomed. If the choices of young people about personal and sexual relationships are cause for alarm, the ways of resolving the alarm and improving the relationships will need to be worked out within the framework of this redefinition of adulthood and of this extension of adult rights to earlier ages.

3. *A trend toward respect for diverse cultures and ways of life.* A third trend that affects the redefinition of male-female roles and relationships in contemporary America is that toward a less homogeneous American culture, toward the granting of esteem and respect for more diverse ways of life. In part this is a trend in which ethnic groups are encouraged to preserve some cultural identity and distinctiveness of life patterns. Assimilation is no longer equated with equality of opportunity or with justice; it may even be a violation of the rights of identity and privacy. In the realm of sexual mores, this trend toward cultural pluralism has the implication that equal rights for women, youth, and cultural groups may override any previous social and ethical advantage in having a single standard for society with respect to the patterns of courtship, marriage, and family life.

In view of the great mobility and instant communications that characterize American society today, any trend that combines openness to varied ways of life with easy movement from one to another will give rise to new problems about the care and control of the immature, the mentally ill, and the socially deviant (terms that present new puzzles for clarification) and about the protection of those who are their victims. While the trend toward respect for diversity of culture thus seems worthy of encouragement, its realization in our time also presents enormous problems of implementation if its effects are not to be predominantly destructive. This task is accentuated by the fact that a change of culture so fundamental will be heavily resisted—even violently resisted—by people who do not accept the ideal of cultural pluralism, do not discern their own guilt in violating it, or cannot accept the pace or impact of the changes it brings in tow.

4. *A trend toward individual autonomy.* A fourth trend affecting the changing mores of man-woman relationships is a growing thrust of moral autonomy and moral responsibility upon the individual, as opposed to the family or the community, for a larger proportion of significant choices. This trend amounts to a new division of labor in moral decision-making. In times past, a much greater part of the choices of policy and principle guiding a person's life was done for him by his family or his community. He had no genuine option of choosing what he thought was the best alternative about his rights of protest, his use of drugs, his choice of mates, even his choice of vocation or of residence. These

were set for him either by rules or expectations which had overbearing strength. Increasingly today we expect the individual to decide things. In college, less and less of his curriculum is prescribed; and he must even choose among curricula. In work, the variety of routes open is legion. The family takes less and less of an influential role than before and is viewed as oppressive if it imposes a solution. At the same time the government has begun to take responsibility for the support of the aged, for the insuring of health and medical services, for assurance of employment or of a minimum economic base for living—functions once carried by the family. These trends, countervailing in some respects, converge in setting the individual free from constraints of the family. For example, some college youth today—children of affluent parents—have severed relationships with their parents and applied for welfare funds while asking their colleges to treat them as "full need" applicants for financial aid.

The cumulative result of these four tendencies in moral outlook is, in our view, a more significant factor in the revolution in man-woman relationships than are such new social patterns as "swinging," "the arrangement," and coed dorms, which are discussed later in this chapter. Singly and in the abstract, each of the trends seems unexceptionable. Combined and applied among people of varying maturity and knowledgeability, they present an unprecedented challenge to both young and old, men and women, individuals and groups, families and their communities. This challenge is further complicated by technological trends and by demographic and other social changes which will enter into our discussion of family, marriage, and courtship. The profundity of the challenge, we believe, will be missed unless it is understood essentially as one arising from the need to implement trends which are ethically both important and right and which can only lead to great harm if they are not provided with applications that are sensitive to the many other values which enter into the life of any social being in modern technological society.

TECHNOLOGICAL, DEMOGRAPHIC, AND OTHER SOCIAL CHANGES

Interacting with the trends just cited are numerous other social changes. Some of these affect the worth[3] experienced by individuals

---

[3]The expression "worth experienced by individuals" refers to the whole of what these individuals experience as valuable, including in this case the effects of the social changes not only upon the individuals' satisfaction with themselves and what happens to them, but also with what happens to others.

through consequences of the technological change; e.g., the effects of technological progress in medicine upon the effects of sexual encounters. Other changes are taking place in attitude, modifying what happens and the evaluation of what happens by those affected. For example, changing attitudes toward religious authority have apparently caused a relaxation of various prohibitions of contraception, with resultant changes in the use of contraceptives, in the evaluation of large families, and in the role of sex in marriage.

It is extremely difficult to estimate which of these technological, demographic, and other social changes are likely in the long run to bear most significantly on the evolution of better patterns of male-female and adult-child relationships. Even the classification of these changes into a manageably small list of major ones presents unresolvable difficulties. Instead of attempting a definitive list, then, we offer only enough examples to suggest how to go about examining this type of information in appraising today's options.

1. *Changes affecting health and length of life.* These range from the effects of new methods of contraception to the lengthening of life by improvements in nutrition and medicine. Of the former, Vance Packard writes, "For the first time in human history, men and women now have an assured way to separate the recreational from the procreative function of coitus. The British demographer Richard Titmuss has suggested that birth control has done more to emancipate women than their gaining the right to vote."[4] Packard cites some young unmarrieds as thinking that prior to our having effective contraceptives we merely made a virtue of necessity in sanctifying chastity.

Abortion is no longer the hazardous, expensive, or (in some states) the illegal operation it once was. Life expectancy at birth now exceeds seventy years in the United States and is even greater in France, England, and Sweden. A person who has reached twenty years of age may expect to live, if he is average, until almost the age of ninety. With this lengthening of life goes a prolongation of vitality, good health, and good looks. Physically youth are maturing earlier (girls start menstruation three and a half years earlier than a century ago), and the end of fertility is extended for women into the fifties.

2. *Changes affecting mobility, productivity, and access to resources.* Never before in history have men moved so far, so fast, or so often. Never before have they produced so much per worker or consumed so much per person. These changes apply peculiarly to the industrialized

---

[4]Vance Packard, *The Sexual Wilderness: The Contemporary Upheaval in Male-Female Relationships* (New York: Pocket Books, 1968, 1970), p. 17.

countries. The automobile has often replaced the parlor as the scene of courtship. In a broader view the new mobility breaks up the closeness of large families, separates the father more often from his family for a large part of the working year, uproots families with more frequent shifts of job, and exposes people more often to different cultures and subcultures. Movement increases anonymity, which contributes to the trend toward leaving more and more to the decision of the lone individual, loosed from religious, community, and family scrutiny and sanctions.

Eli Ginzberg of Columbia University has made studies of manpower mobility and predicts that we will become "metropolitan-type people" with diminishing ties and commitments to neighbors and friends.[5] One newspaper, for example, told of a Montgomery Ward manager who had moved twenty-eight times in a twenty-six-year marriage. The report claimed that such "corporate gypsies" are increasingly common.[6]

The growth in output of goods and services in America has also significantly affected conditions of family and marital life. Such differentiation and specialization in production and distribution has occurred that the contemporary home has a radically altered economic function. It is now a service station, not a production center.[7] Within the home, the roles of family members are accordingly altered. Children are no longer as essential as before to family income, nor as accustomed from their early years to tasks crucial to family well-being. Young men are more often supported in the first years of marriage by the wife's income than even half a century ago. Women can often serve the family's economic status more effectively in a job away from home than as manager of hearth and brood. The family income, while still at poverty levels (reckoned somewhat differently than two decades ago) in a significant proportion of the United States population, is for others likely to call for less deferral of gratifications than typified the life of the pre-World War II generations. The family recreations are less often at home and less often with mixed generational gatherings, as the specialized commercial options and mobility permit everyone to have his first choice of entertainment. Combining mobility and access, the family members have less need of one another for either the necessities or the amenities, except that father and mother must in many cases foot the bills longer than used to be the case.

Child care, once uniquely the function of the family, is increasingly provided elsewhere. For the mother without husband or independent

---

[5] Quoted by Packard in *The Sexual Wilderness,* pp. 19–20.
[6] *The Sexual Wilderness,* p. 20.
[7] Ibid.

income some form of day care is necessary to permit her to earn a living. In the affluent, mobile family the traditional mother may either bring in babysitters or place the child in a nursery or kindergarten. For the liberated husband and wife it is feasible to employ full-time help, to place the child away from home, or to use day-care centers under public or private auspices.

3. *Changes in education and leisure.* With health, long life, affluence, and mobility go time and means to learn and play as never before in human history. Both education and leisure activities are less and less the responsibilities of the home. At the same time the largest proportion of economic activity in human history is currently being devoted to schooling and to an unprecedented variety of commercially provided diversions, hobbies, entertainment, travel for rest and recreation, and so on. What is more, the things that happen at school and at play are no longer the traditional ones that parents knew but involve many novelties, many imports from other cultures, and even revivals from times unknown to the immediately preceding generation. With these changes there has come a tendency for recreation and education to become segregated by age groups. Once the little red schoolhouse mixed many grade levels, and the country dances and the church socials involved all age groups. Today we have teen centers, senior citizens clubs, activities for young marrieds, and all manner of further subspecializations by age and sex.

4. *Changes affecting the content of work.* Work is, of course, enormously more specialized than a century ago. The proportion of jobs in farm and factory is declining as "human service occupations" increase. The proportion of workers who commute to work is rising, and the average distance commuted continues to grow. For people in increasingly automated work, the job satisfactions seem generally to decline. At the same time a growing portion of persons whose work is nonroutine seem to become involved in the competitive rat race of trying to get ahead, to achieve honors or record accomplishments, or to make extraordinary earnings. In all of this, work is separated almost entirely from the home, an increasing strain is put on the home, and in a growing proportion of families home is a bedroom (and possibly part-time dining room) to which more than one earner returns weary at the end of a hard day and leaves early for long weekend holidays. Or alternatively, home may be an unhappy, tense, or deprived environment that suffers by comparison with the work scene or constricts the freedom available on the street, in the school, or on the job.

5. *Other changes in attitudes.* Complicating further the effects of the changes in ethical outlook and in technology are other interacting changes in the prevailing attitudes of our society. Some of these pertain

directly to abortion, homosexuality, premarital sexual relationships, childlessness, expectations of a partner in marriage, and so on. Others bear only indirectly upon these matters but have to do with the weight and influence of religion or the home, the willingness of people to sanction by law what they believe is right or good, the relative importance of present pleasures and future consequences, and so forth. Some of these will emerge sharply when we turn to specific disputes about what is happening in the relationships among men and women inside and outside of marriage.

CHANGING PRACTICES IN MARRIAGE AND SEX

On an August 24, 1971 television program the interviewer asked his guest, a woman newspaper columnist, to comment on the saying that "This is the last married generation." The columnist thought the statement an apt one, descriptive of what is occurring, not in legislation or explicit societal adoption, but in the cumulative effect of thousands of individual decisions. These decisions include a growing proportion of divorces to marriages; a rapid increase in the numbers of couples who live together without entering into a formal marriage contract; a growth in the proportion of formal and informal separations in proportion to marriages; among nondivorced and nonseparated couples, a rising proportion who in varying degrees define the marriage as allowing for freedom to find sexual partners or companionship in other quarters; and a growing proportion of young people who, though not in a coupled living arrangement outside of marriage, obtain sexual satisfactions through casual relationships which were formerly less common and more widely frowned upon.

What are the facts about these alleged changes in social practice? A study of "swinging" (having sexual relations as a couple with at least one other individual) by Gilbert D. Bartell explains its roots in American culture and doubts that it generally provides its participants a gain in companionship or in sexual satisfaction.[8] Most swingers, he reports, are middle class, "respectable," white suburbanites, numbering an estimated one million in America today. He likens the suburban wasteland to the sterile Arctic habitat of the wife-swapping Eskimo. The sterile environment, he concludes, leads some people to try group sex simply to relieve boredom. Others hope it will make them feel young, avant-garde, and sexually desirable. Moreover, swinging is "in

---

[8]Gilbert D. Bartell, *Group Sex: A Scientist's Eyewitness Report on Swinging in the Suburbs* (New York: Peter H. Wyden, 1970).

keeping with American cultural patterns: to be popular, to have friends, to be busy."[9] Psychoanalyst Net Littner is reported to hypothesize that "couples who swing are incapable of intimate relationships even with each other and use wife swapping 'as a safety valve that keeps intimacy at a level each can tolerate.'" Whatever the explanations, Bartell finds that weariness and disillusionment are the common sequel. To avoid intimate relationships, swingers normally swing only once with the same couple, hence must be constantly searching for "great" rather than "moldy" partners, and eventually tire of the effort. More important, however, is that, having acted out adolescent fantasies, many find the reality not up to the fantasy. "Besides, there is generally a loss of self-esteem and identity, and an absence of commitment to partners whom they may well never see again. This total non-involvement represents the antithesis of sexual pleasure.'"[10] Bartell doubts that swinging really benefits anyone very much, but he found little evidence that it caused marital discord or breakup among the couples he studied.

A second novel phenomenon of recent years is coeducational dormitories in college. Unlike swinging, coed dorms seem generally to provide heterosexual companionship with the result of a relative reduction of intercourse, compared with campuses stressing segregation of sexes. As reporter Betty Rollins put her findings: ". . . both from what we observe and from what people tell us, the big message is: there seems really to be less sex in a setup like this than in a sexually segregated one."[11]

This is hard to prove, as the reporter admits, especially with snooping prohibited; but reasons for the claim make sense. One is that the kind of familiarity in groups which coed living fosters breeds nonromantic friendship. A girl becomes less a sex object, more a friend. Another explanation, offered by Stanford psychologist Joseph Katz, is that an "incest taboo" develops; the girl seems like a sister and the boy a brother. Also the sustained association means that consequences of action are present and remembered; as a result one becomes prudent. College deans report that some students who wanted coed living one year do not want it the next. Their needs change, or their experience with the implications leads them to reassess it. Thus while there is a growing proportion of colleges with coed living groups on or off of campus, the change no longer looks like a stampede in this direction.

The "arrangement" is a third contemporary deviation from the traditional norm in American marriage. It is known by many names: super going steady, student cohabitation, an unstructured relationship, and

---

[9]*Time*, 8 February 1971, p. 51.
[10]Ibid., pp. 51–52.
[11]*Look*, 23 September 1969, p. 22.

so on. One person moves in with the other, and the specific terms of their living together usually are not defined. "While in some instances super-steady-going may lead to marriage," says a reporter, "in others it may turn out to be a welcome ounce of prevention. 'When I saw him every day,' reports a University of Colorado co-ed, 'I realized I just couldn't marry him.' But the breakups can be traumatic. 'It was like a divorce,' says a recent Berkeley graduate. 'She is reluctant to try again.' "[12] Common law marriage, of course, is nothing new to the American scene; but the arrangement differs. Dr. David Powelson, chief of the psychiatric division of student health service at the University of California at Berkeley, said that "stable, open nonmarital relationships are pushing the border of what society is going to face in ten years."[13]

A 1968 feature in *Life* concludes its wide-ranging report on different views of the arrangement by stating a consensus of studies by Drs. William Simon and John Gagnon (Indiana University Institute for Sex Research, who conducted a survey of twelve hundred students at twelve colleges), Dr. Ira L. Reiss (University of Iowa), Dr. Joseph Katz (Stanford, Institute for the Study of Human Problems), and Drs. William H. Masters and Virginia E. Johnson (authors of *Human Sexual Response*). Elements of the consensus were: "1) the sexual revolution is real, but 2) its extent is highly exaggerated. Measured in terms of promiscuity . . . it is simply a myth. Promiscuity does exist, of course, and has its visible and highly vocal supporters. But promiscuity was not invented by the current college generation, and the evidence indicates that it is no more common than it ever was." The summary continues, "The more important changes in student sexuality are seen in attitude rather than behavior. 'If behavior has not altered in the last century as much as we might think,' says Dr. Reiss, 'attitudes have—and attitudes and behavior seem closer today than for many generations.' "[14]

What goes into the new attitudes? Sexual activity is appraised more as one ingredient of an entire relationship than as an isolated act. For example, a girl may consider it permissible to sleep with a man she loves or intends to marry, but quite immoral to neck or pet indiscriminately with casual dates. The average coed has shed some inhibitions about premarital sex but reflects, according to Dr. Katz, "not so much a decline in moral codes as a change in their contents."[15] The greater willingness of the female has made the male less rather than more promiscuous. He too tends to seek longer-lasting relationships that offer security.

---

[12]"Unstructured Relations," *Newsweek*, 4 July 1966, p. 78.
[14]William A. McWhirter, "The Arrangement," *Life* 64 (May 31, 1968): 68.
[13]Ibid., p. 79.
[15]Ibid.

Dr. Masters says flatly that the double standard on campus is dead. Some data tend to corroborate this view. The proportion of coeds experiencing premarital sex has risen phenomenally in the last two decades, while that of males has remained about the same. A sizeable number of students of both sexes maintain virginity throughout college. A good many never even date. But other data do not bear out Dr. Masters' claim. Males still have sex more frequently and more promiscuously than females. Many men still treat women as sex objects, while college women rarely view men so simply. The disparity between men and women in both attitude and behavior seems, nevertheless, to be diminishing. The *Life* feature suggests that it might even vanish were it not that women do not want it to vanish. One wonders whether in the time since this article was published, or within a few more years, the disparity will lessen further as the press for women's liberation gains ground.

Speaking of the real meaning of the arrangements as currently practiced, Dr. Simon sees them normally functioning as stable, informal marriages rather than as experimental sexual unions. The erotic component in them is "surprisingly small," he says. The partners claim to be "not sleeping together, but living together." They are conventionally monogamous, do not swap partners, and act much like old married folks.[16]

The overall effect of the changing college mores is seen by Dr. Reiss as one of greater permissiveness, greater frankness, and greater equalization of sexual behavior patterns of men and women. Dr. Masters adds to the decline of the double standard a forecast of healthier, more open sexual attitudes, less promiscuity than ever, and stronger male-female relationships. Drs. Simon and Gagnon see sex as playing a less significant role in human relationships in this new context. All acknowledge, however, that forecasting the future of these relationships is hazardous.

Still different from swinging, coeducational living, and the arrangement are many of the communes, which currently seem to be in a revival stage. One estimate placed their number in the United States at between eight hundred and twelve hundred in 1970.[17] The term *commune* suggests unrestricted sharing of property and possibly of partners in sexual relations. The press may also have given an impression in the last decade that communes are largely an invention of hippies. In fact, the communal movement is probably best understood in the terms

---

[16]Ibid.
[17]Herbert A. Otto, "Has Monogamy Failed?" *Saturday Review*, 25 April 1970, p. 24.

raised at the outset of this chapter. It is a movement back to the large family and toward regaining companionship in the family and in marriage; greater depth in caring among family and marital participants; economies on some costs to permit outlays on others; and variety of age, sex, and personality among the intimate group. Undoubtedly some communes have a strong thrust toward sexual freedom, but others are as "straight" as can be. Different communes have widely different rules or customs about property rights, sexual relations, joining or leaving, and so on. Generally the choice for membership in a commune involves weighing advantages of the kinds just listed against certain losses of privacy and of freedoms of other kinds, for example, disposition or acquisition of property, use of one's income, and mobility. Herbert A. Otto, a fellow of the American Association of Marriage Counselors, attributes the short life-span of many communes to four major "disintegrative pressures that fragment intentional communities": disagreement over chores or work and resulting disillusionment about unfulfilled obligations, interpersonal conflicts (frequently fueled by exchange of sex partners and resultant jealousy), problems related to economic survival, and hostility of surrounding communities.[18]

WHAT IS AND WHAT OUGHT TO BE IN MARRIAGE

So far we have talked about what the changing attitudes and practices are. But what should they be? As we have repeatedly said, what is may not be what ought to be. Nor is what society generally approves likely to coincide with what would be best. The very freedom that increasingly is accorded to individuals in our society to decide for themselves, with fewer constraints of law and with relaxing sanctions from the social mores, puts a heavier burden of decision upon the individual.

Perhaps the best way to address the "should" question is to spell out the types of issues that require decision. These are, as we see it, primarily issues concerning one's assumptions about the right and the good, and not so much issues of fact and relationship, although both kinds are involved. Several illustrations of each type of issue suffice here; our discussion questions at the end of the chapter will raise additional examples.

The first type of issue is that of assumptions about the right and the good. Consider, as a first example, a capsule statement of a Catholic view of the trends just described. In Catholic thought marriage is a sacrament which creates a union of husband and wife. The central

---

[18]Ibid., p. 25.

function of this union is procreation, and the enjoyment of sexual relations is to serve that end, not the pleasure of the partners for its own sake. Only in that relationship are sexual relationships considered right. Attempts to prevent conception are prohibited, because they interfere with the purpose of marriage. Attempts to end pregnancy after conception are viewed as murder, for the fetus is a living human being. Moreover, the Church feels that the state ought to enforce at least the sanction against murder and ideally provide a climate supportive of the ideals of the Roman Catholic religion in matters of spiritual law, because that religion is the one true faith and the temporal authority is rightly subordinate to the spiritual in those matters of primary spiritual concern.

This capsule statement greatly oversimplifies the subtlety and complexity of Catholic thought. For one thing, there is much disagreement among Catholics concerning the rightness of interpreting the judgments about abortion and contraception as implications of Catholic philosophy or theology in a binding sense. Also, the line of thought implicit in the capsule statement and connecting the conclusions to dogma is not a matter of Catholic consensus. Even calling these ideas "assumptions" seems unfair to some adherents of the ideas, who see them as revealed truth. Nevertheless, the ideas stated represent the beliefs of some Catholics and illustrate the range of issues about assumptions governing one's view of what should be an ethic of sex and marriage.

The "assumptions" in the above capsule statement which one must confront in sorting out his own convictions deal with the rightful source of sanction for a marital or sexual union, the rightful functions or purposes of such a union, the rightness of extramarital sexual intercourse, the rightness of enjoying sexual relationships outside of marriage, the criterion of personhood and life (implicit in speaking of abortion as murder), the rightness of a church's determining moral standards for (1) its own members or (2) others in its society, and the rightness of a state's enforcing church regulations (1) in a culturally homogeneous society or (2) in a culturally or religiously pluralistic one.

A quite different example of the sources of controversy about the right or best ways of regulating sexual behavior and marital relationships can be seen in two extracts from the news media. The first has to do with the teaching of sex. According to Fred M. Hechinger the Christian Crusade and the John Birch Society in 1969 had adopted the slogan: "Is the schoolhouse the proper place to teach raw sex?"[19] The

---

[19] Fred M. Hechinger, "Storm over the Teaching of Sex," *New York Times*, 7 September 1969, Education section.

Rev. Billy James Hargis commented to a rally of Conservative Americans in Boston that, "I don't want any kid under 12 to hear about lesbians, homosexuals and sexual intercourse. They should be concerned with tops, yo-yos, and hide-and-seek." He saw the drive to provide sex education as "part of a gigantic conspiracy to bring down America from within," because he saw such education as advocacy of "free love, loose morals, and liberal permissiveness."[20]

Columnist Harriet Van Horne feels that the sexual revolution is given much too good a press and not enough searching analysis. Conceding many changes resulting from higher education for women, higher incomes, urbanization, growing slums, low quality schools, the pill, and the decline of parental and church authority, she asks why we do not also mention the "increasing vulgarization of sex by the mass media and the wanton misreading of Freud" on the dangers of repression. Sex outside of marriage, as all those television programs are at pains to tell us, is no longer premarital or extramarital sex. It is simply sex for its own sake, for pleasure without responsibility. Ms. Van Horne insists that it is a bogus claim to say these developments can lead "the turned-on generation toward a more meaningful, more rewarding way of life."[21] She also feels that they are false prophets who argue that there are no immoral persons or amoral societies, but only different moral systems. For instance, she cites as immoral persons the mate-swappers who number, if the count includes groups from comarital foursomes to clubs of over one hundred, a total which she records as at least five million people. Ms. Van Horne quotes J. I. Simmons, author of *It's Happening*, in a breezy summation of wife-swapping: "Acquaintances and friends become fleeting lovers, then acquaintances again. Strangers meet and become momentary bedmates or soul mates, then dance off to another partner, another scene."[22] Why, asks Ms. Van Horne? It will not do just to say that "kids just aren't scared of sex any more." Why are they not, she asks? Perhaps the health hazards are gone, though some of the data are not so reassuring. The emotional and spiritual dangers are acute, however, especially because our time and our circumstances make people reluctant to get involved, to know and share the sorrows and the problems of other human beings. Many who try to appear happy and free are, in fact, lonesome and lost; "they need love desperately and sex is not doing anything for them. Sex is destroying them. . . . Too

---

[20]Ibid.
[21]Harriet Van Horne, "A Commentary by Harriet Van Horne: The Sexual Revolution—in Living Color," *McCalls* 95 (October 1967): 46.
[22]Ibid., p. 150.

much sex, too little love; result: a sad, lost, disturbed human being."
Why do so few experts emphasize this point in their proclamations of
a sexual revolution?[23]

These reports and commentaries by Fred Hechinger and Harriet Van
Horne challenge assumptions both of value and of fact. They raise
many questions: whether unconcern for others may play a larger role
in the sexual revolution than the concern for more meaningful relations; whether promiscuity rather than more meaningful mating relationships may be more widespread than is admitted by the researchers;
whether the researchers have injected their own value biases into their
surveys, resulting in invalidity in the findings; whether the plea for
respect for divergent moral systems may actually be a plot to undermine
the strength of the society; whether the preoccupation of mass media
with the sensations of the sexual revolution may be having the effect of
promoting irresponsible faddism; and what the actual consequences of
these changes will be when we really begin to understand them adequately.

Some people will be able to answer readily the questions about what
ought to be thought and done because they place the highest priority
on a few quite specific moral postulates. For example, if one defines
abortion as murder and murder of any type as absolutely taboo, then
one does not need to settle the many interrelated issues of fact about
the other consequences of prohibiting abortion; the moral finding is
clear. Of course a similar decisiveness is open to people with opposing
postulates who enjoy a similar single-mindedness and assurance about
their moral stand. If the right to make one's own choice is so high a
moral priority that it matters little what the effects of that choice are
upon others as long as the intent was not to harm others, then a wide
range of individual decisions receives moral approval.

We agree with neither of the views stated in the preceding two paragraphs. What follows is addressed primarily to people who, like us, live
with various degrees of uncertainty about both the facts and the moral
postulates. What can and should they do? In our opinion they must
and should recognize their own uncertainty as a fact, and should also
recognize that some issues, such as those here discussed, are unavoidably complex. Although we are obligated to know the facts when we can
reasonably do so, and to stand by what are right principles when they
can be established as well-grounded, it is not always possible to be certain on either fact or principle. Under those circumstances, a candid
admission of uncertainty may be the healthiest moral condition open
to fallible men. It does not follow that they may suspend action. In

---

[23]Ibid.

such weighty and difficult issues, action must and should occur as risk-taking. Due care should be exercised to avoid not only foolish risks but also the foolishness of inaction that has the certain effect of creating an avoidable degree of net detriment to society. One step that can contribute to responsible conduct in risk-taking is that of weighing alternatives. To illustrate this idea, let us sketch here two general alternatives to simply saying "yes" or "no" to existing conventions and practices in marriage: one approach going from specific types of ethical problems to a redesign of institutions governing marriage, family, and sexual relationships; the other approach starting with a new overall conception of these institutions and then approaching specific types of problems in a way that carries out the new conception. We will then suggest a third alternative that makes limited and complementary use of each of the first two approaches.

One way of dealing with the issues is to take a specific problem and try to see the whole of it. Consider, for example, unwanted pregnancies and the laws on abortion. Many a legislature today is studying its own laws on abortion and trying to find a socially acceptable set of changes that will on balance achieve less heartbreak, less social damage, and a more lawful and humane society in respect to this particular problem area. The usual outcome of such a legislative study is neither a complete rejection of current customs and ideas nor a complete endorsement of them, but a more complex policy which amends present regulations and practices in response to some demands for reform and reaffirms other traditions in recognition of their continuing usefulness. This approach can be applied to any number of specific problems of similar magnitude, with the hope that, as the solutions are reached and synchronized or reconciled with one another, the overall result will be a better set of institutions and practices governing marriage, family, and sexual relationships.

A second approach to dealing with the same range of issues is to conceive a whole new set of institutions governing these relationships, not an easy prospect to arrange. As the preceding discussion makes clear, we think that none of the practices or arrangements thus far discussed has the comprehensiveness or depth to govern marriage, family, and sexual relationships within American society. This conclusion may seem better warranted if we look briefly at a possible redefinition of marriage that would have this scope and combine the following elements:

1. The fulfillment of companionship needs might become the defining basis for marriage.
2. The following needs, once thought to be the responsibility of a marriage, might be assigned as responsibilities to other loci in society:

a. Economic support—this could be the responsibility of the individual himself, of his parents, or in the last resort of the social welfare system.
b. Sexual satisfaction—this might normally go with companionship in marriage but by mutual consent could be viewed as an individual's responsibility to be met in other ways.
c. The procreative needs of society—these might normally be served in marriage, converting the marriage to a small family, but might also be arranged by genetically planned unions outside of marriage, with child care a function of other social institutions.
d. The care of children—this might be a delegable responsibility of parents, who would pay for the care but might have it provided by public or private group or individual arrangements. Or child care might be a state function.
e. Allocation and exercise of property rights—this might become entirely a matter of contracts and wills.
3. Customs and laws now viewed as definitive of moral expectations surrounding marriage might be amended accordingly:
a. Entry into marriage by periods of trial of compatibility (as in the Scandinavian countries and in some informal arrangements in this country) might become normal.
b. Formal entry into marriage might become a more clearly contractual matter in which the expectations of the relationship and the conditions of its dissolution might be less uniform and more explicit from couple to couple than today. In effect this would amount to an individualization of marriage contracts.
c. Abortion might be legalized along lines being tested in New York State today, thus removing the probability of an unwanted procreative function of a marriage.
d. Exit from marriage (now by divorce or separation) might become a matter of choice by either party, subject to legally or morally sanctioned rights of both parties and enforceable by administrative or judicial procedures in equity.
e. With the development of marriage as more clearly a private contract than of a question of public morals, the regulation of marriage by government would become more a matter of guarantees of due process and of basic rights than one of enforcement of a particular code stating what a marriage should be.

The point of spelling out this illustrative alternative to marriage as it used to be known is not to advocate that alternative, but to illustrate the approach to clarifying the ethical choices which confront our society in respect to marriage. In addition to disagreeing with some of the specific features of this particular redefinition of marriage, we are skeptical about the wisdom of attempting such a complete overhaul of an institution as a "package deal." The exploration of such alternatives, however, can be fruitfully used to debate the long-run vision of needed social change. This vision, if clarified, may make it easier to find immediately beneficial changes that are less sweeping in scope and consequences than the new institution.

When we find fault with an existing institution, we are able to see its various dysfunctional effects readily—effects which often result from its interactions with the particular circumstances and institutions of the time. We must keep in mind, however, that it is not so easy to predict what the effects and interactions of a new kind of institution in unknown future circumstances would be. Would the pattern just outlined encourage prolonged dependency of children upon parents, or an enlarged burden of social welfare costs? Would it increase conflict in marriage because of the diversity of contracts and the lack of a common pattern of socially sanctioned expectations? Or would it increase the stability of marriages and the serenity of family life by facilitating good initial unions and prompt termination of unions gone awry?

In appraising a whole new way of life with respect to marriage and family, we would need to probe some questions of a subtlety rarely addressed in decision-making in times past. Consider, for example, the bearing of potential "future shock" upon such a change. Even people who think themselves liberated cannot change in their emotional makeup as rapidly as their rhetoric demands. If, as one coed reported, "hopping in and out of bed" with different mates is not as fulfilling as she expected, what is the reason? Is she a victim of socially ingrained taboos that she intellectually rejects, or is the nonfulfillment the result of a deeper linkage of sexual joy with organic needs for care and security and companionship? What if man's organic needs actually conflict with one another in the sense that, quite apart from social conditioning, we are inherently incapable of getting all that we want or need in respect to all of them? In that event different cultures provide the means of responding to different weightings of these needs. For example, if some people, by virtue of either social conditioning or organically conditioned need, have a significantly greater need for security than others who show a greater drive toward individual autonomy, they may have the most rewarding lives if they live in different communities or cultures which reflect their respective needs. Since the variety of cultures is limited by factors of size and numbers of people and requirements of the viability of a culture, then some cultural taboos are warranted ways of assuring that the values needed by individuals attuned to that culture must be protected from individuals who do not understand those connections. For example, people who need and want a certain level of economic resources are obliged to accede to cultural taboos which protect capitalization and which require deferral of some gratifications in order to achieve the conditions for producing those gratifications.

These probing questions are leading some humanistic psychologists to a "new recognition of the many dimensions and possibilities of monogamy," Herbert A. Otto reports. The efforts to get away from monogamy have disclosed that it can have satisfactions and fulfillments that are difficult otherwise to achieve.

At the same time, if monogamy is to survive as the predominant pattern of American society, that pattern will differ from earlier ones: the marriage will normally be an evolving relationship, built by love and understanding into a developing, flexible union that makes for the growth of each of the partners, for enjoyment of the relationship in its new forms as they emerge, and for responsiveness to the changing social environment.

These are high expectations: an evolving, loving, flexible union responsive to environmental change! Is it reasonable to expect so much of either individuals or an institution? In reply we may ask whether there is a better option, for polygamous or "unstructured" arrangements appear from experience to date to make even heavier demands upon maturity and flexibility of the partners in most cases. Even many who have thrown off convention and tried these arrangements opt afterward for less demanding or more supportive monogamous relationships. Among those who have from the outset chosen the conventional marriage, many have been able to adapt to contemporary social pressures. A growing number of others have, instead of abandoning the one-to-one marriage, turned to new ways of gaining and giving help. New forms of counseling have evolved. New types of supportive groups have been formed, some springing from religious associations, others from relationships to institutions of higher education, and others from other roots.[24] There is, we believe, a growing awareness that more can be expected and realized in marriage than past experience has commonly shown and that, given this new vision of possibilities, the means are beginning to emerge for both individuals and communities to support a new quality of marital and family life.

We do not view the present turmoil surrounding the institutions of marriage and family as a sign of a breakdown in American society. We see instead an extremely trying but promising reevaluation of institutions, a gradually growing clarity as to the many values that are affected and must be nurtured in these institutions, and a capability in

---

[24]"Has Monogamy Failed?" p. 62.

our society for struggling with the problems thus raised while we go on acting upon divergent postulates and conflicting opinions concerning the facts. As a society we will probably neither postpone specific reforms while we wait for a consensus upon a grand reform nor will we declare a moratorium on grand visions in order to concentrate entirely upon fixing up the specific breakdowns. We will go on working at both ends of that option, hoping that each effort will aid the other. And that is probably as it should be.

QUESTIONS AND PROJECTS

1. What is your own appraisal of the effects upon both the individuals and American society of (1) swinging, (2) coeducational living, (3) the arrangement, and (4) communal living groups? Are there unanswered questions in your own mind about the facts or the merits of these situations? How do these uncertainties bear upon your judgment of the right and wrong of these matters?
2. Although, as this chapter mentions, the means of preventing and curing venereal diseases are enormously improved since 1930, there continue to be press and research reports of high rates of these diseases. To what causes would you attribute these findings? Given these facts, what social policy would you recommend for reducing the incidence of such diseases?
3. There are people who call any form of polygamy or group marriage promiscuous. Yet anthropologists report many forms of marriage, more often rooted in economic and social needs than in sexual gratification. Westermarck reacted sharply to the labeling of these customs as "promiscuity":

   After examining in detail all the cases which are known to me of peoples said to live in a state of promiscuity, I have arrived at the conclusion that it would be difficult to find a more untrustworthy collection of statements. Some of them are simply misrepresentations of theorists in which sexual laxity, frequency of separation, polyandry, group-marriage or something like it, or absence of a marriage ceremony or of a word for "to marry" or of a marriage union similar to our own, is confounded with promiscuity. Others are based upon indefinite evidence which may be interpreted in one way or another, or on information proved to be inaccurate. [*A Short History of Marriage.* (New York: Macmillan Co., 1962), pp. 7–8]

   In what ways do you regard the anthropological record as relevant to the ethical appraisal of current deviations from formally sanctioned monogamous marriage forms?
4. This chapter suggests that our society may need a redefinition of marriage and of the law underlying it. Do you agree? If so, how would your

favored redefinition differ from the one proposed? If not, what alternative do you favor? Why?
5. Do you concur with our view that the state of marriage and family in our society should not be viewed as a breakdown of morals? How would you support your own judgment on this question?
6. Do you think that the double standard is disappearing? Should it? How would you relate an appropriate recognition of sexual and individual differences to your answer about having a single or a double standard?
7. Congresswoman Shirley Chisholm recently cited statistics showing that eighty-two percent of employed women are in clerical, sales, factory, farm work, or service occupations; only six percent are medical or health workers, and five percent are managers, officials, proprietors. Yet the Department of Labor, she said, finds women more reliable and less absent from their jobs than men. "What is the reason for their preponderant employment at the lower level positions and pay scales?" she asked. "Quite simply, it is discrimination. . . . Women are sick and tired of being told: 'See how far you've come? You've come a long way, Baby.' . . . The truth of the matter is that the top policy-making positions within the American establishment remain in the hands of white males who are not responsive to the needs of the poor, minorities, or women." ["Of Course Women Dare," Address to Concurrent General Session I of the 27th National Conference on Higher Education (Chicago, March 7, 1972), p. 5.]

Do you concur with this criticism of the "American establishment"? What response to the cited conditions do you advocate? Why?
8. In the Democratic National Convention of 1972 Gloria Steinem and Bella Abzug played influential roles, both in increasing the voice and power of women within the convention and on the choice of candidates and the contents of the party platform. They also, however, came under attack from Betty Friedan, who helped launch the women's liberation movement with her book *The Feminine Mystique,* and who charged them with believing that "man is the enemy" and thus trying to create a war between the sexes. "The assumption that women have any moral or spiritual superiority as a class or that men share some brute insensitivity as a class—that is male chauvinism in reverse; . . . it is in fact female chauvinism, and those who preach or practice it seem to me to be corrupting our movement for equality and inviting a backlash that endangers the very gains we have won these past few years," she said. (F. S. Swertlow, reporting an interview in "Woman vs. Woman: Who's a Female Chauvinist?" *Washington Post,* 23 July 1972, p. E17.) Steinem and Abzug denied the charges. At issue, in part, are questions as to how past injustices can be mended and how discriminatory attitudes ingrained in the culture and in both men and women can be rooted out. What do you view as the most needed steps toward genuine equity among men and women? Support your view with an analysis of the roots of inequity which the new steps must remove.
9. College regulations about being out at night and entertaining guests of

the other sex in one's room often differ for men and women. Should they? If so, in what respects, and why? If not, what problems do you see in creating a congenial environment for dormitory living while according the rights of visiting and freedom of movement which you advocate?

10. Some colleges and universities are getting out of the business of being landlords and parents to students. Should they? For all students? What practical and ethical problems do you see in the alternative resolutions of this question?

11. Students often complain about the dating customs on campus. They say there is pressure to "go steady" after only one or two dates, whereas they would prefer to date a number of different people and to be able to date more than twice without being viewed as a steady. What do you think the custom should be? What needs and concerns should be respected by the patterns of dating?

12. In the discussion of the arrangement and of coed dormitories, it was implied in the discussions mentioning Drs. Katz, Masters, Simon, and Reiss that some students today are freer than before regarding premarital sexual intercourse, but stricter on one another about not even petting unless there is more than sexual gratification involved. What expectations do you favor as (1) campus social policy, and (2) your personal standard on these questions?

13. A bill passed by the legislature of the state of Connecticut would have permitted divorce from a spouse who was confined to an institution for mental care for a period of five years, even though there were temporary interruptions in the confinement. In his veto message, Governor Abraham Ribicoff said in part: "When people marry, they realize that there are potential periods in their lives when illness or other misfortunes may come their way. The marriage vows, 'in sickness and in health' should have meaning. . . . It would indeed be a terrible society where a person could toss aside a wife or husband because serious illness may come their way. Such a philosophy would be contrary to the teachings of all of our great religions and a contradiction of the ethics of Western society. If a person should be so callous as to disregard such normal and human considerations, the state should not lend encouragement to such callousness by allowing a divorce." Do you agree with the governor, or with the legislative majority, and why?

14. An increasing proportion of women plan to work outside of the home after their marriage, with the exception of short leave periods to bear their children. Do you approve of this idea for your own marriage and for others? What considerations do you think ought to be taken into account in the arrangements for marriages with two careers outside of the home?

15. A few years ago a royal commission in England, after two years of official inquiry, declared equal wages for women unsound. The commission of five men and four women based its opinion on three main conclusions: that performance in the lower wage-earning classes is

unequal; that equal pay would result in the long run in a lowering of standards of pay for both men and women; and that the married man with a family would be at an economic disadvantage in the community. On the other hand a considerable number of persons believe that there should be equal pay for equal work and no discrimination. Should family obligations for members of either sex be taken into consideration in arranging pay schedules? Do you agree with recent laws that require equal pay for equal work?

16. In the *Washington Post*, 5 June 1970, pp. B1 and 4, columnist Nicholas von Hoffman wrote:

> For an unknown, but undubitably large number of people, marriage isn't a comfort, a source of companionship or a means of sexual satisfaction. But they adhere to their affliction out of concern for their children, anxiety as to what other, probably unhappily married, people may say, or perhaps out of an undifferentiated sense of fear about changing their social status.
>
> The lucky ones continue to believe that marriage is a God-made sacrament; they, at least, can feel that the suffering of a joyless domesticity has religious merit. The rest of the unhappily married mitigate the pain with alcohol or make unsatisfactory trysts in motel rooms or pay good money to shrinks and marriage counselors in hopes that these professionals can voodoo them into liking what they hate. [Used by permission of the *Washington Post*.]

Von Hoffman proposes "abolishing the standard marriage form" and designing a marriage agreement that differs for each combination of parties. What social policy would you recommend for avoiding or dealing with the conditions he describes? Do you think his picture is overdrawn?

17. Some questions about the form that marriage and family should take turn upon the issues of which elements of our individual needs are of biological origin, which are of physiological origin, which are socially conditioned, and which spring from the interaction between these. What, if any differences between male and female roles in marriage do you think have legitimate roots in the physiological?

18. Some quite specific ethical questions, such as whether an unmarried girl may rightly obtain an abortion, turn upon more general ethical postulates, as pointed out earlier in this chapter. How do you think the soundness of these postulates ought to be decided? For example, how should one decide under what circumstances an abortion is a murder and under what circumstances the taking of life of an unborn child is a justified choice among otherwise unavoidable evils?

19. This chapter does not discuss current issues about the view we should take on homosexuality. What questions of fact and of ethical postulates do you see as critical in determining your personal view and a set of social policies with respect to homosexual behavior? For example, how can you best decide whether to view homosexuality *per se* as normal

and healthy or as a matter of illness or criminality? And if you take either view, what bearing does that view have upon your view of civil rights and the political rights of homosexuals?

20. Reference is made to the fact that different cultures and subcultures work from different postulates about what is good or right. How can a national community embracing quite different cultures respect them without creating unhappiness and unpredictability in marital and family life? An African government is reported recently to have recognized Christian, Buddhist, and Animist patterns of marriage as equally legitimate under its law. Should individuals in such a situation be required to opt for, and abide by, the whole of one or another of these codes?

SUGGESTED READINGS

Bach, George R. and Wyden, Peter. *The Intimate Enemy: How to Fight Fair in Love and Marriage.* New York: Avon Books, 1968.

Bartell, Gilbert D. *Group Sex: A Scientist's Eyewitness Report on Swinging in the Suburbs.* New York: Peter H. Wyden, 1970.

Bell, Robert R. *Premarital Sex in a Changing Society.* Englewood Cliffs, N.J.: Prentice-Hall, 1966.

Calderone, Mary. "It's Society That Is Changing Sexuality." *The Center Magazine* 5, no. 4 (July-August 1972):58–68.

Cuber, John F. with Harroff, Peggy B. *Sex and the Significant Americans: A Study of Sexual Behavior Among the Affluent.* Baltimore: Penguin Books, 1965.

Duvall, Evelyn Ruth, and Hill, Reuben, *Why Wait Till Marriage?* New York: Association Press, 1965.

Ellis, Albert. *The Art and Science of Love.* New York: Lyle Stuart, Publisher, 1965.

Fletcher, Joseph. *Morals and Medicine.* Boston: Beacon Press, 1960. Paperback. See chapters dealing with contraception, artificial insemination, sterilization.

Grummon, Donald L. and Barclay, Andrew M., eds. *Sexuality: A Search for Perspective.* New York: Van Nostrand Reinhold Co., 1971.

Hathorn, Raban; Genné, William H.; and Biell, Mordecai. *Marriage: An Interfaith Guide for All Couples.* New York: Association Press, 1970.

Landis, Judson T. and Mary G., eds. *Building a Successful Marriage.* 4th ed. Englewood Cliffs, N.J.: Prentice-Hall, 1963.

Masters, William H. and Johnson, Virginia E. *Human Sexual Response.* Boston; Little, Brown & Co., 1966.

McCary, James Leslie. *Human Sexuality: Physiological and Psychological Factors of Sexual Behavior.* New York: D. Van Nostrand Co., 1967.

Neubeck, Gerhard, ed. *Extra-Marital Relations.* Englewood Cliffs, N.J.: Prentice-Hall, 1969.

Noonan, John T., ed. *The Morality of Abortion.* Cambridge, Mass.: Harvard University Press, 1970.
O'Neill, Nena, and O'Neil, George. *Open Marriage: New Life Style for Couples.* New York: M. Evans & Co., 1972.
Otto, Herbert A., ed. *The Family in Search of a Future: Alternate Models for Moderns.* New York: Appleton–Century-Crofts, 1970.
Packard, Vance. *The Sexual Wilderness: The Contemporary Upheaval in Male-Female Relationships.* New York: Pocket Books, 1970.
Reiss, Ira L. *Premarital Sexual Standards in America.* New York: Free Press, 1964. Paperback.
Sagarin, Edward, ed. *Sex and the Contemporary American Scene.* Vol. 376. The Annals of the American Academy of Political and Social Science. Philadelphia: The Academy, 1968.
Spock, Benjamin. *A Teenager's Guide to Life and Love.* New York: Simon and Schuster, 1970.
Sussman, Marvin B., ed. *Sourcebook in Marriage and the Family.* Boston: Houghton Mifflin Co., 1963.
Wiseman, Jacqueline. *People As Partners: Individual and Family Relationships in Today's World.* San Francisco: Canfield Press, 1971.
Wynn, John Charles, ed. *Sexual Ethics and Christian Responsibility: Some Divergent Views.* New York: Association Press, 1970.

21
CULTURAL PLURALISM AND RACIAL JUSTICE

"We have left the comfortable land of assimilation and have been thrust into the outer darkness of ethnicity, and every tool that we have to gather information to find our way was designed for a world of assimilation and integration. Our government, our economic system, our educational system and the basic documents of our society are built on other premises than those which we are coming to recognize today." This was spoken by Vine Deloria, Jr., a Sioux Indian, to a Smithsonian Institution symposium[1] on protest and change. His thesis was that the melting-pot concept of America is dead. One reason is the awareness that respect for persons is not genuine unless it also embodies respect for their cultures. Assimilation melts away distinctiveness of cultures, making an amalgam, a single new monolithic culture. If integration of races and cultures means assimilation, if it means a melting-pot world, then it does not respect differences of culture but destroys them. According to this idea, only those persons who fit into the new amalgam can be respected. However, the acceptance of assimilation as an ideal is declining, for choice is at the heart of individuality and personality, and assimilationism denies such choice. A homogenized world would be a world without the most crucial choices of all, the choice of life style and of the context within which one can work out his individuality.

Deloria was saying something further also—that the American majority has imposed upon its minorities an ethnically colored culture

[1] November 20, 1970.

which suppresses them, denigrates their intelligence and worth, and denies them the opportunity of other citizens to integrity in their personal and cultural development. As Michael Kernan argues, the ideal of the melting pot is in practice not a culturally neutral ideal but gives respect only to a dominant subculture into which all others are expected to "melt." The very ideal of the melting pot is thus undemocratic in conception and oppressive in its implementation; those with power imagine themselves as servants to public demand but are clothed by institutions and customs which securely shield them from hearing and heeding the groups which do not already share the values and priorities of the powerful.[2]

At the very moment when federal authority is increasingly used to enforce desegregation, ethnic minorities are beginning to have spokesmen who demand "their own turf." We do not want to be incorporated into your society, they say. Nor do we want you intruding uninvited upon our territory, for we want our own music, our own dialect in our own schools, our own ways of organizing our business and our community life. We cannot have these if we are admitted into your society and its institutions only on your terms. If we enter on those terms, only our color is preserved. Our character and our ways of being are surrendered and exchanged for yours. And we find yours not to our tastes, even in some respects offensive to our sense of right and good.

How can people who see their cultures as so unmixable, so mutually conflicting, live together in mutual respect? Are the conflicts and the contrasts as sharp and as pervasive as Deloria and Kernan see them? And if they are, are we condemned to dominate or destroy one another rather than live together in peace? In a time when men can no longer effectively live apart within a nation's boundaries and soon within the planet's confines, these are critical questions. The questions involve a tangle of subquestions about the concepts and the conduct of education, government, justice, the arts, even the styles and priorities of life.

On college campuses the clash between the ideal of assimilation and that of cultural pluralism began to emerge in America in the mid-1960s. Campuses which had previously admitted only token proportions of Negro, Mexican American, Puerto Rican, or American Indian students started to have sufficient clusters to generate small enclaves of "Blacks," "Chicanos," or other ethnic minorities with an emerging self-definition of their own. The blacks considered Negroes as "Uncle Toms." Those minority students who shared the dominant values of their campus felt that their race was being discredited by their new compatriots'

---

[2]Michael Kernan, "Dissecting Sociologists," *Washington Post,* 21 November 1970, pp. C1 and C2.

militancy and their rejection of accepted standards. Hostility rose, both within the racial groups and between the new clusters and the dominant cultures. Demands crystallized: for black studies programs; for admission of larger proportions of black students; for black faculty to teach those students; for funds to finance both the students and the programs; and for autonomy in the selection of faculty, the certification of studies, and the screening of students. Sometimes the demands were polite requests. Sometimes they came with threats of bombing and burning. As they met with response, generally affirmative though often scaled down and accompanied by critique of the militants' methods, the campuses began to experience counterattack both from the surrounding community and from within. The community insisted upon law and order even if it meant denial of the essence of the demands for self-determination and a new approximation to justice. Within the university, the counterattack often centered upon the reassertion of traditional standards of scholarship and intellectuality, and the contention that the new programs and procedures were an abandonment of the universal values inherent in higher education.

These developments on college campuses coincided with a critical point in the belated effort of federal authorities to enforce the 1954 ruling of the Supreme Court on desegregation of public elementary and secondary schools. A new Civil Rights law of 1964 was interpreted to forbid black dormitories in college as well as segregated bus stations and country clubs. Governor Wallace of Alabama found himself a bedfellow of black militants in resisting the federal directives on racial integration. From the perspective of federal administrators, there was no difference between separatism that was self-chosen or imposed by segregationists: it was forbidden by law in public facilities and in enterprises using the public monies. From the perspective of the rising ethnic groups, the difference between Southern segregation and self-determining ethnic groups was the difference between oppression and freedom.

Faced with the overwhelming force of majority public opinion and federal authority, the advocates of ethnic self-determination began to explore alternative strategies. Some turned to extreme violence: bombing, kidnapping of officials, shoot-outs in court and on the streets, rioting. Others sought to join the forces of different minorities, from ethnic groups (blacks, Chicanos, Appalachian whites, Puerto Ricans) to women's liberation, in order to redefine the fight as one for revolutionary change in the inherently repressive and oppressive institutions of the dominant society. Still others chose a definition of self-determination much closer to a strategy of making room for individual distinctiveness within a basic pattern of cultural assimilation. Yet another strategy argues "the necessity of working the system, of using for our own goals the levers it provides, the issues that are current and the temporary coalitions we can form with other groups within it." But it also holds to "our authentic and legitimate anger with the system."[3] In short, it seeks to preserve ethnic identity within a coherent but pluralistic society.

The campus-community encounter about cultural pluralism is a microcosm of the larger issues of coexistence of cultures in cities, nations, and world at large. The encounter cannot be adequately described from within any one of the conflicting points of view. To hear from them all, however, will be necessary if we are to experience the meaning of a society of relatively distinctive and autonomous subcultures which must nevertheless interact in vital ways if they are to survive and serve the fulfillment of all the members of our society.

DISCRIMINATION IN AMERICA TODAY

The meaning of the aspiration toward a just and pluralistic society can hardly be understood without at least a glimpse of the chasm which separates present-day America from that goal. More than one hundred years after the Civil War and almost two decades after the Supreme Court's historic ruling on school desegregation, the ethnic minorities are still far from achieving justice or equal rights. In explaining its decision to prepare a special issue, "Black America, 1970," *Time* said: "This remains the biggest single problem in America, and its greatest shame."[4] Unless these conditions are rectified, our civilization may destroy itself in violence and repression.

What are the dimensions of this injustice? And what are the directions of change with respect to it? Studies abound concerning these questions. In differing forms, they tell much the same story. In jobs and income, for example, the gap between black and white is very large, though less than one and two decades ago. The median family income for Negroes rose from 54 percent of that of whites to 60 percent between 1965 and 1968. It was much higher in the North Central and Western states and lower elsewhere. The proportion of Negro families below the poverty level (if defined as $3,553 for a nonfarm family of four in 1968 dollars) dropped from 48 to 29 percent between 1959 and 1968. The wages of blacks tend to run considerably lower than those of whites. The black person with four years of high school has a lower average earning than that of the white with only eight years

---

[3]Sterling Tucker, *For Blacks Only* (Grand Rapids, Mich.: William B. Eerdmans Publishing Co., 1971), pp. 206–207.
[4]6 April 1970, p. 13.

of elementary education. Because of lower pay and more seasonal or part-time employment, black families often need two or more wage earners to accrue as much as white families with only one employed member. (In the country as a whole today the average household has 1.7 wage-earners.)

In housing, black Americans pay more rent than whites for similar housing and are much more likely to live in substandard buildings, in slums, and in high density areas. Poverty and racial discrimination have both worked as barriers to open housing or to equal access to the same housing on equal terms. Governmental efforts have often backfired or worked out to worsen the situation though presented initially as intended to remedy the discrimination. For example, since World War II the federal government has financed only about eight hundred thousand urban dwelling units while insuring the financing of some ten million suburban homes.[5]

Segregation and discrimination continue to characterize education, where in some respects the opposition to racial equality has been less and the support for integration stronger than in housing. As of 1970 some 75 percent of Southern black children still went to schools that were 95 percent or more black. Still 40 percent of Southern black children were in partly integrated schools, (including many with less than 5 percent of whites) as compared with only about 1 percent in 1964. This report signifies a ten-year delay in the South in getting under way with school desegregation after the 1954 Supreme Court order. The recent change has been rapid but still has a long way to go. At the same time the North in some respects is beginning to resist school integration more overtly than ever before. Poverty, discrimination, and segregation combine to plague minorities in education. As this decade began, only about 58 percent of black children completed eighth grade, as compared with 73 percent of white children. Only about 40 percent of black teen-agers graduate from high school as compared with 62 percent of whites. About 6.4 percent of undergraduates in college are black. While blacks make up some 11 percent of the population, they account for an estimated 1 percent of doctoral candidates, and less than 3 percent of either law students or medical students.

When injustice strikes, the police and the courts should be a source of redress. But for blacks "law and order" seemed in the late 1960s a shorthand message promising repression of the black community. They are arrested three to four times more frequently than whites and, once arrested, are more likely to be jailed rather than bailed, convicted than acquitted, and likely to get heavier sentences for the same offenses.

---

[5]Ibid., p. 53.

Poverty is again a factor: few blacks can afford skilled lawyers. The victims of black crime are also mostly black; for example, black women are eighteen times as likely to be raped as whites.

Low income, poor education, bad housing, and uneven justice are major factors in spawning the further problems of the city ghetto. There are almost as many black drug addicts as white, though there are nine times as many whites in the population. There are more than six times as many illegitimate children per thousand blacks as whites. There are over three times as many fatherless black households as white. Black admissions to public mental institutions are double those for whites. Though white suicide rates are more than double those for blacks generally, the black male rate in big city ghettoes has been estimated as double the white because of "a sense of despair, a feeling that life will never be satisfying."[6]

Although not every phase of American life is as bleak as these crucial ones of jobs and income, housing, education, legal justice, mental health, and family cohesiveness, the marks of segregation and discrimination rooted in race are everywhere. Segregation has not even been rooted out of the churches, though it is diminishing sharply. Interracial dating is increasing, but statistical studies on the point are scarce. Some sports (golf, skiing, tennis, and auto racing) are still almost exclusively white, although in the major American sports (baseball, football, basketball) the black athlete has come to the fore rapidly. Progress is being made in the number of Negroes holding elective public office (mayors, legislators, school-board members, law-enforcement officials, and so on) and in voting power. The voting increase, however, was less than a million by the 1968 presidential election (from 6,345,000 in 1966).[7]

The pattern of discrimination has varied from race to race and from one ethnic group to another, but racial prejudice is deep in the culture.

RACIAL DIFFERENCES AND SOURCES OF TENSION

Racial tensions have disturbed human relations for many years. When there are observable physiological differences, problems tend to be accentuated. Certain writers maintain that there are superior and inferior races. Since the superior race is a later product of evolution, crossbreeding tends to produce progeny of a lower type, they argue. According to many of these writers, the Nordic is the white man par excellence; but when he mixes with inferior groups, the result of the

---

[6]Ibid., p. 65.
[7]Ibid., p. 27.

union is a race that reverts to a lower type. Consequently, they vigorously condemn racial mixture and the melting-pot theory.[8]

Most anthropologists and students of racial problems, however, tell us that there are no pure and unmixed races existing at present, since all peoples at an earlier or later time appear to have undergone some racial mixture. There is no evidence that inter-mixture produces an inferior type. Similar intellectual capacities and emotional attitudes are found among all groups of people. The association of race—considered as a group of hereditary, biological traits—with certain customs and cultural traits may result from historical circumstances and cultural diffusion.[9] Some writers, in addition to pointing out that "all human beings are hybrid as this term is used by geneticists," indicate that there is evidence that the crossing of different strains may result in a "greater occurrence of hybrid vigor."[10] Identification of races by such criteria as texture and color of skin or hair, nasal form, stature, and shape of head or eyes is only approximate, because there is much overlapping. The differences are caused in part at least, by long periods of selection under diverse environmental conditions.

An examination of the evidence indicates that, if there are differences between racial groups, they are slight. One race during one period may have a few more men of exceptional ability than another race, but the great masses of people in any two racial groups are comparatively equal. It is also well to keep in mind that the status of a race at any particular time is no sure indication of its possibilities. Only recently have certain Western peoples been in the vanguard of civilization. When we consider national groups, this fact is very clear. Witness the status of Japan a few generations ago and just prior to World War II. Whatever the difference between racial groups, it is evident that the difference between individuals in any one racial group is very much greater. There is certainly no justification for contending that all the members of one group are superior to all the members of any other group. Anthropologist Stanley Diamond states that:

---

[8]See the writings of Madison Grant, Lothrop Stoddard, Edward A. Ross, Wesley Critz George, Carleton Putnam, and Audrey Shuey, and the racial views of the Nazi leaders of Germany and the leaders of the apartheid movement in South Africa.

[9]See the books of Franz Boas, R. H. Lowie, R. E. Park, Francis J. Brown and Joseph S. Roucek, Ralph L. Beals and Harry Hoijer, G. E. Simpson and J. M. Yinger, Charles Marden and Gladys Meyer, and Gunnar Myrdal. For a reply to those who say that some races are inferior, see *Race and Intelligence*, Melvin M. Tumin, ed. (New York: Anti-Defamation League of B'nai B'rith, 1963.)

[10]Ralph L. Beals and Harry Hoijer, *An Introduction to Anthropology* (New York, MacMillan Co., 1953), p. 75.

All of the historical and psychological evidence scrutinized by anthropologists leads to one conclusion: there is no differential capacity for the creation and maintenance of culture on the part of any population large enough to be sensibly called a race, in the traditional sense of that term. Mongoloids, Negroids and Caucausoids have been physically and culturally inter-fertile throughout the history of modern mankind. Moreover, none of these groups is exclusively associated with any given cultural phenomenon. Nor has any genetically based differential capacity in intelligence among these major populations ever been established. On the contrary, the doctrine of racial equality is fully supported by scientific and historical inquiry.[11]

PREJUDICE: ITS ROOTS AND ITS EFFECTS

In an earlier chapter we listed prejudice among the obstacles to thinking. Here we need to ask what the basis of prejudice is, and why it is found in some form among men everywhere. While particular or specific prejudices are acquired during the process of our development and training and are not born in us, a propensity to prejudice is found in man's self-centeredness, self-interest, and self-love. A number of writers, including philosophers, theologians, and historians such as Arnold Toynbee, have called our attention to the problems created by self-centeredness in man's life. Each man tends to see himself as the center of the universe and to regard his own interests as primary.[12]

Prejudice is thus in a sense part of the primordial nature of man and part of the struggle between the self and the nonself. It is one side of man's nature—an aggressive self-assertiveness—that easily becomes hostile when anything gets in its way and frustrates its desires. If anything can rightly be called "original sin," it is this tendency for each man to see himself as the center of the world.

A prejudice is a mental bias that, when not kept in control, leads one to make a judgment in advance without examination of the evidence. After it develops and becomes set, it is "absolutely rigid against all rational assaults; it flows around and by-passes the facts; it passes through argument and refutation, however sound and convincing, as though they did not exist."[13] Since prejudice is based on deep, internal, emotional elements in man's nature and is not arrived at through

---

[11] Stanley Diamond, "A Statement on Racism," *Current Anthropology* 4 (June 1963): 323.

[12] In the discussion of prejudice, discrimination, and segregation that follows, the authors have been influenced by the excellent discussion of these topics by Kyle Haselden, *The Racial Problem in Christian Perspective* (New York: Harper & Row, Publishers, Torchbook, 1964).

[13] Ibid., p. 79.

rational processes, it is difficult to uproot it by intellectual appeals and the marshaling of evidence.

Prejudices are of many kinds: racial prejudice, class prejudice, religious bigotry, social snobbery, rabid nationalism, and so on. Note the following "in-group" and "out-group" relationships in which the "superior" in-group scorned the "inferior" out-group: Greeks and barbarians; Jews and Gentiles; Christians and pagans; Nazis and non-Aryans; whites and Negroes. This list could be indefinitely extended. Prejudices arise and are directed most easily toward those who differ from us. For this reason prejudice can develop readily in the realm of race relations, especially when there are visible differences. If we are not accustomed to people of different color, physique, speech, and habits, we feel a sense of strangeness and sometimes antipathy in their presence. Race prejudice is closely related to class prejudice and is intensified by economic competition. If John Doe, a member of the white race, loses his position and it is filled by a member of his own race, he may feel resentment but no racial prejudice. On the other hand, if John Smith, a Negro, gets his position, not only does John Doe feel resentment against his successor but he may show this resentment in an attack on John Smith's race.

Where there are differences of race, class, or religion, we tend to make hasty generalizations. After an unfortunate experience with one person we may transfer our resentment to those who associate with that individual or to the groups to which he belongs. After a trip around the world one man had a strong dislike for the Chinese but admired the Japanese because of pleasant contacts he had made in certain Japanese cities and an unfortunate experience he had had in a Chinese port.

For most people racial prejudice arises from contact with other people who are themselves prejudiced or from some unfortunate contact with a member of another race. Children are given prejudices by hearing the remarks and observing the attitudes of parents, nurses, and other children. If they are told that they must not associate with Jews, Italians, Orientals, or Negroes, or if unpleasant names are used in describing those groups, prejudice is almost certain to arise. Slogans often create unwholesome attitudes in people, and even "innocent" racial jokes reinforce these attitudes.

Racial prejudice is one of the most serious evils in our social life. Under its emotional drive, men attempt to justify cruelty, violence, and numerous other forms of inhumanity. Laws may be flouted, and the administration of justice may be made ridiculous. In their misdirected zeal to attain a superior status, the members of one racial group may disfranchise the citizens of another race and even encourage the continuance of ignorance and of wretched social conditions.

When prejudice is present, the way has been prepared for discrimination—the denial of rights or privileges on grounds that are irrelevant as far as the fundamental nature of man is concerned. Thus we find some men paying taxes, defending their country, helping build its institutions and services, and then being excluded from voting, from many municipal services such as libraries, schools, parks, golf links, swimming pools, and the like, and from many places catering to the public such as hotels, motels, and restaurants. Then, to justify discrimination, fictions are built up, such as that all Negroes are natively inferior and therefore incapable of participating fully in the functions of society, that all Orientals are deceitful and not to be trusted, or that foreigners are unclean and therefore to be avoided.

Stereotyping goes along with prejudice and discrimination and, in attributing to all members of the group characteristics that have been observed (or imagined) in only one or a few, denies the individuality and uniqueness of the members of the group. Such an approach is an assault on the integrity and personality of the individuals in the group so maligned and a denial of the sacredness of personality. By means of stereotypes the frailties and vices of some are applied to the group as a whole.

Whereas discrimination has to do with the separation of people from things and conditions to which they are entitled, segregation is the isolation or separation of one people from another people on the basis of irrelevant circumstances. It has to do with the right to belong, and it separates people on the basis of capricious and arbitrary considerations. To separate the sick from the healthy for purposes of treatment, children or young people from adult society for purposes of education, professional societies from society in general so that they may carry on their special functions is normal and moral. There are many relationships from which we can exclude people because they do not qualify—from our family circle, from a flying club if they have no knowledge and experience in this field, from a university if they do not meet entrance requirements. However, to exclude people from groups merely on the basis of skin color, race, or national origin is to segregate them for conditions that are irrelevant and over which they have no control. Such exclusion is immoral and unjust. If people meet all the conditions for belonging to a group—a church, a union, a political party, a profession, and the like—to exclude them on the basis of race is a denial of the rights of personality and is damaging to the inner being of both those who exclude and those excluded.

Many people in our society do not stop to realize the injustice and cruelty they needlessly and perhaps thoughtlessly inflict by going along with, or failing to protest against, an entrenched power structure that prevents the members of various minority groups from developing their capabilities as persons. If the public schools, libraries, hospitals, and churches in a community were destroyed by fire, tornado, or other disaster, such people would say that they had suffered a great misfortune, perhaps even a calamity. Yet these same people sometimes deprive a section of the community of the use of these facilities because of race alone.

A CHALLENGE TO A RACIST SOCIAL ORDER

As the conscience of America has gradually begun to awaken to the injustice of using irrelevant conditions such as racial identity as a basis for excluding people from opportunity or denying them rights, and as some of the most blatant forms of discrimination have been beaten back in some places, a deeper form of discrimination has been disclosed: namely, the habit of defining the conditions for opportunity and rights in a way that has the effect of racial discrimination. When such conditions pervade the institutions of a society, it is "racist." If, for example, admission to college is subject to the condition of scoring high on tests that give an advantage to people of suburban schooling and affluent families, which schooling and families are denied to some by virtue of circumstances arising out of earlier or continuing racial bias, then the institutional patterns of college admission are racist. If access to superior elementary and secondary schools is available only to those who live in certain neighborhoods, and access to those neighborhoods is cut off or restricted by the history of racial prejudice in the area, then our society operates a racist system in that respect. If advancement in the building trades rests upon seniority, and the history of the building trades is one of craft unionism which in turn mirrored the racial biases of earlier decades, then job opportunity in that field is colored by a racist system.

Some of the racist structures of our whole society are inadvertent. For example, relative to their share of the population, a very small proportion of Negroes, Chicanos, and American Indians are doctors or lawyers (the same applies to many professions). No one wants to be represented by an unqualified lawyer or treated by an inadequately trained physician. So the professional standards of these groups have, in effect, limited the entry of ethnic minority groups which have had limited access to medical and law schools, which in turn selectively choose the most accomplished graduates of colleges. Eventually this chain leads to the racist patterns of access to schools and colleges.

Other of the racist structures of the society are deliberate. Some professional schools have deliberately denied or restricted entry to

Jews at times. The same applies to blacks. When such deliberate patterns combine with the inadvertent ones, the effect is overwhelming. Moreover, the inadvertant patterns are much harder to attack and remove than are the more direct and public forms of discrimination.

Awareness of this problem has grown sharply among minority groups and among their majority advocates during the past decade. With that growing awareness there has grown a conviction that the entire social order must be redesigned if prejudice is to be rooted out and justice given a chance. Redesign is too tame a word for the feelings of some: they call for revolution, either in a sweeping nonviolent overthrow of the structure and leadership of the society, or by whatever means necessary—a euphemism in some usages for organized violence.

By far the largest body of advocates of fundamental social reform is found among people who would be repelled by the idea of using organized violence to achieve the end. The concern about racism, for example, came to the 183rd General Assembly of the United Presbyterian Church in May 1971. This is certainly no radical forum. A committee report called "A Study of Racism and Repression" pointed out that racial inequality and injustice must be viewed in a larger context. The committee recounted that in the late 1960s "forces in the Black and Brown communities... began to raise critical questions concerning the viability of the political and economic systems of the United States in which racism had become institutionalized and beyond the remedy of the orderly processes of law."[14] Similarly Preston Wilcox of Afram Associates, a consulting firm in community development, contends that the master-slave relationship continues to be enforced under the camouflages of professional-client, supervisor-worker, teacher-student, policeman-citizen, and judge-offender relationships. By attributing current injustices and problems to social class differentials or by assuming as a white prerogative the responsibility for alleviating the condition of blacks, he says, we deny the reality of racism and thus entrench it. We justify the pattern by defining blacks as in need of training, as unqualified, as without credentials, as inexperienced. We do so, he argues, because we have a need to be superior, which is, of course, a deep-seated root of bias. So deeply rooted are this pattern and this need, he concludes, that "the myth of white supremacy is essential to the American scene."[15]

If, as these so divergent sources concur, the specific injustices here

---

[14]Quoted in Valerie Russell, "The Justice Question—What's It All About," in *Justice in America* (New York: National Student YWCA), p. 1.

[15]Preston Wilcox, "Social Policy and White Racism," *Social Policy* (May/June 1970): 42.

cited are generated by an underlying system, then removal of one set of specific injustices will simply be followed by regeneration of other and perhaps graver forms of oppression. For example, as minorities have assumed power in some major metropolitan areas, political boundaries are sometimes enlarged to diminish the influence of the minority vote. As the poor begin to be provided competent legal services by hard-hitting, well-trained cadres of young attorneys, the young attorneys come under attack, their licenses are threatened, the source of their funds is diverted or put under different leadership or a different agency. As the courts begin to take notice of injustice that once went unchecked, their power to clean out the evil is checked by racism rampant within police forces and law enforcement agencies. As these problems are attacked, the cry arises that law and order are threatened.

SEARCHING FOR A WAY TOWARD RACIAL JUSTICE

What should be done about bias and injustice that pervades a society and persists as does racial bias in America today? A consensus on this question is far in the future, if possible at all. Yet the "territory" within which to seek it and act for it may be getting clearer. A first step in that direction is one of elimination of some options.

For a time in the late 1960s a substantial number of both white and minority people entertained the idea that a violent revolution in America might be the only hope for racial justice. Their reasons were expressed in many different ways, often violent and vituperative. In its most cogent form, however, the argument was twofold: (1) Many Americans believed in or wanted racial inequality. Though it was but is no longer considered right to admit to such bias, the revolutionaries contended, the fact is that it is rampant. The evidence was the groundswell of response that emerged when any figure such as George Wallace found a language and a style in which the bias could be openly expressed without explicitly violating the social taboos. (2) Almost all but the oppressed minorities benefit from the fruits of discrimination. When pressed to surrender these unearned spoils, they fight the change, either knowing their tainted gain and being unwilling to forego it, or blind to its roots and acting as unwitting instruments of the oppression.

This argument for violence, however, seems to have lost the day. And the reasons for this defeat, also subject to many different formulations, can be put in a few summary propositions.

1. A violent minority cannot win. As a sheer practical matter, the majority has overwhelming numbers, and it has overwhelming resources

with which to suppress. Both the police and the military can be counted upon to suppress any organized violence that reaches dimensions threatening the social order. Both have seen measures to cleanse their bias during the past decade, and the military has probably been the more aggressive in such efforts; but the very advocates of minority violence are the first to accuse these agencies that enforce order of being ready to align themselves on the side of a prejudiced social order.

The impracticality of violent revolution would suffice to turn most people against it. Also, our society is increasingly committed to nonviolence. This may seem a strange saying in a culture of which it is said that "Violence is as American as apple pie." Yet the trend of evolution of our society is toward methods of solution of social problems that at least avoid massive killing and armed clashes. Tolerance is increasing for letting property be destroyed rather than kill to prevent the loss. Such attitudes seem to run ahead of performance, in part probably because the means of achieving resolution of conflict without violence are still little understood. As recent events make clear, the threat of violence unites the biased and the unwitting beneficiaries of bias in the concern for safety and security. Indeed, the ethnic minority communities themselves suffer most from the violence, and in a time of some gains in income, housing, schooling, and other areas of inequality, they are reluctant to risk these gains. Moreover, the black community does not in its majority any more believe in such violent rebellion than does the white community.

2. While neither the white nor the black community in America can be viewed as pacifist, there are growing minorities which turn increasingly toward reliance upon nonviolence. Martin Luther King, Jr. gave his life for this cause and, in spite of his martyrdom, or because of it, second thoughts have echoed some of his own last words. Those who take up violence, he pointed out, as Jesus and Gandhi had said earlier, turn it upon themselves and their own. Violence, moreover, is by its nature a use of irrelevant arguments to win one's own way. It creates a habit that is contagious and can utterly destroy the foundation upon which complex social problems can be solved; namely, the analysis of their causes and the rooting out of those causes. This point, rather than pacifism as such, bears most cogently upon the search for a way toward racial justice. Violence does not help us find that way. We must get onto it without further waste of time and resources.

If violence is no answer, what then? Nonviolence is really only a name for the array of all other possibilities, and it is clear that more of those possibilities are blind alleys than not. Where are we to seek for a better way?

There is widespread agreement among ethnic minority leaders, who otherwise differ radically, that their peoples should gain control over the internal affairs of their own communities. This objective is seen, for example, as calling for blacks to choose their own leaders, to identify the decisions themselves which only they can make, to gather their own data about themselves and about the larger society, and to do so on terms and about questions and within frameworks of their own choice. The objective also calls for gaining a variety of forms of power: for example, greater economic power through more employment at better paying jobs, through ownership, or through changes in the laws that affect the distribution of income and the control of public resources; greater political power and influence through voter registration, election of public officials, enlargement of access to appointive positions, more effective caucuses, and so on; greater intellectual influence through more widespread and better education, through leadership roles in education, through scholarship that influences the major modes of thinking of the culture, and the like.

The same strategy is proposed also for other ethnic minorities. Self-determination, however, will not and cannot be given to people; they must generate it. Others can and should do what they can to facilitate this change. Freedom, however, in the nature of the case, is not something one is allowed to have but is a right and a way of being and thinking that one exercises oneself.

The proposed empowerment and enfranchisement transcends the type of arguments that used to rage between liberals and Marxists as to whether the vote or the dollar controls. Without money, votes can be toothless. Without votes, economic resources can be diverted from their intended ends. Moreover, the holds on influence and power must be made to work together. Thus empowerment is many-faceted. The way toward equality is not simple or even clear. It has to be invented not only with great energy but also with great imagination and with powerful aid from information and analysis of causes and connections.

There are, however, dilemmas about how to empower and enfranchise the minorities. For example, does enlarging the power of some diminish that of others? There are ways of sharing means and power which surely have this effect. If the minorities fight one another over a limited pool of federal funds, they not only diminish one another's shares but also use up much of the share in their conflict. If they conceive their task as one of taking away from the majority to gain their own due, this strategy is limited in its yield by the willingness of the numerically superior whites to share in this way. But if their strategy is to enlarge the pool of resources to be shared among all by a form of society that uses its full potential and yet to share more equitably, then they both allow the majority to welcome the change and gain for themselves both quantitatively and proportionately more.

A second dilemma has to do with how to bring about enfranchisement in a still racist context. In the late 1960s an effort was made at federal level to attack some of the roots of this systemic bias through community action programs in which it was required that at least one-third of the voting members of boards with control over use of federal funds would be elected by low-income people to be served by the programs. In city after city, the intent of this legislation was defeated by a variety of responses and tactics, some of which were well intended but as devastating to the purpose as if they had been deliberately meant to oppress.

A third dilemma about achieving self-determination has to do with the fact that today self-determination, as we said at the outset of this chapter, is not just a matter of individual rights but also one of cultural rights. In a complex and highly interdependent society, no one is altogether free of others. Self-determination occurs within interdependence, which qualifies the independence involved. The self-determination sought, of course, is the same that other citizens enjoy or should enjoy. One problem with this goal is that some of the present options exercised by the majority are sources of the injustice to minorities and should be eliminated. For example, a developer with large capital can buy up large blocks of inner city housing, influence zoning authorities to grant favorable zoning, and raze homes without replacement, with severe hardship and injustices to those affected. A second difficulty with interdependent self-determination for ethnic groups is the problem of how to achieve equality of benefits and cultural pluralism at the same time. Consider a controversy which in 1972 had reached a high pitch—that about school busing in both Southern and Northern metropolitan areas. Because the inner city is racially segregated, some federal judges have ruled that school districts must be treated as if they embraced a large enough area to permit racial balance by busing black pupils to schools in predominantly white areas of housing and vice versa. Since desegregation was found to be itself a cause of discrimination, and discrimination a factor in producing poor education, some courts hold that the right to equality in education requires this action under the present circumstances. The counterarguments are loud and complex. Whatever resolution the immediate issue may have, there are those who contend that in the long run it will be necessary, instead of tackling issues like school segregation and slum problems one by one, to undertake comprehensive planning of metropolitan areas. In a recent television story about the Richmond, Virginia busing decision, for example, one commentator contended that a model solution can be seen in the new town of Columbia, Maryland, which has neighborhood schools of interracial makeup with better than average education, peaceful conditions, and mutual benefit for the different racial groups. But this solution depends on the fact that the city was planned from the outset to be "open" on housing and to have schools centrally located in neighborhoods which are naturally interracial. If this answer was widely adopted, would it make for the end of distinctively black subcommunities? Or would black consciousness and black self-determination be possible for the wider Negro "community" even though this was not expressed by separatism in housing or schooling?

Race is not a relevant basis for the determination of opportunity or rights, we say; yet it is relevant to one's identity both as an individual and as a member of a cultural group. What then is the way toward racial justice and racial equality? It will be nonviolent in essence, whatever episodes of violence may mark the struggle. It will function by means of empowerment of the minorities, but a mode of empowerment that for the most part enlarges opportunity and fulfillment for all rather than diminishing some for the benefit of others. It will face and meet the dilemmas of interdependence, of reconciling individual priorities and choice of identity with the potentialities of cultural diversity. It will meet the practical problems of using some of the structures of a racist society to dismantle those other structures that perpetuate the evil. This will not be a sunny, blissful, easy, or pretty path. It will be strewn with costs and casualties. But it is a path that must be taken.

QUESTIONS AND PROJECTS

1. What specific forms does racial discrimination take in your community and on your campus? What explanations or justifications are offered for each of these forms of discrimination? Which of the justifications seem to you to express bias? Which reflect racism in the structures of the society, as distinguished from direct and overt bias? What do you see as the most effective ways to attack the discrimination in the light of your analysis of its nature and causes?
2. This chapter draws its illustrations of racial discrimination largely from the conditions affecting blacks in the United States. Choose another ethnic minority, such as Chicanos, American Indians, or Puerto Ricans in the United States, and prepare an analysis of the effects of discrimination upon that group.
3. In the recent book *Why Can't They Be Like Us? America's White Ethnic Groups* (New York: E. P. Dutton & Co., 1971), author Andrew W. Greeley argues that self-created ethnic "turfs" may be legitimate and helpful means of fostering pluralism and diversity in the society. Naomi

Bliven contends, on the contrary, that such ghettoes, whether imposed or self-elected, create "multiple apartheid," tucking people into "ethnic and racial Bantustans" where there is not diversity, but homogeneity. Ethnicity, she argues, has been a refuge of the second-rate. Loyalty to one's own kind is "an insufficient virtue." ("E Pluribus What?" *New Yorker,* 20 November 1971, pp. 225–226, 228–229.) How do you view this issue? If self-chosen "territory" creates worse problems than it solves, how would you seek to preserve the values of cultural pluralism and of respect for one's own ethnic roots and identity? If ethnic turf is on balance good, how can it be prevented from fostering racial isolation and new forms of bias rooted in ignorance, noncommunication, and unfamiliarity?

4. A recent essay, "On Being White in America" (in *Interact,* bulletin of the Columbia, Maryland Cooperative Ministry, 1972) discusses the difficulties of being a member of a dominant majority and wanting to live without racial bias. The position of the white man adds up, one black woman said, to having no soul at all, no sensitivity, conscience, goodwill, or human decency. What do your peers experience as their own problems resulting from the built-in biases of the society?

5. Vivian W. Henderson, President of Clark College in Atlanta, has written: "One of the dilemmas . . . faced by predominantly Negro colleges is that the social and racial context within which they were founded and nurtured . . . is of a passing order." For most of their duration they have functioned within "a social structure built upon concepts of racial dualism, racial segregation, white supremacy, and racial inferiority of black people." ["The Black College: A Look Down the Road," AACTE Bulletin 24, no. 8 (November 1971): 1.] Dr. Henderson argues for a continuation of these colleges, but with a redesigned, still distinctive purpose. How do you analyze the values and the disadvantages of colleges which, though open to all, serve a predominantly minority clientele of one ethnic origin? Are the advantages and disadvantages substantially different for college students than for elementary school children? Why do you appraise them as you do?

6. In testimony before the Senate Select Committee on Equal Educational Opportunity, Dr. Kenneth B. Clark of the College of the City of New York contended (April 20, 1970) that segregated schooling is more damaging to white children than to minority group children. There is, he said, "an increasing minority of white youngsters that are rebelling against all the values they see as favored by a hypocritical establishment that preaches democracy and imposes the cruelty of racial segregation." Segregated schools, he continues, destroy the moral sensitivity of white children. (*New York Times,* 21 April 1970.) Do you find evidence of these two problems (rebelliousness against all values and diminished sensitivity) among your own peers? In view of the difficulties encountered in desegregating schools, how do you think the deleterious effects of segregation should be attacked? What steps would you favor with regard to further or faster desegregation?

7. The Kerner Report [Report of the National Advisory Commission on Civil Disorders (New York: Bantam Books, 1968)] stated: "This is our basic conclusion: Our nation is moving toward two societies, one black, one white—separate and unequal." Neil H. Jacoby of the Center for the Study of Democratic Institutions sharply disputed this conclusion: "If you look at equality in terms of civil rights—in terms of school integration, voting participation, office-holding and that sort of thing—the indisputable facts show the same movement *toward* equality." (*A Center Occasional Paper*, December 1970.) Another commentator saw the trend toward separatism as one of sentiment and self-definition rather than one of specific economic and social discrepancies. What is your estimate of the trend toward or away from equality and separatism today?
8. Interracial marriages were, as of the late 1960s, still forbidden in eighteen states, according to the *New York Times*. Attorney Andrew D. Weinberg has estimated that there are about fifty thousand Negro-white marriages in the United States. Dr. Thomas L. Brayboy, a psychiatrist, contends that deep-seated psychological sicknesses underlie the majority of black-white marriages today. The roots of these problems, he said, are in white guilt and fears and Negro desire for revenge. As race relations improve he expected the proportion of healthy black-white marriages to increase. How could a couple estimate the likely impact of bias in the environment upon their own marriage? How could they avoid or mitigate unwanted conflicts in the marriage that were caused by racism in the environment?
9. Will Herberg contends [*The Intercollegiate Review* 7, no. 5 (Summer 1971): 207–214] that talk of racism will get us nowhere in remedying racial injustice. The Negroes should, he insists, be viewed as simply the last of the great masses of immigrants (in this case immigrating within the country into cities). Other immigrant groups have moved upward socially into middle class equality by slow accumulation of means and status, and their racial distinctiveness (as with Sicilians, Japanese, and others) has ceased to be a concern once they became "our type of people." He contends that governmental paternalism hinders, rather than helps, such upward mobility. What likenesses and differences do you see between the situation faced by black "immigrants" and others? Whether you agree or not with Herberg's suggested strategy, what evaluation do you make of a policy that treats an ethnic minority (whether American Indians or Negroes or some other) as a ward of the state?
10. Critics of the United States frequently make its racial inequality the first target of their criticism. Make a study of one or more countries (1) recently experiencing racial strife for the first time, or (2) reputed to be almost entirely free of racial bias. See if such a study can throw light on the causes of racial injustice in the United States.
11. Herbert J. Gans has proposed that the key problems of poverty, segregation, and municipal decay will not be solved until we end majority rule, or, to be more exact, adopt a pluralistic democracy. Such a democracy would temper majority rule by adopting measures that systematically

prevent the tyrannization of minorities by majorities. It would also incorporate the outvoted minorities into positions of political influence in ways that assure increasing responsiveness of governments to the diversity of citizen interests. He proposes specific means to those ends: abolishing the seniority system in legislatures, requiring greater accountability of administrative agencies on criteria of adequate service to diverse groups within the population, funding election campaigns by the government, eliminating gerrymandering of the poor and black, and having governmentally financed opinion polls run regularly on every major issue. (*New York Times Magazine*, 3 August 1969, pp. 12–28.) What measure would you see as furthering such a program? What would be the major obstacles to its effectiveness?

12. A recent report (*U.S. News and World Report*, 24 January 1972, p. 31) states that the South has passed the North in racial integration of public schools. A survey by the U. S. Department of Health, Education and Welfare showed that the eleven Southern states have fewer Negroes in all-black schools and more in predominantly white schools than do the other states. This is reported to be a drop of from 68 percent to 9 percent in all-black schools since 1968. How do you appraise the significance of this change?

SUGGESTED READINGS

Altman, Robert A. and Snyder, Patricia. *The Minority Student on the Campus: Expectations and Possibilities*. Berkeley: University of California, Center for Research and Development in Higher Education, 1970.

Baldwin, James. *The Fire Next Time*. New York: Dial Press, 1963.

———. *Nobody Knows My Name*. New York: Dial Press, 1961.

Barbour, Floyd B., ed. *The Black Power Revolt*. Boston: Porter Sargent, 1968.

"Black America 1970." Special Issue. *Time*, 6 April 1970, pp. 13–100.

Bontemps, Anna W. *100 Years of Negro Freedom*. New York: Dodd, Mead & Co., 1961.

Brink, William, and Harris, Louis. *The Negro Revolution in America*. New York: Simon and Schuster, 1964.

Campbell, Angus. *White Attitudes toward Black People*. Ann Arbor: University of Michigan, 1971.

Clark, Kenneth Bancroft. *The Negro Protest*. Boston: Beacon Press, 1963. James Baldwin, Malcolm X, and Martin Luther King talk with Kenneth B. Clark.

Gordon, Albert I. *Intermarriage: Interfaith, Interracial, Interethnic*. Boston: Beacon Press, 1964.

Gordon, Milton M. *Assimilation in American Life: The Role of Race, Religion, and National Origins*. New York: Oxford University Press, 1964.

Greenberg, Jack. *Race Relations and American Law.* New York: Columbia University Press, 1960.
Grier, William H. and Cobbs, Price M. *Black Rage.* New York: Basic Books, 1968.
Haselden, Kyle. *Racial Problems in Christian Perspective.* New York: Harper & Brothers, 1959; Torchbook ed., 1964.
Isaacs, Harold R. *The New World of Negro Americans.* New York: John Day Co., 1963.
Jacobs, Paul. *Prelude to Riot: A View of Urban America from the Bottom.* New York: Vintage Books, 1968. Sponsored by the Center for the Study of Democratic Institutions.
Killian, L. M., and Grigg, C. M. *Racial Crisis in America.* Englewood Cliffs, N. J.: Prentice-Hall, 1964.
King, Martin Luther, Jr. *Stride Toward Freedom: The Montgomery Story.* New York: Harper & Brothers, 1958.
———. *Why We Can't Wait.* New York: Harper & Row, Publishers, 1964.
Kronus, Sidney. *The Black Middle Class.* Columbus, O.: Charles E. Merrill Publishing Co., 1971.
Lewis, Oscar. *LaVida: A Puerto Rican Family in the Culture of Poverty—San Juan and New York.* New York: Vintage Books, 1968.
Lomax, Louis E. *The Negro Revolt.* New York: Harper & Row, Publishers, 1962.
Malcolm X. *Autobiography of Malcolm X.* New York: Grove Press, 1966.
Marden, Charles, and Meyer, Gladys. *Minorities in American Society.* 2nd ed. New York: American Book Co., 1962.
Montagu, Ashley. *Race, Science and Humanity.* New York: D. Van Nostrand Co., 1963.
Moreland, Lois B. *White Racism and the Law.* Columbus, O.: Charles E. Merrill Publishing Co., 1970.
Myrdal, Gunnar. *An American Dilemma: The Negro Problem and American Democracy.* Rev. ed. New York: Harper & Row Publishers, 1962. New preface by Gunnar Myrdal and a review of recent developments by Arnold Rose.
Seale, Bobby. *Seize the Time: The Story of the Black Panther Party and Huey P. Newton.* New York: Vintage Books, 1970.
Sherman, Richard B, ed. *The Negro and the City.* Englewood Cliffs, N. J.: Prentice-Hall, 1970.
Silberman, C. E. *Crisis in Black and White.* New York: Vintage Books, 1964.
Terry, Robert W. *For Whites Only.* Grand Rapids, Mich.: W. B. Eerdmans Publishing Co., 1970.
Thomas, Piri. *Down These Mean Streets.* New York: New American Library of World Literature, Signet, ed. 1967. (Deals with Puerto Ricans.)
Tucker, Sterling. *For Blacks Only: Black Strategies for Change in America.* Grand Rapids, Mich.: Wm. B. Eerdmans Publishing Co., 1971.
Tussman, Joseph, ed. *The Supreme Court on Racial Discrimination.* New York: Oxford University Press, 1963.
United Nations Educational, Scientific and Cultural Organization. *The Race*

Question in Modern Science: Race and Science. New York: Columbia University Press, 1961.

van den Berghe, Pierre L. *Race and Racism: A Comparative Perspective.* New York: John Wiley & Sons, 1967.

Waddell, Jack O., and Watson, O. Michael, eds. *The American Indian in Urban Society.* Boston: Little, Brown & Co., 1971.

Young, Whitney M., Jr. *Beyond Racism: Building Our Society.* New York: McGraw-Hill Book Co., 1967.

22
THE LIMITS OF LIFE AND ABUNDANCE

A HUMAN PREDICAMENT

The useful and uplifting items around which industrial man has built his life—detergents, Mustangs, the Sunday *New York Times*—turn out to choke his lakes, clog his lungs, and overflow his vacant lots. The harsh lesson is that ecological sanity may require an end to economic growth.

A Dead Earth or No Growth?

So say the ecologists, according to Peter Passell and Leonard Ross in a review of five recent books about the choices involved in having a good earth.[1] Some economists, represented by Edwin G. Dolan, argue that, on the contrary, we do not consume too many things, but we produce them in the wrong way. Because air and water have been free, producers dumped wastes without charge. If they had to pay for pollution, however—and the technology for abatement is already well developed— they would clean up their habits. The price of a livable environment, Dolan contends, is not an end to growth, but "an end to freeloading."[2]

---

[1] Peter Passell and Leonard Ross, "How Much Will the Sweeper Charge and Who Will Pay Him?" *New York Times Book Review,* 17 October 1971, pp. 6–7.

[2] *The Economic Strategy for Environmental Crisis* (New York: Holt, Rinehart & Winston, 1971). Quoted by Passell and Ross, "How Much Will the Sweeper Charge?"

In contrast author Richard Neuhaus contends that ecologists see only the damage caused by economic growth, but they disregard the people it helps. Thus far the only force that has substantially improved the condition of the poor in America has been economic growth. If you eliminate economic growth, you eliminate the hope of economic justice.[3]

The hope of ongoing growth is misconceived, in the view of Donella and Dennis Meadows and two colleagues. The world will stop growing or die, they say. They think that they have shown by computation of the consequences of present world growth rates that such growth would create its own end within one hundred years, or possibly fifty. Within that time, the Meadows team holds, there will likely result a sudden and by then uncontrollable decline in the production of industrial goods if present growth rates continue. Resulting starvation, illness, and other causes will reduce the population. To avoid this result it will be necessary to accept a lower standard of living: one computation estimated it would be necessary to reduce per capita expense to only $1,800, which is half of the present U.S. average and about the same as Europe's, but three times the world's present average. There would have to be equality in food distribution, fewer goods designed for longer life, more services, and universal access to birth control.

The Meadows team's computations derive from a computerized model of the earth's environment. Jay Forrester made the first such model for presentation to the Club of Rome, a group of seventy-five people (including industrialists, educators, civil servants, and others) concerned about man's future. The Meadows then were asked to head a study group at the Massachusetts Institute of Technology to refine the model. The resulting models start with assumptions about the relationships between available resources, industrial output, food, pollution, and population. By projecting the results of their interplay, calculation shows the implications of the assumed relationships. The models are thus useful for forecasting possible consequences of different public policies aimed at controlling these relationships.

The computer models' "predictions," however, are not to be taken as true forecasts. For example, the Meadows model based upon "no great changes in human values nor in the functioning of the global population-capital system as it has operated for the last 100 years"[4]

---

[3]Richard Neuhaus, *Ecology and the Seduction of Radicalism*. (New York: Macmillan Co., 1971). Quoted by Passell and Ross, "How Much Will the Sweeper Charge?"

[4]Allen Kneese and Ronald Ridker, "Predicament of Mankind," *Washington Post*, 2 March 1972, p. B9; a review of Donella H. Meadows, Dennis L. Meadows, Jorgen Randers, and William W. Behrens III, *The Limits to Growth* (New York: Universe Books, 1972).

permits population, capital, and pollution to grow exponentially while available resources are held in fixed supply. In the past, however, resources have been expanded by new technology as demand grew. This resource expansion, it is true, cannot go on indefinitely. But in the Meadows model, assuming an indefinitely expansible land and resource base, it is assumed that pollution cannot be cut to less than a fourth of the current amount per unit of production. This assumption, say critics Allen Kneese and Ronald Ridker, is most unlikely to hold. The problem of the limits to growth, then, is a genuine and critical problem. Thus far, however, we really do not know enough about the interrelationships among the crucial factors to project reliably either what will happen or how it might best be controlled.[5]

Is There a Way to Survive?

The wastes of human life, unless recycled, poison the environment for life. As population grows and as the abundance of the average person's consumption increases, the effluent of this abundance poisons the air, the water, and the land. The earth is like a spaceship and we are its astronauts. The resources and the quarters, once thought to be beyond exhaustion, are actually quite small. And even this space and these limited means of life-giving nourishment and sustenance can be so used up, cluttered, and polluted that life could cease to be possible within the capsule.

In theory recycling offers a way out. On a space ship the occupants use a combined strategy of stockpiling and recycling in order to survive until they can be resupplied. The air in a spaceship can be reprocessed on board, cleansed of some of its surplus carbon dioxide and other poisonous wastes, resupplied with oxygen from reserve tanks (the stockpile), and piped back to the users. Similarly some of the water can be reused.

The limitations of these tactics, however, are severe. The larger the stockpile, the greater the costs, the greater the likelihood of breakdown of the system, and the greater the technical problems in building a sufficiently large system to sustain all of the recycling and storage requirements. For the earth the stockpile itself can be replenished in only the most modest ways by energy received from the sun. The problem of recycling is essentially one of creating a self-sustaining system which purifies and reconverts to usable and nonpoisonous form the wastes that would otherwise kill.

The reduction of consumption also offers a second option with some

---

[5]Ibid., pp. B1, B9.

effect in reducing pollution. When an explosion knocked out one of the reserve tanks of oxygen on the flight of Apollo XV, the astronauts adopted a regimen which lowered their metabolic rate in order to reduce the consumption of oxygen. These and other tactics enabled them to survive. For humanity on earth, a similar strategy could mean a restriction of diet, of motion, perhaps of body size. Mankind might become a hibernating species, and his technology might do such things as concentrate upon substituting communication by satellite for travel to face-to-face meetings, or the conversion of raw materials on site to their ultimate usable form in order to reduce pollution from transport.

An obvious third strategy for reducing pollution is to reduce population. The chief source of pollution is man. At present, however, the talk is not of reducing population, but of arresting the rate of its increase, or at most of zero population growth. We are not far from the time when it was morally obligatory to "be fruitful and multiply," and there are still cultures today in which this is the rule of survival and of a good life. Today we debate the right to abortion; tomorrow we may debate the right not to have an abortion, the right to give birth on a planet which cannot permit everyone who chooses to do so to reproduce his kind.

What then are the limits of the abundant life? And which of these options for coping with pollution are the least objectionable or the most attractive? The purpose of this essay is to open inquiry about what the questions involve and how they might be addressed in such a way as to focus effort upon the most promising alternatives.

A MATTER OF PRIORITIES

The problem of finding the best among the alternatives about how many people should have what kind of life in the future of the earth can be seen as one of strategic choice and timing of priorities. If the achievement of some desired objective is seen as having a certain priority and if the avoidance of its unwanted but interlocking result is also seen as having a priority, then a strategy is required for finding and effecting the optimum conditions possible with respect to those two interacting factors.

What are the principal types of priorities that must be weighed in seeking a strategy for human survival and for an abundant life? Certainly one critical priority is that of sustaining the viability of the planet. Survival is a precondition of all other values in life on this earth. If it is possible not only to sustain a viable planet but also to enhance the livability and the quality of the environment, this objective would also have a high priority because of all the other realizations of worth for which it is a precondition. To achieve these ends, however, is to incur costs, and the choice of costs is a crucial ethical matter. For example, in the federal budgets of the next five years should the needed expenditure for equalization of opportunity in education, for improved health care, for the eradication of racial injustice and economic exploitation be sacrificed for the purpose of reducing pollution? Would it be better to limit the production of automobiles and close certain parts of the cities to automobile traffic as a measure to control environmental degradation, rather than to permit unlimited car production but require the installation of expensive pollution control devices on each car?

Justice, Affluence, and Survival

We believe that an increased rate of progress toward economic and racial justice ought to be made a priority on a par with survival. Any further enhancement of the quality of life should be sought only in ways that also contribute to the rectification of injustices rooted in racial bias and economic inequities. For example, if federal resources are to be made available for the capitalizing of new towns, those new towns should be required to meet stringent objectives about desegregation, about the proportion of low cost housing built and maintained, and about the management of in-town transportation to reduce pollution accumulations. The priorities, in a word, need not be set against one another if social objectives are conceived as integrally interrelated and are implemented in ways that contribute to the entire set of ends which are given highest priority.

To take this approach, however, is not to put an end to the moral dilemmas posed by the limits of an abundant life. Who has a right to define and choose these social objectives? How shall and should the component objectives be weighted as the debate develops about the specific terms of those objectives? Since it will not be possible to reduce the values of the alternatives to mathematically calculable figures in which the best will be the largest figure, clearly and unanimously recognized by all "rational men," what role should these efforts toward rationalization have in the choice of alternative social objectives? To what extent should these be settled by federal, state, and local governmental authorities? And to what extent should they be left to individual choice or to nongovernmental institutions to determine? We shall return to this last type of question in chapter 23. Here let us consider the main options for the control of pollution and the enhancement of the environment.

THE CONTROL OF POPULATION

"The world's population is increasing at a rate which renders distress, famine, and disintegration inevitable unless we learn to hold our numbers within reason,"[6] said Dr. Vannevar Bush, former president of the Carnegie Institution of Washington. "About Asia," Phillip Appleman quotes a student returned from a study tour, "what I remember best is not its history, but its misery."[7] Dr. Paul Ehrlich stated in 1968 that a minimum of 3.5 million people would starve to death in that year. The result of continuing population growth at present rates is, he insists, mass starvation. Currently the world population (now around three billion) is expected to double in thirty-seven years. The doubling time has dropped from one million years when population first reached about five million (around 6000 B.C.) to one thousand to two hundred to eightly and now to thirty-seven.[8] This is, however, no mere explosion, as Gordon R. Taylor adds, for in an explosion the particles lose speed as they move outward from the point of explosion. On the contrary the population growth is continuing to gain speed. The consequences will be not merely hunger and starvation. The balance of nature could be so radically altered as to make life impossible for man in anything like his present numbers. Man depends upon the lives of other animals and plants, and these upon still others. Not only the feeding cycle must be maintained, but also the cycle that regenerates the air. This whole network of relationships is at risk.[9]

There is scarcely any disagreement today among informed persons as to the great danger in the population explosion. Only the school of thought that says we can produce enough to meet the needs for food, air, sustenance of organic functioning, and a rewarding life for ever-growing numbers might be said to differ on this issue. And even that school of thought acknowledges (1) the necessity of timing the population growth to correspond with the growing capability to sustain the people and (2) the fact that growth will be limited not only by the state of technology needed to sustain life but also by physical and other limits (e.g., the aggregate heat generated by new levels of life and civilization cannot exceed certain levels without endangering life). This most optimistic view is represented by Edward Higbee and R.

---

[6]Philip Appleman, "What the Population Explosion Means to You," *Ladies Home Journal* 80 (June 1963): 59.
[7]Ibid.
[8]Paul Ehrlich, *The Population Bomb* (New York: Ballantine Books, 1970), pp. 17–18.
[9]Gordon Rattray Taylor, *The Doomsday Book* (Greenwich, Conn.: Fawcett Publications, 1970), pp. 14–15.

Buckminster Fuller who, in looking at the future, emphasize, not the notion of limits, but that of balance and harmony, of man's living within nature and adapting his institutions to "the organic web of life." They argue that we can accomodate an ever-increasing population on earth, but only by increasing urbanization and industrialization on a world scale. To make this accommodation "the individual must be specially processed.... The more complicated and productive the synthetic habitat becomes through technological development, the more complicated becomes the acculturation process." This new synthetic city environment made by man will require that its people be also "properly man-made."[10]

This vision of the future good is almost as frightening to many critics as is the prospect of nonsurvival. Edward Abbey, for example, sees the Higbee vision as one of treating the earth as sheer raw material to process and keep alive "the human and semihuman mollusca teeming and proliferating within their plastic urban shells." Abbey thinks that most people want just the opposite and rightly so: "not more urbanism and industry, but less; not a larger population but a smaller; not a rejection of agrarian values but a recovery of them; not a divorce from the natural world but a re-union with it." If that means even destroying "the technological apparatus" to escape the technocrats' trap, then destroy it we should," Abbey insists.[11]

Alternatives to Population Growth

That control of population is a must in our future, then, is agreed. But there is no agreement about the vision of future good toward which we should aim. There is no agreement concerning the degree or scope of danger, the timing of its onset, or the risks involved in different courses of action we might take. There is no agreement as to what values should be sacrificed or risked in order to have a needed margin of safety for man's survival with a form of life worth sustaining. There is no agreement about the needed margin of safety or the level of risk that should be run in order to have the right probability of optimum gain or minimum hazard to the ideal future. There is further disagreement about the specific hazards mankind will encounter and what to do about each of them. Finally there is sharp disagreement about strategies and tactics for coping with the different dangers, and this

---

[10]Edward Higbee, *A Question of Priorities* (New York: William Morrow & Co., 1970). Quoted by Edward Abbey, "How to Live on This Planet Earth," *New York Times Book Review*, 19 April 1970, p. 3.
[11]Ibid.

discord abounds even among those who agree in large measure about the nature of the future good man should be seeking. Let us spell out in more detail some of these disagreements about ends and means. They are intricately entangled with one another, and rather than separate them artificially, let us take examples of the views of specific individuals or groups which highlight the conflicting outlooks.

On July 29, 1968, Pope Paul VI issued the encyclical *Humanae Vitae* (*Of Human Life*), renewing the prohibition against all artificial forms of birth control. The encyclical reaffirms the position of the Roman Catholic Church that the prime function of marriage is procreation, and that the use of any artificial form of birth control is an unnatural interference with God's will and way. To non-Catholics who deny the Catholic "axioms" or "revealed truths" about God, the role of the Church in transmitting these truths, and its idea of the function of marriage, the encyclical can be dismissed with a challenge to the bases of the axioms and the axioms themselves. A person who views himself as a faithful Catholic, on the other hand, cannot differ on some of these points without, in effect, excommunicating himself.

Dr. John Rock, clinical professor emeritus of gynecology at Harvard Medical School and co-developer of a contraceptive pill, sees himself as a faithful Catholic with complete confidence in the Church as a transmitter of the mind of God. But Dr. Rock was stunned and saddened by the papal encyclical. Parenthood, he agreed, is a matter of family responsibility which involves raising the children to be rational adults and tending to their health, educational, and growth needs. That task, however, cannot be done without restraint on population growth. Famine, atomic war, or other such disasters are inhumane ways to restrain population growth. And the encyclical presses toward such outcomes. The papal ruling, he forecast, would be a painful blow to Latin American countries, which are among the poorest, and to families of Western Europe. Dr. Rock viewed the pill as an adjunct to nature, not as an unnatural thing. He considered the papal ban similar to the Church's treatment of Galileo in the seventeenth century—the Church, as it now acknowledges, mistakenly interpreted the scientific hypothesis of the earth's revolving around the sun as the denial of a dogma of religion.[12]

This type of disagreement about both the future good and the means toward it is not confined to Catholics. In other continents and cultures other forms of this discord abound. Various religious grounds for the prohibition of contraception or abortion exist, and other cultural taboos

---

[12]Kathleen Teltsch, "Encyclical Stuns Dr. Rock," *New York Times,* 4 August 1968, pp. 1–2.

enter into the reluctance to control population in these ways. The very idea of restricting the size of families runs counter to long-standing notions of the ideal society. We believe that one key to the realization of the view of the future good for man is a change of cultural ideals toward the acceptance of limits on family, tribal, or national growth. The ideal need not be the same in all religions, cultures, or nations. Pluralism of ideal can still prevail, but it should fall within limits that assure human survival while other elements of the different religious and cultural ideas of life are also preserved intact. This outlook of ours is not subject to proof. It is, in effect, a proposal for risk, presented to others in the hope that by reasoning and acting together (and sometimes in conflict) we may discover a way that permits survival with treasured options for life in the future.

Among the explosive forms of disagreement about the future are some which deal with the extent to which certain freedoms, certain options about crowding and closeness to nature and living space, will be part of the human future. Here our preference (we hope it is not mere prejudice) is for a future which permits some people to choose Buckminster Fuller's mass cities of synthetic structures while other people choose a life close to a relatively unmanaged natural environment. Within what bounds such a future is possible and whether it is even possible at all are questions in dispute.

A further type of disagreement, also bearing upon the key issue of the ideal to be sought in balancing costs against possible future benefits, is about the proportion of resources which our society should put into arresting pollution or preventing the further rise of pollution as compared with the proportion to be put into rectification of present patterns of injustice. This situation poses direct competition in some public policy issues. For example, in the next federal budget there will be appropriations to assist with racial integration of the schools, to equalize the quality of education in racially different schools, to equalize job opportunities and job success, to improve housing for the poor, to support legal services for the poor, and so on. There will also be appropriations to support environmental quality controls on automobiles, on atomic energy plants, on pesticides, and on other items. On a few quite specific matters—e.g., rat control in the inner cities—the mitigation of inequalities goes hand in hand with the attack upon environmental pollution. On most specifics, however, the two demands will compete with one another.

There are ways of combining the problems of inequality with those of environmental quality which avoid or minimize this competition or even enhance the fight against inequality with the weapons that improve the environment. For example, a plan to redevelop the entirety of metropolitan Hartford, Connecticut has been worked out by joint effort of the many governmental jurisdictions, a private developer, and the business and community leadership. The plans would require enormous capitalization, but they would yield a city which operated more economically than the present Hartford; which reduced its unemployment, crime rate, racial segregation and discrimination, and other inequities; and which improved the human services available through educational institutions, recreational facilities, health and medical institutions, family support and individual counseling services, and the like.[13] In part, then, the resolution of such conflicts ought to be sought in a vision that minimizes the idea that these aspirations must conflict in practice. In part, the resolution is in the complex conceptual and technical work of inventing the means by which the aspirations can in fact be achieved conjointly. We see such visions and such applications as within our reach. A first step toward them is enlisting advocates of the different objectives in an effort to think out together the different ways in which the objectives might all be served. The subsequent steps involve finding politically acceptable plans that show progress within tolerable costs.

A further type of disagreement brings us back sharply to the statistics of population growth. Exactly how much time do we have in which to make and put into effect the needed new efforts to limit population, to protect and enhance the environment, and to move against existing injustices? In 1965 a former adviser to the governments of India and the Philippines predicted, according to press reports of a meeting of the American Chemical Society, that there would be famine of serious proportions in the 1970s. "The worst famine in history is just around the corner, and more than a billion persons in Africa, Asia, and South America face starvation,"[14] he warned. This fate, he added, will fall first upon China, India, and Pakistan in the 1970s, then will rapidly extend to other millions in Egypt, Iran, and Turkey, and within ten years will spread to Africa and Latin America. While this scientist saw the control of the birth rate as the ultimate solution to the threat of starvation, he felt that his control could not be instituted rapidly enough to avert the famine. Therefore he argued for enormous efforts to increase food production along with a simultaneous drive to lower birth rates.[15]

---

[13]The American City Corporation, *The Greater Hartford Process* (Columbia, Md. and Hartford, Conn.: The Corporation, 1972).

[14]John Nuveen, "The Facts of Life," *The Christian Century* 83 (August 10, 1966): 51.

[15]Ibid.: 50–51.

Ehrlich estimated the present rate of population doubling in thirty-seven years, as we said earlier. Within nine hundred years this rate would yield sixty million billion people or about one hundred persons per square yard of earth surface, land and sea included. Ehrlich proposed in 1968 a nine-year period for finding a solution to the population crisis. His reason for this proposal on timing is largely that famine is imminent, and that it is not only intolerable in its toll of death and misery, but it also brings in its train social upheaval that may undermine the capability even to use the means we have to fulfill human needs.[16] Controversy about the timing for meeting the population problem leads in turn to conflict about the needed outlays of money and effort for coping with this problem. Delay in attacking population growth gives more time to muster funds but increases the magnitude of problems to be resolved and thus enlarges the costs of attacking those problems.

This sketch of issues centering upon population growth is by no means complete, but it makes clear the interrelatedness of the problems of population growth with other human problems. Both the ideal to be sought and the means of seeking it are bound up with other issues. Even a prudent approach to coping with the issues, not to speak of one that seeks some measure of wisdom, would therefore try to see the interrelated problems as a whole.

Let us now turn to another facet of the question of the limits of life and abundance, namely, that pertaining to other causes of environmental degradation and to their consequences and cures.

A Problem With No Technical Solution

In his presidential address to the Pacific Division of the American Association for the Advancement of Science, Dr. Garrett Hardin took the position that the population problem has no technical solution. A technical solution, he said, is one that requires "a change only in the techniques of the natural sciences, demanding little or nothing in the way of change in human values or ideas of morality." Most people who agonize about population growth seek to avoid the disaster of overpopulation without wanting to give up any of the good things we now enjoy or much of the still greater goods we might soon obtain. Hardin compares this problem with a perfectly played game of tick-tack-toe. If opponents understand that game perfectly and if they abide by the rules, no one can win. Only by abandoning the game can anyone win.

---

[16]*The Population Bomb*, pp. 36–45.

So it is with the game of having all the goods we want and letting everyone multiply his kind as he wants: no one can win if we continue to define the choice in those terms.[17]

Population tends to grow exponentially, each increment adding to the number reproducing. As resources per capita cease to be accessible in equally rapid increases and to be put into the forms needed, the per person share of goods must decrease. Even if space would hold the increases, space is no escape. "A finite world," Hardin states, "can support only a finite population; therefore, population growth must eventually equal zero."[18]

It is important to grasp the reasons for this conclusion, for if conclusive, they force us to seek a way out of the population problem by a new choice of game rules, that is, by a new choice of value priorities, a new morality. The primary agenda then becomes one which concerns the value priorities which will make up this new morality, within which the technical problems for implementation of that morality can then be debated and worked out. A first reason for the necessity of limiting population growth to a zero rate is that mathematically it is not possible in a finite system to maximize the values of all of a set of two or more variables at the same time.[19] Given finite means and given that each variable requires means for its increase, as the values of one variable rise, the values of the other must be adversely affected. For example, if population is one variable and food per person is another, and if total food supply is limited in amount at a certain level, then it is not possible to increase both population and food per person indefinitely within that given limit of food supply. A second reason derives from biological relationships. To live an organism must have energy from food, air, and water. It uses the energy to maintain itself and to "work," since work is required for all forms of activity or enjoyment. As we increase population, given limited energy, we force the work calories per person to approach as near to zero as possible, if there are to be enough for everyone; that is, we approach the level of no mobility, no gourmet meals, no sports, and so on. In traditional terms of ethical theory Bentham's goal of the greatest possible pleasure for the greatest number is not possible if it is interpreted to mean unlimited increase of the numbers of people to be pleased. If the appearance of

---

[17]Garrett Hardin, "The Tragedy of the Commons," *Science* 162 (December 13, 1968): 1243–1248.

[18]Ibid., p. 1243.

[19]J. von Neumann and O. Morgenstern, *Theory of Games and Economic Behavior* (Princeton: Princeton University Press, 1947), p. 11. Cited by Hardin.

atomic energy seems to remove this problem of energy limits, Hardin points out that it merely shifts the problem to one of dissipation of the energy expended.[20]

Up until today no culture has solved the problem of so weighting the things wanted that these desires can forever be fulfilled. To solve this problem we must devise a set of values that enables the population to be prosperous and have a growth rate of zero. Given the practical aspects of bringing the population growth rate to zero, this objective means setting a figure larger than the present world population as an initial target, at which point no further growth would occur or some decline might occur, or any further growth allowed would be at a rate at or beneath the rate of increase of the capability to provide energy and dissipate its effects without damage to the system.

A further implication of this outlook is that individuals cannot be free in this ideal or near-ideal situation to make any and all choices that they wish. Of course, no individual is free in this unlimited sense today, but the restrictions will probably have to be more complex and pervasive in the future. It is true that further technological progress may open up options that do not exist today and in this sense expand human freedom. But this will be a more disciplined form of freedom—one can hope not just socially disciplined, but in large measure self-disciplined—than we have known before.

There are small as well as large examples of the problem of redefined priorities and of the consequent limits upon, and extensions of, human options. For example, if unlimited visitors were permitted to the National Parks, while the population grows exponentially, the visitors would overrun the parks, erode and destroy their amenities, and defeat everyone. There are alternative ways to deal with the problem, but all of them require some balancing of access to the parks and of options in its use with limits of the amount and timing of access. A particularly urgent example of new priorities for an enhanced and viable environment is that of the control of pollution because it interacts with the demands for more employment, more income, and more consumption by more people. In essence the problem is that without both general and specific limits upon an individual's and a group's options, we "turn the world into a cage"[21] and "foul our nest."[22]

Let us consider two examples of the risks of environmental pollution: ecological disasters and chronic sources of pollution.

---

[20]"The Tragedy of the Commons," p. 1243.
[21]*The Population Bomb*, p. 14.
[22]"The Tragedy of the Commons," p. 1243.

ECOLOGICAL DISASTERS AND CHRONIC POLLUTERS

Dr. David Price of the United States Public Health Service said in 1959 that it is now possible for something to corrupt the environment to the point that man might join the dinosaur as obsolete. "And what makes these thoughts all the more disturbing," he said, "is the knowledge that our fate could perhaps be sealed twenty or more years before the development of symptoms."[23] This ultimate disaster could happen by a single error or accident, or by the cumulative effect of chronic polluters. The line between the two is not clear. For example, an international incident might trigger an atomic attack, occasioning retaliatory atomic bombing, and touching off directly or indirectly a chain reaction which would make the planet either uninhabitable or nearly so. The famous novel *On the Beach* dramatized that situation. Another possibility is that repeated testing of atomic weapons combined with a few nuclear accidents related to peacetime uses and possibly including leaks from stored pools of nuclear wastes might create a fatal level of radiation in the course of years. Various combinations of catastrophic incident and chronic accumulation of radiation could do the damage.

The danger from accumulating radiation is not simply its direct potential for killing. The nuclear industry was recently estimated to cost some twenty-four thousand added cases of cancer annually. Underground nuclear explosions are said to trigger earthquakes and tidal waves. An earthquake started in this way might be the mechanism that would release stored radioactive wastes, as was warned in 1966 about the Hanford (Washington) site of this country's radioactive waste storage.[24]

Another potential disaster is the "heat death." In the first half of the twentieth century the earth underwent a marked rise in temperature relative to the immediately preceding decades. Then an unexpected change downward occurred, and some scientists began to fear a new ice age. The resulting studies and debates have increasingly caused scientists to look at the whole earth as a single system of energy and material transfers. If life is to persist, these transfers must balance out at levels permitting survival. Between heating and cooling trends, the greater danger appears to be from heating. According to different estimates, man's activity currently accounts for a net heating up of between 1/2500 and 1/25 of the proportion of energy reflected back into outer space from the earth's surface (reflection of solar heat is

---

[23]*The Doomsday Book*, p. 15.
[24]Sheldon Novick and Dorothy Cottrell, eds. *Our World in Peril: An Environment Review* (Greenwich, Conn: Fawcett Publications, 1971), pp. 136–202.

the major portion). A ten percent increase would make the North and South Poles into tropical areas and would render the present tropics uninhabitable except for lizards and insects. Such a change could be produced within twenty-six years according to one scientist.[25] The fact that variations in estimate are so large shows the extent of present human ignorance of just what causes the prevailing climate. A few things are known: a rising proportion of carbon dioxide in the atmosphere produces a "greenhouse effect," heating the air; a rising pollution from dust particles causes cloudiness, reflecting the sun's heat outward and cooling the area below; waste heat reinforces the heating trend. Other factors, still unidentified, seem to be causing other fluctuations in the temperature. In our ignorance we could be triggering an ice age or a heat death well before we were aware of the clues that would permit a forecast in time to reverse the fatal trend.

There are, of course, many other hazards: oil spills, accidents with weapons of biological or chemical warfare or with large supplies of hazardous industrial materials, cumulative effects of vapor trails of supersonic transport, cumulative effects of automobile emission pollution, overuse of electrical and other forms of energy relative to supplies for sustaining the standard of living or relative to tolerable levels of resulting pollution, industrial wastes that kill lakes and streams, uncontrolled wastes emptied into the waterways from urban complexes, residues from accumulating pesticides and from toxic chemicals used in industrial production, and so on. To see the essential nature of the ethical dilemmas confronting us, it is not necessary here to make a full catalog of either the dangers or the possible resolutions of them.

Life depends upon a delicate balance among literally thousands of elements which make up the air, water, soil, and radiation, which can be seen as a balance of matter and energy of many kinds. As long as human numbers and activity had only an inappreciable effect upon the proportions and distribution of these elements, the viability of the planet was essentially unaffected by human choices. This is no longer the case. Moreover, it will be, relative to the risks, a long time before we know enough to know which of our choices are having which of the crucial effects.

WHAT DOES IT MEAN TO CHOOSE LIFE?

In the face of both enormous danger and great ignorance, what is a right ethical response to the limits of life and abundance on the planet

---

[25]*The Doomsday Book*, pp. 55–75.

earth? First, it seems to us, it is important to recognize that the problems of environmental quality and human survival are not merely technical problems but involve choices of value priorities, choices of alternative ways of life. This point has been argued earlier in this chapter.

Second, it is important to recognize that ethical principles (which are forms of expression of value priorities) are incomplete unless they contain a statement of the functional relationship between the values expressed and the state of the system of human and natural relationships to which the principles are meant to apply. The commandment "do not steal" was enunciated in the context of a nomadic economy in which certain possessions were directly related to survival; in that context stealing was a much more serious offense than when a high salaried suburban dweller is robbed of goods worth a few hundred dollars. As Hardin puts the point, "the morality of an act is a function of the state of the system at the time [the act] is performed."[26]

A striking example of the ignoring of the "system-sensitive nature of morality" by traditional ethics can be seen in the implications of the Universal Declaration of Human Rights about family size. In late 1967 this statement was agreed upon by some thirty nations:

> The Universal Declaration of Human Rights describes the family as the natural and fundamental unit of society. It follows that any choice and decision with regard to the size of the family must irrevocably rest with the family itself, and cannot be made by anyone else.

Given the dangers of overpopulation discussed earlier, Hardin asks, "how shall we deal with the family, the religion, the race or the class (or indeed any distinguishable and cohesive group) that adopts overbreeding as a policy?" Hardin phrases the question in terms of a group seeking its own aggrandizement, but the question applies as well to groups seeking some good for all mankind of which they see themselves as the essential bearers or witnesses. The principle proposed by the United Nations group can hold only if the family exercises its right as a qualified right, requiring respect for other rights and for the systemic consequences of the options chosen in the exercise of the right to procreate.

A further implication of the system-sensitive nature of morality is shown by Hardin's argument that "conscience is self-eliminating" under contemporary conditions. The argument is: the people who respond to appeals of conscience to restrict breeding will thereby reduce

---

[26] J. Fletcher, *Situation Ethics* (Philadelphia: Westminster Press, 1966). Cited in Hardin, "The Tragedy of the Commons," p. 1245. But Fletcher's particular inferences and judgments do not follow from the principle, which seems unexceptionable.

their progeny, and those who do not respond will multiply. Thus the conscientious gradually disappear. A system relying upon individual conscience thus eliminates itself and "works toward the elimination of conscience from the race."[27] Hardin argues further that we put the conscientious man in a double bind by appealing to his conscience to solve social problems today. If he does not respond, we condemn him for irresponsibility. If he does respond, we secretly condemn him for a simpleton who can be shamed into self-denial while the rest of us exploit the opportunities to take more than our share. This process actually endangers the mental health of those to whom it is applied, according to Bateson.[28]

A person of conscience need not give so simplistic a response to such pleas. He can work on the system of morality and the system of population control as well as upon his own practices within his family. If he knows the hazards of the double bind, he need not be their victim. Nevertheless, the Hardin argument points the way toward a new sophistication that man needs in the defining of the meaning of conscientious conduct and in the actual exercise of individual choice.

This example of the system-sensitive nature of morality points to a third principle that might be used in responding to the problem of environmental quality and human survival. This problem presents an opportunity that can be effectively met only by concerted action of many individuals and groups. Concerted action implies social pressure and even coercion. That is, individuals and groups exert coercive effect upon others by their individual decisions, both to procreate and to consume. It is not unethical to respond with coercion. Coercion, however, can take many forms; and only those that yield greater possible net benefits among the options foreseen can rightly be approved. Given a problem that involves as many variables as does that of environmental quality, simplistic solutions are sure to fail. What is needed is a complex set of incentives and disincentives, exercised as consciously as possible by people upon one another in order to get this net benefit. For example, both the assessment of taxes (e.g., upon automobiles to finance pollution control development) and the abatement of taxes (e.g., allowing tax deductions for investment in pollution control) are coercive incentives not only upon the initially taxed person or corporation but also upon those to whom this added cost is passed along. A third principle might thus be put in this way: A systemic problem of morality such as that of environmental quality control requires for its

---

[27]"The Tragedy of the Commons," p. 1245.
[28]G. Bateson, D. D. Jackson, J. Haley, J. Weakland, *Behavioral Science* 1 (1956): 251.

resolution concerted action among the types of people affected and a complex solution reflecting awareness of the many factors interacting in the nature of the problem.

A fourth suggestion seems also to be in order. In a highly complex world of many people and intricate problems, we are sometimes stimulated to adequate action only when a great alarm arises about enormous dangers. The atmosphere of alarms, however, is not normally the best climate in which to find the best solutions to complex problems calling for widespread cooperation. Moreover, in attacking problems and dangers arising from old ways or new circumstances, it is possible to overlook new options and opportunities which might by-pass entirely the roots of the old problems. It would be better, then, to work from a vision of the possibilities within reach of present aspirations and means than to concentrate upon removing unwanted problems.

In the matter under consideration here, a vision is needed, not merely of the way toward human survival, but of the way toward an enlargement of human fulfillment resulting from a more productive relationship between man and his environment. From this vision we can then work to identify which threats are most important and urgent and which opportunities need most quickly and vigorously to be sought. In our view this vision cannot be the work of a single individual or of a small group, though each of these can contribute stimulus and conceptions for the larger numbers of individuals and groups who must be involved. The larger involvement is essential to an adequate vision's being developed that reflects the diversity of human aspirations and the diversity of human conditions. That larger involvement is also essential if the commitment is to be engaged and the vision brought to fulfillment. It is for those who study this chapter, if they agree, to begin to contribute to the construction of those models of the future from which might emerge a new human consensus. They can also enlist others in the task and in the actions that will make it more than an intellectual game.

QUESTIONS AND PROJECTS

1. "The individual who pollutes the air with his factory and the ghetto kid who breaks store windows both represent the same thing. They don't care about each other—or what they do to each other". Daniel P. Moynihan closed a recent television special "Cities Have No Limits" on that pessimistic note. Is not caring the correct diagnosis of these two polluters? Are the causes and motivations of their polluting the same? What do you recommend be done about such polluters?
2. For years many countries in Europe and the Americas have dumped

chemical wastes at sea. In 1971 one of Holland's largest chemical and plastic companies chartered a tanker, the *Stella Maris*, to dump a cargo in the Atlantic midway between Iceland an Ireland. Many countries protested; and the *Stella Maris*, unable to refuel at foreign ports and pursued by minesweepers, returned to Rotterdam to await the completion of a three million dollar incinerator. An international agreement (convention) on such matters has been drafted for signing at a United Nations Conference on the Human Environment. What provisions would you recommend for inclusion in such a convention? In justifying your recommendations, how would you provide for economic development as well as for pollution control? Would you seek to arrest economic growth?

3. The governing council of a Maryland county recently announced a freeze on building permits because of an anticipated overload which further building would create upon the sewage disposal system. Developers and citizens protested that the county had committed itself to their building plans earlier and was responsible for having timely arrangements for sewage disposal. There was even a threat that the county might be sued for the economic losses involved in failing to be ready for its implied commitments to industry and housing development. A similar instance is reported from New York State (*New York Times*, 3 October 1971, p. 62). What questions do you think should be dealt with in agreements to sell land, to permit building, and to permit industrial development? How will the home buyer, moving into an area for his new job, be protected from being unjustly frozen out or from suffering excessive costs if ecological concerns are also to be protected?

4. A newspaper report states that ninety percent of the noise of jackhammers can be easily suppressed by inventions that would add only fifteen percent to the cost of the tools. A noise tax might create the incentive to install the muffling. Because of the noise caused by a new highway, the Board of Education of Elizabeth, New Jersey was awarded $164,-119.00 in late 1971 for air conditioning, the sealing of windows, and the like. A school in Birmingham, Alabama, was awarded $500,000. Other awards have gone to a hospital, a game preserve, and a vacation area. (*New York Times*, 3 October 1971, p. 66.) What public policy would you recommend as a guideline for noise abatement requirements? Can a similar policy apply to such diverse sources as jet planes, minibike race tracks, loud high fidelity radios and record players, and highway traffic?

5. Some years ago Congress passed a law establishing a Redwood National Park to preserve the remnants of virgin redwood forest in California. As of 1972 the park still does not exist. Obstacles have included delaying tactics of some state officials and activities of some lumber companies seeking to make a quick profit before the forests are inaccessible. What strategy can you recomend for preserving irreplaceable species of plant or animal life? Will present methods suffice?

6. The Environmental Defense Fund is a coalition of scientists, lawyers, and other citizens who want to protect environmental quality through legal action and public education. The EDF sues environmental of-

fenders. For example, in 1969 it filed suit against the United States Army Corps of Engineers to stop construction of the Cross-Florida Barge Canal which threatened to destroy the Oklawaha, one of the few wild rivers left in the East. Would present laws on environmental quality suffice if such aggressive enforcement efforts were universal? What is your view of the desirability of using lawsuits as a means of fostering improved practices in curbing pollution or destruction of natural environment?

7. In a number of eastern states there are conservation commissions at community (county or city) level. In Ipswich, Massachusetts, such a commission acquired marshland to prevent a drain-and-fill operation. Yale Professor David M. Smith contrasts the zoning commission, which defines what is barely tolerable, from the conservation commission, which works for what is desirable in environmental conditions. What factors would determine the usefulness of such a commission in protecting and improving the environment in your community?

8. Edward B. Fiske, Religion Editor of The New York Times since 1968, quotes the French anthropologist Claude Levi-Strauss in saying that solving the ecological crisis will require nothing less than a "spiritual revolution as great as that which led to the advent of Christianity." Primitive religions believed all natural objects endowed with life and respected them, while Christianity made it possible, according to historian Lynn White, Jr. "to exploit nature in a mood of indifference." [Quotes from Edward B. Fiske, "Saving the Earth: A Challenge to Our Religious Traditions," *Redbook Magazine* (June 1971): 78, 180, 182, 186]. In spite of Judeo-Christian themes of reverence for the created world, the tradition's stress on man's high place in creation has led him to treat plants and animals as having value only as they satisfy human needs—a view that may now seem suicidal. The individualism of our tradition may also have to give way. Theologian Scott Paradise has also argued that warmaking sustains a gap between rich and poor and a disregard for the environment destroyed and will have to give way in a world that seeks environmental health. How do you appraise the relationship of religious values to human capability of living by an ethic that will permit human survival? Which of the values of your own religious tradition would require change or reinforcement for such a relationship to exist?

9. Dr. Norman Borlaugh, a Nobel prize winner in plant genetics, known as father of the "green revolution," denounced "hysterical environmentalists" at a world wide gathering of the United Nations Food and Agricultural Organization. He was attacking the advocates of bans on DDT and other pesticides. Claiming that DDT has saved more than a billion lives and killed no one, he argued that the ban would raise food prices four or fivefold and reopen the dangers of malaria. On the other hand, in a sequel to Rachel Carson's *Silent Spring,* Frank Graham, Jr. cites other scientists in further documentation of the dangers of the pesticides. The *New York Times* chides Dr. Borlaugh for being "apparently unaware" of DDT's worst offense: it is becoming ineffective anyway by wiping out

its victims' predators while they themselves build up resistance. (Claire Sterling, "Do Benefits of Pesticide Outweigh Potential Harm?" (*Washington Post,* 18 December 1971, p. A14). How should a layman go about forming his own judgment concerning the public policies he should support about this complex issue, given the disagreement among scientists and environmentalists?

10. In January 1972 the town of Everett, Washington, was threatened with the closing of the pulp plant. George Weyerhauser explained that his plant could not meet the state and federal anti-pollution mandates and still make money. The town of fifty-five thousand already economically depressed from Boeing aircraft layoffs would lose three hundred thirty more jobs. The chamber of commerce had hoped to save both the pulp plant and a paper-production complex by establishing a city-owned lagoon and finding industrial use for the reprocessed waste. But the paper firm got a state extension of its permit to dump into Puget Sound and thus did not want to share the costs of a more expensive waste disposal system with the pulp plant. How would you design social policy and governmental functions to avoid the type of dilemma Everett faces in choosing between jobs and environmental pollution? (*Washington Post,* 23 January 1972, p. A3).

11. Suppose that it had been agreed in the General Assembly of the United Nations that population growth of the world should be brought to a zero rate within ten years. If you were among those responsible for implementing the decision, what would you advocate as the primary strategies for achieving the objective? Explain the rationale of your choice of strategies.

12. In the projections of the future which were reported by the Meadows Team in *The Limits to Growth* for the Club of Rome's project on the predicament of mankind, the assumptions used about population growth, resources, abatement of pollution, per capita consumption, and the like were different from what will actually occur on these variables. If you were supplying assumptions for the calculation of the future, what would you put into the computer on the four variables just listed for (1) what is most likely to occur if no major fight to reduce environmental pollution is made, and (2) what you think ought to occur?

SUGGESTED READINGS

American Friends Service Committee. *Who Shall Live?* New York: Hill & Wang, 1970. A Report prepared for the committee on the moral and social dimensions of the population problem.

Calder, Nigel, ed. *The World in Nineteen Eighty-Four.* 2 vols. Baltimore: Penguin Books, 1965

Caldwell, Lynton Keith. *Environment, A Challenge to Modern Society.* Garden City, N. Y.: Doubleday & Co., 1971.

Commoner, Barry. *The Closing Circle.* New York: Alfred A. Knopf, 1971.
Dansereau, Pierre, ed. *Challenge for Survival: Land, Air and Water for Man in Megalopolis.* New York: Columbia University Press, 1970.
De Bell, Garrett, ed. *The Environmental Handbook.* New York: Ballantine Books, 1970.
Ehrlich, Paul R. *The Population Bomb.* Rev. ed. New York: Ballantine Books, 1971.
Ewald, William R., Jr., ed. *Environment for Man.* Bloomington, Ind.: Indiana University Press, 1967.
Glass, David C., ed. *Environmental Influences.* New York: Rockefeller University Press and Russell Sage Foundation, 1968.
Graham, Frank, Jr. *Since Silent Spring.* Boston: Houghton-Mifflin Co., 1970; paperback by Fawcett Publications, Greenwich, Conn., 1970.
Helfrich, Harold W., Jr., ed. *Environmental Crises: Man's Struggle to Live with Himself.* New Haven: Yale University Press, 1970.
Higbee, Edward. *A Question of Priorities.* New York: William Morrow & Co., 1970.
Little, Charles E. and Mitchell, John G., eds. *Space for Survival.* New York: Pocket books, 1971.
McHale, John. *The Future of the Future.* New York: George Braziller, 1969.
Novick, Sheldon and Cotrell, Dorothy. *Our World in Peril: An Environment Review.* Greenwich, Conn.: Fawcett Publications, 1971.
Rienow, Robert and Leona. *Moment in the Sun.* New York: Ballantine Books, 1967.
Sherrell, Richard E. *Ecology: Crisis and New Vision.* Richmond, Va.: John Knox Press, 1971.
Taylor, Gordon Rattray. *The Doomsday Book.* Greenwich, Conn.: Fawcett Publications, 1970.

23
GOVERNMENT FOR THE PEOPLE

America faces a growing crisis of government. Citizens look to their government for security, for justice, and for services that exceed the ability of private individuals or groups to provide. Yet in all three of these matters today, controversy rages about the performance of the agencies of government in America. Sometimes the controversy centers around what functions the government should perform. For example, should it plan and control the economy, or should it merely regulate abuses within an otherwise private enterprise system? But most often the controversy has to do with the adequacy and fairness with which an acknowledged function is performed. In his book *Crime in America*[1] Ramsey Clark has charged that in its most direct contacts with crime —prevention, detection, apprehension, conviction, and correction—the American system of criminal justice fails miserably.

Spelling out his charge, Clark, a former attorney general of the United States, says that most crime is never reported to police; in four out of five cases reported no one is arrested; and of the serious crimes reported, barely one in nine leads to conviction. With such a poor record of detection, apprehension, and conviction, efforts at prevention are undermined. All of these defects add up to only one conviction for every fifty or more serious crimes. Only one-fourth of those convicted go to prison. Most of those who go to prison will later commit other crimes. Given that prison, instead of rehabilitating, often moti-

---

[1] Ramsey Clark, *Crime in America* (New York: Simon & Schuster, 1970).

vates and schools its inmates for further crime, a marked increase in convictions under present conditions might actually increase rather than decrease crimes.

It is not our purpose in this chapter to propose an answer to any of the current controversies about the performance of government in America. We will seek rather to put them into a perspective within which the controversies could become resolvable.

THE FUNCTIONS OF GOVERNMENT

The social and political institutions under which men live profoundly affect their lives: their outlook, their character as individuals, and the struggles and rewards they experience. The state is that one of the social and political institutions which exercises final authority within a society, determining in turn the division of labor and authority among other institutions and among individuals. The authority of the state is exercised by its government. It tells a person that he must do some things and refrain from doing others. It imposes penalties for infraction of its laws and regulations, though imperfectly, as we have seen. Even before an individual is aware, the government has registered his birth and regulated the conditions of his survival and early education. Later it takes part of his income for its services to him—all too much and inequitably levied according to current political charges —and as population increases and society grows in affluence and complexity, the agencies of government regulating us increase in number and multiply their regulations.

Do these proliferating governments and regulations minister to the realization of human personality as they should? Do they respect and fulfill the main human rights? How might they do so better? A "no" to the first two of these questions gains an easy majority, but agreement on the third is hard to find.

Who Should Rule?

Historically the majority opinion has favored strong government in the hands of "the right people." Thus Plato favored what we would call a rule of aristocracy. In *The Republic* he dreamed of a government by philosopher kings. In *The Statesman* and *The Laws* his aristocracy was differently composed. In the wars between kings and nobles of Europe the issues have concerned the right people and the territory to bring under their rule rather than the need for strong central authority. From Machiavelli to contemporary fascists, the state has been seen as rightly resting on force. For some it was an end in itself. For others, its end was material prosperity. For still others, it was to glorify their race, kind, religion, or way of life. But for all of those favoring a totalitarian state, unlimited in its power, the end was so important that statecraft was exempt from the ordinary rules of morality: individuals and groups were of worth only as they served the ends of the state.

A more complex version of the commitment to strong rule by the right people is held by Marxists. The right form of government, according to Marxist-Leninist views, differs in different stages of the development of society. Under capitalism, they say, the state is an instrument of power held by the owners of property and capital to keep the workers and the general population in subjection. Marxists seek to bring to power the leaders of the proletariat who will exercise dictatorship through a transition to a subsequent stage of society. In this transition the state may crush opposition, collectivize industry and agriculture, and manage both state and economy to do what its leaders know is in the true interests of the people. According to this doctrine, a further stage is to come in which the state will wither away and there will be peace and abundance for all. In practice, to date, Marxist-oriented states have been dictatorial in rule, with either a small elite exercising control or at times with a single dominant figure such as Joseph Stalin.

There stands another tradition which is best exemplified in the recent history of Great Britain and in the United States and Canada. This newer tradition denies that there is such a thing as the right people who should hold a near-absolute sway over others, even when those people intend the good of all. Because of this conviction the tradition seeks to limit the powers of government and to create institutions and customs which make these limitations effective. We will call this the tradition of political democracy.

Why are there no right people to rule? No matter who comes to power, he will be (1) fallible in his understanding, (2) limited in his capacity to be fair and equitable to all, (3) limited in his capability to carry out his understanding and his sense of right, and (4) restricted by the inertia of whatever course of improvement for society he may undertake to follow.

Some reformers acknowledge these difficulties and conclude that no one should rule: government, they say, is unnecessary; force in itself is evil; and state compulsion should be eliminated. In place of the state, voluntary associations of people should combine for the realization and protection of their common interests. Freed of state compulsion, the natural goodness of men might find expression. Historically, however, the failure of people to obtain and use the franchise has not meant an end of the state, but an assumption of its control by a self-selected dictatorship or aristocracy.

If the elimination of the state is not feasible and no one should rule absolutely, who should rule and under what limitations? The majority of the people should rule, according to one definition of democracy, and their power should be exercised through their representatives. But this power should be limited by a guarantee of minority rights. Lincoln's phrase expressed this aspiration as one of "government of the people, by the people, for the people." To continue the majority in effective control, this type of government limits terms of office, divides the powers of government among governing authorities (e.g., among legislative, judicial, and executive branches), and provides for popular checks through such vehicles as referendum, recall, impeachment, constitutional rights, and voluntary associations which compete with the government in some tasks and act as a check or watchdog in others.

Does majority rule happen, however? Throughout most of the history of the United States, the majority has not been enfranchised: women, Negroes, unpropertied, the poor, the uneducated, and the young. Gradually the vote has been extended to the people in this country, and the issues concerning the genuineness of majority rule have become subtler ones: Do the people have the facts? Do they understand the issues? Will they take the trouble to know and to vote? In some countries, where an attempt has been made to inaugurate majority rule quickly, the results have been sometimes unsatisfactory, sometimes tragic.

What Should Government Do?

Even those who favor strong central government recognize that the government should limit its decisions to a manageable list of key concerns. As societies have evolved from tribal forms to feudal and then national ones, the need to limit central governmental functions has grown clearer, and the difficulty of doing so and still assuring justice, order, and well-being to the society as a whole has become greater. Reacting to the arbitrariness of kings and to the self-serving habits of aristocracies, some thinkers urged as early as the seventeenth century that the state should be confined in its functions to the protection of life, liberty, and property and to the maintenance of peace and order. This view gained adherents in the eighteenth century in the Western democracies and reached the height of its acceptance in the nineteenth century. Adherents of this *laissez faire* doctrine held that each individual knows his own best interests and should be left alone to follow them. Government, they thought, tends to kill initiative and progress.

The laws of natural selection and the economic laws of competition and supply and demand should not be interfered with.

In the context of majority rule, however, at least as *majorities* were then defined and enfranchised, this outlook gave rise to serious injustice and abuse. As a result, there was a growing insistence that the state provide more adequately for equality of opportunity, for protection against economic disaster, and for other services or protections which cannot be provided as well by private efforts, either by single individuals or by large enterprises. Beginning with the provision of such things as roads and utilities, our governments have gone on to provide schools, emergency relief in disaster, unemployment insurance and sometimes jobs, security in old age, park and recreational services, help in conservation of natural treasures, subsidies for agricultural and industrial production or for limiting production, measures to protect health and advance knowledge, and legal aid to those unable to afford it. As a matter of practical politics, the *laissez faire* position is dead, though efforts are still made to move back toward it or to arrest the trend toward more comprehensive governmental responsibility for the well-being of all citizens. Working against any such movement are the growing complexity and interdependence of people and institutions, both within the country and among the states and nations. The interdependence and the speed and volume of interactions across state and national boundaries require a growing regulation of interstate and international relationships. This regulation must be premised upon some purpose, and no purpose short of general order, justice, and well-being seems to make sense.

Again, however, government cannot do everything. Thus as the need for an overall ordering of human society becomes undeniable, the need for a division of labor in the service of human needs also becomes unavoidable. The controversies surrounding this division of labor are many. For example, Congress is considering a "war powers act" intended to redistribute power between the president and the Congress with regard to the making of war. The issues are both substantive—disagreement about whether or in which cases to wage war—and procedural—who should have the right to declare war if majority rule is to be preserved. To take a different example, the division of labor in achieving racial desegregation arouses controversy both between states and federal government and between the judiciary, the executive, and the legislative branches of the federal government. A third example is that of financing higher education. The greatest resources for doing so are with the federal government, but historically the responsibility for providing higher education has been shared by the states and private institutions. If the great resources of the federal government were dramatically tapped for higher education, would there result strong federal control and a monolithic national system of colleges and universities? How can the needs for equal opportunity and for diversity of types of higher education (in philosophy, educational methodology, and content of learning options) be reconciled with the need for academic freedom and vigorous intellectual debate of fundamental ideas and outlooks?

The resolution of these issues of who should govern and what functions the different levels and branches of government should perform is best approached through a recognition of both emerging principles and emerging conditions that affect the application of the principles. The principles express value priorities or ethical imperatives which, however, when taken in abstraction from specific circumstances or applied unskillfully in those circumstances, can conflict with one another. The resolution of the issues requires a design of action to express the principles in a net betterment of the life of the people of the time and a foundation for an equitable opportunity for those to come. For example, a certain predictability in the ordering of society is a prerequisite to all other goods, so the principle may be enunciated that government must provide for this order. At the same time, a person who has all the major choices of life imposed upon him has lost one of the most precious ingredients of life, one distinguishing the values open to human life from those of other animals. Hence, a principle fostering human freedom may be stated as a demand upon all governments. To be more precise as to how the demands for order impinge upon and must be limited by the demands for freedom will require reflection upon the specific social situation. In chapter 22 we discussed the conflicting demands for economic growth and for enhancement of the natural and social environment. Any controls upon economic growth in the interests of the environment will limit individual freedom and corporate opportunities in certain respects in order to enhance individual well-being and choices, thus freedom, in other respects. In that chapter we discussed possible ways to resolve this particular type of conflict. That resolution, whatever it may be, should define in part some ground rules of government for our society in the immediate years ahead.

Another pair of principles that enter into American governmental development has to do with popular consent and equal justice before the law. Not every society is posited upon the goal of equal justice as we understand it. Even in our society the meaning of the goal and the willingness of popular majorities to support changes in implementation of the goal are matters of struggle. For example, for what concept of nondiscriminatory treatment of people of different races can legislators and executives obtain popular consent? Political democracy is based upon the view that popular control (consent) over major issues of policy is desirable. Two reasons can be given for this view. First, in the absence of other reasons one person has as much right as another to decide how the society should be governed. Second, even if some persons are not as informed or wise as others in their exercise of this right to govern, in the long run the decisions will be both better made and better enforced if leaders are obliged to obtain and sustain popular consent for major policies and priorities of government. This obligation upon political leaders forces at least some measure of educating of the electorate. This educating and the exercise of popular voice generate popular cooperation in making the policies work and must be fostered because policies cannot work in any case if they are poorly understood in a complex, interdependent society where enforcement must depend heavily upon intelligent, informed collaboration. By implication this discussion suggests that justice will lag where the mass of people are ignorant, prejudiced, or misguided in their values.

A further pair of potentially conflicting principles of governmental development concerns the duty of government to seek to better the life of the people and the duty of government to protect the property of the people and to sustain the order upon which they have come to expect the society to function. On the one hand, consider the need to wipe out or at least substantially reduce poverty, and on the other hand, the interrelatedness of this poverty with the social order which has enabled others to accumulate the wealth and the means to amass it. Many of the most effective ways to reduce or abolish poverty would seriously and adversely reduce wealth and the access to further wealth on the part of a portion of the population.

These conflicts of principle cannot be resolved in the abstract. Some governments seek concretely to subordinate concern for the growth of individual freedoms to the concerns for equity, health, and other values. We suggest that in theory it is possible to enhance the realization of all these values—order, freedom, consent, justice, betterment of life— if none is permitted to override all others. In practice this theory can be put into effect by study and by public deliberation resulting in the redesigning of the institutions and practices of the society. Each of the chapters in this book concerning applied ethics illustrates the kinds of information, analysis, and weighing of values required to reach such redesigning of concept and practice.

In the remaining pages of the chapter, we shall consider some additional areas of dilemmas in the functioning of government for the benefit of the people. The first of these has to do with the allocation of funds in the federal budget. The second discusses the obligations of individuals who are government officials. The third has to do with the limitation of the powers of the state with respect to the individual who disobeys laws. These cases will be studied as symptomatic of the larger problem of reconceiving the functions of government and the rights of individuals in seeking a good life within a larger, more complex, and more rapidly changing world.

SOCIAL PRIORITIES AND THE FEDERAL BUDGET

In 1970 the National Urban Coalition proposed a blueprint for changing national priorities.[2] It chose the federal budget as the vehicle for examining these priorities because that budget reflects the single most important body of priority decisions made by a public agency in the course of a year. The coalition called its proposal *Counterbudget* because it reflected a counterproposal to the congressional budget priorities. The proposed priorities were six: (1) full employment with a high level of economic growth and minimal inflation, (2) equal opportunity for all citizens to take part in the life of America and in shaping its governmental decisions, (3) a guarantee of basic necessities and income, (4) a better balance of revenues between federal government and state and local governments, (5) national security, and (6) economic assistance to less developed nations.

To achieve these six goals in the way desired would have cost more than the coalition could advocate because of the level of taxes which that cost would have required. A choice had to be made between an ideal outlay on these goals and a tolerable level of taxes. With a less-than-ideal total budget the coalition had to choose how best to spend the limited resources provided. It put the highest priority upon assuring everyone the basic necessities of life, stressing health and housing. It also advocated income support in cash (resulting in phasing out food stamp programs), for such aid enables a family to allocate its resources according to its own priorities.

Rather than trace all of the coalition's main recommendations we can see the point of its call for a debate of national priorities by taking note of a few hard choices it had to face. For example, the choice was made to put more effort on ending poverty, reforming education, and improving state and local governmental services than on environmental protection and restoration. Outlays for transportation were not increased, and a shift of $1.8 billion was recommended from outlays for highway programs to work on mass transit. The coalition recom-

---

[2]Robert S. Benson and Harold Wolman, eds., *Counterbudget* (New York and Washington: National Urban Coalition and Frederick A. Praeger, 1971).

mended a decrease in total spending for agricultural programs and an increase in spending for rural industrial development. Its largest suggested reduction in spending was for national defense and military assistance even though it placed national security as the second priority in order of importance, for its analysis revealed defense programs that contribute little to national strength or even reduce safety by fueling the arms race.

Overall the National Urban Coalition recommended an increase of spending by the federal government, but not all of this funding was to go for existing programs. In many areas the coalition called for new programs, reform of existing ones, and sometimes elimination of old ones. Thus their proposed federal budget reflected priorities in part through shifts of funds, and in part through changes of suggested activity.

Counterbudget brings into focus some of the abstract issues we have just discussed. Consider, for example, the question of the function of the government in furthering the well-being of citizens. Both the budget actually passed by Congress and the one proposed by the coalition involve a division of labor between government and people in achieving the well-being of individuals and families. The two budgets, however, divide the labor differently between state and federal governments (with a federal role in *Counterbudget* aimed at more uniform minimum standards for income maintenance) and between government as a whole and the individual family (with more stress on affirmative incentives rather than penalties to induce effort by the private individual to improve his own income).

To further reflect the fact that government through federal budgeting settles priority issues between different ethical concerns, some examples proposed in *Counterbudget* follow. In reference to the issue of population and pollution control, *Counterbudget* reflects the hard choices required if such control is to be substantial. The proposal puts a top priority on ending poverty in America, as officially defined, by 1975. Because of the priorities given to education and to improvement of state and local governmental services, the outlays proposed for environmental protection and restoration increased by only $1.8 billion for the first year. The resources for this purpose nevertheless would triple between 1971 and 1976 according to the proposal, and this level was thought to be sufficient "to prevent further deterioration of the environment and to set up the structure for dealing comprehensively with pollution after 1976."[3]

One of the most complex and controversial areas of the *Counter-*

---

[3]*Counterbudget*, p. 14.

budget recommendations is that of economic policy. This is an area of decision-making that illustrates with utmost clarity the way in which the ethical and the practical interlock, and the way in which technical knowledge is essential, but not sufficient, to make crucial choices that will affect the quality of life in the years ahead. The coalition argues for increased federal revenues derived from new tax measures plus a strong rate of economic growth, and for full employment by 1976 (defined as less than four percent unemployment). To get these results it proposes a combination of federal government measures: (1) sizeable budget deficits in 1972 and 1973, (2) creation of a large public service employment program, (3) a monetary policy assuring liquidity (easier credit on money), and (4) a real growth rate in the gross national product of more than five percent per year until 1974 and at least four percent per year thereafter. A key technical problem in putting such measures together is that of avoiding a runaway inflation. To do so the coalition advocates price-wage guidelines and possibly price and wage controls. Since this recommendation was made, such controls have actually been put into effect. If the coalition's economic measures were to work, they would yield much larger tax income to the government by virtue of enlarged incomes to individuals and enterprises. Even so, however, additional tax measures and increases in tax rates would be necessary to pay for these changes.

We said at the beginning of this chapter that the United States is involved in a growing crisis of government. The nature of this crisis has been specified with the aid of the example of the federal budget. The choices just outlined are only a small fraction of those required in the making of the federal budget. Some of these choices can have momentous effect, their consequences spreading throughout the society and affecting sharply the opportunities and the restrictions which people encounter. Some of the choices are urgent; gross injustices call for immediate redress and correction, and trends that have enormous effect and are very difficult to alter must be changed now or it will be harder and costlier to do so later. Many of the choices are, in a sense, unavoidable; that is, not to decide at this time is also a decision to let the current conditions and trends continue, and they are admittedly characterized by a great deal of defect and injustice. In addition the choices are interconnected in very complex and technical ways. They cannot be settled by resolutions of good will or declarations of sound principle. They involve problems which in many cases call for new knowledge if adequate means are to be devised for resolving the old difficulties without creating new and possibly worse ones. But they also are often questions in which both knowledge and good will combined will not resolve the question as to what ought to be done.

That question is often one of weighing alternative sets of good items against one another. For example, one "package" might include reduced poverty, better schools, lowered military activity, and higher taxes (as the coalition proposed); another might include improved health services, greater efforts in crime prevention and control, expanded scientific research, and more attention to control of environmental pollution. Each package would include other items as well. No one can possibly know precisely what would be the best set of measures to be embodied in the federal budget for any given year. Yet the effort must be made, because of the urgency and gravity and unavoidability of choosing, to reach decisions which embody awareness, responsiveness to peoples' needs and concerns, and informed effort to foresee consequences.

It would be hard to justify a judgment about whether the quality of decision-making in such matters as the federal budget is better or worse than it was, say, fifty years ago. Perhaps the present sense of crisis is in part a result of greater awareness of the social forces shaping our lives and of the degree of ignorance and powerlessness with which we are confronting these forces. If so that very awareness is a change for the better and may in turn make possible some needed improvement in decision-making processes. In addition, however, the crisis results from the greater numbers of people affected, the diminished social consensus about what is desirable and good, and larger effects that can be produced by virtue of technological developments and the size of federal interventions possible, the growing rate of social and technological change, and the continuing and in some respects increasing unpredictability of the future. These factors must be recognized and mastered in greater measure if people are to have a choice in their own destinies. To master them in any significant degree is to place new demands upon ourselves as citizens and upon our representatives and employees in government.

THE GOVERNMENT AND MORAL STANDARDS

Most governmental officials are honest and desire to serve the public interest. Most of them give effective and efficient service and deserve more recognition than they receive. Even honest officials, however, can easily fail to distinguish clearly between their private interests and the public interest. They sometimes find it difficult to determine what morality in office really is. These difficulties are compounded by the rapidity of change in government and society.

Some students of government believe that standards of public morality have been steadily rising, even though they may not be improving as rapidly as the times or the need for higher standards demand. Though there are occasional slumps or dips in the long-time trend, our standards in political life, at least at the national level, are probably higher today than at the beginning of this century and certainly much higher than in colonial days. We are slowly developing a concept of general welfare that gives us "a working pattern for public ethics."[4] At one time public office was quite generally viewed as a means to wealth. Later there was a time when "private profit by public servants at the expense of the general welfare" was considered corrupt, but private profit which accompanied public service was considered proper. The new principle that is being established is that "private profit by public servants, whether or not it is achieved at the expense of the public welfare, is corrupt."[5]

Standards of public morality influence and are influenced by standards of private morality. The public expects a higher standard of government officials than of private citizens. We condemn public servants for behavior that is a fairly normal part of business and private life. We condemn and turn from office the official who takes a bribe. The public, however, tends to overlook and usually fails to punish the one who offers the bribe.

A minority of governmental officials have carried on practices that have lowered the prestige of government and its officials. Anyone who scans the newspaper headlines of recent years will find accounts of tax scandals, voting frauds, political decisions influenced by means of gifts, protection for underworld characters, and shady business deals involving public agencies. Some officials do not clearly see the issues involved and fall into unethical practices through ignorance. A small number may consciously use political office to promote their private interests.

Ethical Problems of Administrators

The pressure on administrators or other public officials to lower their standards or to engage in corrupt practices comes from many directions and may be very strong.

> In the Federal Government, the forces that would drive public servants from the straight and narrow path of virtue center chiefly upon a limited area, the area in which Government is heavily "action-laden." This is the area in which there are big economic stakes, where the

---

[4] Estes Kefauver, "Past and Present Standards of Public Ethics in America: Are We Improving?" The Annals of the American Academy of Political and Social Science, vol. 280 (Philadelphia: The Academy, 1952); pp. 1–8.
[5] Ibid., p. 7.

decisions of legislators and administrators directly affect the business, or the property, or the income of particular groups or individuals. The abuses of discretion or the exploitation of power are most serious chiefly where the Government is dispensing valuable rights and privileges, constructing extensive public works, spending vast sums for military supplies and equipment, making loans, granting direct or indirect subsidies, levying taxes, and regulating the activities of privileged monopolies or economic practices in which there is a public interest.[6]

These action-laden areas, with the same pressures, are found in state and local governments.

Public officials may have their integrity undermined by accepting gifts that put them under personal obligation to the donor, by accepting expensive entertainment that may lead to a gradual shifting of loyalties; by past ties or the hope of future employment that tend to influence decisions; and by involvement in private business interests in such a way that their loyalties are divided.

With these and other dangers in mind Senator John F. Kennedy, speaking on ethics in government at a Midwestern college shortly before he became president, gave eight basic principles that he expected to use as guidelines in his new administration. The list of principles was an attempt to inform prospective federal appointees what would be expected of them, and what they have a right to expect from a government dedicated to the public interest. The list, somewhat abbreviated, is as follows:

> First, no officer or employee of the Executive Branch shall use his office position for financial profit, or reveal to others for their advantage confidential information acquired through his position, for he serves as a trustee for all the people.
> Second, no officer or employe shall engage in any business transaction with—or hold any financial interest in—or accept any gift, favor, or substantial hospitality for himself or his family—from any enterprise or person who is doing business or seeking to do business with that unit of the government which he serves or is able to influence....
> Third, all gifts which cannot appropriately be refused—such as gifts from public organizations or foreign Governments to the President of the United States—shall immediately be assigned to the Smithsonian Institution or other Federal agencies for historical, scientific or welfare uses....

---

[6]*Ethical Standards in Government.* A Report of a Subcommittee of the Senate Committee on Labor and Public Welfare. Washington, D. C.: U. S. Government Printing Office. See also *Code of Ethics for Government Service,* House Document 103 of the 86th Congress (Washington, D. C.: U. S. Government Printing Office, July 1958).

Fourth, no Federal appointee to any public regulatory agency shall represent any view other than the public interest. . . .

Fifth, no member of any such agency, and no person who assists in its decisions, shall entertain any ex-parte communication from any person—including political pressure or requests originating within the Executive or Legislative branches—concerning any case or other proceeding which is determined solely upon matters of record, unless that communication is made a part of the record and every party at interest is given an opportunity to reply. . . .

Sixth, all appointments, both high and low, will be made on the basis of ability—without regard to race, creed, national origin, sex, section or occupation. . . .

Seventh, senior positions in the State Department, the foreign service and the Defense Department shall be filled by the best talent in both parties. . . .

Eighth, preference in appointments will be given to those willing to commit themselves to stay on the job long enough to apply what they learn.[7]

Ethical Problems of Legislators

While some of the recommendations made above would apply to legislators as well as to administrators, there are special problems which legislators face. Some of the problems dealt with in this section will nevertheless also apply to executive and administrative officials. One problem that often has serious implications is the very high cost of running for elective offices, especially in national and state governments and sometimes in county, municipal, or other areas of local government. Campaign funds and workers have to be secured, and many of the large donors expect favors in return for their help. These favors may be jobs for themselves or friends, special legislation, contracts, subsidies, loans, insurance, or other privileges. The pressure to grant such favors explains in part why gambling and other antisocial practices are at times tolerated by officials in large cities.[8]

Other moral problems facing the legislator include the following: Shall the legislator vote according to his best judgment of the public interest at stake, in line with party policy, or with popular sentiment in his constituency? How shall the legislator conduct himself in dealing

---

[7]"Text of Kennedy's Address in Ohio on Ethics in Government," *New York Times*, 18 October 1960, p. 30C.

[8]See reports of the Special Senate Committee to Investigate Organized Crime in Interstate Commerce (Estes Kefauver, Chairman), *The Kefauver Report on Organized Crime* (New York: Didier Publishers, 1952); for a brief discussion, see "Robert Kennedy Defines the Menace," *New York Times Magazine*, 13 October 1963, p. 15 ff.

with congressional investigations?[9] Party interests may be involved. There have been many demands for a fair code and for reforms in this field. Again, how shall the legislator deal with administrative agencies or bureaus when his constituents ask for aid in obtaining favorable decisions on issues in which they have an interest?[10]

A number of high officials in government have recommended that legislators and administrators make a public disclosure of their private incomes. Such publicity, it is believed, would be a deterrent to improper conduct. In order to free themselves from private economic interests, some officials have voluntarily sold their stocks and bonds and have placed the money in investment trusts or have used it for other purposes. Some officials have voluntarily disclosed the nature and amounts of their income.

Various proposals have been made for codes of ethics for legislators, administrators, and other special groups of public officials. These codes are comparable to the codes of various professional and business groups. Good will alone is not enough. Men who face special or unique problems need to know "the rules of the game"—that is, just what is considered right and what wrong. Such codes, if kept up to date, made fairly specific, and used as the basis of disciplinary action, can be useful guides for conduct and powerful means for maintaining high moral standards.

A United States Senator presented in his testimony before the Subcommittee on Ethics the following "Decalogue for Members of Congress."

1. In the same sense in which a judge debars himself from decisions in which he has a direct personal financial stake, so I shall debar myself from fully legistlative decisions, or, if I take action or choose to vote I shall fully disclose the nature of my interest.

2. I shall never use my office to exert extra-legal pressure over the decisions of executive or administrative agencies.

3. I shall treat witnesses who testify before committees on which I sit with courtesy and fairness, following self-imposed limitations which for centuries have been the hallmark of the judicial process.

4. I shall not abuse my privilege of Congressional immunity; I shall not say things on the floors of Congress that I am not prepared to say outside, nor shall I betray the official confidence of the Congress, or of any committee thereof.

---

[9]For a code of practice for legislative investigations, see Erwin N. Griswold, *The Fifth Amendment Today* (Cambridge: Harvard University Press, 1955), pp. 45–48.

[10]See Paul Howard Douglas, *Ethics in Government* (Cambridge: Harvard University Press, 1952), ch. 3, for suggestions about how to deal with these and related issues.

5. I shall not indulge in personal vilification of any kind, but I shall not hesitate to criticize public figures and public policies with determination and courage whenever facts of public nature justify such criticism.

6. I shall not vote on any issue without an attempt to consider the voiceless interest of the unorganized in our society.

7. I shall strive constantly to interpret interests of my constituents in the perspective of the total national interest.

8. I shall try to be loyal to the promises of my political party, and thus to strengthen party teamwork and party responsibility in the Congress.

9. I shall not waste my own or my colleagues' time with irrelevant and inconsequential talk in committee or on the floor.

10. Whether as a member of the majority or minority, I shall attempt in my actions and words to educate and clarify, never to obscure or confuse.[11]

THE GOVERNMENT AND THE INDIVIDUAL

The government shapes our lives in the large by such instruments as the federal budget and its foreign and domestic policies. It also metes out justice or injustice to individuals one by one. "The achievement of justice," wrote Justice Hugo Black in 1966, "is a problem which, in the final analysis, depends on what kind of government and laws control society."[12] It is all very well and good to have a society with a chosen form of government, a representative democracy for example, and with foreign and domestic policies which are deemed sound. These arrangements still do not suffice to assure justice to the individual. "An urban dweller who is unfairly taxed because of the votes of a malapportioned state legislature, or a young man who is drafted because he participates in an antiwar protest, or an injured plaintiff who must settle a negligence claim for less than its value because he cannot afford a trial delayed for years by crowded court calendars—to these individuals the law has become the method of frustrating rather than fulfilling the high moral purposes of democratic government."[13]

Of the many problems which could throw light upon the functioning of government in the achievement of individual justice, let us consider examples from the controversial arena of the citizens who confront

---

[11] William Benton, "A Decalogue for Members of Congress," *New York Times Magazine*, 12 August 1951.

[12] Hugo L. Black, Foreword in *Confronting Injustice*, Lenore Cahn, ed. (Boston and Toronto: Little, Brown & Co., 1966), p. xi.

[13] Norman Redlich, Introduction in *Confronting Injustice*, p. xv.

customs, laws, or governmental policies which they believe unwise or immoral.

When Is Civil Disobedience Justified?

A citizen who confronts an allegedly unjust act of government presents both himself and the government with moral issues. Consider first his own choices. They are of four types. He may take the attitude that while he does not believe the judgment of the majority to be wise or just, he will accept the decision, since he accepts the pattern of government used in creating the law or the governmental act, and the issue is not so grave or his certainty of his own rightness so great that he can rightly put his judgment over that of the persons duly appointed to govern.

A second option is for him to obey the law while he protests against it and works to have it rescinded or amended. He may choose this course because he deems the injury or injustice not great enough to outweigh the impairment of respect for the law in general that would result from his disobedience of this specific law.

If the law requires something that a person judges to be grossly unjust or immoral, he may choose a third course of action: he may protest and at the same time disobey the law openly. In such a case the protester may make clear why he is breaking the law, and he may present himself to face the legal consequences of the action. In the case of refusal to pay taxes the result may be merely the confiscation of some of his property. In a stand for national independence or religious liberty, the risk may be that of life. This option is usually a choice for nonviolent resistance. It may turn out to be a choice of martyrdom, as it did with Gandhi and Martin Luther King, Jr.

This third option, civil disobedience, is distinguished from the previous two which do not involve a violation of law, and from the fourth, rebellion, which violates the law with the intent of overthrowing the government. *Civil disobedience,* as here defined, is a deliberate and open violation of law with the intent to protest or correct a wrong within the prevailing framework of government. A peculiar form of civil disobedience occurs when there is a state or local law in conflict with some federal law, constitutional principle, or federal court decision. In this situation civil disobedience from the perspective of local law may merely be lawful protest under federal law, but this finding cannot be firm until the protest is made and the case settled by the courts. Such was the case with many acts to desegregate buses, schools, lunch counters, and public facilities in the United States from the late 1950s until today.

The fourth course open to a citizen confronting an unjust law is that of rebellion or revolution—truly an option of last resort, which normally involves a commitment to violence. This was the method used by the early American colonists. It has been recognized in British, American, and some other systems of thought. In *Two Treatises of Government* (1690), for example, John Locke set forth the classical theory of representative government that found expression in the United States Declaration of Independence and the Bill of Rights in the Constitution. From this point of view there is a "law behind the law," a higher law than the formally enacted law of the community. Popular consent is an essential grounding of government, and the rights of individuals must be protected by the state if it is to be legitimate. Some of these rights, according to Locke, are inalienable. The state does not create these rights; it is bound to recognize and protect them. When rulers abuse this mandate, when governments become tyrannical and systematically unjust, or when rulers subordinate the rights and well-being of citizens to the individual or class interests of the rulers, citizens have the right to resist and rebel. Although the costs of such measures of rebellion as well as the risks of failure are so great that only a grave and systematic pattern of injustice could warrant the cost and the risk, the principle so eloquently expressed in the Declaration of Independence stands:

> We hold these truths to be self-evident, that all men are created equal, that they are endowed by their Creator with certain unalienable Rights, that among these are Life, Liberty and the pursuit of Happiness. —That to secure these rights, Governments are instituted among Men, deriving their just powers from the consent of the governed.—That whenever any Form of Government becomes destructive of these ends, it is the Right of the People to alter or to abolish it, and to institute new Government, laying its foundation on such principles and organizing its powers in such form, as to them shall seem most likely to effect their Safety and Happiness. Prudence, indeed, will dictate that Governments long established should not be changed for light and transient causes; and accordingly all experience hath shown, that mankind are more disposed to suffer, while evils are sufferable, than to right themselves by abolishing the forms to which they are accustomed. But when a long train of abuses and usurpations, pursuing invariably the same Object, evinces a design to reduce them under absolute Despotism, it is their right, it is their duty, to throw off such Government, and to provide new Guards for their future security.

The fact that either civil disobedience or rebellion may be ethically warranted leaves open the questions of whether a particular instance of either is warranted, and what the government in question may or ought to do in dealing with the dissidents. Societies that openly and consistently respect the right of civil disobedience and revolution seldom experience revolutions, though they may lead a more tumultuous life than other societies with respect to demonstrations, protests, and litigation. Theorists of political democracy contend, further, that the quality of life—including liberty, security, and well-being—is better fostered by a society respecting dissent, even civil disobedience, than by one which denies such civil rights. "Americans should revolt at the thought, not of revolution, but that future Americans might ever mildly submit to a denial of their equal rights, without revolution."[14] From this viewpoint the upsurge of civil disobedience in the United States in the 1960s reflected a need for substantial changes in the social institutions and practices. The civil disobedience movements were adaptive responses to a condition of overdue reforms, notably in racial injustice and in nationalistic war-making.

Notwithstanding the need for change many of the protests, demonstrations, and confrontations could by no means be equated in clarity and magnitude of the evil or in hopelessness of alternative recourse, as some civil disobedients have urged, with the cause of the early Christians refusing to worship the Roman Emperor, with Gandhi's movement for independence, or with such nearer causes as those of the sit-ins against segregation or the conscientious objectors to military service. Also many of the organized expressions of dissent in the 1960s lacked the coherence of purpose and strategy that would characterize an effective approach to civil disobedience. For such a strategy the dissenters would be obliged to address themselves, not simply to the need for social reform, but to such questions as these:

To what serious injustice or major opportunity for betterment in the laws or in their application are we speaking in our civil disobedience?

Why do we think that there is no reasonable prospect for remedy within the laws?

What alternative strategies for gaining our end have we considered, and why are the costs, risks, and prospects of our chosen course thought preferable to those of the alternatives? What demands of due care in weighing these choices have we followed in our decision?

What is there in the convictions and interests of our opponents and of noncommitted bystanders to which we can appeal with a reasonable expectation that our case will eventually affect enough of them to grant its success?

What is the basis in our own convictions for construing this cause

---

[14]Alfred J. Snyder, *America's Purpose* (Philadelphia: Declaration Press, 1937), p. 157.

and this strategy for pursuing it as requiring civil disobedience on our part? Does our understanding of our own motives support this conviction?

How does our effort comply with our own conviction that the grievous wrongs we protest are best resolved within the legal framework of the society? On what basis would we be willing for others of differing, but equally vehement, conviction to use our own methods of seeking change and communicating concern?

On what views of the facts and of social process do we believe that our effort will indeed produce the intended effect? If the effort requires a commitment to nonviolence, will we in fact be able to adhere to that commitmnt?

Perhaps it will be argued that no one with enough moral passion to risk civil disobedience or rebellion can weigh the choices as rationally as these questions suggest. Perhaps too it will be argued that the choices themselves are not subject to resolution in such rational terms. Yet a decision of such moment is unlikely to be a matter of sudden impulse and, if impulsively made, is even less likely to have the outcomes intended. However far our actual ability to deliberate may be from ideal, an awareness of what is involved in an adequate deliberation can be used to reduce the error and arbitrariness that might otherwise pertain. From a longer perspective, if effective rights of dissent are to quicken the ethical responsiveness of the society and inform its evolution, the users of those rights must be responsible enough in their exercise that on balance this type of salutary effect must in fact normally result.

Viewing the question of what to do about civil disobedience from the perspective of the law enforcement authorities, a similar circumspection seems required. Attempts to suppress violently the peaceful protest of manifest injustice can only build rage in a widening public about both the original injustice and the compounded injury of police response to protest. So it was, for example, with the Selma marches and the earlier efforts at desegregation in Montgomery, Alabama. So it was with the British treatment of Gandhi and his followers and the earlier treatment of the American colonies. So it is in the still unresolved racial strife of the Union of South Africa. Sometimes the law enforcers' reaction to law violation creates a greater wrong than is involved in the matter they are seeking to regulate, as when the penalties for the use of alcohol and more recently of marihuana threatened to generate mass evasion and growing disrespect for law enforcement. Yet the degree of breakdown of law enforcement cited by Ramsey Clark at the outset of this chapter seems clearly incompatible with the purposes of security and well-being of society for which we establish government at all.

The law enforcers too must ask their questions, including the following:

On what basis of public consent and support for the purpose and specific form of this law can we proceed in enforcing it?

How can we maintain the order, security, and well-being of the public in other respects while working out the means of enforcing the particular law that is being protested?

How can our mode of enforcement be so managed as to respect the legal rights of the protesters?

If the enforcers themselves see the laws they are enforcing as in some ways defective, how can they maintain their respect for law in general and their morale and effectiveness in law enforcement while insisting upon a publicly acceptable way of either obtaining compliance with the defective laws or getting them altered?

When protesters are ingenious in drawing sympathy but cannot persuade the public that they are right in their objective, how can enforcement be so managed as to respect both the public sympathies and the public purpose?

In recent years there seems to have been a rash of new issues in the domain of governmental intrusion upon the rights of individuals or, phrased differently, of individual and group objections to governmental efforts to administer society. For example, some Congressmen and some federal employees have felt obliged as a matter of public duty to disclose secret governmental documents, allegedly in violation of the law, because these documents disclosed that other government leaders were engaged in treasonable or at least gravely wrong use of their offices—the Ellsberg case, for example, concerning unauthorized disclosure of contents of The Pentagon Papers is still in the courts at this writing. A number of journalists have been taken to court for refusing to disclose the sources of their information. They claimed the right to protect these sources as a necessary condition of the ability of the press to perform its public function, to be a watchdog upon the government and upon any and every other institution that might use secrecy to hide its exploitation of others or its unethical performance of a task. A major attack has been launched upon the efforts of various governmental agencies to investigate matters which the attackers construe as within the constitutionally protected privacy of the individual. A case recently received court judgment that would assure the rights of prisoners to communicate with the press.

Not all of these instances of clash between governmental and individual rights and prerogatives have involved civil disobedience, as earlier defined, although some have been settled short of such acts only because the protesters were willing to go to that length if necessary to gain redress. Embedded in the overall phenomenon are almost inexorable social trends forcing us toward new practices and new institutions for regulating the balance between individual freedoms and social controls in an increasingly mobile, complex, interdependent, and affluent society. This phenomenon confronts us with a paradox. People venture in the name of greater good to unseat a law or a custom that has as its own warrant its supposed utility for the greatest good. We meet this paradox with a counter-paradox. To assure both freedom and order we entrust government and the enforcement of law to representatives, whose means we then limit by sanctioning counter institutions and rights which they may not throttle or abridge. Small wonder that government today moves into crisis.

The United States of America was founded in rebellion. Dissent has cost us dearly, but it has also enlarged our freedom and multiplied its fruits. Even so grievous injustices still persist, and important possibilities of human dignity and fulfillment remain unrealized. The law and the present social order can never be seamless garments of right. They must constantly be judged and be in the process of alteration in the light of moral standards external to the law. To make these alterations in a society as complex and changing as today's will require, both in policy-making and priority-choosing on the one hand and in relations between the government and the individual on the other hand, a wider and more complex participation of citizens than present institutions have managed. Sometimes this participation will take new forms of confrontation and dissent. The confusion and disorder, however, need not be seen as a period of decline. The last decade is probably better understood as a period of struggle out of which can emerge both an enlargement of the functions of government and a strengthening of the roles of citizens and of nongovernmental institutions in holding the government within boundaries that respect and support the rights of the citizen and of voluntary associations of people. Whether this development will in fact occur will be determined in part by citizen understanding of the possibilities and citizen initiative in making those possibilities come to be.

QUESTIONS AND PROJECTS

1. Many people complain that they are powerless to influence national policy. In some cases they lack the vote. In others they cite other causes for not having their due share of influence. In still others they seem to want their view to prevail even though a majority opposes it, and in some of these last cases the majority view is indeed an unjust policy. What changes would you advocate in present United States'

policies as to (1) who may vote and (2) how, in other ways, the individual citizen can influence legislation? What objections to your reccommendations would you anticipate? Why do you think the objections are inconclusive?

2. In a changing society the old ways tend to become unjust because they do not take account of differences in the values experienced by those affected under changing circumstances. Not all of the old ways need changing, however, to adjust equitably to any given set of social changes. Normally the victims of change are people who are also among the less influential members of the community. Various ideas have been advanced for remedying this difficulty as well as ongoing injustices through federally subsidized legal services, ombudsmen financed by public funds, "watchdog" agencies (e.g., for consumer protection), privately organized lobbies and advocates (e.g., Common Cause, the American Civil Liberties Union, the National Association for the Advancement of Colored People, and the like). What do you view as the most effective ways to cope with this problem? Are there new measures you would recommend? By what criteria would you judge such efforts?

3. If you were in a position to determine the federal budget for the next five years, what would be your top ten priorities? Why? What major changes of policy would be needed in order to make your priorities effective? Would any of these priorities or policy changes involve a change of function for the federal government? If so, how would you justify that change?

4. How do you account for the fact that in some elections less than fifty percent of those entitled to vote actually do so? What should be done about this condition? Why do you think that your proposal would be of benefit?

5. In 1963 the Supreme Court of the United States handed down a decision holding that state boards of education violate the Constitution when they write or approve prayers for students and impose or promote them by public authority. A controversy immediately arose and amendments to the Constitution were proposed as means of permitting prayer and Bible reading. Some claimed that the court decision encouraged atheism and secularism, that all the Constitution forbade was the establishment of any specific religion or church group, and that the principle of separation of church and state was not the issue. Opponents of the proposed amendments to put "God in the Constitution" said that, while the proposed amendments were designed to aid religion, they might actually undermine it. Voluntary prayer and Bible reading could still be encouraged and, in any case, the principle of separation of church and state has been a great help to the growth of religious groups. Some religious leaders, politicians, and the press supported each side of the question. Clarify the principles involved in this dispute and explain where you stand on the issue and why.

6. From time to time there are filibusters in the United States Senate to prevent passage of some bill. For example in the spring and early sum-

mer of 1964 a filibuster against the Civil Rights Bill lasted for weeks before it could be ended. More recently filibusters have been used to block confirmation of presidential nominees to the Supreme Court and to prevent certain anti-war resolutions in Congress. Discuss the filibusters from the point of view of democratic rights and ethical principles. You may wish to consult the *Reader's Guide to Periodical Literature* for recent articles on the filibuster, or such books as Joseph S. Clark, *Congress: The Sapless Branch* (New York: Harper & Row Publishers, 1964).

7. Give your reaction to the following statement, indicating whether you think it is as sound today as when it was first made: "If a man murders another man and is seized by a mob and lynched, the first man is a criminal but the mob are conspirators and rebels, as well as assassins; for by depriving the murderer of his right of trial and conviction by a jury of his peers and of sentence carried out according to the terms of the law, they have defied the whole system of constitutional government, and if they go unpunished they have weakened it and exposed it to further contempt. If a striker throws a brick through a factory window or beats up a strikebreaker, he should be arrested and dealt with as the law decrees. But if a mob of vigilantes drags him out of his house and attacks him and threatens his life, the vigilantes are the dangerous revolutionaries and the striker by comparison is a mere petty lawbreaker." [Freda Kirchwey, "A Plea for Democracy," *Journal of the American Association of University Women* 29 (October 1935): 4.] How do you distinguish between justified civil disobedience and criminal vigilantism?

8. Many important telephones in Washington are reported to be "monitored" —conversations are recorded or taken down by a stenographer who is on an extension telephone. One reason given for this practice is the fear that an outside recording can be "doctored" and used as evidence in a hearing, investigation, or a dispute over what was said or not said. One man is reported to consider the use of these precautionary measures a moral obligation, to protect his own reputation and that of others. Comment on this practice. Is someone who is having his conversations monitored and recorded under obligation to inform the person at the other end of the line that the conversation is being monitored?

9. A Cleveland judge once sent a man back to the Ohio Penitentiary because of a legal technicality. Another man confessed, one hundred thirty-seven days after the conviction, that he had committed the robbery for which the man was serving time, but the law denies a new trial unless the new evidence is filed within one hundred twenty days after conviction. Raymond B. Fosdick in *American Police Systems,* [Reprint Series in Criminology, Law Enforcement, and Social Problems, no. 53 (Montclair, N. J.: Patterson Smith, 1969)] chapter 1, tells about various cases in which criminals were let off because of some minor technicality. For example a man convicted of assault with intent to kill was freed because the copying clerk omitted the letter *e* in the word *malice*. What do you think of the practice of permitting such technicalities to destroy the intent and the spirit of the law?

10. The authors have on file a number of newspaper accounts of men who were released from prison after having served some years for crimes they did not commit. One served three, another thirteen, and still another seventeen years. Not all men in prison are guilty of the offenses for which they were jailed. Prepare a defense of your view on the following questions: Has the state met its full responsibility when it has freed an innocent man? Is a pardon by the governor or a public apology sufficient? Private persons are liable for injuries they inflict even if they are unintentional; should the state hold itself similarly responsible and compensate the injured person?
11. From time to time the newspapers have reported cases similar to the following: A citizen of one state in the United States went to another state, started with little or nothing and, by working hard for fourteen years, built up a prosperous business and established for himself a reputation for honesty and fair dealing. People in the local community in which he lived thought highly of him, and when he had to return to his native state, the local newspaper said: "He has established a reputation as a man of his word, liberal, successful, enterprising. . . . He has always cooperated in the general interest of community affairs." The man in question had no choice but to return to his native state because he was a fugitive from justice. Fifteen years earlier he had been convicted of killing a policeman while intoxicated. He had been sentenced to twenty years in prison but had escaped after one year. Is the attempt to force him to serve additional years in prison upholding the dignity of the law or is it vindictive justice? What good can the remaining nineteen years in prison do for this man or for society? In a number of similar cases the governors have immediately pardoned and freed the person involved. Do you approve?
12. In some states a person registered as a Democrat may vote in the Republican primary, and vice versa. In some cases in which their own candidate was sure of winning their own primary, voters have "crossed-over" to vote in the other party's primary with the intent of electing the weaker of that party's candidates. In this way voters hoped to help their own party's nominee win in the general election. The crossing-over is entirely legal in some states. What is your view of the ethics of the practice?
13. The problem of gifts, entertainment, and the acceptance of other favors has perplexed legislators and other governmental officials for many years. Where do you think the line should be drawn and why? One writer suggests that trouble may begin with acceptance of the first cigar. John Quincy Adams said that his principle was to refuse all presents offered him as a public man. Senator Paul Douglas said he would return any gift that cost more than $2.50. Charles E. Merriam is reported to have said that a bottle of whiskey given to an official was a friendly gift, whereas a whole case was a bribe. Another public figure is reported to have said that he would accept a ham up to eleven pounds, but nothing over that weight. For a political novel by a writer who has covered many

phases of national politics, see Allen Drury, *Advise and Consent* (Garden City, N. Y.: Doubleday & Co., 1959).

14. What is the ethics of ghostwriting? Mr. A. claims that the practice, widely used by politicians, endangers democracy by deceiving the citizens (audience or readers). It is also an evil, he says, because the man for whom the speeches are written need not think through the problem he is discussing. Mr. B. defends the practice because the politician does not have time to do the research himself and prepare all the talks he is expected to give. Most speakers, he says, go over the manuscript and make changes to suit themselves.

    In the 1964 Convention of one party in the United States, a candidate for nomination for the presidency sent a letter that was a blistering attack on the leading candidate. Later he admitted that it had been written by the staff and that because of the pressure of events he had not read it. What should he have done?

15. Should a legislator attempt to discover all the facts in connection with an issue and then use his own best judgment and conscience in recording his vote, or should he be guided by the best judgment or majority sentiment of the voters who elected him? Representative John Vorys once said, "I am extremely cautious about calling political decisions moral issues. On the other hand . . . no Congressman or Senator should cast a vote he knows is wrong in order to be reelected." William Benton, "The Big Dilemma: Conscience or Votes," *New York Times Magazine,* 26 April 1959, p. 12.

16. Members of certain religious sects—for example Jehovah's Witnesses—have scruples about saluting flags. Yet we want citizens to be loyal and patriotic. There are a number of cases on record of students in public schools being expelled for refusal to salute the flag. Discuss these incidents in the light of both moral and legal principles.

17. Is it wise to prevent citizens from traveling in some foreign countries? Three presidents—Truman in 1952, Eisenhower in 1956, and Kennedy in 1963—called for freer travel across international frontiers as a means of removing suspicion and fear as potential causes of misunderstanding and war. Yet in the sixties travel to some foreign countries was prohibited. Read Henry Steele Commager, "Passport Barrier: 'It Must Come Down,'" *New York Times Magazine,* 20 October 1963, and indicate what restrictions you would set, if any, to requests for passports.

18. Can you foresee a situation in which you personally would take part in an act or movement of civil disobedience? If so on what bases would you make the decision? If not for what reasons do you exclude this option?

19. The growth of government and the proliferation of regulations have led some commentators to predict an inexorable decline of personal freedom. Do you see an alternative to this future that is feasible? If so, sketch its main features and explain why you think it both feasible and desirable. If not, what appraisal do you make of the worth of life under the conditions you foresee?

20. Have we in the United States and some other Western countries gone

too far in making illegal not only crimes like murder, robbery, arson, and rape in which there is a victim and which no society can tolerate and still survive but also other acts such as gambling, prostitution, homosexual practices between consenting adults, and the use of drugs where there is no consensus? Two teachers at The John Jay College of Criminal Justice claim that police actions against these latter acts are "counter productive" in that they cause more crimes than they prevent, overburden the police courts, endanger the civil liberties, and lead to widespread corruption. Do we tend to overburden the law and neglect other means of social control? How far can we go in legislating morality? See Alexander B. Smith and Harriet Pollack, "Crimes Without Victims," *Saturday Review* 54 (December 4, 1971): 27-29.

SUGGESTED READINGS

Allen, Francis A. "Civil Disobedience and the Legal Order." *University of Cincinnati Law Review* 36: nos. 1 and 2 (Winter-Spring, 1967): 1–38, 175–195.
Bedau, Hugo Adam, ed. *The Death Penalty in America*. Garden City, N.Y.: Doubleday & Co., Anchor Books, 1964.
Brandt, Richard B., ed. *Social Justice*. Englewood Cliffs, N.J.: Prentice-Hall, 1962.
Clark, Ramsey. *Crime in America: Observations on Its Nature, Causes, Prevention and Control*. New York: Simon & Schuster, 1970.
Dahl, Robert A. *Modern Political Analysis*. Englewood Cliffs, N.J.: Prentice-Hall, 1963.
Douglas, Paul H. *Ethics in Government*. Cambridge: Harvard University Press, 1952.
Fortas, Abe. *Concerning Dissent and Civil Disobedience*. New York: New American Library of World Literature, Signet Books, 1968.
Frankel, Charles. *High on Foggy Bottom: An Outsider's Inside View of the Government*. New York: Harper & Row, Publishers, 1969.
Freidrich, Carl J., and Chapman, John W., eds. *Justice*. Yearbook of the American Society for Political and Legal Philosophy. New York: Atherton Press, 1963.
Gordis, Robert. *Politics and Ethics*. Santa Barbara, Calif.: Center for the Study of Democratic Institutions, 1961.
Hart, H. L. A. *Punishment and Responsibility: Essays in the Philosophy of Law*. New York: Oxford University Press, 1968.
Hills, Stuart L. *Crime, Power, and Morality: The Criminal Law Process in the United States*. San Francisco, Calif.: Chandler Publishing Co., 1971.
Kaplan, Abraham. *American Ethics and Public Policy*. New York: Oxford University Press, 1963.

Keeton, Morris. "The Morality of Civil Disobedience." *Texas Law Review* 43 (March 1965): 507–525.
Macfarlane, Leslie J. "Justifying Political Disobedience." *Ethics* 79 (October 1968): 24–55.
Moberly, Sir Walter. *The Ethics of Punishment.* Hamden, Conn.: Shoe String Press, Archon Books, 1968.
National Advisory Commission on Civil Disorders. *Report of the National Advisory Commission on Civil Disorders.* New York: New York Times Co., 1968.
Power, Paul F. "On Civil Disobedience in Recent American Thought." *The American Political Science Review* 64, no. 1 (March 1970): 35–47.
Prosch, Harry. "Toward an Ethics of Civil Disobedience." *Ethics* 77 (April 1967): 176–192. See also *Ethics* 77 (July 1967): 311–313.
Rucker, Darnell. "The Moral Grounds of Civil Disobedience." *Ethics* 76 (January 1966): 142–145.
Schooler, Dean, Jr. *Science, Scientists, and Public Policy.* New York: Free Press, 1971.
Somigel, Erwin O., and Ross, H. Lawrence. *Crimes against Bureaucracy.* New York: Van Nostrand Reinhold Co., 1970.
Stokes, Anson Phelps, and Pfeffer, Leo. *Church and State in the United States.* New York: Harper & Row, Publishers, 1964.
Swomley, John V., Jr. *American Empire: The Political Ethics of Twentieth-Century Conquest.* New York: Macmillan Co., 1970.
Thomas, S. B., Jr. "Authority and the Law in the United States, 1968." *Ethics* 79 (January 1969): 115–130.
Turk, Austin T. *Criminality and Legal Order.* Chicago: Rand McNally & Co., 1969.
Walzer, Michael. "The Obligation to Disobey." *Ethics* 77 (April 1967): 163–175.
Warren, Earl. *A Republic, If You Can Keep It.* New York: Quadrangle Books, 1972.

24
WAR AND THE QUEST FOR PEACE

The problem of war in the thermonuclear age is one of the most urgent of the moral questions facing modern man. The problem is incredibly complicated, and men of intelligence and understanding hold different positions in part because of our inability to predict the future with any certainty. New inventions or discoveries may change conditions with great rapidity, or a change in the world situation may cause us to interpret problems in a different frame of reference. We are not concerned here with technical knowledge about nuclear energy and weapons or with the strictly scientific and engineering problems involved. The control and use of nuclear energy is much more than a scientific issue. It is a moral and human problem of the first order. Decisions regarding its use will affect man's social, political, and economic relationships and may well determine the course of history and the fate of all mankind.

THE ROLE OF ATOMIC ENERGY

Once man had very little control over land, sea, or air, or the other processes of nature. He stood in awe before them and was forced to adjust his life to their demands. Throughout history man has been gaining more and more control over nature. At first the rate of progress was very slow. Then changes came at an accelerating pace until, within the last few decades, man has released power so vast that the difference between previous explosives and atomic explosives is a factor of more than a million.

New discoveries and inventions and new sources of power tend to spread out their effects and lead to changes in all phases of human living. The discovery of fire was used for comfort and progress, but also for destruction. The invention of gunpowder helped destroy feudalism in Europe and usher in a new type of society. The invention of printing was an important element in the rise of modern civilization. The microscope led to great change in medicine; the telescope did the same in astronomy. Other inventions like the steam engine led to the industrial and technological revolutions, which have changed all phases of society. The new sources of energy released in our time appear to make these earlier advances pale into relative insignificance.

Now a single twenty-megaton H-bomb is said to deliver "more explosive power than that of all the weapons used by all nations for all purposes during all the years of World War II."[1] We are told that one of the thermonuclear or hydrogen bombs could destroy any city in existence. In addition to complete destruction over something like a hundred square miles, the radioactive fallout might settle on an area of many thousands of square miles and make this area uninhabitable for a considerable time. "After a test of a larger H-bomb at Bikini, there were several injuries and one death due to the exposure of the small crew of a Japanese fishing trawler well over a thousand miles away."[2] We have moved in a few decades from a condition of power scarcity to a condition of power surplus and potential overkill. Weapons of destruction have piled up so fast that the balance-of-power principle of the last century has been replaced by a balance-of-terror strategy, in which the threat of massive retaliation and total annihilation is stressed as a deterrence to enemy attack.

The development of Intercontinental Ballistic Missiles (ICBM) is now the form of weapon posing the most danger. These have been developed by the "superpowers" in such quantity and with such increasing sophistication that the overkill potential is even greater. This in turn has led to a huge development of antiballistic missiles.

Fortunately there are some signs that at least a small degree of progress in disarmament is taking place. First, the test-ban treaty of 1963, then the two agreements that President Nixon brought back from his Moscow visit in the late spring of 1972, plus some easing of tension

---

[1] David Rittenhouse Inglis, "The Nature of Nuclear War," in *Nuclear Weapons and the Conflict of Conscience*, John C. Bennett, ed. (New York: Charles Scribner's Sons, 1962), p. 43.

[2] Ibid., p. 44.

in the cold war have brought renewed hope. The Moscow agreements contained a treaty to sharply limit defensive antiballistic missiles and an agreement to freeze current levels of missiles for five years. The strategic-arms-limitation treaty (known as SALT) is only a first stage which is supposed to lead to a much more comprehensive agreement in arms control on the part of the great powers. If such control becomes a reality, it could lead to a great lessening of tension to say nothing of the release of money for constructive purposes. At present, armament control by agreement is something worth working for, even though progress in this field is slow in coming.

There remains of course the possibility of the spread of atomic weapons to many other nations. Such an event could lead to hysterical fear of an atomic war, especially if this development were in the hands of an irresponsible totalitarian power. However, this danger could be somewhat reduced if the larger powers can gain a realistic sense of the need for control.

Another danger in the present situation is that there will always be the possibility (some would say the probability) of war breaking out in one or more of the following ways: (1) War by accident, through failure or mistake of some official or mechanism, or even by a strategically placed official who becomes nervous and loses his head. (2) War by miscalculation, when one side to a dispute misjudges the point at which the other side would take a stand, refuses to be pushed further, and uses any and every means to defend national interests. (3) A small or limited conflict or war which gets out of bounds and flares into an all-out conflict.

In an age when many nations are stockpiling atomic weapons, the leaders of any particular nation may not know the source or cause of an explosion that takes place in its territory. Against whom or what will that nation retaliate? We have reached the point where imagination and clear thinking on an unprecedented scale are needed to avoid war and utter catastrophe. Many people, including atomic scientists and leaders in many nations, are telling us that securtiy and escape from war may be gained only through effective international control. One who reads recent literature dealing with atomic energy is impressed with the constant demand for its strict international control. This goal, it appears, depends on the development of ethical standards that are higher than most "practical men" have been prepared to accept in the past, for themselves or for their nation.

We have been considering the impact of nuclear power in the whole field of armaments and war. Let us not forget or underestimate the fact that nuclear power has many peaceful uses of very great promise. How can this vast power be released and used for the promotion of human welfare? There is already, we are told, a power surplus for destruction. The moral challenge in view of the possibilities before us is tremendous and urgent. Research in the everyday peacetime uses of atomic energy is being pursued in a growing number of countries. Space does not permit us to discuss at any length the potentially very great industrial, agricultural, medical, and other uses of atomic energy. Early enthusiasm, however, has been reduced somewhat by the problem of the safe disposal of radioactive waste. In industry electric power generated from the new source of energy can furnish power for various means of transportation and for factories. Radioactive materials or radioisotopes have many uses. In the field of agriculture the new discoveries may change our crop patterns, improve the fertilizing of crops, and enable us to preserve food longer. In medicine the gains are great in the areas of both diagnosis and treatment. Certain types of cancer, for example, yield to irradiation, and radioactive iodine in the thyroid gland is used to treat thyroid disease. These are just a very few of the ways through which atomic energy can be a boon to men and women.

WAR AS AN ANCIENT INSTITUTION

War as a means for settling disputes between groups of people, from kinship groups to nations, goes back to the dim, distant past. There are records of primitive man using stones, clubs, spears, and bows and arrows for weapons. With the domestication of animals and the development of agriculture, the defense of territory and economic gain, along with political conquest and prestige, came to play increasing roles as motivating factors in conflicts. The use of the horse, the chariot and the fortification of cities appeared somewhat later. Conquest led to the centralization of power and the rise of dynasties and kingdoms and what have been called "universal states," such as Egypt, Mesopotamia, Persia, China, India, Mexico, Peru, and later Greece and Rome. These states dominated considerable areas of the earth. The story of the discovery and use of new weapons and tactics, such as gunpowder and firearms, the airplane (fighters and bombers), and nuclear energy is too long and involved to relate here, but it is fairly well known and may be found in books dealing with the history of warfare.

The beliefs of men regarding war have varied greatly. In ancient Greece men generally accepted war between the city-states and between the Greeks and the "barbarians" as part of the order of nature. Heraclitis said that "All things come into being and pass away through strife." The Hebrew Old Testament includes many passages in which God is viewed as leading his people in warfare. The existence of war continued to be an accepted fact during the Roman era and the medieval period in the West. Catholic thinkers, including St. Thomas Aquinas, while asserting that peace was the end to be desired, called on monarchs and princes to defend the state and the faith. They drew a distinction between a just and an unjust war, a distinction defended by some recent writers.[3]

With the growth of secular nationalism in modern Europe, war came to be regarded by many as necessary and inevitable. The more extreme view is sometimes called Machiavellianism because Machiavelli (1469–1527) in *The Prince* not only viewed the state as resting on force with material prosperity its conscious aim but also believed that the ordinary rules of morality did not apply to affairs of state. Less extreme views of war were expressed by Thomas Hobbes, John Locke, and Baruch Spinoza. In the nineteenth century, especially in Germany, war came to be viewed as a positive means of national revival. The outlook of certain philosophers, including Hegel, Fichte and Schopenhauer, may be included here. Nietzsche, whose views were influential, glorified war and the dangerous life. To this list we should add a large group of militaristic writers and political leaders whose doctrines, with racial overtones, were taken over by the German nazi and Italian fascist leaders.

The views that war is naturally caused by an innate, aggressive instinct in man and that it will continue unless the instinct is redirected or sublimated have been revived in the last decade by Robert Ardrey and Konrad Lorenz.[4] Ardrey is a dramatist and popularizer of the work of others; Lorenz is a student of animal behavior. While both men recognize the elements of learning and adjustment to conditions, they believe that the instinctive drive is the most important factor. This thesis has been vigorously challenged and refuted by various anthropologists, zoologists, and other scientists[5] who point out that human beings adapt to their group's traditional way of life and that warlike behavior is the product of the institutions and the history to which the individuals have been conditioned.

In disregard of the evidence given by many scientists of the destruc-

---

[3]See Paul Ramsey, *The Just War: Force and Political Responsibility* (New York: Charles Scribner's Sons, 1968). For a criticism see Donald A. Wells, "How Much Can 'The Just War' Justify?" *Journal of Philosophy* 66 (December 4, 1969): 819–829.

[4]Robert Ardrey, *The Territorial Imperative* (New York: Atheneum, 1966); Konrad Lorenz, *On Aggression* (New York: Harcourt, Brace & World, 1966).

[5]See M. F. Ashley Montagu, ed., *Man and Aggression* (New York: Oxford University Press, 1968).

tive nature of modern war, there are those who seem to believe that war is needed for eugenic purposes, for population control, and for a healthy economy, believing that only war solves the problem of inventory. Large sections of the population have a vested interest in preparation for war—the big corporations with billion dollar contracts for weapons, the big unions with large numbers of workers in defense plants, and the great number of persons trained in the arts of war. More than two hundred retired officers, including more than a score of generals and admirals, are reported to be on the payroll of one large aircraft corporation. Military men sit on the highest councils of state and have a powerful influence on congressmen and on foreign policy. Certainly on many questions of state the military establishment has been granted the highest priorities.

EFFORTS TO ACHIEVE PEACE

Like warfare itself criticism of war and efforts to achieve peace reach far back in history. The founders of the great world religions have been opposed to war, and pacifism has been found among adherents of Buddhism, Hinduism, Confucianism, and Christianity. Some prophets among the Hebrews looked forward to a time when men would mold their spears into pruning hooks and their swords into plowshares and would no longer know war. Among the early Greeks opposition to war was found mainly among the Stoics. The early Christians stressed nonviolence and refused to bear arms, but this stand, along with that of the Stoics, was abandoned when certain emperors embraced Stoicism (Marcus Aurelius) or Christianity (Constantine). Christians in the medieval period sought to apply principles of justice to the conduct of war and to set limits to it in practice. Various religious sects or groups of Christians, such as the Anabaptists, Mennonites, and Quakers, have refused to bear arms. In the twentieth century sentiment against war has been growing among Protestant denominations as well as among Roman Catholics. Recent popes have called upon men and nations to seek peace.

In each century of the modern era some powerful voices have been raised against the excesses and folly of war. Erasmus in the sixteenth century said that man is born for love and service to his fellowmen, and thus his duty is to strive to put an end to war. Hugo Grotius in the following century laid the foundation for international law. During the seventeenth and eighteenth centuries various proposals for peace were set forth by Jean-Jacques Rousseau and Immanuel Kant.

During the nineteenth century in both Europe and the United States unofficial and official peace movements were calling for the arbitration of disputes and the strengthening of international law. Between 1843 and 1904 seven International Peace Congresses (unofficial) were held in various cities in the Western world. The First Peace Conference at the Hague met in 1899, attended by a hundred official delegates from twenty countries, and set up a Permanent Court of Arbitration which had considerable success in handling cases submitted even by the great powers. The Second Peace Conference at the Hague in 1907 set up a Court of Arbitral Justice and an International Prize Court. A considerable number of peace organizations and foundations were organized before and after World War I. Many books, such as Norman Angell's *The Great Illusion* (1908), were contending that war had become so destructive of life and all social and economic values that men no longer should engage in it.

After World War I the peace sentiment grew and led to the founding of the League of Nations and other movements for collective security. The Covenant signed in 1920 called on members not to resort to war until the League had spent nine months in attempts to settle the dispute. Between 1921 and 1932 the League was able to stop a number of small wars. It was not very effective, however, because some powerful nations including the United States refused to become members. The Kellogg-Briand Pact of 1928, another attempt at peace, called on its sixty-three member states to "renounce war as an instrument of national policy."

World War II was followed by the United Nations. The Charter pledged its members to settle their international disputes by peaceful means so that peace, security, and justice would not be endangered. It also called on its members to give the United Nations armed assistance in any acts it takes to enforce the Charter. This provision was put into effect in 1950 in the Korean War.

On August 6, 1945 a new age was ushered in with the release of the power in the atom. As a result of two world wars and the coming of the nuclear age an increasing number of governments and peoples have declared that modern types of warfare and civilization are incompatible and that we will have to give up one or the other. The issue appears clear that we need to create more effective instruments of peace and to educate the general public to support them. Whether man has the moral and intellectual insight that is needed is yet to be determined. Dwight D. Eisenhower, the commanding general in World War II said, late in his second term of office as president of the United States, "There is no alternative to peace."

The revulsion against war is spreading rapidly among young people but is by no means confined to the young. The problems of recruiting young men to engage in war and of keeping morale and discipline in the armed services may force the nation's leaders to rethink the whole question of war. There appears to be a real conflict between loyalty to conscience and convictions and to patriotism when presented as a willingness to fight.[6]

IS PERMANENT PEACE POSSIBLE?

Can we achieve permanent peace with freedom and justice? One of the most important, if not *the* most important moral and social issue of our time, has to do with the relationship of states or nations to one another. Are we destined in the near future to move into an era of peace, international understanding, and goodwill, or will more terrible wars threaten the future of our civilization and perhaps of mankind? For the first time in human history, man has the power to change his own nature and even to destroy all life. War has now become the ultimate absurdity.

The dropping of two atomic bombs on Japan in 1945 not only brought World War II to a sudden and decisive end but changed the nature of warfare itself, as we have seen. Unless we can revise our old-fashioned ways of thinking and acting, overcome our cultural lag, bring our morals up to date, and apply them to the new conditions that we face, the new power may destroy us. The release of atomic energy has caught the world unprepared and incredulous. Truly, modern man is obsolete.

In a world that demands clear thinking and courageous living, too many people fool themselves with dangerous illusions. Among the fallacious ideas are the notions that our form of government will save us, that democracies are safe if the citizens stay at home and give their attention to their own affairs, that science alone can save us, that progress is inevitable, and that we do not need to concern ourselves about the future. The events of the past few decades should be enough to convince anyone of the fallacy of these clichés. The view that man is a fighting animal and that wars are therefore inevitable is an even more persistent notion. War, in our opinion, is a phenomenon that can be eliminated. It is a social phenomenon like dueling and slavery. Just as these have been eliminated from most of the earth's surface, so war can be eliminated. In fact war already has been eliminated from considerable areas—in the fifty states in the United States and among the nations within the British Commonwealth, for example. Disputes arise between these political units, but no longer do the peoples even dream

---

[6]B. Drummond Ayres, Jr., "Army Is Shaken by Crisis in Morale and Discipline" *New York Times*, 5 September 1971, pp. 1, 36.

of settling these disputes by warfare. People, however, do tend to become belligerent when threatened, and especially when their emotions are stirred by aggressive leaders. This has happened in various countries in the twentieth century.

An especially obstinate fallacy is the view that the nation-state is the last stage of social evolution and that nothing must be done to impair the sovereignty of the nation. The nation is not the last and highest expression of social evolution. The times in which we live call for some form of world community and government, since a world of competing and unrestrained national sovereignties is a world of conflict and periodic wars. The world is too interdependent for any nation to be the exclusive judge of policies and actions, especially when its national interests are involved. While nationalism and patriotism can be good, they can also be perverted and overemphasized. They can lead to the belief that the state can do no wrong.

A dangerous practice, one that tends to lead directly to war, is the old game of power politics. It is closely related to the concept of national sovereignty, and it frequently takes the form of economic imperialism. Either economic or political considerations may be dominant, but the result is much the same. The drives for power and strategic position, for prestige, for sources of raw material, and for markets have been major causes of war. During the last few decades ideological factors or wide differences in social philosophies have added to world tension.

Few people today want war. Intelligent men of goodwill the world around are hoping and working for peace. The issue that faces our nation and other nations is: How are we most likely to get peace? There are two schools of thought among those who claim they want peace. One group insists that the way to get peace is to make the nation strong: to maintain a large army, navy, and air force; to acquire strategic bases; and to develop the new methods of warfare, such as the atomic and the bacteriological, so that other nations will fear us and, fearing us, not dare attack us. Members of this school of thought do not necessarily oppose the creation of international machinery for settling disputes, but they are likely to oppose an abridgment of national sovereignty.

The other school of thought emphasizes instruments for the peaceful settlement of disputes and an effective world organization. Adherents of this school hold that if we plan for war, we are likely to have war— and they have little trouble citing illustrations from history in support of their contention. Logic seems to be on their side too. How can we expect a nation to be secure by being stronger than any other nation? Obviously, only one nation can be the strongest at any given moment. All nations want security. Can each one achieve it by being stronger than any other? If one nation becomes the strongest for a time, must not some other nation overtake it if it is to become secure in its turn? When other nations fear, they too begin to arm to the teeth and to combine against those whom they fear. This creates a vicious circle which has led to war in the past and is likely to do so in the future. Fear and the desire to be strong lead to national rivalry, then to power politics and imperialism, and finally to war.

The same thing holds true psychologically. When men prepare for war and think of war, they tend to create war. That is the danger in what is known as the military mind. When men live in a warlike atmosphere, the tinder is always there and a small spark may easily ignite it. Two men may quarrel over a trivial thing. Under ordinary circumstances the matter will blow over or be settled in some peaceful way. But let those same men quarrel while each holds a loaded gun in his hand and the chance for a peaceful settlement is much less.

In an age in which scientific discoveries are taking place so rapidly, how can we have any assurance that we can always be the strongest nation? Types of warfare become obsolete almost overnight. The atomic scientists tell us that any advantage we may possess today is likely to be temporary. They tell us also that an attempt to keep our knowledge secret is likely to stifle scientific development, so that we may eventually be left behind. Scientists from many countries assisted in the release of atomic energy.

Also if we are to think and plan for another war, we shall need to spend most of our resources on preparations. We shall have to disperse our cities. We shall have to give up a considerable part of our freedom to some overall authority so that we may be able to act quickly and unitedly.

Thus many people fear that preparations for an atomic war can lead to an armament race and eventually to a war of annihilation that may set civilization back centuries if, indeed, it does not end our type of civilization. Power is too great and the world is too interdependent for intelligent men to permit the world to drift into another war. The crucial question before our age is whether the new power in our hands is to be used for constructive medical, social, and industrial purposes or be poured out in new rivers of blood and new avalanches of human destruction. Writing before the release of atomic energy, Quincy Wright said, "In the most recent stage of world civilization war has made for instability, for disintegration, for despotism, and for unadaptability, rendering the course of civilization less predictable and continued progress toward achievement of its values less probable."[7] Arnold Toynbee

---

[7]Quincy Wright, *A Study of War*, vol. 1 (Chicago University Press, 1942), p. 272.

claimed that "warfare is the commonest cause of breakdown of civilization during the four or five millennia."[8] If this has been the effect in the past, what is likely to be the result in the atomic age?

To avoid misunderstanding, let us state here that we are under no illusion that we will discard our armaments overnight, or that one nation will do it alone. That is not the most important problem at the moment. We do need to have a general lowering of armaments in all countries, as we discussed earlier in this chapter. It appears not only foolish but actually immoral to spend so much money on weapons of destruction when we might be using the money for constructive purposes, such as the promotion of health, education, a higher standard of living, and cultural development along many lines. The important matters at present include inspection and international control of atomic energy, so that individuals or nations that might wish to use it for destructive purposes will be curbed; the strengthening of the United Nations; and the promotion of goodwill and understanding among the peoples of the world.

Among the paths to war are power politics and aggression, ideological conflicts, bigoted nationalism, competitive armament races, economic imperialism, and monopolistic trade practices. We can help eliminate war as we change conditions that beget war. In the face of aggression a nation may have to resist, but there are alternative ways of resisting and the choice should be made for a way that strengthens the prospects of justice and peace in the long run. Among the paths to peace are the growth of transnational or international organizations to promote cooperation among the nations, the general reduction of armaments, a growing sentiment in opposition to war, the growth of democracy, and the maintenance of full employment and a sense of security and well-being on the domestic scene.

We have pointed out above that the nation-state is not the last stage of social development and that the twentieth century is demanding some form of world community and order. Probably the nation-state is not destined to pass away. Just as it was superimposed on the family, tribe, or clan, thereby eliminating tribal warfare, transnational or international institutions need to be established as a step toward the elimination of wars between nations. The United Nations is a step in this direction. The world is so interdependent that acts in any one part of it affect the peoples in the rest of it.

If the world is to attain peace with justice and freedom, regional organizations, such as the Organization of American States, the Atlantic Treaty Organization, and the European Economic Community, will be

---

[8] Arnold Toynbee, *A Study of History*, vol. 3 (London: Oxford University Press, 1934), p. 150.

needed to give attention to strictly regional problems. World organizations will be necessary to give attention to issues that concern men everywhere or that are too far-reaching and important to be handled even by regional groups. While some new organizations may be needed, it appears that the most promising hope for the future is supporting and strengthening organizations now functioning and at least partially effective.

The opening paragraphs of the Charter of the United Nations include these statements: "We the people of the United Nations, determined to save succeeding generations from the scourge of war, which twice in our lifetime has brought untold sorrow to mankind, and to reaffirm faith in fundamental human rights, in the dignity and worth of the human person . . . to establish conditions under which justice . . . can be maintained, and to promote social progress and better standards of life in larger freedom . . . have resolved to combine our efforts to accomplish these aims."

The United Nations provides a code of international conduct as well as machinery for giving it practical effect. It has exhibited considerable adaptability to changing conditions and needs; it is neither an ineffective and loose league nor a menacing superstate. Failure of our nation to support it would mean relinquishing responsibility for leadership in the quest for peace and perhaps even the shift of influence to the enemies of freedom. If peace is to be secure, a strong world public opinion and a strengthening of the peace-keeping machinery of the world, including United Nations police forces, would appear to be necessary.

A detailed discussion of the organizations or machinery for the promotion of peace is not possible here. The alert student, however, should keep informed regarding these developments. He should remember, too, that while organization is important, the spirit, the attitude, and the living faith that men hold are of even greater importance. While the accident of birth makes a man a member of a nation, he is also a member of humanity. He can be loyal to mankind without being disloyal to his own state and his own kindred. When a man feels that the rights of other groups are as sacred as those of his own group, he is approaching moral maturity.

A former assistant Secretary of State has said, "Moral force does not move mountains, but it moves men to action, and by their action mountains can be moved—and civilizations built or destroyed."[9] There is a moral obligation facing men of intelligence and goodwill to make a strenuous effort to transform the present international system into one

---

[9]Ernest A. Gross, *The United Nations: Structure for Peace* (New York: Harper & Brothers, 1962), p. 125.

that will be more effective in maintaining peace with freedom and justice for all.

REVOLUTION AND VIOLENCE

Up to this point we have been discussing war and peace in relation to states or nations. In recent years, however, our attention has been drawn to the internal conditions of our country where violence—almost warfare and revolution—has become increasingly apparent. We cannot consider peace within the world as secure without peace within nations. We therefore conclude this chapter with a statement on revolution and violence in our society.

Our age, as we have seen, has been called the atomic or nuclear age, the space age, and the age of automation and electronic computers. These, however, are only the outer or more obvious changes taking place. In addition to the scientific and technological transformations, there are vast social, political, and cultural changes and, perhaps even more basic, a revolution in ways of thinking and in values and standards of behavior. A revolutionary period is one in which the rate of change is markedly more accelerated than it is in normal times.

Revolutions are not all of the same kind. Let us look at two different ways of distinguishing between the kinds of revolutions that occur. First, consider the difference between intended and unintended revolutions. Some revolutions are planned, intended, and depend on the use of force. These are the violent conflicts between two groups of people. These intended revolutions, such as the American, French, and Russian Revolutions, are crises usually caused by the stupidity of some group that refuses to change in the face of new conditions, and by injustices and the resulting resentment in another group. In such a situation one group is resisting an abuse of power by another group and is attempting to force a social, political, or economic change. Our world has witnessed many revolutions of this type.

The unintended revolutions, on the other hand, steal up on us unawares, since they are relatively slow and peaceful. A series of inventions, for example, which included the steam engine, eventually changed the nature of Western civilization and that change is now spreading all over the world. Later technological revolutions were of a similar nature. Whether we wish to think of the industrial and technological revolutions as still under way and speak of new stages in these revolutions, or whether we prefer to use new terms to describe the new age of nuclear power, space, and automation is immaterial.

There is also a difference between revolutions that affect one or only a few segments of society and those that appear to be all-inclusive. Some revolutions are centered in one area of society and may be localized in space—that is, they are primarily political, economic, racial, educational, religious, or the like. They may occur without open conflict and they may be intended or unintended. At other times the changes may be all-inclusive in that they affect many institutions and basic social attitudes, ideas, and the conditions of life of people in general.

All over the world, large groups of persons are in revolt against the old order with its inequalities and injustices. People are dissatisfied with colonialism, imperialism, and racial intolerance. They are revolting against political systems that lead so frequently to conflicts and war, against economic systems that leave many destitute in the midst of plenty, and against interpretations of life that take from it all meaning and significance. The revolutionary movements in our world, coupled with the release of atomic energy, have created an unprecedented situation.

To explain the changes in our world as caused by communism, as a few people do, is to grasp at a simple explanation and fail to understand what is happening in our world. Revolutionary changes in many areas are the cause of the conflicts, and communism has arisen as one of the efforts to interpret and direct these changes. Communism, however, has added to the violence and confusion.

One exceedingly disturbing fact of our time is the upsurge of violence not only in war but in everyday life. Reliance on force is self-destructive and is evidence of the failure of the constructive elements in our civilization. Violence is not something new in American history; from early days we killed Indians and enslaved black men. We have had rebellions and civil war and even some of our labor conflicts have led to violence. In our time we have witnessed the growth of individual and group violence in the form of muggings, rape, murder, assassinations, riots, and terrorist activities of a wide range. In many areas of the country people are afraid to walk out at night and, in some areas, even in the daytime. People have been buying firearms at an alarming rate and watchdogs are in great demand. Lord Harlech, a former British Ambassador to the United States, has said that violence in the United States has become a world scandal.

A large majority of our population is composed of decent, lawabiding, sensitive persons who are concerned about the rapidly rising crime rate and the recourse to violence. How can we explain the disturbances of our time and what can we do about them? This is a moral problem that should be of concern—a concern leading to action—on the part of all thoughtful citizens. In the first place, some violence is caused by the presence in our society of many persons who have become antisocial because of conditions that have left them selfish, bitter, and even brutalized. They turn to violence when they cannot get what they want in peaceful ways. Some causes are the failure of homes, schools, churches, and our penal and correctional institutions. Second, some crime and violence is occasioned by repressive conditions that people refuse to tolerate. "Repression," said Woodrow Wilson, "is the seed of revolution." When reactionaries gain control of society and attempt to stifle all change and progress, sooner or later there will be violent explosions of repressed rage and resentment. Third, violence is likely to break out when there are great injustices that men are unable to remedy by peaceful means. These injustices as well as their repression are sometimes called the quiet types of psychological, social, or institutionalized violence that involve pressure, manipulation, and threats of many kinds where physical force is not openly used. Fourth, for decades the mass media have emphasized violence and brought it vividly into the homes, as we pointed out in an earlier chapter. This has had a pervasive influence and gives the impression that such activity is commonplace and normal. Fifth, for almost a generation we have been at war so that many young persons have not known an era of peace. Military training has tended to habituate people to the use of firearms and to killing. Finally, an individual who lacks convictions, a scale of values, or any reasonable basis for making choices is likely to experience anxiety, lack of identity, and powerlessness. He easily becomes a drop-out from society and the end result may be violence. Our society desperately needs a moral and an educational revolution, because the basic cause of our disorder appears to be an emphasis on a false order of priorities that lead man to prize wealth, power, speed, and bodily comforts and not the development of the inner man and the growth of the person in an orderly society.

QUESTIONS AND PROJECTS

1. What are some of the problems we face as a nation seeking to make democracy effective on the home front and seeking peace and justice in international affairs?
2. How would you answer the following questions?
    (1) Are we more secure or more insecure now that we have a large supply of atomic and hydrogen bombs?
    (2) To what extent is the doctrine of national sovereignty obsolete, or is it as valid as ever?
    (3) Are there any human or natural rights of man that are above national rights? If so what are they?
    (4) Is it ever possible for us to have the law on our side while ethics is against us?

(5) Has the charge that since World War II there has been a gradual abdication of moral judgments in relation to military decisions any real basis in fact?
3. What is meant by "the military mind"? Does a member of the armed services necessarily exhibit this outlook? In an address early in 1961 Dwight D. Eisenhower referred to a "military-industrial complex" against which we need to be on guard, since "its total influence—economic, political, even spiritual—is felt in every city, every statehouse, every office of federal government." Later, in discussion with a reporter, he said, "We are being recast in new molds, turning out a generation of Americans with totally different morals, ambitions and ways of doing things." ["Juggernaut," *The Nation* 195 (October 13, 1962): 211-212]. See also Fred J. Cook, "Juggernaut: The Welfare State," *The Nation* 193 (October 28, 1961): 277-328; Walter Millis, "Puzzle of the Military Mind," *New York Times Magazine*, 18 November 1962, p. 33; Robert N. Ginsburgh, "The Challenge to Military Professionalism," *Foreign Affairs* 42 (January 1964): 255-268 and James A. Donovan, *Militarism, USA* (New York: Charles Scribner's Sons, 1970).
4. Evaluate the statement that there is now no alternative to peace except utter destruction. See *Speak Truth to Power* (Philadelphia: American Friends Service Committee, 1955).
5. Is it possible, as has been suggested, that the principle or attitude "What I have, I hold" may in some situations be as immoral as the attitude "What you have, I take"? Discuss the problems involved in the adjustment of resources and territory to changing conditions in the world. What would appear to be the moral approach to such problems of international relations?
6. The United Nations Convention on Genocide is an effort to outlaw acts intended "to destroy in whole or in part, a national, ethnic, racial, or religious group." The United States delegates joined in a 50–0 vote in favor of a resolution which urged all states to speed ratification. After the vote the delegation said that its vote for the resolution was "not a commitment as to the timing of action by the United States" and was not to be interpreted as authorizing propaganda in favor of the convention in the United States. To date no vigorous effort has been taken to secure United States ratification of the agreement, even though a majority of the member nations of the United Nations have ratified the agreement. Comment on the consistency, integrity, and moral leadership of the United States in this matter. See William Korey, "On Banning Genocide," *World* 1 (September 26, 1972): 28-32.
7. There are many recent incidents in the area of international affairs that raise important questions in the field of ethics. What are the moral issues in each of the following: the Eichmann capture and trial [Yosal Rogat, *The Eichmann Trial and the Rule of Law*, Santa Barbara: Center for the Study of Democratic Institutions, 1961]; the war-crimes trials [Joe J. Heydecker and Johannes Leeb, *The Nuremberg Trial* (Cleveland, O.: World Publishing Co., 1962)]; and the invasion of Cuba in April

1961 [*Time* 77 (April 28, 1961): 19–23]. For the U-2 case (1960), the Pueblo case (1968), and the release to the press of the Pentagon papers (1971) revealing a distortion of reports of the progress of the war in Southeast Asia, see references on p. 341. Books, articles, and press accounts of these events and others are available.

8. Do we need an international code of ethics for space, or at least some principles that can be applied in space travel and exploration? Do frontiers extend into the sky and, if so, how high? If one nation claims the right to observe another nation from the air, does it have an obligation to permit that nation to fly over its territory? Is air espionage legal—and ethical? See Harlow Shapley, "Stars, Ethics and Survival" and Edward L. Long, "Ethical Problems in the Space Age," *Religion in Life* 30 (Summer 1961): 334–344, 366–373; F. B. Schlick, "International Law in Outer Space," *Bulletin of the Atomic Scientists* 18 (November 1962): 2–6.

9. What ethical problems are involved in the moon program? The program has both staunch supporters and serious critics. The cost is estimated at between $20 and $40 billion. Scientist Warren Weaver tells us that with this money we could give every United States teacher a ten percent raise in salary for ten years, give "ten million dollars to each of 200 small colleges"; offer fellowships for seven years at $4,000 per year for 50,000 young scientists; create ten new medical schools with gifts of $200 million each; build and endow universities for 53 new underdeveloped nations; create three foundations similar to the Rockerfeller Foundation; and have $100 million left to inform the public about science. [Blake Clark, "A Job for the Next Congress: Stop the Race to the Moon," *Reader's Digest* 84 (January 1964): 75–79]. See also Lawrence Galton, "Will Space Research Pay Off on Earth?" *New York Times Magazine*, 26 May 1963, p. 29; Arthur C. Clarke, "The Uses of the Moon," *Harper's Magazine* 223 (December 1961): 56–62: Lillian Levy, ed., *Space: Its Impact on Man and Society* (New York: W. W. Norton & Co., 1965); S. Fred Singer, "Exploring Space in the Seventies," *Bulletin of the Atomic Scientists* 26 (November 1970): 22–23.

10. Can you work out some ethical principles applicable to fallout or air raid shelters? Is self-preservation the first law of war and peace, or are there higher laws? In building shelters some people are trying to keep them secret. Others say they plan to admit as many neighbors as possible. One man started a discussion that brought comments from people far and wide when he said, "When I get my shelter finished, I'm going to mount a machine gun at the hatch to keep the neighbors out if the bombs fall. I'm deadly serious about this." [*Time* 78 (August 18, 1961): 58.] A series of four editorials on "Shelters, Survival, and Common Sense," *Saturday Review* 44 (October 21 to November 25, 1961) may be helpful.

11. How do you explain the fact that "friend" and "foe," the "good fellows" and the "bad fellows" change so frequently on the world scene? For example in 1945 the United States, Russia, China, Poland, and Czecho-

slovakia were allies, and Germany, Italy, Spain, and Japan were their enemies. If one takes a list of allies and enemies in World War I, in World War II, and then in the 1970s, he notices some amazing shifts. What is likely to be the situation in another decade or two?

12. How do you explain the growing amount of violence in the sixties and early seventies? Work out a program that you think might help in reducing the amount of violence in America. You may wish to consult a statement by the Editors of *McCall's Magazine* in the article "What Women Can Do To End Violence in America," *Saturday Review* 51 (June 29, 1968): 18–19.

13. Most wars of history have been between men in uniform carrying weapons. Civilians have been killed mainly when they got in the way of the battle. In World War II both sides waged war upon noncombatants—saturation bombings, fire bombings, and the use of atomic bombs against two cities. A second novel precedent resulting from World War II was that losers, but not victors, may be tried as war criminals even though atrocities were committed on both sides. Soldiers have previously been tried for murder, robbery, rape, and other crimes committed during periods of occupation. Now they are being tried for crimes against civilians committed during combat operations. What are the moral implications of this trend?

14. At My Lai in the war in Vietnam, old men, women, and children were massacred although they offered no resistance. In the trial of the lieutenant in charge, who claimed he was only following orders, the evidence nevertheless seemed clear, and the verdict of the court was that he was guilty. There was a public outcry against the verdict and President Nixon intervened and the Secretary of Defense ordered the lieutenant removed from the stockade. The prosecutor wrote to the President and said among other things: "To believe . . . that any large percentage of the population could believe the evidence . . . and approve of the conduct . . . would be as shocking to my conscience as the conduct itself, since I believe that we are still a civilized nation." If such be the case, he continued, then the war "has brutalized us more than I care to believe. . . . How shocking it is if so many people . . . have failed to see the moral issue . . . that it is unlawful for an American soldier to summarily execute unarmed and unresisting men, women, children, and babies. But how much more appalling it is to see so many of the political leaders of the nation who have failed to see the moral issue, or having seen it, to compromise it for political motive in the face of apparent public displeasure with the verdict." (For the full text of the letter written by prosecutor Captain Aubrey M. Daniel III to the President, see "Calley Prosecutor Asserts Nixon Undermines Justice," *New York Times*, 7 April 1971, p. 12.)

Here are questions the reader should ponder: When atrocities occur in war, who is mainly responsible or guilty—the individual soldiers, the officers in charge who have given orders, the war system, or the general public that supports war as a method of settling disputes? Are atrocities committed only by soldiers with small arms (hand weapons) or are those engaged in mass killing of a different nature (artillery shells, bombs, napalm) equally responsible or guilty?

SUGGESTED READINGS

Arend, Hannah. *On Violence.* New York: Harcourt, Brace & World, 1969.

Bennett, John C., ed. *Nuclear Weapons and the Conflict of Conscience.* New York: Charles Scribner's Sons, 1962.

Bondurant, Joan V. and Fisher, M. W., eds. *Conflict: Violence and Non-Violence.* Chicago: Aldine Publishing Co., 1971.

Bottome, Edgar M. *The Balance of Terror: A Guide to the Arms Race.* Boston: Beacon Press, 1971.

Cousins, Norman. *In Place of Folly.* Rev. ed. New York: Washington Square Press, 1962.

Foreman, Harry, ed. *Nuclear Power and the Public.* Minneapolis: University of Minnesota Press, 1970.

Gross, Bertram M., ed. *Social Intelligence for America's Future.* Boston: Allyn & Bacon, 1969.

Gross, Ernest. *The United Nations: Structure for Peace.* New York: Harper & Brothers, 1962. Published for the Council on Foreign Relations.

Hocking, William Ernest. *Strength of Men and Nations.* New York: Harper & Brothers, 1959.

Hofstadter, Richard, and Wallace, Michael. *American Violence: A Documentary History.* New York: Alfred A. Knopf, 1970.

King, Edward L. *The Death of the Army.* New York: Saturday Review Press, 1972.

Lapp, Ralph E. *Arms beyond Doubt.* New York: Cowles Book Co., 1970.

McClintock, Robert. *The Meaning of Limited War.* Boston: Houghton Mifflin Co., 1967.

Mills, C. Wright. *The Causes of World War Three.* New York: Simon & Schuster, 1958.

O'Brien, William V. *War and/or Survival.* Garden City, N. Y.: Doubleday & Co., 1969.

Ramsey, Paul. *The Just War: Force and Political Responsibility.* New York: Charles Scribner's Sons, 1968.

Rubenstein, Richard E. *Rebels in Eden: Mass Political Violence in the United States.* Boston: Little, Brown & Co., 1970.

Stackhouse, Max L. *The Ethics of Necropolis.* Boston: Beacon Press, 1971.

Taylor, Telford. *Nuremberg and Vietnam: An American Tragedy.* Chicago: Quadrangle Books, 1970.

United Nations Association. *The United Nations in the 1970s: A Strategy for a Unique Era in the Affairs of Nations.* New York: The Association, 1971.

INDEX

Names of authors whose books are listed only once for review under *Questions and Projects*, in the *Suggested Readings*, or in footnotes, are not included in this Index.

Abbey, Edward, quoted, 477
Abortion, 355, 428, 431, 436, 438, 439, 440, 446, 474
Abundance, questions regarding, discussed 471–491
Achan, story of, 41
Adler, Mortimer J., 19
Administration of justice. *See* Justice
Adulteration, 383, 389
Adventure in the realm of morals, 232–238
Advertising, 243, 300, 312; business and, 383; cases concerning, 168; mass media and, 282, 399, 400, 403, 406, 409, 410, 416
Agreements, 25, 39, 40, 59, 113, 128, 238; working, 129
Agriculture, 10, 241, 243, 524. *See also* Farmers.
Aiken, H. D., quoted, 156
Alcohol, 279–282

Alexander, S., 180
Alienation, 17, 214, 383
Altruism, 73–74, 152. *See also* Selfishness.
American Association of University Professors, 304
American Bar Association, 357, 358, 362; code quoted, 358–359
American Civil Liberties Union, 303, 315–316
American Federation of Teachers, 364; code of, 364–365
American Indian, 450
American Medical Association, 353, 370; code quoted, 353–354
American Society of Newspaper Editors, code quoted, 404
Amusements, 277, 278; puritan view of, 277
Analysis of ethical language, 31, 34, 109–131
Anger, effect of, 95, 289

Index / 541

Animals, 12, 172, 183
Anshen, Ruth Nanda, 188
Anti-loitering legislation, case, 26–27
Anxiety, 289
Appleman, Phillip, 476
Aquinas, Saint Thomas, 194, 220, 224, 525; quoted, 194–195
Aristippus, 151–152
Aristotle, 34, 92, 112, 114, 115, 160, 192–194, 298, 321, 332; quoted, 192, 193
Arnold, Thurman, quoted, 410
Arrangement, the, 427, 432–434
Art and the artist, 11, 14, 15, 260
Art student, case, 102–103
Artificial insemination, 184, 187, 231, 355
Assimilation, 426, 449–450
Assumptions in living and morals, 89
Athletics. *See* Amusements.
Atomic age, 7, 521–532
Atomic bomb, 522–523
Atrocities, in war, 538
Attitudes, 120–123, 130, 131, 320, 400
Audrey, Robert, 525
Augustine, Saint, 66, 220, 323, 330
Authority, 10, 11, 27–28, 34, 108, 222; appeals to, 47–49; experimentation and, 232, 234, 235; when justified, 34, 47–48; when not justified, 48
Automation, 231, 323, 375
Autonomy, principle of, 139–140, 426
Axiology, 253. *See also* Value and values.
Ayer, A. J., 31, 116, 117–118, 119; quoted, 118

Bacon, Francis, 299
Bandura, Albert, quoted, 410
Banning of books and speakers, 305–306
Banting, Frederick G., 347

Bartell, Gilbert D., quoted, 431, 432
Beals, Ralph L., quoted, 455
Beauty, 65, 252. *See also* Art and the artist.
Belief, crisis of, 15
Benson, Robert S., quoted, 500
Bentham, Jeremy, 115, 152–154, 162, 165, 166–167; quoted 154. *See also* Hedonism.
Benton, William, 518; quoted, 507–508
Bergson, Henri, 180–182, 185; quoted, 180–181
Better Business Bureau, 386, 387
Bible, 41, 48, 56, 57, 292, 322; as authority, 222, 223; and Judeo-Christian ethical ideals, 218–225; on justice, 54–58; quoted, 55, 56, 57, 221, 223, 224; reflecting moral development, 41, 48, 56
Bill of Rights, in United States Constitution, 302, 305, 309, 311, 510
Biological engineering, 182, 231
Biological factors in conduct, 72–73
Birth control, 428, 435–436, 478
Black, Hugo, quoted, 317, 508
"Black America" *(Time)*, quoted, 452–453
Blacks, 450–453
Blanshard, Brand, quoted, 81, 125
Bliven, Naomi, quoted, 466
Borlaugh, Norman, 490–491
Bradley, F. H., quoted, 164
Brandeis, Louis, quoted, 316
Brayboy, Thomas L., quoted, 467
Bribery, 384, 504
Broadcasting, 405–411; cases concerning, 419–420; codes quoted, 408–409
Brunner, Emil, quoted, 223
Buber, Martin, 216
Buddhism, ethics of, 30, 92, 97, 113, 325
Bush, Vannevar, quoted, 476

542 / Index

Business and business ethics, 11, 241–244, 346, 348, 374–397; cases concerning, 99, 394–397; criticism of, 379–385; efforts toward improvement of, 385–388

Bussing of children to achieve integration, 29, 366, 464–465

Butler, Joseph, quoted, 51, 160

Cabot, Richard C., quoted, 267, 329–330

Calvin, John, 66, 220

Capitalism, 210–211, 375–378, 495. *See also* Business and business ethics.

Carson, Rachel, quoted, 173

Categorical imperative, Kant's view, 136; rejected, 179

Catholicism. *See* Roman Catholic Church.

Celibacy, 145–146

Censorship, 301, 305, 306, 402, 411–414, 415, 416–417

Changing social order, 1, 11, 48, 211, 231, 234, 240–243, 311, 375, 533–535

Character, 70, 80, 320–327

Cheating, 381, 384; cases of, 248, 368

Child care, 429

Children, 407–410, 411, 419, 429, 453

Chinese scholar, quoted, 369–370

Chisholm, Shirley, quoted, 444

Christian Church, 46, 48, 221–222. *See also* Protestantism *and* Roman Catholic Church.

Christian ethics and Christians, 30, 58, 92, 113, 195, 209, 213, 220–225, 322, 526

Civil disobedience, 509–514; questions and cases regarding, 515–519

Civil liberty, 215, 298–299

Civil Rights Acts, 298–299

Civilization, 1, 3, 9, 10, 11, 220, 252; and issues of peace and war, 530, 533

Clark, Kenneth B., quoted, 466

Clark, Ramsey, 493, 512

Clergymen, 369, 370–371

Climate, effect on behavior, 70

Cohen, Jerry S., 382; quoted, 385

Collective bargaining. *See* Labor and labor organizations.

College campuses, 427, 450, 451; coed dorms, 427, 432

Commager, Henry Steele, 61–62, 518

Commercialism, 345–347; in athletics, 278; in the professions, 345–346, 348, 356, 360–361

Commitments, need for, 24, 25, 200–201, 203, 238, 299

Common-carrier liability, 266. *See also* Due care.

Communication, ethics and the means of, 399–421

Communes, 434

Communism, 2, 6, 312, 380, 402, 534; ethics of, 209–213; moral code of, quoted, 212

Compassion, law of, 97

Compensation, form of self-deceit, 335; for victims of criminal violence, 267

Competition, 14, 180, 497; in athletics, 277, 278; in business as a moral problem, 377, 388, 390. *See also* Capitalism *and* Profit and the profit motive.

Compromise, 238–240; cases regarding, 248–249

Conditioning, 71, 72

Conflict of interests. *See* Double morality.

Conformity, pressure for, 307

Confucius and Confucianism, 30, 67, 97, 113; virtues of, 326

Confusion, about standards, 1–19

Conscience, 49–52, 134; cases concerning, 61–62; development

of morality and, 49–52, 59, 60; elements in, 49–51. *See also* Duty and duties.
Conscientiousness. *See* Responsibility.
Consensus, a lost, 1–19
Consequences, in relation to motives and means, 98–102, 104, 141, 144, 147, 154, 264
Constant, B., quoted, 149
Consumer's cooperative movement, 380
Consumer's interests and groups, 392, 393, 416
Contraception, 428, 436
Convictions, 15, 17, 24, 52, 239, 511–512, 535; working, 126–129
Cooperation, 39, 69, 95, 128, 171, 174, 176, 180, 323, 394
Corporation, 241, 242, 243, 244, 375, 377, 385, 386, 391, 403, 526; cases concerning, 37, 395–397; lawyers and, 357; responsibility of officials of, 243, 244
Counterbudget and priorities, 500–503
Courage, 95, 141, 142, 193, 244, 321, 322, 337, 338
Courts, 45, 46, 47, 55
Courtship, 423–424, 427, 429
Cousins, Norman, quoted, 407
Cox, Harvey, 169, 225
Creativity, 91, 197
Crick, Francis, quoted, 16
Crime and criminals, 4, 10, 55, 493–494; and the mass media, 407–410, 412, 415. *See also* Justice, administration of.
Criticism, 312–314; attempts to suppress, 312, 344–345; importance of, 313–314, 411; of industrial society, 379–385
Cousins, Norman, quoted, 407
Cultural relativism and values, 110–114

Custom, 25, 71, 234, 320; as moral standard, 39–44, 54–59; dealing with unjust, 42–44, 59–60
Customary morality, 39–44

Daniel, Aubrey M. III, quoted, 538
Darwin, Charles, 115, 170, 171–175, 185, 198; quoted, 172–173, 174, 175
Davis, Bertram H., quoted, 304
Deception, 329–335, 383–385; cases involving, 339–342. *See also* Truthfulness.
Decisions in federal budget, 503; necessity for, 23, 24, 37, 251
Dehumanization, 383
Delinquency, 10, 73, 276
Deloria, Vine, Jr., quoted, 449
Democracy, 2, 45, 299, 314, 394, 402, 495, 496, 498–499; in relation to freedom, 314–315
Democritus, 151
Deontological ethics, 133–148, 222. *See also* Formalism.
Deshumbert, Marius, 180
Determinism, 76–79, 215. *See also* Freedom of choice.
Dewey, John, 34, 92, 115, 196; quoted, 53, 80, 164
Diamond, Stanley, quoted, 455–456
Diehl, Harold S., quoted, 284
Disarmament, 522–523; strategic-arms-limitation treaty, 522; test-ban treaty, 522–523
Discrimination in race relations, 452–458, 459, 464
Dissenters, 510, 511, 513
Divorce, 431, 440; cases concerning, 445
Dobzhansky, Theodosius, 72, 182–184, 188; quoted, 182, 183, 184
Dolan, Edwin G., quoted, 471
Dostoevski, 214; quoted, 125
Double morality, 247, 345–346, 424–425
Douglas, Paul, 507

Douglas, William O., quoted, 304, 316
Drinking. See Alcohol.
Druggists, case concerning, 371
Drugs and drug addiction, 4, 284–289, 384; cases concerning, 294, 295, 371
Due care, 144, 262–267, 299, 439; cases of lack of, 268–269, 384–385; necessity of exercising, 237
Dueling, code of, 55, 60, 66, 241
Duty and duties, 221, 251, 262–267; conflict of, 145, 240; as fixed by the group, 59; in Judeo-Christian ethics, 222; in Kant's philosophy, 133–148; *prima facie*, 147–148, 262; and rights, 256–262

Eavesdropping devices, 309–311, 318
Ecology, 180, 186, 471–491; cases regarding, 488–491
Edel, Abraham, quoted, 54, 113–114; and Mary, 54
Education and educators, 2, 11, 35, 36, 299, 304, 362–368, 371, 430; as a right, 254, 258; code of, 363–365; mass media and, 408, 409; problems facing, 365–367. See also Teachers *and* Students.
Ehrlich, Paul, 476, 481; quoted, 481, 483
Einstein, Albert, quoted, 8
Eisenhower, Dwight D., quoted, 306, 527, 536
Ellsberg case and the Pentagon Papers, 513
Emotions and emotional responses, 17, 83, 109, 119, 122, 278, 416; emotive theories, 109–131
Emotive theory in the field of ethics, 109–131
Employment figures for blacks and whites, 452–453
Environmental factors in conduct, 4, 6, 28, 29, 32, 70, 176, 234–235; livable, 471–491, 500–501
Epicurus, 151–152
Equality, principle of, 97; racial, 465; for young adults, 425
Ethical objectivism, 110–114, 125–126
Ethical Standards in Government, 493–514; for administrators, 504–506; for legislators, 506–508
Ethical subjectivism, 110–114
Ethical theory, three viewpoints, 104–105
Ethics, 24; aim of, 24–27; descriptive, 28; language and, 114–126; methods of approach to a study of, 27–32; theories of, 88–247
Ethnic groups. See Cultural pluralism.
Eugenics, 182, 187
Euthanasia, 355; cases of, 205–206
Evil, 48, 90, 196, 274, 275, 314; and human nature, 66, 69. See *also* Vices.
Evolutionary ethics, 67, 170–188, 204; evaluation of, 184–186
Ewing, A. C., quoted, 99–100, 100–101
Exception-making, form of self-deceit, 336
Exercise, value of, 277
Existential ethics, 213–218
Experimentation, 231–238; cases regarding, 247–249; in medicine, 355; in morals, 232–238; in science, 233

Faith, 2, 215, 292, 299, 322
Family, 40–41, 423–447
Far right and far left, 3, 312
Farmers, 7, 11, 243, 524; cases related to, 167–168, 241, 243
Fascism, 2, 213, 312, 380, 402, 525
Fatalism, 76, 215

Fear, 2, 95, 289, 311, 530
Federal budget and its priorities, 500–503
Federal Communications Commission, 405–406, 410, 411, 416–417
Federal Trade Commission, 386, 405, 416
Fees and the professional man, 347–349, 359–360
Fee-splitting, 353, 354
Feral man and human nature, 73
Filibuster, question concerning, 515–516
Finalism, rejected, 182
Fiske, Edward B., 490
Fittingness, 147–148
Fletcher, Joseph F., 395, 486; quoted, 225
Foreigners, treatment of, 55, 58
Formalism, 133, 141; in Christian ethics, 222–223; in customary morality, 41–42; in the ethics of Kant, 135–146
Forrester, Jay, 472
Fosdick, Raymond B., quoted, 516
Fox, Philip G., quoted, 340
Frankel, Charles, quoted, 407
Frankena, William, quoted, 163
Free enterprise, 5, 375–378
Freedom of choice, 75–83, 215; Kant's view of, 140; the problem elaborated, 75–83; terms defined, 75–76
Freedom of thought and expression, 14, 298–319, 413–414; as a right, 258; why so important, 313–315; why in jeopardy, 311–312
Freud, Sigmund, quoted, 50
Frog, example of the, 6
Fromm, Erich, quoted, 187–188, 246
Fulfillment, as a goal, 124, 190–207; as a type of Christian ethics, 223–225
Fuller, Buckminster, 477, 479

Fuller, Edmund, quoted, 14

Gagnon, John, 433, 434
Galbraith, John K., 13
Gandhi, Mahatma, 509, 511, 512
Gans, Herbert J., quoted, 467–468
Gardner, John W., 19; quoted, 16
Garnett, A. Campbell, quoted, 51, 201
Gautama, Siddhartha, 325
Generalization principle, 89, 96–97
Generosity, 140
Genetics, 187
Genocide, 257, 536
Ghostwriting, 518
Gifts and entertainment of officials, 505; questions concerning, 517
Gilman, Charlotte Perkins, case of, 206
Ginsberg, Morris, quoted, 112–113
Ginzberg, Eli, quoted, 429
Goals, 258–261, 337
God, 69, 115, 195, 215, 222, 223, 225; in Christian ethics, 221, 222, 223; and the development of morality, 58; in Judaism, 219, 221; His will as the standard, 47, 76. See also Religion and morality.
Golden mean, 193, 194, 322, 326
Golden Rule, in relation to morality, 97, 245, 264
Good, 1, 2, 35, 114, 116, 118, 146, 226; the common, 35, 152, 416; ethics of the, 143, 146, 147, 223; the highest, 192, 194; in relation to right, 141, 143, 146, 147, 252
Gordon, Leland J., 374
Government, 379, 392, 393, 493–519; and civil disobedience, 509–514; as instrument of social welfare, 260, 427; problems of administrators, 504–506; problems of legislators, 506–508. See also Democracy and State.

Greeks, the early, 10–11, 35, 190–194, 221, 299, 321, 322, 526
Greeley, Andrew W., quoted, 465
Griswold, Erwin N., 507
Gross, Ernest A., quoted, 532
Group morality, 245
Growth, law of life, 247, 476
Guaranteed annual wage, 267
Guidelines, 93, 94; for choice among alternatives, 93–96, 251; for experimentation in morals, 235–238; for federal appointees, 504–506
Guilt, 62, 331; by association, 308

Habit, 68, 71, 241, 320, 416; and custom, 8, 25, 40, 51; as obstacle to thinking, 300; in relation to the virtues, 320–321
Hammurabi, code of, 352
Happiness, 93, 141, 146, 147, 151–169, 192, 203, 321; cases involving, 167–168; evaluation of, as a theory, 157–166; as the standard, 151–168
Hardin, Garrett, 486; quoted, 481–482, 483, 487
Hare, R. M., 262
Harelip, case of boy with, 84
Hargis, Billy James, quoted, 437
Harkness, Georgia, quoted, 225
Harlech, Lord, quoted, 534
Hartford, Conn., plan for community development, 479–480
Hartmann, Nicolai, quoted, 328, 330–331
Hartshorne, Hugh, quoted, 334
Haselden, Kyle, 456; quoted, 228, 246, 415
Health, 273–295, 410, 428; alcohol and, 279–282; drugs and, 284–289; right to, 258; tobacco and, 279, 282–284
Hebb, Donald, quoted, 12
Hebrews, 34, 35, 314, 322, 526; moral development among, 54–58, 218–219

Hechinger, Fred M., 436, 438; quoted, 438
Hedonism, 151–169; evaluation of, 157–166; types of, 152. *See also* Happiness.
Heermance, Edgar L., 350
Hegel, Georg, 196, 198, 209, 210
Heilbroner, Robert L., quoted, 385
Henderson, Vivian W., quoted, 466
Hentoff, Nat, quoted, 305
Herberg, Will, quoted, 467
Heredity and human behavior, 67, 70, 171–172
Higbee, Edward, quoted, 476–477
Highet, Gilbert, quoted, 269
Hinduism, ethics of, 30, 35, 97, 195, 324
Hobbes, Thomas, 152, 177, 291, 525
Hoffman, Nicholas von, quoted, 446
Hoijer, Harry, quoted, 455
Holmes, Oliver Wendell, quoted, 316
Home, 71, 375, 423, 425, 429, 430, 453; as a basic institution, 71; as a right, 259. *See also* Family *and* Marriage and sex relations.
Homosexuality, 431, 446–447
Honesty, 83, 95, 137; cases concerning, 83–84, 149, 332, 339–341. *See also* Truth *and* Truthfulness.
Horney, Karen, quoted, 68
Housing, 453
Hugo, Victor, case from, 149
Human nature, 65–74; cases concerning, 83–85; as a social product, 69, 71; three views of, 66–69
Human values. *See* Value and values.
Hume, David, 117, 134, 135
Hunt, Kenneth, quoted, 175
Huxley, Aldous, 304
Huxley, Julian, quoted, 245

Idealists who supported self-realization, 196
Ideals, 10, 42, 247, 251. *See also* Principles *and* Virtues.
Indeterminism, 76
Individual autonomy, a recent trend, 426–427
Individualism, 255, 260, 376, 377; in business and government, 255; in relation to rights, 255, 260
Industrial revolution, 8, 18, 210, 375
Industrial society, 10, 11, 374–398; chief virtues of, 323, 376–378; criticisms of, 379–385; efforts to improve, 385–388; unethical practices of, 383–385
Inequality of power, risks, wealth, and work, 380, 390
Inglis, D. R., quoted, 522
In-group, 241–244, 245; in race relations, 457; and selfishness, 245–247
Injuries, 90, 262
Institutions and institutional ethics, 17, 18, 71, 241, 242, 343–371, 441, 494; need of criticism of, 313, 314; test of, 255; when justified and when not, 392
Insurance, health and medical, 292–293
Integration, racial, 366, 450–451, 468
Intellectual freedom. *See* Freedom of thought and speech.
Intelligence, 58, 59, 80, 83, 89, 95, 141, 174, 237–238, 337; obstacles to, 299–301
Interdependence, 242, 344–345
International control, need for, 522, 531
International law, 7, 527, 531–532
International organizations, 531–532. *See also* United Nations.
Intolerance. *See* Prejudice.

Intoxication, 280
Intuitionists and intuitionism, 118, 133–134, 146–148
Inventions, effects of, 8, 522, 533. *See also* Technology and technological changes.
Irrationalism, 16, 50
Isenberg, Arthur, quoted, 4
Islam, 30, 92, 113, 327

Jackson, Robert H., quoted, 316
Jacoby, Neil H., quoted, 467
Jaspers, Karl, 216–217
Jefferson, Thomas, quoted, 302
Jesus of Nazareth, 220–224, 314; ethics of, 220–224; quoted, 56, 97, 220, 221, 223
Jews and Judaism, 30, 92, 113, 195, 209, 213, 215, 222, 224–225, 393; ethics of, 218–219
Joad, C. E. M., quoted, 74–75, 131, 157
Johnson, Oliver A., quoted, 148, 226
Johnson, Virginia E., 433
Jones, Stacy V., quoted, 8
Journalism, 243–244, 404
Judeo-Christian tradition, 10–11, 92, 96, 179, 209, 214, 252
Judgments, elements in, 109–110; moral, 25, 27, 108–111
Justice, 44–47, 92, 96, 148, 182, 244, 454, 493; administration of, 54–58; as a virtue, 321, 322, 337, 338; in Judaism, 218–219; Plato's view of, 191–192

Kant, Immanuel, 133–149, 160, 166, 177, 526; evaluation of the views of, 143–146; moral philosophy of, 134–146; quoted, 51, 80, 97, 99, 136, 137, 138, 141
Katz, Joseph, 433; quoted, 432–433
Kaufman, Walter, 177
Keeney, Barnaby C., quoted, 17
Kefauver, Estes, 506; quoted, 504
Kennedy, John F., quoted, 505–506

Kernan, Michael, quoted, 450
Kerner Report, quoted, 467
Kierkegaard, Sören, 115, 164, 199, 209, 214, 215–216
Killing, 10, 110, 122, 173, 205, 206, 243, 412; cases dealing with, 149, 205, 206; modern means condemned, 243; among primitive groups, 41
King, Martin Luther, Jr., 462, 509
Kirchwey, Freda, quoted, 516
Knowledge, 8, 15, 34–36, 58, 65, 95, 147, 183, 225, 263, 502; and freedom, 80, 82, 83, 89. See also Intelligence and Wisdom.

Labor and labor organizations, 7, 11, 246, 389, 390, 391, 402, 526
Ladof, Nina Sydney, quoted, 306
Laissez Faire doctrine, 11, 183, 376; and the state, 260, 376, 496, 497; virtues of, 323
Language, 82, 182; and types of meaning in ethics, 114–122
Laws, 10, 267, 514; and civil disobedience, 509–514; dealing with unjust, 509–514; in relation to morals and professional ethics, 349–350; natural, 47, 67, 75, 176, 180; statutory, 37, 44–47, 59, 314, 320. See also Justice, administration of.
Lawyer, 345, 346, 357–362; cases concerning, 369, 370, 371. See also Legal ethics.
Leake, Chauncey D., quoted, 279
Legal ethics, 357–362; code of, 358–359
Lehmann, Paul L., quoted, 223
Leisure, 430; right to, 259
Lenin, Vladimir, 211
Lewis, C. I., quoted, 25, 126, 158, 159–160
Leys, Wayne, A. R., 29, 200
Liberty. See Civil liberty and Freedom of choice.

Life, limits of, 471–488
Lindgren, Henry Clay, 335
Lindstrom, Carl E., quoted, 401
Linguistic analysis, 204
Literature, 12, 14, 260
Littner, Ner, quoted, 432
Locke, John, 134–135, 152, 510, 525
Lord, E. W., quoted, 395
Lorenz, Konrad, 525
Love, 14, 69, 71, 90, 92, 94, 137, 197; Christian ideal of, 221, 223, 225, 322, 338; right to, 259; romantic, 423–447
Loyalty, 9, 10, 11, 18, 41, 142, 145, 201, 203, 226–227, 239, 240, 246, 249, 251, 337; in Christian ethics, 221–222, 224, 322; oaths of, 304, 317; selfishness masquerading as, 345; and the virtues, 142, 201
Luther, Martin, 66, 220, 223
Lying, 10, 137, 243–244, 329; cases concerning, 84, 149, 339–341; Kant's view of, 137. See also Self-deceit and Truthfulness.
Lynching, question concerning, 516

Machiavelli, 177, 495, 525
McLuhan, Marshall, quoted, 416
McWhirter, William, A., quoted, 433
Man, 77; as a being of worth, 197–198; distorted view of, 11; Plato's view of, 191–192; social nature of, 197–199. See also Persons and Self.
Mao Tse-tung, 209
Marcel, Gabriel, 216
Marcuse, Herbert, quoted, 3
Maritain, Jacques, 188
Marmor, Judd, quoted, 273
Marriage and sex relations, 423–447; cases concerning, 443–447; interracial, 467; new designs for, 431–435; problems in con-

nection with, 435–443; trends in, 424–427
Marx, Karl, 115, 209–213
Marxism and ethics, 209–213
Marxism-Leninism, 495
Maslow, Abraham, 188; quoted, 9
Mass media, 18–19, 282, 312, 399–421, 439, 535; cases concerning, 418–421
Masters, William H., 433, 434; quoted, 434
May, M. A., quoted, 334
Mead, Margaret H., quoted, 423
Meadows, Donella and Denis, 472, 473
Meaning, 77, 238; and use of language, 31, 114–126, 130; of life, 226
Means, 98–104, 144, 211; cases concerning, 149; in Kant's philosophy, 142–144; in relation to motives and consequences, 142–144, 211
Medical care, 292; methods of, 293
Medical ethics, 345, 346, 352–357; cases concerning, 369, 370; code of, 353–354; new trends and problems in, 354–357; and public interest in, 354, 356–357
Medieval age, virtues of, 66, 323
Mencius, 327
Mental health, 289–292
Mercy killing. See Euthanasia.
Merriam, Eve, quoted, 410
Metaethics, 105, 114–130
Mexican American, 450
Military-industrial complex, 6, 327, 382–383, 526
Milk, cases concerning, 241; infected, 243
Mill, John Stuart, 115, 152, 155–157, 161, 165, 166, 198; quoted, 155, 156, 301
Milton, John, quoted, 301
Minister. See Clergymen.
Minority groups. See Cultural pluralism.

Minow, Newton D., 420; quoted, 407–408
Mintz, Morton, 382; quoted, 385
Misprision, 269
Mixed system in society, 378–379
Mo Tse, 326
Mohammed, 327. See also Islam.
Monogamy, 434, 442. See also Marriage and sex relations.
Monopolies, 256, 379, 381, 404, 417, 505, 531
Montagu, Ashley, 187, 525; quoted, 13–14, 67, 187
Montgomery, Edmund, 180
Moon, ethical questions concerning landing a man on, 537
Moore, G. E., quoted, 116, 148
Moore, Harry H., quoted, 370
Moral judgments, 37, 108–111; inescapable, 24–27. See also Morality.
Moral law in Hinduism and Buddhism, 324, 325; in Kant's philosophy, 135–145
Moral obligation. See Duty and duties.
Moral relativity. See Relativism.
Moral standards brought up to date, 240–245; how to test, 88–104; methods of approach to, 27–33; primitive, 40–48, 54–58
Morality, 33; development of, 39–60; reflective, 53, 59, 231–247; theories of, 88–247
Morgan, Arthur E., quoted, 264–265
Morgan, C. Lloyd, 180
Morgenstern, O., quoted, 482
Morro Castle incident, 266
Moslems, 327. See also Islam.
Motion Picture Association of America, production code quoted, 412; rating symbols, 413
Motion pictures, ethics of, 399, production code of, 412–413
Motives, 93, 98–100, 104, 320; central in Christian ethics, 220–

221, 222; Kant's view of, 99, 141–144; in relation to means and consequences, 98–100
Moynihan, Daniel P., quoted, 488
Muller, Herbert J., quoted, 4, 384
Mumford, Lewis, 19, 382; quoted, 12
Munn, Allan M., quoted, 83
Murder. See Killing.
Mutual aid, 39, 180

Narcotics. See Drugs and drug addiction.
National Association of Broadcasters, 408, 409, 410, 411
National Association of Manufacturers, 2, 389
National Council of Teachers of English, pamphlet quoted, 306
National data bank, 311
National Education Association (NEA), 363; quoted, 363–364
National health plans, need for, 292–293
National Safety Bureau report, 384–385
National Urban Coalition, 500–503
Nationalism. See also State and Fascism.
Natural laws, 47, 67, 75, 176, 180, 255, 376, 381; and human welfare, 176–177. See also Nature as the standard.
Natural rights, 376. See also Rights.
Natural selection, 183, 376, 497
Naturalistic fallacy, 116
Nature as the standard, 170–188
Negligence, cases of, 268–269. See also Due care.
Negroes in the United States, 450–452; cases concerning, 466–467. See also Blacks and race relations.
Neo-orthodoxy, 222–223
Neuhaus, Richard, quoted, 472

Newspapers, 243, 400–405; cases concerning, 417–418
Niebuhr, Reinhold, quoted, 68–69
Nietzsche, Friedrich, 115, 177–180, 185, 199, 214, 216, 525; quoted, 178, 179
Nihilism, 179
Nixon, Richard M., 522, 538; quoted, 287
Noise, cases concerning, 37, 489
Nonviolence, 462, 512, 526
"Nordic myth", 454–455
Nuclear energy, 521–524, 530
Nuclear test ban treaty, 128, 522–523
Nuveen, John, quoted, 480

Objectivity, 214, 237
Obligation, 41, 181, 251, 262–267. See also Duty and duties.
Obscenity, 409, 412, 415
Occult, interest in, 16
Ofstad, Harold, quoted, 82
Organ transplant, 231
Oriental ethical ideals, 30, 34, 92, 97, 324–327
Orthogenesis, rejected, 182
Orwell, George, 304
Osgood, Charles E., quoted, 12
Otto, Herbert A., 334, 442; quoted, 435
Ought, 77, 118, 119, 154, 159, 163
Out-group, in race relations, 241–244

Packard, Vance, quoted, 428, 429
Pain, 55, 71, 90, 153, 166, 176, 275, 276
Paradise, Scott, 490
Pascal, Blaise, quoted, 52
Passell, Peter, 471
Patriotism, 529, 530, 531
Paulsen, Friedrich, 329
Peace, conferences, 526–527; efforts to achieve, 526–528; fallacies regarding, 528–529; quest for, 521–539

Pentagon Papers, 267
Persons, 90; as ends in themselves, 89, 90, 138, 143; unique qualities of, 89–92
Philosophy of life, 292
Physician. See Medical ethics.
Plato, 34, 92, 95, 114, 115, 177, 190–192, 198, 214, 321, 322, 494
Pleasure, 71, 151–168, 175–176. See also Utilitarianism and Happiness.
Pollution, 4, 6, 32, 245, 273, 374, 471–495
Pope Paul VI, 478
Population, problems of, 8, 9, 231, 472, 476–477, 491
Positivism, 16, 116, 213
Poverty, 453, 454
Powelson, David, quoted, 433
Power politics, 529, 531
Predestination, 76
Prejudice, 248, 456–461; as an obstacle to thinking, 300; and race relations, 456–461
Pressure groups, 389, 391–392
Price, David, quoted, 484
Price fixing, 384
Primary groups, 241–242, 343
Principles, 25, 89, 320; brought up to date, 240–244; for moral experimentation, 235–238; for officials of government, 505–506; for periods of social change, 393–394; of selection in field of values, 253–254
Priorities, 19, 471, 498, 535; federal budget and, 500–503; types of, 472–491
Pritchard, H. A., quoted, 146
Privacy, 258; and data banks, 311; invasion of, 318
Private property, 242, 255, 260, 376, 377–378; owned by passive agents, 242; and rights, 255, 260; when ethically defensible, 378

Profession, defined, 347
Professional ethics, 343–371; relation to morals and to law, 347–350; why codes are necessary, 350–351
Professionalism, 245–246, 344–345; and amusements, 278
Profit and the profit motive, 375, 376, 377, 382, 390, 403; cases concerning, 395, 396, 397
Progress, 42, 179, 261, 454, 475; and compromise, 239–240; and experimentation, 234, 239
Projection, 335
Promiscuity, 433, 438, 443
Promises and promise keeping, 146, 148, 262
Propaganda, 243, 279, 300, 312, 402, 406; as an obstacle to thinking, 300
Property. See Private property.
Prostitution, 138–139
Protestantism, 66, 215, 222–224, 393, 526; and the virtues, 323. See also Christian ethics and Christians.
Protestors, 513–514, 533–535
Psychological basis of behavior, 71
Public opinion, 392; as an obstacle to thinking, 300, 303
Public ownership, 379, 403
Public versus private interest, 345–349, 414, 417, 503–508
Puerto Ricans, 450
Punishment, and the courts, 45–47, 49, 55; for corporate evils, 242–244, 383–385; among primitive groups, 45–47. See also Justice.
Puritan view of amusements, 277; virtues emphasized by, 323
Pusey, Nathan M., quoted, 303

Quigley, Carroll, quoted, 346

Race relations, 43, 366, 449–469; cases concerning, 465–468; prejudice and, 456–459

Radhakrishnan, S., quoted, 92
Radio, 7, 399, 400, 405–411; code of, 409, 410. See also Broadcasting and Mass media.
Raju, P. T., 92
Ramsey, Paul, 525
Randall, Richard S., quoted, 415
Rationalism, 115
Rationalization, 335
Ray, Marie Beynon, quoted, 292
Reason and the moral order, 50, 82, 142, 196, 197, 213, 225; in Aristotle, 193, 194; in Kant, 134–136, 142, 143; in Plato's ethics, 95, 191. See also Reflective morality.
Recreation, 277, 430; and health, 277; right to, 259
Recycling as a way out, 473
Redlich, Norman, quoted, 508
Reductionism, 16, 186
Reflective morality, 53, 88–105, 226, 231–247; case as example of, 102–104; experimentation and, 232–238; freedom and, 81–82, 299
Reflective thinking, 81, 90. See also Reflective morality.
Reformation, 48, 223
Reich, Charles A., quoted, 5–6
Reiss, Ira L., 434; quoted, 433
Relativism, 60, 110–114, 130
Religion and morality, 30, 200, 218–227; world religions, 322–327
Renaissance, 48, 152
Repression, 274, 452
Responsibility, 41, 57, 130, 215, 242, 247, 261, 263, 388; collective, 242, 247, 388; and freedom, 80, 82, 83; among primitive groups, 41, 57. See also Due care.
Retaliation, law of, 54
Revolution, 5, 18, 211, 234, 383, 461, 510, 511, 514, 533–535, 538. See also Communism and Industrial revolution.
Ribicoff, Abraham, quoted, 445
Riesman, David, 13
Right, 1, 2, 88–105; defined, 90; ethics of the, 143–144, 146, 222; problems of right and wrong, 25–26, 82, 94. See also Morality and Ethics.
Rights, 15, 41, 251–270, 391, 424; Bill of, 302, 305, 309, 311, 510; human, 254–262; natural, 255, 315; of students, 365–366; and values, 254–260
Rock, Dr. John, quoted, 478
Rollins, Betty, quoted, 432
Roman Catholic Church, 194, 215, 224, 393, 526; and birth control, 435–436
Roosevelt, Franklin D., 258
Roosevelt, Theodore, 386
Ross, Leonard, 471
Ross, William David, quoted, 146–147
Rotary International and the promotion of ethical codes, 388
Rousseau, Jean Jacques, 67, 134, 526
Royce, Josiah, 115, 149, 196
Russell, Bertrand, 116, 117
Russell, Valeria, quoted, 460

Sartre, Jean-Paul, 216, 217
School. See Education and educators and Students.
Schopenhauer, 177
Schroeder, John C., 201
Schweitzer, Albert, 175
Science and scientists, 2, 10, 13, 48, 89, 122, 232, 233, 530; in relation to moral judgments, 32–33, 34
Secondary groups, 241–242, 343
Security, 493; right to, 259, 260, 307
Segregation and segregationists, 43, 184, 451, 454, 458, 464
Self, 13, 16, 72, 74, 78, 90, 202,

216; characteristics of, 91–92, 197, 201, 202, 203; freedom and the, 79–83
Self-consciousness, 58, 72, 82, 83, 89, 91, 197; as essential to freedom, 77, 79–80
Self-control, 42, 83, 95, 152, 191, 193, 244, 282, 321, 322, 337, 338
Self-deceit, 335–336. *See also* Truthfulness.
Self-determination as a right, 463, 464
Self-determinism, 76, 79
Self-fulfillment. *See* Self-realization.
Self-interest, 152, 156, 244, 245, 246, 346, 348–349, 376, 392–393; in relation to competition, 376–377. *See also* Selfishness.
Selfishness, 18, 66, 69, 95, 152, 158, 275; and altruism, 73–75; of groups, 245, 348–349
Self-realization, 190–207; as the standard, 190–202; evaluation of the theory of, 202–204.
Self-sacrifice, 39, 74, 171, 176, 179
Service clubs, 386, 387–388
Service motive as adopted by the professions, 347–349
Severeid, Eric, quoted, 402
Sex and the mass media, 408–410, 412, 415
Sex relations. *See* Marriage and sex relations.
Sharing, 323; in control of the conditions of life, 259–260
Shaw, George Bernard, quoted, 370
Simmons, J. I., quoted, 437
Simon, William, 433; quoted, 434
Simpson, G. G., quoted, 180
Situation ethics, 225
Six methods of approach to a study of ethics, 27–34
Skepticism in morals, 4, 12, 30, 112
Skinner, B. F., quoted, 13

Slaves, treatment of, 55, 58, 138
Sleep, value of, 276
Smith, Richard Austin, quoted, 384
Smoking and human welfare, 282–284, 409
Snow, C. P., quoted, 3
Snyder, Alfred J., quoted, 511
Social change. *See* Changing social order.
Social Darwinism, rejected, 182–183
Social planning, 381–382
Socrates, 30, 114, 151, 156, 177, 214
Sovereignty, 11
Space age, 8, 231
Specialization, 15, 35, 89, 198, 241–242, 344–345, 354, 368, 375
Speer, Robert E., quoted, 330
Spencer, Herbert, 67, 115, 170, 175–176; quoted, 176
Spengler, Oswald, 4, 5
Spinoza, 79, 196, 525
Sportsmanship, 294. *See also* Amusements.
State, 11, 48, 176–177, 191, 257, 310, 315, 494–519, 531; cases concerning, 515–519; and civil disobedience, 509–514. *See also* Democracy.
Stealing, 10, 244, 486; modern forms of, 244, 486
Steenbock, Henry, 348
Stereotyping in race relations, 458
Sterilization as a moral problem, 184, 187, 355
Stevenson, Charles, 116, 120–122; quoted, 121–122
Stoics, 196, 526
Strike, right of teachers to, 366–367
Struggle for existence, 171–174, 180, 183
Students, 304–305; rights of, 306, 365–366. *See also* Education and educators *and* Youth.

Students' Right to Read, quoted, 306
Subjectivism, 16, 110–111, 215
Sublimation, 291
Submarine, case concerning, 206
Suffering, 274–275
Suicide, 137, 149, 454; for a cause, 205, 206
Sumner, William Graham, quoted, 112
Supreme Court. *See* United States Supreme Court.
Surgeon General, report on smoking, 283
Survival of the fittest, 173, 175, 176, 184, 185, 376–377; and the environment, 474–475
Swertlow, F. S., quoted, 444
Swinging, 427, 431–434
Sympathy, 39, 69, 97, 137, 175, 176, 179, 180

Taxes and priorities, 500–503
Taylor, Gordon R., quoted, 476, 484, 485
Taylor, Richard, 76
Teachers, 344, 362–367; cases concerning, 368; and civil liberties, 304–306; ethics of, 362–368; problems facing, 365–367
Technology and technological changes, 3, 10, 213, 382–383, 503; as affecting family and home, 427–431
Teleological theories, 148, 151–247
Television, 8, 399, 400, 405–411; effect on children, 409–411
Teltsch, Kathleen, 478
Thermonuclear age, problems of, 521–532
Thomas, George F., quoted, 221
Tillich, Paul, 64; quoted, 68, 214
Time reviews, quoted, 5
Time-Louis Harris Poll, quoted, 9–10
Tobacco, 279, 282–284

Tobin, Richard L., quoted, 416, 417
Totalitarianism, 213, 257, 310, 495
Toynbee, Arnold, 456; quoted, 227, 346, 530–531
Trade associations, 386–387, 388–389, 391, 408
Trade union. *See* Labor and labor organizations.
Tradition of the sea, need for changes in ethics of, 62, 84–85
Traditional codes and values, 10, 32, 59, 114, 343; problems not covered by, 231, 486
Truman, Harry S., 293; quoted, 302
Truth, 35, 36, 91, 149, 161, 252; cases concerning, 248, 332, 368; degrees of concern for, 333; right to know the, 356
Truthfulness, 137, 140, 149, 161, 321, 328–336; as absolute or relative, 329–333; cases concerning, 248, 332, 339–341; need to be brought up to date, 243–244; and self-deceit, 333–336
Tucker, Sterling, quoted, 452
Tufts, James H., quoted, 53, 80
Turgenev, quoted, 201

United Nations, 46, 256–257, 402, 486, 489, 491, 527, 531, 532, 536; Charter quoted, 532, 536
United Presbyterian Church, report quoted, 345–346, 460
United States Bill of Rights, 302, 305, 311, 510
United States Constitution, 255, 268, 302, 305, 309, 425
United States Declaration of Independence, 255, 273, 311; quoted, 510
United States Department of Health, Education and Welfare, Report to Congress on Alcohol and Health, 281
United States Supreme Court, 243,

302–303, 304, 316, 412, 451, 515
Universal Declaration of Human Rights, 256–257, 486
Universality, principle of, 96–97, 144–145
Utilitarianism, 151–169; evaluation of, 157–166; of Bentham and Mill, 153–157. *See also* Happiness.
Utility, principle of, 153–154

Valenti, Jack, quoted, 413
Value and values, 2, 9, 11, 17, 24, 65, 89, 94, 111, 122, 179, 212; grounding of, 252–253; principles of selection, 253–254; in relation to rights and duties, 251–270; as subjective or objective, 110–112
Van Horne, Harriet, 438; quoted, 437
Vices, 92, 142, 193, 320–321
Violence, 1, 2, 4, 12, 13, 14, 16, 17, 18, 19, 234, 383, 451, 452, 461, 462, 465, 533–535, 538; and the mass media, 407, 408, 409, 412, 415
Virtues, 92, 113, 142, 147, 175, 178–179, 193, 201, 224, 320–341; of a business society, 324; conventional approach to, criticized, 336–338; new, needing emphasis, 244
Vocations and vocational ethics, 343–371

Wage, guaranteed annual, 267; a living, 258
Wallace, George, 451, 461
War, 2, 3, 4, 383, 521–539; efforts to eliminate, 526–532; as an institution, 524–526; paths to, 531
Warburg, James P., quoted, 246–247, 367
Warnock, Mary, quoted, 115, 126

Warren, Justice Earl, quoted, 10
Waste, 471, 473; by experiments of incompetents, 237; in the industrial system, 374, 381–382, 391, 485; radioactive, 484; of resources, 245, 381, 471–473, 483–485; from sickness and disease, 274–275
Weatherhead, Leslie D., quoted, 227–228
Weaver, Warren, quoted, 233
Weinberg, Andrew D., quoted, 467
Welfare, human or social, 37, 146, 224, 226, 236–237, 238, 243, 244–245, 263, 504
Wellman, Carl, quoted, 123
Wells, Donald A., 525
Wertham, Frederic, quoted, 409–410
Westermarck, E. A., 117; quoted, 51, 443
Western civilization, 2, 220; two impulses behind education in, 34–36. *See also* Civilization.
Whitehead, Alfred North, 34, 92; quoted, 7, 64
Wilcox, Preston, quoted, 460
Will of God, 47, 226, 227–228
Will to live, 91, 94, 177, 178
Will to power, 178, 216
Wilson, H. H., quoted, 168
Wilson, Woodrow, quoted, 535
Wiretapping and monitoring, 269, 307, 309, 310, 318
Wisdom, 93, 152, 183, 191, 321, 322, 338
Witkin, Jacob, 348
Wittgenstein, Ludwig, 116, 117
Wolman, Harold, quoted, 500
Women, equal rights for, 424–425
Women's Liberation Movement, 444, 451
Work, 375, 390, 427, 430; an element in happiness, 291; as a right, 258–259; unequal distribution of, 380–381
Workers, 389–390, 391

World order. *See* Peace *and* United Nations.
World organizations, 529, 531–532
Worship, right to, 260
Wright, Quincy, quoted, 530
Wright, W. K., quoted, 138–139

Wrongdoing, new forms of, 243–244

Youth, 3, 8, 9, 11, 16, 26, 407–410, 411, 419, 425–426, 427, 453